THERE'S
ALWAYS
WORK
AT THE
POST
OFFICE

The
University
of
North
Carolina
Press
Chapel Hill

THERE'S ALWAYS WORK AT THE POST OFFICE

African American Postal Workers and the Fight for Jobs, Justice, and Equality

PHILIP F. RUBIO

Designed by Jacquline Johnson
Set in Baskerville MT
by Keystone Typesetting, Inc.

The University of North Carolina Press
has been a member of the Green Press
Initiative since 2003.

Library of Congress Cataloging-in-Publication Data
Rubio, Philip F.
There's always work at the post office: African
American postal workers and the fight for jobs,
justice, and equality/Philip F. Rubio.
p.   cm.
Includes bibliographical references and index.
ISBN 978-0-8078-3342-1 (cloth: alk. paper)
ISBN 978-0-8078-5986-5 (pbk.: alk. paper)
ISBN 978-0-8078-9573-3 (ebook)
1. African American postal service employees—History.
2. African Americans—Employment—History. 3. Postal
service—Employees—Labor unions—United States—
History. I. Title.
HE6499.R82 2010
331.6'396073—dc22   2009049091

TO
EVERYONE
WHO HAS EVER
MOVED THE
MAIL

CONTENTS

ILLUSTRATIONS

PREFACE

From 1980 to 2000 I worked for the U.S. Postal Service (USPS). I enjoyed most of the experience, especially working as a letter carrier, meeting and serving the public every day. I began my career in Colorado as a PTF (part-time flexible) clerk at the Denver Bulk Mail Center (BMC), making eight dollars an hour—more than twice what the post office was paying starting workers a decade before. And when I left the post office I was a full-time letter carrier in Durham, North Carolina, earning about twenty dollars an hour. Other benefits included paid annual and sick leave, a choice of government-sponsored health plans, and a full retirement pension for those who served at least thirty years.

From the first day I was hired I was keenly aware of being a beneficiary of the Great Postal Wildcat Strike of 1970 that forms a key part of this narrative. The results of that brave action by thousands of postal workers across the country meant that my coworkers and I now had relatively secure jobs, could belong to a union with full collective bargaining rights, and could earn enough to buy a home and help pay to send our kids to college.

When I started work in February 1980 with other new hires in Denver, I first had to take a strength test (clerks and mail handlers had to heft an eighty-pound mail sack). I also had to sign agreements that I would not strike, did not belong to organizations that advocated the government's overthrow, was a high school graduate, and was not a convicted felon. From there each of us was on a ninety-day job probation en route to a potential USPS career as a "regular" full-time career appointment.

The Denver BMC was huge, resembling factories where I had worked. Mail handlers loaded and unloaded trucks. Clerks electronically and manually processed parcels as well as moved bundles of bulk mail from conveyor belts into big dusty gray sacks divided by zip code. It was all monotonous work. But talking and socializing made it go faster. And there was also a culture of resistance to mandatory overtime and other controversial management practices. One supervisor on the bulk mail belt seemed particularly intent on ordering me to work faster. I must have looked pretty discouraged, because an older black clerk waited until the supervisor left after yet another tirade to tell me with a grin: "They'll ride you your whole ninety days [probationary period], and then even after that—until you 'make regular.' But once you 'make regular,' they can't get you out of here with a crowbar!"

He was right. "Making regular" meant full-time work guaranteed at forty hours a week (PTF status only guaranteed you twenty hours of work over a two-week period, although I rarely worked less than forty hours a week. There were also "casuals" appointed for ninety days at roughly half pay, and "temporary employees" known as TES appointed for one year.) And "making regular" allowed a postal employee to "bid" on an open position within one's craft, whether clerk, carrier, mail handler, maintenance, motor vehicle, or any other, depending on one's "seniority" or hire date. But "making regular" also afforded postal workers a certain amount of civil service due process job protection, which I also enjoyed from union membership—first with the American Postal Workers Union (APWU), and later the National Association of Letter Carriers (NALC) after I transferred to the letter carrier craft in the fall of 1980. Letter carriers' work culture included trying to gain some control over their work environment, such as finding more efficient ways to deliver their routes other than the way they were arranged on the metal route cases. Every day saw a dance of disputes and negotiations with supervisors over how much mail to "curtail" (hold back) or deliver that day (first class mail was never curtailed) —as carriers would often request overtime or help from those on the "overtime desired list." On the other hand, there was also a sense that labor and management were on the same team, racing against time to sort and deliver people's mail as soon as possible, in spite of often impractical official procedures.

In 1988 I moved with my family to North Carolina, where I first worked in the Raleigh post office before transferring to nearby Durham. The stations I worked in averaged around fifty employees. They featured constant talking and joking among workers to help relieve boredom and break the tension of getting the mail put up in a few hours before carriers had to go deliver their routes.

The post office has a highly unionized and well-educated workforce. Despite the history of anti-union laws and attitudes in the South where I now lived (North Carolina has the lowest unionization rate in the nation), I was impressed by the amount of union influence at the post office in Raleigh and Durham that resembled what I had experienced in the more union-friendly North and West, both at the post office and in manufacturing. I was glad to see workroom floor life governed by the same labor-management contract that also dictated our raises, benefits, and work rules. Our elected union shop stewards were there to file grievances if necessary, and in general represent workers—who also found their own ways to negotiate each workday with management, whether individually or collectively.

But it was in Durham, where I worked as a letter carrier from 1990 to 2000, that I noticed how many of my black coworkers—about 50 percent of the local workforce—made up a workplace community. It was a community that socialized inside and outside of work, welcomed new African American employees, and included many college graduates. Their jobs were also made possible in large part due to the pioneering efforts of the historically black National Alliance of Postal and Federal Employees (NAPFE).

When I left the post office in 2000 to pursue a Ph.D. in history at Duke University, I found that I could not entirely leave the post office behind. I wanted to learn more about the black labor and civic tradition that I had seen at the post office yet found absent in the historical literature. I wanted to write a history of black postal workers, their activism and influence on the post office and its unions, as well as the significance of government employment in the making of the black community. After almost a decade of research that included thirty-one oral history interviews and countless conversations with current and former postal workers, I have still only scratched the surface of this little-told but important story.

This story is also a lens through which we can view an even larger picture of struggle, accommodation, and change over time at the post office.

I'm not an African American, but I wanted to relate this story that is uniquely black as well as all-American, and one that has touched me personally. As I write this, the post office is suffering huge deficits due to the economic recession, multiple communication and delivery alternatives, and escalating operating costs. In response, the USPS has felt compelled to raise postal rates, cut retail service hours, close many offices, encourage veteran employees to take early retirement, and consider eliminating Saturday delivery. The post office and its unions, which black postal workers did so much to help transform, are vital but threatened American institutions. I write this book with fervent hopes that future histories of those institutions will be written as ongoing chronicles, not epitaphs.

ACKNOWLEDGMENTS

In researching and writing this book I owe debts of gratitude to many people, starting with the most profound debts I owe my mentors Charles Payne, Thavolia Glymph, Barry Gaspar, Raymond Gavins, John French, Peter Wood, Edward Balleisen, Robert Korstad, Lawrence Goodwyn, Paula Giddings, Karin Shapiro, Jocelyn Olcott, and the late Jack Cell, all at Duke University, for helping me complete my training as a historian.

The University of North Carolina Press provided me with so much valuable direction, especially editor-in-chief David Perry, associate managing editor Paula Wald, editorial assistant Zach Read, copyeditor Eric Schramm, editor Mary Caviness, and the anonymous readers. Thanks also to my mentor Charles Thompson at the Duke Center for Documentary Studies (CDS), along with Rhonda Jones and other colleagues at the CDS.

There would have been virtually no story without oral history and telephone interviewees, including Countee Abbott, John Adams, and Dorothea Hoskins; Sam Armstrong and Samuel Lovett; Eleanor Bailey, Joann Flagler, Frederick John, Carlton Tilley, and Gregory Wilson; Felix Bell Sr.; William H. Burrus Jr.; Don Cantriel; Willenham Castilla; C. C. Draughn; Vivian Grubbs; Joseph Henry; Douglas C. Holbrook; Walter T. Kenney Sr.; Jimmy Mainor; Al Marino, Frank Orapello, and Vincent Sombrotto; Raydell Moore; Cleveland Morgan; James Morris; Noel Murrain; James Newman; Richard Peery; Jeff Perry and Richard Thomas; D. James Pinderhughes; George Booth Smith; Donald P. Stone; Daisy Strachan; and Tommie L. Wilson.

In Washington, D.C., invaluable research guidance, resources, and encouragement were provided by National Alliance of Postal and Federal Employees historian Paul Tennassee; historians Candace Rush and Nancy Dysart at the National Association of Letter Carriers; communications director Sally Davidow at the American Postal Workers Union; historians Megaera Ausman and Jennifer Lynch and librarian Earl Arrington at the U.S. Postal Service archives and library; and the Library of Congress staff. In New York, I could not have done without the help from archivists Gail Malmgreen, Erika Gottfried, Evan Daniel, and Kevyne Baar at New York University's Tamiment/ Wagner Archives, as well as the staff at the Schomburg Center for Research in Black Culture. In North Carolina, I was aided by the staff at Duke University libraries; the History Department and Shepard Library at North Carolina Central University (especially archivist André Vann); and the staff at the University of North Carolina–Chapel Hill libraries.

I received fruitful feedback from my friends in Duke's African and African American Studies Program (AAAS) dissertation-writing group: LaNitra Walker Berger, Niambi Carter, Erica Edwards, Reena Goldthree, Alisa Harrison, LaShaune Johnson, Gordon Mantler, Charles McKinney, and Stephane Robolin. Thanks to Tiana Mack for transcribing help. Generous funding was provided by Duke's Department of History, AAAS, CDS, and Graduate School; the Mellon Foundation; the American Historical Association; and North Carolina A&T State University, where I am also grateful for my colleagues' encouragement and support.

I am eternally grateful to Paul Jackson and Barbara Pikos; Philip Jackson and Kimberly Gladman; Matthew and LaNitra Berger; and Judy Bellin for putting me up while I was conducting research. Thanks also to colleagues and mentors at the Duke history department, AAAS, and CDS for intellectual and moral support; David Barber, William Chafe, V. P. Franklin, Blair Kelley, Max Krochmal, Jeffrey Ogbar, June Patton, Jeff Perry, David Roediger, and Orion Teal, all of whom read and commented on chapters, spinoffs, and versions of chapters; and those who provided references, connections, and resources, including Emile and Myrna Adams, Steve Alston, Leah Platt Boustan, Carl Cruz, Peter Derrick, Ajamu Dillahunt, Nishani Frazier, Mindy Fullilove, Barbara Gannon, Aryn Glazier, Robert Gabrielsky, Wellington Cox Howard, Amity Kirby, Jennifer Lee, Jimmy Mainor, Henry McGee Jr., James M. McGee, Jacquelyn Moore, Paul Nagle, Charles M. Payne, Nelson Peery, Richard Peery, Jeff Perry, Frank R. Scheer, Anne Firor Scott, Donald Shaffer, Clarice Torrence, Jenessa Kildall, Wendell Haynes, and Jonathan Wallas.

Thanks to my friend Lance Hill for recommending UNC Press as a publisher. Much love to all my former coworkers at post offices in Denver, Colorado, and Durham and Raleigh, North Carolina (with a special shout-out to West Durham Station!), and to family members for their encouragement—especially my wife, Paula, for her patience and moral support!

ABBREVIATIONS

AFL	American Federation of Labor
APWU	American Postal Workers Union
BMCS	Bulk Mail Centers
BSCP	Brotherhood of Sleeping Car Porters
CIO	Congress of Industrial Organizations
CORE	Congress of Racial Equality
CRC	Civil Rights Congress
CSC	Civil Service Commission
EEO	Equal Employment Opportunity
EPA	Equal Pay Act
GPO	General Post Office
LIUNA	Laborers International Union of North America
MBPU	Manhattan-Bronx Postal Union
NALC	National Association of Letter Carriers
NAPE	National Alliance of Postal Employees
NAPFE	National Alliance of Postal and Federal Employees
NAPOC	National Association of Post Office Clerks
NAPOGSME	National Association of Post Office and General Services Maintenance Employees
NARLC	National Association of Rural Letter Carriers
NARMC	National Association of Railway Mail Clerks
NASDM	National Association of Special Delivery Messengers
NASPOE	National Association of Substitute Post Office Employees
NFPOC	National Federation of Post Office Clerks
NFPOMVE	National Federation of Post Office Motor Vehicle Employees
NNC	National Negro Congress
NNLC	National Negro Labor Council
NPCU	National Postal Clerks Union
NPMHU	National Postal Mail Handlers Union
NPTA	National Postal Transport Association
NPU	National Postal Union
NRLCA	National Rural Letter Carriers Association
NUL	National Urban League

PCEEO	President's Committee on Equal Employment Opportunity
PCSW	President's Commission on the Status of Women
PWA	Postal Workers of America
RMA	Railway Mail Association
SNCC	Student Nonviolent Coordinating Committee
UAPOC	United Association of Post Office Clerks
UFPC	United Federation of Postal Clerks
UNAPOC	United National Association of Post Office Craftsmen
UNIA	Universal Negro Improvement Association
USPS	U.S. Postal Service
WAPU	Washington Area Postal Union

CHRONOLOGY

1775	First Continental Congress appoints Benjamin Franklin first postmaster general of United States.
1794	Congress establishes U.S. Post Office Department.
1802	Congress restricts mail carrying to "free white persons." Postmaster General Gideon Granger cites negative example of successful Haitian Revolution.
1810	Congress restricts letter carrying to "free white persons."
1825	Congress restricts all mail "conveying" to "free white persons."
1863	Congress inaugurates free nationwide city mail delivery.
1865	Congress removes bars to blacks in post office.
1883	Pendleton Civil Service Act establishes Civil Service Commission with examinations to replace patronage system in government hiring.
1884	71 percent of postal workforce consists of local postmasters.
1889	Formation of National Association of Letter Carriers from remnants of Knights of Labor associations.
1891	United National Association of Post Office Craftsmen, commonly regarded as "company union," forms out of merger between United Association of Post Office Clerks, a former Knights of Labor affiliate, and National Association of Post Office Clerks.
1900	Chicago Post Office Clerks' Union No. 8703 becomes first union of federal employees to affiliate with American Federation of Labor.
1902	President Theodore Roosevelt issues "gag rule" forbidding postal employees from lobbying Congress for improved wages and working conditions.
1903	Formation of National Association of Rural Letter Carriers.
1905	Formation of National Postal Mail-Handlers Union.
1906	Formation of National Federation of Post Office Clerks, which protests gag rule and joins AFL.

1909	President William Howard Taft imposes another "gag rule" that bars postal workers from answering questions from congressional committees.
1912	Lloyd-LaFollette Act removes "gag rules" and allows government workers to join unions but forbids them from striking. Formation of all-white Railway Mail Association out of old National Association of Railway Mail Clerks, which formed in 1906.
1913	Black railway postal workers form National Alliance of Postal Employees, a nonexclusive union for black railway postal workers barred from white unions (later opened to all postal crafts in 1923). President Woodrow Wilson orders segregation of federal office buildings in nation's capital, including post office.
1914	President Wilson directs CSC to require that federal government job applications include photographs.
1917	NALC joins AFL, as does RMA. NALC Dallas convention votes to admit Jim Crow local branches known as "separate charters" or "dual charters."
1919	NALC Philadelphia convention overturns "dual charters."
1932	National Association of Substitute Post Office Employees, integrated leftist union, forms to advance rights of postal "subs."
1934	NASPOE March on Washington, with the goal of improving wages and working conditions of "subs." Formation of integrated, leftist Postal Workers of America, probably communist-affiliated "dual union" (folded in 1937). Congress of Industrial Organizations postal union organizing, 1938–1940s.
1939	Hatch Act bans government employees from partisan political activity.
1940	CSC abandons photo applications and other forms of discrimination after President Franklin D. Roosevelt issues Executive Order 8587.
1941	NALC national convention votes once again to allow "dual charters."
1941–46	Committee on Fair Employment Practices conducts investigations, holds hearings, and makes recommendations on eliminating workplace discrimination in war industry and

government service after President Roosevelt's Executive Order 8802.

1947　President Harry Truman's government employee "loyalty program," Executive Order 9835, leads to purge of postal employees accused of being communists.

1949　RMA becomes NPTA (National Postal Transport Association).

1954　NALC and NFPOC vote at their national conventions to charter no more Jim Crow branches and locals and to study their abolition entirely.

1955　President Dwight Eisenhower issues Executive Order 10590 prohibiting discrimination in federal employment and establishing President's Committee on Government Employment Policy. AFL-CIO merger.

1957　Civil Rights Act of 1957 passes, weakened considerably by jury-trial amendment that allows all-white juries to acquit whites accused of violating voting rights of African Americans. Amendment supported by NALC.

1958　"Boston Tea Party" walkout of NFPOC by Progressive Feds faction that in 1959 becomes National Postal Clerks Union, and in 1960 becomes National Postal Union.

1960　NPTA drops "Caucasian only" constitutional clause. Passage of Civil Rights Act of 1960. First national convention of Negro American Labor Council, of which National Alliance is a charter member.

1961　President John F. Kennedy issues Executive Order 10925 abolishing discrimination in federal contracts and setting up President's Commission on Equal Employment Opportunity. Kennedy's Executive Order 10980 establishes President's Commission on the Status of Women. NFPOC merges with UNAPOC and NPTA to become United Federation of Postal Clerks (UFPC).

1962　President Kennedy issues Executive Order 10988 recognizing unions for federal employees (including postal unions) and allowing union elections and limited collective bargaining. To qualify, unions must certify they do not practice discrimination based on race. Recognition of unions on national, regional, and local basis, graded according to election results: exclusive, formal, and informal. Separate gender pay registers abolished in post office following ruling by Attorney

General Robert F. Kennedy. NALC eliminates remaining segregated branches.

1963   President Kennedy issues Executive Order 11126 reinforcing
PCSW. Congress passes Equal Pay Act of 1963. National Alliance and NPU members participate in March on Washington for Jobs and Freedom.

1964   Civil Rights Act of 1964 passed, including Title VII abolishing
job discrimination and providing for affirmative action.
States ratify Twenty-fourth Amendment to Constitution
abolishing poll tax, which Congress had passed in 1962.

1965   NAPE becomes National Alliance of Postal and Federal Employees, expanding coverage to include all federal employees. Passage of 1965 Voting Rights Act. Leslie Shaw of
Los Angeles appointed as first African American to head
large urban post office.

1966   Huge volume of mail combined with personnel shortage
creates major backlog at Chicago post office, just a month
after its first African American postmaster, Henry McGee,
is appointed to head that office. John Strachan appointed as
first African American postmaster of New York City.

1967   Brief postal worker "sick-out" in Newark, New Jersey, during
Christmas mail rush.

1968   Government-appointed Kappel Commission issues report recommending that post office be reorganized as government
corporation to increase efficiency and cut costs. NALC, UFPC,
and NPU national conventions vote to reexamine their "no-
strike" constitutional clauses.

1969   Brief "sick-out" in July by New York postal workers at
Knightsbridge and Throgs Neck stations in Bronx. National
Alliance threatens to strike if only "exclusive" and not "for-
mal" recognition is allowed for federal employee unions.

1970   Nationwide wildcat strike breaks out at midnight on March
18, beginning in New York City. About 200,000 postal
workers in dozens of cities participate over eight days,
mostly in the Northeast, Midwest, and Far West. President
Richard M. Nixon calls out troops from National Guard,
army, navy, air force, and marines in a failed attempt to
move mail in and out of New York City. Troops called out in
Detroit but never leave armory. Later, President Nixon signs

the Postal Reorganization Act, creating present-day quasi-government corporation, U.S. Postal Service.

1971   First full collective bargaining agreement with four remaining postal unions, including NALC, National Rural Letter Carriers Association, NPMHU, and newly created American Postal Workers Union. Latter was formed out of merger of NPU, UFPC, National Association of Post Office and General Services Maintenance Employees, National Federation of Post Office Motor Vehicle Employees, and National Association of Special Delivery Messengers. National Alliance left out of collective bargaining agreement and continues work as equality-advocacy organization. Threatened postal wildcat strike in New York City by NALC and APWU called off. Postmaster General Winton M. Blount announces plans for building Bulk Mail Centers in mostly white suburbs.

1972   Title VII amended to allow, among other things, government employees to file antidiscrimination class action lawsuits. Charlotte, North Carolina, black postal workers file suit against post office for discrimination in promotions. Coalition of Black Trade Unionists formed, including members of APWU, protesting AFL-CIO neutrality in presidential election. They back candidacy of Senator George McGovern (D-S.D.) and oppose Viet Nam War and President Nixon's anti-integration policies.

1974   "Battle of the Bulk" wildcat strike at New York/New Jersey BMC.

1978   Wildcat strikes at BMCs in New York, New Jersey, and San Francisco. Elected to NALC national office, Vincent Sombrotto team institutes union reforms.

1980   Elected to APWU national office, Morris "Moe" Biller team institutes union reforms.

1981–84   NALC and APWU negotiate with USPS as Joint Bargaining Committee.

2001, 2004, 2007   William H. Burrus Jr. is elected as first African American president of APWU.

THERE'S
ALWAYS
WORK
AT THE
POST
OFFICE

INTRODUCTION

You know a lot of people don't talk about the history of the
post office when it comes down to blacks. This [the post office]
was a saving grace for the blacks, and most blacks in the
post office back in the early years in the forties and fifties and
early sixties, they were educated—master's degrees, some of
them had law degrees, and stuff like that.

—CLEVELAND MORGAN, New York
City letter carrier and 1970 rank-and-file postal wildcat
strike activist, New York Letter Carriers Branch 36,
National Association of Letter Carriers

In February 2003 I gave a lecture on black postal worker history to an audience
of about eighty mostly young, black undergraduates at North Carolina Central University in Durham. Few of them had seen or even heard of Robert
Townsend's 1987 film satire of Hollywood racial stereotypes called *Hollywood
Shuffle*. So they had no reference point for the funny line from the film that I
chose for the title of this book. Repeated several times during the film as a kind
of black folk adage (either as "There's work at the post office!" or "There's
always work at the post office!"), it was also popular among my black coworkers at the West Durham post office in North Carolina in the 1990s. But
when I asked how many of the students had relatives working for the post
office, the majority raised their hands, as if to confirm the film's aphorism and
serve as a reminder of the historical significance as well as continuity of postal
work in the black community.[1]

Why study the post office? Not only has it been vital to black community
development, but black postal worker activism changed the post office and its
unions. This is a dynamic history, one that involves narratives of migration,
militancy, community, and negotiation—and all at a workplace that African
Americans saw as being inclusively, not exclusively, theirs. It is a story that
crosses boundaries of labor, left (broadly defined as socially progressive activity), and civil rights history. While black postal worker history has been
mostly ignored in historical texts, there is an extensive oral tradition (for the
most part unrecorded) of blacks in the post office. It was not until I left the post

office in 2000 after twenty years of service (mostly as a letter carrier) and began to research this topic that I heard and read compelling and representative narratives about blacks in the post office such as the ones that follow.

Actor and human rights activist Danny Glover's parents were postal workers as well as activists in the historically black National Alliance of Postal and Federal Employees (NAPFE, the National Alliance, or simply "the Alliance"), in addition to being active in the National Association for the Advancement of Colored People (NAACP) branch in San Francisco.[2] Heman Marion Sweatt, the law school applicant who filed suit and whose name appears as the plaintiff in the U.S. Supreme Court's landmark 1950 decision *Sweatt v. Painter* that forced the University of Texas law school to integrate, was a letter carrier and member of both the National Alliance and the NAACP. (Sweatt's father was a founding member and lifelong activist in the National Alliance as well.) The stepfather of *Plessy v. Ferguson* plaintiff Homer Plessy was Victor Dupart, a postal clerk and Unification Movement activist in late nineteenth-century New Orleans.[3] The father of William Monroe Trotter—co-founder of the 1905 black civil rights group Niagara Movement—was James Trotter, a runaway slave who became a Union Army officer, musician, published author, and postal clerk in Boston from 1865 until 1882, when he resigned after a white man was promoted over him. The father of NAACP executive secretary Walter White was an Atlanta letter carrier.[4] Mortimer Weaver, the father of Robert C. Weaver—the first African American appointed to a Cabinet position—was a Chicago postal clerk.[5] Historian Barbara Jeanne Fields's godfather (who had been a roommate at Howard University with her father) was a postal worker in Washington, D.C.[6] Poet June Jordan's father—Panamanian-born Granville Jordan—worked as a postal clerk in New York City.[7] Filmmaker Spike Lee's grandfather, Jack Shelton, a Morehouse College graduate who was married to a Spelman College graduate and schoolteacher, took on a career in the Atlanta post office.[8] Historian John Hope Franklin, who later married Aurelia Whittington (whose father was a railway postal clerk and whose mother was a teacher), was born and reared in the Rentiesville, Oklahoma, post office that also served as the family home while his father, attorney Buck Colbert Franklin, the local postmaster, was trying to start a law practice.[9] Congressman Charles Rangel from New York and Coleman Young, the first African American mayor of Detroit, were both postal workers.[10] Tuskegee Airmen Hiram Little and Percy Sutton (the latter later elected Manhattan borough president) were postal workers.[11] Letter carriers in Montgomery, Alabama, employed their knowledge of mail routes to divide the city into grids and organize a massive carpool that contributed to the success of the famous bus boycott of 1955–56.[12] The noted Savannah, Georgia, civil rights leader Westley W. Law carried mail from 1949 into the 1990s, defiantly noting that "for about 30 years they have been trying to get rid of me."[13] Amzie Moore, the well-known local civil rights leader of the 1950s and 1960s, got a job in 1935 as a postal custodian in Cleveland, Mississippi, and kept it until his retirement in 1968 despite attempts to fire him for civil rights activism. Historian and sociologist Charles Payne has pointed out that in Moore's case, postal work was considered "a high status job for a Black man in the Delta," which also afforded him some amount of protection from official reprisal.[14] In the early 1960s comedian and civil rights activist Dick Gregory worked at the Chicago post office during the day while polishing his comedy act at night.[15] Richard Wright worked at the Chicago post office in the late 1920s into the early 1930s as he was trying to launch a career as an essayist and novelist. In fact, Wright's novel *Lawd Today*, posthumously published in 1963, was written between 1932 and 1937 and based on his experiences as a postal worker as well as his observations of what he called the broken dreams of his black coworkers: "They want to become doctors and lawyers, but few make the grade. So most of them practice the three A's—autos, alimony, and abortion," he concluded.[16] Harry Haywood, a leading organizer for the Communist Party of the United States of America (CPUSA), also worked for the Chicago post office after serving in World War I and was active in the black nationalist leftist Phalanx Forum study group.[17] James Ford, head of the Harlem section of the CPUSA in the 1930s and its 1932 candidate for vice president of the United States, had a historical connection to the post office, according to historian Mark Naison: "After graduating from college [Fisk University], Ford served in the Signal Corps in France during World War I, where he participated in protests against the jim-crowing of black troops. But his most disillusioning experience came when he returned to the United States to find that the only white-collar job he could get was a position in the Chicago Post Office. Ford joined the Chicago Postal Workers Union and through it the Communist Party." Hubert Harrison, the legendary West Indian socialist and black nationalist leader, worked for the post office in New York City from 1907 to 1911, and was a member of the National Federation of Post Office Clerks (NFPOC) Local 10, American Federation of Labor (AFL).[18]

Jazz percussionist/vocalist Vicki Randle (an "out" lesbian and the first woman to play with the Tonight Show band) recalls that her jazz pianist father, Norvell Randle, had a full-time postal job in the 1950s and 1960s when rock 'n' roll was pushing jazz musicians out of the nightclubs: "It was the jazz musician's motto in L.A.: There's always work at the post office." The Los Angeles post office was also where legendary jazz bassist Charles Mingus worked between 1949 and 1950 when he was in between bands and trying to pay bills. (He also worked at San Francisco post office in 1946–1947 and at the New York City post office in 1952.)[19] And finally, Freddie Gorman, singer-songwriter for the 1960s Detroit Motown singing group called The Originals, was a letter carrier who began his career with the post office in 1957, and is today best remembered for the 1961 hit song he wrote for the Marvellettes titled "Please Mr. Postman."[20]

These histories are not unique or coincidental but rather representative stories that locate black postal workers in an elevated black community status similar to that once occupied by mariners through the nineteenth century and Pullman porters in the twentieth.[21] There is a distinct historical connection between the black community and the post office, one that informs the creation and transformation of the modern post office and its labor force. "Though there are no accurate statistics," reported an article in the November 1949 issue of *Ebony* magazine, "it is generally conceded that Negroes [in the post office] have a higher educational level than white postal employees. As a result, the post office has often been called 'the graveyard of Negro talent.'" That gloomy metaphor notwithstanding, the *Ebony* article, like the examples previously cited, collectively point to the post office in fact as a place "risen" from the graveyard, so to speak—as both an avenue of black mobility and incubator of black struggle. Indeed, the same article went on to declare that black postal workers had also come to enjoy "community prestige" with this secure government job: "Today more than ever Negro talent is getting a chance to win a status in the post office never before attainable."[22] The popularly conceived middle-class status that postal work signified among blacks enabled not just individual advancement and capital accumulation, but the potential for labor and civic mobilization as well.[23] Black postal workers generally and Alliance members in particular were instrumental in the expansion of the working-class base of the NAACP during and after the Great Depression. Historian Adam Fairclough reveals not only external challenges to the NAACP from the Congress of Industrial Organizations (CIO) and the CPUSA during the 1930s, but internally as well, frequently by young black members with ties to the labor movement:

> In the South, postal workers like [civil rights activist] W. W. Kerr became key figures in orienting the NAACP more closely toward the labor movement. Black postal workers comprised, along with longshoremen and Pullman porters, the aristocracy of black labor. In the flattened class structure of black America, moreover, postal workers enjoyed a level of pay, prestige, and job security that places them in the middle class rather than the working class. They were, in fact, unique among black wage earners: federal civil service regulations protected them from arbitrary dismissal and gave them

some means of redress against discrimination. Post Office jobs were highly prized, and they attracted some of the best-educated blacks, including people who aspired to be teachers, journalists, and lawyers. By 1940, postal workers led many of the NAACP's largest Southern branches, including Norfolk, Mobile, and New Orleans.[24]

Combining oral histories with written narratives by union and management sources, this study of black postal workers takes stock of some of the most active labor and 1960s civil rights activists during World War II, the early Cold War years, and the 1960s civil rights movement. It constructs a holistic rather than fragmented view of black, left, and labor histories. It also rejects the AFL-CIO as the "default setting" for a study of unionism at the post office. After all, some of the most significant postal union activity occurred independently of that federation and its antecedents. (The same can also be said of left activism occurring outside the CPUSA.) And evidence in this study points to the overall importance of workplace activism by public workers—just now receiving attention in a field heretofore focused on factory workers.

It is surprising how little scholarship has been generated on black postal workers. The very useful history of the American Postal Workers Union (APWU) that was written by John Walsh and Garth Mangum, *Labor Struggle in the Post Office: From Selective Lobbying to Collective Bargaining*, subsumes the struggles for equality by black postal workers and their allies as part of the overall struggle for union recognition. One of their two pages devoted to black postal workers even contains this understatement: "The century-plus story of the black American battle for equal rights in the Postal Service could be the subject of a book in itself."[25] For its part, *Carriers in a Common Cause*, the well-written official history of the NALC by M. Brady Mikusko, devotes only two pages to black letter carriers. Blacks also receive spare attention from the handful of scholarly articles that deal with the 1970 nationwide postal wildcat strike. There is not a single history written of the largely black National Postal Mail Handlers Union (NPMHU). And the official history of the National Rural Letter Carriers Association (NRLCA) makes no mention of blacks in their union.[26] By contrast, National Alliance histories have been extensively chronicled, both by their resident historian Paul Tennassee as well as members themselves, including A. L. Glenn, *History of the National Alliance of Postal Employees 1913–1955*; O. Grady Gregory, *From the Bottom of the Barrel: A History of Black Workers in the Chicago Post Office from 1921*; and Henry W. McGee, *The Negro in the Chicago Post Office*.[27] And recently some fine internet scholarship has been posted by the USPS and the U.S. Postal Museum on their respective websites chronicling the African American experience at the post office.

In this book, I examine the ways black postal workers influenced the debates among postal labor unions: industrial vs. craft unionism, rank-and-file democracy vs. top-down power, and narrow economic vs. broader social justice demands—especially those for equality. In doing so I have tried to write a narrative where blacks are central, not peripheral to the history of the post office and its unions. As historian Vincent Harding puts it: "Black history moves out of the context of the experiences of black people in America and judges America on the basis of our experiences. That is the only way in which the society can be judged by black people. Even other people are now learning that the proper way to judge the nature of the American experience is by the way in which the most downtrodden of the society have been treated."[28]

This book also follows the lead of labor historians who combine union history with workers' social history. Michael Honey emphasizes both oral history as well as the visible activity of unions and their frequently extensive archival evidence. For their part, Leon Fink and Brian Greenberg caution against a union-centered approach: "An institutional study may generally overemphasize the minority of formally 'organized' workers and ignore the experience of the vast majority of people employed outside the realm of unionism. There is, as well, in union histories, the tendency by sympathetic scholars or in-house chroniclers to accept at face value the union's own assumptions about its past. Union hagiography thus regularly exaggerates organizational and contract 'victories' while it rarely penetrates the organization's inner tensions."[29]

THE HISTORICAL SIGNIFICANCE OF AFRICAN AMERICANS IN THE POST OFFICE AND ITS UNIONS

In the early morning hours of March 18, 1970, postal workers in New York City walked off the job and threw up picket lines, which in turn inspired postal workers all across the country to do the same. All told, for the next eight days over 200,000 postal workers stopped or slowed the mail in dozens of cities and towns, defying federal law and their own unions to conduct a "wildcat strike" (one not officially authorized by a union) against woefully inadequate pay and benefits, although deeper grievances also lay behind the action. President Richard M. Nixon called up U.S. Army and National Guard troops in New York City in an unsuccessful attempt to move the mail. Union officials finally convinced their members to return to work by assuring them that satisfactory agreements with the administration had been promised. The strikers' bold autonomous direct action, which enjoyed widespread public sympathy, resulted in Congress passing the Postal Reorganization Act in August 1970 that replaced the U.S. Post Office Department with the quasi-governmental corporation United States Postal Service (USPS), whose unions—by now also reorganized—had full collective bargaining rights (but still not the right to strike).[30]

How did a federal government labor force, divided for years by multiple (and generally conservative) craft unions with Jim Crow locals in the South, and historically deprived of the legal right to strike, suddenly stage and win the largest nationwide wildcat strike in U.S. labor history—one that has stunningly escaped scholarly scrutiny? Studying black postal worker insurgency in the mid- to late twentieth-century United States helps us answer that question. I argue that black postal worker agency, emerging historically from their leading position within the black community as well as within labor and human rights movements, was a crucial factor in the success of that strike.

The current interest in public sector unions by labor historians is long overdue, although those unions are still not in U.S. history textbooks. Overall, private sector workers "at the point of production" remain the standard for studies of the labor movement.[31] But looking at black postal workers' role in postal history leading up to the 1970 strike reveals the importance of public sector workers and their growing militancy in the late twentieth century. Labor historian Paul Johnston has this to say of public union organizing: "Public workers' movements are shaped by—and in turn shape—the distinctive context within and against which they operate: public organization. Consequently, their demands, their resources, and their historical roles differ in important ways from those of private sector labor movements. Public workers' movements are constrained to frame their demands as public policy. . . . Thus the public worker's movements that swept American cities in the 1960s and 1970s must be understood as part of the ongoing conflict over our urban agenda."[32]

This book argues that a leading role was played by black postal workers in the United States labor movement and black freedom movement, and that they were influential in shaping today's post office and postal labor force in this country. Black postal workers functioned as a kind of transmission belt or mediator between the black middle and working classes that actually put them in both classes in terms of community status and activism. Black postal workers also exercised a similar mediating role between civil rights, labor, and left movements. Their perspectives had much in common with the left-labor activism of the times, contrasting sharply with the dominant conservative, and American nationalist, white male craft orientation of the AFL. And many black postal worker activists often took militant stances in addressing social as well as economic concerns, both at the workplace and in society. Black postal workers' perspective—especially in the case of NAPFE—was unique in making the fight for equality primary.[33]

At the same time, not all black postal workers were militant, class-conscious, trade union and civil rights leaders. This book avoids romanticized generalizations that "blacks always played the leading role." But it also rejects the opposite tendency—that somehow common struggle over time inevitably produces interracial unity and black assimilation into white institutions. Blacks at the post office played a variety of roles over the years, from resistance to accommodation. One would expect to see that kind of diversity within any population group, especially given the fact that blacks had made the post office a "niche job" for so long. But the denial of equality in that same "niche job"—at the same time that whites were rewarded with caste privileges—in fact helped spark a greater tendency toward class consciousness, militancy, and equality among African Americans than whites, in addition to black nationalism.[34]

The historical availability of postal work to African Americans compared to the private sector also encouraged them to force changes in postal work life in addition to using postal jobs as launching pads for social mobility and activism. Henry W. McGee, longtime National Alliance and NAACP activist, postal labor scholar, and the first black postmaster of Chicago, put it this way: "Because of racial discrimination in the general work force, blacks could not get the usual jobs as office workers or what was generally known as white collar jobs. They were often barred from the skilled trades like plumbing, electrical and construction. As a result of this discrimination, the post office became a haven for blacks. The only other good paying jobs that blacks held were hotel waiters and Pullman porters."[35]

For years the post office had commonly been considered a "safe" job for blacks because of exclusion by both white capital and white labor in the private sector. Often college educated and active in the black freedom movement, black postal workers were uniquely situated in a government service where strikes were illegal, but white "hate strikes" were nonexistent; where multiple unions diffused worker unity, but also white supremacy; and where the absence of any collective bargaining agreements until 1962 also meant that predominantly white unions could not exercise exclusive control over workers as they did in private industry. Postal union papers and publications, civil rights organization correspondence, black newspapers, and oral histories reveal how black postal workers and their allies made the best of a white supremacist landscape. This was notwithstanding the post office's history of white-advantaged hiring through craft segregation, ignoring high-scoring black applicants through the "rule of three," and the job application photograph used until 1940. In fact, these racial screens were mitigated somewhat by the civil service entrance exam at which black applicants generally excelled. And black postal workers' challenge to white supremacy, anticommunism, and craft union conservatism over several decades helped pave the way for the postal strike of 1970.

In this book I have borrowed the term "civil rights unionism" used by historians Michael Honey and Robert Korstad to describe left antiracist union interventions against Jim Crow unionism by members of the CIO and the CPUSA in the mid-twentieth-century South. I argue that civil rights unionism—defined by Honey as "a unionism engaged simultaneously with striving for decent jobs and equal political and legal rights"—is actually part of an older and broader black protest tradition.[36] Few black postal workers or their allies were known to have been members of the CPUSA or the CIO. But black postal worker-activists and their formations were stronger and more consistent civil rights union role models than the CIO or the CPUSA. In the post office, civil rights unionism has been embodied in the National Alliance and the National Postal Union (NPU, 1959–1971), as well as the efforts of black postal workers and their allies in the AFL-CIO postal unions to break Jim Crow.

Key to African Americans' leading role in the struggle for jobs, justice, and equality at the post office was the fact that from the very beginning of their service after the Civil War, black postal workers had to fight their way into the post office and its unions. Once inside those larger institutions, black postal workers behaved both as a critical mass as well as an influential minority. Black postal workers were a highly educated workforce, and black veterans' military service tended to spur a growing political awareness and militancy within the post office. Despite often being relegated to second-class status in the post office and its unions, black postal workers enjoyed a social backing in the black community along with a social and fraternal network that included the National Alliance, black newspapers, the Prince Hall Masons, and civil rights organizations like the NAACP, the Congress of Racial Equality (CORE), and the National Urban League (NUL). They also had access to a nationwide network of unions with headquarters in Washington, D.C., in addition to a huge strategically situated unionized postal workforce in New York City. The black labor protest tradition found important allies among white left-labor sectors of postal unions—often college-educated white postal workers who came into the post office during the Great Depression with a left labor perspective.

The National Alliance was a marriage between the black labor protest tradition and the black civic tradition. The former tradition was working class–conscious, militant, and pro-equality. The latter combined black grassroots and black elite advocacy for black community concerns as well as universal democracy in a tradition that historically has constituted, in the words of sociologist Fredrick Harris, "a participatory norm that is similar to yet distinct from the participatory norm of mainstream civic life." The activity of black members of predominantly white postal unions, by contrast, was both militant and circumspect, but often drew inspiration from the activity of the Alliance to which many simultaneously belonged.[37] Black postal worker activists joined postal craft unions for pragmatic and political reasons. They joined the Alliance for civil rights and labor advocacy; and the NAACP and black civic organizations for civil rights advocacy and race pride. Their objective, like that of the black freedom movement as a whole, was support, security, and social change. Alliance president James B. Cobb put it this way in an August 1955 news release: "As we bring the light to America, born of our suffering inured patience, and give it the stamina, the result of our labor-induced endurance—they [our union's founders] would want it that way. They knew that America is the home of the brave—the home of the brave who would forever have it free."[38]

There is a need for the literature of the civil rights, labor, and left movements in the United States to better integrate the histories of those three movements. Popular arguments in the literature of those movements have tended to (1) construct the civil rights movement as one dominated by the black middle-class and less concerned with economic issues than it was with social status; (2) view white supremacy in the labor movement as primarily the result of worker manipulation by capitalist elites, thereby ignoring the autonomous exercise of white privileges by white workers; and (3) focus on the CIO, the CPUSA, and "interracial unionism" based on common economic grounds, while downplaying independent black radical activity that was usually but not always leftist. Yet there has also been a recent shift toward unifying the narratives—which ultimately owes a great debt to the work of W. E. B. Du Bois. The experience of black postal workers argues for a more nuanced and holistic approach to American social movement history than generally seen. The evidence indicates that white supremacy, not the Cold War, was the primary culprit that weakened the postwar black-left-labor alliance, contrary to what many historians have argued.[39]

This study examines black postal workers' agency as a way of looking at the development of the modern post office and the modern postal labor movement, focusing especially on the campaign for equality. World War II was a crucial era for that campaign, as a dramatic increase in black postal employment combined with organized civil rights activism. In the early 1940s postal jobs had become more factory-like, while more advancement opportunities outside the post office opened up for black professionals. There was a higher level of black postal worker militancy on the shop floor. Black women entering the postal labor force during this period helped fuse middle-class traditions with the new working-class militancy. In addition, black male postal worker—

headed households did not achieve middle-class economic and social status solely based on their position and income: that status was also enhanced by black women spouses who often worked as teachers or other professionals.[40]

On the other hand, white supremacy and anticommunism posed special problems to the success of progressive social movements generally during this period, especially the labor movement, and, for our purposes, the multi-union postal labor movement. "Jim Crow" and "McCarthyism," I argue, were not only distinct, repressive mechanisms of government or right-wing labor leadership. Nor were they some kind of virus that "killed" the nascent 1940s progressive black-left-labor coalition. They were also white reactionary social movements. The survivors of the black-left-labor coalition who advocated combining demands for economic justice, social equality, and worker autonomy found themselves in a minority in the organized labor movement. But their voices were not entirely muted. In fact, they played significant roles in the emerging civil rights and Black Power movements of the 1960s.

The black community-based fight against white supremacy in the post office and its unions embraced the more inclusive *industrial* (as opposed to the more narrow *craft*) approach. Leading black and white union activists did much to advance not only black postal workers and the postal labor movement in particular, but also both labor and civil rights movements in general. The roadblocks imposed by white management and white labor on black employment and advancement in the private sector made the post office and other federal work a kind of "migration magnet" for blacks from the rural and urban South as well as the Caribbean, all coming to the urban North, South, and West. This resulted in a mix of black nationalism, labor radicalism, uplift, and trade unionism operating within the post office and its unions.

In constructing a narrative of how blacks led the fight against white supremacy (and not merely "discrimination" or "segregation"), this book pays close attention to how the mechanisms and language of white supremacy were framed in the post office—from the first federal law in 1802 that banned black workers by restricting postal work to "free white persons," to the mid-twentieth-century postal unions that either tolerated Jim Crow locals or actually contained "Caucasian only" clauses in their constitutions. White supremacy was not something simply "imposed" by capitalist or government elites, but was often demanded by many white postal workers and their unions. The historical critique of white supremacy by black postal worker activists, however, is part of a long-standing black intellectual tradition that influences this study.[41] Black postal workers, like black workers generally, created an organized labor alternative. Through their activism they gave primacy to the fight for equality within the overall campaign for workplace justice in the United States.

Black initiative played a major role in the events and organizational choices leading up to the dramatic 1970 nationwide postal strike, out of which emerged the present-day USPS along with full collective bargaining rights for the major postal unions. It was no accident that the 1970 strike was strongest in major cities of the Northeast, Midwest, and Far West that had substantial traditions of black labor, black community, and left labor activism—including some postal union "women's auxiliaries" that engaged in political organizing.

On the surface it appears to have been no coincidence that the South, with its history of Jim Crow locals and anti-unionism, was the weakest link in that strike. In fact, strike activity in the South was minimal—owing in large part to other factors as well, such as loyalty to anti-strike national union leadership, fewer economic privations relative to other regions, and less militancy in their history. But significantly, black and white postal workers throughout the South debated and took strike votes. Furthermore, the historical southern black social activist tradition contributed in large part to the ultimate success in the struggle against white supremacy in the post office and its unions in all regions. The cross-regional experience of black postal workers highlights the problem of dichotomizing North and South in the black freedom movement as a conflict between, respectively, black nationalism versus nonviolent integrationism, or labor versus middle-class activism.[42] Black postal workers were instrumental in the struggle for equality and democracy in unions and workplaces by challenging white postal workers to break with conservative union leaders in a labor movement crippled by anticommunism and a white supremacist status quo.

On the surface, the 1970 Great Postal Wildcat Strike was just over wages. But economic demands alone have rarely proven sufficient to provide long-term unity for workers divided along lines of white privilege and black discrimination. Workers who fight to improve working conditions—including risking their jobs to engage in a wildcat strike—often act from a wide range of motives not always articulated. Strikes generally represent stronger stuff than simply the struggle to improve wages and benefits. And that is especially true of autonomous, risky actions like wildcat strikes.[43] Small acts of resistance on the shop floor and dissent expressed in postal union journals or at national conventions preceded the "big event" of the 1970 nationwide postal wildcat. The radical option of illegally striking came from a variety of sources that had historically campaigned for union democracy, equality, and full collective bargaining.

The activism of black postal workers nationally forms the backdrop of this study, although special emphasis is given to New York City and Washington, D.C. The experiences of both cities were unique and yet both also played a significant part of the 1960s social upheaval. New York City's strong protest traditions were based on a fusion of northern and southern U.S. combined with European and Caribbean cultures. Concentrating on New York City in this study is based in part on its strategic location as a major artery for commerce, finance, and postal business. But it is also home to the largest industrial postal union local in the world. New York City has a rich history of influential radical, black protest, and workers' movements, including unions in the public sector. The state of New York enacted a civil rights law in 1918 and was the first to ban employment discrimination in 1945. New York City later saw an increase in public employee organizing in the 1950s with the liberalizing of city labor laws.

But Jim Crow also lived in New York—in hotels, nightclubs, and even at the post office retail counter.[44] With Harlem popularly conceived as the black capital of the world in the 1920s during the heyday of the Universal Negro Improvement Association (UNIA), New York operated as a kind of migration magnet not just for the South but for the Caribbean as well. New York City has also helped set the tone for the rest of the country in labor and left political movements even as it was also absorbing the migration of people and ideas. It was home to the national office of the NAACP, a major UNIA chapter, and the National Negro Congress (NNC). A. Philip Randolph's Brotherhood of Sleeping Car Porters (BSCP)—another important black civil rights union—originated in New York City. There was a contradictory mix of both political borrowing and exclusion among black, white, labor, and radical groupings. And the 1970 nationwide postal strike that began in New York City was the product of years of agitation and conflict that galvanized postal workers throughout the rest of the country.[45]

I also focus on Washington, D.C., as a border (or "transitional" southern) city, as well as a nationally contested site over democracy and equality based in large part on its "southern-ness": its history as a center of the antebellum slave trade from its 1800 creation until 1850; the practice of enslaving blacks in that city until the Civil War; its disfranchisement of "free blacks" after President Thomas Jefferson's 1802 order; and Jim Crow from Reconstruction to the 1960s. Washington, D.C., also hosts a large black community with a historically activist intellectual center in Howard University—widely regarded as one of America's premier historically black colleges and universities.[46] For years the nation's capital hosted the largest, most prominent NAACP branch and the national headquarters of the post office and its unions; in addition, as a movement site it has local significance and national symbolism.[47]

CHAPTER I CHRONICLES THE historical background of black postal workers from the Civil War to 1940, as black military service veterans began fighting to create a tradition of federal government employment for blacks, established their own postal union (National Alliance), and found footholds within predominantly white postal unions. Chapter 2 examines the upsurge of black postal worker activism against white supremacy in the post office and its unions during the World War II era. That activism employed lobbying, petitioning, and collective action to cause the collapse of discriminatory entrance devices like the civil service application photograph, and challenged segregated postal union locals as well as the old guard conservative leadership of the National Alliance.

Chapter 3 looks at how black postal worker activists confronted white supremacist repression in its newest anticommunist incarnation in the post office and the predominantly white postal unions. Chapter 4 focuses on the "McCarthy era" of the early Cold War that saw official repression of left, labor, and civil rights groups. The chapter examines divisions within the left, labor, and black freedom movements over issues of anticommunism, white supremacy, and democracy, and looks at why black antiracist postal labor activists were especially vulnerable to government harassment and job termination.

Chapter 5 examines how challenges by left-leaning black and white militants to Jim Crow union locals, discrimination at the post office, and the repressive loyalty oath in the era of the *Brown* decisions and AFL-CIO merger led to significant events like the 1958 NPDOC convention walkout by progressives over issues of democracy and integration. Chapter 6 looks at how in the 1960s black people and their allies both inside and outside the post office and its unions finally caused Jim Crow union locals to collapse, as they challenged all forms of white preference in postal work life.

Chapter 7 examines black women's transformative effects on the post office and its unions in the mid-1960s as a result of lobbying, direct action, executive orders, and congressional legislation. Chapter 8 looks at how "civil rights unionism" in the Alliance and NPU made equality and democracy important agenda items at a time when postal workers were also becoming more frustrated over low pay and poor working conditions. Yet what drew those two union allies together also made them competitors for black members.

Chapter 9 studies the influx into the post office of young people, women, veterans, and especially African Americans in the late 1960s, the growing tensions over poor pay and working conditions, and emerging tensions between not only postal management and labor but also between the leadership and rank and file of postal labor unions. Chapter 10 discusses how African Americans played a leading role in the 1970 nationwide postal wildcat strike that also saw rank-and-file disaffection from leadership of both predominantly white and historically black postal unions.

Chapter 11 and the Epilogue examine the aftermath of the strike as a mixed victory. Rank-and-file striker militancy did more than win pay demands and challenge bureaucratic unionism. It also helped accelerate the process by which the U.S. Post Office was transformed into the USPS quasi-government corporation that many in Congress had previously promoted against postal union preferences. The unions reluctantly supported the USPS's creation in exchange for full collective bargaining rights that excluded the National Alliance. The struggle for equality within the bargaining units was now led by black postal workers in other unions, although the Alliance is still a key part of the struggle against discrimination at the post office, especially through its handling of Equal Employment Opportunity (EEO) cases. The Conclusion argues that black involvement was key not only to the success of the 1970 postal wildcat strike, but also to reform in the post office and its unions going back many decades. That reform was largely a product of the interaction of black-led rank-and-file militancy and civil rights unionism.

CHAPTER ONE

WHO WORKED AT
THE POST OFFICE
(BEFORE 1940)?

William Harvey Carney ran away from slavery in Norfolk, Virginia, while still a teenager. Using the Underground Railroad in the early 1850s, he made his way to New Bedford, Massachusetts, less than twenty years after the famous black abolitionist Frederick Douglass arrived there in 1838 following his own escape from captivity in Maryland. (Carney's father had also escaped, then bought his family's freedom and moved them to New Bedford.) William Carney found work on the New Bedford docks where Douglass had earlier been denied work by white ship caulkers who threatened to strike if he was allowed to work. Both men had taught themselves to read while in slavery, and Carney was preparing himself for the ministry when the Civil War broke out in 1861. Blacks in Massachusetts began lining up to volunteer but were prevented from enlisting until after President Abraham Lincoln's Emancipation Proclamation of January 1, 1863, which he was compelled to issue, in part, due to battlefield losses, white soldiers' desertions, and pressure from abolitionists like Douglass. (Douglass in fact helped organize the Union Army's famous 54th Massachusetts Infantry Regiment, with its all-black soldiers commanded by white officers.) There is evidence that Carney knew both Douglass and Douglass's son Lewis. Carney and the younger Douglass both volunteered for the 54th, and Carney was the standard bearer for the regiment. Carney survived the disastrous assault on Ft. Wagner, South Carolina, with an injury, but managed to retrieve the U.S. flag dropped by the first standard bearer shot during combat. For this action Carney became the first African American to be awarded the Congressional Medal of Honor for heroism in the Civil War—although not until 1900.

In 1869 Carney was still walking with a limp from his war wounds as he embarked on a career carrying mail for the U.S. Post Office in New Bedford (just a few months after James B. Christian was hired in Richmond, Virginia, making him the first known black letter carrier).[1] Carney carried mail for thirty-two years. His name appears as founding vice president on the original

William H. Carney delivering mail in 1890 on his route in New Bedford,
Massachusetts. A letter carrier for thirty-two years, Carney was also vice
president of the New Bedford NALC Branch 18. During the Civil War, he was a
sergeant and flag-bearer with the Union Army's 54th Massachusetts Regiment,
later becoming the first African American to receive the Congressional Medal
of Honor. Note his Union Army greatcoat worn over his postal uniform.
Courtesy of the Carl Cruz Collection, New Bedford Historical Society, Inc.

March 20, 1890, charter of New Bedford Branch 18 of the National Association of Letter Carriers (NALC), founded in 1889 at the Milwaukee annual meeting of Union Army veterans known as the Grand Army of the Republic.[2]

But there was not always work at the post office for African Americans like Carney and Christian. Opportunities for free waged labor for blacks at the post office only began officially in early 1865 as the Civil War was ending, with the Union military forces crushing the white supremacist slaveholding Confederacy.[3] Black postal worker activism began at that time among Union Army veterans, former slaves, abolitionists, and free blacks from before the war, as blacks began working as "generation one" letter carriers, clerks, and postmasters. They were supported in those efforts by some white postal workers and government officials. But they also met much resistance from many others determined to keep the post office and its unions segregated. For the next eighty years, black postal workers—as individuals, in civic groups and unions, or within the predominantly white postal unions—led the fight for equality, combining civil rights unionism and grassroots militancy that would transform the post office and its unions.[4]

WHEN POSTAL WORK WAS WHITE ONLY

The post office "was the largest public enterprise in antebellum America," notes economist Kelly Barton Olds.[5] Olds's study does not discuss black employment or black discrimination. But it does reveal the post office's function as a patronage magnet: "By mid-century it employed 20,000 individuals. . . . In 1831, three-fourths of all civilian federal employees worked for the Post Office. By the time of the Civil War, this fraction had risen to almost five-sixths. Almost all of these employees were deputy postmasters or clerks."[6] And they were white without exception. In *North of Slavery: The Negro in the Free States, 1790–1860* Leon Litwack mentions some of the earliest references I have found to black postal workers, tracing obstacles to black employment in the post office to before the Civil War.[7] Litwack notes that before 1865 blacks were legally barred from working at the post office, although after 1828 enslaved blacks were occasionally allowed to handle mail under white supervision.[8]

What was the objection of whites to blacks working in the post office? It was born of the same fear that compelled the white slaveholding South to censor the mails and intercept antislavery tracts: concern for the security of the slaveholding states.[9] Postmaster General Gideon Granger's 1802 letter to a Senate committee chairman summed up white fears of blacks working for the post office, as Litwack summarized: "Negroes constituted a peril to the nation's security, for employment in the postal service afforded them an opportunity to co-ordinate insurrectionary activities, mix with other people, and acquire subversive information and ideas. Indeed, in time they might even learn 'that a man's rights do not depend on his color' and transmit such ideas to their brethren."[10] Granger's anxiety was provoked by the successful rebellion of enslaved Africans in the French Caribbean colony of Saint-Domingue, which would become the free black republic of Haiti in 1804. Congress obliged Postmaster Granger by including in its 1802 law governing "Public law and Post-Roads" a section that proclaimed that "*no other than a free white person* shall be employed in *carrying* the mail of the United States," making whites who violated that law subject to a fifty dollar fine.[11] The subsequent 1810 post office law borrowed that section from the 1802 law practically verbatim.[12] At that point, according to Litwack, Congress was excluding blacks from carrying the mail within a context of legislation restricting the rights of free blacks overall, but also within what he describes as a "sometimes conflicting and even chaotic federal approach."[13] Fifteen years later Congress shortened yet also broadened the provision to declare that "*no other than a free white person* shall be employed in *conveying* the mail," while at the same time reducing the fine for white violators to twenty dollars.[14]

In 1828 Postmaster General John McLean allowed that black labor might be permitted to move mailbags from stagecoaches into post offices under white supervision.[15] That same year also saw the election of Andrew Jackson as president and, with his administration, the inauguration of the spoils system in federal government service. In essence this was a form of "white affirmative action," rewarding those who had helped in the preceding election to bring the Democratic Party to power, despite the effects on morale and performance when political affiliation of any kind superseded professional competence. Similar to the spoils system, both the 1810 and 1825 federal postal laws were constructed as restricting postal work to "free white persons only." Their wording implied black exclusion in creating an exclusively white occupation, with whiteness serving as the basis for government service. It is significant that this was one of the first labor laws of the United States (if not the very first) and that it represented a fearful white elite reaction to the successful Haitian Revolution.[16]

ABOLITIONISTS IN AND OUT OF UNIFORM

"Once let the black man get upon his person the brass letters U.S.; let him get an eagle on his button, and a musket on his shoulder, and bullets in his pocket," predicted black abolitionist leader Frederick Douglass in 1863, "and there is no power on the earth or under the earth which can deny that he has earned the right of citizenship in the United States."[17] There was a symbolic confluence of black men finally being allowed to bear arms for the Union Army in 1863 following President Lincoln's Emancipation Proclamation and the beginning of free city mail delivery throughout the United States. The end of the war saw many blacks, including Union Army veterans, begin to work at the post office. The Union Army uniform—like that of letter carriers—signified citizenship, manhood, and personhood in a country that had only a few years before denied that blacks had any "rights which the white man is bound to respect," in the words of the infamous 1857 Supreme Court *Dred Scott* decision.[18]

"Black men and women were routinely rejected for federal employment until 1861," writes historian Jacqueline Jones, "when Boston's William Cooper Nell received an appointment as a clerk with the United States Postal Service."[19] Cooper's date of hire is actually listed in official post office records as 1863. But this still makes him the first known black postal worker appointed in the United States. (Individual post office records for this period do not indicate race or gender, forcing historians to use other means, such as newspapers and letters.)[20] According to historian Dorothy Porter Wesley, Nell was an abolitionist whose activism led to his being appointed the first black postal clerk and government employee by white abolitionist Boston Postmaster John Gorham Palfrey, who in doing so defied federal Jim Crow postal law—with apparently no repercussions. Just a year before that appointment, Nell had been living in New York City helping to organize the fight against that state's anti-black suffrage property qualification.[21] While I have not found evidence of abolitionists targeting the exclusionary 1810 and 1825 post office employment laws, there is an indication of at least the beginnings of such a campaign the year following Nell's appointment. In early 1862, Massachusetts senator Charles Sumner, an abolitionist and Republican, proposed legislation to allow blacks to carry the mail in Washington, D.C., only to see Representative Schuyler Colfax (R-Ind.) tie it up in committee, claiming there were no petitions or popular outcries for blacks to be admitted to the post office. (Later that spring, Nell would write to Sumner protesting post office prejudice.)[22]

John W. Curry, probably in the fall of 1868, became the first known black postal worker appointed in Washington, D.C.—just three years after the white citizens of that city had voted 6,951 to 35 against black suffrage in a referendum.[23] Only six years before, Washington had seen slavery banned by an act of Congress, with compensation being offered to slaveholders of up to $300 for each slave.[24] Curry, like Nell, was a political activist for black public education, and joined the new D.C. Branch 142 (chartered in 1895) of the NALC—the first of today's postal unions. Curry worked as a clerk, messenger, and sexton

John W. Curry, first known black postal worker hired in Washington, D.C., ca. 1870. Official records suggest he was first appointed in 1868 as a clerk, and then worked as a letter carrier from 1870 until his death in 1899. He was probably a charter member of NALC Branch 142, founded in 1895. Courtesy of *Postal Record*, National Association of Letter Carriers, AFL-CIO.

before spending most of his career as a letter carrier from 1870 until his death in 1899. Along with other newly appointed black postal workers, he owed his employment to a bill authored by Senator Sumner that passed on December 19, 1864, and was signed into law the same day as the one establishing the Freedmen's Bureau, providing land and relief to former slaves—March 3, 1865—and forty years to the day of the last federal law restricting mail delivery to whites. The new law stated emphatically that "no person, by reason of color, shall be disqualified from employment in carrying the mails, and all acts and parts of acts establishing such disqualification, *including especially the seventh section of the act of March 3, eighteen hundred and twenty-five*, are hereby repealed."[25]

Many blacks and abolitionists joined the Union Army during the Civil War. Given the substantial rates of Union Army veteran entry into the post office generally, at least some of the first black postal workers were Union Army veterans, probably many of them postmasters.[26] William Carney, along with William H. Dupree and James Trotter, were three prominent examples of early black Civil War veterans becoming postal employees. Dupree served with the 55th Massachusetts Infantry Regiment during the war, and afterward became manager of Station A in Boston's South End.[27] Trotter was a runaway slave from Mississippi who joined the black 55th Massachusetts Infantry regiment, and was one of its few black commissioned officers. In 1865, according to historian Stephen R. Fox, Trotter returned to Boston where he and other black war veterans received clerk appointments in the Boston post office.[28]

The experience of these and other early black postal workers suggests an absence of any substantial white postal worker resistance to black entry into the post office after the Civil War, compared to blacks' experience in the private sector. In fact, white letter carriers in Newark, New Jersey (doubtlessly including members of another original NALC branch, Branch 38), in 1893 refused an invitation to ride in a local bicycle rally because their black co-worker, Louis A. Sears, was denied entry despite having pioneered bicycle mail delivery in that city.[29]

William Carney was also just one among a growing number of black NALC officials. Scipio A. Jordan was the Arkansas state vice president, and the Little Rock Branch 35 corresponding secretary was Howard H. Gilkey. In Memphis, Tennessee, David W. Washington, probably the first black letter carrier in that city, was the first president of Branch 27, formed in 1889. Washington, described as a "substantial" citizen by the famous newspaper publisher and civil rights activist Ida B. Wells, also served as Sergeant-at-Arms at the NALC's first annual convention in Boston in 1890, where he represented Branch 27. Thomas H. Moss, Branch 27's recording secretary, was also a businessman who owned People's Grocery. A good friend of Ida B. Wells, Moss and two of his employees were lynched in 1892 by a white mob incited by a white business competitor. No mention of this crime, however, was made in the NALC's monthly journal, the *Postal Record*, that in the meantime had begun running a "humor column" that evoked the popular white supremacist blackface minstrel stage: fake reports to Postmaster General John Wanamaker by "Peter Dobson, colored, the erudite and distinguished postmaster of Coon City, Mississippi," and titled "Affairs at Coon City." Invoking white prejudices and anxieties of black upward mobility, the reports employed familiar white tropes of imagined black middle-class pretensions, undermining progressive steps the NALC was taking in recruiting blacks.[30]

Blacks also began serving as postmasters after the Civil War, many having been Republican activists rewarded by elected Republican candidates. James W. Mason was the first such appointment in Sunny Side, Arkansas, in 1867, one of 123 known black postmasters from Reconstruction to 1900, out of almost 500 known blacks in the post office and in 1,400 political offices overall in the South.[31] Anne Dumas of Covington, Louisiana, in 1872 became the first black female postmaster—one of twelve in the 1800s. And the first known black female postal worker was Eliza Ridgely, a laborer in Washington.[32]

Most blacks still lived in the South at the end of the nineteenth century.

With 71 percent of all postal jobs in 1884 belonging to postmasters, black postmasters in southern communities especially threatened the institution of white supremacy.[33] Violence often resulted, as Leon Litwack points out: "Not surprisingly, then, when blacks vied for or managed to secure federal appointments in the post office, whites responded instantly and angrily. . . . The black postmaster, like any black official, was out of his or her place, symbolizing political ambition and assertiveness that could only raise the specter of social equality and mongrelization."[34]

Media accounts confirm black appointments and white hostility from the 1860s through the turn of the century. The *New York Times*, for example, reported that Charles Miller was appointed postmaster of Columbia, South Carolina, in 1869, which local whites found "offensive." The *Times* in 1897 reported an assassination attempt on the life of Postmaster Isaiah Loftin in Hogansville, Georgia, and the murder of Postmaster Baker in Lake City, South Carolina.[35] The *Washington Post*, meanwhile, reported black postmaster appointments in Laverne, Alabama, in 1889 in the first year of President Benjamin Harrison's administration (1889–1893), which also appointed black postmasters in eight South Carolina cities (Charleston, Columbus, Florence, Marion, Bennettsville, Georgetown, Edgefield, and Beaufort), along with Tallahassee, Florida, and Natchez and Vicksburg, Mississippi. In the latter, black Postmaster James Hill reportedly was reluctant to assume his office for fear of attempts on his life.[36]

Similar white resentment and violence drove Postmaster Minnie Cox from her job—her life threatened by whites in Indianola, Mississippi, in 1902. Cox has since appeared as a hero in several black history texts. Rev. David Matthews of Indianola told an oral history interviewer in 1995 that blacks "were admirers of Minnie Cox and what she accomplished" in her ability to perform her official duties despite white harassment. As Matthews put it, the black community was proud of Minnie and her husband Wayne Cox, a banker and railway postal employee who, with Minnie, established the Penny Savings Bank in Indianola. Both were college graduates, "wise people" who bought and retained land in the face of Jim Crow restrictions.[37] Minnie Cox's appointment in 1891 during the Harrison administration made her one of the earliest black female postmasters. She left her office in 1902 after white mob violence was threatened against her by Governor James K. Vardaman and others, but President Theodore Roosevelt refused to accept her resignation and suspended Indianola's mail service until 1904.[38]

Minnie Cox was no isolated case, though, as Leon Litwack points out. The same whites who saw Cox's job status as a "menace to white civilization" also

Minnie Cox (pictured ca. 1900) was appointed postmaster of Indianola, Mississippi, in 1891 but resigned in 1902 after local white residents petitioned to have her removed. Some even threatened her life. In 2009 Congress named the post office in Indianola after her. Courtesy of Wellington Cox Howard.

Wayne Wellington Cox (pictured ca. 1900), husband of Minnie Cox, was a railway postal clerk, educator, businessman, banker, and farmer in Indianola, Mississippi.
Courtesy of Wellington Cox Howard.

forced African American letter carrier John Harris from his job carrying mail in rural Georgia. (He claimed with pride to have been the first to do so in that state.) Harris recalled that the congressman who got him fired told him that "he thought a white man should have the job." Black postal employees who survived purges, threats, and violence became tenacious symbols after the Republican Party's political power was crushed in the South after Reconstruction, although their survival also made them lightning rods for yet more white threats. Whites desired Harris's job, where the salary had been raised from a menial job category paying only $30 a month to $75 a month. They wanted him and other blacks restricted to the lowest occupations.[39] Yet the post office in the post-Reconstruction South became a contested site: black postmaster appointments actually rose during that period. And black postal employment later survived the purges of the first two decades of the twentieth century, especially in the South.[40]

Looking back on the 1920s, historian Anne Firor Scott recalls growing up in Athens, Georgia, and thinking then that "all mailmen were black" because those were the only letter carriers she remembers seeing. Her childhood memories are instructive. According to A. L. Glenn's work on the historically black National Alliance of Postal Employees (NAPE), Athens by the 1920s had already seen two black postmasters appointed by President Ulysses S. Grant for two terms, another by President William McKinley for four years, and like many Georgia post offices of any size, Athens for years employed blacks as both clerks and carriers. In 1921 blacks made up the majority of the NALC Gate City Branch 172 in nearby Atlanta.[41]

Postal-related upward mobility was also a black family affair. Hartford Boykin, born in 1922 in Wilmington, North Carolina, told an interviewer in 1993 how his father had been a railway mail clerk and letter carrier there before moving to the ministry. Hartford himself carried mail from 1947 to 1970, married a teacher, and later served as an administrative law judge involved in black civic and social clubs like the Masons and Elks. He described growing up in his integrated middle-class neighborhood: "My father made a decent living . . . above and away from my people. . . . In my area you had professional people . . . mostly teachers, letter carriers . . . pullman porters."[42] But Republicans were less than reliable allies for blacks in the South. Abe Whitess, a former slave from Bay Minette, Alabama, told a Works Progress Administration interviewer in the late 1930s how after emancipation, he became "chairman of the Republican party in Baldwin County here, but when the [white] Republicans got in they made the white gem'mun [gentleman] what took my job [as] postmaster. . . . I votes for Mr. [Franklin D.] Roosevelt [Democratic president, 1933–1945] now."[43] Similar to strategies pursued by blacks during slavery, blacks after the Civil War employed a multi-pronged strategy that exploited whatever openings they could find among whites, whether they were abolitionists, government officials, private elites, or fellow union members.

AFRICAN AMERICANS, THE FEDERAL GOVERNMENT, AND THE WHITE UNIONS

The first letter carrier associations had begun in New York City in 1863—the same year that free city mail delivery began in the United States. The Railway Post Office (RPO) began a year later. The RPO was part of a significant development not just for government service, as postal scholar Vern Baxter has noted, but also as a vehicle for the growth of advertising and publishing as publicly subsidized private industries.[44] The Civil War and Reconstruction heralded both black employment in the post office as well as the birth of the modern postal service and its unions. Postal unions emerged by the turn of the century. For years they would operate in a milieu that was contentious, chaotic, and contradictory: lobbying public officials while also battling them over working conditions and wages in addition to challenging other postal unions for representation rights. White management and white labor, however, often found common cause in treating black postal workers as a "problem." Should they be hired? If so, in which job categories should they be allowed to work? And should they be able to join white unions, restricted to Jim Crow locals, or the all-black National Alliance?[45]

The first blacks to be appointed to various postal crafts and supervisory positions represented not just individual breakthroughs but also collective black defiance of the previous "white-only" postal employment law, in a long, uneven, though very familiar struggle.[46] W. E. B. Du Bois's characterization of Reconstruction as "a splendid failure" perfectly captured how quickly social change can be won and then crushed, especially during that particular revolutionary historical period. It was remarkable that African Americans found work at the post office, and that some became members of integrated union branches.[47]

Union Army service was embedded in the formation of the very first national postal union where blacks were included as members and officers. The NALC grew out of the 1889 Milwaukee encampment of the Grand Army of the Republic—the national fraternal organization of Union Army veterans. A leading role in the NALC's formation was also played by postal unionists in New York City who had previously tried to bring the NALC into the Knights of Labor when the latter was in decline. For their part, postal clerks in New York

City established the first citywide postal clerks union in 1888, which in 1890 became the National Association of Post Office Clerks (NAPOC). Two notable black charter members were Augustus "Gus" Richmond, secretary of the Little Rock local, and Henry F. Thompson, "1st Vice-President" of the Detroit, Michigan, local.[48]

Postal workers nationwide, especially African Americans, found the passage of the 1883 Civil Service Act (also known as the Pendleton Act) establishing the Civil Service Commission (CSC) mostly good but with some drawbacks. The previous spoils systems of party patronage established in 1829 by President Andrew Jackson had resulted in frequent turnover and thus diminished quality in postal service. Appointments to postal crafts were replaced in 1883 with merit examinations, and black college graduates in particular seized the opportunity. Uneven availability of race-based statistics indicates some progress —but with certain caveats. Historian Paul P. Van Riper found that black federal employment overall rose from .57 percent to 5.86 percent between 1881 and 1910, although figures based on postal historian Jennifer Lynch's research indicate that new appointments of known black clerks and carriers dropped dramatically from 1890 to 1900, but rose for politically appointed black postmasters.[49] Congress was also not showing as much interest in postal workers as career rather than as political appointees.[50]

Black applicants faced an additional dilemma. If they scored high on the civil service examination, they still faced rejection by the "rule of three" that allowed personnel officers to pick one of three applicants from each batch of applications for a postal position (or any other civil service position).[51] In practice, then, the "merit" examination was not color-blind despite representing an improvement over patronage. Ironically, blacks were still winning postal appointments even as they were losing voting rights. Louis J. Harper, a National Alliance founder from Atlanta (and the son of a railway postal clerk), recalled entering the service in 1889 and serving under ten presidents beginning with President Benjamin Harrison: "When President Grover Cleveland, near the end of his first term, by Executive Order placed the R.M.S. [Railway Mail Service] under Civil Service, the republicans allowed the order to remain, but held up its execution some 6 months. During this time a democrat would be removed and a republican given his place."[52] His words reinforce the observations by historian Rayford W. Logan concerning Republican Party Reconstruction survivals in the South, and point to blacks' continued use of the old political patronage system as an alternative path to federal employment that still favored whites.[53]

When Woodrow Wilson, a southern Democrat, became president (1913–1921), he surrounded himself with other arch-segregationists like *Raleigh News and Observer* publisher Josephus Daniels (whom Wilson appointed Secretary of the Navy), Secretary of the Treasury William McAdoo, and Postmaster General Albert S. Burleson of Texas. On April 11, 1913, with no objection from Wilson during a secret Cabinet meeting, Burleson ordered the separation of blacks from whites in the Washington, D.C., post office, as did McAdoo in the Treasury Department. The newly formed NAACP led a petition drive protesting Wilson's segregation policies and joined with other African American activists in calling for meetings with the president in 1913 and 1914. In November 1913 they presented Wilson with a petition bearing 20,000 signatures protesting segregation. The following year Wilson was again confronted at a White House meeting by an angry delegation of African American activists led by 1905 Niagara Movement co-founder William Monroe Trotter. Wilson replied that separating black and white federal employees was "for their own benefit," and abruptly ended the meeting after Trotter retorted that white prejudice, not "friction," was responsible for the new Jim Crow regime.[54]

The new federalized Jim Crow system of the Wilson administration represented an extension of policies begun under the previous administration of President Taft, who dared not risk appointing any black postmaster who might be opposed by white southern elites. White southern congressmen had unsuccessfully tried to pass legislation segregating the civil service both in 1913 and 1914, thus making the executive branch the hero of the segregation movement. But almost forgotten in this whole shameful episode was a grassroots campaign by white federal workers to segregate their workplace.

Calling themselves the National Democratic Fair Play Association, they held mass meetings and circulated petitions and letters warning of "UnDemocratic, UnAmerican, and UnChristian" conditions where whites would be forced to work with "greasy, ill-smelling" blacks. Their first barrage of letters (including one sent to Wilson himself) began four days *before* the 1913 cabinet meeting, where Burleson first announced he was segregating the post office. In 1914, as if answering their pleas, the Civil Service Commission (with Wilson's support) required that photographs accompany civil service job applications, the declared purpose being to prevent "impersonation." In fact they were used to screen out black applicants. No postal union other than the National Alliance protested.[55]

Yet despite Wilson's efforts to purge blacks nationwide from the post office, blacks in Chicago—numbering over 500 by 1910—enjoyed a certain amount of political protection by a local congressman as well as elevated black community social status. Black postal workers in Chicago collectively organized the black civic group Phalanx Forum in 1910. It grew out of the Appomattox Club, the name of which evoked the courthouse in Virginia where Confederate general Robert E. Lee surrendered to Union general Ulysses S. Grant on April 9, 1865. But the Appomattox Club was soon eclipsed by the National Alliance, formed the same year that Wilson lowered the Jim Crow curtain in government service.[56]

THE NATIONAL ALLIANCE: BIRTH OF A
PREDOMINANTLY BLACK INDUSTRIAL POSTAL UNION

Blacks found work at the post office in most of its job classifications: clerks, carriers, special delivery messengers, laborers, custodians, and motor vehicle mechanics. But it was blacks' exclusion from their most highly populated postal occupation—the railway mail service clerk—that inspired the formation of their own union.[57] There exists no better depiction of what railway mail work was like than its portrayal in Richard Wright's novel *Lawd Today*. Posthumously published in 1963, three years after the black novelist's death, it was based on his work as a clerk in the Chicago post office in the late 1920s and early 1930s. The dilemma faced by the novel's protagonist, Jake Jackson, should be recognizable to any postal clerk who has worked in manual mail sorting:

> His attention centered on his scheme rack, a little honeycomblike wooden case before which were piled hundreds of tiny white cards. *Lawd, I ain't fooled with that scheme in almost a month now. And I got to go up and pass a test on it in about two weeks.* Merely to think of it made his head feel heavy. He had to learn that scheme, learn where each card went, and when it went where it went, and on what train. *Let's see now. Six o'clock sweat. Chicago and Evans. 15. Number 2. Except on Sundays. . . .* He frowned. . . . *Where do that Danville and Carbondale go?* He could not remember. And he had nine hundred little white cards like that to commit to memory.[58]

What made such tasks especially challenging to black railway clerks, according to former Chicago postmaster and postal labor historian Henry W. McGee, was the tendency by postal management to assign blacks to the hardest and least desirable runs. Yet the railway clerk—already vanishing as a craft by World War II and practically extinct by the 1960s—was considered at one time an elite job in the post office. This was not just because of the skill required to sort mail based on memory of complicated schemes, as they were called, as well as to throw and catch mail bags as the trains rushed through the stations. It also had to do with mobility they enjoyed, as with Pullman porters. Along with the handling of official government dispatches, the job itself gave black clerks a kind of federal imprimatur. But that job was also a battleground as white clerks took the best runs and excluded blacks from their union.[59]

Using a catcher arm, a Railway Mail Service clerk grabs a mailbag from a mail crane as his train passes by in 1913. Whites forced many blacks out of jobs as railway mail clerks when steel railroad mail cars like the one pictured here began replacing the more dangerous wooden ones. In 1912 whites voted to segregate the union of railway mail clerks, the Railway Mail Association. This led to the 1913 founding of the predominantly black National Alliance of Postal Employees. © 1913 U.S. Postal Service. Used with permission.

For these black postal workers in particular, black pride and white prejudice were both "part of the job." In 1912 the Railway Mail Association (RMA) excluded blacks, and whites now began driving many blacks from railway mail jobs as working conditions improved—a common pattern in American work life.[60] Historian Paul Tennassee notes that the opportunity for blacks to "escape from the option of the neo-slave, agricultural fields" also meant dangerous working conditions aboard wooden railway cars. Yet white workers squeezed blacks out of railway clerk jobs as soon as the new, safer steel railroad cars replaced the old and dangerous wooden ones in 1913. This in turn led black railway mail clerks to form their own union—the National Alliance.[61]

The National Alliance was founded as a nonexclusive black railway postal employees' union in 1913 after the RMA excluded blacks in its 1912 constitution.

In 1923 the Alliance extended an invitation to postal employees of *all* crafts.[62] Even with elements of black middle-class uplift mixed into this brand of industrial unionism, the Alliance was more pro-working class than any white union —which is to say, it stood for the interests of the entire working class. The story of the Alliance epitomizes black resistance to white supremacist postal management and unions in the first part of the twentieth century. That early resistance set the stage for increased activism by black postal workers with the coming of World War II.

The origins of the Alliance were in the turn of the century "Progressive era"—typically associated with the growth of white middle-class reform organizations but also radical labor organizing. That era also saw heated debates over custom, law, and identity over race and immigration: who was "white," and who was "American"? The Ku Klux Klan, whose original heyday was 1866 to 1871, was reborn in 1915. But there was also a rise of black middle-class activist reform organizations like the NAACP, the NUL, black college student fraternities and sororities, historically black colleges, as well as black nationalist organizations like the UNIA.[63]

The National Alliance borrowed from black middle-class reformism, black nationalism, as well as left industrial union organizing. The Alliance's first members and officials tended to have more education than the typical postal worker of that time, just as black postal workers tended to have a higher educational background than whites generally. Unlike other postal unions they made their primary task the fight against white supremacy in the post office and its unions. The Alliance's first constitution in 1913 proclaimed: "Any regular employee or certified substitute of the Railway Mail Service, who shall conform to the requirements of the charter and the ritual and obey the laws of the Alliance, may become a member."[64] The Alliance's "ritual" opening of meetings and "initiation" of new members proclaimed "the principles of liberty, equality, and fraternity," affirmed the need for "helping each other financially" and doing whatever was deemed necessary "for keeping apace with this progressive age," concluding: "Let us grasp every opportunity that makes for the advancement of our welfare *as a class* and for the improvement of our condition in the service."[65]

The Alliance's initiation also referred to "Comrades" working for the "betterment of our condition socially, educationally." While this initiation was expressed in gendered terms like "upright men" and "one band of brothers," the organization was not gender-exclusive. In 1922 Bertha Bonaparte and Lillian Wood—probably the Alliance's first female members—joined its branch in New York City and soon became leading branch activists.[66] And while most late nineteenth and early twentieth-century unions began as "mutual benefit associations," there was particular significance to the fact that most of the original Alliance members belonged to the black Prince Hall Masons. Article II of the Alliance's constitution declared the "object of this alliance is to conduct the business of a fraternal beneficiary organization." As Felix Bell, a Mississippi Alliance official told me: "Most Alliance members were . . . also Masons. . . . In order to know who a true brother was . . . someone you could trust, . . . [organizational secrets] were carried by the black railway clerks. . . . The Masons had a secret handshake, and so, if you were a Mason, and you could do the secret handshake, then I felt comfortable with passing this information on to you. . . . That's how the Alliance was organized."[67]

The National Alliance was a unique independent black labor organization led by college-educated intellectuals. While they were politically to the left of most of the predominantly white organized labor movement, the Alliance, like most postal unions, operated within accepted middle-class mores of negotiation rather than confrontation with management. And in terms of education, its first president, Henry L. Mims of Houston, a Howard University graduate, was more the rule than the exception.[68] As Paul Tennassee writes: "For many young African Americans who got the opportunity to be railway mail clerks, after graduating from secondary school, college or university, it was an adventure and opportunity." Howard Law School provided many graduates who would lead the Alliance.[69]

Belonging to the Alliance also gave many black activists an opportunity to fight for both civil rights and labor rights. Paul Ortiz's examination of the Jacksonville, Florida, Alliance provides us this significant example by a black union promoting not just economic but also *political* advocacy: "In the final week of May, 1919, members of the Jacksonville branch of the National Alliance of Postal Employees, a union of African American railway mail clerks, met at the home of A. J. Gillis, a senior clerk, for their monthly meeting. . . . The clerks' union was able to call upon its members to risk the dangers of engaging in politics in the Deep South because the union had woven together personal relationships of trust and reciprocity that allowed members to survive Jim Crow."[70]

Labor unions in general have traditionally been weakest in the South, in large part due to a long history of white supremacy, along with state and corporate violence. That weakness was later fortified with federal authorization in the 1947 Taft-Hartley Act's anti-union "right-to-work" laws that became endemic to the South.[71] And mainstream postal unions have always been strongest in the Northeast and Midwest. But the National Alliance began its first chapters in the South, where most black railway mail service workers lived, before it moved north. It held its 1913 founding convention in Chattanooga, Tennessee. Several subsequent conventions were also held in the South. The initial call to form the Alliance began with a group calling itself the Colored Railway Postal Clerks in Houston—a site of significant black industrial union and civil rights organizing. Its narrative of "founding fathers" from the thirteen mostly southern delegations comprising what they called the "thirteen original colonies" suggests both a patriotic American and a parallel black nationalism.[72]

In sharp contrast to the Alliance, Progressive-era influence on the labor movement was not just reformist and middle class but often white supremacist.[73] The establishment of the all-white RMA the same year the Lloyd–La Follette Act recognized postal labor unions provides us with a good example of the self-imposed limitations of the early twentieth-century American labor movement. Meanwhile, by removing previous presidential gag orders imposed on postal workers to not petition Congress with their grievances, the Lloyd–La Follette Act also enabled postal workers to organize and represent workers, although they could still not strike.

Those previous gag orders had represented responses by Presidents Theodore Roosevelt and William Howard Taft to postal organizing. And the Lloyd–La Follette Act itself was a reaction to railway mail workers protesting speedup of work after routes were combined and crews were cut. This could have been a good opportunity to organize solidarity among black and white postal workers on the railroads. But instead, white postal workers chose to organize an exclusive union to replace and exclude black workers in favor of whites.[74]

New York and Washington, D.C., were at the center of these black postal worker struggle stories. The New York City branch of the National Alliance was chartered in 1922, several years after West Indian socialist and black nationalist Hubert Harrison was fired from his postal job in that city for political reasons. Harrison, who ran a study group of other black postal worker intellectuals while working at the post office from 1907 to 1911, was a member of the National Federation of Post Office Clerks, or NFPOC, New York City Local 10—a local founded in 1910 that included black charter members.[75] While no direct connection has been established between the Alliance and Harrison, it could be argued that the Alliance's development as a black alternative union drew on Harrison, UNIA founder Marcus Garvey, the Industrial Workers of the World (IWW), the NAACP, and the NUL for a mixture of left, black nationalist, and black middle-class reformist influences.

Caribbean immigrants were also an important part of the black nationalist activist resurgence in Harlem in the World War I era, as historian Winston James points out, and were attempting to join the postal workforce as well.

Hubert Henry Harrison (pictured ca. 1910), from St. Croix, Virgin Islands, was a black nationalist and socialist leader in Harlem, as well as a postal clerk and member of NFPOC New York Local 10 from 1907 to 1911. He also organized a study circle of activist black postal workers. After Harrison publicly criticized Booker T. Washington's accommodationist ideology, friends of Washington arranged with the post office to fire Harrison on trumped-up charges in 1911. Courtesy of the Hubert H. Harrison Papers, Rare Book and Manuscript Library, Columbia University.

With Garvey convicted and imprisoned for mail fraud in 1925 and then deported two years later, the surviving New York City UNIA branch, among other things, landed postal jobs for blacks and handled discrimination grievances, performing similar functions as the Alliance, the NAACP, and the NUL. (The NAACP and NUL had their national offices in New York City.)[76]

In Washington, D.C., black postal workers first petitioned for a National Alliance branch there in 1914. By 1925 the nation's capital had become the organization's national headquarters. The decision to establish a national headquarters of the National Alliance in Washington, D.C., represented a coincidence of factors: (1) Washington, D.C., had become the site where postal unions lobbied the government for reforms; (2) it represented the center of the railway mail service and the post office nationally; (3) it saw black letter carriers barred entirely from the NALC Capital City Branch 142 there, as well as segregated in D.C.'s NFPOC local; (4) it was a "transitional" southern city with many Jim Crow features; (5) it had an established black middle class; and (6) it was the home of Howard University and its law school, both of which provided many graduates to the Alliance and other black activist organizations. Howard's ongoing supportive relationship with that union made the Alliance unique among all American unions.[77]

The first National Alliance convention outside the South was held in 1929 in Detroit. Within a few decades of its 1913 founding, so many workers from other postal crafts were joining that the Alliance was hearing complaints that its original railway mail members were being neglected. More black workers were migrating to cities looking for jobs in all regions, especially with the onset of the Great Depression in 1929. In southern cities and towns, arbitrary white local restrictions determined whether blacks would be excluded from either or both of the letter carrier and clerk crafts. That erratic patchwork highlights the inconsistencies of an irrational system. Most important, those restrictions were established on the basis of which jobs whites deemed to be inferior so that they could claim the superior jobs. Outside the South blacks joined most postal crafts but also found some occupational segregation.[78] Between the world wars, however, several factors made postal work accessible for blacks, including urban migration, political patronage, independent unions, and black civic organizations. In 1931 historians Sterling Spero and Abram Harris observed:

> In some occupations, however, such as the government services where the political power of the employees counts quite as much as their economic strength, independent Negro organizations have played a role of some importance. This is particularly true of the postal service where the Negro is

an important factor in most of the large northern offices. The entire postal service employed 25,390 Negroes in 1928, about 9 percent of the total force. In Detroit Negroes constitute about 16.4 per cent of the postal staff. In Chicago, they constitute 31 per cent; in New York 16 per cent. They are thus unmistakably a force to be reckoned with. Though the regular unions of postal workers such as the clerks and letter carriers have large colored memberships, the Negro workers have felt that their interests could be served best by supplementing the work of the regular organizations with associations of their own. Almost every city where Negroes are employed in significant numbers has a colored postal employees' benefit society or club, purely local in scope, which aims to consolidate the political power of the Negro worker and to guard his interests before the local postal officials.[79]

Spero and Harris also pointed out that the National Alliance had organized 2,453 black postal workers in all branches of service by 1929. An organizing rate of less than ten percent does not seem very high, leading A. L. Glenn to call his organization "pitifully weak from a national point of view" during this period.[80] Yet even during its early organizing years the Alliance's activities suggest that it formed an active minority of the postal labor movement. While some branches were small and characterized by chronic infighting, others like Atlanta's managed to attract large numbers of eligible postal employees as early as 1919. Within a decade, the Alliance had absorbed many local black postal social clubs.[81]

In 1929, the National Alliance successfully secured an appointment in the postmaster general's office of a black official for black postal worker affairs, although during the 1920s it had not received "the same official recognition in Washington which has been accorded the white unions," according to Spero and Harris (which they ascribed in part to official indifference, but mainly Alliance passivity).[82] Spero and Harris concluded that black independent unionism was only successful during this period in occupations that were either all-black or at least predominantly black.[83] The rejection by the Alliance to overtures from the American Negro Labor Congress (ANLC, dominated by the Communist Party of the United States of America, or CPUSA) in 1925 does not in itself mean the Alliance had no interest in the CPUSA's radical "dual unionism," but that it attached greater importance to maintaining an independent black union.[84]

Also key to this independent black labor protest tradition exemplified by the Alliance was the role of black supervisors in the fight for equality. The Alliance campaigned for an increase in black supervisors, many of whom belonged to the Alliance. This contradicts standard labor movement practice in the

United States where supervisors have historically (and logically) been treated by labor as management representatives and enforcers of labor discipline. (The only other postal union that included supervisors was also widely considered a management-friendly "company union"—the United National Association of Post Office Craftsmen, or UNAPOC—that merged in 1960 with the NFPOC.)[85]

But the National Alliance was a unique organization that defied easy categorization. It was closely allied with both the NAACP and black labor and socialist leader A. Philip Randolph, founder of the Brotherhood of Sleeping Car Porters (BSCP) in New York City in 1925. During this period the Alliance functioned as a kind of "labor NAACP"—using negotiation rather than confrontation with postal management and postal unions. Although it did include leftists, the Alliance never defined itself as "left." The Alliance's commitment to a democratic working-class movement contrasted sharply with the exclusionary white supremacist labor rhetoric common in the AFL during this period.

The Alliance also maintained a social base among black social organizations and the middle class.[86] In that way it embodied both black labor and civic traditions. The organized labor movement generally restricted itself to economic concerns, but the National Alliance put equality first. Their monthly *Postal Alliance*, founded in 1914, listed their "Objectives" below the masthead, fusing black civil rights unionism with public sector labor pride: "To keep the membership informed as to what is going on in the Postal Service; improve our efficiency for the good of the service and to show that Negroes form an integral part of American civilization, and need no peculiar arrangements set aside for them to hold any certain positions within the Government service, but they are entitled to the same equality of opportunity as other citizens to play their part in the function of our National Government."[87]

A. L. Glenn's history of the National Alliance shows individual members and local branches throughout the country involved in the fight for equality in the post office and society. Throughout the 1910s, 1920s, and 1930s, new chapters applied for membership at a rapid rate, especially in urban areas, including Houston, Detroit, Jacksonville, Atlanta, New York, Chicago, Los Angeles, Memphis, and St. Paul, among others. By 1923 eleven national districts including thirty-four states and the District of Columbia had been approved.[88] In 1916 the National Alliance voted to become a contributing member of the NAACP.[89]

Alliance members also belonged to local social and civil rights activist organizations of black postal workers like the Ebony Club in Kansas City, Kansas; the Appomattox Club in Detroit; and the Phalanx Forum in Chicago. The latter, according to CPUSA activist Harry Haywood, became dominated after

World War I by young veterans like himself and students who were interested not in the old "conservative crowd of social climbers and political aspirants," but who were more interested in conducting study groups on "the current campaign of white racist propaganda [and] how to counter it on the basis of scientific truth." In 1927 the Alliance incorporated the Phalanx Forum and its 1,500 members along with "mutual welfare" black postal worker clubs from Philadelphia, Cincinnati, and Cleveland.[90] Black World War I veterans in the post office also pushed the Alliance to be more aggressive, resulting in an increase in lobbying and litigation, according to Glenn.[91] In 1922 the Alliance urged branches "to present their written grievances for presentation to postal officials. Scores of briefs were prepared. These covered cases and subjects submitted by the membership as well as specific issues of general interest, among which was the prevalent photo requirement for identification, failure to promote senior Negro clerks in the R.M.S., and the policy of keeping Negro clerks off the N.Y. and Wash[ington, D.C.] RPO and other trunk lines and not promoting our eligibles on lines out of Washington southward."[92]

FIGHTING JIM CROW UNION BRANCHES AND LOCALS

Jim Crow union branches and locals were not anachronistic institutions marginal to the overall labor struggle, including the post office. Separate, unequal, with black branches and locals subordinate to white, they epitomized white supremacist choices that organized labor had made that fractured worker unity. Those choices included a disinterest in organizing black workers and elevating them to union leadership. But segregated branches and locals were also battlegrounds. The debates over their existence revealed starkly different assumptions among postal unionists—both spoken and unspoken—concerning white privilege, patriotism, and labor peace and prosperity. The two largest predominantly white AFL postal unions—NALC and NFPOC—tolerated Jim Crow locals.[93]

How successful were blacks within the white unions in fighting Jim Crow branches and locals? Black postal union activists helped inject the civil rights movement into the labor movement—and vice versa. It is instructive, for example, to see Mississippi NAACP leadership from the 1930s to the 1960s often coming from black postal unionists like attorneys Carsie Hall and Jack Young. "There was an unspoken gentleman's agreement during the early '30s," Willenham Castilla, veteran Jackson, Mississippi, National Alliance, NALC, and NAACP activist told me. "The whites would work inside [as clerks] blacks would work outside [as carriers]. . . . I guess they [whites] felt a certain superiority working inside. . . . But when times got tough they [whites] disregarded that . . .

agreement, and the whites were working inside *and* outside." According to Castilla, blacks ran the NALC Mississippi Association, based in western Mississippi towns like Jackson, Natchez, Vicksburg, and Yazoo City. Black postal workers in Mississippi were "the backbone" of the NAACP, in part because "the local [postal officials] couldn't fire them so easily." But why did most black postal workers in that state belong to both the Alliance and the NALC? "The NALC was a good labor union," he replied, "but the Alliance was in the forefront of civil rights for blacks."[94]

Black postal unionists fought separate branches and locals throughout the twentieth century. The NFPOC probably began with Jim Crow locals, although their monthly journal did not acknowledge them until World War II.[95] And the NALC apparently first recognized Jim Crow branches at their 1917 national convention in Dallas, where they voted to allow what were euphemistically called "additional" charters segregated by race. They did so after hearing whites' arguments that segregated southern branches would provide economic advantages by enrolling more white southern (and D.C.) carriers, whom they argued would only join a white branch, and enroll more black carriers who might otherwise be excluded from an existing all-white branch.

But it was in fact a northern delegate—from Detroit Branch 1—who put the pro–Jim Crow resolution on the floor. With support from President Edward J. Gainor, the resolution passed after a short but dramatic debate, despite a moving speech by P. M. E. Hill of Branch 986 in Yazoo City, Mississippi, invoking equality, faith, patriotism, and workers' internationalism:

> Mr. President, I regret that I must arise as an American citizen and a member of the greatest organization in the world which seemingly is purely democratic and stands for all men, to defend myself as a black man to be separated from other Americans just because I was born black. . . . I was in Argentina, where they had an organization of this kind, and there were [no separations]. . . . When the great [postal union] convention met in Canada no such action as this was taken. . . . I was in the Spanish-American War. . . . I have a boy now who is in the trenches in France. . . . I hope you gentlemen who I know are all Christians will remember that the Lord said, "God is no respecter of persons." I believe in the proposition of all men up and no man down, and this is wrong.[96]

Hill's speech drew applause, but his side lost. Yet two years later "separate charters," as they were first referred to in 1919, were suddenly repealed at the Philadelphia convention. What happened in two years to change so many minds? Looking back sixteen years later was J. F. Morgan, NALC Constitution and Law chairman, as he now spoke against a new "separate charter" resolution at their 1935 convention: "At the [1917] Dallas convention we had it [the constitution] amended so as to provide for dual charters. Following that, on November 5, 1917, a [residential segregation] case came up in Louisville, which was sent to the U.S. Supreme Court, and the U.S. Supreme Court decided that all segregation laws were unconstitutional. Following that decision, the Association did not issue any dual charters, and at the Philadelphia convention, in 1919, we had the dual charter provision of our constitution stricken out."[97]

This was a remarkable about-face. A limited challenge to *Plessy v. Ferguson* (1896) that was *Buchanan v. Warley* (1917) was seen by NALC delegates in 1919 as demanding the abolition of their segregated branches.[98] But Morgan neglected to credit the floor revolt against Jim Crow from black and white carriers at both the 1917 and 1919 conventions. In 1919, two delegates from the mostly black Jacksonville Branch 52—Joel C. Dawkins and I. A. Ross—led the charge against Jim Crow branches. And it was an abashed white New York Branch 36 delegate, P. J. Vandernoot, who revealed that at the 1917 convention he had promised Hill he would speak against the Jim Crow resolution, but President Edward J. Gainor had warned him he would only recognize southern delegates speaking on that issue. But thinking now about Hill's wartime speech made Vandernoot break his silence and speak against segregated branches.[99]

During the first half of the twentieth century, the content of most NALC convention resolutions reflected narrow craft concerns—from everyday working conditions to opposition to the movement for one big postal union. Yet for years after the 1919 vote, these conventions were also persuaded against readopting Jim Crow branches in large part by the testimony of P. M. E. Hill. Combining arguments from the Bible and Reconstruction-era Republican citizenship ideology and rhetoric, the indefatigable Hill was heard in conventions and read in letters opposing separate charters and white supremacist union policies in general. For years, in fact, Hill was one of only two regular convention delegates from the entire state of Mississippi in addition to being NALC state vice president.[100]

In all these NALC convention debates the National Alliance loomed in the background. In Spero and Harris's account of the twenty-sixth annual NALC convention at El Paso, Texas, in September 1927, for example, black carriers helped defeat a resolution that they maintained was brought by white carriers urging blacks to join the National Alliance as a way to induce blacks to leave the NALC. The convention, Spero and Harris noted, resolved that no organization would be permitted within the NALC, "especially a group known as the Postal Alliance [National Alliance]."[101]

Spero and Harris were essentially right. But there is more to the story—including the mystery as to whether blacks helped sponsor the resolution as some whites accused. The all-white Houston Branch 283 brought a resolution suggesting Houston blacks join the Alliance. After the Resolutions Committee recommended rejection, Houston delegate Homer E. Switzer disavowed it: "When this resolution was placed upon this floor it was done by the colored carriers themselves. In Houston, Texas, we have no colored carriers in our organization. The colored carriers do not seek membership, knowing that it is a cause of friction from past experience, and that if they were in our organization it would cause disruption in seeking of official honors. This was thoroughly discussed in Texas, and it was endorsed and agreed to by all colored carriers and white carriers, that some condition of this kind must be taken up whereby there would be no dissension in our ranks."[102] Switzer even suggested that a discussion, possibly even a negotiation, had occurred before the convention that included Alliance members, although the Alliance never acknowledged such a meeting. It is doubtful the Alliance would have agreed that the Houston NALC should remain Jim Crow, even if that would have assured the Alliance more members. The resolution's language looks even more suspicious with its appeal to white supremacist fears of "black domination":

> Whereas the conditions in the south, as well as the entire Association of the United States, in respect to the colored members of the National Association of Letter Carriers, in that in many of the Branches the colored members have come to majority, and, therefore, places them in authority, causing a disruption in the ranks of the membership. . . .
>
> Whereas their strength in voting has proved without question in those Branches that white letter carriers have been compelled to either withdraw their membership or take the embarrassment of being defeated to positions of local officers and representation in our National Conventions. . . .
>
> Whereas the higher-minded and considerate colored carriers have recognized these conditions, and desiring to avoid any future trouble have instituted an organization for the colored civil service employees, which is known as the Postal Alliance [*sic*].[103]

The resolution concluded by asking that the convention go on record endorsing the "Postal Alliance" (National Alliance) with "appeals to all colored carriers to avail themselves in its membership in order that peace may be preserved in the service."[104] Two black delegates who were not buying this as a pro-black resolution immediately spoke in opposition and ultimately helped defeat the resolution, with one also expressing some sympathy for the Alliance. The speakers were R. M. Casey from Memphis Branch 27 and P. M. E. Hill.

President Gainor attempted to kill the resolution before Hill and Casey had a chance to denounce its larger implications, but they insisted on having their say. Hill's address included a poignant postscript to remarks he had made a decade before on his son's military service:

> I think in this resolution there is something every Branch and every carrier ought to fully understand. We have colored carriers in our Branch, Memphis has several, Pittsburgh has several, and almost every Branch in the State of Mississippi and many other places in the South have them. They have just as much right to come to this convention as any white man. . . . This very resolution states than whenever colored people get in the majority they will run things, rule or ruin. It says the higher-minded colored people have joined the Postal Alliance [*sic*]. Those that are not higher minded have not joined. That thing in itself is an insult to every colored man. . . .
>
> I am an American citizen, I have fought for all the institutions and for everything that is progressive in America. I was in the Spanish-American War, *I had one son killed in the World War*, and I have stuck by this country. . . .
>
> You recollect when I made a speech on this colored charter down in Dallas [in 1917]; all this stuff was done away with [at the 1919 Philadelphia convention]. This is nothing but the colored charter revived.[105]

Then Casey took the floor and began: "I am against the word 'colored' but I have to use it just now." The National Alliance, he reminded his audience, was formed by black railway postal clerks who were excluded from "the Railway Postal Clerks *White* Association, as I may call it."[106] Casey blamed Switzer for the resolution, despite Switzer's disavowal, and backed Hill's attack on white supremacy and its attempts to drive blacks from the NALC:

> In New Orleans there are 175 colored carriers who cannot join the Association because it is in the white men's possession. The man from Houston says where we are in a majority we do not allow the white men to join. That is not true. You say we are keeping you out: why, you are keeping us out every chance you get. Is that right, gentlemen? We want to show you that we do not discriminate against any man because of his color. When men . . . present sugar-coated resolutions to kick us out of the National Association of Letter Carriers, where are we going?
>
> Brother Hill told you that we are citizens of the United States. *According to the Constitution, I am as white as any man in here.* . . . We have no advantage in this country; we have no States in our charge; no cities are in our charge.[107]

A New York delegate's counter-resolution was then unanimously adopted. It did not address the issue of blacks leaving for another organization but rather opposed "the organization of any group within the membership of the N.A.L.C, especially the Postal Alliance [National Alliance]."[108] Once again a black-led opposition to Jim Crow unionism in this AFL union had remarkably triumphed—during the same decade that the BSCP was fighting to be admitted to the AFL. It was also several years before the NAACP made labor organizing a priority, and just a few years after the apogee and collapse of both the Ku Klux Klan and the UNIA as viable national movements. Yet for black letter carriers, their struggle in the NALC had just begun. At the 1935 Cleveland convention, white southern delegates brazenly tried to pass a constitutional amendment that would amend Article II, Section 1 to read: "In cities where there is in employment a sufficient number of both colored and white carriers for each group to maintain a separate Branch, they may if so desired by the majority members of each group form two distinct Branches."[109] Speaking in support of the Jim Crow amendment, white delegate R. F. Stevens of College Park, Georgia, tried to pull from the Bible what he called the "beautiful story" of Abraham and Lot to justify the segregation of branches. Besides refuting Stevens on constitutional grounds, Hill challenged the Georgia delegate's scriptural expertise by asserting that "Abraham was the religious man and Lot was the sinner," and that their dispute had nothing to do with color. The Jim Crow resolution was defeated again, politically and theologically.[110]

Four years later, during the 1939 NALC convention debate in Milwaukee over reintroducing "separate" charters, Hill attacked pro-segregation delegate J. M. Bistowish of New Orleans for citing separate churches as a basis for segregating union branches. Combining black religious and abolitionist traditions, Hill thundered: "*Who divided the church, but the devil?* (Laughter.) And he [Bistowish] called your attention to the segregation down in the South. Who did that but the devil? And what did we do to alleviate that kind of segregation? We took up arms and fought against it."[111] The "devil," according to Hill, was white supremacy—whether it was in the House of the Lord, the House of Labor, or American society as a whole. Opposing that devil was a black freedom movement with roots in nineteenth-century abolitionism. Hill evoked what could be called a "Union Army Americanism" that defied the post–Civil War national white reconciliation that abandoned blacks to southern white supremacy. He linked the modern movement for equality to Frederick Douglass and other abolitionists' plea that future generations remember that the Civil War was fought over slavery.[112] ("Slight of stature and weighs but 100 pounds" is how the *Chicago Defender* described Hill in a September 15, 1923, report on the NALC's national convention that week in Providence, Rhode Island. Significantly, there was nothing slight about his capital accumulation, as they noted that Hill "is reported to be the wealthiest letter carrier in the country. He is said to have amassed $100,000 by buying and selling cotton.")[113]

Meanwhile, Bistowish was making his case for separate branches on the basis that southerners had no choice but to abide by segregation: "the custom and tradition handed down" to them. "We have the Jim Crow law," Bistowish frankly admitted. But his understanding of Jim Crow law was something that was set in stone: "We have to abide by that law, as well as you have to abide by your own laws in your cities. New York has more or less of segregation—the Harlem district. Chicago has the same thing in the southern part of Chicago. It is voluntary, and ours happens to be mandatory, but you have the same thing."[114] In Hill's corner against Bistowish and the segregationists was Horace H. Scott of Richmond (a dual Alliance-NALC member), who along with Ft. Smith, Arkansas, Branch 399 delegate John T. Barret unsuccessfully moved to table the matter. In addition, Hill had support to quash the Jim Crow amendment from whites, like Resolutions Committee member Hugh S. Noonan and Chicago's Barney Bernstein, who earned applause and boos with his impassioned invocation of the Reconstruction amendments—which he had also done at the 1935 convention. Now in 1939, Bernstein angrily declared: "This little baby pops up every two years, clothed in new clothes. It is not designed for the purpose of anything but hate."[115]

The vote was taken and "separate" charters in the NALC were defeated once more. Surprisingly for the NALC, the convention also voted for a resolution from Detroit Branch 1 opposing discriminatory civil service application photographs.[116] Just as surprisingly, the NFPOC also in 1939 voted at their national convention in Houston to abolish the discriminatory photograph applications at the prompting of radical left Brooklyn Local 251.[117] Meanwhile, Jim Crow unionists changed the language of their proposed amendments from "separate charters" to "second charters," although "separate" and "dual" charters continued in use in convention debates and published accounts.[118]

BLACKS, WHITES, AND RED UNIONS

Many white left-leaning postal workers took active stances in favor of equality during the 1930s. Within left postal unions they were more inclined to be able to make that policy than they were within the conservative AFL postal unions. Yet white leftists also shared a "white blindspot" with conservative white workers in not acknowledging the salience of the issue of equality, as well as how their rallying cry of "one big postal union" had actually originated with the National Alliance.[119] During the late 1930s the Alliance carried on conversations with the CIO and its left-led unions nationally, but did not work formally together in coalition with them. There is evidence, however, of black involvement in the left postal unions that may have been noticed by the Alliance— which for its part became more assertive in forging ties with organized labor in the 1940s.[120]

The Great Depression of the 1930s brought a higher level of militant working-class mass protest to the postal labor movement, as it did to the labor movement as a whole and to predominantly working-class black communities.[121] For example, the 1935 Harlem riot represented a black protest against police brutality and economic exploitation, along with white Harlem business owners' failure to hire blacks.[122] City officials' concern with the riot's causes led them to hire economist Charles Lionel Franklin as a researcher, as he noted in the preface of the book that he wrote based on his study.[123] Franklin's 1935 study included a brief but revealing look at black postal workers in New York. Not only does it show black public workers (especially postal workers) joining unions at a substantial rate (2,250 out of 17,900, or 12.6 percent of all public workers; and 500 out of 3,000, or 16.7 percent of the liberal Local 10 of the NFPOC-AFL), but blacks also formed nearly a third (350 out of 1,200, or 29.2 percent) of the Postal Workers of America (PWA) Local 9, New York Postal Workers (NYPW).[124]

Little information is available on the PWA, but what one finds is tantalizing. One example is this quote from PWA national organizer Ronald Fishbein: "Our union believes in industrial unionism, so that all workers are given a chance. I guess the A.F. of L. will not issue us a charter because this is one of our fundamental principles."[125] Franklin meanwhile observed that Local 9's vice president was a black woman, that it had five black "delegates" (shop stewards) who were also organizers, and that "Negro members are on the whole active and interested."[126] According to one recent researcher, the PWA was suspected by mainstream postal unions of being a CPUSA-inspired dual union (probably true). But given the black radical labor protest tradition, the PWA's attraction of black workers should come as no surprise.

The PWA, established in 1934, was supported by the CPUSA but collapsed in 1937 as most of its members—employed as substitutes ("subs")—returned to or joined the mainstream unions as their working conditions improved. As the CPUSA political line had changed by 1935 to one that now opposed dual unionism, the CPUSA apparently made no effort to save this or any other dual union.[127] Oddly, this union that was one-third black provided little coverage in its newsletter to discrimination issues, made few references to the National Alliance, and did not even acknowledge the National Alliance as the originator of postal industrial unionism.[128]

Another union that may have been a CPUSA dual union was the National Association of Substitute Postal Employees (NASPOE), which encouraged members to belong to mainstream postal unions in its efforts to get those unions to represent substitutes. Both the NASPOE and the PWA were integrated and apparently did not tolerate Jim Crow in their few southern branches.[129] In 1934 there was a remarkable mass action led by the NASPOE, where about 600 "substitute" postal workers—members of the NASPOE and including many African Americans—marched in the bitter cold in the nation's capital on January 24 to protest the Roosevelt administration's civil service hiring freeze.[130]

White postal activists on the left also described being influenced by black worker activists at the time. Max Epstein, a retired New York City postal unionist, shared this recollection in 1976 during an interview with colleague and fellow postal retiree Arthur Ryland, an African American: "I happened to attend a political party meeting that was functioning at that time; not one of the regular political parties; it was somewhere in Brooklyn and a delegation of local negro people came; I remember they were dressed like construction workers. And they asked a very frustrating question: can we get them jobs? Well in the '30s, getting a job for anyone was like winning the million dollar lottery now, and especially for negro workers; and I remember that as the most frustrating experience that I ever felt."[131]

Epstein's words suggest a left party meeting in Brooklyn. What he described was part of a larger national scenario where white leftists were often being moved to action by the experience and demands of black workers and activists.[132] His remarks, in fact, immediately followed Ryland's memories of moonlighting as a jazz piano player at Harlem "rent parties" that were thrown to help pay the rent of African Americans who were unemployed or underemployed and short of money. Ryland then observed that by contrast "the only people who had a decent job were the people who worked in the post office, and these were people who had education without portfolio. Doctors, lawyers, people with half an education went into the postal service for security."[133] While he may have been speaking in general terms, in the context of his conversation and experience, Ryland was probably speaking mainly of blacks at the post office, although his remarks also suggest a bond between black unionists and white labor radicals.[134]

Mainstream conservative AFL postal unions, postal management, and government officials all considered the leftist NASPOE and PWA to be a nuisance.[135] For its part, even the CIO never managed to make significant inroads into organizing postal or government labor unions. Yet the concept of "one big postal union"—first introduced by the National Alliance—later became the watchword for left-labor postal activists including the Progressive Feds of the

NFPOC in 1946, the breakaway NPCU (National Postal Clerks Union) in 1959, and many members of the NALC and APWU toward the end of the century. The CIO did establish postal union locals in the industrial cities of Detroit, Boston, Pittsburgh, and San Francisco that helped carry a radical tradition forward from that period into the era of the 1970 national postal strike. What historian David Roediger calls "nonracial syndicalism" (the notion that integrated workplaces and unions were enough to unite black and workers) was not enough to sustain CIO organizing in manufacturing. There is no reason to believe that it would have been successful in the generally conservative postal craft unions.[136]

Seen in the minutes kept by NFPOC Brooklyn Local 251 as well as the UNIA papers in New York City during this period is the extent of coalition between labor, black nationalist, civil rights, liberal, and left groups around a number of domestic and international issues in New York City. Many if not most of those attending the Local 251 meetings and passing resolutions against the poll tax, lynching, Jim Crow locals, and the 1935 Italian fascist invasion of Ethiopia were Jewish (including the leadership), and probably only a small number of members and leaders were black. Local 251 (seen moving to the left during this period) sent a delegate to the 1940 National Negro Congress (NNC) convention. The NNC, until its breakup, included communists, socialists, liberals, and black nationalists. Of the names included on the inaugural 1936 NNC Presiding Committee—alongside other leading black labor and civil rights activists— was Snow Grigsby, Detroit civil rights activist, National Alliance member, and future editor of its journal *Postal Alliance*. Elected to the 1936 NNC Executive Council were Grigsby and Jerry O. Gilliam, then president of the Alliance.[137]

Local 251 had friendly relations with both Alliance and the NAACP. It also sent money to the Abraham Lincoln Brigade and the National Lawyers Guild —groups that enjoyed close relations with the CPUSA. It is quite possible that some of these Branch 251 members were communists, as was charged by Karl Baarslag—a former Branch 251 member who turned anticommunist witch-hunter in 1945. Baarslag cited as evidence their establishment of a "Culture Club" in 1931, their increasing attacks on timid craft unionism, and their calls for "ONE BIG UNION." Local 251 did resemble in that sense a CPUSA-influenced CIO local. Yet its minutes reflected both support for and opposition to CPUSA-dominated postal unions in the 1930s, even as it shared many of the same programs and positions as the CPUSA. Even their decision to send a delegate to the NNC convention in 1940 (where the CPUSA dominated and took over that organization) was made "with the express instructions that this delegate shall confine his activity to general labor and federal labor problems."[138]

Black and white left postal activists often put their higher education to use in union activities. "College boys" was a popular derisive term used by supervisors to describe many white left-labor postal activists in the 1930s. (I have found no evidence of anyone using that expression to refer to black college graduates in the post office, let alone that term's gender bias, suggesting either a "white blindspot" or the fact that black college graduates working at the post office were seen as nothing new.) Collectively, these postal worker intellectuals often brought a left political awareness along with writing and speaking skills. White left postal workers were more inclined to ally themselves with black postal workers in the fight for equality in the post office and its unions.[139]

The disproportionately high numbers of blacks in the left postal unions, photographs of integrated militant demonstrations, and articles written by whites against lynching and racist postal hiring practices suggest a friendlier terrain for blacks in those unions than in the conservative unions. But left union concentration on economic issues reveals a white blindspot in both organized labor and the left that compelled many black postal workers to join the Alliance—and the Alliance itself to remain autonomous rather than merge with other unions.

THE FIRST EIGHT DECADES OF
BLACK POSTAL WORKER ACTIVISM

With free labor defined as "white" in the early republic, postal labor was explicitly constructed as "free white" labor from 1802 to 1865 by federal statutes. After the Civil War, as blacks fought for full citizenship rights, postal employment represented a paradox for them. On the one hand, it served as a dramatic validation of that citizenship by making them representatives of the federal government. Postal job opportunities represented a relative oasis for blacks in a desert of American white occupational exclusion. Yet blacks still had to fight to get hired, and once inside they found occupational and union segregation and discrimination. Black postal workers within the NALC and NFPOC during this period functioned as small but vocal and influential minorities.[140]

Before 1940 black and left postal activists fought to extend union protection to all postal workers. The fight for equality was the linchpin in all the struggles of black postal unionists during this time. Prominent in that struggle was the National Alliance, born out of black radical left-labor politics, black fraternal orders, black middle-class reformism, and in opposition to Progressive-era segregation and white paternalism. The Alliance assumed a leadership role comparable to that of the BSCP. It represented black postal workers and built alliances with civil rights, left, and radical labor movements during the Great Depression. Black postal worker activists practiced civil rights unionism and rank-and-file union advocacy within a variety of organizations, including the independent industrial National Alliance; the short-lived or marginalized left postal unions of the NASPOE, PWA, and CIO; and the AFL postal craft unions—sometimes holding multiple union memberships. Putting equality first, these activists embodied organized labor's best possibilities.

CHAPTER TWO

FIGHTING JIM CROW
AT HOME DURING WORLD WAR II
(1940–1946)

"I SAW UNCLE TOM DIE"

It was July 1943, and James B. Cobb, president of the Washington, D.C., branch of the historically black NAPE was not satisfied with the gains he and his organization had made for black postal workers since 1940 in breaking down barriers to employment and promotion. Discrimination in the post office and its unions was still the norm. Meanwhile, the Durham, North Carolina, native, former tobacco factory worker, and Howard University graduate had won election as president of the Alliance's largest branch in 1941—the year the United States entered World War II on the side of the Allies that had begun fighting back against the invading fascist Axis powers in 1939. Cobb had won on the ambitious platform of "Complete integration throughout the Post Office."[1]

In 1940, the year before his election, a victory had been achieved in the longtime campaign led by the National Alliance and the NAACP to abolish the civil service application photographs that had been routinely used by the post office since 1914 to screen out black applicants. But now Cobb offered his assessment that it was time for the Alliance to "redefine itself with respect to its relationship" with the post office. "Our status is not much more than a Company Union," he charged, "and the limits of our action is conference and petition." He proposed this alternative: "We need, also, some sort of relationship with other labor groups, as an independent organization. There should be developed a keen interest in all labor legislation, and in return the labor movement would have more than a passing interest in our labor problems. It can be done and yet retain autonomy."[2]

Cobb was proposing a decisive shift in National Alliance strategy that also seemed risk-free: doing outreach while maintaining organizational independence. The sentiment in that direction had actually already been building over the past year and more. Chicago NAPE president Ashby Carter predicted at the

James Cobb (center), a prime mover in the 1940s connecting the National Alliance with organized labor, was elected president of the National Alliance's D.C. branch in the 1940s and then national president in the 1950s. He is shown here at his installation banquet as president emeritus in the late 1960s, with then–National Alliance president Ashby Smith (left) and Ranson Jones, president of District Four (Alabama, Mississippi, and Tennessee). Courtesy of the National Alliance of Postal and Federal Employees.

end of 1941 that in the coming year "the Negro postal employee will . . . reassert his right to a 'square deal.' "[3] The new editor of the *Postal Alliance*, the National Alliance's national monthly journal, was veteran Detroit civil rights activist Snow Grigsby, who was elected in 1940. Two years later he began featuring more radical coverage on labor and civil rights issues than ever before.[4]

Grigsby published a call for the Alliance to take on roles more oriented to confrontation and coalition: "In 1942 the Postal Alliance must become more active and closer related to the civic organizations of the communities, national Negro organizations, and the Associated Negro Press," in addition to accelerating their lobbying and legislative efforts.[5] Grigsby published news of black postal workers' protests against discrimination, most strikingly seen in this September 1942 article: "Because of widespread unrest among Negro postal employees caused by discrimination, president L. F. Ford of the N.A.P.E. found it necessary to call his [Executive Committee] to meet in Washington Aug. 21–23, 1942, to appear before the F.E.P.C. [Fair Employment Practices Committee] to present many complaints from all sections of the country, of discriminatory practices against Negroes. . . . The N.A.P.E is determined to break down racial discrimination in the postal service. Conferences with high postal officials gave President Ford much encouragement for a new deal."[6]

The National Alliance in Chicago had already petitioned the FEPC to investigate post office discrimination as early as January 1942, when FEPC officials held hearings in that city. But this new burst of black postal labor activism throughout the country compelled Alliance union officials to become even more engaged. Black postal workers began demanding faster results in the fight against discrimination almost a year before the post office and other government employees were formally covered under the second version of the FEPC. What black postal worker activists wanted to know was this: if government-contracted defense industry could be covered by the FEPC, why not also government workers?[7] While postal workers were forbidden by law to strike, their confrontations with management (although on a much smaller scale) paralleled the impatience of workers in private industry who saw the war being used as an excuse by management to diminish their bargaining power over working conditions and economic demands. In fact, given the widespread use of white wildcat "hate strikes" during this time in the private sector—despite the no-strike pledges promised by the AFL and CIO—it was even fortunate in a sense for black postal workers that strikes had not been part of postal labor culture.[8] Meanwhile, James Cobb, Snow Grigsby, and other Alliance officials were responding to membership demands to shift from being a civil rights advocacy group to a labor union. In doing so Alliance officials also initiated membership "welfare and education" training programs.[9]

James Cobb's 1943 declaration in the *Postal Alliance* mirrored growing black militancy across the United States. African Americans confronted white supremacy in both the public and private sectors. They also expressed alienation with the idea of being asked to unite in the nation's antifascist war "with a mop and a broom" (to quote a popular phrase then) while Jim Crow still ruled at home. In Harlem, black postal workers had taken part in a successful united community bus boycott in 1941 that had, like many similar protests, forced changes in the hiring of blacks. The Harlem rebellion in the summer of 1943 expressed blacks' frustration over continued unemployment, police brutality, and the steady flow of capital out of Harlem.[10] Cobb's call for a shift in strategy was in part a response to mass grassroots protest at the endurance of white supremacy in the United States and especially within the post office. The next section of his 1943 article, titled "No Recognition Proves Disastrous," contained his reflections on the June 20, 1943, "race riots" in Detroit, in which he noted that 34 were killed—including 24 blacks and 10 whites—with over 800 injured, 1,833 arrested, and millions of dollars of property damage:

> I have just finished reading the editorial of the Wayne County Democrat and the Detroit Labor News, both giving their views on why the Detroit streets ran with blood. It was all because public officials failed to recognize the existing and growing problems of Detroit and the U.S.A. in general. . . .
>
> No doubt a few members of the old school will say that the editor should not mention the Detroit affair in the Journal, but some have not realized the fact that whatever effects [*sic*] the Negro's jobs or living conditions in Detroit, Michigan, Detroit, Texas, or Detroit, Mississippi, effects [*sic*] the membership of the N.A.P.E. Not only the N.A.P.E., but labor in general and the whole framework of Democracy.[11]

The National Alliance, meeting in St. Louis for their national convention on August 16, 1943, saw the sudden collapse of what Cobb called the old "representational culture" of negotiation between the Alliance and postal management. With the convention theme "Equal Opportunity for the Negro in the Postal Service," guest speaker St. Louis Postmaster Rufus Jackson managed to not only greet but also quickly antagonize his audience. He did so by refusing to consider their complaints against his post office's segregated cafeteria—the very site where he had invited the convention to have lunch that day. Just two years earlier, a young black postal worker, Leslie Green Jr., had refused to sit in the back of that cafeteria. When the manager physically confronted him, Green decked him. When Green then met with Postmaster Jackson, Jackson himself tried to goad Green into a physical fight.[12]

Now, as a kind of climax, the 1943 Alliance convention minutes read like a well-scripted drama. Delegates debated how to respond to this latest insult. Some were fearful of repercussions to the St. Louis Alliance members. A few rationalized Jim Crow as the law of the land. Lillian Wood of New York then spoke for a growing militant activist tendency with this rhetorical question: "If you accept hospitality at the back door, will that not mean that we also approve the segregation policy of the St. Louis Post Office?"[13] In the middle of this debate the sergeant-at-arms abruptly announced that Jackson had arrived to speak. Jackson entered, began his speech by joking about the hot weather, and mentioned the scheduled tour. Then, alluding to the controversy over his post office's segregated cafeteria, he changed tone and defiantly declared before finishing his speech that "we of St. Louis don't need any advice and counsel from outside influences." But as Jackson was leaving, Alliance past president Jerry O. Gilliam reminded him: "We are different from other Post Office organizations. We have many things other than Post Office matters to consider. . . . The Negro can't get as many jobs as white men although our efficiency rating often is higher. . . . We are playing our part in America, and dying on the fields of battle."[14]

The Alliance certainly *was* unlike other postal unions: their resolutions included opposition to Jim Crow in the military; support for anti-lynching legislation; praising black-owned life insurance companies for providing employment and capital for the black community; and gratitude to the postmaster general for making promotions and assignments based on seniority and merit, not race or other considerations.[15] After Jackson left, the convention picked up where it had left off, with anger visibly rising among the delegates. Delegates were now overwhelmingly in favor of boycotting the lunch and tour. The question being debated was simply over whether to send a delegation to Jackson to lodge a formal protest in person, or send it by mail. (The resolution to send a delegation won.) The differences were predominantly tactical: those voting "yes" argued for a delegation, while those voting "no" were mainly delegates who favored mailing a protest petition to Jackson as well as to the postmaster general (which they claimed would send a stronger message). There were only a few who objected to taking any action at all. Arguing for a written response, Marian C. Whittaker from Detroit made this organizational contrast: "The CIO removed their group from St. Louis to Buffalo on account of discrimination. If a white group can do that, is there nothing that we can do?" Meanwhile, the president of the Washington, D.C., branch and the Alliance's chaplain, Reverend Alexander Taylor, prophetically urged convention delegates to consider the history they were making: "I am known as a minister, but I also believe in militancy. I agree with all of the previous speakers who have said that we should fight, and let the Postmaster know that we, as a body, will not tolerate the kind of procedure he is putting on the people here. . . . We are not fighting for ourselves, but rather for our progeny."[16]

The drama continued as the Alliance's delegation (Ashby Carter, Jesse L. Robinson, and Arthur J. Chapital) reported back later that week on their meeting on August 19, where Rufus Jackson had been joined by Assistant Postmaster Maher and two postal inspectors. The postal management group had provided the Alliance's delegation with a merry-go-round of excuses: (1) there was no discrimination in the cafeteria—separate seating by race was merely customary; (2) the postmaster general's June 2, 1943, condemnation of discrimination in post offices nationwide applied only to *work* areas; and (3) the Service Relations Council was in charge of cafeteria policy and they were dominated by white postal workers. Jackson concluded the meeting with the threat that if no discrimination was found in the St. Louis post office, "the ones making the charges will answer to him." When the convention delegates heard that news, they quickly moved and voted to approve the report and send a copy to the postmaster general requesting that he take action against the segregated cafeteria. "We want to see that if Rufus Jackson persecutes anybody we will sue him and run him into the river," angrily declared Jerry O. Gilliam. Even outgoing president Lafayette Ford, who had previously told a reporter that he thought it would have been better to "go through the Post Office and then protest," now proclaimed to the convention: "We are going to fight this thing to the very end."[17]

The September 1943 issue of the *Postal Alliance* reported the delegates' determination: "A substitute motion was offered to cancel the tour and instead, send a committee to call on the postmaster. The forces of reaction were dead! Thus one great postmaster was 'buried' by a national convention—the eulogy was by Jerry O. Gilliam of Norfolk." In October, convention delegates were still talking about the significance of the action they had taken. District Eight president Elmer Armstead of New York wanted no one to miss the significance of their defiance that day (and in doing so he could not resist drawing a parallel with the protests that had greeted British Prime Minister Neville Chamberlain's 1938 appeasement of German dictator Adolf Hitler's territorial conquests in Europe): "Never before has any service organization . . . taken so firm a stand on that most controversial of all issues and policies— DISCRIMINATION. Never before in the history of the Alliance has an official of the Department . . . been put so completely on the spot as it was in St. Louis by the determined and outspoken attitude of the men and women of that convention on the discriminatory practices in the St. Louis post office. This also serves notice on future Alliance officers—*there will be no appeasement*. We are determined to be ceaseless in our efforts to make a reality of those famous words inscribed on the walls of every Supreme Court: EQUAL JUSTICE UNDER LAW."[18]

But it was Henry W. McGee, NAPE convention delegate and first vice president of the Chicago branch, who most succinctly summed up the new spirit of black postal worker resistance when he wrote in September: "*I saw Uncle Tom die*. The place was the Pine Street Y.M.C.A. The time was the Wednesday morning session of the 12th Biennial Convention of the National Alliance of Postal Employees."[19] This dramatic mass action against Jim Crow was noticed by the Council of Negro Organizations of St. Louis and Vicinity. They passed a resolution four days later commending the Alliance for its "protest against the segregation and discrimination practiced at that office against its Negro employees."[20]

This was a watershed moment in the history of the Alliance. Combining the spirit of CIO labor direct action protest and NAACP anti–Jim Crow social and legal protest, Alliance convention delegates were proud to have performed like a grassroots black civic action group. The upsurge of black postal worker activism during and after World War II was part of a larger national trend among blacks that challenged white supremacy with tactics of lobbying, petitioning, and direct action. Black postal worker's activism caused the collapse of the discriminatory civil service photo application, as they also presented testimony before the FEPC, confronted Jim Crow union locals in the predominantly white postal unions, and challenged conservative leadership members of the historically black postal union.[21]

Black-led progressive postal union elements also had to overcome both active white supremacy and white indifference, with much of the struggle's leadership emerging from black postal workers in the South or those who had migrated north. A pioneer in this struggle was the National Alliance along with its monthly journal the *Postal Alliance*. While not abandoning their tactics of lobbying and negotiating with government officials who constituted postal management, Alliance activists of the 1940s broke with past conservative tendencies by confronting discriminatory practices and policies in addition to requiring activist training of all their members.

DEATH OF AN UNEQUAL PHOTO OPPORTUNITY

The civil service application photograph had been an inviting target for the Alliance to challenge white supremacy in the post office since its origins in President Wilson's administration. But with the world now embroiled in war against global fascism, that Jim Crow system in the post office became especially vulnerable to challenge. "Today we stand between two worlds. The world of yesterday is rapidly dying," declared an article in the June 1941 *Postal Alliance* that was given the ironic title "Making America Safe for Democracy." Six months before the Japanese attack on Pearl Harbor and America's entry into World War II, the writer decried the hypocrisy of this "re-birth of national patriotism" in military recruitment and defense industry hiring that also saw white employers, white government officials, and white workers all attempting to exclude blacks. The writer was the Reverend Adam Clayton Powell Jr. of the Abyssinian Baptist Church in Harlem—a longtime friend of the National Alliance.[22]

This was not the typical union journal coverage one would read in 1941, but it was typical of the Alliance and other black unions like the BSCP. For example, the January 1942 issue of the *Postal Alliance* featured a copy of a Civil Service Commission (CSC) examination ratings report for Harold P. Douglas, an African American postal job applicant from New Orleans. It was dated April 20, 1936. The fact that he was African American was evident from his photograph attached to the report—which in 1936 was still a required part of the civil service application.

A copy of Douglas's ratings report along with the photograph occupied a full page of the *Postal Alliance*, which they ran as a vivid reminder of what discrimination looked like in the years before the application photograph was abolished. The entire page was a reprint from the *New Orleans Sentinel*, a black newspaper, and included this editorial caption that began with an imagined quotation that perfectly captured the post office's rejection of Douglas's application: " 'Mr. Douglas, your 96.40 per cent examination rating is not enough to get you a job.' Harold Douglas, shown above, is one of the 11 Negroes who made high averages in [civil service examinations but were not] appointed to that position because of race."[23]

The *Sentinel* was a sister newspaper to the *Alliance* in more ways than one: it was founded in 1940 by a black civic association called "The Group" that included black postal workers like John E. Rousseau Jr., the Alliance's District Four secretary and also local NAACP board member.[24] The government's stated purpose of the application photograph had been to "prevent impersonation."[25] But blacks exposed both its white supremacist intent and its everyday use as a major obstacle to black postal employment, along with the "rule of three." While all postal applicants were required to submit application photographs, white applicants enjoyed the privilege of not being rejected on that basis.[26]

As a result of twenty-seven years of steady pressure, primarily from the National Alliance and the NAACP, the application photograph requirement was finally abolished by President Franklin D. Roosevelt's Executive Order 8587 of November 7, 1940.[27] Roosevelt signed the order on a Thursday, just two days after Election Day, while newspapers throughout the country were proclaiming his landslide victory over Republican challenger Wendell Wilkie and speculating what a third Roosevelt term would look like.[28] This executive order—announced six days later—was not even covered in the mainstream media in the days that followed. There was also no mention of the event in the *Union Postal Clerk* of the NFPOC, nor in the *Postal Record* of the NALC, despite the fact that both unions had voted for the abolition of the application photograph at their respective 1939 national conventions. But Roosevelt's order was noted in the *Postal Alliance* and other black press outlets like the *Crisis* and the *Pittsburgh Courier*. They all praised that reform while criticizing the persistence of Jim Crow in the post office.[29]

Meanwhile, the 1930s had also seen a dramatic rise in the hiring of letter carriers and clerks. Postal employment and postal revenue both shot up in the

1940s, particularly after World War II. The post office had run large annual deficits since 1921. But it suddenly enjoyed large surpluses from 1943 to 1945. Total postal employment, which barely moved from 1926 levels of 329,050 until World War II, began a steady rise until it reached 517,690 in 1949, almost a two-thirds increase.[30] The peak of railway mail in 1930 began yielding to federally subsidized air mail slowly and incrementally until rail service was phased out in the 1960s.[31]

Roosevelt's New Deal administration had already been compelled to create more federal jobs by labor strikes, civil rights activism, massive unemployment, and widespread unrest. But the New Deal had also been a mixed benefit for blacks. It actually widened the gulf between black and white employment opportunities, wealth, and life chances.[32] And absent the strike weapon, government workers had to be cautious in disputes with management.[33]

During the Roosevelt administration, according to historian John Hope Franklin, black employment in the civil service (including the post office) rose from "about 50,000 in 1933 to approximately 200,000 before the end of 1946." Most of these jobs were in urban areas, and most of these jobs were not considered "skilled."[34] With barriers to black postal employment like the application photograph (until 1940) and the "rule of three," it is remarkable that so many blacks were hired at all. Black postal employment actually dropped from 8 percent in 1925 (approximately 22,000 out of 300,000 employees) to about 5 percent (roughly 18,000) in 1940, the year the application photograph requirement was abolished.[35]

In 1940 the nation was emerging from the Great Depression in large part due to heavy production of war materials. This meant more jobs for the millions who had been unemployed.[36] Inside the post office, meanwhile, a number of social and economic issues were being contested. Lagging pay along with monotonous and dangerous working conditions were constant themes in postal union literature, as were challenges to the entrenched union leadership by people like Henry W. McGee. McGee, who rose from postal clerk and Alliance activist to Chicago Alliance president to eventually becoming a supervisor and later the first black postmaster of Chicago in 1966, noted in his 1961 University of Chicago master's thesis about major changes in work at the wartime post office: "Beginning with World War II the tremendous explosion of the volume of letter mail and parcel post made the post office even more of a factory operation than an office function."[37]

In 1945, at the post office and elsewhere, returning black veterans wanted better jobs and working conditions along with full democratic rights in recognition of their service. Neil McMillen's oral histories of Mississippi black World War II veterans included letter carrier and NALC member Dabney Hamner, who, after having just faced combat in Europe, had no patience for the Mississippi white man who told him that "he was still just a nigger." Hamner responded by knocking the man down.[38] Another World War II veteran, Sam Armstrong, a letter carrier and Alliance member in Miami, told me of returning home from the war in Europe still in his Army uniform and sitting toward the front of a city bus. He recalls the driver telling him: " 'Soldier, I'm sorry but you have to go in the back of the bus.' Now this hit me harder than any other one incident that might have happened to me. . . . I didn't move." Fighting for democracy abroad while denied it at home made a lasting impression on him.[39]

Many blacks coming into the post office during and after World War II, besides demanding equal treatment, also had professional aspirations. But all were probably aware of the job's elevated status in the black community. Economists Leah Platt Boustan and Robert A. Margo note: "By 1940, 14 percent of all blacks earning above the national median worked for the postal service. The earnings of the average black postal worker placed him in the top five percent of the black weekly wage distribution and at the 70th percentile of the non-black distribution in that year." Furthermore, Boustan and Margo point out, of all black postal workers at the time, "28.1% had at least some college education, compared to 4.9 percent of the black population as a whole."[40]

As black postal workers became more aware of both the recalcitrance and vulnerability of Jim Crow, many were no longer content to use middle-class protest methods of negotiation and petition even as those methods continued to still bear fruit. Henry W. McGee in his study noted that black women entering the post office during this time brought a combination of enthusiastic union activism along with middle-class civic group organizing experience, while newly hired black men tended to be more working-class in origin and outlook, regarding the Alliance "more as a union than as a civil rights organization." With postal jobs now available for bid by seniority, there was more of a need for the Alliance to act like a labor union. But with discriminatory practices still a daily reality, the Alliance had to also continue advocating as a "middle-class" civil rights group.[41]

FIGHTING JIM CROW UNION BRANCHES, AGAIN

Segregated unions were never unique to the post office. Many AFL unions by the 1940s (including the NALC and NFPOC) either segregated or excluded blacks outright, and even some CIO unions tolerated segregated locals. The failures and successes of mid-twentieth century civil rights postal unionism can be gleaned from battles over Jim Crow union branches and locals, the battleground often being the floor of the biennial union conventions. This era saw many Alliance members belonging to both the Alliance and one of the postal craft unions, either to combine black pride and postal craft or to effect policy changes from within the craft unions. Within the NALC and NFPOC, blacks argued against Jim Crow branches and locals in the South. The establishment and maintenance of Jim Crow locals exemplified black's second-class treatment in the postal unions and were a microcosm of the U.S. political process as a whole. Black unionists, often from the South and with multiple memberships, played the leading role in resisting Jim Crow at the union hall. But victories won by Jim Crow unionism during and after the war years challenge assertions by historians today that the 1940s birthed a viable black-left-labor coalition suddenly crushed by anticommunism just as victory was in sight.[42]

While denunciations of Jim Crowism and comparisons of that system with European totalitarianism were more frequent at the NFPOC conventions than at those of the NALC, voices were also raised in protest within the NALC. An NALC *Postal Record* article written almost a half-century later succinctly summed up what was then being claimed by defenders of the resolution supporting "separate" or "dual charters" (as Jim Crow branches were euphemistically known): that they were essential because without them, potential black members might otherwise be lost to the National Alliance.[43] The argument was even advanced in 1941 by some of these same "dual charter" supporters that to defy southern white "custom" would not only alienate white members but also deny black letter carriers access to union membership, and therefore second-class union membership for blacks was better than their union disenfranchisement. It was no secret that the NALC also felt competition from the Alliance for black carriers and their union dues. A white supporter of the "dual charter" amendment disingenuously warned that black carriers in Georgia would go unrepresented if not allowed an NALC "dual charter." But since the Alliance had already organized black carriers in Georgia, these "dual charter" advocates were really recommending a "raid" on Alliance branches.[44] This victory for Jim Crow NALC branches came at their 1941 Los Angeles convention—almost a year after the Civil Service Commission had dropped photographs and references to race from its applications.

Unlike readers of the *Postal Alliance*, letter carriers reading the NALC's *Postal Record* during the 1940s rarely found any discussion of potentially "embarrassing" issues such as discrimination against black postal workers.[45] The photographs in the 1940s *Postal Record* were almost exclusively of white male letter carriers and their white female spouses belonging to the NALC women's auxiliary. Discrimination and segregation were issues that this organization consistently avoided, as the NALC proved to be a major obstacle to Jim Crow's elimination at the post office. While there was much comment on the global and national war effort (personified especially against Hitler), issues of "race" or "racism" were rarely discussed. There was no mention, for instance, of President Roosevelt's significant Executive Order 8802 banning discrimination in war industry as a result of A. Philip Randolph's threatened 1941 March on Washington.[46]

The September 1941 NALC convention hosted influential politicians like Rep. Robert Ramspeck (D-Ga.), chairman of the powerful House Civil Service Committee. Keeping Ramspeck happy was clearly on the minds of many delegates. The proposal for separate charters was brought by the Georgia state delegation—more specifically, the branch from his hometown of Atlanta. Concern was expressed about what Ramspeck would think if the measure were defeated. Letter carriers in 1941, after all, like all postal and other federal workers, did not yet enjoy collective bargaining rights, and were forced to depend on the kindness of politicians like Ramspeck to pass beneficial legislation. (Ironically, in 1940 Congress had passed a civil service reform law that he authored called the Ramspeck Act, which included nondiscrimination provisions for the first time in federal law.)[47]

The entire proceedings of that convention were transcribed and published in the October 1941 *Postal Record*, and the debate over "separate charters" is revealing. First, the item was removed from debate as a simple resolution in favor of its consideration as a much more serious and permanent constitutional amendment. In the course of that debate, the words "white" and "colored" were each used only once. Speakers instead utilized euphemisms like "one race" and "another race." Those who supported the white southern position on dual branches alluded to traditional "peculiarities" of the South and the inability of "the races" to get along. The fact that the Committee on Constitution and Laws approved this latest "dual charter" amendment gave it an official imprimatur, thereby making future opposition a formidable undertaking.[48]

Yet judging from applause and cheers recorded on both sides of the debate (right down to the amendment's ultimate approval), it was a divided convention that approved by voice vote the Jim Crow separate charters over the impassioned objections by delegates like Barney Bernstein of Chicago and B. P. Newman from Jackson, Mississippi, along with Ray Lieberman and Pete Craig of Detroit.[49] Newman and Craig were both African Americans and also active members of the National Alliance.[50] Craig asked, "How can you determine which Branch is subordinate?" and compared this proposal to "methods . . . by dictator nations." He pointed to the counterexample of "Jacksonville, Fla., once separated . . . brought together in harmony, and are now functioning together," and closed with this appeal: "May I ask, brothers, that you not undermine democracy," calling on them to "unite America into one fair land of democracy and brotherhood."[51]

Despite the loss to Jim Crow unionism, this 1941 NALC convention debate reveals that black letter carriers apparently formed a majority in Atlanta and elsewhere in the South, including New Orleans and parts of Virginia and Mississippi. This suggests that there were indeed black postal labor political survivals dating from Reconstruction and the period immediately following it. The Mississippi state NALC convention had just been held on June 6, 1941, at the historically black Jackson College (which became Jackson State University in the 1960s).[52] The state association, in fact, was all black, according to black postal unionist and civil rights activist Willenham Castilla, who was a member of both the NALC and the Alliance during the 1950s.[53]

The white supremacist myth that blacks and whites in the South had to be kept separate because they "could not get along" could have been put as follows: "We can't get along with blacks on any terms that would threaten white supremacist tradition and ritual."[54] But during the 1941 national convention debate, B. P. (Ben) Newman questioned the NALC's "logic" of proposed separate branches made up of blacks and whites who presumably could not "get along" but yet under a separate related amendment were supposed to be able to agree on a common governing council.[55] According to the report of the forty-fourth Mississippi state NALC convention held at historically black Jackson College (now Jackson State University) in 1941, Newman, "one of Branch 207's oldest and most dependable members, was elected by acclamation." Leading black activists from this NALC branch also served as local Alliance and NAACP leadership. This was a southern black wellspring of civil rights unionism in the postal labor movement, and it threatened Jim Crow.[56]

After twenty-two years of rebuffing separate charters, it might seem strange that the NALC convention would suddenly cave in to Jim Crow proponents in the midst of a global war where the enemies of the United States espoused ideologies of fascism and racial supremacy. The convention majority deferred to Jim Crow in large part from financial considerations, combined with a desire to pacify angry white southerners as well as recruit black letter carriers —and their dues. Considerations of equality and unity yielded to arguments that the South had "peculiar" institutions and contained people who somehow could not "get along" and therefore required separation—for whites to decide, of course. In the end, the NALC acquiesced to a growing movement of white southern apartheid. Serving as a barometer of organizational indifference, the months following the stormy convention debate saw only four letters addressing Jim Crow charters in the *Postal Record*'s regular monthly

"Branch Items" section, including three from white southerners in support of the resolution. The only opponent was the Norfolk branch scribe: M. E. Diggs, an African American and also an Alliance member.[57]

The NALC had become even more solidified as a conservative trade union—possibly in part as a reaction to rising militant industrial egalitarian unionism in the post office. Even the resolution calling for an AFL-CIO reunification had been resoundingly defeated by the convention after outgoing president Edward Gainor—to much applause—declared his thoughts on the ongoing rift between the estranged labor federations: "Now the fact of the matter is—well, take, for instance, our own National Association of Letter Carriers, and we immediately see how overwhelmingly important is the idea of craft organization."[58] While William Doherty's election as NALC president in 1941 ostensibly indicated the passing of the conservative old guard to a more progressive activist leadership, the approval of separate charters at this convention contradicted his progressive ascendancy. If anything, separate charters sadly now secured the NALC's place among the most reactionary AFL elements that saw craft work as non-industrial and "white."[59]

But black letter carriers in the NALC remained among the most active progressive unionists in addition to being advocates for equality. In his *Postal Record* article decrying how the NALC had "surrendered to the spirit of fascism" with its 1941 adoption of Jim Crow branches, M. E. Diggs also listed the ongoing issues that remained to be addressed, among them "longevity, optional retirement, abolition of the speed-up system, salaries in keeping with the rising high cost of living, seniority, etc." Diggs also wondered why his all-black Norfolk branch had been generally ignored for its stands on postal labor issues: "We here were and are much disappointed to note that the convention Postal Record does not give either our Virginia State Association or this Branch 525 credit for any of the resolutions sent in. They covered practically all the subjects reported by the resolutions committee, and then some."[60]

By contrast, the NFPOC had evidently tolerated dual locals for some time. The fight for equality at their 1941 national convention in St. Louis is a similar story as that of the NALC but with an interesting twist. The group photograph taken at their 1941 national convention reveals a number of African American delegates. Like the NALC's *Postal Record*, the NFPOC's *Union Postal Clerk* articles during this era were also almost exclusively concerned with (1) postal matters; (2) the ability of organized labor to mobilize around the war effort; and (3) refuting the image of labor as unpatriotic and strike-prone that some of their members complained was being promoted by the mainstream media.[61]

The organization as a whole, like the NALC, was proud to be affiliated with the AFL. Yet, unlike what one might have seen at an NALC convention during the 1940s, the NFPOC passed resolutions opposing discrimination in the defense industry and the post office, as well as calling for the abolition of the discriminatory poll tax. In April 1941, as the March on Washington Movement (MOWM) was gathering steam for pressuring President Roosevelt to open up defense jobs to blacks, the NFPOC Chicago Local No. 1 met and adopted a resolution that was published in the *Union Postal Clerk* the following month. It called upon "the President of the United States and the commissioners of the defense program to see that these firms which are making millions of dollars by producing munitions which are being paid for the Government of the United States are forced to stop this willful discrimination against these worthy citizens of the United States."[62]

This resolution No. 902, dubbed "Discrimination in Defense Industries," was cosponsored by Brooklyn Local 251.[63] Another resolution titled "Discrimination Against the Negro" and sponsored by Cleveland Local 72 was intended to "instruct our delegates to the [upcoming] convention of the A.F. of L. to work for the abolishment of the discrimination against Negroes."[64] And one more resolution—this one from New York City Local 10—was passed condemning "persecution of minorities."[65] The debate on the Cleveland local's "Poll Taxes" resolution to abolish the poll tax prompted a white Florida delegate to rise and urge its passage because of the many poor whites he claimed were disenfranchised by it (he made no reference to the anti-black bias of that law still popular in southern states at the time). The resolution passed.[66]

The clerks' union was clearly putting itself on record against bias and prejudice against African Americans—outside the union. Yet when presented with a concrete opportunity to fight discrimination in their union, the NFPOC fell on its face at that convention. The Cleveland local had moved to challenge Jim Crow locals with their Resolution No. 888: "Resolved, That the convention assembled oppose the continuance of the Jim Crow policy in our Federation and that all P.O. clerks be eligible to belong to the one Local in their city, and that all present dual Locals be done away with, and that dual Locals be merged, democratically, under the supervision of the National Executive Board."[67]

But similar to what happened at the NALC convention that same year, the NFPOC resolutions committee backed what they called "separate locals." The majority of the convention voted in agreement, thus continuing to endorse Jim Crow, as the Cleveland local had bitterly noted.[68] Three years later at its Indianapolis convention, again with the "non-concurrence" of the resolutions committee, the NFPOC dismissed Local 251's proposal to "consolidate dual locals." There was no debate other than President Leo George's defense of Jim Crow locals as being a local matter for members who "feel that they are promoting the interests of their members."[69]

Postal union conventions historically have featured discussion and debate on issues pertaining to work and union-related matters. But highly charged political debates over segregated union branches and locals also took place during the twentieth century. This photograph of the NALC national convention in August 1974 in Seattle, Washington, features the delegation from Washington, D.C., Branch 142, originally integrated at its 1895 founding, then segregated between 1948 and 1961 after the 1941 convention sanctioned Jim Crow branches. Courtesy of *Postal Record*, National Association of Letter Carriers, AFL-CIO.

But a black NFPOC delegate, Henry McWright of Cleveland (also vice president of the Cleveland Alliance branch), speaking on behalf of an antidiscrimination resolution approved earlier, must have made Jim Crow's defenders squirm as he compared racism that he had seen in both the South and Ohio to European fascism. He concluded with an allusion to the debate over Jim Crow locals: "There are some things that I hope will be bettered in the future, at the next national convention, but I won't dwell on that now."[70] And Earl A. McHugh, another Cleveland delegate, took issue with two white southern defenders of the poll tax, calling it racist and antidemocratic. The applause and passage of the resolution must have irritated southern white delegates. Two of them rose to record their opposition (Alabama and Georgia), and two white Alabama delegates asked other delegates to refrain from raising "these things."[71]

Wartime had unleashed productive forces in the United States as well as agents of social change in the black community, of which black postal workers were an integral part. But as blacks were moving forward, white majorities of the postal unions were moving backward, as were most American unions, acquiescing in racial and political repression at the workplace. Black postal workers, who for years had fought their way into the post office, continued to struggle for equality within its unions.

THE FEPC: "AN NLRB ON NEGRO DISCRIMINATION"?

The FEPC represented a wartime forum for black postal workers to present grievances against both their employer and the postal unions for maintaining systemic white preferences. As more blacks entered the post office, the fight was transferred from the one against the now-defunct application photographs to other standard black exclusionary devices like the "rule of three."[72] Following Executive Order 8587 that abolished the application photographs, President Roosevelt issued Presidential Memo 63, which asked postal officials to pay extra consideration to black applicants. In effect this was a precursor to modern affirmative action policy and law, and as such it also slightly offset "rule of three" exclusions of blacks.[73] While postal workers had fewer options in terms of job protest actions, the fact that black postal workers had a higher overall educational level provided many of them not only a civil service examination advantage, but also gave them an edge in filing complaints, including those to the FEPC. That black labor groundswell was cited in a September 29, 1943, memo from FEPC examiner Alice R. Kahn to FEPC commissioner John A. Davis: "Summary of WPB Report on Detroit." Kahn's memo discussed efforts made by grassroots "Negro organizations, unions and liberal groups" working with the FEPC to overcome white management and labor resistance to black employment and occupational advancement in a city with a labor shortage: "The government, to enforce its attitude has created the FEPC which is in effect, 'an NLRB on Negro discrimination.' The minority group division of WMC [War Manpower Commission] will attempt to solve problems of discrimination before they refer cases to FEPC. . . . Negroes emphasize the need for government compulsion to eliminate unfair practices."[74]

This upbeat assessment by an outspoken, lower-level FEPC official referred to the FEPC as a corrective even as it acknowledged the failure of the 1935 National Labor Relations Act failure to protect black workers—something that labor historians today are still slow to acknowledge despite considerable evidence accumulated by Herbert Hill and others.[75] Alice Kahn also documented in her memo how a coalition had formed to challenge white supremacy in Detroit in reaction to the worst race riot in U.S. history just three months before. She further noted black historical memory from Reconstruction—that the federal government would protect black citizenship rights with force if necessary.[76]

The FEPC itself was a product of President Roosevelt's Executive Order 8802 of June 25, 1941, banning discrimination in the nation's defense industry. Roosevelt's order came in response to the threatened July 1 all-black march on the nation's capital by the MOWM, led by A. Philip Randolph against defense industry and military service discrimination. Randolph called off the march as a result of the order, although he was criticized by many in the MOWM for doing so and allowing Roosevelt to duck the unresolved issue of Jim Crow in the military.[77] Black postal workers had been part of the organizing effort for the 1941 March on Washington, and were among those filing complaints with the FEPC—part of the nationwide challenge to employers and white labor unions. (New Orleans Alliance members protested local job discrimination to Roosevelt just three weeks after he issued EO 8802.)[78] The FEPC was the first such organized pro-equality effort by the federal government since Reconstruction, and many activists helped fight to revive it as a permanent committee after its 1946 demise.[79]

FEPC investigations often made corporate, government, and union targets nervous or defiant while simultaneously encouraging pro-equality activists. Roosevelt's EO 8802 provided for an FEPC under the Office of Production Management to prevent discrimination "in industries engaged in defense production."[80] If the gains that were being made by early 1943 were sluggish, the language in Roosevelt's subsequent Executive Order 9346 of May 27, 1943, communicated an even greater sense of urgency, based on a very real labor shortage: "WHEREAS the successful prosecution of the war demands the maximum employment of all available workers regardless of race, creed, color, or national origin." The new order moved the FEPC to the Office for Emergency Management and broadened its scope to include government agencies, like the CSC. By now, the FEPC had become a symbolic battleground between pro– and anti–Jim Crow forces.[81]

Black postal workers did not wait until the new executive order was broadened to include them. By early 1942 they were demanding that Alliance leadership present their grievances to the FEPC. But the CSC managed to blunt most of these grievances and the FEPC was of little help in overcoming them. During this wartime "window," however, the FEPC opened some doors for black postal workers. This was despite the fact that they often found themselves either passed over for hiring or promotions once inside the post office—even in cases where they had greater seniority.[82] The threat of being "last hired, first fired" when peacetime came applied not only to blacks in private industry but also in federal employment, which under the War Service Regulations of the CSC had made all appointments temporary after March 16, 1942.[83]

Black postal worker activists also successfully pushed for a seniority system to halt the exclusion of blacks from supervisory positions despite longer service, job qualifications, and college education. The campaign for more black postal supervisors, according to Henry W. McGee, was not just symbolic but practical—the expectation being that black supervisors would be responsive to the needs of black postal workers where whites were ordinarily not.[84] In general, despite the limits inherent in filing complaints with the FEPC, the National Alliance, aided by favorable regular coverage in black newspapers, began putting its new "welfare and education" program to good use in applying pressure to the post office and its majority-white unions, as seen in this 1944 *Postal Alliance* report: "The welfare front was given new stimulus with the advent of the F.E.P.C. The *California Eagle*, Jan. 20, 1944, gives this story in part: 'Probe of Los Angeles postoffice begins. . . . Four conferences were held with officials of the Los Angeles postoffice. Results were immediately recognized in changes in assignments.'"[85]

There was also grassroots activist work at the post office. In the February 1944 *Postal Alliance*, Curtis W. Garrott reported the influence black postal workers had on whites in Los Angeles: "White clerks in ever increasing numbers are now aware of the fact that *labor in a white skin cannot liberate itself as long as labor in a black skin is branded*. They need us and we need them. We are convinced that prejudice has been fostered by a small group of financially powerful, fascist-minded individuals for the purpose of dividing and conquering, that they might be in a stronger position to exploit more thoroughly the common people. A number of white employees believing in racial equality, and seeing the danger of disunity as a result of this Jim Crow policy, worked with us in this fight. (Reference is to non-employment of Negroes in the postoffice cafeteria.) As a result of this unity the racial bar was ended."[86]

Black workers combined the struggle against Jim Crow with the global antifascist war to exert pressure on both the federal government and their white coworkers to abandon white supremacist policy. This was contested terrain, to be sure. Unfortunately, the obstacle of white supremacy ensured that the major postal unions would rarely take the necessary steps to ensure labor solidarity.[87] Meanwhile, a prominent advocate for a permanent FEPC was the *Postal Alliance*. Its editor Snow Grigsby, along with Rev. William H. Peck and Rev. Charles A. Hill, had been part of the new group of militant NAACP activists in Detroit that included working- and middle-class blacks opposed to Henry Ford's paternalism in which many black middle-class leaders, especially ministers, had acquiesced over the previous two decades. Grigsby and Peck (joined later by Hill) organized the Detroit Civic Rights Committee in 1933, which, according to historians Jeanne Theoharis and Komozi Woodard, "lasted for close to ten years, during which time it challenged racist hiring practices of the Detroit Board of Education, the Post Office, the Fire Department, and the Detroit Edison Company."[88]

Years later, historian Richard Thomas interviewed Grigsby, who remembered what had motivated him and other NAACP members to found a rival civil rights organization in Detroit: "I wasn't tied down . . . you have to go through so many different channels and you have to observe national policy. We made our own policy here. It was local."[89] Grigsby in fact was responsible for an upsurge in public sector employment for blacks in Detroit, as historian Thomas Sugrue notes: "Perhaps the most promising area of opportunity for blacks in postwar Detroit was government employment. In 1935, only 202 of Detroit's 23,684 municipal employees were black, and in 1940, only 396 of 30,324. By 1946, blacks comprised a remarkable 36 percent of city employees. . . . In part the reason for the movement of blacks into city work resulted from the efforts of civil rights activist Snow Grigsby and his Civic Rights Committee, who put pressure on the city government to hire African Americans throughout the 1930s and early 1940s."[90]

There is no doubt that Congress's 1946 abandonment of the FEPC left a legacy that included the ongoing campaign for a "Permanent FEPC"—one that drew many left-leaning white postal worker activists right up until the establishment of the EEOC (Equal Employment Opportunity Commission) under Title VII of the 1964 Civil Rights Act. Even after the collapse of the federal FEPC, there arose a number of state FEPCs beginning with New York in 1945. These states had some power to compel corporations, government, and unions to comply with antidiscrimination provisions.[91] The National Alliance supported and helped lead the grassroots fight to revive the FEPC.[92]

WORKING-CLASS LEADERS

Black postal workers held memberships in movements of the political left, organized labor, and civil rights. Their multifaceted role reveals a continuous thread alongside an abrupt leap connecting the black, labor, and left struggles of the 1930s to those of the 1940s and late 1950s.[93] The 1940s generation of black postal worker activists were also part of the generation that actually named the movement "civil rights"—both narrowly defined as equality before the law, as well as more broadly as full social, political, and economic equality. The argument by John Hope Franklin and others that the 1940s was the incubator of the modern black freedom movement is a cogent one, exemplified in black postal labor history.[94]

The previous circumspect lobbying of postal officials and members of Congress by the National Alliance during the 1920s and 1930s gave way to a younger generation of union activists oriented toward more confrontation than negotiation. Many of these younger activists even favored uniting with the CIO. But the new generation was also encouraged by previous pro-equality efforts, as Paul Tennassee notes: "The pre–second world war leaders . . . were able to have eliminated the use of photographs for civil service jobs, bought a headquarters in the nation's capital, established the union in virtually all the States and inserted the union in the civil rights movement. The union was institutionalized in spite of a world war, a severe depression, segregation, discrimination, lynching, and alienation."[95]

The 1940 abolition of the discriminatory civil service application photograph enhanced the post office even more as an employment magnet for African Americans. Yet obstacles to equal opportunity remained in force, including the "rule of three," barriers to promotions and certain crafts, tolerance of southern segregated union locals, and the segregated facilities in many post offices throughout the country. Those obstacles were reminders that Jim Crow white supremacy was national, not just southern, and that the victory over the application photograph was just the first round in a new battle.

Black postal workers' agitation within their historically black union or allied with non-blacks in the predominantly white unions—often enjoying black middle-class support—was unique. Historian Martha Biondi notes the growing unity between black middle and working classes around organizing blacks into trade unions in Harlem: "Both college graduates and unskilled laborers had a stake in shattering the occupational ghetto that consigned the majority of Black workers to personal service jobs, regardless of their level of education. The support of Harlem's middle-class leadership for social democratic, prounion politics created a deeply enabling environment and a broad push for social change."[96]

Black interclass cooperation was combined in the Alliance with its balancing act of civil rights advocacy and militant trade unionism. Black worker radicalism in New York City was part of a long tradition of radical left, labor, and black nationalist politics in a city that also headquartered the national NAACP office. The World War II era saw a massive black migration to urban areas at the same time that black veterans were returning from the war with new expectations. Meanwhile, many black, left, and labor groups often acted in coalition, and workers acted in concert. Campaigns for black employment —using the federal FEPC as well as similar state and local initiatives after it expired—occurred while the CIO was actively recruiting black workers: "In 1948 one million African Americans were members of trade unions," notes Biondi. "In this era when unionized blue- and white-collar employment was becoming a stepping stone to a middle-class lifestyle, autoworkers and meat-packers, nurses and postal workers, displaced the 'talented tenth' as agents of Black community advancement."[97]

Key to the growth of the southern-born National Alliance were strong urban northern branches like New York City, Detroit, and Chicago—prob-ably the most unionized of any of the Alliance's branch cities.[98] The move-ment of blacks from the rural South to the urban North (as well as to the urban South and West) was not just a demographic but a *social* movement that included Coleman Young leaving Tuscaloosa, Alabama, and Snow Grigsby leaving Chatsville, South Carolina (both for Detroit)—or James Cobb leaving Durham, North Carolina, for Washington, D.C. Auto plants and the post office were important black job migration magnets. Blacks asserted agency through mass migration, writes Richard Thomas: "These southern migrants, who to many black southern and northern leaders were but faceless and poor souls to be guided and taught the ways of urban civilization, were destined to become the catalyst that would set into motion the rapid urbanization of nearly static, black urban communities."[99]

The national structure of work and organization in the post office and its unions had a unifying effect on postal workers at the same time that white supremacy created divisions among them. Black postal workers, especially in the National Alliance, made *all* post office and postal union business their concern. The elimination of white privilege barriers like the application pho-tograph and other bars to black postal employment opened the post office even more to an "in-migration" of blacks from rural and urban, college-educated and veteran backgrounds. Collectively, their demands for equal job treatment paralleled their demands for the right to vote and upward social mobility. Black postal workers succeeded in breaking down discriminatory postal policies utilizing a similar interest convergence to what was accom-plished by the MOWM in defense industries. Unfortunately, black postal workers failed to win enough white support in the predominantly white postal unions to defeat Jim Crow branches and locals during this period.

No one in postal management forced any white postal workers into institut-ing or maintaining Jim Crow locals in the NALC, NFPOC, and NRLCA: it was something many of them chose. Public sector workplaces, like those in the private sector, were crucial theaters where Jim Crow and other forms of white supremacy were not just contested by blacks and their white allies, but rein-vented by white supremacists as well. Where the civil rights, labor, and left movements began splitting apart as a tenuous coalition during this period came in large measure from the unwillingness of most unions to challenge and defeat white supremacy.

Black postal workers, however, were among those at the forefront of that struggle. They had joined other African Americans active in the civil rights and labor movements. In the postal labor movement they worked within their own black independent union or the predominantly white ones. Sometimes they were members of the former consciously intervening in the latter. Never prematurely declaring victory nor despairing of setbacks, they claimed victories over the civil service application photograph and segregated postal facilities, while protesting the abandonment of the FEPC as well as Jim Crow's inroads into the NALC and intransigence in the NFPOC.

CHAPTER THREE

BLACK-LED MOVEMENT
IN THE EARLY COLD WAR
(1946–1950)

"I recall before I went away to World War II, before '45, I joined the NAACP in Times Square station because I believed that this is a good organization. . . . I never joined a political organization, let's say I was almost, almost many times. But I could not accept the dogma that said 'This is it' and you may not question it. You know if you were in the Communist Party, at that time I know, if you had a falling out with somebody or a disagreement, they would attempt to destroy you."[1] Those candid memories by postal union activist Milt Rosner were recorded by oral historian Dana Schecter in 1976. Rosner, who was white, was comparing what he and many others considered the rigid, sectarian practices by the CPUSA to the NAACP that "organized" him at the post office. In the 1940s Rosner was also a member of NFPOC's New York City Local 10. The NAACP—where he found a political home—was itself undergoing a "growth spurt" of mainly black working-class membership and perspective that also continued to attract white allies like Rosner.[2] But that rising level of protest by the NAACP, the NAPE, and others against Jim Crow was arrayed against an institution far from dead. In fact, Jim Crow was stiffening its resistance and broadening its appeal.

Anticommunism—which by 1950 was popularly termed "McCarthyism" after its archetypal advocate Senator Joseph McCarthy (R-Wisc.)—formed a key part of that right-wing reaction, with white supremacist "Americanism" a core value. The federal government was concerned with its image in its postwar battle with communism for global hegemony in what came to be known as the Cold War. Yet black postal workers were more vulnerable than whites to domestic anticommunist campaigns. This was largely because the fight for equality was seen by many Americans as subversive.

Historians continue to debate the Cold War's role in the civil rights movement. For example, Mary Dudziak posits U.S. government political vulnerability, while Carol Anderson thinks the NAACP lost ground following World War II to southern white supremacist red-baiting and so was forced to scale back its "human rights" struggle into a weaker one for "civil rights." I would combine those two ideas to argue that the NAACP compromised its more comprehensive "human rights" focus but was still able to use "civil rights" as a weapon to shame the United States into making progressive public policy changes. Looking back, "civil rights" seems a more narrow focus than "human rights." Yet in everyday use it often carried the same meaning, much as "Jim Crow" in early 1940s popular parlance meant not just segregation (as it came to be by the mid-1950s) but all forms of white supremacy.[3]

Nevertheless, anticommunist reaction severely set back the black-left-labor coalition that had been forming and which black postal workers had been trying to effect. It was not just heavy-handed Cold War–era government repression that fractured that coalition, however, but a reactionary coalition of opposition that included white unionists. In turn, the NAACP and the CIO tragically made themselves junior partners of anticommunist racial liberalism, while the CPUSA practically wrote the script for its own demise and triumph for its accusers with its rigid (when it was not vacillating), secretive, pro-Soviet, and often sectarian political perspectives. In spite of all these problems, there were survivors from that shipwrecked coalition that included black postal workers who made social and political equality a primary goal of labor struggles, and economic equality a priority for civil rights struggles.[4]

Scholars today also debate precedence versus continuity in tracing back to the 1940s a number of important and enduring issues: the origins of the 1960s civil rights struggle, serious defeats and compromises in the cause of organized labor, a chilling anticommunism that set a new benchmark for state political repression, and a new social contract with the working class that included a substantial differential between the relative wealth and opportunity of blacks and whites.[5] This origins debate serves to remind us that there has always been a black freedom movement, and that modern versions of it can trace their ideas and tactics to prior struggles.[6] But it is just as important to avoid creating a simplistic construction of continuity between the 1930s–1940s movements and what sociologist Aldon Morris calls the "modern civil rights movement" of the 1950s–1960s.[7] Class, ideological, and tactical differences have also been overemphasized in some histories of the black freedom movement. Historian Richard Thomas, for example, critiques Robert Korstad and Nelson Lichtenstein's study of 1940s Detroit for their "class emphasis [that] ignores the organic, communal ties inherent in the larger community building process. . . . The fact that black workers by the thousands joined the traditional NAACP speaks volumes for their faith in a traditionally middle-class organization."[8]

In addition, there are some conundrums that most labor histories avoid dealing with, including the campaigns by black workers for more black supervisors, the complex relationship between black workers and black elites in the civil rights movement, and the frequent white worker and white union official acquiescence in white supremacy.[9] As useful as historical studies by Harvard Sitkoff and Adam Fairclough have been on the severity of McCarthyism in creating an activist drought between the 1940s and the 1960s movements, their claims (along with those of Aldon Morris) of sharp movement breaks are overstated. Morris does convincingly point to the uniqueness of what he calls the "modern civil rights movement" of the 1950s and 1960s that he argues "broke from the protest tradition of the past" by using mass nonviolent disruption of white supremacist institutions.[10] But in doing so he also establishes 1950s southern-based nonviolent direct action organizing outside the workplace as normative of the civil rights struggle. Viewed from the perspective of those living in the 1940s, however, "now was the time" (to borrow the title of a popular 1940s bebop jazz instrumental by black jazz saxophonist Charlie Parker). The movement operated on a number of fronts. It combined lobbying with lawsuits, nonviolent direct action, boycotts, strikes, as well as urban rebellions against white supremacy.[11] Black postal workers were active in those campaigns.

There is a problem, however, with the popular argument that primarily blames the Cold War for the collapse of the 1940s black-left-labor coalition during what some have called the "long civil rights movement" running from the 1930s to the 1970s and beyond. The "blame the Cold War" theory constructs an undifferentiated black-left-labor coalition arising in the 1930s, maturing in the 1940s to its high-water mark in the Progressive Party 1948 presidential campaign—only to be crushed by the early 1950s, primarily through government repression, thus giving rise to a black middle-class church-based civil rights movement that abandoned economic issues. This argument fails to acknowledge two important factors: (1) the crucial role played by the majority of white workers and their union officials in opposition to that budding coalition—or at least their acceptance of the status quo; and (2) the pro-working-class civil rights movement survivors of McCarthyism. I argue instead that white nationalism successfully combined with anticommunism to weaken that coalition—fragile as it actually was (although black postal workers and their white allies were among those who kept some of those civil rights–labor coalition efforts alive). Furthermore, the three-decades-plus "long civil rights movement" concept that accompanies the "blame the Cold War" theory is problematic given the average six-year life expectancy of social movements that historian E. P. Thompson once pointed out. Historians Sundiata Keita Cha-Jua and Clarence Lang have rightly questioned this "long civil rights movement" thesis "because it collapses periodization schemas, erases conceptual differences between waves of the BLM [Black Freedom Movement], and blurs the regional distinctions in the African American experience."[12]

In addition, historians of private sector unionism like Thomas Sugrue, Earl Ofari Hutchinson, George Lipsitz, and David Roediger have noted the growing conflation of white supremacy and anticommunism, the conflicted role of the CPUSA, and the importance of blacks initiating coalitions. With Herbert Hill they have surveyed white supremacy's salience in the 1940s among white workers, many of whom bear much of the blame for the failure of that coalition. And even the CPUSA was not always a reliable ally of the black freedom movement, thus making CPUSA influence questionable as a way of validating past black-left-labor coalitions.[13]

Compared to private sector unions, most postal unions like the NALC and the NFPOC were craft-based AFL affiliates. There was only a marginal presence of either the CIO or the CPUSA in all postal unions. But that did not stop the National Alliance from taking stands that were stronger, more consistent, and often to the left of the CPUSA. Despite class differences within the black community, black workers and the black middle class were in many ways on parallel, not opposite tracks, as the "blame the Cold War" argument often suggests. The Alliance combined the working-class "for itself" and the black community "for itself"—class contradictions and all. They were part of a black radical tradition that often borrowed from but was not dependent upon the CPUSA. In the 1940s black freedom movement, black postal workers helped maintain a priority on economic issues, and were also part of a class-conscious alternative to the conservative white labor movement.[14]

Black postal worker activists confronted white supremacy in the post office, postal unions, and federal government during the early Cold War. In that struggle a significant role was played by (1) black returning military veterans; (2) black women who desired to stay in the post office and make their temporary wartime jobs permanent; (3) black men and women with college degrees and formal connections with the black freedom movement; and (4) blacks who belonged either to the historically black National Alliance, or predominantly white unions like the NALC and the NFPOC. Black postal worker activists found white allies in labor and management who were inspired by a growing postwar protest against what some called America's "white problem." A broad movement that increasingly identified itself with what is called "civil rights" issues often took place outside the range of the CIO and the CPUSA, especially in the postal labor movement, where unionists were politically active, the CIO and CPUSA being practically nonexistent, and unions were dominated by predominantly white, conservative, craft-dominated AFL affiliates. In the 1940s, Jim Crow postal unionism had to contend with civil rights postal unionism.

Black postal workers were instrumental in keeping alive demands to reinstitute the abandoned FEPC after World War II as part of the overall fight for equality. Near the end of that war, a significant percentage of postal workers were military service veterans. By 1948 most postal employees were veterans.[15] Many black veterans entered the post office as a result of pressure from civil rights groups in the 1940s. But it was not until 1948 that the administration of President Harry S. Truman (1945–1953) began to lean on the CSC to investigate complaints of discrimination in the post office. (Ironically, this came one year after Truman instituted anticommunist loyalty hunts to purge radical federal employees, many of them black, from government service.) This was the same CSC that Arthur W. Mitchell, a black Democratic congressman from Illinois, had in 1938 called the "most rotten" of all agencies. During the FEPC's tenure the CSC had insisted on the right to police agencies under its jurisdiction. Despite the order by Treasury Secretary Hans Morgenthau banning all segregation and discrimination in his department in 1942, the post office was slow to respond. The Alliance, for example, had to start campaigns against segregation in postal cafeterias to prompt the postmaster general to finally order such segregation abolished in 1943.[16]

In 1945 returning black veterans became more active in the civil rights movement. Like all veterans, they were able to gain greater access to the post office through veterans' hiring preferences that had existed since the end of the Civil War but were now even more pro-active.[17] In addition, the application photograph was dead, and the Army's infamous "Negro Quota" (no higher than 10 percent black) was formally buried with President Truman's 1948 Executive Order 9981 banning segregation in the military, enabling more blacks to move directly from military to postal service.[18] But the Veterans Preference Act and the Servicemen's Readjustment Act (or "GI Bill") of 1944, like programs of the New Deal and subsequent Fair Deal programs of President Truman, did not lift all boats equally, so to speak. White veterans in general received more veterans' benefit advantages than blacks for college, new jobs, and buying homes.[19]

The postwar period saw the post office hiring more women, including African Americans. This differed from the trend seen in private industry, where women who were hired during the war were laid off in favor of returning male veterans. Among the 4,500 black employees of the New York City post office, for example, the *Postal Alliance* in 1948 celebrated the hiring of "hundreds of Negro women."[20] However, the post office as a work site continued to be masculinist, similar to most public and private sector workplaces. It was con-

National Alliance District One (Texas and Louisiana) Auxiliary convention, 1978. Rosemary Ventress, district president, is seated on the far left. Postal union auxiliaries were able to engage in many political activities that their postal worker spouses were prohibited from doing under the 1939 Hatch Act. The Alliance Auxiliary was also actively involved in civil rights work. Union auxiliaries across organized labor, formerly called "Women's" or "Ladies" Auxiliaries, now typically include both men and women and are simply called Auxiliaries. Courtesy of the National Alliance of Postal and Federal Employees.

structed in large part by male-preference hiring, which included extra points given to veterans (usually male) on the civil service exams and gender-specific job registers. Few if any women can be seen in the major postal union journals of that time serving as local officers, convention delegates, or even appearing in photographs—with the exception of the women's auxiliaries.

By contrast, the National Alliance in the 1940s saw a marked increase in women postal workers taking activist roles. For example, the December 1948 *Postal Alliance* printed a photograph of the seventh annual convention of the West Coast's District Ten, where twelve of the twenty-seven delegates were women.[21] What also made the Alliance unique was the social activist role played by the women's auxiliaries that accompanied their middle-class uplift orientation. Whether these black women were professionals (usually teachers or nurses) or homemakers, their meeting minutes often included discussions of involvement in civil rights activity such as voting rights and resisting "red-baiting" (accusations or implications of cpusa membership). It is curious that, despite the Hatch Act's severe curtailment of all government workers' political activity, this did not create a lobbying front by major postal union women's auxiliaries, with one exception: the Alliance was an inheritor of the historical black struggle for voting rights.[22]

In 1946, the *Pittsburgh Courier* highlighted the overall differences between the National Alliance and the largest of all the postal unions, the nalc. The latter

Rowena Hairston, from Columbus, Ohio, was a longtime civil rights activist and former president of the National Alliance Auxiliary. She was first elected national Auxiliary president in 1956, then again in 1975, and again in 2004. Courtesy of the National Alliance of Postal and Federal Employees, 2005.

at their national convention that year rejected resolutions abolishing Jim Crow branches, opposing lynching, and calling for the restoration of the FEPC. By contrast, that same year the National Alliance's regional convention in Norfolk, Virginia, went on record protesting layoffs of women postal workers (especially black women) who had been given "war service appointments," arguing that they should keep their jobs "on the basis of their ability instead of their race, color, creed, or sex."[23]

African Americans—including postal workers—made use of the FEPC and fought for its survival even after the collapse of the March on Washington Movement in 1943. Mass rallies called "Negro Freedom Rallies" or "Save FEPC Rallies" were held in New York's Madison Square Garden every year from 1943 to 1946. A mass organizing meeting had been held in New York in 1942, and in 1950 a "Civil Rights Mobilization" saw 5,000 delegates representing fifty-five organizations descending upon Washington, D.C., to lobby for civil rights legislation, including a permanent FEPC. Black postal workers, especially in the National Alliance, played a key role in these mass events.[24]

The National Alliance also made a point of praising New York postmaster Albert Goldman for hiring and promoting more blacks (including black women) in that city's post office since 1934: "Qualified applicants for seasonal work are accepted regardless of race or color and no top eligible has ever been passed over for appointment to the classified service. . . . The New York City Post Office also maintains the largest group of Negro employees and Negro supervisors in the entire Post Office Department. Here the Negro has gradually obtained recognition and advancement has been rapid. No other Postmaster has seen fit to utilize the ability of the Negro employee."[25]

To punctuate the point, a photograph of Postmaster Goldman with several dozen black male and female postal workers holding elevated postal positions (clerk-in-charge or foreman) was positioned atop the article, with the caption, "Object Lesson in Civil Rights in the Post Office."[26] The "lesson" contained in the photograph was that struggle, not charity, especially by an autonomous black union, yielded pro-equality results at the workplace. Not only was there mass civil rights activity in the 1940s, but it benefited from a good deal of initiative by northern blacks—including black postal workers who refused to dilute demands for equality in their attempted alliances with the predominantly white organized labor movement. For black postal employees and other workers, as Richard Thomas points out, "the NAACP had rocked their cradle and fought their battles long before the white-dominated labor movement had any use for them."[27]

As editor of the *Postal Alliance*, Snow Grigsby's local radical activism for equality was writ nationally as organizations like the National Alliance put pressure on the Truman administration. The January 1948 *Postal Alliance* featured articles with titles like "Securing These Rights in the Post Office" and "Little Progress in the Segregated School System." Subsequent issues were devoted to the FEPC and other local "civil rights" struggles both inside and outside the post office. These articles reflected branch activism as well as an organizing tool used by Grigsby and the national organization.[28] President Truman needed black votes from all parts of the country to carry him to his famous upset victory in the 1948 election over Republican challenger Thomas E. Dewey.

That kind of black voting clout would not have been possible without the U.S. Supreme Court's *Smith v. Allwright* decision in 1944 that banned the exclusive white Democratic Party primary that operated in Texas and throughout the South. Historian and sociologist Charles M. Payne argues convincingly that "a better case can be made for *Smith v. Allwright*" as a Supreme Court decision that "inspired more civil rights activism" than the better-known 1954 *Brown v. Board of Education* decision. The *Smith v. Allwright* lawsuit originated in the 1940 Houston NAACP chapter, in which the National Alliance was actively involved. Meanwhile, outside of Texas, Alliance activist John LeFlore of Mobile, Alabama, was just one of many black postal worker activists involved in voter registration after that 1944 decision, when the national office of the NAACP made that work a priority.[29]

Another prominent black National Alliance activist testing *Smith v. Allwright* in his home state was John Wesley Dobbs in Georgia. A postal clerk who had attended Atlanta Baptist College (later to become Morehouse College), Dobbs was Grand Master of the Prince Hall Masons in 1932 and founder of the Atlanta Civic and Political League in 1934. In 1946 he became active in forming the Atlanta Negro Voters League (and All-Citizens Registration Committee) that registered 18,000 blacks to vote in Fulton County within a two-month span that year, influencing local elections and driving white supremacist governor Eugene Talmadge to distraction. Dobbs was also part of a movement to force Atlanta's mayor, William Hartsfield, in 1948 to hire eight black police officers in that city.[30]

INSPIRING MORE WHITE ALLIES

The end of the 1940s saw black postal workers enlisting aid from white workers and management officials in the fight against Jim Crow, especially on the floor of postal union conventions. Similar to labor conventions of private industry unions, these conventions typically make policy decisions, conduct elections, and serve a ritual reaffirmation of purpose, including rousing speeches by sympathetic elected politicians, officials from other unions, and even management officials. But Alliance conventions were unique. In August 1947, delegates to the Alliance's convention in Cleveland heard this frank admission from Los Angeles postmaster Michael D. Fanning, a former letter carrier and NALC member who in 1945 had replaced Mary Briggs (against whom blacks had made numerous complaints of discrimination):[31]

> As a member of the so-called Caucasian race, whatever that means, I feel very humble as I stand here before you people of another race. . . .
> . . . I have a tremendously deep and sincere feeling that all of us white people owe to our darker brethren not just a sense of equality under the law—that you already have, but we owe an apology for the manner in which we and our fathers have treated you and your fathers for the past several generations. . . .
> *You may begin to see now what I mean when I say that this whole thing is a white problem.* I know it's a white problem because I, as a white man, am on my way to a solution of it. I know it seems extremely unusual that we have 11 supervisors in this office who are Negroes, but remember this: None of them is yet in an executive capacity, other than the station superintendents, and there are 250 supervisors in that office who are not Negroes.[32]

The *Postal Alliance* reported an overwhelming response: "Needless to say that a standing ovation was given Mr. Fanning."[33] Black postal worker activists took help from wherever they could get it, whether it was from white unionists or management officials like New York's Postmaster Goldman or Los Angeles's Postmaster Fanning. The Alliance praised these two especially as positive role models. While Fanning's speech to the Alliance might be dismissed by some as preaching to the choir, his remarks reflected his practice—to an extent. But just as New York Alliance activist John Adams would recall Goldman for his part as being more pragmatic than principled, Raydell Moore, who had been a black NFPOC activist in Long Beach, California, in the 1950s, later recalled that Fanning was not exceptional but rather "average" on the question of equality.[34] Goldman and Fanning, then, were part of a broad postwar tendency or coalition that recognized the need to abolish Jim Crow nationwide for reasons that included both moral imperatives and the need to maintain labor peace, given the large and growing number of African American workers at the time.[35] This egalitarian coalition had maintained some momentum in the late 1940s, but so had the forces of reaction. For example, efforts to overturn the NALC's 1941 "separate charter" provision were invariably defeated, as the *Postal Alliance* observed in 1948.[36]

For its part, the NALC's November 1948 *Postal Record* informed its members

Raydell Moore in 2001. After serving in the armed forces, Moore began working in the post office in Long Beach, California, and joined the Long Beach NFPOC local in 1952. He was part of the 1958 NFPOC split and later held the top offices in both the Long Beach NPU and the California NPU (1964–71) before becoming APWU National Representative in 1971 and Western Regional Coordinator in 1977, serving on the APWU National Executive Board. Moore was also a 1970 postal strike veteran and became a specialist in processing EEO cases for union members. Courtesy of Raydell Moore.

with a scant one-paragraph entry that the convention had turned back the effort led by the black Norfolk Branch 525 to abolish separate charters. Despite the efforts of black carriers and their white allies, Jim Crow had become the NALC status quo. The only public post-convention comment within the NALC on that convention resolution appeared in the December 1948 *Postal*

Record, written by Leon Samis on behalf of New York City Branch 36, noting among the highlights of the convention: "Actions which displeased: . . . Tabling resolution denying the award of a convention to any city practicing segregation. . . . Failure to rescind dual charter policy."[37] Yet despite the dual (or "separate") charter policy, photographs of the 1948 NALC convention in the *Postal Record*, in contrast with past conventions, now showed many more black letter carrier delegates than ever before, including a few serving as national and local officers.[38]

Meanwhile, the *Postal Alliance* published its own account of the anti–Jim Crow resolution defeat in their November 1948 issue, describing it as a "heated session" in which the convention defeated resolutions banning separate charters and keeping conventions out of segregated cites. The integrated branch resolution, the *Postal Alliance* reported, was brought by the New York branch along with eleven other northern branches. (It also noted that a black New York delegate, Herman Wooley, questioned the so-called "subversive elements" ban, which did pass.) The *Postal Alliance*'s source for this information was the *Pittsburgh Courier*.[39]

But the Alliance could just as easily have asked for a report from its own members who were also serving as NALC convention delegates. The 1948 NALC convention delegate roster, for example, included the names of John W. Lee of Newport News Branch 609; plus Carl Christian and M. E. Diggs of Branch 525, Norfolk's black branch. All three were also Alliance members. Diggs had just the year before been appointed to the Alliance's Constitution Revision Committee, and was referred to in the January 1947 *Postal Alliance* as "a man of action. . . . He is very active in the Alliance as well as in the National Association of Letter Carriers. He knows what the score is and what is to be done."[40]

Diggs really was a man of action. According to the 1948 NALC *Postal Record* convention issue, it was his branch (and probably Diggs himself) who brought the unsuccessful pro-integration resolution to the floor. "What is democracy except equality?" he demanded during the floor debate that featured black versus white southerners on the issue of separate charters.[41] When Diggs submitted his final report to the 1948 convention as state vice president for Virginia, he chronicled his travels around the state to local branches "in the interest of the N.A.L.C. and . . . winning the fight for improvement of working and salary conditions for letter carriers."[42]

Throughout the 1940s the *Postal Alliance* and the black press regularly kept tabs on the NALC and other postal unions. The Alliance seems also to have at least tolerated their members simultaneously belonging to other postal unions —even praising it on occasion if their members were using that dual membership to work from within the predominantly white postal unions. But the

National Alliance also took a very dim view of their members or any black postal workers enabling Jim Crow unionism. So it seemed very strange indeed that the November 1948 edition of the *Postal Alliance* should include an article titled "Attention Letter Carriers Special Meeting!" that in fact was an invitation to join the new Washington, D.C., *segregated* black NALC branch.

The article was printed verbatim as a press release, not sold as an advertisement nor endorsed by the Alliance. President Doherty himself, the article announced, would be there to charter Branch 4022 of the NALC: "YOU owe it to yourself to become a member of this great AMERICAN institution," it gushed. It is possible that this was a flyer not intended for publication but that the *Postal Alliance* had found and printed as a piece of evidence to fire up its readers—as Jim Crow branches never received anything but scorn from the Alliance. On the contrary: the *Postal Alliance*'s coverage of the NALC convention that appeared on the same page not only reported the NALC's reaffirmation of Jim Crow branches and the convention's segregated social activities in Miami, but added that black carriers in the nation's capital refused to join the NALC until their Jim Crow locals were banned.[43]

But the most astonishing thing about the "Special Meeting!" article was the fact that those signing themselves as its "Special Organizing Committee" were seven leading black members of the National Alliance and the NALC (several if not all holding dual memberships)—from New York and other cities. They included well-known civil rights postal unionists like John W. Lee of Newport News; left activist John H. Turner of Brooklyn; Charles B. Davis of Chicago; Clinton G. Hopkins of Philadelphia; and from New York City NALC Branch 36, two elected officials: John R. Gibson and Carlton S. Davis, along with Branch 36 member Noel D. Morrell. Lee and Turner are known to have been Alliance members, but some or all of the aforementioned may have been as well.

On the same page where their names were listed there also appeared an angry protest letter written after the meeting had been held, signed "The Washington Negro Letter Carrier Movement Group" and titled "A Message To Our Fellow Letter Carriers." It denounced the "24 to 30 men" who had been present at NALC Branch 4022's inaugural meeting September 17 as having committed "an unpardonable, inexcusable crime . . . against themselves, their fellow workers, and the equal rights program advocated by the President of the United States."[44]

This controversy was just beginning to heat up. In May 1949, an angry front-page article appeared in the *Alliance Leader*, the New York City Alliance branch's monthly newspaper, written by its former president John L. Stokes, who had just been appointed to "Clerk in Charge," a management position. Provocatively titled "Uncle Tom's Chillun" and printed in the *Postal Alliance* that same month, Stokes's article credited *Postal Alliance* editor Snow Grigsby for having "exposed" the "Jim Crow Letter Carrier Branch in Washington." Given the National Alliance's policy of opposition to segregated union branches, Stokes could not understand why "the matter has been allowed to cool off." Stokes stirred the fires by reprinting the names of the "Special Organizing Committee" in case anyone had forgotten. He even evoked images of antebellum plantation slaves, slave owners, and overseers, derisively imagining out loud the seven black letter carriers catching the train for the nation's capital wearing jeans and bandanas, happy to furtively meet in the postmaster general's reception room with the founders of D.C.'s new Jim Crow branch, whom he dubbed "Marse Doherty and Cap'n Lepper." Stokes, already furious that NALC national president William Doherty had been involved in establishing a new separate black branch (in the nation's capital, no less), expressed particular outrage at Philip Lepper, NALC Branch 36's liberal president, for betraying Branch 36's historical opposition to NALC "dual charters."[45]

I have found no further evidence of internal debate or recriminations within the National Alliance over the collusion by some of its own members in establishing a Jim Crow NALC branch in the nation's capital—including those who would later take part in the nationwide campaign to abolish Jim Crow branches. "Working from within" is the only logical reason I can surmise why seven black union activist letter carriers would help set up a Jim Crow branch—in cooperation with both liberal and conservative white NALC officials.

But the strong and apparently unanswered charges of collaborationism published with editorial approval by two of the Alliance's principal organs demonstrate the seriousness with which the organization took the struggle against Jim Crow. Stokes spoke for National Alliance historical activism when he declared: "If we fail to fire a broadside at this evil of dual charters and permit the perpetrators of such treachery as was demonstrated in the establishment of the Jim Crow Letter Carrier Branch in Washington, D.C. to go their merry way without the caustic criticism their action deserves, then we are failing in our duty to our own constituents and the Negroes of this country."[46]

Meanwhile, for the NFPOC, the issue of Jim Crow locals had reemerged at their 1946 Milwaukee convention. Charles O. Maxwell, a black delegate and future local vice president from New York Local 10, joined other Local 10 delegates in sponsoring resolutions against discrimination in the armed forces and lynching, both of which passed. (For the previous two years Maxwell had also been a vice president with the New York City National Alliance branch.)

Another "Progressive-Fed" local—Brooklyn Local 251—successfully sponsored a resolution against Jim Crow locals and black exclusion by AFL affiliates (which included the NFPOC).[47]

But the resolutions committee once again—just as it had in 1941—opposed a resolution barring "dual locals" in their own backyard, because, as the convention report said, it "felt that the loss of dual Locals would be a loss to the membership." At that point delegates from Washington's black Local 148—Ernest C. Frazier, Royal R. Robinson, and Lawrence C. Winters—brought a compromise measure at the "suggestion" of national president Leo George. It included a condemnation of dual locals as "inconsistent with liberal thinking and present-day social progress," combined with a caveat against "reforms introduced from above without preliminary process of agitation and education." They recommended an "amicable solution for abolition of dual Locals wherever they exist between officials of such Locals, and no separate charter shall ever again be granted." The NFPOC resolution was adopted as a gradualist "compromise" with Jim Crow not unlike one that would later be proposed by some black NALC delegates to the NALC national convention in 1954. Yet the issue was not raised at the NFPOC's 1948 convention—not even as part of the new "Progressive Program" for more union democracy.[48]

Jim Crow in 1948 was far from being a fading southern institution in the labor movement, and in fact it was enjoying new strength in both the NFPOC and NALC. In the latter case, President Doherty himself during the 1948 convention debate over Jim Crow branches boasted how his recent efforts in helping to establish those branches throughout the South had netted 673 new members.[49] Southern white delegates like Lucius Cowan of Hattiesburg, Mississippi, Branch 938 no doubt appreciated the gesture, as Cowan resurrected the hoary charge of how white carriers in Jackson had been denied membership by blacks until separate charters were instituted. But now three white delegates from the new all-white Jackson Branch 3835 were seated, while no members—black or white—from Jackson's original Branch 207 (formed in 1891) were anywhere to be seen.[50]

After a Cleveland delegate had challenged the propriety of Doherty speaking on behalf of Jim Crow branches, Doherty retorted: "There is going to be order." In defending the "success" of the "separate charter situation," Doherty invoked the biblical "sins on both sides" expression three separate times, most revealingly here: "I supposed it has been debated endlessly in all democratic forms of government since long before the War between the States or the Civil War. *It is just one of those things.* I say definitely that there are sins on both sides of this question and the figures speak for themselves." Segregation, while only recently institutionalized in the NALC, had become in Doherty's narrative part of an old tradition that had existed "long before" the Civil War (Doherty making sure to include the preferred Confederate term "War Between the States").

Had Doherty really just tried to rationalize both slavery and Jim Crow as some kind of venerable American democratic institutions? Dangling visions of white regional reconciliation before his listeners, Doherty reimagined Abraham Lincoln's famous oratory with this symbolic use of the letter carrier's uniform: "It is impossible to prevent *a house divided against itself* unless you bring every man who wears the blue-grey uniform of a letter carrier into the ranks of the National Association of Letter Carriers," he declared. He added that the NALC was "the only organization that represents letter carriers," effectively denying the Alliance's existence. Doherty also invoked another standard catchphrase in arguing that the union did not discriminate based on "race, creed, or national origin." The white supremacist movement in the NALC was reaching its peak in the same year that southern Democrats (known as "Dixiecrats") threatened to permanently bolt the party. Interestingly, of the eight cities that had instituted separate charters, all were in National Alliance strongholds. In nearly all those cities, the old branches were now all black while the new branches were all white—Washington, D.C., being the most notable exception with its new all-black branch. In D.C. and other cities where whites did not form their own branch, they often forced blacks out of the old branch and simply took over, contradicting Doherty's "sins on both sides" narrative.[51]

The real problem here was not "southern tradition" or black animosity but rather the NALC's support for white privilege. Nevertheless, for Doherty the extra income from new members' dues money, plus the placating of white southerners, made the controversial policy worthwhile. Unfortunately, most delegates ignored the unity plea by Claude E. Sullivan from Atlanta's black Branch 172: "We need to stand together regardless of whether we are white or black."[52] They voted to uphold the status quo in the NALC as they did in the NFPOC—with internal division along racial lines proclaimed as the price of promoting labor peace and prosperity.

LABOR UNION OR "MINI NAACP"?

The National Alliance combined civil rights work and labor unionism—a unique marriage that was not without its problems. But it was an identity that also gave it considerable influence in both the civil rights and postal labor movements. If there were political differences between the National Alliance and the NAACP, they were not aired openly. Nor can they even be seen in correspondence between the two organizations. Yet the former was far from being a clone of the latter despite their similarities and overlapping membership. The National Alliance's emphasis on economic and political issues—especially equality—grew in the late 1940s. And it paralleled the pro-labor rank-and-file upsurge in the NAACP. For example, during his speech given to the Alliance's August 1947 national convention, Howard University law school dean George M. Johnson had demonstrated a current within the 1940s black freedom movement that identified economic issues as key, as he declared: "The National Alliance . . . is essentially a labor organization . . . not just another social organization with only an incidental interest in national labor problems."[53]

The Alliance's legal and lobbying efforts both paralleled and intersected those of the NAACP in fighting discrimination—as well as pushing the latter to support economic equality. Black postal workers who were NAACP members also called on the national office to support economic issues. Los Angeles postal supervisor John T. Hall, who served on the local NAACP branch's "Pay-raise committee" as well, wrote an April 1, 1948, letter asking NAACP executive secretary Walter White and the national office to endorse a congressional bill raising postal salaries (for which the NALC had been actively lobbying): "Almost two-thirds of the employees of our local post office are Negroes. Working in this capacity affords many of them the opportunity of holding decent and dignified positions. . . . Many postal employees are among our most faithful and loyal membership campaign workers. . . . We are most desirous to have the endorsement and support of the N.A.A.C.P. We fully realize that our [pay raise] problem is not one of racial prejudice and discrimination. We do feel, however, that by all groups working together, when the opportunity presents itself, will come one step closer helping us solve many of our problems."[54]

Historically, black unions like the National Alliance did not limit themselves to black postal workers' concerns, but addressed the needs of the black community as well as the entire working class. Without collective bargaining power, however, both black and white postal unions labored under the same lobbying and grievance representation limitations. What each postal union chose to do within those limitations was different, especially relating to the issue of equality. And most postal unions did tend to confine themselves to postal matters.

But the National Alliance was also working in coalition with other liberal organizations to pressure President Truman. The Alliance and additional groups also exploited Truman's multiple election year challenges in 1948: from his own left wing; from Republican candidate Thomas Dewey; from the left in Progressive Party candidate Henry Wallace; and from the right in States' Rights Democratic Party ("Dixiecrat") candidate Strom Thurmond.

Truman was especially competing for black votes. Less than two weeks after he won the Democratic nomination on July 15 (with a party civil rights plank strong enough to provoke the all-white Alabama and Mississippi delegations to walk out, and thus lead to Thurmond's candidacy), Truman on July 26 issued Executive Order 9981 integrating the military, while Executive Order 9980, titled "Regulations Governing Fair Employment Practices Within the Federal Establishment" set up the Fair Employment Board (FEB) to help eliminate discrimination in hiring, treatment, and promotion in the federal government. The overwhelmingly Democratic black vote was decisive for Truman's narrow victory in November in large part due to such civil rights policies.[55]

Besides the presidential election, three black-led actions undoubtedly had some influence on Truman's bold but belated pro-equality initiatives, including one that he himself had convened. First of all, the National Alliance was one among many civil rights and black labor groups to praise the 1947 report issued by the President's Committee on Civil Rights, titled *To Secure These Rights*. The report was prepared by a committee made up primarily of leaders of the New York City civil rights establishment as a result of a 1946 executive order by President Truman.[56] As historian Martha Biondi points out, far from being a mere elitist exercise, the report reflected "the influence of the New York civil rights movement" with its call (as she puts it) for "the total abolition of racial and religious segregation and discrimination in the United States."[57]

National Alliance president Ashby Carter issued a lengthy response to the report in his "Statement on Civil Rights by the National Alliance of Postal Employees," published in the February 1948 *Postal Alliance*, and "supervised" by Bertram ("Bert") A. Washington, president of the Cleveland branch and also a member of the leftist Civil Rights Congress (CRC), serving here in his capacity as chair of the Alliance's Civil Rights Subcommittee of the Education Committee.

President Carter made a number of concrete proposals, calling for the repeal of the anti-labor Taft-Hartley Act and the House Un-American Activities Committee; the "distribution of land to landless agrarians"; and the elimination of Jim Crow in the military. He pointed to the "antagonism" between communism and fascism in the world, the need for civil rights for labor, and the need for rights to be secured "by those who are deprived" of those rights, and he made a connection between the President's Committee report and the Alliance's experience. In New York, Cleveland, Detroit, Los Angeles, and other northern and western cities, Carter noted, blacks could be found working as postal clerks, carriers, and supervisors, whereas in southern cities they were often relegated to custodial jobs and barred from clerical or supervisory positions. "Thus," he concluded, "as the President's Committee points to the effects of the mores of a community, we can attest to the direct relationship between the level of integration and the level of Negro employment in the postal service of that community."[58]

The second initiative compelling Truman's 1948 civil rights executive orders can be seen in the April 1948 *Postal Alliance*, as it positively reported A. Philip Randolph's March 31 declaration before the Senate Armed Services Committee. If the military was not desegregated, Randolph promised, "I personally will advise Negroes to refuse to fight as slaves for a democracy they cannot possess and cannot enjoy."[59]

The third initiative occurred on July 22, just four days before Truman's executive orders. A national civil rights conference of "25 national labor, civil rights, fraternal, Negro, and religious organizations" was called by the NAACP and included the National Alliance. It assembled in Washington, D.C., and issued a press release demanding military desegregation, revival of the FEPC, abolition of the poll tax, desegregation of public accommodations, anti-lynching legislation, and immigration reform.[60] This 1948 civil rights conference led to the January 15, 1950, National Emergency Civil Rights Mobilization (NECRM) to revive the FEPC. Ironically, its "mass civil rights mobilization" of about five thousand activists marching on Washington represented the ascendancy of lobbying and litigation by the coalition's liberal anticommunist leadership, while nonetheless keeping economic demands prominent in the overall civil rights struggle.[61]

Legal strategies both complemented and clashed with mass organizing in the movement, especially at the local level. For example, prominent Chicago Alliance official Henry W. McGee in his autobiography recalled how his 1946 election as NAACP branch president represented victory over the "silk stocking crowd" who had opposed both his postal worker status and his grassroots civil rights movement strategy. As he put it: "There were differences over whether the branch should spend more on legal services than on mass protests and demonstrations."[62]

McGee followed Ashby Carter into the presidency of one of the National Alliance's biggest branches, Chicago, with Carter becoming head of the national organization in 1945. "Under his leadership," wrote McGee of Carter, "*the Alliance grew in numbers and redirected its focus on being more of a labor union than just a mini NAACP fighting discrimination.*"[63] Yet they were still more than just a labor union in that they assigned top priority to the fight for equality. National Alliance members initiated numerous grievances, complaints, and anti–Jim Crow lawsuits. The latter included the landmark U.S. Supreme Court decision *Sweatt v. Painter* in 1950 that forced the University of Texas law school to admit a previously barred black applicant where no comparable black law

Heman Marion Sweatt, a letter carrier, active National Alliance and NAACP member in Houston, and son of one of the Alliance's founders, was the plaintiff in *Sweatt v. Painter* (1950), filed against the University of Texas law school for denying him entry based on race. He won his case in the U.S. Supreme Court and was subsequently admitted to the law school. Courtesy of the Dolph Briscoe Center for American History, University of Texas at Austin, 1948.

school existed. The National Alliance proudly backed Sweatt: "This 'Sweatt Case' may well prove to be 'IT' in setting the Negro on the road to full Civil Rights," the *Postal Alliance* exulted in its January 1950 issue.[64]

The original lawsuit was filed in 1945 by Heman Marion Sweatt, a Houston letter carrier and National Alliance activist whose father had been one of the founding members of the Alliance. But the *Sweatt* case was more than just a single plaintiff being guided by the NAACP Legal Defense Fund (LDF). It demonstrates the combined and conflicting grassroots and lawsuit strategies among civil rights groups in the late 1940s and early 1950s.[65] While it is important to contrast the NAACP's national office attempts to channel the civil rights struggle into litigation and lobbying, Sweatt's case also highlights the poverty of historical debates separating civil rights grassroots organizing and litigation into opposing strategic camps.

Heman Marion Sweatt giving a speech at a National Alliance Fourth of July picnic, possibly in Houston and probably related to strategy for defeating Jim Crow segregation. Courtesy of the Dolph Briscoe Center for American History, University of Texas at Austin, 1948.

Heman Sweatt, for example, supported the NAACP national office's legal strategy of attacking segregated education while other Houston NAACP members disagreed with it. Carter Wesley, a black civil rights attorney and publisher of the black newspaper *Houston Informer*, argued that "if whites insisted on segregation, we would demand equality." Wesley finally quit the NAACP over those differences in 1947—just three years after having been part of the NAACP's victorious legal team in defeating the white primary in *Smith v. Allwright*.[66] Two months later, NAACP chief counsel Thurgood Marshall, realizing that the case was, in Judge Archer's words, "wide open," wrote excitedly to William Hastie, his former co-counsel on the *Smith v. Allwright* case, that "whether we want it or not, we are now faced with the proposition of going into the question of segregation as such. I think we should do so because even if we don't take the case far, we at least should experiment on the type of evidence which we may be able to produce on this question."[67]

The kind of evidence that Marshall suggested would later prove critical in winning the 1954 *Brown* case: testimony from psychologists, historians, and anthropologists denouncing the "evils of segregation" and asserting that "there is no difference between folks," as Marshall put it.[68] For his part, however, Sweatt's public comments after the decision bearing his name emphasized the fight for equal facilities over fighting segregation. Furthermore, in a 1946 private letter to Walter White, Sweatt even stressed "the advisability of divorcing my personal identity" from the case because of his leftist politics: "Very frankly, I have agreed with the opinions of so many persons accused of being communistic that I loathe to deny that I am one," he confided. Sweatt also noted minimal black working-class hostility to the Soviet Union because of Jim Crow in the United States, and he approvingly quoted Richard Wright's *Native Son* protagonist Bigger Thomas: "Yeh, go head and get tough with Russia—I hope you (The United States) gets the hell beat out of you."[69]

Fortunately for White, always anxious to keep left politics out of civil rights struggles, the mainstream media in the United States apparently never heard those words from Sweatt or they would have had a field day with them. In fact, after the case had been won in 1950, Marshall sent Sweatt a letter of praise, predicting that he would serve well as an "Ambassador of Goodwill" (an interesting metaphor) once Sweatt got into law school.[70] But it is unfortunate that Sweatt's voice has been muted for so many years as a mere plaintiff, when he was in fact an outspoken radical left activist postal worker.

Another high profile case in point was that of John LeFlore, a Mobile, Alabama, letter carrier, National Alliance member, NAACP branch president, and, like Sweatt, a grassroots activist. The January 1947 *Postal Alliance* noted LeFlore's exoneration on charges of violating both the Hatch Act and Civil

Code for "unusual political activity," which consisted of trying to register blacks to vote in Alabama the previous February. The article noted that Le-Flore had been defended by Philadelphia attorney William C. Jason Jr., the national welfare director of the Alliance, and exonerated by a December 6, 1946, verdict: "In other words, it was established that what Mr. LeFlore did was not part of a political campaign, but was merely a part of a general social movement in behalf of the voting franchise of colored people in the State of Alabama without regard to their party affiliations."[71]

For his part William Jason, according to Paul Tennassee, was part of the insurgent group that took the Alliance in a more activist direction in the early 1940s, where litigation was seen as just part of the overall strategy to defeat Jim Crow. While the NAACP national office did in fact adopt a legalistic strategy by the time they took the *Sweatt* case, the National Alliance did not, even though they availed themselves of the NAACP's legal help. They also duplicated the NAACP's lobbying strategy that already was an intrinsic part of postal union life for all postal unions.[72] The differences in emphasis between the Alliance and the NAACP over fighting the loyalty hunt, promoting mass mobilization, and emphasizing economic issues lends credence to Henry W. McGee's assertion that the Alliance in the 1940s actually shifted from being a civil rights organization to a labor union when it began fighting to represent black postal workers in competition with other unions.[73]

Yet the Alliance also continued to chronicle and advance its own civil rights advocacy tradition, suggesting more fusion than transformation. For example, the July 1950 *Postal Alliance* feature article on Heman Sweatt noted his predecessors: the 1917 *Buchanan v. Warley* decision that involved an ordinance in a segregated neighborhood and a black letter carrier in Louisville; and *McGhee v. Sipes*, companion to the landmark 1948 *Shelley v. Kraemer* decision banning racial restrictive housing covenants, which had as one of its plaintiffs (as the *Postal Alliance* proudly noted) "Mrs. Orsel D. McGhee . . . a clerk in the Detroit Post Office."[74] Litigation originating with postal workers involved plaintiffs like Heman Sweatt who often did much of their own case research. Furthermore, the Alliance and other black working-class and middle-class organizations put an even greater emphasis on the campaign for a permanent FEPC than did the NAACP national office, thereby exerting pressure on the latter to do the same.

The *Postal Alliance* in 1950, for example, published resolutions by the Prince Hall Masons' national conference that sounded more pro–working class than those of most U.S. labor unions at that time. The Masons, the Benevolent Protective Order of the Elks of the World, and other black fraternal orders were not organizations peripheral to the Alliance. They were, in fact, the important social and civic organizations to which many of their members and other black postal workers belonged.[75] Ashby Carter, National Alliance president, in his capacity as Grand Master of Illinois Prince Hall Masons, had put his name at the top of the list of other Grand Masters in a 1950 Prince Hall Masons national conference resolution castigating Congress for its failure to enact civil rights legislation (FEPC, fair housing, anti–poll tax, anti-lynching), and attacked the post office's loyalty program as "dangerous to the true concept of American ideals."[76] "America has never produced a traitor who was a Negro," the resolution continued, invoking heroic black Revolutionary War patriots like Crispus Attucks, Peter Salem, and the organization's namesake. They opposed both communism and fascism while declaring their "determination to labor incessantly and assiduously for the elimination of every imperfection now existent on the American scene."[77]

Meanwhile, after having sensed in 1948 that the country was in danger of lurching to the right, and still smarting from the catastrophic effects of Truman's loyalty oath, *Postal Alliance* editor Snow Grigsby had actually greeted Truman's 1948 election with relief, opining that now there was a chance that Congress might pass "[anti] Poll Tax, Anti-Lynching, and other Civil Rights Laws." After all, Grigsby noted, the past two years had seen "hysteria, the reactionary propaganda has permeated the country that the Republicans were going to take over and there would be another depression and the minority groups that have worked in governmental service would be fired in order to make room for others when the Republicans took over."[78] Neither Grigsby nor anyone could have known then that Jim Crow would be destroyed only after two more long and painful decades.[79]

Blacks in the mid-1940s were still optimistic and determined, like the Los Angeles black postal worker cited earlier who reported growing white support for equality as a key component of emerging labor solidarity. At the end of the 1940s, however, many were anxious that a move to the right would set back earlier gains. By 1950, the black-left-labor coalition (such as it was) was tenuous. Yet D.C. was still a national lobbying center for postal unions and civil rights forces, and in New York communists and liberal anticommunists regained a working relationship within the local labor movement.[80]

The black press, including the new Chicago-based monthly magazine *Ebony*, continued to support the struggle of black postal workers in the late 1940s. *Ebony*'s November 1949 issue praised black postal workers—especially the National Alliance—for carving a niche of struggle and achievement out of a government agency founded on white privilege and black discrimination. It also called attention to the official support that civil rights efforts were gaining, such as the Senate probe of "Jim Crowism" in southern post offices led by

John T. Risher, "the first Negro to be appointed an investigator for a Senate committee."[81] The Truman administration by 1950 backed labor and civil rights, but was still also curtailing civil liberties.[82]

Alliance leaders did a balancing act of praising Truman's halting steps against Jim Crow while criticizing his anticommunist measures—at the same time their members wanted to be both a strong labor union *and* civil rights organization. Black postal workers combined congressional lobbying with NAACP activism to maintain pressure on Jim Crow at the workplace and union hall while doing their best to dodge McCarthyism. In 1947 the National Alliance had begun its "welfare and education drive" and fought separate civil service exams given to white and black applicants in Atlanta, Norfolk, and Portsmouth—cities with strong Alliance and black NALC branches.[83] That same year, President Truman's Executive Order 9835 called for loyalty investigations for federal employees—and it especially targeted black postal workers.[84]

CHAPTER FOUR

FIGHTING JIM CROW
AND MCCARTHYISM
(1947–1954)

A March 19, 1949, letter from Winston-Salem, North Carolina, NAACP branch officer Charles A. McLean to NAACP labor secretary Clarence Mitchell included this observation concerning the recent hiring of two black "sub-carriers" (substitute letter carriers) in that city thanks to efforts of the NAACP national office: "These are the first Negro carriers in Winston-Salem, N.C. in about a half century," exulted a grateful McLean. His comment suggests that blacks filled that occupation up until the turn of the century, when they were blocked by the combined action of white labor, management, and government, possibly at about the time of the notorious North Carolina white supremacy campaign that culminated in the 1898 Wilmington coup and racial massacre.[1]

McLean's letter represents just one example among many of black institutional memory of fighting for government jobs in the post-Reconstruction South. It also reveals the weight of black labor and its allies forcing the post office to open its doors to black hiring, promotion, and fair and equal treatment. Just a few months before, the NAPE noted that for the first time "in almost a half-century" two black clerks were hired at the Memphis post office. This was in a city where in 1889 black letter carriers were charter members and officers of NALC Branch 27 that included a black marching band. But whites split the branch by color in 1946.[2]

The landmark hiring of blacks in these two large southern post offices came during the same period when the predominantly black Food, Tobacco, and Agricultural Workers (FTA) union of the CIO was red-baited in both Winston-Salem and Memphis and, as a result, workers were losing their jobs. Black postal workers in a number of cities also lost their jobs to this national anticommunist witch-hunt aimed at silencing dissent, in which the CIO, NAACP, and other liberal organizations participated. The "purging" of blacks from government service (supported by liberals and conservatives) was no coincidence, as their antiracist activism made them targets. Their removal also constituted a threat to blacks' middle-class status and civil service job protection that enabled many of them to work as community activists.[3]

Black postal workers fought at the post office and in their unions for civil rights, labor rights, and civil liberties after World War II. The period from 1950 to 1954 is commonly known as the era of McCarthyism, based on the political harassment campaigns led by its namesake, Senator Joe McCarthy (R-Wisc.). But McCarthy's "extreme" anticommunism was no anomaly. Rather, it was an outgrowth of public policy and law with roots in the World War I era that had now revived itself with a vengeance with the establishment of the House Committee on Un-American Activities (known as HUAC) in 1938. In 1940 FBI Director J. Edgar Hoover, a veteran of those earlier "red hunts," began liberally stretching presidential directives as he pursued "subversive" activists who were not just communists and fascists, but also members of civil rights and union organizations. Among the most devastating anticommunist public policies of this period was President Truman's 1947 Executive Order 9835. Known as the Federal Employees' Loyalty Program, it was designed to combat "infiltration of disloyal persons" in the federal government.[4] Yet anticommunism was not the silver bullet that derailed the black-left-labor coalition, but it did derail its successful ability to make a solid connection with Jim Crow political and social activism.

Beginning in the late 1940s, postal unions and management typically reacted to the national hysteria with anticommunist convention resolutions, investigations, and even job termination (known in the post office as "removal from service"). Among the postal unions, only the National Alliance challenged both McCarthyism and Jim Crow. Black postal workers and their allies (including members of other postal unions) still fought white supremacy in a similar fashion as they and their counterparts had during World War II. Now they were invoking the Korean War, the negative example of communist totalitarianism, and American democratic traditions in order to try to shame their opponents. Their status as government employees paradoxically made black postal worker activists (especially Alliance members) both targeted and protected, and their combination of militant labor and civic traditions allowed them to speak out and maintain dialogue with government officials throughout this repressive era.

By 1950, white supremacist and anticommunist politicians across the United States often made common cause in trying to stifle labor and civil rights groups, even as some of those same politicians were moderating their traditional white supremacist language to broaden their appeal nationally. Meanwhile, McCarthy's name became synonymous with government or other institutional persecution of anyone suspected of communist political tendencies, disloyalty to the United States, or even association with people or groups deemed disloyal. McCarthyism in the private sector saw corporations and unions discharging those accused of being members of the CPUSA or any affiliated organizations. In the public sector, McCarthyism signified government agencies spying on, harassing, and indicting workers and private citizens whose activities were deemed by government officials to be left-wing. These same agencies simultaneously encouraged private citizens to spy on their neighbors and coworkers, and generally spread a climate of fear that somehow progressive public policy advocacy fostered communism.

The Cold War turned to actual warfare in the Korean peninsula from 1950 to 1953. At the same time, anticommunism was responsible for the CIO's 1949–1950 expulsion of ten of its left-leaning unions for "disloyalty" to the United States. This translated into one-fifth of its membership and one-third of its leadership, including many workers of color and many of its most pro-equality members. A similar action was taken by the NAACP. Leading those expulsions were liberal anticommunists like Walter Reuther of the United Auto Workers–CIO and the NAACP's Roy Wilkins, who assumed the position of executive secretary in 1953 with the sudden death of Walter White. Left CIO postal unions—never very populous or influential—were even fewer and more scattered by now. Meanwhile, William Doherty of the NALC and Leo George of the NFPOC were typical of AFL trade unionists who tended to see the struggle for equality as divisive and the fight for civil liberties suspicious. Black postal workers who held membership in civil rights, labor, and left organizations thus found themselves navigating a political minefield where McCarthyism was considered mainstream. But National Alliance members belonged to a unique organization that was willing to defend their left political views, unlike the NALC and NFPOC. And opponents of Jim Crow, McCarthyism, and anti-democratic practices in the NFPOC became so alienated with their union that they seceded from it in 1958.[5]

LOYALTY HUNTS AND PURGES

Campaigns led by blacks around the country to open up postal jobs once reserved for whites coincided with a right-wing drive to purge left political dissent, especially in the government service. Labor and civil rights groups were cutting off their left wings and compromising civil liberties in order to avoid government repression, while the same government was taking halting steps toward backing civil rights in a nation's capital still ruled by Jim Crow. The city was thus described in *To Secure These Rights*, the 1947 report of the President's Committee on Civil Rights: "For Negro Americans, Washington is not just the nation's capital. It is the point at which all public transportation into the South becomes 'Jim Crow.' If he stops in Washington, a Negro may dine like other men in the Union Station, but as soon as [he] steps out into the capital, he leaves such democratic practices behind."[6]

The National Alliance had been fighting segregation and discrimination throughout the country, but loyalty hunts put them on the defensive. In the labor movement, even the AFL had initially opposed the loyalty hunt. The CIO similarly opposed it, but also used it to purge its most militant sector either for alleged communist activity or refusing to sign the Taft-Hartley 1947 loyalty oath for unions. By 1950 the Alliance was virtually alone among labor unions in calling for the hunt's abolition. The NAACP meanwhile was purging suspected communists—often refusing to help persecuted members if they were suspected communists. Both Jim Crow and McCarthyism had the upper hand: the federal government was hostile toward protest petitions that were being submitted to the United Nations against white supremacist violence, and the major postal unions still tolerated Jim Crow locals in the South.[7]

Despite the appearance in the late 1940s of *To Secure These Rights*, the Fair Employment Board (FEB), the abolition of Jim Crow in the military, and positive responses to the fight for equality among many white postal union members (especially in the NFPOC), a national shift to the right was marked by hysteria over who was a "loyal American." Unions generally became more conservative in their demands upon management, even though strikes continued unabated from their postwar high of 1945–1946.[8] The CPUSA and the left were marginalized by mid-century at the same time that left politics were still promoted and discussed, albeit cautiously—including among civil rights and postal union activists.

By 1950 even the NAACP had lost members and was focused primarily on legal campaigns. Yet NAACP grassroots activity continued to challenge its "old guard." It has become axiomatic to regard Cold War government repression, aided by capital and anticommunist labor, as a virtually unopposed bulldozer crushing progressive movements. But a more nuanced story reveals black postal workers playing a leading role among civil rights activists challenging loyalty hunts and workplace purges that particularly affected them.[9] In a somewhat contradictory fashion, the National Alliance in 1948, for example, argued that it was not opposed to rooting out communism but objected to the trampling of civil liberties and loss of organizational autonomy, although it had worked with communist-dominated CIO unions.[10] The Alliance also spent the next several years objecting in print to the enforcement of Truman's loyalty hunt and called for its abolition at a time when few labor unions were doing so. This was based both on principle and on the fact that many Alliance members were being purged from the post office on the basis of their political activism.[11]

These were both familiar and uncharted political waters. W. E. B. Du Bois in his 1949 congressional testimony had noted the similarities between contemporary white supremacist anticommunism and nineteenth-century opposition to abolitionism.[12] More recently, Martha Biondi has highlighted the vulnerability of black postal employment during these postal purges:

> The assumption that antiracism was evidence of sympathy for communism permeated loyalty investigations. Indeed, advocacy of racial equality was an official justification for heightened scrutiny of the employee. . . . To gauge the influence of the loyalty program it is necessary to appreciate the critical importance of government jobs to middle-class formation for African Americans. There were over 150,000 African American federal employees, a sharp increase from the prewar era. *The largest single employer of African Americans in New York City in 1949 was the postal service.* Its more than 4,500 Black workers [about 15% of the total postal workforce of 30,000], according to a Harlem journalist, "represent a stable part of the community and enjoy excellent community standing." Several owned valuable Harlem properties and apartment buildings, indeed "many of Harlem's most prominent citizens, judges, ministers, physicians and business men look back with pride to the days when they punched the Post Office time clock."[13]

Cold War repression contributed to conservatism and silence by white unions in contrast to the black press, black labor, and civil rights groups. The latter groups during this period provide a different narrative, but one that is also not monolithic. Black-organized unions like the National Alliance were concerned with issues of equality, civil liberties, working-class unity, and progress, while the black press and civil rights groups advanced those issues in a more circumspect manner, particularly defense of communists. What stands out here is a greater willingness by black unionists to take chances and make larger political connections than the NAACP national office, then headquartered in New York City. For example, in a typical case, letter carrier Fred H. M. Turner of Brooklyn, who had been president of the local NAACP and NAPE branches, was indicted in 1948 for having been a member of the National Negro Congress (NNC) in the 1930s when it was still a legal organization. He was ultimately cleared by the loyalty board in large part due to public support, but Biondi points out that many postal workers also indicted on spurious charges were not so lucky.[14]

Large numbers of black postal workers became victims of government anticommunist hysteria based on suspicion of CPUSA membership or reading its newspaper, the *Daily Worker*; being seen attending a left event; belonging to a "subversive organization" (of which there were dozens listed by the attorney general); or speaking out against government policy. Many of those harassed *were* left activists. But the harassment was aimed not just at communists and leftists. It confronted entire organizations like the National Alliance as well as at selected leftists and liberals, primarily to create fear and distrust among those who might think about engaging in pro–civil rights activity or associating with those groups or individuals. Charged with disloyalty, for example, was Bert Washington, Cleveland Alliance branch president, NAACP official, NFPOC Local 72 official, and member of the Civil Rights Congress (CRC) and the defunct NNC. Acknowledging membership in the latter two organizations, Washington used his postal loyalty board hearing in 1948 to not only assert his innocence but to also charge the post office and Cleveland NFPOC locals with discrimination. He further argued "that it was the N.A.P.E.'s fight for Negro job rights in the post office and against racial discrimination that led to the disloyalty charges."[15]

Since the early Cold War the AFL, CIO, NAACP, and many government officials had fretted openly over communism's targeting blacks for recruitment.[16] The national office of the NAACP under Executive Secretary Walter White's direction hoped to gain civil rights concessions from the government in return for supporting U.S. foreign policy, and many times the NAACP waffled on defending the civil liberties of accused communists, including NAACP members. By contrast, the Alliance made a point of principle never to divorce the issues of civil liberties and civil rights, even if the Alliance was circumspect on the overall question of "loyalty." NAACP official correspondence shows the NAACP's national office frequently called upon to act by their members and local branches, while privately discussing how to make inroads in the black working class, especially among postal workers. Unfortunately, the NAACP's policy of fighting discrimination but not anticommunism was reflected in its ambivalence toward fighting the nationwide black postal worker purge of 1948.[17]

Organizational correspondence relating to that purge was exchanged between the NAACP, the National Alliance, and the black press on the same theme: blacks were being "removed" nationwide from post offices for alleged disloyalty in the wake of President Truman's loyalty purge.[18] Those fired included, for the most part, black postal workers in Cleveland, Philadelphia, Washington, D.C., Chicago, Detroit, Brooklyn, Newark, and Santa Monica, California. The *Chicago Defender* also noted that the Cleveland purge included six white clerks: "Government unions and NAACP are fighting this thing which looks like a pattern aimed at Negro and Jewish government workers."[19] Dur-

Bertram A. Washington, Cleveland NAPE branch president, ca. 1948. Washington was also an NFPOC Local 72 official and was active with civil rights and left organizations. He fought (unsuccessfully) President Harry Truman's loyalty purge that, from 1947 to 1953, resulted in the firing of numerous federal employees for "subversive activities," including himself and many other postal workers, most of whom were African Americans active in civil rights issues. Washington later went to work as an organizer for the United Electrical Workers. Courtesy of Vivian Grubbs.

ing this flurry of politically motivated postal firings, on October 21, 1948, William G. Nunn, managing editor of the *Courier*, wrote to NAACP public relations director Henry Lee Moon, requesting help from the NAACP:

> I talked with [acting NAACP secretary] Roy Wilkins today concerning the loyalty purge of Negro postoffice employees. I understand from Roy that the president of your Santa Monica branch was accused and suspended because of alleged disloyalty but, because of pressure, his suspension was lifted. . . . As you know, Negro postal workers who have been members of the National Alliance of Postal Employees for years and who have fought discrimination and segregation in the postal service are being eliminated in Cleveland, Philadelphia, Detroit, and, we understand, Chicago. We are going all out in an effort to protect these men and we would like a positive expression from the NAACP . . . supporting our position.[20]

Henry Moon, seeing the extent of black postal worker civil rights activism and resistance to the postal purges, sent an excited memo on November 1, 1948, to Roy Wilkins, suggesting the possibility of the NAACP representing black postal workers who had been unjustly fired: "The postal employees have from the outset been among our most loyal supporters," he wrote, "and I believe that we ought to be able to increase our influence and support among these workers if we undertake an effective campaign in their behalf."[21] Articles denouncing the postal "disloyalty purge" appeared in the *Courier*, the *Defender*, and the *Cleveland Call and Post*, another leading black newspaper.[22] The January 1949 *Postal Alliance* quoted part of the NAACP's resolution against government loyalty hunts recently passed by the NAACP Executive Board: "The NAACP will intervene in loyalty cases where the whole charge or a part thereof is based upon a) Race or color of the persons or person involved, b) Membership or activity in the NAACP, c) Membership or activity in any co-ordinating group approved by the National Office of the NAACP."[23]

But suddenly on January 18, 1949, NAACP labor secretary Clarence Mitchell sent NAACP chief counsel Thurgood Marshall a "Confidential" letter:

> Dear Thurgood: Yesterday I met with Louis B. Nichols, who is in charge of the Federal Bureau of Investigation because of J. Edgar Hoover's illness. We were discussing the FBI practice of asking colored persons whether they associate with white individuals and vice versa in loyalty investigations. Mr. Nichols denied that the FBI followed this practice. . . . The most important thing which came out of the conference, and which is somewhat disturbing, I am giving to you in confidence. Mr. Nichols said with great assurance that some of the Cleveland postal employees are definitely members of the

Communist Party and the FBI has their membership cards . . . . In view of these new developments, I believe that it would be very important for you to discuss the situation with Dr. [N. K.] Christopher [Cleveland NAACP branch president] and Charlie Lucas [Cleveland NAACP branch executive secretary] to determine whether we need to restudy our commitments in the Cleveland cases.[24]

NAACP national leaders, in other words, considered abandoning the purged black postal workers based on FBI "evidence" of Communist Party membership. Coincidentally, that very same day Bert Washington was writing to Marshall, announcing the formation of the Federal Employees Defense Committee to back a civil suit against U.S. Attorney General Tom Clark, Postmaster General Jesse Donaldson, and others, testing the constitutionality of Truman's loyalty oath. Washington and twenty-five other postal workers who were suspended pending "removal" for "disloyalty" had retained former Assistant U.S. Attorney General O. John Rogge, and Washington wanted to know what the NAACP's position would be. (The NAACP at Washington's prodding did support his civil suit appeal to the Supreme Court in 1951.)[25] Was the NAACP craven here and elsewhere on anticommunism, and, if so, was it justifiable? Adam Fairclough makes this observation: "An evaluation of anticommunism . . . might soften the sometimes harsh judgments that have been rendered on the anticommunism of the NAACP. During the McCarthy years, survival became the name of the game; the NAACP survived."[26]

Meanwhile, the National Alliance, while fighting the disloyalty campaign as antidemocratic and unconstitutional, proclaimed their loyalty by announcing that it reserved the right to purge from its ranks anyone whom it found to be disloyal to the United States.[27] Alliance national president Ashby Carter linked Truman's "loyalty program" to Jim Crow in this 1948 statement: "Members of our organization in several cities have been cited to show cause why they should not be separated from the postal service for alleged disloyalty to their government. We realize that Jim Crow is a venerable old bird, but we insist that taking pot shots at him is not disloyalty to America."[28] The Alliance was a unique organization in sticking to its agenda of black social and working-class advancement with a combination of caution and defiance.[29]

THE NATIONAL ALLIANCE VS. MCCARTHYISM

The Alliance was virtually alone among postal unionists fighting McCarthyism. McCarthyism combined successfully with Jim Crow unionism, provoking black postal workers and their allies in the black press and civil rights groups to fight that toxic mix. McCarthyism and Jim Crow were antidemocratic and elite-controlled, yet also mass-based white-identified social movements that existed not separately but in close harmony.[30] One of the greatest contributions made by historian Ellen Schrecker to the study of McCarthyism has been her explosion of the popular notion that government agencies like the FBI, HUAC, Senate Internal Security Subcommittee (SISS), and McCarthy's Permanent Investigating Subcommittee of the Government Operations Committee conducted the repression on their own. Schrecker shows that without anticommunist networks and mass support or acquiescence in anticommunism—similar to that which sustained Jim Crow—the FBI was in danger of its anticommunist campaign becoming stalled in the late 1940s.

At the post office, the NFPOC was a case in point.[31] Members of the NFPOC's New York City Local 10 and Brooklyn Local 251 had become vulnerable targets because of their past and ongoing support for progressive causes, including civil rights and opposition to loyalty oaths, despite their public pronouncements that rejected communism. In fact, Local 10 President Ephraim "Frank" Handman and another officer were suspended from the post office on loyalty charges in 1950. Yet the NFPOC's *Union Postal Clerk* during this time included articles and convention speeches consistently supporting the fight against communism in the labor unions, including its own.[32] Emblematic of the NFPOC's cowardice was the April 5, 1949, "Loyalty Case No. 99" set before Postmaster General Jesse M. Donaldson, "In the Matter of the Loyalty of Mr. Murray Hochberg," a New York City postal clerk accused of alleged CPUSA membership—which Hochberg denied. NFPOC president Leo George's appearance at the hearing, listed officially as being "on behalf of the respondent," was only nominally so. The "strongest" argument George raised in Hochberg's defense was the possibility of mistaken identity. Hochberg, he noted, "is a rather common name for a lot of people of the Jewish race." Harold Buckles, a congressional aide whom local union officers had asked to help, had this reaction: "The transcript is incredible. I doubt very much that the attorney ever read the [loyalty case] regulation, and somewhat that Donaldson has ever read it. . . . Hochberg's own statements formed the basis of a fairly intelligent inquiry into the question of union-busting. . . . There certainly seems to be an undue dwelling on Hochberg's national derivation, his faith, and the spelling of his name."[33]

The National Alliance had a similar reaction to that of Buckles, and one quite different from that of the NFPOC. Elmer E. Armstead of the Alliance's New York City branch wrote an angry rebuttal in the August 1951 *Alliance Leader* to the New York City NFPOC local that displayed those differences. The NFPOC's July edition of its monthly *New York Fed* had pronounced that it was the "only postal union" in New York. Armstead had no trouble filling up an entire page reminding the *New York Fed*'s editor, William J. Karp, and his readers that the Alliance had in fact pioneered seniority agreements with the post office in addition to standing by its members accused of disloyalty. This, he said, was in sharp contrast to the "Feds" national president Leo George urging his organization to "soft pedal" the issue while its own members were being investigated, harassed, suspended, and even removed.

But then Armstead dropped the ultimate bombshell. Not only did he chastise the *New York Fed*'s editor as a fellow worker for his lack of labor solidarity; he also shamed him as a fellow "Fed"! In criticizing the NPFOC, Armstead disclosed his own dual membership—favorably comparing the Alliance to the CIO's most militant recent traditions: "Dear Brother Karp, For the past twenty years of more, I have prided myself on being a labor man . . . to withstand the onslaughts of a reactionary management that would completely enslave the mass of working people into a state of complete peonage. It was this thinking that prompted my application for membership in 1937, first, to the National Alliance of Postal Employees, and then, The National Federation of Post Office Clerks. . . . It gave me a sense of security to know that I was a member of both of these militant organizations, one a craft organization, the other a sort of CIO."[34]

While the *Postal Alliance*, like most black press outlets, criticized communism, it did not engage in that hallmark of anticommunism, red-baiting (accusing) any progressive cause, organization, or individual of having ties or sympathies to the CPUSA or its politics. In some cases the National Alliance expressed honest reservations about the CPUSA's politics, while in others it behaved opportunistically to avoid suspicion or guilt by association.[35] But the Alliance provided only an appearance of anticommunist antiracism that was, in fact, policy for the NAACP. Like most black media sources, the *Postal Alliance* backed W. E. B. Du Bois and Paul Robeson in their struggles with the federal government.[36] (Black periodicals shared articles, the *Postal Alliance* being an integral part of the black National Newspaper Publishers Association.)[37]

Ironically, no other postal union besides the Alliance praised Rep. Robert Ramspeck (D-Ga.) as "one of the more liberal products of the State of Georgia in public life" because of his public criticism of McCarthyism's unfair targeting of innocent federal employees in 1951. In fact, the 1951 Alliance convention was markedly different from the one they held in St. Louis almost a decade before. In contrast to the insult they had received in that city in 1943 by their host, Postmaster Jackson, this time their host, the Houston postmaster, "received an ovation, due largely to his breaking all Southern precedents in appointing a Negro as supervisor in the post office, and scores of Negro clerks."[38] Howard University law school still loomed large in the Alliance, symbolized by D.C. branch president James B. Cobb—a Howard graduate— becoming national president of the Alliance in 1953. In fact, both the 1951 and 1953 conventions were addressed by representatives of Howard Law School who praised the Alliance's continued existence as a black union and its struggle against Jim Crow and McCarthyism.[39]

The end of 1950 also found National Alliance welfare director William Jason cleared by the U.S. government of disloyalty charges, although the January 1951 *Postal Alliance* predicted "the chapter is still unfinished." In the February 1952 *Postal Alliance*, Jason bitterly noted that even as his loyalty was being questioned, Robert E. Lee's picture in a Confederate uniform still hung "in a place of honor" at the U.S. military academy at West Point, and Confederate flags were flown by white G.I.s fighting in Korea. Jason warned: "The standard of loyalty moves toward unprotesting, unswerving loyalty to discrimination and segregation. To those standing guard against integration, equality of opportunity and full citizenship rights for our 10% of the population, every threat to these vestiges of slavery is subversion and disloyalty. To speak against white supremacy will soon be disloyalty itself."[40]

Another round of purges, however, began the following year that hit black postal workers particularly hard.[41] Over the protests of Robert Ramspeck, William Jason, and many others, President Truman in April 1951 signed Executive Order 10241, now making it easier for the government to fire suspected "subversive" employees. No longer did government employers need "a reasonable basis" to remove them. "A reasonable doubt" as to the employee's loyalty was sufficient. In December, the federal Loyalty Review Board even decided to reopen and cite 565 "borderline" disloyalty cases. In January 1952, letters of proposed removal were sent to all the Alliance members who had already been cleared during 1949 and 1950—including Jason. In April 1952, Jason sued the federal Loyalty Review Board and won.[42] In June of that year he accompanied eight other Alliance members to the NAACP convention, including Frank Barnes of Santa Monica, California, who was another purge victim, later to be reinstated with back-pay the following year along with thirteen other postal workers (mostly Alliance members). Their presence must have played a significant role in tempering the NAACP's previous anticommunist declarations, as the 1952 national convention passed a resolution protesting government targeting of antiracist activists on disloyalty charges. They also called for loyalty oaths to be restricted to "security sensitive agencies" and not trample the constitutional rights of federal employees.[43]

The following April 1953, newly elected president Dwight D. Eisenhower, a Republican, issued Executive Order 10450, replacing President Truman's Executive Order 9835. It even included language similar to the NAACP resolution in apparent response to their protests. But the Alliance cautioned that the order did not leave the post office out entirely from security dragnets.[44] And when the September 1953 *Postal Alliance* celebrated the fact that the National Alliance had won $37,000 in back-pay for twelve fired black postal workers (all Alliance members), it also noted that "new charges now loom."[45] Indeed, as John Walsh and Garth Mangum point out, the Eisenhower order's switch from "reasonable doubt" to "reasonable grounds" actually made it *easier* for the federal government to dismiss employees suspected of "disloyalty," as it reserved the right to conduct searches in all government agencies for "security risks."[46] Less than two years after Eisenhower issued his "Security requirements for Government employment" EO 10450, an editorial in the November 1954 *Union Postal Clerk* reported some astonishing figures contained in the CSC's recent report on Federal Employee Security Programs. Enforcement of the "national security" provision of EO 10450 had already resulted in 6,926 job separations of federal employees (2,611 terminations and 4,315 resignations—presumed forced), including 715 postal workers (292 terminations and 423 resignations). Of those 715 postal workers separated from service, only 197 even had background files of suspected "subversive" activities or associations. What helped the Alliance survive this continuing repression was its political lobbying power.

With so much timidity, treachery, and repression in the air, it is no wonder that there was a kind of grim stoicism in the framing of early 1950s *Postal Alliance* articles and National Alliance speeches. President Ashby Carter's last convention speech in August 1953 pointed to the Alliance's position in the "vanguard" of the civil rights struggle, and praised Welfare Director Jason's "Operation Contact" that had begun on Labor Day the previous year. Borrowing military language, this "operation" was similar to other postal unions' bipartisan lobbying but unique in its emphasis on democracy and equality. The purpose of the "operation" had been to inform the two 1952 presidential candidates—Eisenhower and Governor Adlai Stevenson (D-Ill.)—of the Alliance's positions and their expectations following the election. The Alliance was not alone in this respect: "Leadership conferences on Civil Rights comprising 20 other national organizations were held frequently in this election year," they reported. "The N.A.P.E. was, as usual, in the forefront with able leadership." The Alliance and the black press stepped up criticism of organized labor's obstructionism in the fight for equality as new (and competing) black labor federations were emerging.[47]

While I have seen no *Postal Alliance* coverage of the founding convention of the NNLC that began in Cincinnati on October 26, 1951, at least one high-ranking Alliance member attended and was also a leading member: Bert Washington of Cleveland, who later helped lead the successful 1952–1954 nationwide campaign against Jim Crow at Sears, Roebuck and Co.[48] Former CPUSA member Nelson Peery provides a compelling inside look at the NNLC and his friendship with Bert Washington, whom he writes was a fellow Party member who was not only removed from the post office in 1951 for his political activities, but expelled from the CPUSA in 1953 along with Peery and other black members who insisted on staying in the NNLC. Washington went on to become a field organizer for the United Electrical, Radio and Machine Workers of America (UE) until his death in 1960, according to his daughter, Vivian Grubbs, who told me that "a lot of people were blown away" by political repression during this time. (Grubbs herself became a union activist, inspired by her father's activity.)[49]

Regardless of the number of Alliance members drawn to the NNLC, radicalism existed within the Alliance even as it sought to maintain official political neutrality and win more allies. One such ally was NFPOC Brooklyn Local 251, a union that on occasion socialized with the New York Alliance. Local 251 provides some historical continuity with the labor and civil rights struggles of the 1930s and 1940s, as seen in one of their 1952 local resolutions passed: "Whereas, the incumbent National Officers of the N.F.P.O.C. over a period of many years have displayed an ineptness, lack of militancy, disregard of Convention mandates and a deplorable lack of foresight. . . . Resolved: That Local 251 reiterates its endorsement, support, and approval of the Progressive Group in the N.F.P.O.C."[50]

The following month, among the twenty-one resolutions reflecting the militancy that Local 251 decided to take to the state convention were these two: "Civil Rights" and "Discrimination and Segregation within A.F. of L." Local 251 became progressively alienated with the NFPOC on issues of democracy, civil rights, and civil liberties—right up until the 1958 NFPOC convention walkout that they and other militant locals would lead.[51] Meanwhile, *Postal Alliance* columns in the mid-1950s warned that white resistance against civil rights was growing, including from within the trade unions. But Senator McCarthy's downfall the same year as *Brown* provided grounds for civil rights optimism.[52]

Support, acquiescence, or opposition to anticommunism did not rule out differences in popular expressions of loyalty during the "Red Scare" of the 1950s. Public expressions of anticommunism ranged from enthusiastic and conformist to perfunctory. Even those in progressive social movements who did not want to risk repression or marginalization were often seen paying at least lip service to anticommunism almost as an obligation—at the same time circumspectly asserting an alternative patriotism. There were real differences between these latter expressions and those for whom "patriotism" and "loy-alty" meant not making demands for their civil or labor rights. Anticommunists owned the political terrain in the 1950s, whether in labor, government, or management. Those who were red-baited by anticommunists in the postal labor movement included both unrepentant leftists and anti-white supremacists. And they did not give up.

THE PRICE OF RESISTANCE

The actual collapse of the system of Jim Crow white supremacy, like its rise, was not orderly. Its contentious demise was framed by the domestic battle over McCarthyism and the global challenges of anticolonialism and communism.[53] In the post office and its unions, the struggle over Jim Crow reflected debates in the larger social arena. Black postal workers—the majority of whom were union members—continued to make the fight for equality primary at the U.S. Post Office. Paradoxically what made African Americans vulnerable in the post office to loyalty purges also protected them.

The post office by now was not a new entry point for blacks but a "niche" job, where the Alliance was the largest postal union in Washington, D.C., and Chicago. In the fifties, one could say that there indeed was "always work"—along with repression and worker activism—at the post office for African Americans.[54] In the Baltimore and Washington editions of the *Afro-American* as well as other black newspapers, for example, social and political activities by black postal workers were always news. These were, after all, prominent community members working for the federal government.[55] In 1951 the *Washington Afro-American* published two instructive articles on black postal workers less than three months apart. On June 9, columnist Woody L. Taylor informed his readers that a "Civil Service spokesman" had told him "that this is an excellent opportunity for persons interested in getting into post office work to do so." The message Taylor was relaying suggested a serious labor shortage at the post office: "The Post Office Department and Civil Service are making an urgent plea for applicants to post office clerk jobs," he announced. Both of these federal agencies, Taylor noted, had complained of having "not nearly enough applications" to fill job vacancies.[56]

But just a little over two months earlier, a March 31 article in the same paper had reported that Alliance past president Jerry Gilliam—then also president of the Norfolk NAACP branch—had felt compelled to publicly deny ever having been a member of the CPUSA. (It was as if the post office were saying to African Americans: "There's work at the post office if you don't challenge Jim Crow and McCarthyism!") Gilliam in fact was responding to accusations made the previous December by HUAC that he was a member of a communist front group called the National Committee to Defeat the Mundt Bill.[57] The bill was named for Sen. Karl Mundt (R-S.D.), who, besides authoring the 1951 bill to ban the CPUSA, would go on to proclaim in Congress the following year that communists could be identified as those who were "supporters of any dogma or doctrine which will weaken or nullify States rights [a common euphemism for segregation]." To that latest salvo of red-baiting and race-baiting (accusing someone of supporting civil rights), National Alliance president Ashby Carter had this disdainful response: "Communists, in an endeavor to latch on to an espousal of our rights as citizens, are late. Our grandfathers began the struggle long before Mrs. Stalin was old enough to even think of conceiving her little boy Joe."[58]

Gilliam's dilemma was no isolated case. There were a number of articles in the black press during this period, including in the *Postal Alliance*, that dramatized how much black postal worker activists were being singled out for repression by anticommunist witch hunters in the post office and in Congress. The black press also reported that the workers were resisting these witch hunts, while speculating that the motives for the purge came from white supremacist attempts at intimidating anti–Jim Crow labor activists.[59]

For many white southerners, according to Ellen Schrecker, the anticommunist crusade offered them "a respectable way to defend segregation" and regain the offensive by linking "outside agitators" with the CPUSA, "which had consistently pushed for racial equality, gave the segregationists new allies as well as a more modern rationale for their campaign against the civil rights movement." Without missing a beat, the SISS chairmanship that Senator Pat McCarran (D-Nev.) had previously used for anticommunist witch hunting in the early 1950s was in 1955 passed along to plantation owner and arch-segregationist Sen. James Eastland (D-Miss.). In a joint effort between the FBI and southern officials, Schrecker notes, the SISS "sought to expose the connections between the civil rights movement and the Communist party. That such connections were unimportant made little difference."[60]

Battles over Jim Crow and McCarthyism converged at the post office and its unions during the era of the anticommunist witch-hunts, the 1954 *Brown* decision, the 1955 merger of the AFL and CIO, and President Kennedy's executive orders on labor and civil rights in the early 1960s.[61] During this period, popular movements mobilized to attack Jim Crow and McCarthyism at the grassroots and in the courts. At the same time, they treaded cautiously for fear of being red-baited for doing any kind of progressive work. Jim Crow and McCarthyism, after all, were not just discrete state-sponsored repressive campaigns. Rather, they were mass-based interlocking systems that enforced conformity of political thought and action, and reinforced the system of white privilege and black discrimination. The ways in which black media along with black left trade unionists like the National Alliance and their allies in the major postal unions dealt with anticommunist repression help remind us of the diverse points of view that actually existed in the left, labor, and civil rights movements of the 1950s.

Unfortunately, in reaction to earlier scholarship that unfairly deemed all communists during that period as manipulative, opportunist spies and traitors, much of today's scholarship romanticizes them as the most conscious (albeit mistake-prone) of all left activists who were unfairly persecuted and betrayed by other progressive groups. The implication here is that all criticism of communists by civil rights groups like the NAACP was misplaced and must have been motivated by fear of McCarthyism, desire for survival, or competition with the Communist Party. It has even become axiomatic to see the purge, persecution, and betrayal of communists from the CIO and NAACP as the downfall of the fight for equality in organized labor, extinguishing hopes for a black-left-labor coalition.

But as appalling and self-defeating as those purges indeed were, the evidence is thin that such a coalition was really viable in the face of Jim Crow's tenacity throughout the 1940s. Political survivors, meanwhile, learned to employ more circumspect strategies under these repressive circumstances. Paradoxically, the Cold War that split the labor movement and repressed some of its most dedicated activists also created conditions where civil rights activists—including many college-educated black postal workers and civil rights unions like the National Alliance—developed the tactic of using the Cold War to advance the fight for equality.[62]

President Ashby Carter of the National Alliance died suddenly in 1953 and was succeeded by James B. Cobb. It was the same year that also saw the decentralization of the post office from total management concentration in Washington to the growth of more regional administration.[63] The Alliance noted how that change would have an impact on its ability to lobby in Washington.[64] Washington was then the epicenter of McCarthyism, as the anticommunist witch hunt focused especially on government employees and the alleged communist threat to national security from within government service. It was also the hub of the Civil Rights Congress, which among other things fought to reinstate 130 fired postal workers in that city—most of them black.[65] In the early 1950s the mainstream media and most of the black press rarely offered anything more than tepid criticism of McCarthy. But the largest black newspaper in the region, the *Afro-American*, expressed its contempt for those who race-baited and red-baited left-leaning black activists like Paul Robeson and Mary Church Terrell, while the *Postal Alliance* criticized McCarthyism and still managed to maintain respected status in the community, among social movements, and with the federal government.[66]

By 1953, Alliance activists like Jerry Gilliam of Norfolk and Elmer Armstead of New York City were also prominent figures in national civil rights organizations like the NAACP. Their activities frequently appeared as news items in the black press, right along with whatever new legal fights were being led by "Mr. Civil Rights," as Thurgood Marshall was popularly known.[67] However, McCarthyism also crippled social movements in New York City and elsewhere. Nationwide, NAACP membership remained flat, although its income rose largely because of southern repression, as Jack Greenberg, a leading former NAACP attorney points out. But as Martha Biondi notes, the NAACP also lost members because Roy Wilkins was determined to eradicate the NAACP's left.[68]

The Alliance, on the other hand, was proud to be one of the few labor or civil rights organizations to directly confront McCarthyism. The May 1954 *Postal Alliance* contained a triumphant article accompanied by a photograph taken at the law offices of Alliance attorneys Rufus Watson and Howard Jenkins. Vic Sparrow, the president of the National Alliance's Philadelphia branch, was shown presenting back-pay checks to six postal employees (five black, one white) "who had been suspended for alleged disloyalty." Also present at the ceremony was William Jason, who had fought two attempted removals by the post office for "disloyalty."[69] In the 1950s blacks once again had to fight to hold on to the niche they had carved out in government service, relying primarily on their own efforts. The confluence of struggles against McCarthyism and Jim Crow accelerated changes and contradictions in the post office and its unions in the 1950s, and Jim Crow union branches and locals in the NALC and NFPOC became targets for civil rights postal unionists.

LAST GASPS OF THE JIM CROW BRANCHES

The last successful defense of Jim Crow postal union locals by white union activists came in the middle of the McCarthy era and two years before the U.S. Supreme Court's *Brown* decision banning public school segregation. Defenders of Jim Crow branches and locals demonstrated no sense that their institutions were about to collapse, nor suggested any awareness of irony in praising white separatism as both democratic and nondiscriminatory. But black postal workers and their allies—including Alliance members with dual memberships "working from within"—continued their assault on this white self-imposed racial divide in the postal unions.

In the NFPOC, no progress had been made between the 1946 convention—

which agreed to study the issue of Jim Crow locals—and its 1952 convention. At the 1952 convention in St. Paul, Minnesota, New York Local 10 proposed Resolution No. 1005 to "make a determined effort to bring about the consolidation of existing dual locals." The resolutions committee concurred, amending it to require that "officers of the dual locals involved cooperate with one another in drafting a definite plan that will bring about an eventual consolidation."[70] That diluted language appears to have been in deference to the all-white segregated Washington, D.C. Local 140, as a member of the Committee on Organization indicated in his remarks from the podium.[71] But despite the conciliatory wording, Local 140 president Carl Malone suggested that the amended resolution was unnecessary. Malone claimed to have in operation a satisfactory "joint council" between his local and Local 148 representing African American postal clerks. Malone then yielded the floor to delegate Robert Bates from Local 148. Bates, who in 1958 would play a pivotal role in the radical walkout from the NFPOC in part over this issue, noted that this "Joint Council" had been mandated by the 1946 Milwaukee resolution, and concurred with Malone: "Mr. Chairman, I want to confirm more or less the statement made by Mr. Malone. . . . I think these two organizations are making definite progress toward solving their own problems and I feel that this resolution should be rejected because it is not necessary." With vocal support for "dual locals" from a black delegate (despite Bates's "more or less" caveat), those favoring abolition of Jim Crow locals had their legs cut out from under them. D.C. delegate John Crickenberger (white) agreed with Malone and Bates, adding, in familiar segregationist language: "We are all working to that end, but we like to do it in our own way and take our own time."[72] After more discussion (which included Vice President Francis Filbey objecting to having to deal with Baltimore's black local because it contained only one person, a supervisor) the resolution was rejected. Jim Crow lived still in the NFPOC.[73]

Meanwhile, in New York City at the NALC September 1952 convention, the battle over Jim Crow branches was on again. President Doherty and the Board of Laws continued to throw their weight behind Jim Crow branches, just as they had at the 1948 convention in Miami. White members from various regions for the most part rose to back those branches, or at least table the proposed amendment to the NALC Constitution banning "dual charters" that had been brought by delegate Philip Lepper. Lepper, who was white, was a national executive board member and president of the NALC's biggest branch, New York City Branch 36. By all accounts he was also a gifted and influential orator. "Can there be compromise with human rights?" Lepper plaintively asked. "Can we search our souls and find any reason why one shall be given separate but equal rights rather than equal rights itself? . . . Can we compro-

Letter carriers in Mobile, Alabama, 1956. City carriers sorted mail into delivery sequence by hand until the late twentieth century. Note the integration of the workroom floor and that most letter carriers were black—belonging to the NAPE branch, the NALC Branch 551, or both. In 1962, Mobile's segregated NALC branches were merged: Branch 551 (black, with 147 members and national convention representation) and Branch 3789 (white, with 64 members) together became Branch 469. © 1956 U.S. Postal Service.

mise the very fact that . . . shoulder to shoulder, men of all creeds, men of all colors and men of all religions are supporting the bulwark of democracy in a far hell-hole of this world, bombed and bombed, with planes overhead, their sleep disturbed, fighting for the democracy that we are enjoying here?"[74]

Lepper was followed by two black delegates, both of whom took President Doherty to task for his 1948 "sins of both sides" speech. Claude E. Sullivan from Atlanta's black Branch 172 prefaced his attack on Jim Crow branches with praises for the convention's host city: "While here I have seen democracy in action. . . . May God bless New York for that . . . !" Taking up Doherty's biblical rhetoric (reminiscent of P. M. E. Hill in 1939), Sullivan challenged

Doherty's lack of evidence: "He said nothing about sin in the other house. If there was sin on our side of the house, he said nothing about it." Sullivan continued to methodically rebut Doherty and other defenders of Jim Crow branches. Doherty and others had collectively insisted on the necessity of separation because of some southern regional peculiarity whereby the "races" historically could not get along.[75]

But Sullivan had a startling reply: "We, as Branch 172, will take anybody, regardless of race, creed or color," he said, noting: "Just a few years back, we took in nearly 100 white carriers in our branch." Only one of those white carriers remained, he continued, employing the historically familiar positive black cultural archetype of the white "race traitor," a kind of Old Testament prodigal son returning home to seek forgiveness: "We have in our branch today, a Mr. Chambers, a white carrier. He came to our branch and said, 'I have seen where I have done wrong,' and he was the man who instituted the whole thing in the white branch of coming into our branch, attempting to take over, and when they found they couldn't take over, they stepped out again through nonpayment of dues."[76]

L. H. Chambers was the white letter carrier whom Sullivan used as a dramatic role model to prove his point that prejudice and "poor race relations" were nonsensical white supremacist inventions. It is not known if Chambers was actually seated in the audience as a delegate with Sullivan's black Branch 172 at this convention—as in fact he had been in 1948.[77] Backing up Sullivan's speech was Max Butler from New Orleans's black Branch 3866, who called for abolition of the "so-called precious 'traditions' of Jim Crow" that he observed were "fast disappearing with the march of American progress." Butler pointed to the humiliation that his branch endured, not only in having had its invitations to white carriers rebuffed, but also facing criticism from "various other labor organizations as well as the press of our city for accepting such an undemocratic way of getting into a service organization." Butler said he had seen "hundreds" of black New Orleans letter carriers refuse to join the NALC's black Branch 3866.[78] He also remembered Doherty's words in 1948. This time he used them against him: "We agree with our National President's remarks made at past conventions: *'That every man wearing the blue gray uniform should be entitled to memberships in the N.A.L.C., regardless of race, color, creed or national origin,'* but is it right to expect a man to be morally and duty-bound to join an organization with the positive knowledge that the only branch open to him will forever be a second-rate one in the eyesight of his postmaster? The answer is an emphatic no."[79]

Nevertheless, the vast majority of NALC convention delegates in 1952 chose to side with speakers from both the South and the North who employed appeals to economic benefits and southern exceptionalism. "It is an overwhelming vote to this convention that the committee is sustained," announced Doherty to cheers and applause, "and I so rule." Sullivan bitterly retorted: "I want you to know that we shall ever and ever and on and on fight until this wrong is righted."[80] Black letter carriers from Virginia asked for a suspension of the rules that would allow a vote to freeze any new "separate charters." Delegate Frank B. Harris of Norfolk echoed Philip Lepper's wartime invocation, noting that "as long as young men die, white and Negro, as are dying in Korea now, and then you deny any one of those men, or any set of those people any privileges that this country can give, then we are not true to our trust." Harris's appeal was impassioned, drawing on Thomas Jefferson and quoting from Abraham Lincoln's Gettysburg Address, concluding: "Fellow delegates, one hundred years from that finds us so stupid as to be arguing the same question now." Many in the audience booed him. Someone called the question. The body voted once again to sustain the Jim Crow status quo.[81] The *Official Proceedings* recorded that the convention then went on to other business. But the NALC's *Postal Record* later reported that "a spirited discussion" had been held on dual charters.[82] In fact, as the *Postal Alliance* reported, "pandemonium broke out" over the proposal to dissolve the dual charters that the NALC still maintained in seventeen cities. When those dual charters were upheld, black letter carriers staged a walkout.[83] Protest actions like these led by black postal workers in the early 1950s were accompanied by the rhetoric of inclusion. For its part, the Alliance's defense of civil liberties while claiming political neutrality represented an insistence on black autonomy, even as it made the Alliance a particular target for government repression. Jim Crow affirmed separate and unequal union representation as well as unequal postal job opportunities that were not limited to the South. But despite assumptions of permanence by their defenders, Jim Crow postal unionism, like McCarthyism, was enjoying its last hurrah.

CHAPTER FIVE

COLLAPSING JIM CROW
POSTAL UNIONISM IN THE 1950S
(1954–1960)

They had finally done it. Two hundred delegates had walked out of the August 1958 convention of the NFPOC in Boston protesting the lack of union democracy and the Jim Crow locals still in the South. Over the next three months, Local 231 in Staten Island, New York; and Local 65 in St. Paul, Minnesota, seceded, followed by the NFPOC National Executive Board suspension of eight other urban "Progressive-Fed" locals in New York, Philadelphia, Brooklyn, Boston, Los Angeles, Detroit, Minneapolis, and Newark. By February 1959 the first issue of the *Progressive* announced "Hail New Union!" as the dissident locals had begun to form a new postal union.[1] Now they were meeting in May as the National Postal Clerks Union (NPCU) in the nation's capital. The inaugural May 1959 issue of the *Progressive* (the national newspaper of the NPCU that became the National Postal Union or NPU a year later) proudly quoted its guest speaker, Robert L. White, president of the D.C. branch of the NAPE: "I am glad to see this organization formed . . . [fighting conditions] which we have opposed for many years, you are acting democratically to get fair and equal union representation for all postal employees."[2]

During the interim between the August 1958 walkout—the "Boston Tea Party"—and the February 1959 formal split, the dissident NFPOC locals had postponed secession pending possible reconciliation. Meanwhile, New York Local 10 filed what was probably its last NFPOC letter of protest on November 10, followed by its last NFPOC resolution. The latter they sent to President Cline House, the executive board, and AFL-CIO president George Meany. The resolution, related to that letter, was issued against the *Union Postal Clerk* for publishing, in both their October and November issues, two mutual job trade/transfer advertisements that allowed clerks desiring transfers to self-identify as "white." Local 10 officials protested that this violated both the AFL-CIO Constitution and New York state antidiscrimination law.

But by the time President House had responded to the letter on November 17 and promised to look into the matter, he had already suspended the Staten

Island local for being the first to walk out of the Boston convention. The next day the St. Paul local seceded. Many more urban and largely black locals followed. By February 1959 the dissidents had taken out over one-fifth of the NFPOC's membership.[3] Three months later, two hundred enthusiastic delegates were meeting as the NPCU, representing 115 locals from twelve states and the District of Columbia. Article 10, Section 1 of the NPCU's constitution proclaimed: "There shall be no more than one local of this Union within any one postal installation."[4]

The National Alliance and the NPCU were among the few actively pro–civil rights unions in organized labor by this time. The price of the NPCU's secession from the NFPOC and the subsequent taking of progressive political positions included being red-baited and (ironically) accused of practicing "dual-unionism" (organizing outside recognized labor federations) by government officials, the NFPOC, and AFL-CIO officials. Charges now raged back and forth. Accusations of communism and "dual-unionism" from the NFPOC were countered by charges of "sellout" by the NPCU.[5]

The Alliance and NPCU (that changed its name to National Postal Union, or NPU, in 1960) both resembled militant pre-1950s civic labor unionism that related to community as well as job issues—only more so. The political stands that these two organizations took on equality, democracy, and loyalty were unique in organized labor and made them continued targets for red-baiting and race-baiting by their opponents who were committed to the status quo. How had progressive postal activists broken the 1950s reactionary logjam in the postal unions and the post office itself? As we will also see in this chapter, Jim Crow in the NALC died a slower death beginning in 1954 and ending in 1962 as activists in that union kept up their campaign against segregated southern branches in spite of stiff opposition. But as for the NFPOC, after having tried to bottle up that same issue for a whole decade and more, how did that union suddenly explode in 1958 in large part over Jim Crow locals? In the case of both unions, a dedicated core of black activists—similar to others in the civil rights movement as a whole—both created and took inspiration from momentum they saw building with favorable Supreme Court decisions, presidential executive orders, and grassroots direct action. This was despite the fact that they were operating during one of the most politically and socially repressive social eras in American history: the 1950s.

COMING THROUGH THE 1950S

The early 1950s had seen the rise of the "Progressive Feds" within the NFPOC, partly out of alienation from a national organization that tolerated Jim Crow locals in the South. Some New York City clerk activists involved in left-labor postal activity in the 1930s were part of this important trend embracing democratic union procedures and rejecting "dual locals" and other forms of discrimination.[6] In retrospect one can follow the trajectory of alienation by many of these "Progressive Feds" from the NFPOC—from their first national newsletter on January 23, 1952, to the first national newspaper of the NPCU in 1959. But it was an uneven growth that must have involved some struggle even within the insurgent NFPOC Progressive caucus from 1952 to 1958, as not everyone had the same commitment to abolishing dual locals within that caucus.[7]

In the 1950s many left-leaning activists in the labor and civil rights movements were becoming impatient with the plodding pace, bureaucratic process, and muted activism of their respective organizations. Black postal workers had a unique vantage point of being actively engaged in both of those movements. Their activism in the period of the U.S. Supreme Court's 1954–1955 *Brown v. Board of Education* school integration decisions and the 1955 AFL-CIO merger put pressure on postal unions to abolish Jim Crow postal union branches in the South, and the government to abolish antidemocratic labor practices like the loyalty test. Those challenges to Jim Crow solidified the place of the National Alliance as an important black civil rights industrial labor union. Debates over segregation accentuated political differences within the NALC and also led to the 1958 NFPOC walkout by politically progressive postal clerks. Crossover between labor and civil rights struggles also saw black postal workers fighting segregated schools and disenfranchisement, while the civil rights movement supported black postal workers in their campaigns to democratize the post office and its unions.

Meanwhile, the National Alliance and the NPU coalesced outside the AFL-CIO as militant, industrial, independent partners—as well as competitors. All postal unions—the majority as of 1955 now in the AFL-CIO—were more or less on equal footing with no collective bargaining rights. And the Alliance was still a very effective and strong advocate for black postal workers. Despite their overall optimism, however, the Alliance saw increasing competition from other postal unions for members, even as it cautioned black postal workers that white supremacy still lived in the post office and in those unions. Competing demands echoed throughout the postal union movement, ranging from demands for higher wages to protests over oppressive working conditions and to tentative discussions of merger into "ONE BIG UNION" (often capitalized in the fashion of the old IWW). While the Alliance had always supported the "one postal union" idea in principle, writers for its monthly journal cautioned against being swallowed up by predominantly white craft unions that historically displayed questionable commitments to equality.[8]

Black postal workers during this period steered multiple courses against Jim Crow and McCarthyism from within the different postal unions and the NAACP. Alliance activists lobbied under the umbrella of both the civil rights and labor establishments, making good use of civil rights public policy such as President Eisenhower's Executive Order 10590 in 1955. That order, which replaced the Fair Employment Board with the President's Committee on Government Employment Policy (PCGEP), proclaimed that "this policy necessarily excludes and prohibits discrimination against any employee in the Federal Government because of race, color, religion, or national origin."[9] Still, change came slowly. But slow changes drove impatience for more change.

BLACK OPTIMISM IN BLEAK TIMES

It seems strange today to read optimistic narratives by African American activists, including those in the postal unions, suggesting the imminent fall of Jim Crow. This was a decade that in retrospect looks bleak, with intense, widespread white resistance to emerging civil rights law and public policy. But black activists were then often heard expressing a guarded optimism.

This was also a time when most white trade unionists (including postal unionists) hailed the AFL-CIO merger of 1955. For its part, the National Alliance was warning that organized labor's merger (or reunion) did not guarantee equality and democracy for black workers, or anyone else for that matter. But while the Alliance was protesting anti-black activity in the postal unions, it was also meeting with progressive members of local clerk and letter carrier unions, especially in New York.

Generally speaking there were plenty of good reasons for activists in all progressive social movements in the 1950s to be afraid, pessimistic, and even depressed. Looking back on the early 1950s four decades later, Karl Korstad, a white former organizer for a North Carolina tobacco workers' union, compared the widespread optimism within progressive social movements in the 1940s to the despair of the early 1950s:

By 1952, it was apparent that the goals we had set for ourselves [organizing black and white industrial labor unity] in the heady days after the war's end would not be realized. In fact, in 1952 it looked like the world might be heading toward World War III. At home anticommunist hysteria made progressive political action all but impossible. I couldn't help but feel that the leaders of the CIO were partly to blame, abandoning, as they did, their role as the leader of the progressive postwar coalition and seeking security as a minor partner in the Cold War coalition of Democrats and Republicans. As a result, today's unions have become, for the most part, harmless ghosts of the living organizations they once were.[10]

A more hopeful assessment, however, was provided in April 1953 by National Alliance president Ashby Carter, who wrote almost poetically in the *Postal Alliance* just four months before his death: "We have gone through a Winter of despair, darkness and defeat. Now, with unswerving Faith in the belief that Good eventually overcomes evil and with the certain knowledge that Light dispels darkness, we face a Future that is the promise of Easter—A Spring bursting forth in all its glory, giving new Life to our suffering hopes and worthy aspirations."[11] That same issue included an article with a photograph of Baltimore Alliance members presenting a petition to Senator John Butler (R-Md.) protesting bias by the Baltimore postmaster and demanding more hiring and promotion of blacks in the post office.[12] In February 1952, Ashby Smith had already launched his "Civil Rights Trail" column in the *Postal Alliance*. Smith, a Chicago attorney, journalist, and former postal clerk, listed both victories and losses in the overall fight for equality in a column that would run regularly until 1961 when he became Alliance president. His first column began with this vow: "Every month we will use this space to bring to you all the 'ups and downs' of Civil Rights and Race Relations that have come to our attention."[13]

In July 1953, Smith reported the following significant activist events: the white bus drivers' strike in Baton Rouge, Louisiana, protesting a city ordinance that had integrated its buses; the House of Representatives rejecting an amendment that would have abolished Washington, D.C.'s segregated schools; an anti-discrimination strike at a Campbell's Soup Company plant in Camden, New Jersey; the U.S. Supreme Court decision upholding the D.C. civil rights coalition's struggle against that city's discrimination laws; and the veto by Illinois governor Stratton of what he called "thought control" loyalty oath bills.[14] The August column defiantly concluded: "And so goes on to Atlantic City where the National Alliance of Postal Employees will regard for the fullest implementation of Civil Rights for all of God's children."[15] No matter how discouraging the current news often sounded, Smith always emphasized the movement's gains, frequently employing Cold War metaphors to describe the freedom struggle in the South. At times he even assumed a triumphant tone suggesting a completion of Reconstruction, as he declared here in February 1956 during the Montgomery bus boycott:

> 1956—The year of the Cold Civil War—from the United States, Southeast strident inflammatory voices are raised in agonized protest against the "threats" to their "way of life" posed by the recent decisions of the United States Supreme Court and the Interstate Commerce Commission.

For those who travel the Civil Rights Trail, 1956 may be the "Year of Provocation." If our ears are attuned only to the sounds emanating from the remnant [southern] states, we may easily be deceived into believing that the whole advance of civil rights has been halted in its tracks, that the long fight for human freedom has been in vain. . . . *Their screaming is naught but the measure of their frustration; their defiance but the last despairing mark of their impotence.*[16]

The National Alliance was not alone in its optimism in the 1950s. Articles in the *Postal Alliance* and other black media outlets predicted the imminent end of Jim Crow, chronicling both the victories and setbacks in the struggle. One of the first of these early civil rights celebrations came in 1950 following the *Sweatt v. Painter* Supreme Court victory.[17] Six years later, in December 1956 a young civil rights leader in Alabama, Dr. Martin Luther King Jr., along with National Alliance president James B. Cobb, spoke at the First Annual Institute on Non-Violence and Social Change in Montgomery. Just a month before, the Supreme Court had struck down segregation in public transportation, sealing the victory of the Montgomery bus boycott. King alluded to God having used Montgomery "as the proving ground for the struggle and triumph of freedom and justice in America." But he also issued this profoundly perceptive warning: "Now it is true, if I might speak figuratively, that old man segregation is on his death-bed. But history has proven that social systems have a great last minute breathing power."[18]

King's caution notwithstanding, how do we account for such overall black optimism in the midst of a national climate of conservatism, repression, and fear? Social movements dialectically change in response to changing material conditions. Drawing inspiration from mass spontaneous activity, they tend to ebb and flow from the organized core to the mass movements. For example, the 1950s civil rights movement, with roots in 1940s activism and that was now focused primarily on overturning segregation, did not truly emerge as a nationwide mass movement until the 1960 wave of black student sit-ins and the founding of the Student Nonviolent Coordinating Committee (SNCC).[19] Studying black postal unionists—especially their confrontations with the labor movement—gives us a dynamic picture of that movement still in motion in the 1950s among black workers. Articles and reports in the *Postal Alliance* during this period reveal a black intellectual working-class activist center organizing, petitioning, protesting, and agitating in small numbers in between periods of mass uprisings.[20]

"There does appear to be a cleavage in our national thinking that is pulling us into opposite directions," Ashby Smith wrote in his "Civil Rights Trail" column in the July 1953 *Postal Alliance*, "but this is not strange or new in a

National Alliance members lobbying members of Congress, ca. 1950s. Logan Carter, president of the Philadelphia branch, stands at the right in a hearing room packed with other Alliance members from Philadelphia, Washington, D.C., New York City, and Virginia. Courtesy of the National Alliance of Postal and Federal Employees.

nation that scorns policy and theory and goes blithely along its pragmatic way."[21] Public political pronouncements in the twentieth century by black postal worker activists—whether as a minority in the major postal unions or in their own union—often had the weary sound of speakers keenly aware of the long history of racial oppression in the United States. Yet they also spoke with a sense of social change being imminent, despite many past betrayals. There was more reason to be optimistic because of the *Brown* decision than any pledges of solidarity by white organized labor. Did *Brown* break the spell of McCarthyism? Martha Biondi argues that it did and adds: "McCarthyism postponed the climactic overthrow of Jim Crow. Over and over again, African American leaders and others in the late 1950s described pent-up and overdue anger, tension, and frustration. The Brown decision in 1954 pierced the heavy gloom and restored a sense of forward motion."[22]

Biondi's argument that McCarthyism gave Jim Crow new life when it was in serious trouble assumes that there were forces poised to overthrow Jim

Crow before 1950. But anticommunism was in large part white supremacy dressed up in patriotic clothes. Anticommunism also became an adopted ideology, not solely an instrument of repression. Had there been no Cold War, the long-standing tradition of white supremacy would have found another patriotic defense of its institutions. With the two major postal unions—the NALC and the NFPOC—maintaining Jim Crow locals even during the antifascist World War II in deference to the demands of their white southern membership, it is hard to imagine momentum building to dismantle those locals *after* the war, although progressive forces never stopped trying to do so.

Which was more tenacious and enduring: white supremacy or anticommunism? I would argue the former. Biondi's argument for the *Brown* decision's "piercing the gloom" is well taken, but it could be countered that the movement received more of a boost from the angry nationwide black rallies and demonstrations resulting from the 1955 lynching of Emmett Till, a black Chicago teenager, by whites in Mississippi. The movement renewed itself in part through memory of mass activism of the 1940s in which the National Alliance played a leading role. The 1950s revival tended to unite black working and middle classes. Black postal workers were a transmission belt in tackling economic *and* social issues.[23]

Historians Dona Cooper Hamilton and Charles V. Hamilton in fact reveal how civil rights groups were committed to a "dual agenda" of social and economic equality. That dual agenda was suggested by NAACP executive secretary Roy Wilkins in the early 1960s, as organized white labor both battled and coalesced with black-led civil rights groups: "It must be understood that all organized bodies have their primary and secondary purposes. The primary purpose of the NAACP is to combat discrimination against Negroes. The primary purpose of labor organizations is to protect the wages, hours, and working conditions of its members. Civil rights activity for them is desirable but must be secondary. Inevitably these differences in emphasis will produce tensions in greater or less degree."[24]

For their part, the National Alliance advanced both civil rights and labor struggles. But it also cautioned against complacency in the late 1950s when the progress of the established civil rights movement in the South slowed. The *Postal Alliance*, like other black newspapers, eagerly published articles throughout the 1950s and early 1960s that revealed a growing nationwide activism. For example, the voter registration drives were a constant source of news in black newspapers, including the *Postal Alliance*. Black postal workers were instrumental in many of those drives.[25] While 1955 found the Alliance calling itself "the second most effective civil rights organization in America" (deferring here to the NAACP), the 1960 wave of black student sit-ins in the South inspired the *Postal Alliance* to recommend that its members become more engaged in the growing *mass* civil rights struggle—whether it was with the NAACP, SNCC, SCLC (Southern Christian Leadership Conference), or CORE.[26]

THE *BROWN* DECISION AND JIM CROW POSTAL UNIONS

The 1954 *Brown* decision provided room for black postal workers and their allies to apply more pressure on Jim Crow postal union locals. In the case of the National Alliance, it was a key part of their overall strategy to combat white supremacy in the post office and its unions. The Alliance took an unequivocal abolitionist stand, in contrast to those arguing from within the predominantly white postal craft unions who often combined circumspect language with moral imperative. National Alliance members with dual membership in those unions continued their intervention in those unions' internal debates.

The NALC and NFPOC meanwhile had both upheld Jim Crow locals at their respective conventions in 1952. But just two years later, in addition to approving a broad civil rights resolution, the NFPOC Cincinnati convention approved Resolution 908-A, "requesting that our National officers make a determined effort to bring about the consolidation of existing dual locals," while also passing Resolution 907-A, "favoring inclusion in ranks of the Locals of the N.F.P.O.C all postal clerks whose eligibility is established in our national constitution, regardless of race, color, or creed."[27] A bulletin titled "The 'Progressive Fed's' Report of the NFPOC in Convention at Cincinnati Ohio" later excitedly announced: "A spirited discussion accompanied the eventual adoption of a resolution banning discrimination in membership, particularly one calling for action leading toward the elimination of dual locals."[28]

An even more far-reaching resolution against segregated branches was passed that summer by the NALC. What happened in two years to make the NFPOC and NALC commit to eventually abolishing separate union branches and locals? Anti–Jim Crow resolutions in both unions were passed just a little more than three months after the U.S. Supreme Court's landmark May 17, 1954, *Brown v. Board of Education* decision that abolished statutory segregated public education. That decision invoked the Fourteenth Amendment in overturning the principle of "separate but equal" enshrined in *Plessy v. Ferguson* that had legalized Jim Crow since 1896.[29] A moral imperative was starting to gain ground in the unions thanks to a growing mass movement for equality.[30] Yet neither the NALC nor the NFPOC in the 1950s devoted any journal space to discussing discrimination and segregation in the post office. It would have been hard to predict based on reading those journals before the summer of 1954 that Jim Crow branches and locals were about to suffer a severe blow.

Besides inspiring the growing civil rights movement, *Brown* also provoked a good deal of negative white working-class reaction. The *Brown* decision in fact changed the focus for many of Jim Crow's advocates from ideological warfare to a terrorist war against equality. With the Cold War in full swing, the anticommunist card was still playing so well that by 1959, *Postal Alliance* editor Snow Grigsby felt compelled to write that the Alliance "had always been anticommunist," although any longtime reader would have been hard pressed to find that assertion in the *Postal Alliance* at any time during the previous decade.[31] Jim Crow and McCarthyism together still checked labor and civil rights militancy well into the 1950s.

Meanwhile, in an era of growing national liberation movements in the developing world, clear anticolonialist references and metaphors can be found in the *Postal Alliance*, such as this one in 1960, quoted from the National Alliance's District Eight convention, where President James B. Cobb declared: "The floors of some post offices may look like Liberia, but in the floors above, where policy is made, they look like any office in a manufacturing concern in Vicksburg, Mississippi." Cobb was talking about the average urban American post office, making an implicit comparison between segregated Mississippi and apartheid South Africa (both of which they referred to elsewhere on a regular basis). His choice of Liberia as a metaphor in this case, however, is both interesting and instructive. Liberia, founded in 1821 as a colony of freed African American slaves, became an independent republic in 1847, remaining so even as most of Africa was still colonized by Europe throughout much of the twentieth century. The Alliance, which identified with African independence movements that were actively throwing off colonialism at the time of Cobb's speech, was in turn proud of its own organizational independence.[32]

By contrast, blacks in the NALC and NFPOC were minorities within unions that did not make equality a priority. Narratives from blacks in the NALC and NFPOC typically combine circumspection and angry revolt. If the Alliance was a pro-equality activist organization, and the NALC and NFPOC were targets of their war on white supremacy in postal unions, then the splitting of the NFPOC in 1958 and the complete abolition of Jim Crow postal union locals by 1962 would become two important major results of the Alliance's civil rights unionist influence.

The end of the line for Jim Crow branches in the NALC began with its September 1954 NALC convention. The convention itself was winding down by Friday the third, the last weekday before the Labor Day weekend. Millions of

Americans including government employees would be getting the following Monday off for the Labor Day national holiday as letter carriers from across the United States were meeting at their thirty-ninth convention in Cleveland. Many were listening to a speech that Friday morning by Robert Ramspeck, former Georgia congressman and Civil Service Committee chairman, now vice president of both Eastern Airlines and of the Air Transportation Association. According to the October 1954 *Postal Record*, Ramspeck declared that the government should pay higher rates to the airlines in recognition of the post office's increased use of airmail and air parcel post.[33]

That same day, the NALC Board of Laws came forward to make their report. "Dual charters" were no longer buried in convention business as a late-appearing resolution, as had often been the case in the past. This time the *Postal Record* reported with unusual solemnity: "One of the most important decisions before the convention was first on the Board of Laws agenda—the question of separate charters." The Board of Laws changed its previous official "disapproval" to a "neutral position" on the amendment that nine branches had drawn up, calling for the elimination of separate black and white branches. The branches proposing the amendment were an interesting mix of branches that included the "hometown" of the *Brown* decision, Topeka, Kansas, Branch 10; along with Branch 36, New York City; Branch 11, Chicago; Branch 704, Tucson; Branch 3866, New Orleans; Branch 27, Memphis; Branch 4022, Washington, D.C.; Branch 38, Newark; and Branch 525, Norfolk. All four southern branches were African American, and included carriers who held memberships in both the National Alliance and the NALC. The amendment to Article 2, Section 1 proposed by all these branches made this explicit, unequivocal declaration: "No letter carrier shall be denied membership in any branch because of race, creed, color, or national origin. All existing second charter branches shall be dissolved and all members working under the supervision of one postmaster shall automatically become members of the original charter branch."[34]

What was proposed was the abolition of the remaining seventeen Jim Crow branches and all future ones (Jim Crow branches euphemistically referred to as "second charters" in Article 2, Section 1). But delegate Claude E. Sullivan from Atlanta's black branch moved to strike the abolitionist amendment and substitute a compromise.[35] Chicago delegate John T. Kinsella seconded Sullivan's motion, and President Doherty summed up Sullivan's amendment as one that preserved existing dual charters while preventing future ones.[36]

Immediately objecting to this amendment was delegate Clarence Acox from New Orleans's black branch. Acox argued for the original motion. Respectfully disagreeing with Sullivan, yet obviously disappointed with the compromise amendment, Acox declared: "I speak here today, carrying out the

The NALC Memphis Branch 27 Marching Band in 1954, the year the NALC voted not to admit any new Jim Crow branches. This was Memphis's original NALC branch, chartered in 1889 as an integrated branch, but it became all black when whites seceded in the 1946 national convention to form the segregated Branch 3856. The two branches were reunited as Branch 27 along with other remaining separate branches in 1962. Courtesy of *Postal Record*, National Association of Letter Carriers, AFL-CIO.

mandates of my branch, in favor of the original amendment, and not in favor of the amendment submitted by the dear Brother to my left." He noted that Doherty was also an AFL vice president and had gone on record at that body's 1953 convention as supporting complete union integration: "We, being employees of the federal government . . . we set the pattern for all workers throughout America," Acox added. Acox further attacked as spurious arguments advanced by Jim Crow's defenders that a significant loss of membership dues money would result if "dual charters" were abolished. He noted how many *blacks* avoided the NALC because of its Jim Crow policies:

> I would just like to quote a few figures.
> In the city of Washington, D.C., there are 802 Negro carriers, of which only 22 are members of the National Association of Letter Carriers, which is ridiculous. *The reason they give for this is that they do not care to be affiliated with a Jim Crow federal workers union.*

In the city of Houston, Texas, there are more than 500 Negro carriers, of which only 22 members of the National Association of Letter Carriers, and I think that is pathetic. . . . In my own city we only have 35 per cent of our potential members. I just wanted to let you know that the National Association of Letter Carriers would not lose financially as I have heard it rumored around.[37]

The convention heard a motion for tabling by a white delegate from Miami and a second by a white delegate from Nashville. That motion lost by a close vote of 578–499. The Sullivan amendment was called and it won on a voice vote. The convention quickly moved on to other business.[38] It was a victory, to be sure, but a qualified one. A potential bold stroke had been modified into one that preserved this racist relic of the NALC's recent past while agreeing to halt its reproduction. But why would Sullivan, who was black, champion a weaker amendment to the original resolution that would have banned *all* dual charters? Despite the momentum that had built up in the NALC from the *Brown* decision in May to put the organization on record against segregation, there was still some resistance. Sullivan was probably proposing a compromise to make passage more likely and start the process of desegregation by first taking Jim Crow branches out of the NALC constitution. By 1954, blacks were a small but increasingly vocal minority in the NALC, which had been loath to dissolving dual charters since reenacting them in 1941. Sullivan's tactic was one of "half a loaf is better than none." He also revealed a personal stake in passing this amendment immediately while they had some momentum. Movingly, he told an applauding 1954 convention that his compromise was offered in the spirit of unity: "I am an old man, and I have been a member of this Association for thirty-three years. . . . So if we will get rid of this thing, I can die in peace."[39] A blow had been struck against Jim Crow, although existing "dual charters" would not be abolished for almost another decade.[40]

Prior to this convention, the first branch to back the original anti–Jim Crow amendment, ironically, was Branch 4022—the black D.C. branch.[41] The other branch to publish its support for that amendment before the convention was black Branch 525 from Norfolk, which included National Alliance members. There were a number of dual Alliance-NALC members in attendance at this historic convention, in fact, including W. C. White of Jacksonville Branch 52; T. C. Almore, delegate-at-large from Mississippi; and John W. Lee of Newport News Branch 609.[42] The close vote on tabling the original resolution suggests that Sullivan's compromise—approved on a resounding voice vote—was probably necessary to produce a victory, albeit a weaker one. But the *Postal Alliance* had no public criticism of Sullivan for his gradualist strategy. Nor did it even mention any division among the anti–Jim Crow forces. Instead, it captioned the event "Dual Charters get first blow," and praised the New York, Brooklyn, and Detroit branches for fighting Jim Crow.[43]

Despite the fact that union conventions are typically attended by the most active members, they are not always the most active shop floor organizers. Nonetheless, delegates could typically be heard representing their local branch members' mood and activities as well as speculating on the impact of the various proposals made to the national body. Clarence Acox's earlier observation was significant: black letter carriers in Washington, D.C. (and presumably those in Houston and his native New Orleans) were refusing to join the NALC as a way of protesting Jim Crow. He did not have to add what everyone knew: the National Alliance represented competition with the NALC as well as a refuge for black letter carriers.[44]

While the *Brown* decision did not make separate union locals illegal, Jim Crow opponents now saw themselves armed with a federal anti-segregation imprimatur to begin their dismantlement: the NALC erasing segregation from their constitution (without banning existing Jim Crow branches) and the NFPOC agreeing to now study the matter. Both took tentative steps that angered white southern delegates—but not enough for substantial numbers to leave. At the same time they left blacks and their allies encouraged yet frustrated. In the *Postal Record* there were no comments on the *Brown* decision throughout the rest of 1954. There was only one mention of the historic elimination of the NALC's segregation clause. Not surprisingly, it came from a New York Branch 36 delegate, Leon Samis, who cheered the "deletion, after 13 long years, of [*sic*] constitutional clause which had permitted dual charter branches in the N.A.L.C."[45] There was also growing interest in both unions concerning the pending AFL-CIO merger—possibly a factor in the NFPOC and NALC votes against Jim Crow. Black labor and civil rights leaders expressed both praise and skepticism of the merger because of the AFL and CIO's mixed track records on equality.[46]

"IN THE AREA OF CIVIL RIGHTS LIES THE HARD NUT"

In 1955, the heads of the AFL and CIO were holding joint meetings to effect merger before holding their first unified convention in December of that year. UAW-CIO leader Walter Reuther publicly promised that a commitment to equality would be a prerequisite for the CIO merging with the AFL. More blacks considered joining the predominantly white postal unions now, and some urged the National Alliance to apply to the AFL-CIO for affiliation. As an industrial union the Alliance had long advocated in principle merging all postal unions while insisting on its own autonomy. The 1955 AFL-CIO merger effectively made most postal workers (the vast majority having previously belonged to AFL affiliates) members of the newly merged labor federation. Yet about a quarter of all black postal workers (as National Alliance members) were still outside the AFL-CIO. Had the Alliance joined the CIO in 1953, it is possible that it would have become an AFL-CIO affiliate two years later, and become embroiled in federation battles over equality that would have put it in a distinct yet highly vocal minority.[47]

In 1956, National Alliance president James B. Cobb expressed his frank opinion in the *Postal Alliance* concerning the popular debate around merger. Speaking both as a labor leader and legal scholar, he carefully weighed arguments on both sides—then added this caveat: "I fear that many of us have a heady feeling of future gains derived from the wine of promise. . . . But, in attempting to assess the impact of this action, we can look to history and its information and to ourselves for the role of self determination." In contrast to other postal unions that invariably sanctified the memory of white supremacist trade union leaders like Samuel Gompers, Cobb looked at past promises of labor federations—from the 1866 National Labor Union to the AFL—as abandoning blacks whenever white members demanded it: "History further points out that organization of Negroes and the granting to them of equal opportunities has long been a union principle. However, that principle has often fallen under the pressure of expediency. Today, that question haunts the leadership as well as those of us who hold to democratic principles. Our bitter experience, attributive to the violation of these principles, demands reading of the fine print."[48]

Cobb acknowledged that he saw "the merger as a necessary and logical event paralleling the growing concentration of business and broadening power of government in our economic lives."[49] While appreciating opposition to racial discrimination by Walter Reuther and AFL-CIO president George Meany, Cobb nonetheless noted that white supremacy at the local level undermined any stated commitment to equality. "In the area of civil rights lies the hard nut," mused Cobb. Then he argued: "With powerful unions such as the machinists, the carpenters, the plumbers, the railroad workers and others, I cannot visualize complete dedication and mobilization to the cause of freedom of opportunity for everyone."[50]

This summed up the Alliance's civil rights unionism: equality was central to the workplace and society, but white labor had failed to fully commit itself to that task, so the Alliance should remain independent. For that matter, were AFL-CIO leaders fully committed to *all* American labor? In 1956 its president George Meany told the NALC Minneapolis convention that "one thing about the American trade union movement is that it is basically American. We do not consider and we do not concede that there is any such thing as a labor class in America."[51] This strange-sounding remark reflected Meany's brand of narrowly conceived and minimally combative "business unionism." It also underscores the analysis by historian Edmund Wehrle that the AFL-CIO supported full employment that was tied to the nation's Cold War military buildup, and consistently downplayed any hint of labor's dissatisfaction with capitalism.[52]

Meanwhile, after the second *Brown* decision in 1955, white "massive resistance" (named after Virginia senator Harry Byrd's noncompliance strategy) began accelerating after that decision allowed school districts to integrate not immediately but "with all deliberate speed."[53] White resistance to *Brown* was not just organized and promoted by the white elites and white middle class. There were also significant elements of white organized labor, including many white postal workers. This resistance, like the still-existing Jim Crow branches, was now a source of embarrassment to the leadership of the postal unions and AFL-CIO leadership.[54] The backpedaling on equality by postal union leadership that had also supported the *Brown* decision resembled the CIO's late 1940s abandonment of its Operation Dixie campaign, during which time it actually recognized some Jim Crow locals in the South.[55]

By comparison, the Alliance had backed the 1957 Civil Rights Act during the same year as the Little Rock, Arkansas, white riots and school integration crisis. That summer, National Alliance members were protesting at their convention against the NALC joining with the United Mine Workers and the railroad brotherhoods backing Senate Majority Leader Lyndon Johnson's (D-Tex.) "jury trial amendment" to the 1957 civil rights bill. That amendment, objected the Alliance, was part of a deal to obtain support from conservative Republicans and southern Democrats for a proposed postal pay raise. The civil rights bill was supported by the Alliance and other civil rights groups as a weak but necessary first step toward stronger legislation. But the Alliance and civil rights groups also protested the final product of this bill: (1) its "heart," known as "Part III," banning public accommodations segregation, was eliminated; and (2) traditionally all-white southern juries under the "jury trial amendment" were effectively allowed to acquit whites charged with violating the civil rights of African Americans, especially the right to vote. The cover and inside page of the October 1957 *Postal Alliance* showed National Alliance delegates at their July national convention in Atlanta lining up behind a floor microphone to angrily denounce the NALC's support for the jury trial amendment. The *Postal Alliance* editorialized against the NALC and other unions that supported that provision. They also reprinted a column by pundit Drew Pearson in the *Washington Post* that described Johnson's lobbying for that amendment to get his bill passed and the unions that supported it. The NALC especially, said Pearson, was "desperately anxious to pass a pay-raise bill. It must be OK'd by Senator Olin Johnston (D., S.C.) and his Postoffice Committee. So, Johnston agreed to make postal-pay increases the first order of business before his committee and keep it there until passed—if the postal workers in turn, would woo Republican senators over to the jury-trial amendment."[56]

Senator Johnston had been a frequent guest at NALC conventions. A leading member of the Senate Post Office and Civil Service Committee, he had also been a prominent backer of the 1956 anti-integration "Southern Manifesto" that counted nineteen senators and eighty-three representatives among its signers (all but four southerners signed it). Four of these were members of the House Post Office and Civil Service Committee, including James Morrison (D-La.), who in 1962 would author the postal worker pay raise bill.[57] Johnston's opposition to civil rights was never noted in the *Postal Record*, nor was Morrison's. But Drew Pearson made this observation: "It was this big push by labor which really rescued Lyndon Johnson on the jury-trial amendment." Ironically, Pearson noted, organized labor "lined up with part of exactly the same Dixie-GOP coalition which put across the Taft-Hartley Act. It was Senator Taft and Northern Republicans who worked out the long-standing coalition whereby the South voted against labor and Northern Republicans voted against civil rights."[58] An October 1957 *Postal Alliance* editorial was both short and blunt, and posed this rhetorical question concerning what it called the NALC's bargain for a pay raise bill: "Are a few more dollars worth the price of freedom?"[59]

Meanwhile, frustrated with the NFPOC's maintenance of dual locals, militant locals led by New York Local 10 walked out of the NFPOC convention in 1958 over issues of democracy and discrimination in that organization. Convention resolutions from their 1954, 1956, and 1958 conventions reveal uncanny resemblances to the congressional debates over slavery in the decades preceding the Civil War, where tenuous compromises ultimately gave way to southern secession. But unlike the Civil War, in the case of the NFPOC it was the *anti*-white supremacists who were seceding. In 1956, two years after the NFPOC's Cincinnati convention had mandated merger talks between "dual locals," a South Carolina–sponsored resolution attacked the new president of the AFL-CIO, of which the NFPOC was now a part. Evoking the southern anti-abolitionist gag orders of the 1830s, their resolution accused President George Meany of making "political speeches," no doubt referring to his 1955 speech in favor of the *Brown* decision. It failed to garner support from the resolutions committee or the convention. But it reflected some of that southern "massive resistance" in the postal unions.[60]

Starting a new round of attacks on Jim Crow unionism in both 1956 and 1958, convention resolutions were placed by black and white NFPOC members from New York and Washington, D.C., calling for "abolition" of dual locals, as well as for support of civil rights legislation. For many if not most of the NFPOC's "Progressive Feds," segregated southern locals symbolized a lack of democracy and equality in their union. The battle was on again. At the 1956 NFPOC convention in Chicago, Locals 10, 148, and 251 brought resolutions calling for national officers to step up the efforts at dual local abolition. They did the same at the NFPOC 1958 convention in Boston. After a local referendum to merge the two D.C. locals failed by a lopsided margin, Robert Bates and two colleagues from D.C.'s black local 148 joined once again with New York Local 10, Brooklyn Local 251, and the New York State Federation to bring combined resolutions calling for the NFPOC to merge all its dual locals. The failure of the 1958 NFPOC convention to abolish Jim Crow locals (with four new ones in fact applying for membership) was one of several major conflicts over union democracy that provoked a walkout by its more radical members.

In 1958, after a referendum to merge the two D.C. locals failed, Robert Bates and two colleagues from that city's black NFPOC local sponsored two separate resolutions calling for the national organization to merge their city's dual locals as well as any Jim Crow locals remaining in the NFPOC. The failure of that resolution to pass the convention was one of several major conflicts over democracy and militancy that provoked a walkout by that organization's more radical members. The *Progressive Fed* monthly newsletter had now grown to a tabloid format, and its March and April 1958 issues included, among other things, news of a proposed referendum for "one man–one vote" in the NFPOC; a photo of a long picket line of CIO postal workers in San Francisco protesting President Eisenhower's veto of postal pay raises (about half of the pickets were black); and a photo of Sam Taylor, the African American president of the former UPW-CIO Detroit postal local taking his organization into the NFPOC—just months before the "Boston Tea Party" walkout.[61] That August 1958 Boston convention protest by "Progressive Feds" against Jim Crow locals and the general lack of democracy in the NFPOC, however, was a dramatic new development.

Over the years there had been little love lost between the National Alliance and the NFPOC (or "Feds" as they were popularly known). But many black and white, liberal and socialist "Progressive Feds" had worked with the National Alliance over the years, particularly in New York City. In 1956, the Alliance had condemned the NFPOC white local in D.C. for voting against merging the black and white locals in that city. And just a few months before, the *Postal Alliance* had reprinted a *Washington Afro-American* editorial defending the Alliance against charges by the NFPOC that they were outmoded and racially divisive. That editorial included this familiar observation: "Labor history proves that when the chips are down no white dominated labor union, matters not how lofty its purposes, will fight for its colored membership as well as representatives of its own."[62]

Alliance D.C. branch president Robert White's greetings to the breakaway NPCU's first convention in D.C. in May 1959 represented vindication for the Alliance as well as their stamp of approval. The convention was hosted by the newly formed NPCU affiliate, the Washington Area Postal Union (WAPU)—one that counted among its members clerks from both of the former separate branches of the Washington, D.C., NFPOC—the white Local 140 and the black Local 148. Yet many former "Progressive Feds" remained with the NFPOC. They included members like Carl Malone, president of Local 140, who had spoken at the NFPOC 1952 convention in favor of dual locals like his own; or Chicago Local 1 president George Wachowski, who once condescendingly told former Chicago National Alliance president Henry McGee: "I am opposed to dual unionism. I think the Alliance should stick to purely racial matters and leave the trade union function to us."[63] Another well-known former "Progressive Fed" who did not affiliate with the NPCU was Francis Filbey, a national NFPOC officer from Baltimore. On the other hand, those joining the new union included many black and white NFPOC members whose politics for the most part were to the left of most of the AFL-CIO.

Robert White's guest speakership at the NPCU founding convention was historically significant. In 1953 the National Alliance had contemplated accepting the CIO's invitation to join that organization, but ultimately declined rather than risk losing its autonomy. A *Cleveland Call and Post* reporter assigned to cover the Alliance's August 1953 convention noted that, in its refusal to join the CIO, the Alliance had pointedly "called attention to the fact that the N.A.P.E. is the only Federal organization in the nation to wage a court battle on behalf of its 'purged' members."[64] But here in 1959 President White was praising the arrival of the NPCU as another democratic, progressive, industrial, explicitly anti-white supremacist postal workers union like the Alliance. The *Progressive*'s page of convention photographs made sure to visually capture this unity by prominently including one of Robert White taken alongside James Hopkins of the WAPU.[65] *Progressive* articles from that point on often evoked the old CIO—as editorials condemned prejudice by the post office and its unions, proclaiming that "we speak with a united voice."[66] But the NPCU was different from the old CIO unions that saw industrial unionism in itself as the cure for racial workplace divisions. The NPCU instead constructed a program that combined aggressive recruitment of workers of color with explicit challenges to racism in building postal industrial unionism.

Despite their solidarity, however, the two unions were also competing for members, with the Alliance declaring that they spoke not just for black workers but also as black workers. The *Postal Alliance*, for example, along with other black media, covered black workers' walkout of the October 1959 UAW convention "in protest to the convention's handling of the civil rights issue."[67] The following year, the Alliance helped A. Philip Randolph and other black trade unionists organize the first Negro American Labor Council convention meeting in Detroit during May 28–29, 1960, which counted 1,000 black unionist delegates, including forty Alliance members. It also featured a speech given by Little Rock, Arkansas, NAACP activist and regional director Daisy Bates, famous for her work with the Little Rock Nine fighting "massive resistance" to integrate Central High School in 1957. This was a convention that was glowingly reported by the *Postal Alliance* in its June 1960 issue.[68]

Whether black postal workers were affiliated with the National Alliance or one of the predominantly white postal unions, in the 1950s they often found themselves engaged in both civil rights and labor activism that frequently brought them into conflict with the post office as well as postal unions like the NALC and the NFPOC. The National Alliance's emphasis on both equality *and* labor rights became the resolution to the problem of conflicting interests between civil rights and labor organizations. As the fourth largest and one of the most influential postal unions by 1960, the Alliance stood as a model for black postal workers in whatever affiliation they chose. There are two compelling quotations taken from the *New York Alliance Leader* during this decade that evoke W. E. B. Du Bois's famous 1903 quote about the "two-ness" of being black in America, and suggest the role that these activists saw for themselves:

> The Negro in the Government Service finds himself (or herself) occupying a dual role. 1. A Government employee and a Negro Government employee. 2. An American citizen and A Negro American citizen. This dual status is bound to create problems difficult in their solution, and calling for careful evaluation before action is committed in either direction. All legislation should be carefully studied, as Civic problems; both local and National; and a careful appraisal arrived at before decisions are made. In plain language, each side of our bread should be examined carefully to determine on which side there is more butter.[69]

Along the same lines, a few months later the *Alliance Leader* editorialized: "The Negro in Government service must of necessity maintain dual standards of evaluation in all pertinent matters, for not only is he a Government employee, but also a Negro one; similarly, he is an American citizen, but also a Negro American. We did not create those distinctions. They were thrust upon us."[70]

The *Postal Alliance* was unique among postal union journals in the way it informed its membership—including its use of reprints not only from the black and left press but also the *Journal of Negro History*. In that sense it was an intellectual as well as activist organ, and was more to the left than any mainstream black newspaper. And while other postal union journals tended to train only its officials in legal and contract matters, the *Postal Alliance* made that information available for all their readers, encouraging all members to be activists.[71] Toward the end of 1953, Alliance president emeritus Jerry O. Gilliam, the Norfolk, Virginia, civil rights leader and Alliance member since 1916, had been appointed the first National Organizer for the NAPE as a means of "conserving and increasing our manpower," possibly in reaction to or in anticipation of competition from other postal unions for their black membership.[72]

One dramatic example of the Alliance's self-identity as a civil rights union came in 1959 when a black newspaper implicitly challenged its militancy. A March 7, 1959, *Pittsburgh Courier* editorial titled "White Citizens Councils' Unionists" charged that white supremacists led many AFL-CIO locals in the South, that AFL-CIO national labor leadership was doing nothing to stop this "Ku Klux element," and furthermore that the absence of "Negro labor organization" proved the "bankruptcy of Negro labor leaders." The Alliance, which frequently reprinted articles from the *Courier*, was incensed at what it considered to be an insult. An open letter to the *Courier* was published in the March 1959 *Postal Alliance* from Alabama Alliance member John W. King, who pointed out that the Alliance had in fact been *very* active against Jim Crow unionism since 1913: "The Alliance has fought and is fighting with our every resource job discrimination in the Postal Service. . . . We are organized on the same pattern as the C.I.O., having adopted this plan of membership in 1924, which precedes the C.I.O. in its use of same by quite a span of time. We have been using methods which Rev. M. L. King, Jr., has come to term 'Non-Violent.' . . . We have spear-headed efforts on behalf of all Postal workers, such as: decent salaries though other postal organizations, such as the Letter Carriers Association, have been awarded the lion's share of the credit."[73]

Three key themes can be read here from this southern black postal unionist consistent with typical Alliance rhetoric backed up by regular practice: nonviolent civil rights activity; a history of industrial unionism even before the CIO; and leadership on "bread and butter" craft issues such as salaries. All the more significant is the fact that this rebuttal was issued during a lull in civil rights movement mass activity from 1957 to 1960. Jim Crow postal unionism began to collapse in 1954, which in turn encouraged many black postal workers to remain in or even join the major postal unions instead of the Alliance. The Alliance in turn warned black postal workers that their only security lay in exclusive NAPE membership.

"WHY THE ALLIANCE?"

The opening up of the mostly white postal unions and the decline of overt occupational segregation in the post office ironically hampered the organizing ability of the National Alliance in the North as black postal workers joined other unions, causing concern among Alliance activists. "Many times have I heard the question asked, 'Why the Alliance?', by well meaning fellow work-ers," wrote James Hill of the New York City branch in the October 1954 *Postal Alliance*. "In a city like New York where there are no apparent racial barriers to membership in postal organizations, the uninformed may feel that his inquiry is in order, but is it?"[74] New York Alliance president Elmer E. Armstead similarly wrote in the June 1954 *Alliance Leader*: "We of the Alliance know that segregation and discrimination in the postal service is *not entirely related to or confined to the southland*. . . . Segregation and discrimination is everywhere as is evidenced by a recent happening on our Eastern seaboard where it was found that employees of that office were being given different consideration in as-signments and promotional opportunities on the basis of race and national origin."[75]

Meanwhile, long-time New York Alliance activist official John Adams proudly told me of his individual as well as the branch's collective civil rights activism, both at the workplace and in society, symbolized in the fact that Russell Crawford—editor of the branch newspaper in the mid-1940s—was also president of the Harlem NAACP.[76] Alliance civil rights and labor activists were surrounded by like-minded black civil rights unionists. For example, teachers' union local members fought against Jim Crow in the New York City public schools as well as in their own national union, the American Federation of Teachers. (This period also saw an organizing surge by another public sector union: the leftist hospital union District 1199.)[77]

"Surprisingly," notes Martha Biondi, "New York City was one of the first places in the nation where the *Brown* . . . ruling sparked a push for integration." Biondi sees that spark as being set by a February 1954 speech by Dr. Kenneth Clark, the black psychologist whose testimony was critical to the success of that case when it was finally decided. Dr. Clark, described by the *Alliance Leader* as "one of the leaders of the movement" to end segregated schools in the city, denounced the damage done by segregated schools to black school-children, speaking at a mass conference of the Intergroup Committee on New

York's Public Schools at the New Lincoln School in Manhattan on April 24. That conference, featuring over forty organizations like the National Alliance, the NAACP, the National Urban League, and various community and parents' groups, "requested" that the Board of Education investigate segregated schools that discriminated against "Negro and Puerto Rican pupils."[78]

According to Biondi, community campaigns in New York for equality at this time found few white allies.[79] Besides local NAACP city branches that were more radical than the national office (New York Alliance president Elmer Armstead at one time also headed the Harlem NAACP), labor and social activist organizations campaigning for equality included the Harlem Trade Union Council, the Urban League, the United African Nationalist Movement, and the Harlem Trade Union Committee. The Alliance saw its public service mission fulfilled both at the post office and in society, expecting active involvement from its members.[80]

The post office was undoubtedly the biggest employer of African Americans in New York City by mid-century. In the nation's capital by 1950, points out legal scholar Richard Kluger, Washington, D.C., had 46,000 African Americans working for the federal government: one in every three African American jobholders, many of them working for the post office. Washington, like New York, had seen a boom in twentieth-century black migration, mostly from the South but also from the Caribbean. The prospect of government, domestic service, professional, and skilled jobs became a magnet for black migrants from around the country and the Caribbean, as well as the opportunity for higher education at historically black Howard University. Washington's black population more than doubled to 280,000 between 1930 and 1950, with 65,359 arriving between 1940 and 1950, making the city 35 percent black. By 1960, D.C. was 53.9 percent black, with blacks holding 66.3 percent of all postal jobs, plus the highest rate of postal supervisors of any city in the nation: 14.9 percent.[81]

Washington's black elite was in control of the NAACP and other civil rights organizations as well as Howard University, the latter especially furnishing both professionals for black communities and other historically black colleges around the country as well as lawyers for the black freedom movement. Yet there was also a lively grassroots movement that often challenged that elite leadership. The lodges and clubs of black men and women offered some opportunities for the working class to mix with the middle class in organizations that were social activist. Black postal workers, part of the working class because of their relationship to the production of goods and services, were also middle class in their education, part-time professional statuses, and community status and self-identity. Jim Crow segregation in D.C. encouraged black congregation, as the old saying went. Former Alliance D.C. branch president Tommie Wilson from Mississippi also described the D.C. post office as being just as segregated as that of his home state. James Pinderhughes, a member of the NALC segregated black Branch 4022 in that city, said that blacks were typically barred from promotions, and white business customers often demanded to have white letter carriers deliver their mail.[82]

The Alliance made good use of its national office in the nation's capital to also advocate for nearby southern branches. In North Carolina, despite the longtime Alliance presence in Raleigh and Charlotte (and more recently Greensboro), Durham—with its strong black middle-class and black industrial working-class protest traditions—did not begin hiring black postal workers until after the *Brown* decision as a result of Alliance pressure.[83]

The narrative of black Army veteran and college graduate George Booth Smith becoming Durham's first black letter carrier and among the first black postal workers is a revealing story of black resistance, Alliance "clout" in the nation's capital, and low-paid black professionals taking postal jobs and becoming labor and civil rights activists. Smith recalls that while earning his bachelor's and master's degrees in library science at historically black North Carolina College for Negroes (NCC, now North Carolina Central University) in Durham in the late 1940s and early 1950s, the noted black activist C. Elwood Boulware, a professor of mathematics, would give students time off to take the postal exam. Despite high test scores, blacks were never called. But Smith kept noticing whites who had taken the test with him now carrying mail. By the mid-1950s, Smith, who had worked at libraries in Oklahoma, Virginia, and in nearby Raleigh, was tired of commuting:

> So after a while, I went back to see Postmaster Allen, and he told me: "These jobs weren't for niggers, these jobs were for white high school graduates, why you want to come up here with a master's degree?" And then I got mad, and there was a fellow who was in the National Alliance of Postal Employees came through here and he knew Summerfield, he worked in Washington, D.C., so he made arrangements for me to see Postmaster General [Arthur] Summerfield, and I went up there and sat in his office and told him what had been said. . . . So he told me to "get that SOB on the phone down there in Durham." . . . He told him that he was "sending Mr. Smith back to Durham: if he doesn't have a job when he gets back there, we'll have a new postmaster [in Durham]." . . . I'm just kicking my heels up in the office. I came back to Durham Sunday, had a certified letter waiting, asking if I was available to work. I went up on Monday, and Postmaster Allen "just happened to have an opening" for a clerk/carrier.[84]

New York City and Washington, D.C., were both politically active cities in the 1950s. New York City had a high level of unionization among private and public sector employees, along with a good deal of political activism and lobbying. As center of the federal bureaucracy Washington, D.C., was not industrialized and was never considered a "union town." Nonetheless, by 1960 the nation's capital saw approximately one-third of its government employees unionized. The nationwide unionization rate among postal employees was an astounding 84 percent, topped by the NALC with over 90 percent represented by that union in 1963. Most postal unions had by that time also located their national headquarters in Washington, D.C.[85] The campaign in D.C. against segregated and unequal schools in the late 1940s not only brought into sharp focus the racial-economic apartheid that operated in society and government service in the nation's capital. It also revealed the divide as well as potential unity between working-class mass movement and middle-class legalism in that movement.[86]

Meanwhile, the conundrum of all or mostly black organizations like the Alliance fighting for integration—as Alliance historian Henry McGee once put it—was debated in the black press and civil rights movement both before and after *Brown*. The *Postal Alliance* in its September 1956 issue, for example, used the disparity of black and white teachers' salaries nationwide to address the worry over black teachers' potential job loss for with integration. The Alliance—a black union agitating for integration while acknowledging that one day they would not be needed—was ironically arguing here that black teachers should join mainstream teachers unions![87] Something similar was happening in the postal unions.

The bars to blacks being hired and promoted in the post office began breaking in many cities in response to black freedom movement–led agitation. "See, they had a black union [NAPE] and a white union [NALC]. Then most of us [letter carriers] joined the white union, and you began to get more, you know. . . . The white guys, they began to talk, and fraternize with you." That was how retired letter carrier Walter Holmes described change coming to the Charlotte, North Carolina, postal unions by the early 1960s. Interviewed in 1993 by oral historian Karen Ferguson, Holmes, a World War II combat veteran, North Carolina A&T State University graduate, and Mason, also had some representative stories to tell about his career that ran from 1951 to 1981. The stories included seeing blacks with college degrees passed over for management positions in favor of whites with high school diplomas, and customers on his mail route calling the postmaster to complain that "I got a black mailman out here." While he would argue with supervisors who denied him overtime to finish his route when the mail volume was heavy, by contrast he ignored verbal expressions of racism by older white coworkers, recalling a motto he had learned as an officer in the Army: "Take it and grin, as long as they don't put their hands on you."[88]

Meanwhile, in Washington, D.C., and Chicago, the Alliance was still the biggest postal union. In New York and elsewhere it was also large and influential. But it was now facing competition, especially from the independent, industrial, antiracist NPCU—now called the NPU. "It would be ironical indeed," Henry W. McGee wrote in 1961, "if continuing changes in personnel practices by the post office would lead eventually to the elimination of the need for the Alliance, especially in Northern cities like Chicago."[89] Black postal workers—many of them Alliance members—had challenged loyalty hunts, bars to black promotions in the post office, and Jim Crow union locals. But they did not always feel compelled to join or stay with the Alliance, even if they worked with civil rights groups or belonged to black lodges and clubs. For most Alliance members this was their civil rights labor organization. More and more black postal workers were becoming mainly interested in belonging to a strong, effective postal union, whichever one they felt that happened to be.

"It was like the dawn of a new day," said Arthur Ryland in a 1976 oral history interview with Dana Schecter, "with light upon that cold January of 1959 when we went to Washington on the first constitutional convention to set up a constitution." Ryland was recalling the early 1959 meetings of the NPCU (later to become the NPU) following the walkout over issues of local representation and Jim Crow locals by one-third of the delegates just before the adjournment of the August 1958 NFPOC Boston convention. "And I believe this was the beginning of my deep involvement as a [MBPU-NPU] union vice president. . . . And we'd begun without a penny. . . . And we had to go through the people on the [workroom] floor to make a collection." The NPCU wrote into that first constitution, among other things, referendum elections with proportional convention representation and no "dual locals," as the new union, with 25,643 members, grew rapidly to its peak of 80,000—about a quarter of them black postal workers like Ryland. Like the Alliance, the NPCU's members, too, had suffered through loyalty hunt removals, some suspended at the hands of Postmaster General Summerfield with the cooperation of NFPOC officers. "The only thing I can say is that it drew me closer to the union, and it made me fight harder for its continuity," said Ryland.[90]

The same was true also of NALC activists fighting for greater democracy and equality within their union. For them, taking a stand against segregated union branches in the South "was not a popular issue to take," recalled Vincent

Arthur Ryland (left), ca. 1960s. Ryland began working in the post office in New York in 1927. A onetime jazz musician in Harlem, he became a postal union official and activist known for his command of postal regulations and contracts. He was a member of NFPOC Local 10, joined the 1958 convention walkout, and later became a vice president of MBPU-NPU. Courtesy of the Metro Postal Workers Union Photographs Collection, Tamiment Library, New York University.

Sombrotto, then a New York Branch 36 rank and file member (later to become a 1970 strike leader, president of the branch, and president of the national organization). "It was taken up by our branch and in Brooklyn . . . where you had a lot of African Americans working in the branches, and where in the North here they were more or less integrated."[91] Indeed, the National Alliance, whose Washington, D.C., branch president, Robert White, greeted the NPU's first convention in that city in May 1959, now had more company in the struggle.

CHAPTER SIX

INTERESTING CONVERGENCES
IN THE EARLY SIXTIES POST OFFICE
(1960–1963)

"We have no more separate Charter Branches." That simple yet dramatic statement, greeted by applause, was announced at the NALC's 1962 national convention in Denver by its retiring president, William Doherty. Doherty's tenure had begun in 1941—the same year that the NALC voted to allow separate (or "dual") black and white branches throughout the South, over the objections of pro-black NALC activists. Now, the two black and two white members of the Committee on Separate Charters who had been appointed October 1, 1960, at the previous NALC convention were about to read their report on the abolition of segregation in the NALC. Included on that original committee was an African American letter carrier from New York City's Branch 36, Oscar Durant, who had also been an active member of the New York–Bronx branch of the National Alliance. One other African American had served on that committee—Walter Samples from Mobile, Alabama—in addition to three white members: its chair, Lloyd D. Nowak from Oakland, California; Frank Wetschka from St. Paul, Minnesota; and Loy S. Bell from the all-white Atlanta Branch 3837. As Doherty introduced each one to applause from the audience of fellow letter carriers, he joked that they had "worked so successfully that they worked themselves out of business."[1] While the NALC had voted in 1954 to ban any new segregated branches, it allowed existing ones to decide whether to combine or remain separate in any given city. Why the sudden change now, in 1962?

LOBBYING FOR PRO-EQUALITY LABOR LEGISLATION

Postal unions dropped all remaining Jim Crow branches and locals not long after President John F. Kennedy issued Executive Order 10988 on January 17, 1962, providing limited collective bargaining rights for federal employee unions that did not practice racial discrimination. In the space of just a few years, black postal workers and their allies had won important gains in the fight

President John F. Kennedy signs Executive Order 10988 on January 17, 1962, granting partial collective bargaining rights to government employee unions that do not discriminate or segregate. Fourth from the left is NALC president William Doherty. On the far right is National Alliance president Ashby Smith. Courtesy of *Postal Record*, National Association of Letter Carriers, AFL-CIO.

for equality in the post office and its unions. That included the integration of unions, the breaking down of race and gender barriers to all postal crafts and management positions, and the monitoring and enforcement of executive orders and laws relating to equal employment opportunity. The abolition of Jim Crow union branches and locals set the tone for a decade of struggle parallel to that outside the post office.

In the early 1960s, while postal union merger talk was in the air, postal unions were still largely divided along craft lines. But shifts and divisions were already occurring. That shifting became more pronounced with Kennedy's labor and civil rights executive orders that provided limited collective bargaining rights for federal unions as well as disallowed racial discrimination by federal agencies, contractors, or unions. Black postal workers and their allies continued to make the best of their limited representation by litigating, lobbying, agitating, and taking advantage of concerns by organized labor and the

The night they drove old Jim Crow down in the NALC. The NALC Separate Charter
Committee delivers its report on integrating the remaining segregated NALC branches at
the NALC national convention in Denver, September 6, 1962. Members include, from
left to right, Oscar Durant from New York (also an NAPE member); Frank Wetschka from
St. Paul, Minnesota; Walter Samples from Mobile, Alabama; and Lloyd Nowak
from Oakland, California. Courtesy of *Postal Record*, National Association of
Letter Carriers, AFL-CIO.

Kennedy administration that civil rights protests and white supremacist resistance were damaging America's image abroad in the Cold War.[2]

The lobbying power of the postal unions had become considerable by the
early 1960s. The NALC probably had the most clout of any postal union.[3] But
there were a number of others of varying size and influence also trying to put
pressure on senators and representatives on behalf of their respective constitu-
encies, because no federal employees' union enjoyed collective bargaining
powers then. Yet those lobbying for both civil and labor rights numbered
exactly two: the NAPE and NPU.

Of the nine postal employee unions, six were affiliated with the AFL-CIO: the
NALC, the United Federation of Postal Clerks (UFPC), the National Postal Mail
Handlers Union (NPMHU), the National Association of Post Office and General
Services Maintenance Employees (NAPOGSME), the National Federation of Post
Office Motor Vehicle Employees (NFPOMVE), and the National Association of

Special Delivery Messengers (NASDM). Of the three independent unions, two were militant—the National Postal Union (NPU) and the National Alliance. The other independent—the National Rural Letter Carriers Association (NRLCA)—was still largely based in rural farm family networks and federal patronage politics.[4] Following the 1958 split of the NFPOC, what remained merged in 1961 with the United National Association of Post Office Craftsmen (UNAPOC) to form the UFPC. The abolition of Jim Crow union locals early in the sixties removed a major social division within unions, but did not in itself build unity among postal workers or postal unions. And neither the NALC nor the UFPC possessed what the NPU and the Alliance proudly displayed: "one person—one vote" decision making at conventions.[5]

The prior absence of any collective bargaining rights and a national work agreement meant that postal unions still had to lobby Congress for pay and benefit raises, while local union officers bore the brunt of daily issues of labor discipline with local management. As noted by NALC historian M. Brady Mikusko: "In spelling out the rights and obligations of both parties. . . . there was no grievance procedure. . . . [and] the only written document was the *Postal Manual*." Yet federal employee legislation "was imminent," she wrote of this period, because of the widespread acceptance by Democrats and Republicans of the need for federal employee union recognition and collective bargaining. If Jim Crow was an embarrassment to the federal government, so were bad labor relations in the post office—the nation's largest employer.

The postal unions anticipated relief, but only the Alliance and the NPU lobbied for antidiscrimination provisions.[6] How did black postal worker activists convince the Kennedy administration to consider such measures given its lukewarm civil rights stance?[7] November 1960 had seen Kennedy, a liberal, pro-labor Democratic senator from Massachusetts, elected to the White House in a close race over Vice President Richard M. Nixon. The black vote for Kennedy played a significant role in his narrow victory.

Both the National Alliance and the Negro American Labor Council credited their intensive lobbying before the election for influencing Kennedy's issuance of EO 10925 on March 6, 1961, banning discrimination in federal employment and contracting, and EO 10988 in 1962 that extended official recognition to all federal unions while eliminating all Jim Crow government employee union locals.[8] The November 1960 *Postal Alliance* reported that their president, James B. Cobb, appeared on the "Equal Opportunity Panel" at Senator Kennedy's October Conference on Civil Rights and Constitutional Liberties in New York City, and that on October 29, Kennedy's younger brother Robert, his campaign manager, had met in Washington, D.C., with Alliance vice president Ashby G. Smith and research director Charles R. Braxton.

Reminiscent of the National Alliance's "Operation Contact" with the incoming Eisenhower administration just after the 1952 election, Smith and Braxton asked the younger Kennedy for consideration of a new "Fair Employment Policy." They also relayed their general concerns on black postal workers, noted that the Alliance's purview was "the entire field of employee concern including the question of equal opportunity," and included a list of "major proposals," including the following: "A re-evaluation of the loyalty-security cases in the light of the temper of the McCarthy era. The drive for economic equality and the emotion and rigidity that followed." The November *Postal Alliance*, published after the election, was able to refer to Kennedy as "President-elect," reinforcing the optimistic October report that had concluded: "Mr. [Robert] Kennedy commented that the points set forth during the conference would be given sympathetic study. He further assigned his closest adviser to be our continuing communication line after the election."[9]

The National Alliance thought they had the new president's ear, but they nonetheless kept the pressure on. For example, the December 1960 *Postal Alliance* included a letter that President Cobb had sent to President-elect Kennedy that month objecting to the latter's consideration of Senator William G. Fulbright (D-Ark.) as his secretary of state. Cobb noted that Fulbright had been a signatory to the 1956 "Southern Manifesto" by southern senators and representatives that urged white defiance of the 1954 *Brown* decision. Cobb questioned Fulbright's "effectiveness in representing this country and its national purposes in negotiating with the people of the world." Indeed, Fulbright was not nominated, due in part to civil rights movement protest.[10] The *Postal Alliance* during this time wondered aloud what world opinion thought of white supremacists attacking black civil rights demonstrators fighting for democracy.[11]

As pro-active as the Alliance's leadership was, it was also in danger of falling behind its rank and file and even the more cautious NAACP, as seen in this clash between outgoing Alliance president Cobb on the one hand and the Philadelphia NAACP branch leadership on the other. The NAACP had taken up the Philadelphia Alliance's discrimination complaint under President Eisenhower's EO 10590. Earnest Fleming of the Philadelphia Alliance (and a local NAACP board member) had charged that blacks were not being promoted in that city's post office and that his supervisors had retaliated against him for NAACP activity. In 1961, Philadelphia NAACP executive secretary James K. Baker wrote to Cobb, incredulous that he would take the side of the post office, especially when "Total Integration of the Postal Service" was the Alliance's 1961 convention theme. "In my twelve years of doing legal work for the NAACP," wrote Baker, "I must say that this is the most astounding document I have ever seen or heard of coming from a leader of a Negro organization. . . . May I finally add that perhaps you have not lived long enough as a Negro to have any feeling of discrimination as Fleming did, when, in the summer of 1959, the Philadelphia Post Office (which as you know has a huge number of Negro employees), made mass supervisory promotions and included not one single Negro."[12]

Whether Cobb felt chastened by the experience is not known. But this onetime leader of the 1940s Alliance upsurge against its then-hesitant leadership now found himself accused of compromising the fight for equality. Perhaps this came from close contact with postal management of which he was soon to become a part. Yet at the Alliance's 1963 summer Executive Board meeting Cobb had managed to find some of that old insurgent voice in calling for the union to get more involved politically and socially, which is what members of activist branches like New York City were already doing.[13]

Pressure from black postal workers had accelerated changes in the post office and its unions with regard to treatment of blacks. Donald P. Stone, an Atlanta postal clerk and Alliance member who joined the post office in 1958 (and later SNCC), remembers more black supervisor appointments after Kennedy's executive orders were issued.[14] In August 1965, two years after Kennedy's assassination, and just days after the Watts riots in Los Angeles, Postmaster General John A. Gronouski was proudly proclaiming before a Los Angeles Alliance banquet: "Today, we have in the Post Office, Negroes holding positions such as regional postal inspector, personnel director, Board of Appeals officers, assistant to the Regional Director, regional personnel director, real estate officer, medical officer and architect. None of these positions was held by a Negro in 1961 when Executive Order 10925 was issued."[15]

Issued in March 1961, Kennedy's EO 10925 banned discrimination by employers and unions in federal contract work, established a President's Committee on Equal Employment Opportunity (PCEEO), and reaffirmed and expanded EO 10590 that had banned discrimination in federal employment. Soon after Kennedy's order, NAACP executive secretary Roy Wilkins asked Jerry R. Holleman, executive vice chairman of the PCEEO, for a meeting with NAACP labor secretary Herbert Hill: "On behalf of Negro workers, Mr. Hill wishes to file complaints [with the PCEEO]." Holleman replied that he would welcome that meeting, noting: "*We are receiving complaints in considerable quantity and we will be unable to hold hearings on all these. Time will simply not permit it.*" Black postal workers' activism helped induce top-down executive orders that in turn provided them a channel for bottom-up responses that now overwhelmed the administration.[16] President Kennedy's EO 10988 similarly recognized the campaign against Jim Crow postal union locals even as he limited efforts to empower federal labor unions.

As senator, Kennedy had supported the Rhodes-Johnston bill that Representative George M. Rhodes (D-Pa.) had introduced in various forms annually since 1949 without gaining passage. But its chances appeared better than ever with the new Congress and president in 1961.[17] Speeches sympathetic to postal workers were made on the Senate floor in January by Senators Olin D. Johnston (D-S.C.) and Hubert H. Humphrey (D-Minn.). Both used vivid language to highlight the post office's oppressive and outdated management style: Johnston described it as "wicked" and "soul killing despotism," while Humphrey called it "autocratic" with a "Victorian structure." They pointed out that postal unions, denied the right to strike by federal law, were forced to beg Congress for raises and benefits. They described severe morale problems at the post office, offering this bill as relief for problems that compromised the federal government's image as a model employer. With 2.5 million employees, the federal government was the largest employer not only in the nation but in the entire world. Both senators were silent on the issue of discrimination. The bill appeared poised for passage.[18]

But Kennedy had other ideas. In June 1961 he formed the Task Force on Employee-Management Cooperation, whose scope was the same as Rhodes-Johnston. The Task Force itself was not exactly balanced. Postal labor historians John Walsh and Garth Mangum point out that it "was, in effect, a committee of federal employers."[19] The postal unions, however, were allowed to make proposals. Among other things, the UFPC recommended the Alliance be denied union recognition because it was only a "social organization."[20] Besides refuting those hoary charges by the UFPC, National Alliance president Ashby G. Smith (the only postal union president who was also an attorney) made fourteen recommendations having to do with everything from reforming management practice to asserting the right of postal employees to choose their own unions.[21]

The Alliance's testimony played a significant role in the Task Force's findings that ultimately became the basis for EO 10988. When President Kennedy signed that executive order, he trumped the Rhodes-Johnston bill that was still in committee. Postal labor historians have argued that EO 10988 was a diluted version of what might have been a strong federal employees' labor law.[22] Rhodes-Johnston would have granted collective bargaining rights, while EO 10988 did not even contain that term, providing instead "recognition," "discussion," "consultation," and "negotiation." Yet a form of "collective bargaining" was implicit in EO 10988, and even cited in a ten-page conference memo circulated by the New York City postmaster's office in 1962 to prepare local postal officials for this new process. "Remember," the memo counseled in its final section, "collective bargaining is play acting, it's a poker game, it's horse trading."[23]

Given the history of what postal unionists called "collective begging" of Congress for raises and reforms, NALC president William Doherty now went so far as to hail EO 10988 as the "Magna Carta" of federal worker legislation.[24] Yet one of the key provisions of that executive order that most postal labor historians have forgotten was its abolition of discrimination and segregation by federal employee unions.[25] It is highly unlikely that a white supremacist like Senator Johnston would have cosponsored a bill that would have outlawed segregated union locals. Kennedy, however, had been lobbied before the election by civil rights and black labor groups to end Jim Crow in the post office and its unions.[26]

EO 10988 protected federal workers' right to belong to a union. It also forbade federal unions from striking, advocating the "overthrow" of the government, or discriminating based on "race, color, creed, or national origin." It mandated federal agencies to provide an ascending hierarchy of union recognition: "informal," "formal," and "exclusive," all based on preference elections among federal workers. "Informal recognition" required no vote minimum, but only provided for that union's representatives to express its members' views to government agency officials. "Formal recognition" gave a union consultation rights on personnel matters based on winning at least ten percent of the vote. "Exclusive recognition" required a majority vote of any craft and entitled the winning union "to negotiate agreements covering all employees in the unit and shall be responsible for representing the interests of all such employees without discrimination and without regard to employee organization membership."[27] Despite similarities, EO 10988 and Rhodes-Johnston were substantially different. EO 10988 disallowed *any* form of discrimination: "When used in this order, the term 'employee organization' means any lawful association [including] Federal employees and employees of private organizations; but such term *shall not include any organization . . . which discriminates with regard to the terms or conditions of membership because of race, color, creed or national origin.*"[28]

By contrast, Rhodes-Johnston declared federal unions "shall not include any organization which, by ritualistic practice, constitutional or bylaws prescription, or tacit agreement among its members, or otherwise, *denies membership* because of race, color, religion, national origin."[29] Rhodes-Johnston, while banning federal unions from *excluding* black members, said nothing about *internal* union segregation. While segregation always constituted a form of membership denial, it could have been argued, as many unions did, that segregation did not actually deny membership to blacks. (For its part, EO 10988, also known as "Employee-Management Cooperation in the Federal Service," banned Jim Crow locals outright.)

In fact, the Rhodes-Johnston antidiscrimination clause would have applied to no existing postal union. The last postal union to bar blacks from membership was the National Postal Transport Association (NPTA), formerly the RMA until 1948. The NPTA lifted its Article III "Caucasians only" constitutional clause at its September 1960 convention, presided over by its antiracist activist president Paul Nagle.[30]

Finally, Rhodes-Johnston provided for a "winner-take-all" employee referendum system of choosing a national collective bargaining agent for each craft. Had that bill passed, and such an election been held and defeated the relatively smaller independent industrial unions—the National Alliance and the NPU—it would have stripped both of them of any representation, as well as effective civil rights advocacy.

The National Alliance had long objected to the problematic precedent in the private sector of "exclusive" union representation enshrined in the 1935 National Labor Relations Act (NLRA) that historically privileged white unions.[31] Like every other postal union the Alliance expressed cautious praise for EO 10988. Their approval for that order was based upon its prohibition of discrimination or segregation by any federal employees' union desiring official recognition, and their reading that "it very clearly established the fact that no Federal Agency is to operate as a closed shop."[32]

EO 10988, while limiting collective bargaining rights for all postal workers, also avoided "winner-take-all" contests. The Alliance preferred "formal" recognition for *all* unions, however, not divisions along craft lines with the potential for domination by the major unions. They voiced their misgivings over the ambiguous wording of the order's provisions, reiterating their determination to fight for all workers and for equality.

In contrast to their official critical support for EO 10988, however, a D.C. Alliance official felt vindicated participating in the Kennedy administration's March 2, 1962, reading and discussion of the order to the various postal union representatives. Administrative assistant Charles R. Braxton of the D.C. branch vividly portrayed the major postal union chiefs as having "smiles of satiation . . . sweat glands oozing with the pressure of long-restrained greed" in anticipation of learning they were presumably about to take over postal worker representation. No more frivolous talk of "one union," Braxton pictured them saying to themselves, "or this other malarkey these fuzzy headed liberals are always yelling about." Braxton used the divide he saw between the Alliance and the AFL-CIO postal unions to sardonically project his imagining of their selfish expectations: "Today . . . they were going to be rescued from the heat of the Postal Alliance pressures. The Alliance, you know, has only very narrow interests in this thing. Somebody in that organization is always talking about stuff like democracy, equal opportunity." Braxton suggested this gleeful climax: "And then it struck. Eyes snapped open. . . . 'Any organization obtaining exclusive recognition must represent all employees in the craft, whether member or not.' 'This is union busting,' he imagined them exclaiming to themselves, 'You mean we're going to have to fight for everybody?' " Underneath cordial public relations between union leaders, Braxton's narrative highlights splits between the postal unions and the Alliance in the fight for equality. His written rejoinder to AFL-CIO postal unions concerning the Alliance's supposed "narrow" interests was coupled with a bitter rebuke regarding nepotism and corruption: "But the business of running a union involves getting all your relatives on the union pay roll and in the government service using the dues of the membership to foot the bill."[33] Braxton and the Alliance saw flaws but also hope in EO 10988.

The signing of EO 10988 in 1962 signaled the opening of a battle among nearly a dozen unions fighting for "exclusive" national recognition of their respective crafts. Failing that, they would try to at least win "exclusive" regional recognition in the fifteen postal geographic regions, or else "exclusive" local recognition in thousands of post offices across the country. Below the highest, or "exclusive" status, the difference between the lower two—"formal" and "informal"—may seem insignificant and in retrospect might seem to have been "consolation prizes" to be avoided. But "formal recognition" granted rights to "consult," while "informal recognition" only conferred rights to "present." That made a big difference.[34]

The largest postal unions—the NALC and the UFPC—won national exclusive recognition in the summer of 1962 after winning a majority vote among all carriers and clerks, respectively. But this system also allowed postal workers to vote for other unions desiring "exclusive" recognition locally or regionally. The UFPC did win "exclusive" recognition in fourteen of the fifteen postal regions. But the NPU's impressive voter turnout actually left the New York region open, and it also won exclusive local recognition in eleven major urban areas. Its biggest local, the MBPU (Manhattan-Bronx Postal Union), won exclusive local recognition in New York City for clerks and mail handlers. The National Alliance for its part won local "exclusive" recognition elections like the one in Philadelphia for motor vehicle operators. The National Alliance and NPU also challenged the NPMHU in local elections, despite the latter having won national exclusive recognition for mail handlers.[35]

EO 10988, in addition to banning Jim Crow locals, also wound up providing the basis for both the Alliance and NPU to exist as militant, viable alternatives throughout the 1960s, although postal workers generally chafed at EO 10988's limitations and were frustrated at still having to lobby Congress for raises. And in 1963, one year after the first labor agreement was signed between the post

Sam Armstrong, World War II veteran, joined the Miami post office and National Alliance Miami branch in 1949. He worked as a special delivery messenger and letter carrier after the Alliance pressured the Miami postmaster to hire black clerks and carriers. Armstrong served as branch president for twenty years, representing employee grievances and fighting Jim Crow facilities at the Miami post office. He is currently the chairman of retirees for District Three (Florida, Georgia, North Carolina, and South Carolina). Courtesy of Sam Armstrong.

Samuel Lovett from Atlanta, NAPFE president of District Three (Florida, Georgia, South Carolina, and North Carolina), was instrumental in fighting Jim Crow in the post office and its unions in the 1950s and 1960s. Courtesy of the National Alliance of Postal and Federal Employees.

office and its unions, postal workers won the right to the union dues "check off" (paycheck deduction)—a system that private sector unions had enjoyed for years.[36] For the Alliance and NPU, that victory plus local "exclusive recognition" gains around the country represented footholds won.

The year 1962 had found the National Alliance now able to compete for representation nationwide under EO 10988, as Miami Alliance official Sam Armstrong recalled: "And then came Executive Order 10988. . . . And then, *and only then*, did the NALC decide, 'we'll accept [integration] . . . but you cannot go to any social functions.' " At one time, there was even a segregated partitioned cafeteria in the Miami post office until, in the 1960s, he proudly remembers, "the Alliance got that wall removed." Armstrong's friend and Alliance colleague Samuel Lovett came to the Atlanta post office by way of Atlanta University, the army during the Korean War, and Lockheed Corporation. Lovett shared Armstrong's pride in the Alliance's fusion of black labor, civic, and legal traditions: "The Alliance always worked within the framework of the law," Lovett maintained. "It was the [postal] *agency* that worked outside of the law, the situation with segregation and discrimination."[37]

The pressure applied by the Alliance on the Kennedy administration was not as dramatic as A. Philip Randolph's 1941 threat to lead an all-black March on Washington against discrimination and segregation in defense industries and the military. But with the Cold War so much a public relations battle between the United States and the Soviet Union on the world stage, labor relations within the federal government was a sensitive area. Top-down lobbying by the Alliance and the NPU was backed by the encouragement of grassroots organizing and filing of discrimination complaints. Pressure from black postal workers and their allies on the predominantly white postal unions abolished the last of the Jim Crow locals in 1962 and challenged the national unions' exclusive craft control.

ABOLISHING JIM CROW BRANCHES

Activists and events moved quickly after the summer of 1959 when AFL-CIO president George Meany rejected the idea of banning Jim Crow locals within member unions. The following May, black trade unionists (including Alliance members) held the first meeting of the Negro American Labor Council to defeat white supremacy in organized labor. Three months after the council met, the NALC began debating the issue of its segregated southern branches. The AFL-CIO instituted a Committee on Civil Rights at their convention that summer, and the NALC followed suit. All of this was happening against a backdrop of organized black student protests against segregation, mostly in the South.

Alliance members, who had fought white supremacy in the post office and in society, found the students' struggle inspiring. In March 1960, the Greensboro Alliance branch passed a resolution pledging its support for the mass sit-ins in that city against segregated lunch counters launched by four black students at the historically black North Carolina Agricultural and Technical College (now North Carolina Agricultural and Technical State University) that in turn inspired a wave of sit-ins across the South. "I remember it like it was yesterday," C. C. Draughn, a retired postal EEO counselor/specialist (and former clerk and mail handler) told me of those 1960 protests in which he and other Greensboro Alliance members were actively involved, as was his son.[38]

Black postal workers were challenging white supremacy at the workplace when black college students began mobilizing in 1960 against Jim Crow lunch counters and other public facilities. Years later, veteran SNCC leader James Forman pointed out how SNCC challenged not just Jim Crow but also residual

McCarthyism. "Because the Southern students were somewhat isolated from the effects of McCarthyism," Forman theorized in his memoir, "they were not afraid in some ways to take action against segregation and discrimination."[39] Forman then concluded: "By accepting the support of radicals and progressives, we helped to create an atmosphere that made it possible for many people scared by McCarthyism to come out of the woodwork and engage once again in active struggle. SNCC's role in helping to create a climate for radical thought and action was a most important contribution."[40]

Veterans of struggles against Jim Crow and McCarthyism in the old NFPOC, who had left in 1959 over Jim Crow locals and democracy issues and formed the NPCU, changed their name in 1960 to the National Postal Union (NPU) to reflect its industrial character. The NFPOC, for their part, merged in 1960 with the UNAPOC to become the UFPC, and ostensibly abolished all segregated locals. But the NPU, noting its own constitutional ban on Jim Crow locals and its support for the call by President Kennedy's Task Force to do the same, was unimpressed. They charged in July 1961 that "at least one major postal union—the former NFPOC—has dual locals."[41] William H. Burrus Jr., a black military veteran who had grown up in segregated Wheeling, West Virginia, before entering the Cleveland post office in 1958 as a distribution clerk, recalls an astounding historical silence: "The UFPC did not even acknowledge the existence of black locals" that earlier in the twentieth century had flourished in its predecessor NFPOC, said Burrus, later elected APWU national president in 2000. He told me he joined the UFPC before soon switching to the NPU "because I believe in the industrial concept. We had the model of the UAW and the coal miners and the steelworkers union. . . . No matter what one's color, no matter one's occupation, you all were in the same union."[42]

As for the NALC, the process by which separate branches were finally abolished is well documented but still not commonly known. At the NALC convention in Cincinnati in 1960, New York City Branch 36 brought Resolution 110 to the floor calling for the abolition of "dual" charters. Three significant arguments Branch 36 made in support of its resolution were the convention's 1958 commitment to exploring postal union amalgamation; the *Brown* decision precedent; and the integration of southern locals by the newly formed NPCU.[43] Harold Lowe from Branch 40 in Cleveland moved that a "five-man committee" be appointed to carry out the abolition process. At that moment Garrett Taylor from D.C.'s separate black NALC Branch 4022 rose in support and to remind his colleagues of the futility of trying to unite all postal workers as long as their own union was divided by race, adding these prophetic words: "I shall discuss this proposition with candor because it is unanimously felt by the membership of Branch 4022 that your action may easily determine the limits of our efforts to further the cause of the Letter Carrier and his fellow rank and file government worker in the next decade."[44]

The only objection to abolition from the floor came from Ralph Seery, a member of the all-white Norfolk, Virginia, Branch 3947. Seery's branch had been issued a separate charter a dozen years before and now stood to be dissolved into the predominantly black, activist, and much older Norfolk Branch 525. He wanted the resolution ruled out of order on the basis that his branch had been issued a "separate" rather than a "dual" charter. Seery may have remembered when Doherty himself had corrected a speaker in 1948 during that convention's debate on the issue and insisted that their constitution provided for "separate," not "dual," charters.

No one had ever pointed out that the NALC constitution provided for neither "separate" nor "dual" charters but rather the even more euphemistic "second charter," although the actual charter certificates never differentiated between "first" and "second" charters. But in their haste to dispose of Jim Crow charters, nearly everyone speaking had adopted the colloquial term "dual charter," including Doherty, who had always been loath to use it. Doherty—who at the 1948 convention had boasted how his efforts to establish separate charters (including Seery's) had garnered 673 new members—was not in the mood now for any more semantic quibbling: "Well, for your information, there *are* separate charters," he snapped impatiently at Seery, adding, "There are seventeen such charters, and by previous convention action it is impossible to issue any additional so-called separate charters. Does that answer your question?" "It does," replied Seery, getting the point. There were no further objections. The measure passed. The Committee on Separate Charters would now make its appointed rounds, so to speak, of branches that were still segregated in order to try to facilitate their abolition—starting with D.C.[45]

In 2004, when I interviewed James Pinderhughes, a retired black Washington parcel post letter carrier (who later became a supervisor), he told me that his small Branch 4022 met in schools or churches from the late 1940s until the spring of 1961 when it merged with the city's white NALC Branch 142. In my 2005 interview with Joseph Henry, who served as NALC Branch 142 president from 1998 to 2008 and who is also black, he recalled that he came to work at the post office in the fall of 1961 after that city's black and white NALC branches merged, and that he later joined Branch 142 in 1962. He witnessed no acrimony between black and white carriers at that time, but noted that whites begin to use the promotion process to move out of the carrier craft into becoming supervisors.[46]

In its final report at the September 1962 NALC convention, the committee cited mandates to abolish segregation and discrimination from both the NALC and the AFL-CIO. But Thomas Ward, a white delegate from the recently merged Montgomery, Alabama, Branch 106, objected that since 1960 the committee had never left D.C., when he had assumed that they were to travel to all the affected cities and make "a thorough study" of the implementation. "There was much dissension," he complained, while acknowledging that he himself had "merged in good faith." Ward suggested the committee had overstepped its original mandate that had been approved by the 1960 convention to "study" and make recommendations to "consolidate" separate branches "wherever possible," evaluate the "future" of those that somehow could not do so, and even allow for the possible preservation of "the present status quo."[47] What had happened?

Replying for the committee, Nowak noted that a January 31, 1961, deadline had been set by the NALC Executive Council, but the committee had agreed to allow branches more time to work out merger problems. After the committee ran into white resistance in March 1961 during a futile test run trying to merge the two separate branches in the nation's capital, the Executive Council issued a directive on April 14 merging the remaining separate branches—numbering over 5,000 members. Nowak and the committee now praised President Doherty and the Executive Council for having acted well in advance of President Kennedy's EO 10988. They also noted that in cities that formerly had dual branches, membership substantially increased after dissolution, despite dire predictions of "white flight" made by white southerners. (Ironically, it was probably black Alliance members who made up many of the new NALC recruits. It should also be noted that no evidence exists of black NALC branch objections to merger at this or any prior time.)

The committee acknowledged that by "early March of 1961, a number of outside pressures were working toward the abolition of discrimination because of race, creed, color, or national origin in Federal employment." Those included Kennedy's EO 10925 requiring the NALC and other postal unions to file "Non-Discrimination Compliance Reports" and the postmaster general's ban on discrimination in promotions. The committee then observed: "But the greatest pressure came from the denial of contracting authority to any organization practicing discrimination in connection with . . . the Federal Employees' Health Benefits Act. This denial posed a real and serious threat to the health insurance of all members and their families."[48]

Besides D.C. and Montgomery, other branches surrendering separate charters and subsequently merging were in southern urban areas that had traditionally large black populations, were sites of civil rights activism, and in most cases were destinations of varying rates of black migration over the past few decades: Mobile, Birmingham, Jacksonville, St. Petersburg, Albany, Atlanta,

Greenville, Charleston (S.C.), Memphis, Houston, Lubbock, Norfolk, Portsmouth, and Shreveport. All-white branches in New Orleans and Baton Rouge refused to surrender their charters and were abolished with new integrated charters subsequently established in those cities.[49] The NALC's top leadership, having allowed Jim Crow branches for twenty-one years, now moved quickly and decisively against them.

Even before the 1962 convention, NALC officials had been sensitive to charges of being coerced into dropping Jim Crow branches. They protested that in fact President Doherty had proclaimed at their 1960 convention that the NALC had taken steps to abolish separate charters before it was required to do so.[50] But Robert White, who for years as president of the D.C. branch of the Alliance clashed with postal management and unions over segregation and discrimination, would later recall that the major postal unions agreed to disband Jim Crow branches only after Kennedy's executive order outlawed them.[51]

Meanwhile, the relief that Doherty expressed for their abolition stood in sharp contrast to his participation in their maintenance. And there were still some black NALC veterans from the convention battles of the 1940s and 1950s—people like Elliot Peacock of Washington, D.C., and Clarence Acox of New Orleans—who no doubt remembered when President Doherty was on the wrong side of that issue. There were even a few like C. G. Ezzard of Atlanta who had lived to see the reversal of that 1941 convention that allowed Jim Crow branches. Also a witness to change was Claude E. Sullivan of Atlanta, who had vowed in 1952 to "right this wrong."[52] But while black postal workers were encouraged to see these barriers come down (and to also see more black union officers), the Alliance, which had helped lead that campaign, now faced competition for black members and their representation.

COMPETING UNION AGENDAS

Postal union cooperation was hampered by competition. The National Alliance and NPU together charged that the division among the craft unions also underscored their lack of commitment to equality. The NFPOC-UNAPOC-NPTA merger of 1961 made the resulting UFPC double the size of the NPU and a formidable contender for national "exclusive recognition." Despite a close election held in the summer of 1962, the UFPC won "exclusive" rights to represent over double its actual membership of clerks everywhere—except the New York region, where the smaller NPU was victorious. For its part, the NALC handily won national exclusive recognition in the carrier craft, while the NPU and National Alliance both received the less prestigious "formal" recognition nationally along with some local "exclusives."[53] Joseph Henry recalls that after

1962, when the NALC won "exclusive recognition" for the carrier craft, D.C. saw many black carriers who had once only belonged to the Alliance now joining the NALC, or maintaining dual memberships—often out of loyalty to the historically black union. But the successful war against Jim Crow unionism within the NALC owed a great debt to dual NALC and Alliance members like Oscar Durant from New York; M. E. Diggs from Norfolk; Eugene L. Griffin, Edward Allen, and H. L. Belliny from Jacksonville; Alliance president L. W. Dakers from Columbia, South Carolina; Alliance president T. C. Almore from Jackson; Alliance financial secretary Hugh L. Fountain from Richmond; and Harold Goodman from Beaumont, Texas.[54]

After the 1962 nationwide union recognition vote, both the NPU and Alliance were disappointed with the outcome and voter turnout. But they defiantly made the best of the election results. The NPU publicly scoffed at the UFPC's claim of "victory," while the *Postal Alliance* reiterated that the National Alliance's job was to represent their members, fight for equality, and lobby to modify EO 10988. The New York City Alliance branch was even more adamant on the need to fight for changes in EO 10988 than the national office. And the NPU continued their national organizing campaign, highlighting each new city they either took from the UFPC or almost did, especially in the South, reminiscent of the CIO's 1940s "Operation Dixie" organizing drive. The fact that other postal unions were opening up to more black workers posed a challenge for the Alliance, which was still a unique postal union.[55]

For example, the *Postal Alliance* excitedly reported the reactivation of the stalled civil rights movement's direct action protests against Jim Crow—protests that included its own members. With the wave of black student sit-ins in 1960, the *Postal Alliance*, which just four years before had heralded the coming end of Jim Crow and urged its readers to trust legalistic strategies to overturn it, now supported those who defied Jim Crow laws. Vice President Ashby Smith called the black student sit-in demonstrators "rebels with a cause." His "Civil Rights Trail" column chronicled the growing number of black student-led protests. Smith characterized the student rebellion as a legacy of ongoing black protest as well as a break with the moderation of past movements. The student sit-in movement, argued Smith, "differs from the [Dr. Martin Luther] King tactic in some respects. It is carried on primarily, almost exclusively by high-school and college students."[56]

Later, in supporting the 1961 Freedom Rides' challenge to Jim Crow public accommodation laws in the South, Smith excoriated "some northern journalistic 'friends of the Negro' who are afraid that the riders are not exhibiting sufficient patience." Smith even wondered if young blacks did not see their parents as having waited too long: "Those who say 'patience' have totally failed to realize the mood of the persons engaged in this crusade for freedom. Where we of our generation dreamed of, and worked for, freedom from discrimination for our children or grandchildren, the generation participating in the 'rides' are determined that freedom shall come, not only in their day, but also while they are young enough to enjoy it. I would not be surprised if they silently suspect that if we, in our time, had exhibited a bit more impatience, then their job would not be so difficult."[57] This older generation of black labor activists expressed pride in black students, often even deferring to young activists, some of whom were their own children at times needing to be bailed out of jail for engaging in civil rights protests. The latter was a proud recollection of former Durham, North Carolina, local Alliance president George Booth Smith.[58] The putative "Civil Rights–Black Power" generational split that would emerge several years later also saw more cooperation than is commonly credited.

When Ashby Smith was elected national president of the Alliance in August 1961, he announced that he was terminating his monthly "Civil Rights Trail" column in the *Postal Alliance* because of time constraints, not because he believed that victory over Jim Crow had come. On the contrary, while Smith counted with satisfaction the 115 columns he had contributed over eleven years, he cautioned that he had only reported a fraction of the news on the "civil rights" front. The "trail" of progress, he reflected, "has been bumpy and winding." "Seldom, if ever has it found its way direct to its goal." Smith closed with a defiant declaration that contextualized the domestic civil rights movement within the global black liberation struggle: "There is and can never again be a Half-Way-House between slavery . . . and freedom. . . . This message is sweeping across the world from Jackson, Mississippi to Johannesburg, South Africa."[59]

The *Postal Alliance* continued to feature news of the struggle for equality in the post office and the nation with news reports, opinion columns, and reprints from branch newsletters, black newspapers, and the mainstream press. They also stepped up their criticisms of other unions for acquiescence in white supremacy. And sometimes the NPU also did so: "Here are Nine Good Reasons Why Only the NPU Merits Your Vote," declared an ad in the June 1962 edition of the NPU's monthly journal the *Progressive*: "[The NPU] Did not need a Presidential directive to eliminate dual (colored and white) unions and discrimination because of race, color or creed. The NPU's Constitution and Bylaws forbid discrimination because of race, color or creed."[60]

The first labor agreement between the post office and its unions came in 1963.[61] In addition to the new representation statuses, there was also a new grievance procedure that allowed postal workers to remain on the job pending any negative decision made by a mediator, according to postal historian Vern

Baxter. Despite the standard portrayal of EO 10988 as a breakthrough for postal workers, however, Baxter points out that it truly was a "limited collective bargaining" order whose procedures, while hailed by postal unions, were soon "perceived by many workers as mechanisms to neutralize dissent." They had good reason to feel that way, as Baxter explains: "Major issues were nonnegotiable and many issues that were negotiable in 1963 became non-negotiable by administrative fiat in 1968."[62]

The Alliance, meanwhile, continued to consistently connect civil rights at work and in society. The same issue of the *Postal Alliance* in January 1962 that provided deadlines for voter registration and poll taxes in southern states also covered the Pittsburgh Alliance's protest against the maintenance of what they called "lily-white" local postal administrative and clerical jobs in a post office that was one-third black. Longtime agitation by Alliance branches in southern cities like Norfolk and Jacksonville had contributed to Congress's 1962 passage of the Twenty-fourth Amendment abolishing the infamous discriminatory poll tax, with the states providing final ratification in 1964. Virginia was one of the states that kept its poll tax until its abolition. But even up until that time the Norfolk Alliance had defiantly made branch membership conditional on being a "qualified voter," which included paying the poll tax. Also living to see the poll tax abolished were two New Yorkers who were former members of the Jacksonville Alliance branch that had promoted black voter registration in the early twentieth century before that movement was defeated by white terrorism: Wallace S. Hayes, an Alliance and NALC member, Howard University graduate, and later a New York postal clerk; and Alfonso W. Davis, an active New York City Alliance member who had transferred at least two decades before from the Jacksonville Alliance branch.[63]

During this period of social movement upsurge, black postal workers found no guarantees within the normal civil service job protections that often enabled them to perform off-the-job civil rights work—protections typically enjoyed more by professionals than blue-collar workers. Emblematic of black postal workers' role in civil rights and labor struggles were the political firings in 1961 of both Amzie Moore, Mississippi postal laborer and grassroots NAACP leader from 1935 to 1968, and Westley W. Law, a letter carrier for forty-two years as well as president of the Savannah NAACP branch and the Georgia state NAACP. Amzie Moore described to an interviewer what happened after the post office fired him for civil rights activities in 1961:

> On April 1st, I was fired by the Post Office Department here. So I got on the telephone and . . . told [Justice Department official] John Doar I had been fired. John Doar told me to get a plane and come on in to Washington. But I

didn't take a plane, I took a train, a slow train, out of Memphis. It took me twenty-four hours to get to Washington. . . . I came on in, went into see Mr. Doar, a meeting was set up for me and the assistant postmaster general to discuss the reasons for my dismissal. And when they got through checking, there was no apparent reason I got kicked out. So then, they had to call Memphis and tell Memphis to inform the Greenville Post Office that I was reinstated and not to bother me.[64]

For his part, Westley W. Law, hired by the Savannah post office in 1949, was fired on September 15, 1961, for political reasons at the request of U.S. Rep. C. Elliott Hagan (D-Ga.) by Michael Monroney, executive assistant to Postmaster General J. Edward Day. Law was rehired on October 24 following demands by national NAACP leaders and at the orders of President Kennedy. Kennedy even ordered the retraction of Day's subsequent demeaning remarks. Day, pandering to white prejudice, had declared: "I would not want a person with Law's record of conduct delivering mail to my family's home."[65] Interestingly, both Law and Moore conducted their civil rights and labor organizing with no apparent union affiliation or assistance. (One might even call the NAACP their union.) Voter registration was Moore's emphasis, while Law was a direct action protest leader, especially against segregated facilities. Despite harassment, they both worked for a federal agency that was now under public scrutiny.[66]

During the summer of 1963—three years after black student lunch counter protests had spread throughout the South—the *Postal Alliance* reported that President Kennedy had ordered "contract stations" (private enterprises that use government contracts to dispense postal services) to end segregation or lose their contracts. The *Wall Street Journal* article that the *Postal Alliance* reprinted also quoted Kennedy aides and postal officials on the significance of this order as reflecting the president's desire "not only to set an example but directly to influence local actions." (Paul Tennassee observes that Kennedy actually chose the post office as his "laboratory" for equal opportunity policies.)

Other examples of Kennedy's progressive postal policies, as the *Journal* article noted, included the 1963 appointment of Leslie N. Shaw as acting (later permanent) postmaster of Los Angeles, the first African American to head a large urban post office. The *Journal* also pointed out that the administration directed postmasters at the nation's 600 largest cities to "deliberately seek out qualified Negroes for promotion," noting that "the largest employer of Negroes in the U.S." was the federal government. These affirmative action-type steps, it added, were taken "before the recent flare-ups of racial violence and demonstrations."[67]

Although not as vocal as the National Alliance on the question of equality, the NPU also made it a point to attack racism, highlighting its own role as a combatant in that fight. Examples included *Progressive* articles from 1962 and 1963 concerning the difficulties that blacks had registering to vote in Mississippi and a road trip through the South made by white and black postal colleagues who refused to stop anywhere that would not serve all of them together. The NPU also supported the civil rights bill then before Congress, including its FEPC provisions that abolished workplace discrimination. The *Progressive* backed "nonviolent" demonstrations by postal workers as well. It is fair to say that the NPU prided itself in belonging to a "progressive militant" union tradition, distinguishing itself from conservative organized labor.[68] (And the NPU probably had more black officials than any other postal union besides the Alliance.) The July 1963 issue of the *Progressive* also favorably noted the promotion of black postal officials Leslie Shaw and Henry McGee (both Alliance members) as longtime NPU friends. NPU locals grew in Jacksonville, Florida, along with those in Texas and Arizona, with a number of Latinos serving as union officers. To the UFPC's embarrassment, the January 1963 *Progressive* headlined antidiscrimination grievances the NPU had won on behalf of two UFPC members. Triumphantly, the NPU informed their readers that both reinstated workers—Velma Frazier, an African American clerk in Des Moines, and Alfred Gallegos, a Mexican American clerk in Albuquerque—immediately switched to the NPU, since the UFPC had refused to fight their attempted removals by post office.[69]

Black members of other postal unions also engaged in civil rights activity, some having done so since their adolescent years, like letter carrier Cleveland Morgan of NALC New York Branch 36. Born in 1942 in Cuthbert, "a little town in south Georgia," Morgan recalls (like Felix Bell of Jackson, Mississippi, NAPFE) that "we stressed education down there." At age fifteen he was an active member of the NAACP Youth division: "I used to go around, in the '50s, in the woods, [doing] the voter registration, helping people to vote." He emphasized the importance also of the black church, including its music that gave them strength. Northern black labor and civil rights activists were more than mere spectators of a southern civil rights drama but participants in a national movement. Morgan continued his civil rights activism after leaving the South and entering the post office, observing that in the 1960s northern public school students became segregated by neighborhoods that translated into de facto school segregation, with northern racism a "closet case" of neighborhood and job segregation.[70]

Under conditions of discrimination and segregation, labor solidarity remained problematic in general. National unity among postal unions as well remained an elusive goal with the issue of equality continuing to serve as an important barometer. The UFPC had abandoned segregated locals, but continued to attack the Alliance as "segregated" and initiated another controversy in June 1963 when it opposed the promotion of three black clerks as supervisors in the Dallas post office.[71]

But the Alliance and the NPU were not intimidated. They carried progressive unionism from the pre-CIO era into the 1960s labor and social movement upsurge. For example, all postal unions mourned the assassination of President Kennedy on November 22, 1963, and recalled his friendship to labor; but the Alliance and NPU emphasized his civil rights support. The Alliance compared his assassination to those of black civil rights leader Medgar Evers, gunned down at his home in Mississippi; white Baltimore Alliance activist William Moore, shot dead in Alabama during his one-man march through the South for equality; and four black girls killed in a Birmingham church bombing. *Postal Alliance* editor Snow Grigsby argued that vindicating the lives of these martyrs required that all Alliance members must become more politically active.[72] Meanwhile, the NPU's *Progressive* noted: "Civil rights is one of the biggest issues confronting Congress, one in which the late Pres. Kennedy was deeply interested." They summarized the major provisions of the civil rights bill making its way through Congress, most notably: "Fair Employment—Discrimination by unions and employers in interstate commerce . . . would be banned."[73]

Black postal workers and their allies had made the war on Jim Crow unionism part of a larger critique of inequality in the post office and its unions. They successfully exploited the federal government and organized labor's competition on the world stage with communism and national liberation movements, in an interest convergence that finally abolished Jim Crow postal union branches and locals. That abolition, combined with the 1961 establishment of the PCEEO and the 1962 elimination of separate postal gender job registers (discussed in chapter 7), helped set the tone for more militant postal union organizing for the rest of the decade. Despite some white resistance, black postal union activists and white allies continued to bring the civil rights movement into the post office and its labor unions, both from the top down and the bottom up.

CHAPTER SEVEN

BLACK WOMEN IN THE 1960s
POST OFFICE AND POSTAL UNIONS
(1960–1969)

"It is important to note that most of the women coming into the PO [Post Office] are Negroes. Reflecting the conditions in the American economy and the unfair treatment that they have received on the 'outside' down through the years, these women come into the Federal government hoping that they will get a 'fair shake.'"[1] Those words appeared in the May 1966 *Union Mail*, the monthly newspaper of the militant industrial Manhattan-Bronx Postal Union (MBPU), the huge New York local that was the largest in the NPU. The article's author, MBPU executive vice president Philip Seligman, a European American, pointed out that there were over 3,400 women in the New York post office (up from 550 in 1960), and that half of all postal workers soon to be hired were expected to be women. He called for the union to fight sexual harassment and the inadequate training of female clerks, noting: "More significant, is the protest from many of our female members that they receive inadequate indoctrination when they are appointed."[2]

Ten years later, as part of a postal union oral history project by Cornell University, Professor Dana Schecter interviewed Seligman, who had since retired from the post office. The MBPU was now the New York Metro Area Postal Union (NYMAPU) Local 10, the largest in the APWU—itself a product of the 1970 postal wildcat strike and subsequent union merger of clerk and other craft unions. Seligman recalled how legislative and executive orders during the Kennedy administration contributed to the abolition of separate gender job registers and paved the way for a tremendous increase in postal employment for women. He also reflected on how the influx of mostly black women in the 1960s in New York transformed the post office and its unions: "And they brought a new force with them, a dramatic change. . . . The change was a more aggressive change, they wouldn't take abuse, they fought back, they hit back, and it was good."[3]

One of those recently hired militant black women was Eleanor Bailey, who in the early 1970s told a meeting of APWU women activists: "Our group of

Eleanor Bailey, New York City 1970 postal strike rank-and-file leader (MBPU-NPU), in 2004. Now retired, Bailey was hired during a large influx of women—especially African Americans—into the post office in the 1960s and fought for their rights. She was shop steward for thirty-one of her thirty-two years at the post office, promoted women's organization, and later held positions as legislative director, human relations director, and chair of the Trustee Board of New York Metro Area Postal Union Local 10–APWU. Photograph by the author.

'subs' was always 'getting into something.' Challenging the establishment of the P.O. and the union on their policies. We had stewards who we wondered on whose side they were on. I attended meetings just to have the knowledge of the union policies and my rights."[4]

Black women helped transform the post office and its unions in the early 1960s. By advocating for themselves and all postal workers, black women broadened the scope of civil rights unionism. Their entry into the post office was facilitated in large part by presidential executive orders and congressional legislation that represented not only Kennedy's New Frontier anticommunist Cold War ideology and idealism, but its response to the black freedom movement, residual New Deal Democrat advocacy, and competition from communist countries and liberation movements around the world. It was a response that was both politically pragmatic and ideological—an interest convergence where "top-down" met "bottom-up."

Black women entering the post office in the 1960s got help from black

In the 1960s, African American women were hired in increasing numbers, for the most part as postal clerks and mail handlers; shown here are workers in one of the main post offices in New York City. Courtesy of the Postal Workers Union Photographs Collection, Tamiment Library, New York University.

women working in the President's Commission on the Status of Women (PCSW), who argued for and helped facilitate policy change at the top with their intervention. The Kennedy administration, like the AFL-CIO, generally vacillated and had to be dragged kicking and screaming by the black freedom movement to support equality. The subsequent civil rights legislation and executive orders of President Lyndon B. Johnson's administration were legacies of those struggles.

In the 1960s, before and during the upsurge of the predominantly white feminist movement in New York, black postal worker union women were leading campaigns for women's rights at the workplace as well as challenging racism and the anti-worker policies of postal management. The migration of militant young black women into the post office paralleled a similar youth migration into the civil rights movement and progressive social movements in general in the 1960s. Unlike the 1940s, however, women's employment in the post office was now considered permanent, not temporary. The removal in the early 1960s of what might be called "Jane Crow"-gendered postal job registers was somewhat akin to the 1940 abolition of application photographs that the post office had once used to screen out black applicants.[5]

The National Alliance had long advocated for women in the post office, and they were now joined in that endeavor in the 1960s by the MBPU. Unfortunately, scholars have largely ignored black women postal workers, and in fact women generally in the post office, as well as their struggles to enter the post office on an equal basis. There is evidence women carried mail and served as postmasters as early as 1773 and first worked as clerks in 1862, but men's annual salary was two to three times the maximum for women of $600. Hostile to women's presence in part because of their productive performance at considerably less pay, male postal workers helped make the post office a masculinist workplace for many decades, limiting female entrance. An 1870 law allowed the post office to pay women the same salary as men for the same work, but also allowed agency officials to limit job openings to men or women only. For the most part those officials only asked for men. Women were allowed to take the new civil service exams introduced in the Civil Service Act of 1883, but gendered job registers kept their numbers low in the post office and all federal agencies.[6]

The first known black female postal worker was Eliza Ridgely, hired in 1869 as a "laborer" (today called a "mail handler") in D.C., while Anne Dumas of Covington, Louisiana, in 1872 became the first black female postmaster—one of twelve in the 1800s. Most of the first black female postal workers in the late nineteenth century were probably local postmasters. Many others were clerks and laborers. But the 1907 census record reports no women as city letter carriers.[7] Black women letter carriers (twenty-four in the entire nation) first appeared in the 1920 census, putting their entry into that craft sometime in the prior decade, possibly during World War I when more occupations opened up to black women and women in general.[8] The first known black female postal clerk was Mary E. DeLacy of Alexandria, Louisiana, hired in 1879. The first known black female postal unionist was Lillian Wood, a Railway Mail Service clerk who in 1921 helped found the New York City branch of the National Alliance. White women were among the founders of the NFPOC in 1906 and first appeared as NALC convention delegates in 1902, but it is not known when black women began to affiliate with either union.[9]

Postal unions, like most labor unions, also had "women's auxiliaries" that integrated the wives of male postal workers into the social life of the union. In the case of postal workers, we have also seen that with the 1939 Hatch Act limitations on federal worker political activity, these auxiliaries sometimes played important roles in doing political work that postal workers were not allowed to do. Alliance president Ashby Smith's words of praise for their women's auxiliary at the height of the civil rights movement in October 1963 commended their advocacy and fundraising accomplishments of the auxiliary. No other postal union matched the Alliance and NPU for advocacy of women in the post office. In the case of the Alliance, not only did women serve as convention delegates, but they were also assuming local branch presidencies in Indianapolis, Los Angeles, and other cities.[10]

While every postal union has historically emphasized the social and political importance of the auxiliaries, postal unions in the sixties depended highly on the auxiliaries to help with their congressional lobbying. The most active civil rights-oriented auxiliaries were in the Alliance and the NPU. Alliance auxiliary women, for example, marched with CORE in Baltimore for civil rights in 1966, while the Washington Area Postal Union (WAPU) Women's Auxiliary reflected the NPU's civic unionism in its statement of purpose: "To unite women interested in the welfare of the postal employee and his family. To actively promote remedial legislation that will gain for postal employees a better standard of living and better working conditions. To actively promote the education of the membership in the political operations of government and responsibilities and duties of citizenship."[11]

The post office had hired women as temporaries during both World War I and World War II, laying off most of them after the wars ended in favor of returning male veterans and incoming male applicants. It was here as well as in daily postal union life that the National Alliance stands out. The Alliance alone fought after World II to keep women at the post office.[12] Throughout its existence the Alliance took pride in announcing "firsts"—including the first black women hired in particular post offices or management positions.

Lillian Wood in fact was one of the few women in the entire Railway Mail Service, and by 1942 the only one in New York City. Her pioneering, however, was more significant in her role as a union leader. Combined with Henry McGee's recollections of black female postal workers bringing their civic influence into the Alliance in the 1940s, we have also seen how black women like Lillian Wood played a leading role at the pivotal 1943 National Alliance convention debate in St. Louis that defied Jim Crow at that city's post office.[13] One is also struck by the large number of female names on the list of Alliance new members in 1940s and 1950s, as well as those active on union committees. Of the 136 new members that the New York Alliance branch recruited in the first two months of 1945, for example, only 25 were men. In 1959, women filled

15 of 108 branch committee positions in the New York Alliance, including several chairs.[14]

Most women working at the post office before the 1970 strike were occupationally segregated as clerks, although some worked as mail handlers and a few as letter carriers. The hostility exhibited by men toward women at the post office in the 1940s and 1960s is similar to other historically male private and public sector workplaces where men saw women as competition for a male-defined job.[15] And most women worked as clerks rather than carriers up until the 1960s, even though the civil service exam often allowed applicants to choose whether they wanted their score to make them eligible for one or both crafts. Postal workers were required to be able to handle heavy mail sacks up to eighty pounds. Men often expressed skepticism that women could lift that much weight. There were also racial preferences that white supervisors gave white women mail handlers, as mail handler Richard Thomas remembers: "Anytime a white young lady would come in, the supervisor would say, 'Listen you don't want to be a mail handler—you'd rather be a clerk. Why get your hands dirty? Go upstairs, we'll find you a nice typing job.' . . . Black women they would never say anything to."[16]

In 1956, only 92 women (many of them black) carried the mail nationwide. By 1960 that figure had increased to 104, and to 370 in 1965, outpaced by 524 women rural letter carriers. In 1965 women made up 49,880 of the post office's 600,000 employees, 27,616 of whom were clerks. But they also made up an astonishing 38 percent (13,005) of all postmasters in 34,000 post offices. By 1969, the number of women in the post office had almost doubled to 99,168 out of 604,489 employees.[17]

In early 1966 the *New York Daily News* profiled a young black woman, Alice Williams, as a prototypical female new-hire in an article prophetically punned: "Gals Put Their Stamp on the PO: Lady Clerks Are Now Carrying the Mail." The photo showed Williams being trained as a letter carrier at the Church Street Station. The article's subtitle noted the growing occupational shift in postal "women's work" from clerk to carrier, and the text noted the overall social change wrought at the workplace: "It seems that there's a provision in the new civil rights law that says an employer can't say no to a prospective employee just because of his race, color, religion or sex." A postal official acknowledged: "Most branch managers have preferred to keep the women on inside jobs. . . . But because of the increasing volume of mail, and because some of the girls like the work, more and more of them have been going on mail routes." Despite the article's patronizing title and narrative, its citation of Title VII, management pragmatism, and enthusiastic female letter carriers and males "showing the ladies the ropes" reveals an erosion of the masculinist workplace by multiple imperatives.[18]

Passage of Title VII of the 1964 Civil Rights Act with its "affirmative action" provision solidified and united previous legislation and executive orders that had banned discrimination based on race and sex in federal employment. Yet despite smiles on the faces of Alice Williams and Bob Rinaldi, the young white male carrier training her, the women who entered the post office in the early sixties had to struggle with management and many male co-workers who resented their entry, as well as with women already there who did not want to give up paternalistic gender-based job privileges that they previously enjoyed. The struggle for women's entry and equal treatment in the 1960 post office was not an exact parallel of African Americans' postal job migration, but it was similar and had some of the same allies, one of the principal ones being the National Alliance.

PIONEERS IN THE EARLY SIXTIES

Black women in the early 1960s helped force changes in the post office at a time when the civil rights movement, according to Adam Fairclough, was politically pressuring the maddeningly ambivalent Kennedy administration by using dramatic direct action that confronted Jim Crow.[19] The post office was possibly the *only* federal civilian agency to see an entry of large numbers of blacks and women during this period.[20] Black women took advantage of executive orders, congressional legislation, and postal directives that increased the number of women coming into the post office. Many took an active role in union affairs, raising issues of particular importance to women, such as accommodations for childcare; separate women's bathrooms; and the paternalism and harassment on the shop floor by both supervisors and male co-workers.

Scholars of Kennedy's labor and civil rights executive orders, however, have surprisingly often overlooked his Executive Orders 10980 (1961) and 11126 (1963) establishing and reinforcing, respectively, the PCSW. PCSW scholarship frequently forgets the influential black female civic and business leader members who served on that commission and who advocated for black women in particular: Hilda Fortune (New York National Urban League), Maude Gadsen (Beauty Shop Owners Association), Dorothy Height (National Council of Negro Women), Cenoria Johnson (National Urban League), Inabel Lindsey (Howard University), and Gerri Major (Johnson Publications). Combined with Attorney General Robert F. Kennedy's ruling and the Equal Pay Act

(EPA) of 1963, policy steps toward gender equity at the workplace encouraged the mass migration into urban post offices of many young African American women.[21]

Early in 1962, Attorney General Kennedy responded to the PCSW's request for a review of the 1870 law that had created de facto gender-segregated job registers. Kennedy declared those registers invalid, and in 1965 Congress abolished the law altogether. The Post Office Bureau of Personnel, in the January 11, 1962, weekly *Postal Bulletin,* announced that President Kennedy had established the PCSW and ordered "the Civil Service Commission to review Government-wide policies having to do with the opportunities open to women in the Federal service, with a view to amending any such regulations or policies which might tend to encourage discrimination on the basis of sex."

While it would not be until the 1964 Civil Rights Act that race and sex discrimination would be banned in the same piece of legislation, the beginning of equal opportunity public policy based on *both* race and gender was quite possibly first established in the post office. On the next three pages of that January 1962 *Postal Bulletin* was a page-long memorandum titled "Equal Employment Opportunity" directed to "all postal officials and employees" in which it listed instructions for compliance with Executive Order 10925. Women's new federal job rights were now protected—at least on paper.[22]

On May 10, 1962, advertisements from the Board of U.S. Civil Service Examiners significantly if cautiously made explicit invitations for women to apply for postal jobs. The message could not have been any more unmistakable in those ads—all from the New York City area. One ad with bold letters proclaimed: "Serve with Pride and Honor: the U.S. Post Office," coupled with a quotation from President Kennedy's January 30, 1961, State of the Union message: "Let the public service be a proud and lively career. And let every man and woman who works in any area of our national government, in any branch, at any level, be able to say with pride and honor in future years: 'I served the United States Government in that hour of our nation's need.' " This captured the essence of Kennedy's Cold War liberal idealist message that all Americans, especially the young, were part of a domestic and global American reform mission—civil service being a kind of civilian enlistment.

Yet another postal ad announced: "All qualified applicants will receive consideration for employment without regard to race, creed, color or national origin," while adding in bold letters halfway down the page: "Male and female employees will be required to perform the same duties." There was also an ad in bold capital letters that proclaimed new postal jobs "Open to Men and Women, $2.16 to $2.63 an Hour," at the same time forewarning: "Male and Female Employees Are Required to Perform All the Duties of Their Position,"

Post office recruiting "job mobile" in 1968 in New York City. Note that the invitation to apply was "open to males and females" and the description of a "good salary" ($2.95 an hour for carriers and clerks and $2.72 for mail handlers), notwithstanding that many workers in these jobs were on welfare and receiving food stamps. Courtesy of the Metro Postal Union Photographs Collection, Tamiment Library, New York University.

which was repeated again in smaller print. Seemingly addressed especially to women who envisioned a career as a clerk or carrier, the ad cautioned that "Clerks handle heavy sacks of letter mail, paper mail, and parcel post weighing 80 pounds or more," and "Carriers . . . may be required to carry on their shoulders loads weighing as much as 35 pounds."[23]

In Cleveland, William H. Burrus Jr., then in the NPU, saw his sister Billie come into the post office, at a time when women—mostly black, unmarried, and between the ages of eighteen and twenty-five—were "flocking to the post office for employment. . . . Women didn't have any opportunity in the private sector. For them it paid fairly well . . . [and unlike most men they had] the dexterity required [to operate the new letter sorting machines or LSMs]." In addition, recalls Burrus, there were "a lot of conversations going on" between men and women on the shop floor, and that "a lot of marriages ensued after that!"[24]

Meanwhile, MBPU vice president Seligman did more than write in the May 1966 *Union Mail* to protest the absence of safety classes for women new-hires. That same year he also wrote to management requesting classes for women hired as clerks and mail handlers but not given adequate training or time to change to appropriate clothes when changing jobs.[25] Examples of the black female shop floor leaders whom Phil Seligman described as "not taking abuse" were Daisy Strachan (pronounced "Strawn") from the Bahamas and Eleanor Bailey from Long Island, New York.

The daughter of a trade union regatta captain in the Bahamas, Strachan came to New York in 1960 with her husband Leroy, the nephew of John Strachan, New York's first black postmaster and a National Alliance member. Daisy Strachan started working for the post office in 1962, the same year as Executive Order 10988 and a year before the EPA, while Eleanor Bailey started in 1964, the same year the Civil Rights Act was passed by Congress and signed into law by President Lyndon B. Johnson. Both Strachan and Bailey told me that at first men were often hostile to the presence of women on the shop floor and would assign them physically demanding tasks. Said Strachan: "In those days it was very, very hard for females because they had a thing going on [a male shop floor culture] which I was not fully aware of then." But what impressed her was seeing the Alliance confront sexism inside the post office, especially in the mail handler craft. Strachan joined the Alliance in 1965 and did secretarial work for the post office for a period, although she notes that black women generally were not hired for that position. Following that, she trained on the new LSMs. She became a shop steward from 1966 to 1967 at Grand Central Station, after which she had to return to the Bahamas to care for her ailing mother. She would not return until after the 1970 nationwide postal wildcat strike, at which time the Alliance helped secure her reinstatement.

Daisy Strachan said that during the 1960s she was not aware of hostility or discrimination by whites toward blacks at her office—but it was something she heard about while processing grievances. She recalled black coworkers' reactions to her lack of experience dealing with racism in the United States: "People would say 'Oh you're different 'cause you're from the islands.' "[26] Advocating for women's rights on the shop floor saw competition between the Alliance and the MBPU, even before large numbers of women began working in the post office.

In 1960, women did not even have their own bathroom facilities. Yet they were also exempted by management from many demanding physical tasks. Letters and memos circulated during this time reveal that management actually deferred to the MBPU's egalitarian judgment. The MBPU objected to the post office's granting shift preferences to women who wanted to avoid working

John Strachan (far right) during the 1969 New York Truck Terminal (NYTT) inspection. A National Alliance member and jazz musician, Strachan was appointed New York City's first black postmaster in 1966. Here he meets MBPU president Morris "Moe" Biller (center) and Phyllis Dillard (left), a member of the NYTT Recreation and Welfare Committee, along with two others (one unidentified, the other identified only as Kanter). Courtesy of the Metro Postal Workers Union Photographs Collection, Tamiment Library, New York University.

the midnight shift, presumably for family considerations. The MBPU treated this as a seniority issue and had that gender preference quashed. But they also began to advocate for women who were entering the post office and encountering harassment by male managers and coworkers expecting women to do physical tasks that they did not even require men to do.[27] Helping to blunt male resentment and in the process building labor solidarity were black women MBPU activists like Eleanor Bailey.

FROM NEGOTIATION TO DIRECT ACTION

Bailey's story, especially in contrast to those of National Alliance activists like Daisy Strachan and John Adams, reveals just how much the MBPU stood on the

Left to right: Gregory Wilson, Frederick John, and Joann Flagler (a 1970 strike veteran) in 2004. All are NYMAPU Local 10–APWU activists. Photograph by the author.

shoulders of the Alliance in advocating for women's rights, but how much it diverged in its embrace of both rank-and-file and official union militancy with black women taking leadership in shop floor actions. In 1963 Bailey, whose father was a Manhattan postal worker, was a thirty-two-year-old recently divorced single mother from Long Island who had moved to New York City that year, where she had taken several other civil service exams in addition to the postal exam. When the post office called her for a clerk position in Manhattan on Tour 1 (the night shift) in 1964, she took it.

Bailey and other African American postal workers recalled that in those days the postal exam was more difficult than the memorization and identification test that was taken in the early 1980s by two other black members of New York Metro whom I interviewed, Gregory Wilson and Frederick John. It was an exam that Eleanor Bailey and Carlton Tilley (who started work right after the 1970 strike) are proud to have fought to have changed: "At that time," remembers Bailey, "to take a test for the post office, you took a test that lasted four hours. You took a math test [and] . . . English composition." The exam favored college-educated postal applicants: in fact, when Bailey started at the post office, she discovered her dentist (who was black) and other college gradu-

Carlton Tilley came to work at the post office in New York City just after the 1970 postal strike. A former Alliance member who later joined the APWU, he was interviewed at NYMAPU headquarters in 2004. At the time he was the local union's director of human relations and chairman of the trustee board. Photograph by the author.

ates working at the post office as a second job or because they could not yet find work in their profession.[28]

Already working at the post office when Bailey was hired was New York City–Bronx Alliance Branch President John Adams. Adams had taken that long civil service exam in the 1940s, and had also seen blacks with college education and careers spend time working in the post office, including Charles Rangel, later elected to Congress from Harlem, and Percy Sutton, a Tuskegee Airman who later graduated from Brooklyn College Law School and served as Manhattan borough president. Adams, a World War II combat veteran, went to work as a full-time letter carrier at the Radio City Station and became part of struggles by the National Alliance to secure full-time employment in the post office for women during the 1940s and the 1960s.

The first struggle was after World War II to keep women who had been hired during wartime from being laid off. They were largely successful. At that time there were only two African Americans serving in Congress, both Democrats: Rev. Adam Clayton Powell Jr. from Harlem, and William Dawson from

Longtime New York City National Alliance activist official John Adams (second from right), a World War II veteran, special delivery messenger, and letter carrier, was elected president of the branch. He became an EEO specialist and was instrumental in bringing more women into the post office and his union. Adams is shown here in 1965 with other Alliance officials, including president Ashby Smith (center), at a "bon voyage" party for outgoing postmaster general John Gronouski (third from right), who had recently been appointed ambassador to Poland by President Lyndon B. Johnson. Courtesy of the National Alliance of Postal and Federal Employees.

the south side of Chicago. Both men advocated for African Americans and for the National Alliance and helped open up the post office to black hiring and promotions. "We used to meet weekly with Herbert Hill on cases with the Alliance," Adams recalls of the Alliance's close ties with the NAACP, its famous labor secretary and their strategy sessions.[29]

The second struggle for women's postal employment was in the early 1960s, when Adams remembers that the first female letter carriers were hired. But the post office was as unprepared for women's arrival as it was before World War II: "We had to fight to get restrooms for women. We had to convert the managers' restrooms into women's restrooms. Even locker rooms: they had no facilities for women."[30] Around the time Eleanor Bailey was hired, John Adams was promoted to the position of EEO specialist with the post office. He recalled that in 1967, when John Strachan, an Alliance member, was sworn in as the first black postmaster in New York City, Adams handed him a list of thirty names of qualified black applicants who had been overlooked for promotion. They all subsequently received promotions, according to Adams. And Alliance District Eight president Noel V. S. Murrain explained to me that a key part of the Alliance's advocacy work for equality and black promotion was "social lobbying" (dances, pre-Christmas receptions, and scholarship dinners)—even before Alliance members became New York City postmasters, such as Strachan or Vinnie Malloy, New York's first black female postmaster, appointed in 1999.[31]

But black women in the MBPU adopted a more confrontational approach with the post office. The clerk position that Eleanor Bailey took in 1964 was at the giant General Post Office (GPO) in Manhattan. Manhattan's post offices in 1963 were combined with those of the Bronx to become the world's largest post office, employing over 41,000 employees. Bailey was one of a growing number of women applying and getting work at the post office in the early 1960s, which she attributes to both Executive Order 10988 and the Equal Pay Act of 1963 banning gender-based wage discrimination.

By 1960 African Americans already were in the majority of those working in post offices in Chicago, Los Angeles, Washington, D.C., and New Orleans, and were close to half of the postal workforce in Philadelphia, Detroit, Houston, Cleveland, Cincinnati, Memphis, and Atlanta. The Kappel Commission (appointed in 1966 by President Johnson to study problems in postal operations and structure) noted a jump in the percentage of women working at the post office, from 11 to 17.4 percent from 1959 to 1967, with 73 percent of women employees working as postal clerks by the end of this period.[32]

Although by 1972 female postal workers in the New York region made up one of the smallest percentages of women in major urban post offices, their activism in that city was probably more crucial than anywhere else. In 1960 women still made up just over 28 percent of new members recruited into the strong Washington, D.C., and Chicago Alliance branches.[33] In New York, the percentage of women compared to men entering the New York Alliance by the 1960s was 17 percent, slightly lower on average compared to the previous two decades, but still significant. Black women who entered after Kennedy's executive orders, the EPA, and the 1964 Civil Rights Act were, like black men, just as likely to join the MBPU or one of the craft unions as they were the Alliance.

In fact, Eleanor Bailey rose quickly to shop steward, or "delegate," as the

MBPU's stewards were then called. Having grown to 27,000 members by the mid-sixties, the MBPU was the largest local in the NPU. Bailey prided herself in winning most of the grievances she filed based on a thorough studying of not just the union-management contract, but also every management document she could find. And if all else failed, Bailey recalled, chuckling: "A couple of times I made up stuff!"—meaning that she used her universally recognized knowledge of the contract to bluff management by inventing nonexistent contract provisions.

Bailey also teamed up with an Italian American clerk she remembers only as Josephine. Together they confronted male coworkers over gender discrimination in the union and also challenged female workers who resisted doing the same jobs men had been doing for years, especially the more physically demanding tasks. Bailey filed grievances on behalf of other workers—sometimes the same workers she was challenging over male chauvinism. She also led direct action protests demanding childcare and childcare leave for working mothers along with the absence of women's bathrooms at the post office. "Strachan will never forget me with my white mini[skirt] sitting outside his office when we did the bathroom strike!" Bailey laughed, recalling their late-1960s women's protest in Postmaster Strachan's office over the lack of separate bathroom facilities for women: "We wouldn't let anybody in 'til he promised us two more bathrooms."[34]

The Alliance had pioneered the same campaign for women's bathroom facilities just a few years earlier, and kept the pressure up after Strachan was made postmaster. The MBPU added to this effort with letters to Strachan when he was Acting Postmaster in 1966. But what made the MBPU unique was that it encouraged this kind of direct action, according to Bailey, even when she was clashing with other shop stewards of her own union. Most labor unions at that time and even today prefer that its members "work through channels"—that is, restrict their advocacy to established labor-management grievance procedures. This was no less true of the Alliance, which prided itself in its ability to negotiate or send delegations to present grievances to management, including campaigns to increase female hiring and promotion, as well as the development of childcare and separate women's bathroom facilities. As the MBPU became more active, the National Alliance was concerned that their pioneering activist role would be forgotten.

No punishment was meted out by the postmaster to Eleanor Bailey and the other women protesters for their sit-in. But the post office issued a ban on June 15, 1967, on miniskirts and tight-fitting toreador pants worn by some women in the New York City post office. This was during a time when women and their male supporters in the Alliance and MBPU were arguing that the post office needed to liberalize its previous policies of only allowing women to wear dresses or skirts at work. It also reveals the role of expressive culture by newly hired women in postal jobs that did not require uniforms of clerks, then the occupation of most women postal workers.

Eleanor Bailey does not recall the exact date of the sit-in, but it was probably sometime in 1967, possibly before May, but no later than November. Memos and letters exchanged between the MBPU and postal management between May and November of 1967 refer to agreements for adding women's bathrooms and the building of a women's locker and "swing room" in the section of the GPO known as Outgoing Mails. It must have been ironic for Alliance members to see the MBPU announce in its May 17, 1967, *News Flash!*: "This latest achievement ends a struggle of many months duration by our union to obtain decent and adequate facilities for the female employees who to-day are so much a part of our postal life and our union." Not only had the Alliance begun this fight—but the postmaster approving the reforms was an Alliance member.[35]

Women continued to play key roles throughout the Alliance organization. Loraine Huston from the Cleveland Alliance branch was the first woman to have a regular column in the *Postal Alliance* beginning in 1963, although it did not deal exclusively with women's issues. Columns aimed at women finally began appearing in the 1960s in both the New York *Alliance Leader* and the MBPU *Union Mail*. Articles written in support of the PCSW appeared in the *Postal Alliance, Alliance Leader*, and *Union Mail*, in 1963, making the Alliance and the NPU the only postal unions to even mention it.[36]

In D.C., women had held positions as postal clerks for years and were well represented in the Alliance, the city's largest postal union. Women also joined the WAPU, although they were a tiny minority of union officials.[37] The first female letter carrier in the nation's capital since World War II was not hired until 1963, and there were still few of them by the time of the strike in 1970, a situation that soon changed. The February 1963 *Postal Alliance* welcomed Evelyn Craig Brown, a twenty-eight-year-old African American divorced mother of three as "another trail blazer . . . Washington's first lady mailman, as the Post Office calls them. . . . She was assigned as a mail carrier, partially through inadvertence. Needing a job, Mrs. Brown had applied for appointment as a clerk but also filled out an application for a carrier's job. 'I've always been a good walker,' she said. 'This is the perfect job for me.' "[38]

Retired D.C. letter carrier James Pinderhughes remembered Brown as "hard-working." Letter carrier Joseph Henry also remembers her as an excellent carrier, "running dispatch" (driving a truck and collecting outgoing mail). But despite publicity and support from the Alliance for Brown's breaking

Evelyn Craig Brown, hired by the post office in 1963 in Washington, D.C., was the first black female letter carrier hired in the nation's capital since World War II. She was a member of NALC Branch 142. © 1967 U.S. Postal Service. All rights reserved. Used with permission.

gender barriers, she joined the NALC, not the Alliance, soon after coming to the post office. In nearby Richmond, Virginia, in 1969, a young African American clerk named Joyce Robinson who would later be elected APWU Director of Education chose to join the UFPC rather than the Alliance. One of the more conservative postal unions, the UFPC, too, was being pushed in a militant direction by the influx of young people, veterans, blacks, and women.[39] Black women who had in the past overwhelmingly chosen the Alliance were now drawn to other unions. The NPU especially had gained ground on the Alliance on women's rights, principally through its encouragement of women's use of direct action.

BLACK WOMEN'S AGENCY

The entry of black women into the post office, its unions, and all their debates and struggles over work life reminds us that the activist role historically played by black workers in the post office included *both* women and men. From the beginning of the 1960s upsurge in black women's hiring at the post office, they were choosing which unions to belong to and merging their experiences with that of the unions they chose. Their hiring was itself the result of executive orders, legislation, and postal management directives. This was in turn a product of interest convergence and the campaign by the civil rights movement for equality in all spheres of social life. More than a mere job migration, this was literally a working woman's movement.

In New York, arriving in the years just prior to the 1970 strike from southern unionist families were Josie McMillian from Birmingham, Alabama, and Joann Flagler from Kingstree, South Carolina, both of whom, like Eleanor Bailey, joined the MBPU. McMillian's father was a union coal miner, her mother a café cook, both of whom instilled in her the need to fight for labor rights, including the right to withhold that labor. Flagler had attended CCNY and was urged in 1969 by her mother, a domestic worker, to take the postal clerk position when offered because "it's a government job." Flagler joined the MBPU on her first day at work, stating simply: "That was the thing to do. My father was a union person. He was a welder."[40] Daisy Strachan and Dorothea Hoskins, meanwhile, stuck with the Alliance because of its record in the fight for equality. Hoskins picked the Alliance when she came to the post office just after the strike, and Strachan was reinstated in 1972 with the help of John Adams, who was now an EEO specialist. (Strachan also held simultaneous Alliance and APWU membership in the early 1970s.)[41]

The union choices made by black women postal workers were similar to those made by black men during the 1960s and 1970s—a time when the postal unions were opening up to women, dropping color bars, and actively engaging on behalf of women and people of color. Before 1959, the Alliance was the only union to advocate strongly for women at the post office, and much of that advocacy came from black women themselves. The Alliance uniquely combined a labor and civic leadership focus: Daisy Strachan noted her membership in the NAACP, the NCNW, and the National Bahamas Association, and she was also proud of having retired as a Tour Superintendent with the post office in 2000. But women in the MBPU after its formation in 1959 were also activists. "I joined every feminist group there was in New York!" Eleanor Bailey said. The MBPU's emphasis on defending workers on the shop floor put them in an adversarial relationship with management, a battle for which women like Eleanor Bailey were ready.[42]

Women were a significant part of the new workforce that entered the post office and its unions in the 1960s and often rebelled against the snail's pace of reform in the post office. In New York especially they took up issues particular to women along with labor rights in general.[43] In the Alliance and the NPU black women helped develop rank-and-file militancy, in contrast to other postal unions where historically male craft unionism tended to retard militancy. The National Alliance had begun the fight for equality but was now upstaged by an NPU willing to use more adversarial tactics. Black women were entering the post office in greater numbers than ever before and reflecting a diversity of educational, social, and work backgrounds, and with more union choices. The mood of the 1960s brought militancy into the post office along with large numbers of working-class black women.

CHAPTER EIGHT

CIVIL RIGHTS
POSTAL UNIONISM
(1963–1966)

There is no doubt that 1963 was a pivotal year for civil rights activism, and that the NAPE especially was deeply involved, fusing black labor and civic protest traditions. At their 1963 convention in New York City, President Ashby Smith called for convention delegates, including the women's auxiliary, to mobilize in order to secure passage of the Civil Rights Bill. Times had changed, according to Paul Tennassee. Acting Postmaster General Sidney Bishop was the convention's keynote speaker, and, in Tennassee's words, "Virtually, the entire speech was on civil rights as it affected African Americans." A more significant address, however, was given by former Alliance president James B. Cobb, now a postal official: "I'm on the side of management now, I represent the big shots, but I haven't forgotten that my hair is kinky and my skin is black, I haven't completely forgotten those days when organizations in the POD turned their backs and when Bill [former NAPE Welfare Director William Jason] and I tried to go down to have a conference. . . . We have several things to our advantage. We've never had a Caucasian clause, we have never been a craft, and we have been interested in the philosophy of the workingman. We now have a program, which I am grossly identified with, management and employee cooperation and we have had another program of Equal Employment Opportunity."[1] (Three years later, Cobb went even further when he contrasted the Alliance's civil rights unionism with AFL-CIO business unionism in the May 1966 *Alliance Leader*: "In the Civil Rights struggle, how active can a labor union be? This has been the one area where it has been hard to distinguish the Alliance from other civil rights groups, because the Alliance has never failed to pursue this right even beyond the realm of the postal service.")[2]

Cobb, despite his management status, summed up his union's key tenets as a combination of black racial solidarity and working-class advocacy. He did so by invoking his own historical memory of having been both a class- and race-conscious black worker. Whether spurred or chastened (or both) by the criticism he had received in 1961 for abandoning his own members by the head of the Philadelphia NAACP, Cobb now declared the Alliance to be an exemplary model for other unions and the post office, with its historical fusion of black labor and civic traditions.[3]

The National Alliance, however, was still maintaining a balancing act between black labor unionism and black middle-class "civic-ism"—at the same time engaged in (mostly) "friendly competition" with its ally, the militant, industrial, antiracist NPU. The NPU practiced a form of civil rights unionism that might be called "interracial syndicalism"—organizing all workers in one industry and opposing racial and all other divisions and differentials wherever they found them. The Alliance, on the other hand, personified civil rights unionism in making primary the fight for equality, uniting workplace and community struggles, and leading the struggle to unlock the crafts, promotions, and union locals previously closed to blacks. Their important work (and the NPU's) in the labor and civil rights movements has unfortunately been omitted in popular narratives of both movements.

The Alliance during this time pressured the post office to open up the crafts and management positions to blacks, and do away with disciplinary double standards based on race. Many were also active in the campaign to pass the civil rights bill, which Congress passed and President Lyndon B. Johnson signed into law in 1964. The section of the Civil Rights Act the Alliance praised most was Title VII, which made equal employment opportunity the law of the land. But it only received lukewarm support from the AFL-CIO. No mention was even made of the bill or the law in the monthly journals of the other postal unions except the NPU.[4] The Alliance's reluctance to merge with other postal unions or the AFL-CIO was therefore understandable. Yet even within victories there were setbacks for the Alliance and the NPU. In 1963, the year after Jim Crow postal union locals were abolished and postal unions won government recognition, the first national labor agreement was signed between the post office and its "national exclusive" unions that did not include the Alliance or the NPU.[5] In addition, the primary reasons for postal union merger failure during this period were issues of craft autonomy between the NALC and the UFPC, as well as differences between the craft unions versus the industrial Alliance and NPU.[6]

Mitigating the Alliance's ability to function as a full-fledged labor union was its lack of national "exclusive" representation rights. This also hampered the NPU nationally but not in New York, where it enjoyed "local exclusive" rights to bargain directly with management. The Alliance's approach to industrial postal unionism was conditioned on equal opportunity being primary, so they saw union merger as virtually out of the question. They still functioned as a kind of "parallel NAACP" in the labor movement, however, and the congressional and postal management lobbying that characterized all postal unionism meshed well with the Alliance's civil rights agenda. The latter included making demands outside the purview of most trade unions at that time, including affirmative action and other civil rights law and public policy measures that ensured fairness in hiring, job opportunities, and management promotions.

For the NPU, on the other hand, shop floor militancy was as important a practice as lobbying and negotiating, while the fight for equality was an important but not a central part of its agenda, which was democratic industrial unionism. The latter was the sticking point that prevented its merger with the UFPC in the 1960s that would have created a huge postal union with exclusive representation over most crafts. The most promising merger *practice*, however, continued to be in New York City, where, based in part on local unions' civil rights support, the Alliance became both observer and participant in discussions and demonstrations convened by NALC Branch 36 and the MBPU. Yet it was in New York that the Alliance's "pro-black" civil rights unionism came to clash with the MBPU's "color-blind" interracial syndicalism.

NO MERGER WITHOUT EQUALITY

For years postal unionists had debated the merits of uniting all postal unions into one big organization for maximum strength, as opposed to maintaining one's own craft and organization. But a bigger difference both between and within postal unions was not their stance on merger, but their approach to the fight for equality and to what degree they were willing to combat or avoid it. Nationally, the Alliance and the NPU made a practice of confronting that issue, while the other unions generally practiced avoidance. The Alliance made civil rights their main priority more so than the NPU. Yet the NPU took a more militant rank-and-file approach to labor struggles. The two industrial independent allies—both proponents of principled merger—would often clash in 1966, the same year Black Power first appeared nationally as a political and ideological force in American society. Neither union embraced Black Power explicitly, but it nevertheless became the subtext for their differences: was the National Alliance separatist and divisive, or was it the best embodiment of working-class politics in a black labor civic organization?

While national merger between postal unions was problematic, New York City was a different story. Postal unions in that city overall probably practiced more unity in favor of equality than anywhere else. Meetings were held in February 1961 between the local branches and locals of the National Alliance, the NPU, and the NALC, which they all agreed represented joint collaboration toward the formation of "ONE BIG UNION as soon as possible."[7] Yet that summer at the Alliance's Detroit convention, "lively and serious" workshops on that very subject concluded: "Until the status of the Negro, as a citizen of the United States has greatly improved, especially in the Southern States, the National Alliance cannot successfully merge with other unions."[8]

Nevertheless, in 1964, when New York branches of the NPU and the NALC combined to form the Metropolitan Postal Council, the Alliance played the role of interested if cautious observer. They conducted a joint outdoor pay raise demonstration in March of that year at the GPO in Manhattan that was widely deemed unprecedented (although New York NALC and NFPOC had co-sponsored a similar protest rally in 1952).[9] The following year the NPU's *Progressive* exulted: "An historic first was achieved on May 2, 1965 when all Brooklyn postal unions (UFPOC, NALC, Nat'l Alliance and NPU) . . . combined to hold a joint legislative-grievance rally . . . triggered by the fears of . . . the Joint Conference of B'klyn Postal Employees that we were reaching an impasse on . . . much-needed legislation." Individual postal union lobbying always had a mass component, but joint postal union efforts in New York were new.[10]

If the most successful attempts at union merger were centered in New York City and reflected a higher sense of working-class unity than most of the postal workforce, then the least successful efforts were in the South with its history of Jim Crow. The National Alliance, a longtime champion of the industrial model of postal union organization, continued to express skepticism over "one big union" if it meant that the needs of black postal workers would be diluted. But as promising as local postal union unity efforts were, on the national level they seemed to always lose steam because of union competition. Another major cause of the failure of postal union merger was that the same EO 10988 that in 1962 forced unions to integrate and collectively bargain also allowed them to compete for membership and representation.[11]

In the 1950s and 1960s black postal workers had used a variety of tactics including lobbying, litigation, direct action, coalition, black unions, and working within predominantly white unions to challenge and eventually defeat Jim Crow in the post office and its unions. In 1962, the decades-old ritual process of postal union "collective begging" from Congress was ameliorated somewhat with the new limited collective bargaining arrangement. Despite its inadequacies, it also prevented predominantly white unions from exercising exclusive control over the workforce, or conservative craft union leadership from monopolizing union activity.

Furthermore, the new collective bargaining agreements beginning in 1963 allowed the Alliance to compete with the major postal unions under the same 1962 executive order that had overturned Jim Crow postal union branches and locals. In that sense, black postal workers had succeeded where the NAACP and the National Urban League had failed in 1935 to add an antidiscrimination clause to the Wagner Act covering private sector workers and unions. When the UFPC won exclusive bargaining rights for postal clerks in 14 of 15 postal regions, for example, their victory editorial in the August 1962 *Union Postal Clerk* acknowledged in bold type: "Following this certification, the national organizations must stipulate in writing their conformance with the nondiscrimination policy and formally notify the Department of the local organization which will represent them in dealing with the postmaster."[12]

Limited collective bargaining rights encouraged postal unions to compete at the same time that some were making proposals for "one big union." A December 1963 *Postal Alliance* article observed that a "cold war" was going on among postal unions, and questioned why Alliance members would maintain membership in other unions given the hostility expressed by those unions for the Alliance, especially the UFPC.[13] As the two industrial unions in the post office, the Alliance and the NPU were the most vigorous supporters of industry-wide merger. The NPU regularly committed itself to that ideal in the *Progressive*, as did the WAPU-NPU's monthly *Washington Area Postal Employees* newsletter. But the National Alliance was also skeptical of merger based on the other unions' track record on equality, and on its own desire to preserve black autonomy.[14]

The National Alliance continued its criticism of the postal unions and organized labor in general for failing to deal with discrimination and segregation in its ranks, as well as what might be called a "white backlash" to civil rights advocacy and law enforcement. Reminiscent of the 1962 debate with the Baltimore and national UFPC where the UFPC had accused the Alliance of favoring "discrimination" and "mass promotion of Negroes," the Alliance in June 1963 angrily rebutted the UFPC's formal protest filed that year with the CSC. The UFPC opposed the promotion of three black clerks to supervisors in Dallas as "reverse discrimination" (a charge predating today's affirmative action debate using identical terms). A public battle ensued pitting the UFPC and the Dallas mainstream media against the National Alliance and Assistant Postmaster General Richard J. Murphy. The Alliance, Murphy, and the NPU all wondered how the unprecedented appointment of three black supervisors in Dallas amounted to "black favoritism" in a city with 600 black postal workers out of a total postal workforce of 3,000. Murphy even wrote a letter to the editor of a Dallas newspaper protesting the "favoritism" charges. Those black clerks, he countered, not only possessed college degrees, high test scores, and superb performance ratings, but were chosen from "an eligibility list, not a qualification list" that incorporated a number of different factors. Compelling public arguments for black promotion notwithstanding, congressional hearings were held that fall on the UFPC's charges—leading to the post office actually rescinding the three black appointments.[15]

While the UFPC and NPU alternated between trading charges at each other and negotiating over possible merger, the bad blood simmering between the Alliance and the UFPC finally boiled over when the Alliance picketed the UFPC's D.C. headquarters from July 30 to August 1, 1963. This came just a month before the famous March on Washington for Jobs and Freedom, and right in the middle of the UFPC's Legislative Conference (also known as a "Pay Rally"). The Alliance was protesting what they called the UFPC's "opposition to minority group promotions." Two years earlier the UFPC had told the President's Task Force on Employee-Management Programs that the Alliance should be denied union recognition, forcing the Alliance, in the words of President Ashby Smith, to go before the Task Force "to defend the Alliance against the old, tired charge that we were a social organization, not a labor union."[16]

The NPU backed the Alliance's protest in their national biweekly newsletter *Washington Reports*. They echoed the Alliance's charges of "semantic duplicity" contained in the UFPC's advocacy for "seniority" and "merit promotion." The UFPC's "exclusive recognition" of clerks in Mississippi and Alabama, the NPU warned, was bad news for blacks, as there were only two black clerks in the whole state of Mississippi, while in Alabama the UFPC had actually fought black promotion. The NPU found it ironic that the UFPC responded to charges of discrimination by calling for "a merit promotion program" that ensured "equality of opportunity."[17] National Alliance president Ashby Smith was incredulous, and in an October 1963 speech blasted the UFPC:

> Here too, we faced an American myth, the myth that equal treatment and merit promotions prevail in the federal service. It was a myth in 1913 and despite several substantial steps taken in the right direction taken recently by the Post Office Department and followed haltingly by other federal agencies, it still remains a myth in 1963. . . . How false are they who cry that Negroes in the postal service are getting preferential treatment the moment that the historical preferential treatment for whites is breached and a dusky face appears as a level seven [management status].[18]

But there were still many black rank-and-file activists who joined or remained in the UFPC to effect change within that craft union. Walter T. Kenney Sr., for example, was hired in 1954 as a distribution clerk in Richmond. Already active in the Crusade for Voters and NAACP, he would not join the NFPOC because it allowed segregation. Recruited into the UFPC in 1962, he was elected vice president and later president of Richmond Local 199. In 1970 Kenney became the first African American elected national vice president. (He later entered electoral politics and won races for the city council and the mayor's office.)[19]

A highlight of the Alliance's civil rights union coalition building was its charter membership in the Negro American Labor Council that helped organize the March on Washington.[20] The Brooklyn and Manhattan-Bronx locals of the NPU also supported the march and sent representatives, as the NPU continued to hammer the UFPC for lack of commitment to equality. New York City's NALC branches backed the march, but no position was taken on it by the national NALC, UFPC, or any other postal union.[21]

Two years later, the featured speaker at the Alliance's 1965 Los Angeles convention was Dr. Martin Luther King Jr. That convention was held as the Watts rebellion raged August 11–16 in that mostly black district, sparked by police brutality and provoked by poverty, unemployment, and the move by California to limit sections of the Civil Rights Act—especially the right to integrated housing. King spoke before rushing off to meet with Governor Pat Brown.

Gratefully acknowledging the Alliance's history of support for the SCLC and the civil rights struggle since the Montgomery bus boycott, King observed that "Brother Maisel," an Atlanta delegate, was Chief Usher at his church. King was optimistic yet shaken by the Watts uprising, with its dramatization of deep structural inequalities that he felt the nonviolent southern-based civil rights movement had been unable to address: "And this problem right here in Los Angeles now, is indicative of the fact that the Negro huddled up in . . . ghettos all over the country is still frustrated, bewildered, the victim of seething despair because of the continuation of oppression, segregation, discrimination, and economic deprivation. And so our job is a big one in the days ahead, but I can assure you that we will continue to work with the faith that we can solve the problem and that, we as a people can be brought into the mainstream of American life."[22]

In 1965 the Alliance became the National Alliance of Postal and Federal Employees (NAPFE), open to all federal employees. They had decided at their 1963 convention that it would help expand their organization to try and win national "exclusive recognition" in other federal agencies. In 1966 their monthly journal discarded the agency-specific name *Postal Alliance* in favor of the union's longtime popular name, the *National Alliance*.[23] But their black solidarity approach to civil rights and labor issues was in effect even before the Watts rebellion. The April 1965 *Postal Alliance*, for example, reprinted a Cleveland branch newsletter article by local officers Mary F. Guen and John M. Hayes on why the National Alliance still refused to join the AFL-CIO:

The Alliance contends that such affiliation would serve no useful purpose since that very august body faces the very big problem of eliminating some of the many inequities within its own ranks. According to reliable sources, discrimination, segregation, and a marked lack of equal employment opportunities, not only exists within the framework of the big labor unions, but is, in many instances, fostered and perpetuated by them. . . . The Alliance is a *labor* union. It was founded on the principle that equality of opportunity should be a reality for all American citizens.[24]

For their part, neither the NALC's *Postal Record* nor the UFPC's *Union Postal Clerk* made mention of the passage of the 1964 Civil Rights Act, nor the 1963 March on Washington. Of the four major postal union monthlies, only the *Postal Alliance* and the NPU's *Progressive* covered these and other events in the fight for equality. In doing so, they provided a microcosm of organized labor's divide between a minority of enthusiastic black and left-liberal unions versus a majority of AFL-CIO ambivalence. This was especially the case with Title VII that promised enforcement powers against both future and existing mechanisms of discrimination—such as seniority systems that favored white workers.

But the Alliance and NPU also disagreed on how best to fight discrimination. The Alliance saw no separation between civil rights and labor organization roles, while the NPU was primarily concerned with uniting all postal workers.[25] The movement of Alliance officials into EEO work was an example of those two different approaches.[26]

It should come as no surprise that many of the early EEO officials were National Alliance members, as the Alliance had long trained members to be part of the institutional process for equality. New York attorney and Alliance member James Morris finished Brooklyn Law School in the 1950s after having come into the post office in the 1940s as a mail handler and clerk. By the 1960s he was able to put his legal skills to use directly for the Alliance by getting a position as a contract compliance examiner which, as he put it, "was a level 22 [position], which dealt with equal opportunity. . . . And we dealt with that and used the civil rights laws when it was necessary to enforce equal opportunity. A lot of the things we dealt with was where people figured they were discriminated and they would file a EEO complaint."[27]

New York Alliance members John Adams and Dorothea Hoskins were also involved in EEO counseling for postal workers in the same city—as well as for the northeast region. Adams in addition belonged to the NAACP, and Hoskins reported that she worked with CORE and SNCC. In Chicago, Countee Abbott, a postal clerk who was District president of the Alliance from 1968 to 1974, was promoted to EEO specialist and then manager of EEO complaint processing from 1974 to 1990.[28] These were common stories in the Alliance, whose pressure on the Kennedy administration to ban Jim Crow union locals in 1962 logically extended to EEO civil rights law enforcement work beginning in 1964.

Despite failed efforts by the National Alliance, the NAACP, and other civil rights groups to pass a tougher civil rights bill in 1966, their lobbying that year made postal clerk jobs available to blacks in Jackson, Mississippi. Among them was future Alliance official Felix Bell, who got a job in that office three years later, leaving Tougaloo College after his freshman year and taking his civil rights activism to the post office. There he found and learned from black civil rights and labor veterans like Willenham Castilla, who by then had moved up to management—the first African American in his post office to do so. Castilla, a former local Alliance president, former NALC member, and NAACP member and poll watcher, had come to the post office in 1951, the same year B. P. Newman retired. In a symbolic passing of the black freedom movement baton, Newman's Route #1 was taken over by letter carrier and civil rights attorney Carsie Hall, according to Castilla. "Then Robert Moman [took it when Hall retired], then I had it." Castilla also did voter registration work in Alabama and Mississippi in 1966, and gave me a revealing story of how much politicians depended on such grassroots efforts: "One night, LBJ called to our office to ask how many we had registered that day!"[29]

The MBPU, by contrast, was known for its civil rights support—with the Alliance being an actual civil rights labor organization. For example, the MBPU's newsletter *News Flash!* of June 10, 1966, quoted MBPU president Moe Biller's special delivery letter to President Johnson and New York's two senators, Republican Jacob Javits and Democrat Robert Kennedy, "on behalf of 22,000 postal employees" protesting the recent shooting of black civil rights marcher James Meredith in Mississippi. The newsletter also reported the MBPU's executive board vote to make a contribution to CORE and SCLC in support of Meredith's "March Against Fear"—a voting rights march from Memphis, Tennessee, to Jackson, Mississippi. In the words of the *News Flash!* their contribution represented support for "continuing the march from where it was abruptly interrupted."[30] But the two postal unions were now competing for the same pool of prospective black members: the Alliance's emphasis on civil rights unionism versus the NPU's emphasis on interracial syndicalism.

PRO-BLACK VS. "COLOR-BLIND" APPROACHES

Not all black postal workers saw the Alliance as the best way to represent them, even if they had that opportunity locally after the 1962 representation elections. The Alliance had fought for other postal unions to open their doors to blacks while also insisting that no one but the Alliance could adequately represent them. Alliance officials often expressed disappointment in representing "only" one-fourth of all black postal workers in what actually seems like a notable accomplishment.

But many black postal workers felt that other unions could better represent them as workers—either those representing the crafts to which they belonged or the militant, industrial, antiracist NPU. The Alliance countered with its historic commitment to workers' struggles *and* black liberation. President Ashby Smith proudly noted, for example, how during the 1963 New York national convention some delegates "left the hotel at five-thirty a.m. to picket for equal employment opportunities at a construction site in Jamaica, New York."[31] And theirs was the only postal union journal to feature grassroots Mississippi activists Fannie Lou Hamer and Annie Devine in their coverage of the Mississippi Freedom Democratic Party.[32]

Dramatically highlighting the Alliance's "integrated black unionism" was the assassination on April 24, 1963, of a new Alliance member—a white letter carrier from Baltimore named William Moore. Moore was shot and killed by a white supremacist while conducting a solitary civil rights protest walk through Alabama. Moore, who had also been a member of CORE, had participated in the recent CORE-Alliance civil rights protests in Baltimore and made a pilgrimage to Washington, D.C., to try to meet with President Kennedy. The National Alliance was quick to accord Moore martyr status, in contrast to CORE's hesitation to do so. The June 1963 NPU *Progressive* also noted that NALC Branch 36 had donated $100 to the NAACP in Moore's memory, and left-leaning MBPU officers sent CORE a contribution after Moore's murder.[33]

"We had a lot of white members," several Alliance members told me. The existence of white Alliance members like Moore disprove charges from other unions that the Alliance was exclusively black, yet its black identity was always its greatest asset. The oral histories that I conducted with New York Alliance members uncover themes and narratives similar to those that can be read in the pages of the *New York Alliance Leader*. They reveal pride in being labor and civil rights pioneers in the post office, residual disappointment with blacks who did not join the Alliance, bitterness at not being given the same access to new hires as other unions were, and resentment at being called by some a "social organization."

On the other hand, my interview with New York Metro APWU members—equally proud of their own pioneer efforts in labor history—uncovered a combination of respect and irritation with the Alliance in the 1960s. They tended to see the Alliance as an organization that had felt entitled to the black franchise, so to speak, without possessing sufficient power to agitate on behalf of all postal workers. Eleanor Bailey said she was contacted by the MBPU on her first day of work but did not hear from the Alliance until some time afterward.

Meanwhile, the Alliance fought depictions of them by management and other unions as a mere social organization. And EO 10988 both strengthened and weakened the Alliance's status as a labor union, with their national "formal recognition" status lacking the strength and prestige of "exclusive recognition." But even before their "formal" status was revoked by President Nixon's 1969 executive order, many black postal workers (especially in New York) found the NPU, NALC, NPMHU, and the UFPC (about one-third black) to be more viable as labor unions.[34]

The Alliance had become in many ways a "victim of its own success"—to borrow historian Jeffrey Ogbar's observation of late 1960s civil rights movement leadership.[35] Ogbar also avers that during this period there was in fact a break between Black Power and the mainstream civil rights movement. But clashes like these also have a way of finding dialectical resolution, as the 1960s fight for equality at the workplace saw both a coalescing and collision of civil rights and Black Power. As much as the Alliance criticized Black Power as a divisive ideology and practice, in many ways the Alliance symbolized "black power" to black postal workers. Unlike the private sector, blacks at the post office tended not to form autonomous caucuses in the predominantly white unions as long as there was a black union. The "civil rights versus Black Power" collisions that characterized other industries and unions seem to have been minimal in the post office largely because of the Alliance.[36]

There was also a parallel echo between Martin Luther King Jr.'s conversations with SNCC leaders in 1966 over the efficacy of Black Power as a slogan and a similar discussion in the postal unions.[37] Black postal workers I interviewed in the South alluded to whites participating or acquiescing in white privileges. By contrast, black postal workers I interviewed from northern post offices for the most part reported minimal exhibitions of individual white prejudice or craft discrimination. Yet they also observed whites winning promotions based on belonging to "white ethnic" advocacy groups.[38] In trying to explain the absence in postal unions during the late 1960s of the kind of black caucuses found in manufacturing, one might be tempted to argue that postal workers were less militant. But that would be missing an additional explanation. The Alliance drew black postal workers who, if they had no alternative union, or if they worked instead in private industry (as many already had), might have formed or joined a black caucus within the other postal unions.[39]

The National Alliance as a black autonomous union had long been baited as being "exclusively black" and even "separatist" by opponents in other postal unions. At the same time, a growing number of black postal unionists began finding homes in some of those same postal unions. Moe Biller's regular monthly *Union Mail* column in May 1966, for example, used a private conference he had held with two black female MBPU members to fire back at New York Alliance president John Adams who, in his monthly column in the March 1966 *New York Alliance Leader,* had criticized the proposed NPU-UFPC merger because of the UFPC's poor track record on equality.

Biller, stung by accusations of consorting with racists combined with the implication that no postal union but the Alliance could look out for blacks, retaliated by calling the Alliance's attacks examples of "separatism" and "segregation." Biller's main ammunition was the plaintive testimony of the two black female MBPU members. Both had joined the MBPU in December 1965. One woman, whom he called Amy, was the daughter of an MBPU member who had been the first black window clerk assigned to a New York post office outside of Harlem. (A window clerk handles retail and customer service duties at the counter or window.) The other woman, "Mary," told Biller how an Alliance "delegate" (shop steward) in March had suggested that she join the Alliance as they were "the only outfit that knows how to handle your problem." This was Mary's reaction as reported by Biller: "This separatist pitch is the exact opposite of what Americans are fighting for in Alabama, Mississippi, and even here in New York. To me separatism is segregation. *I told him I wanted a union that was color blind*, a union that'll fight for all postal workers."[40]

This must have seemed like a low blow to the Alliance. They were used to accusations of separatism, but not by the progressive MBPU. Competition had now heated up not just over labor representation but civil rights advocacy as well. Throughout the 1960s, the pages of the MBPU's *Union Mail* discussed the fight for equality the same way that the Alliance did: it was a struggle against any form of discrimination and segregation, not a negotiated process. Yet they employed a different approach than the Alliance that lobbied against discrimination, while the MBPU's monthly newsletter emphasized their support for major civil rights events like the 1963 March on Washington, as well as highlighting the work of black MBPU officials. They generally considered themselves exceptional, exemplified in a 1968 report on a conference in New York City titled "The Negro and the Labor Movement." The MBPU's reporter, Vice President Henry Reese, observed that "to the credit of the MBPU, good race relations are not a problem. . . . We've constitutionally [been] a voice and vote for every member, regardless of race, color or creed."[41]

Both Adams and Biller's charges were overheated. But the MBPU's criticism of the Alliance as "separatist" was unfair, as were charges that they did not fight for all postal workers. In fact, they embodied civil rights intervention inside and outside the post office.[42] The *National Alliance*, for example, regularly published news of activist Alliance members. They could be found in Baltimore joining with CORE to picket segregated theaters in 1963; marching in Austin, Texas, with the NAACP for a broad equal opportunity city ordinance in 1964; or picketing in Pittsburgh with other civil rights groups for passage of the Civil Rights Act and against discrimination at the post office in 1964–65.[43] By the mid- to late 1960s, struggles at the post office for the most part could assume integration as a given. The fight to rid the post office of inequality, however, was both a historic and an ongoing struggle.

The National Alliance was part of the civil rights movement establishment. But black postal workers were part of the rank and file of *both* the labor and black freedom movements. The "old hands" in the Alliance supported non-violent direct action while campaigning for improvements in civil rights laws and their enforcement, at the same time that urban, factory, and campus rebellions were breaking out.

Meanwhile, the "master narrative" of the civil rights movement has the Civil Rights Act of 1964 and the Voting Rights Act of 1965 serving as the dramatic climax of a decade of nonviolent civil rights struggle, followed by the late 1960s radical Black Power movement and black urban rebellions somehow unnecessarily provoking white resentment. But actual movement dynamics were much more complex. Following the signing of the Civil Rights Act in July 1964, the Alliance reported on and supported an actual moratorium on direct action "until after Election Day, next November." That was initiated by the NAACP and supported by a broad coalition including the NUL, SCLC, CORE, Negro American Labor Council, SNCC, and District 65, the Retail, Wholesale and Department Store Employees Union. Why? The moratorium was motivated by movement leaders' concerns over the impact of recent urban rebellions and the potential for what was then already being called "white backlash." With the Civil Rights Act signed into law by President Johnson on July 2, this coalition proposed "*a temporary change of emphasis and tactic . . . to encourage the Negro people, North and South, to register and to vote.*"[44] An NAACP telegram was quoted (and presumably supported by the Alliance) in the June 1964 *Postal Alliance.* It urged urban NAACP branch presidents to make "efforts to reach teenagers and young adults in problem areas to avoid racial outbreaks."[45]

But other divisions arose within the Alliance. Its vice president, Wyatt Williams, received a cool reception at its 1965 convention when he charged that SNCC and CORE might be communist organizations. Not only were there negative reactions from the rank and file in opposition to this old-fashioned red-baiting, but many defiantly favored keeping the Alliance's traditional though anachronistic form of address—"comrade"—because it carried no indication of communist orientation, as one delegate proudly put it in a black nationalist vein: "*We have no communistic background, we came from Africa.*" At that same convention, Thomas P. Bomar, who had served as national secretary and district president during the 1930s and 1940s, trumpeted the Alliance's civil rights activism record ahead of all other postal unions, counting as partial evidence thirty-four of thirty-six black supervisors in the Baltimore post office who were Alliance members. Bomar charged that other postal unions lacked interest in processing discrimination cases and almost invariably referred blacks with discrimination grievances to the Alliance.[46] Yet unions like the NPU were handling discrimination cases. And within the Alliance, younger members were interested in a different kind of activism. The Alliance was seeing more interest in rank-and-file militancy.

By the late 1960s, the Alliance remained the historic touchstone of the black postal labor movement in addition to being a key player in both the civil rights and black labor movements. Splits in the civil rights movement did not hurt the Alliance. Despite its close ties to the NAACP, the Alliance remained independent. But the biggest challenge for the Alliance was that more union options were available for black postal workers. The Alliance was a trailblazer for blacks, women, and in fact all postal workers. But in the early 1960s, shop floor militant Eleanor Bailey of Manhattan chose to belong to the MBPU, while Evelyn Craig Brown of Washington, D.C., the first woman letter carrier hired in that city since World War II, picked the NALC to represent her. It was not enough for the Alliance to claim a vanguard role for all black postal workers, as both the unions and the workforce became more integrated.

Many postal workers in the 1960s, meanwhile, including blacks, women, youth, and those who were returning from tours of duty in the Viet Nam War, found Cold War American nationalism increasingly irrelevant when democracy was still not guaranteed at home in the United States, starting with their government job. But especially in smaller southern cities like Jackson, Mississippi, and Durham, North Carolina, instances of segregation and discrimination persisted into the late 1960s and early 1970s. Former Alliance District Four president Felix Bell recalled that the swing room in the Jackson post office had separate water fountains until 1969—the year he started work there. Jimmy Mainor and George Booth Smith told me how NALC Branch 382 in Durham was turning away black letter carriers as late as 1972, directing newly hired black postal workers to join the Alliance instead. Smith remembered the fight it took to remove separate toilets and water fountains in the Durham post office in the 1950s.[47]

A paradox emerges in the memories of black postal workers who endured Jim Crow during this period of its collapse in southern post offices and postal unions. It is a paradox that is also often heard among African Americans who remember this era in U.S. history. Their recollections combine resentment at the system's injustice, astonishment at its irrationality as well as the irrationality of those implementing it, and a defiant as well as bemused reaction to the enforced social separation. But even many of those who were part of campaigns for the integration of American institutions have expressed positive memories of the autonomy of being away from white people. "We didn't care," laughed former postal worker and SNCC activist Donald P. Stone concerning the segregated "swing room" in the Atlanta post office: "We were having too much fun anyway." You could buy pig's ear sandwiches in the black break room, and "that's where we'd have these great checkers games going on."[48]

George Booth Smith, by contrast, remembers the hostility of the Durham post office swing room in the mid-1950s, as when the workers listened to baseball games on the radio and invariably the white postal workers would spew racial epithets if Jackie Robinson was playing. "We looked out for one another," said Smith of his black coworkers. "They didn't want us around; we didn't want to be around. We had more fun by ourselves anyhow! So we stayed to ourselves." And Joseph Henry along with James Pinderhughes remember the D.C. post office in the 1960s as being integrated on the shop floor but nowhere else due to white prejudice. Henry also noted that black civic organizations like the NAACP and the Prince Hall Masons helped settle grievances and advance black promotions in the D.C. post office.[49]

For black postal workers in the North, there were fewer obvious constraints to their professional or social mobility than in the South, which provided more space for unity and advocacy. But this also allowed for more frustration because benefits based on white skin color were better concealed in the North. The decade leading up to the 1970 postal wildcat strike saw white supremacy in the South often hampering the postal worker unity that was germinating in the North. But the greater postal worker unity achieved in the North also created competition between unions for representational rights. Many blacks joined the Alliance for the same reasons as those who joined any union—to have someone represent them in dealings with their employer. The National Alliance embodied civil rights unionism, but by the early 1960s the Alliance was encountering competition from unions that were either likeminded allies or ambivalent former adversaries. "We played the role in both directions," recalled former Detroit NPU president Doug Holbrook of their labor and civil rights advocacy. According to Holbrook, blacks began leaving the strong Detroit Alliance branch for the NPU in 1966 as black visibility in the NPU increased. Betty Littsey, he said, who was a black local NPU official, "signed up a thousand members in one year, most of those from the Alliance and the Federation [UFPC]."[50] Civil rights unionism in the 1960s post office maintained as primary the struggle for equality. But the Alliance now faced a challenge of rank-and-file labor militancy growing among all postal workers, especially African Americans, impatient and angry with postal management and union leaders over poor pay and benefits, often oppressive working conditions, and lack of representation.

CHAPTER NINE

PRELUDE
TO A STRIKE
(1966–1970)

Asked what it was like to work at the GPO in midtown Manhattan in 1968, mail handler and military service veteran Richard Thomas was blunt: "Actually GPO was an embarrassment to the postal service because of the filth. On the outside, it's recognized as the leading post office in the world. The columns there look all romantic and everything. But the inside—the working conditions were horrible. I mean *horrible.* Old wooden floors. Old cement floors. Back then we used to unload trucks. Mail was on the floor so we had to drag the bags. It was like a slave mentality back then. . . . When you worked, you worked like a slave."[1] Born in the Bronx to parents who were union members, Thomas joined the MBPU—"mainly because they had a credit union"—before switching to the NPMHU after the 1970 nationwide postal wildcat strike. He thought the NPMHU could better represent him and other mail handlers in management disputes.[2]

Growing postal worker militancy in the late sixties was primarily a product of frustration and demoralization over economic and work issues, such as Thomas described. That militancy was fueled by the influx into the post office of young people, women, veterans, and especially blacks, who in turn ratcheted up the struggle for equality as a key part of the general campaign by postal unions for workplace reforms. Many jobs had opened up in the post office in 1965 that for the first time made black recruitment a priority, thanks in large part to the gains of the black freedom movement, and in particular the activism of the NAPFE, still popularly known as the National Alliance.

Many newly hired black postal workers were joining other unions, although only the National Alliance and the NPU emphasized rank-and-file militancy as well as the struggle for equality.[3] By the late 1960s postal unions seemed to be on a collision course with the federal government. All postal unions were concerned with the government's stalling on work-life issues, and with insufficient pay raises from Congress that were lagging behind the cost of living. The Alliance and the NPU were especially struggling with their diminished status of

Forty NALC Branch 41 letter carriers dramatize the low pay received by postal workers in 1969 by applying for welfare at the Brooklyn Department of Social Services office. Many postal workers were actually eligible for and received welfare. Courtesy of *Postal Record*, National Association of Letter Carriers, AFL-CIO.

"formal recognition" (as opposed to the "exclusive recognition" enjoyed by the AFL-CIO postal unions) and the slow pace of workplace reform. Meanwhile, poor working conditions and management styles created an overall service dysfunction and notable incidents like the October 1966 Chicago post office mail backlog. This "crisis," as it was later described, became the opening sought by those who wanted the post office taken out of the executive branch and converted into a government corporation. In 1967 President Lyndon B. Johnson appointed the Kappel Commission to investigate the crisis in postal operations and labor-management relations, and proposed that the post office be converted to a federal corporation.[4]

By the end of the decade, Congress and President Richard M. Nixon had continued the Johnson administration's practice of stalling postal pay raises because of inflation, and were now tying them to proposals for a new postal corporation. By 1970 the post office's overall service had deteriorated as it struggled to handle a one-third increase in mail volume while its costs doubled, producing an annual deficit of over one billion dollars a year.[5] Nixon's Executive Order 11491, issued on October 29, 1969 (effective January 1, 1970), made the Alliance's existence even more tenuous. Nixon's order eliminated all representation categories except "exclusive" (dominated by the AFL-CIO unions).

Aside from tensions between government and labor over daily work life and the post office's future, a divide was also growing within the postal unions between bureaucratic leadership and a frustrated rank and file denied the right to strike, full collective bargaining rights, and a living wage. The growing convergence of civil rights unionism and rank-and-file militancy (along with the influence of Black Power) produced widespread alienation and scattered incidents in the year preceding the nation's largest wildcat strike that began on March 18, 1970.[6]

WHAT POSTAL WORK LOOKED LIKE IN THE 1960S

For postal workers generally and blacks especially, work at the post office was simultaneously available, attractive, and oppressive. Twenty-five years after the historic 1970 nationwide postal wildcat strike, President Moe Biller of the APWU said Manhattan post offices resembled "dungeons," with inadequate light year-round. They were suffocating during the summer and chilly in the winter.[7] Throughout the country, job conditions for postal workers worsened. Postal wages were the same nationwide, and thus went farther in small towns, rural areas, and some southern urban areas where the cost of living was lower. No provision was made to increase wages in regions with higher living costs, although some union members from those regions called for the establishment of higher "area wages."[8]

Despite the post office's reputation for providing secure working-class jobs, the sad fact was that lagging postal salaries in the 1960s did not keep up with inflation—especially in northern cities. "Comparability" was an issue for postal workers, especially against other salaries in the public sector. By 1970, for example, the annual starting salary for postal workers at $6,176 was 27.4 percent *less* than sanitation workers in New York City making $7,870, while police and transport workers earned wages over 50 percent higher than postal workers. In pay levels 1–7 (where 93 percent of postal workers were classified) it took twenty-one years for a postal worker to reach top pay. But postal workers were not the only low-waged workers in the country. Many if not most working-class families were just getting by. So despite the stagnant wages, postal jobs were still sought by people who had been looking for work or hoping to move up to something better because it had a reputation for decent benefits, flexible hours, and job security. Blacks also continued to apply for postal jobs after finding private sector and professional jobs closed to them.[9] But low pay combined with increasingly repressive workplace policies created a growing sense of frustration among postal workers who saw workers in both the public and private sectors advancing in salaries and benefits while theirs were essentially unchanging.

A popular misconception holds that unemployment in the 1960s was universally low during those booming economic times. But the June 1963 monthly journal of the NPU local in D.C. reported that 20,000 people in Detroit "had lined up at the Federal building . . . to apply for 60 jobs that the Post Office will fill through a three-hour competitive examination."[10] The unemployment that later ran rampant throughout the country in the 1970s was already hitting urban areas like Detroit in the 1960s, as auto factories and other manufacturers began automating their assembly lines and moving entire plants to the suburbs or overseas. In fact, Detroit's unemployment never dropped below 10 percent during that decade, with blacks making up 60 percent of all jobless. Nationwide, unemployment at the beginning of the 1960s was over 6 percent, dropping below 4 percent by the middle of the decade, but creeping back over 5 percent by 1970. By comparison, black unemployment had remained consistently double that of whites since the Great Depression: it was 11 percent by 1962, with the number of all people of color out of work at 20 percent. The National Urban League found in a 1961 survey of fifty cities that black unemployment was two to three times that of whites: for example, 17.3 versus 5.7 percent in Chicago; and 24 percent versus 11.6 percent in Pittsburgh. New York City was just under the "two to one" marker at 10 to 6.4 percent black to white unemployment.

Yet the 1940s and 1960s also saw expanded economic gains for blacks. It is indicative of both job opportunity and job limitations that those who describe applying for jobs at the post office during this time were also applying for other public sector jobs that were on the rise in urban areas as manufacturing began to decline. Indeed, from 1946 to 1968, public employees more than doubled in the United States from 5.5 million to 11.6 million, or about 40 percent of the workforce.[11]

As a result of civil rights movement campaigns that inspired new legislation and public policy, newly appointed postmaster general Lawrence F. O'Brien in 1965 made a pledge of nondiscriminatory hiring in the 40,000 new jobs that had just opened as a result of the 1965 Retirement and Salary Acts. To demonstrate his commitment, O'Brien empanelled a three-member EEO Task Force that included Henry L. Dixon, a former Alliance member. The December 1965 *Postal Alliance* ran a full-page announcement titled "Take the Federal Service Entrance Examination" that informed its readers: "The year 1966 will be marked by Federal agency efforts to fill their vacancies with Negroes. Special recruiting efforts are being made on Negro college campuses to get Negro students to compete in entrance examinations." The Alliance's announcement praised the government's efforts, but also worried that it would come at the expense of black career postal employees who had their own aspirations for promotions in the post office or other federal agencies. It urged its members to take this exam, assuring them that they could keep their benefits and Alliance membership even if promoted and transferred. As a "civil rights union," the Alliance often "crossed over" from labor union to civic group and back again, serving as both job recruiter and ombudsman for black federal job applicants.[12]

By the 1960s, the actual work that was done at the post office had changed over time in many ways—although in some ways it seemed almost timeless. One notable holdover from the past was manual mail sorting. In 1968 the government-appointed Kappel Commission charged with investigating deficiencies in the post office reported in amazement: "In this electronic era, the basic sorting device remains the pigeonhole case into which letters are placed, by hand, one by one."[13] Salaries were just as antiquated. By the 1960s postal pay raises were lagging behind the rising standard of living. More whites were therefore leaving the post office for better paying jobs and were increasingly replaced by younger and more militant African Americans.[14]

Overall, postal employment by the 1960s increased as the U.S. population grew and became more urban. Black postal employment remained steady at about 20 percent of the workforce. Meanwhile, the 1950s had given rise to bulk business mail (otherwise known as junk mail), the facsimile (fax) machine, and the automated letter-sorting machine (LSM). Similar to the private sector, technological advances at the post office had changed the nature of postal work, especially clerical jobs, leading to layoffs and retraining with each new development. The growth in mail volume in 1943 led Congress to convert the craft of "postal laborer" into "mail handler" that also absorbed tasks once done by clerks. This was one of the lowest-paid crafts, filled mostly by blacks in big cities like New York. With some tedious tasks replaced by automation, a new form of boredom now characterized work at the post office, cited by postal scholar Vern Baxter as a contributing factor to the 1970 postal wildcat strike.[15]

And then there was morale. Government employee pride became increasingly compromised by frequently degrading management treatment. This 1948 postal clerk's perspective on management, for example, could have been

Clerks, probably at the General Post Office in New York City, sorting mail by carrier route in "pigeonhole" cases, 1969. Note the adjustable stools that enable clerks to sit, stand, or prop themselves up while working. Courtesy of the American Postal Workers Union–New York Metro Postal Workers Union Photographs Collection, Tamiment Library, New York University.

said by many postal workers at any time during the twentieth century: "The assumption of the foremen is that everybody is trying to get away with something. A good part of a clerk's life is spent at work where there is constant aggravation, petty pestering and annoyance. . . . Just imagine having someone come around day in and day out picking on you and reprimanding you for things you didn't do or couldn't help doing."[16] Working as a clerk in Cleveland in the sixties, William H. Burrus Jr. describes the "boring, mindless" work of "sifting pieces of paper into a bin," combined with the pressure of having to pass the "scheme" exam: "It was all pure memory. . . . Small cards . . . made out of cardboard, address on the front. . . . 100 of those cards in the proper separation in three minutes, [about] 95–98 percent accuracy: three failures dismissal. . . . You had to 'throw the scheme' every year [until twenty years seniority] . . . so every year your job was on the line."[17]

For their part, letter carriers over the decades successfully resisted "scientific management" time and motion studies of how long it takes to complete each task. Yet they still found their work measured. Indeed, they could be penalized if they did not meet "standards." But overall, the city carrier craft, begun in 1863 during the Civil War, had seen few substantial changes—such as the 1950 cutback in mail deliveries from twice to once daily along with longer mail routes to cut costs. City carrier jobs were less socialized compared to those of clerk and mail handlers, who typically spent only a fraction of their workday at the post office "casing mail" (arranging their route's mail in segmented metal cases). Most of their workday was spent instead delivering mail (and engaging with the public) on their residential or business routes. "Downtown is much easier than the residential district," Chicago letter carrier John Fuller told oral historian Studs Terkel. "I know about 90 percent of the people in the office building. We are on a first name basis."[18]

Part of a relatively elite craft that was mostly represented by a historically conservative union (the National Association of Letter Carriers [NALC]), letter carriers would seem to have been the last workers one would expect to lead a nationwide wildcat strike in 1970. But labor historian David Montgomery notes that even the most privileged craft workers have often confronted management over workplace autonomy. And it was letter carriers who wound up leading the 1970 strike, starting in one of the most militant labor cities in the United States: New York City.[19]

Letter carriers' jobs in urban areas have also been more socialized than in the smaller offices that tend to atomize the postal workforce. In the larger post offices especially, some carriers worked as "routers" casing mail at all hours of the day for other carriers to deliver. Carriers also often worked in team delivery or spent long hours during different shifts casing mail for New York's many business and residential customers. Good public relations, speed, accuracy, and memory were necessary skills for carriers as well as postal retail clerks. Meanwhile, New York City mail handler Richard Thomas spoke of a "class war" with other crafts that often prompted mail handlers (a craft that also saw occupational segregation) to joke: "I'm just a dumb mail handler!"[20]

The job of clerks, carriers, mail handlers, and other postal crafts involved various combinations of tedium and skill—all without commensurate or adequate pay.[21] Despite their differences, most postal jobs, unlike highly socialized factory jobs, included isolation (or independence) as well as social activity and mutual dependence. With thousands of workers in huge facilities like GPO, Grand Central Station, or Morgan Station in Manhattan, it is no wonder that many clerks called them "letter factories."[22] Whether individual or collective, postal worker desire for workplace autonomy clashed with the paramilitary organizational structure of the post office.[23]

Postal worker job rights had improved considerably since the 1930s and 1940s, when postal workers were typically called in and then told to wait, unpaid, until there was enough mail to work, while they filled out attendance cards to show they had arrived at work on time. But postal workers still began their careers in the 1960s as PTFS (Part Time Flexibles, also known as "flexes" or "subs") for months or even years until the number of subs had reached a certain percentage (or "complement") of the local workforce. Then they would "make regular," that is, be "appointed" as "career employees" with forty hours of work guaranteed per week, their pay calculated on an annual rather than an hourly basis.

By the 1960s many "subs" still had to depend on outside income because they were guaranteed no more than twenty hours of work every two weeks. Others found no problem getting forty hours and even overtime. "Regular" status was the most desired, with its forty-hour week, higher pay and benefits, better opportunities to bid jobs and vacations, and job security. But even career postal workers found pay and benefits lacking in the 1960s, especially as inflation became rampant during the Viet Nam War and ate into their already meager salaries. As a cost-cutting measure, the post office tried to move as much mail with as few career employees as possible, often using inadequately trained temporary workers (called "casuals" or, less charitably, "89-day wonders"), hired for no more than ninety days, who were called in during peak mail flows like the annual Christmas rush.[24]

In the mid-1960s, the various postal unions were discussing and debating merger at the same time they were trading political potshots and competing for members.[25] The end of the decade saw the abolition of patronage in supervisor and rural letter carrier appointments that historically favored whites.[26] Meanwhile, the fight by the Alliance against discrimination in discipline and promotions to supervisory positions accelerated in the 1960s against opposition from the UFPC that called its efforts "reverse racism."[27] Fueling worker militancy was the long-standing frustration over low salaries combined with greater salary expectations for performing such an important unionized government job with no right to strike or collective bargaining rights.[28] Johnson administration budget constraints combined with inefficient postal management methods in 1966 provoked a near-shutdown of mail operations in Chicago.

THE 1966 BIG MAIL BACKLOG IN CHICAGO

The main section of *Towards Postal Excellence*, the 1968 report by the Kappel Commission authorized by President Johnson in 1967 to investigate the post office "crisis" and propose solutions to prevent another such disaster from happening, opens dramatically:

> In October 1966, the 13-story, 60-acre Chicago Post Office—the world's largest postal facility—stopped functioning. Breakdowns in management authority and in physical plant paralyzed service in one of the nation's biggest cities and delayed millions of cross-country letters and parcels normally routed through Chicago. The crisis lasted nearly three weeks.
>
> The backlog of mail exceeded 10 million pieces. Railroad cars and trailer trucks clogged approaches to the post office. Millions of citizens were inconvenienced; hundreds of businesses suffered financial losses. With the help of a Departmental task force vested with special authority by the Postmaster General, service was gradually restored, first to letter mail, and then to other classes.[29]

Unions, management, and the government engaged in mutual recriminations over an event that postal unions claimed represented postal management's inept response to the Johnson administration's orders to control inflation. The crisis also came suspiciously just after Chicago's first black postmaster had been appointed, combined with elements of a worker slowdown to protest poor working conditions. The Kappel Commission, named after its head, Frederick Kappel, the retired chairman of the board of directors of American Telephone and Telegraph (AT&T), was made up almost entirely of corporate executives. Postal officials argued that an unrealistic freeze on personnel and overtime hours imposed by the administration combined with an unusual spike in bulk mail volume had contributed to the shutdown, but the commission did not agree. For their part, postal union journals were already reporting how those problems had become standard, were producing low morale, and were even provoking rank-and-file anger. The post office's predilection for utilizing temporary employees with insufficient experience had caught up to them with a vengeance and precipitated this Chicago "backlog," the unions charged. Alarm spread in business and the federal government that such a catastrophe could happen again without "modernization" and "reform": euphemisms for corporatization that made the Kappel Commission's ultimate "findings" along those lines a foregone conclusion.

The Chicago mail backlog of 1966 became a watershed moment in postal labor history, although ultimately the creation of an independent government quasi-corporate "establishment" known as the U.S. Postal Service would not occur until 1970, following eight days in March when postal workers did the unthinkable and went on strike.[30] Almost forgotten in that October 1966 debacle, however, was the landmark appointment the month before of Chicago's first black postmaster, former National Alliance and NAACP official Henry W. McGee. There is also evidence of a Chicago postal worker slowdown to protest cutbacks in overtime and insufficient personnel. Yet the Chicago mail backlog was both understated and overblown. First reported by the *Chicago Tribune* on October 7, 1966, it was not even front-page news in that city until October 14, when Deputy Assistant Postmaster General for Transportation William Hartigan—sent from the post office's D.C. headquarters to help clear the backlog—announced that it had "reached emergency proportions." Four days later the post office imposed a news blackout, then suddenly announced that the crisis had passed. The Kappel Commission report, however, dramatized an issue that had become typical of postal operations yet one that was more problematic to bulk mailers than the average customer.

In the fall of 1966, a sudden large influx of advertising mail hit the Chicago post office hard. It needed to be processed right away. The holidays were looming, but employee overtime had been cut back since July. The workforce included many temporary employees with inadequate training who were unable to process nearly nine million pieces of mostly bulk mail. In the wake of the backlog, postal officials promised to "curb loafing and excessive absenteeism" that included possible "disciplinary action" against 138 employees. Absenteeism at the Chicago post office was higher than the national postal average, chalking up "1,000 or more daily unscheduled absences" out of 26,000 employees. Postal officials could not explain this, but they did complain of workers greatly extending their breaks or even going AWOL. NPU Secretary-Treasurer David Silvergleid flatly rejected that suggestion, noting that management was worsening the morale of career employees with this "crackdown," especially given that over 4,000 of the 14,000 workers at the Chicago main office were temporaries. Indeed, during his personal inspection he reported that temporaries constituted most of the absentee cases. But all reports agree that there was a work slowdown by many Chicago postal workers to protest the backlog and poor working conditions.[31]

Postal management had for some time been stonewalling discussions of working conditions with postal unions, whose rank and file frequently clashed with management on the shop floor and were pushing their union to take stronger stands. Writing in the August 1966 *Postal Record*—just two months before the Chicago crisis—NALC vice president James Rademacher expressed concern with low morale, noting that "longtime workers, and newer career employees, have reached the point of urging strong action, such as demonstration, and even the imposition of economic sanctions." For Rademacher, "economic sanctions" was a euphemism for what he later would call "the strike weapon"—a subject he said could be discussed another time, reminding his readers that striking for federal employees was illegal. Rademacher aptly captured how demoralization affected letter carriers: "They take pride in their efficiency and reliability. . . . Suddenly they are told to curtail mail." The issue of workers' control in this key public sector job was especially crucial. Postal workers best understand the job process and typically become infuriated if blamed for poor performance when management prevents them from "doing their job."[32] In the two months before the Chicago incident, NALC branch scribes wrote to the *Postal Record* to protest similar service deterioration in Alabama, Arkansas, Ohio, New Jersey, and New York. After the crisis passed and Congress voted postal workers only a 2.9 percent annual raise, NALC members openly began talking strike.[33] Ahead of the NALC and other postal unions was the self-described "militant independent" NPU. The NPU was the first to pass a right-to-strike resolution at its summer 1966 convention, its Philadelphia local (evoking famous American revolutionary Thomas Paine) proposing that the NPU "investigate the feasibility of testing the constitutionality of laws forbidding the postal worker *the right of free men* to strike."[34] The Alliance, without discussing the strike weapon, joined other postal unions condemning the post office for causing the backlog. President Ashby Smith, former Chicago branch president, warned in the January 1967 *Postal Alliance*:

> Much newspaper copy in the past few months has been devoted to the growing unrest of the Federal workers with their conditions of employment. This unrest has been directed by employees, not only against management, but also against the union leadership to whom they looked for protection. . . .
>
> As a result the employee-management cooperation program from which so much was expected, is as 1966 comes to an end, an almost non-existent entity. . . .
>
> If the indecision of Congress and the Nation as to whether the postal service shall be treated as a national service or as a profit-making or break-even business, leads to appropriation restrictions that make for such unrealistic tactics as stringent overtime limitations in the face of an ever-increasing volume of mail, is it surprising that the employees are confused, their morale lowered?[35]

While the 1966 Chicago mail shutdown is often cited as the impetus for the modern postal reforms, there has been no discussion in scholarly literature of a possible contributing factor being the appointment of Henry W. McGee as only the second African American to head a major urban post office and the first in Chicago. This was a city where the position traditionally went to a white person of German ancestry with no postal experience but with political connections. It was Henry W. McGee's good fortune—and also his bad luck—

to have been named postmaster in September, just a month before the giant backlog.

Back in late spring, at the annual Alliance congressional dinner in the nation's capital, Congressman Carl B. Stokes (D-Ohio) quoted from an article in the March 17, 1966, *Chicago Daily News* that had made this surprising declaration: "By tradition the postmastership 'belongs' to a German-American." Stokes, an African American, noted the article's references to the fact that "German American organizations in the Chicago area have no intention of giving up their plum." Stokes was incredulous: "Nowhere in the article did it say that the German candidate was the most qualified. . . . Just that he was German!" For white postal management and German American social groups, this coveted postal position was an acknowledged ethnic white entitlement. Irish Americans also occupied high management positions, and an appointment of someone of Irish descent would surely not have produced such outrage as McGee's did among many whites. This was more than just a local problem. Stokes also pointed to the lack of black supervisors in Cleveland and the Cincinnati postal region. And this racial favoritism, he mused, was taking place under the administration of President Johnson, who had committed himself to equal employment opportunity. This was not only undemocratic, concluded Stokes, but wrong "because it militates against the selection of the best man for the job."[36]

Meanwhile, "affirmative action" became the Johnson administration's attempt to enforce equal employment opportunity provisions under the 1964 Civil Rights Act's Title VII. Just a few months before, Johnson issued Executive Order 11246 transferring equal employment opportunity programs for federal employees to the CSC. Significantly, Stokes also referred to the fact that 91,000 out of a total of 92,265 blacks working in the post office made up the lowest pay grades in the post office. They were working, said Stokes, at "levels 1 through 4, with a pay range of $4,000–$6,000." At the same time, the National Alliance saw relief in the appointment of Henry W. McGee—a long-time local president of both the National Alliance and the local branch of the NAACP.[37]

"It was the proudest day of my life when I was sworn in as Postmaster by Postmaster General Lawrence J. O'Brien," McGee recalled later. But McGee also pointed to the "racial politics" relating to the shutdown, something the Kappel Commission had missed: "The delay in naming a postmaster and the speculation that it would be a black caused some turmoil and when I was appointed, there was quite a backlog of mail. Some thought that because a black was about to be appointed postmaster, there was a deliberate effort made to sabotage the operation."[38]

McGee also remembered white upper-level management's defiance of his appointment: "The Director of Operations, Boschelli, who had been Acting Postmaster, walked out the day my appointment was announced. The Director of Management and Support refused to work under me and went on sick leave. . . . This particular supervisor had entered the post office with me as a substitute employee in 1929 and risen fast in supervisory ranks due to his good contacts with Irish politicians. His name was Francis Quinn and he was of Irish descent."[39]

Upon assuming his office, McGee appointed an African American as Director of Operations in a post office that was about 80 percent black. Most black employees, he said, "were happy that one of their own had reached the top. . . . Almost immediately the morale rose and productivity increased."[40] Countee Abbott at the time worked as a Chicago postal distribution clerk and served as a presidential aide in the Chicago Alliance—by now the largest postal union in that city and the largest branch in the Alliance. The Alliance in fact had *increased* its nationwide representation from one-fourth of all black postal workers in 1960 to one-third in 1966, despite having only "formal" rather than "exclusive" recognition, as did the AFL-CIO postal unions. Abbott's observation of McGee's appointment resembles what black postal workers have said of John Strachan's appointment as New York City postmaster that same year: "It made a significant difference to have someone that . . . was a little fairer in terms of selection of supervisors. . . . He started promoting based on qualifications. And actually whites still got promoted but they didn't get promoted in the 80%, 90% that had been previous. Things started to fall more in line with what the makeup of the office was like, not only as it related to blacks, but as it related to women also. Women started getting more promotions."[41]

McGee himself noted that while he did put a stop to racial discrimination, "some black employees had the misguided opinion that things would be easier under my administration and they would not have to work as hard."[42] Yet during the October mail backlog he felt compelled to defend his mostly black workforce against charges of excessive absenteeism.[43]

What constitutes "hard work" is always a bone of contention between labor and management everywhere. But what is revealing here is a divide between civil rights unionism and militancy that became a difficult juggling act for the Alliance: advocating for black workers including their promotion *into* management (thus functioning as a civil rights group) versus representing black workers *against* management (thus functioning as a union). McGee himself, in his 1961 University of Chicago master's thesis on the Chicago Alliance, addressed that contradiction which emerged within the Alliance in the 1940s. And with affirmative action to this day criticized by many as contravening the seniority process, it is also interesting to consider McGee's recollection in that same paper that it was the Alliance in 1945 that had demanded and won the seniority plan still used in the post office in order to ensure fairness and block discriminatory promotions.[44]

Despite speculation by McGee and others that white postal officials who were trying to sabotage his appointment contributed to the 1966 Chicago postal backlog, it is possible that the backlog would have happened had even a white postmaster been appointed. In fact, a white political appointee with no postal experience (as typically had been the case prior to McGee's appointment) might have made a bad situation worse, which likely would have provoked a widespread postal worker slowdown. As it happened, McGee was able to serve as a symbol around which a predominantly black Chicago post office could rally and help end the backlog. In any event, the federal government now had a dramatic incident to argue for a new structure that, from its perspective, would be more cost-effective and efficient and make postal labor discipline less problematic. McGee's appointment, however, did much to start breaking down systemic white privileges in the Chicago post office, as well as inadvertently foster postal worker unity that would erupt four years later against the wishes of all the postal unions' top leadership, including the Alliance.

BLACK POWER UNIONISM?

Did Black Power appeal only to radical black students—as well as black auto workers in Detroit—and somehow skip the post office? While Black Power never established itself in the postal unions as it did in some private-sector unions, it was nevertheless a substantial presence in the post office. By the late 1960s, as Jeffrey Ogbar reminds us, Black Power as a social force had become so powerful among African Americans that even its critics within the civil rights movement often felt compelled to qualify their objections in the late 1960s and early 1970s. But the generation that had come of age during the black postal worker activist upsurge in the 1940s was expressing ambivalence toward this ideology. While much of Black Power writing and oratory seemed divisive and separatist compared to the Alliance's agenda of coalition, equal opportunity, and integration, Alliance members were also used to being called "black nationalists" by opponents. And while most Alliance members shunned separatism, many nevertheless related to the aspects of Black Power that had to do with black race pride and solidarity.[45]

In some ways the Alliance's literature and practice resembled Black Power, despite the widespread rejection of that term by Alliance members like Dorothea Hoskins of New York, who told me emphatically: "We weren't a black power union, we were a *civil rights union*."[46] In part this shift was a reflection of young, college-educated militants rapidly moving into leadership positions in this traditional civil rights labor organization. A broad form of black nationalism was the Alliance's heritage and therefore in some ways a parallel track with the Black Power movement—if not an actual antecedent. Other issues like affirmative action and black promotion further complicate any attempted dichotomizing between civil rights unionism and Black Power. But whatever the Alliance called itself or was called by others, it was committed to civil rights law enforcement. Better known as affirmative action, that public policy challenged systems of historic white privilege and black discrimination—and was linked to the issue of black promotion. With management status traditionally embedded in whiteness, struggles for black advancement challenged the system of racial oppression as an expression of both collective and individual strivings for social mobility, even if those same black supervisors at times treated postal workers unfairly. The conundrum was that management's *class* interests were opposed to those of its workers, and young Alliance members increasingly found that the civil rights unionist focus of their union to be conservative and not militant.

Donald P. Stone, a proponent of an all-black SNCC in 1966, was, like many other black Atlanta postal workers, a Morehouse College graduate who joined the National Alliance and appreciated its advocacy work, but he was increasingly drawn to direct action. A non-active member of the Alliance, he was interested in practical ways of resisting white supremacy—like routinely refusing to give up to whites his seat at the front of the interstate bus when traveling from Alabama to Georgia. Stone had been dismayed seeing the Atlanta black business community co-opt efforts of black students (then called the Human Rights Committee), as in 1960 when they convinced the students to abandon a direct action protest in favor of running a pro-equality ad in the local newspapers.

Besides taking graduate classes at Atlanta University, Stone also took part in the activities of the newly formed SNCC, like the "kneel-in" direct-action protests aimed at segregated white churches. He recalls the day in 1966 when he suddenly quit his postal job to become a full-time SNCC activist: "I was on my way [to work]. I would park my car and you'd have to go through this little depressed community to get to the post office. Really slum conditions. And so SNCC had taken up a campaign there against the landlord. And so I was . . . walking to work one morning, . . . and they were out there marching around. So I started marching around with them. After I got through marching, I went to the post office and handed in my resignation and started working fulltime for SNCC. [I resigned] on the spot, man. I had no idea when I left home that that's what I was going to do."[47]

Stone also recalls that after he left the post office, former colleagues still asked him to represent them in their grievances with management instead of their shop stewards. Interestingly, what Stone considers to have been the conservatism of the Atlanta Alliance was recalled as militancy by its local president Samuel Lovett.[48] But Atlanta was not the only site of tactical and ideological divides in the Alliance. In 1966, monthly issues of the *National Alliance* reported labor and civil rights protests by Alliance members in Baltimore, a CORE stronghold, where the Alliance's District Two convention joined with CORE protesting issues related to "open occupancy [housing], rent control, school budget, and the shooting of [black civil rights marcher] James Meredith."[49] That same year the Alliance continued its work as part of the Leadership Conference on Civil Rights (LCCR), campaigning for a stronger civil rights bill, among other things. How did the Alliance reconcile working both with integrationist groups like the NAACP and the Black Power–influenced CORE?[50]

The Alliance's activists throughout the 1960s, according to its monthly journal, were still for the most part members of the NAACP (and to a lesser extent CORE and the National Urban League). The journal's objectives, like those of the organization itself, had not changed in decades.[51] But by 1968, their longtime ally Rev. Adam Clayton Powell Jr. was calling nonviolence "no longer useful." And he was not alone. There was an upsurge in militant black activism both before and after the April 4, 1968, assassination of Dr. Martin Luther King Jr., when rebellion spread to over one hundred cities. While the Alliance was not an organization that embraced Black Power, there were differing views within the organization.[52]

During their convention in the summer of 1969, Alliance members from District Six (Ohio, Kentucky, and Indiana) heard keynote speaker Charles H. King praise Black Power ideology as beneficial while distancing himself from violence as a movement tactic. King was director of the Gary, Indiana, Human Relations Commission and a former staff member who had quit the 1968 Kerner Commission on Civil Disorders because of its self-imposed restrictions to examine past disorders only. King presented Black Power to his audience as something familiar rather than alien: "The correct function of black power is to improve the condition of black people, and in the process, assist in the liberation of the total society. . . . It is hardly a new concept."[53]

In 1967, echoes of Black Power also figured in a debate between Alliance president Ashby Smith and John White, president of the Baltimore branch that had close ties to CORE. Smith wanted the NAACP to file antidiscrimination lawsuits, while White argued for local "independent action" that did not drain their national treasury with legal expenses.[54] Smith earlier referred to Black Power as "irrational but an inevitable response to intransigent white supremacy.[55] But in 1968, Enormel Clark, the Alliance's Treasurer-Comptroller, wrote a long rebuttal to white conservative writer Eric Hoffer's contention that blacks were unsuccessful because they lacked sufficient pride. Clark's rebuttal included this assessment: "BLACK POWER. It may shock Mr. Hoffer to learn that more and more Negroes are beginning to think along these lines."[56]

Could a labor organization be black nationalist *and* have a "civil rights agenda," as Alliance historian Paul Tennassee has argued? The Alliance never called itself black nationalist. Indeed, they often used the popular critique of black nationalism that called it a "black racist" mirror image of white racism. President Smith, for example, used the occasion of Dr. King's 1968 assassination to denounce both white supremacy and "the immature sophistry of the black nationalists." Yet the Alliance argued to black postal workers that only a black union like the Alliance could properly represent them.[57] On the other hand, for example, Alliance vice president Wyatt Williams did not hesitate in early 1967 to criticize the New York City post office for poor working conditions and slow promotion of blacks in spite of the fact that an Alliance member, John Strachan, was then its acting postmaster.[58] The Alliance was still fundamentally a labor union that doubled as a black civic organization, as *National Alliance* articles continued to blast white supremacy as well as white liberals in the labor movement for obstructing equality and democracy.[59]

By the late 1960s, black-led direct action protests at construction sites, factory floors, and college campuses typically included "affirmative action" compensatory demands, and that term was now often popularly identified with Black Power in the public mind.[60] In 1966, the Alliance expressed hopes for improvement as the government shifted the EEO from the executive branch to the CSC. EEO had become synonymous with affirmative action, which civil rights groups were now describing as consistent with civil rights law enforcement for which they had long struggled. The Alliance dubbed the EEO a "positive program" of equal opportunity for federal employees.[61] Just a year later, the *National Alliance* protested the lack of EEO enforcement.[62]

By 1968, issues of the *National Alliance* (corroborated by subsequent oral histories) confirm the Alliance's support for vigorous civil rights law enforcement, employing stronger rhetoric that was antiracist and sympathetic to Black Power.[63] The Alliance saw no separation between issues of equality, economics, work life, and black "race solidarity." The mid-1960s actually found the Alliance growing rather than shrinking despite the opening of other postal unions to African Americans. The 1940s conundrum that Henry W.

McGee had identified, of the Alliance being a "segregated" union pursuing integration, was not problematic for active Alliance members. Nor was it an issue for those now building the Alliance's biggest branches in the North, the region where Black Power found its strongest expression.[64] Joining the Alliance in itself was a popular expression of black nationalism in its broadest sense. It could be argued that there was no separate black caucus in the post office in the late 1960s because the Alliance still flourished as a viable black labor and civic organization in a public sector occupation.[65]

ANGER AND RESISTANCE ON THE SHOP FLOOR

Urban labor environments like New York City with a history of labor activism had a profound effect on postal labor. Strikes by teachers, hospital workers, and other public employees were part of that atmosphere.[66] The popular image then of the docile postal worker failed to take into account not only the federal employee strike ban deterrent, but also the concentration of power in the hands of union officials who often functioned as lobbyists. Postal workers were by no means merely envious bystanders waiting for their chance, as many had also been active for years, particularly African Americans. Nor was militant black activism an outside influence. Labor and civil rights militancy were typical in the NPU and the Alliance. NALC branches that were pro-equality and pro-union democracy had become lightning rods in that union, especially New York Branch 36 and Detroit Branch 1. Postal union activists were choosing how to resist postal management and even their own union leadership. Possessing limited collective bargaining rights presented the peculiar paradox of postal workers still having to beg Congress for pay and benefit raises, while simultaneously enjoying some measure of workplace representation. Automation came to the post office in the sixties—at the same time the NPU and Alliance were protesting "slum conditions" in the New York post office.[67]

Richard Thomas (whose story began this chapter), like Eleanor Bailey, Joann Flagler, and other young black workers moving into the postal unions, brought a heightened sense of urgency for change. Viet Nam–era veterans resisted management abuse in New York, according to Thomas, and challenged racist white coworkers in the South, according to Alliance member Felix Bell, who went to work for the Jackson, Mississippi, post office in 1969. Thomas worked for the post office in 1966, left for U.S. Army service in Europe, and then in 1968 returned to postal work:

> The post office was the main available job after I got out of the military. And after I used up all of my savings bonds, which was a typical thing to do back

in the 60s . . . I decided to go to the postal service and earn some money there, staying only a brief time, which is what everybody said back then, and then going to the police force. That was my game plan. . . . Black postal workers were basically the majority of the people there only because . . . it was like a drop off point out of the military. . . . You went in and you just continued on with the federal government. We even wore our khaki outfits, our fatigues on the work floor. . . . *Most of us were veterans, and most of us were angry.*[68]

Thomas also alluded to a program called Project Transition (today known as Operation Transition) that the post office and the Department of Defense began in 1968 to make government jobs available for returning veterans. In March of that year, while Thomas and other veterans were making the transition from military life back to the post office, the *National Alliance* published a message from outgoing postmaster general O'Brien informing its members that President Johnson had signed Executive Order 11397, which "provided for transitional appointments with subsequent conversion to career status for certain qualified Vietnam-era veterans."[69]

Meanwhile, the National Alliance held a press conference in New York City along with the NAACP and the National Urban League to publicize their new coalition, the National Equal Employment Opportunity Committee. They criticized O'Brien's allusion to a recent survey that he claimed "demonstrates that the Post Office is maintaining its position as a pacesetter in the field of equal employment opportunity," owing to "a record of 151,961 individuals who make up about 21.7 per cent of the work force" who were people of color. The Alliance objected that unemployment still hit blacks hard and that civil rights laws went unenforced. They claimed O'Brien was not telling the whole story "because the facts are that the tight manpower market and the undesirable working conditions in some federal agencies, particularly in the postal service, have forced the employment of large numbers of Negroes. The facts indicate there just is not anyone else available for the Post Office Department to hire because white people consider the Post Offices in large cities as undesirable places to work. The facts also indicate that the discriminatory system is resulting in the *firing* of an unusually high percentage of minority group employees."[70] As more blacks applied and many whites resigned or quit applying for postal jobs, turnover at the post office reached 25 percent a year by 1967. Management harassment of employees was probably due not only to "tradition" but also to growing postal worker defiance, as public sector workers in general were demonstrating more militancy on the job.[71]

Memphis was a good example of general black worker militancy in the

South. The February 1968 wildcat strike by black sanitation workers affiliated with the American Federation of State, County, and Municipal Employees (AFSCME) led by former sanitation worker T. O. Jones galvanized that city's black community, including postal workers. In fact, Jones had begun organizing in 1960, getting help from O. Z. Evers—a black postal unionist, president of the Unity League of the Binghamton neighborhood, and civil rights activist who had refused to sit in the back of a Memphis bus in 1956 (later filing suit in *Evers v. Dwyer*).

But Evers's initial attempt to affiliate the sanitation workers with the Teamsters Union failed when the latter abandoned them under pressure from the city.[72] In March 1968 Dr. Martin Luther King Jr. was first called in to help drum up national support. The strike ended with a bittersweet union victory a week after King was assassinated on April 4. One of King's Memphis allies had been someone whom historian Joan Turner Beifuss describes as combining labor and community activism: "Rev. Harold Middlebrook, 26, of the strategy committee, was in charge of youth activities. . . . A graduate of Morehouse College, the Atlanta student activities, youth work at Ebenezer Baptist Church with the Rev. M. L. King Sr., and SCLC's Selma campaign, Rev. Middlebrook was an assistant at Judge Ben Hooks' Middle Baptist Church and worked as a clerk at the Memphis post office."[73] Reverend Middlebrook worked at the Memphis post office from 1965 to 1970, where he told me he belonged to both the National Alliance and the UFPC.[74]

While the 1968 assassination of Dr. King and the nationwide black urban rebellion that followed has been often characterized as representing the death of the civil rights movement, this analysis ignores new movements of black-led protest activity that continued for the next several years—including blacks and their allies at the post office and other workplaces.[75] But there was room for both a symbolic honoring of nonviolent social change—such as at the June 19, 1968, Washington, D.C., commemoration of King's legacy (attended by the Alliance and NPU)—as well as a growing rank-and-file impatience, as seen in the pages of the *National Alliance, Alliance Leader*, and *Union Mail*. Of all the postal union monthly journals, King's assassination was only noted by those of the Alliance and the NPU. The *National Alliance* in particular ran editorials, features, and photo captions that included King with Alliance members at past civil rights movement events.[76]

On the other hand, the Alliance did not join the chorus of those blaming Black Power for King's death and the subsequent urban rebellion, as many were doing. For the past two years they had challenged that kind of blaming as part of overall efforts to split the black freedom movement. For example, in

1967, the Alliance had taken exception to nationally televised remarks made by liberal congressman Emanuel Celler (D-N.Y.) that it was "virtually impossible" to get civil rights legislation through the 90th Congress as a result of the antiwar stance taken by Dr. King, Floyd McKissick, and Stokely Carmichael. The Alliance noted similar excuses had been used in 1966 during "Black Power riots."[77]

The Alliance also stepped up its criticism of organized labor, especially after learning that President Johnson had appointed a committee to study the effects of EO 10988 and that AFL-CIO president George Meany had testified that only unions with "exclusive recognition" should be able to collect dues and represent federal workers. Vice President Wyatt Williams and other Alliance officials contrasted the AFL-CIO's professed political liberalism with its continued defense of white privileges in unionism.[78] Symbolic of the divide between the National Alliance and the AFL-CIO postal unions was a 1969 *National Alliance* article reporting that Brooklyn Alliance members were livid that Jack Leventhal, Brooklyn's NALC branch president, had gratuitously blurted to a reporter that black postal worker participants at a local postal pay raise protest were not members of the Black Panther Party. By 1969, the *National Alliance* had also replaced "Negro" with "black" in its pages as the term gained in popularity among blacks generally. The Alliance's rhetoric had become more militant and expressed even more impatience with white supremacy in the post office and its unions. A combination of black racial pride and impatience with white supremacy, repressive management, and bureaucratic unionism was percolating up from the rank and file.[79]

STRIKE DRESS REHEARSALS

Contrary to popular myth, the 1970 postal wildcat strike was not unanticipated, solely over wage issues, exclusively based in New York City, or the first postal wildcat strike—although it was certainly the largest. Black postal workers took part in what might be called "mini-wildcats" in Newark 1967 and the Bronx in 1969. Besides these brief outbreaks, warning signs for the 1970 nationwide wildcat had flashed for years. Postal management even anticipated them. On July 15, 1968, Deputy Postmaster Frederick C. Belen drew up a "Post Office Contingency Plan for Work Stoppages"—a four-page memorandum instructing postal officials to prepare for the possibility of "prohibited concerted action by postal employees or postal unions such as strikes, slowdowns, work stoppages or related picketing." While the memo was meant to counteract management uncertainty as to what procedures to follow "should a work stoppage occur," its timing suggests a response to the "mini-wildcats" and postal union convention outcries that summer that were sympathetic to defying the federal employee strike ban.[80]

In September 1968 the *Wall Street Journal* reported the post office's contingency plan along with the news that the three largest postal unions (the NALC, UFPC, and NPU) had scrapped their respective constitutional "no strike" clauses at their conventions that summer. In fact, the NPU convention in June passed a resolution that authorized a July 1, 1969, strike deadline until President David Silvergleid overturned it as illegal.[81] These were significant events. For the 70,000-member militant NPU to take this strong stand should have surprised no one. But the more conservative craft unions UFPC (165,000 members) and NALC (210,000 members) were now also edging toward what a *Washington Daily News* reporter called "the postal worker revolt."[82] Both the *Journal* and the *News* accounts noted that all three unions had exercised caution by not replacing their anti-strike constitutional provisions with outright assertions of the right to strike.[83] For example, the NALC resolved to "investigate . . . the right to strike" and "study the feasibility" of abolishing the individual "no-strike" oath."[84] And both articles noted pressure on NALC and UFPC officials from younger "militant" members to test the federal strike ban. Yet the NALC and NPU resolutions (and possibly that of the UFPC) were unanimous. UFPC legislative director Patrick Nilan told Congress that postal union leaders were "sitting atop a live volcano."[85]

Responding sympathetically to that rank-and-file restiveness in the May 1968 *Postal Record* was NALC vice president James Rademacher in his editorial, "Urgency of Militant Unionism More Clear Now."[86] Union leaders were being challenged from below, but they were also trying to make this new militancy pay dividends in their negotiations at the top. Virtually buried in the *Journal* article, however, was the report of a local postal worker action that may have contributed to Belen's memo. During the December 1967 holiday mail rush, the *Journal* mentioned in passing, eighty workers staged a walkout concerning overtime in Newark, New Jersey—an NALC, NPU, and Alliance stronghold. It is not clear if other unions besides the NALC participated in that December 17 protest against a cut in overtime hours upon which letter carriers depended for supplementing their income. The *Newark Star-Ledger* reported a picket line of 150 postal workers, including those who came down on their day off to picket the main post office. NALC members initiated and probably predominated among the picketers.[87] It was a sign of things to come.

If the anxiety level was rising among postal officials concerning imminent or actual job actions, the feeling was mutual among postal workers as they watched support grow within the federal government and the business com-

munity for corporatizing the post office. Public proposals by government officials tying reorganization to future pay raises sounded like blackmail to them.
After President Johnson's executive order established the Kappel Commission
to study the feasibility of corporatization, Kappel himself averred it would be
the first step to privatization. The commission's report in June 1968 in fact
proclaimed to no one's surprise on page 2 in bold type: "We recommend, that
a Postal Corporation owned entirely by the Federal Government be chartered
by Congress to operate the postal service of the United States on a self-
supporting basis."[88]

In 1969 Postmaster General Winton Blount launched a propaganda blitz
for postal reorganization under the guise of a "citizen's campaign," while
Congressman Thaddeus Dulski (D-N.Y.) and the postal unions led opposition
to the plan in Congress, arguing for reform, not reformation.[89] Ironically, from
1962 to 1969, postal workers' lobbying had won a few small gains, even as their
pay lagged. Rising expectations pushed postal workers to consider more se-
riously the strike option. Even the UFPC—still accused of being a company
union by the NPU's *Progressive*—saw a growing militancy among its members.
Delegates to the UFPC 1968 convention, for example, had cheered a speech by
a Canadian postal strike veteran. Anger expressed at NPU, NALC, and UFPC
conventions that summer, especially by younger workers, was not directed so
much at the Kappel Commission as it was at the arrogant bargaining posture
of postal management and the failure of Congress to come through with an
adequate pay raise. The heads of the MBPU and NALC Branch 36 had warned of
a wildcat strike in March 1969. Four months later, one actually broke out in the
Bronx.[90]

On July 1, 1969, fifty-six of sixty-two carriers (all NALC members) and sixteen
of seventeen clerks and mail handlers (all MBPU members)—whites, blacks, and
Puerto Ricans—staged a "sick-out" at the Kingsbridge station in the Bronx. It
was the very same day that a woefully inadequate 4.1 percent pay raise was
issued by President Nixon via executive order. It was also the date that the NPU
at its 1968 convention had tried to set as national strike deadline. Being the first
of the month, it was also a day when many government welfare and pension
checks were normally delivered. The following day, sixteen of the thirty-six
carriers working at the Throgs Neck Station in the Bronx also called in sick.

Bronx postmaster Frank J. Viola implemented the post office's contingency
plan that provided for local postmasters to call substitutes, supervisors, and
employees from other stations to help move the mail, as well as to inform the
unions and the striking workers that collective sick calls constituted an illegal
strike. All those who called in at Kingsbridge were suspended without pay
until July 22. That was when Viola lifted the suspensions and dropped all

charges after MBPU president Moe Biller and NALC Branch 36 president Gus Johnson personally appealed to the postmaster general. NALC president emeritus Vincent Sombrotto told me that this is when he really became actively involved in union affairs. Sombrotto noted that the sick-out was actually intended as a "dry run" rehearsal for a larger strike by NALC Branch 36 leadership—who unfortunately distanced themselves immediately from the strikers after they were suspended. But many rank-and-file letter carriers were excited, wanting to know when it would be their turn to strike. The UFPC condemned the sick-out and were ridiculed by the MBPU, who compensated MBPU wildcatter's salaries for the three weeks they were suspended. NALC Branch 36's leadership balked at doing the same until their members demanded that they also help remunerate their members who had gone out. That led to the forming of the Rank and File Caucus in Branch 36 as strike talk began to circulate.[91]

The Alliance had no comment on the walkout: they felt there were other priorities. But then, on October 29, 1969, President Nixon issued Executive Order 11491 ("Labor-management relations in the Federal Service") that among other things revoked "formal" representation for federal unions the following year, thus marginalizing the two most militant postal unions—the NPU and the National Alliance. The Alliance was furious but not surprised at the order, suspecting that the Alliance and the NPU were about to become sacrificial lambs to corporatization and exclusive AFL-CIO representation. Articles in the *National Alliance* reflected frustration and anger over EO 11491. Columnist Lorraine Huston from the Cleveland branch said Nixon's decision meant making the post office a "closed shop."

Huston's words echoed Alliance vice president Wyatt Williams's column the year before that had drawn parallels to 1935 when the predominantly white AFL won the right to exclusive recognition in the private sector with the passage of the 1935 National Labor Relations Act, also known as the Wagner Act. During that earlier campaign, the NAACP and the Urban League had objected that black workers would be shut out of union membership and representation. (The Wagner Act, ironically, also had provided mostly white union organizers with "affirmative action" to regain their jobs if they were fired for union activities.) The Alliance now similarly accused the AFL-CIO of supporting Nixon's move to eliminate progressive independents like itself and the NPU.[92]

National Alliance editor Snow Grigsby voiced the organization's objections in the form of a December 1969 open letter to all elected officials and community groups. Nixon's executive order was harmful, he argued, not only because it revoked recognition of two major independent postal unions, but because "the Alliance, as a labor organization within the Federal Service, is somewhat unique, for it is the only organization which has been an outspoken advocate of equal opportunity, merit promotions, and is concerned about human dignity and justice for all."[93] In that same issue, National Alliance president Smith warned that Nixon's order was intended to eliminate the Alliance and its civil rights advocacy along with other like-minded unions. The Alliance announced that it had helped form a new labor coalition that included the NPU, the National Federation of Federal Employees, the National Association of Government Employees, the National Customs Service Association, and the Civilian Technicians Association. Furthermore, Smith declared that he had been given strike authorization by his national executive board "and that he would use it if the White House doesn't change the order, or if Congress doesn't overrule it." Smith was later criticized by Alliance members for not supporting the March 1970 nationwide postal wildcat, but he may have actually unwittingly contributed to the growing strike fever. The Alliance—one of the last postal unions to discuss striking—became the first to actually issue that threat.[94]

Denied the right to strike, legal "informational pickets" were by this time both an outlet and a source of frustration for postal unionists. Parading with picket signs—an activity traditionally associated with labor strikes in this country—became their dress rehearsal for doing something they were barred from doing by federal law: striking. Pay raise rallies continued throughout the late 1960s in New York City and D.C., and within them the Alliance continued to raise the issue of equal employment opportunity and to question proposals for "one big postal union" given the lack of civil rights unionism by postal unions.[95]

Meanwhile, then-MBPU activist Eleanor Bailey remembers how her union turned annual pay demonstrations from routine affairs into festive protests. In 1967 they had blown whistles while demonstrating in front of the Capitol building. And during May 6–7, 1969, they staged another theatrical protest: "The last year before we went on strike we went down there with 200 pounds of peanuts. . . . We walked around the post office and said 'no more peanuts, no more peanut salaries' . . . We were eating peanuts, the security guards were upset with us, we were eating [peanuts] while passing them out. . . . The rest of the time we'd walk around for about six hours and then come back home."[96]

As often happens in social movements, humor expressed in these public demonstrations channeled anger and frustration. In this case it was directed at chronic low pay and poor working conditions that built up throughout 1969 and exploded in the early morning hours of March 18, 1970. That anger had begun building in 1966 with mail processing breakdowns, followed by the rank and file of postal unions (and some postal union leaders) agitating for the right to strike and engaging in their own spontaneous protests. The unions rejected

Postal workers at the General Post Office in Manhattan protesting "Nixon's nothing" 4.1 percent raise effective July 1. Over 5,000 postal workers in Manhattan and the Bronx took part in this demonstration on June 20, 1969. Courtesy of the Metro Postal Workers Union Photographs Collection, Tamiment Library, New York University.

the proposed corporate model when they realized that it would deny them the right to strike.[97] But on December 16, 1969, a bombshell was dropped on the postal unions with the news that NALC president Rademacher had broken ranks with the other postal unions in secretly meeting with Nixon, making a deal tying a paltry 5.4 percent wage increase to Nixon's plan to corporatize the post office. New York letter carriers were particularly infuriated, remembering Rademacher's appearance in New York in August following the Bronx wildcat strike where he had mocked their militancy, pledging to lead a strike himself if a pay raise was not voted on by Congress. During the Christmas rush, Branch 36 members began talking about striking.[98]

On the post office shop floor, angry young black veterans took the lead in resisting supervisors, oppressive work rules, and poor working conditions. While the Alliance made some gains against the recalcitrance of white management and labor in the fight for equality during this period, they also fell behind the black rank and file. Postal workers' economic and work life situation was becoming more desperate as management ignored their grievances, and as Congress and President Nixon deferred postal pay raises while pushing for a postal corporation to solve issues of management inefficiency and labor strife. Limited collective bargaining powers whetted postal workers' appetite for full collective bargaining rights. The same post office that had once been a proud source of status, especially for black postal workers, had turned into a source of humiliatingly low pay and benefits, as well as a place of oppressive and disempowering working conditions for all postal workers. It was against this backdrop that a fragmented postal labor movement in 1969 would coalesce and explode as a rank-and-file movement in 1970.

CHAPTER TEN

THE GREAT
POSTAL WILDCAT STRIKE
OF 1970

Cleveland Morgan, a black member of New York Branch 36 of the NALC, was among the first to set up picket lines in New York City to kick off the nationwide March 1970 postal wildcat strike (a strike not authorized by one's union). It was a strike that was also illegal because federal employees were still denied that right. Morgan, originally from rural Georgia, came to the post office in 1963 after attending New York University. Besides working at the post office, to help support his family Cleveland also drove cabs and buses. It was typical for postal workers then to work a second job to make ends meet. This was also while he was coming to the GPO at midnight to "box up" mail to deliver the next morning at the Empire State Building with thirty-six other carriers.

At the time of the strike, Morgan was twenty-seven. In 2005 he shared with me his memories of the strike that began at the Grand Central Station (GCS) post office. "We went over to Grand Central; [strike leader Vincent] Sombrotto, some more guys that went over there, put up the [saw] horses [wooden police barricades] . . . and that morning at six o'clock we were picketing. . . . I was a young guy, back then, matter of fact I had two kids, I was walking around before the strike, demonstrating, they called it picketing. I had a shoe with a hole in it. . . . It was history!"[1]

For eight days in March 1970 about 200,000 postal workers—many of them African Americans, and representing almost every postal union and craft—walked off the job in a nationwide wildcat strike led by members of NALC New York Branch 36. Labor historian Aaron Brenner has called the strike not only "the largest strike against the federal government, but also the largest wildcat strike in U.S. history."[2] For the most part it was conducted by people who had never before engaged in such an action. By striking they risked not only job termination but also fines, jail terms, and union dissolution. Their principal grievance was low pay, but poor working conditions and inadequate bargaining rights were also contributing factors. Brenner called the strike "an extraordinary display of rank and file militancy on the part of previously passive

Cleveland Morgan in 2005. Morgan was a New York City 1970 postal strike veteran and an officer in NALC Branch 36, the union local that began the strike. Photograph by the author.

workers."[3] Yet this unprecedented action has not received its due in labor history. The standard narrative of the 1970 postal strike goes little farther than noting that New York City was exceptional as the spark and main locus of the strike, but there was also significant strike activity elsewhere. The problems that ensued after the strike—especially for the militant industrial independents, the NAPFE and the NPU—have also been inadequately studied. And especially absent from labor history is the key role played by black postal workers and how the fight for equality contributed to this remarkable action.[4]

BUILDUP

Postal workers who struck in March 1970, while proud of their government service jobs, had long felt taken for granted. The gap between their expectations and government recognition, especially in the area of compensation, widened to the breaking point in the months just before the strike, facilitated by their union membership. While federal employees overall were about one-third unionized during the 1960s (roughly the same percentage as private sector workers), postal workers, who represented the largest number of nonmilitary federal employees, had an astounding unionization rate of 84 percent in 1961 and 88 percent in 1968—including 98 percent of letter carriers. This was especially remarkable given their lack of full collective bargaining rights or the right to strike. African Americans, who were proportionately more active than whites in private sector unions by this time, were also some of the most active public sector unionists in the post office. Fully one-third of all black postal workers were now represented by the Alliance, and about one-fifth were represented by the NPU.[5]

Postal workers were both highly unionized and well represented in lobbying efforts in Washington, D.C. But both their newly won limited collective bargaining rights and lobbying power shrank in the 1960s. Postal workers still had to request Congress for pay raises and benefits while enjoying some measure of workplace representation. In early 1970, expectations and impatience were rising among all postal workers. Most were dissatisfied about pay, treatment, and their union leadership's ability to negotiate. A district meeting of 1,100 Long Island letter carriers on February 28 called for a March 16 strike. Postal unions for years had cultivated a culture of lobbying from the top as well as from the rank and file, which paradoxically encouraged both worker passivity and activism. Contradictions now grew between postal workers' pride in government service and feelings of betrayal by the government.[6]

Postal workers felt insulted by the administration's minimalist pay offers. Nixon added fuel to the fire in early February 1970 when he deferred their scheduled July 1 pay increase until January 1971 and threatened to veto any pay raise legislation that did not include reorganization of the post office as a corporation. Nixon's postal corporation plan now took the form of a compromise bill approved by the House Post Office and Civil Service Committee on March 12, 1970.[7]

But events and conditions intolerable to postal workers were now moving them in the direction of defying the government and their own union leaders. Receiving inadequate relief from their respective unions in dealing with an uncooperative postal management did not stop protests across postal crafts, including mail handlers. One of the few jobs at the post office officially classified as blue collar, mail handling was a crucial craft in literally moving the mail for clerks and carriers to process despite that craft's relatively small size (13 percent of postal employees in 1968). By 1970 many mail handlers were black military service veterans. MBPU member and army veteran Richard Thomas described how he and his coworkers in New York City dealt with daily issues like supervisor confrontations: "Because of the fact that most people were veterans, they basically took it in their own hands, and *then* called the union. That's the way it was back then. We would argue with the supervisor, refuse to

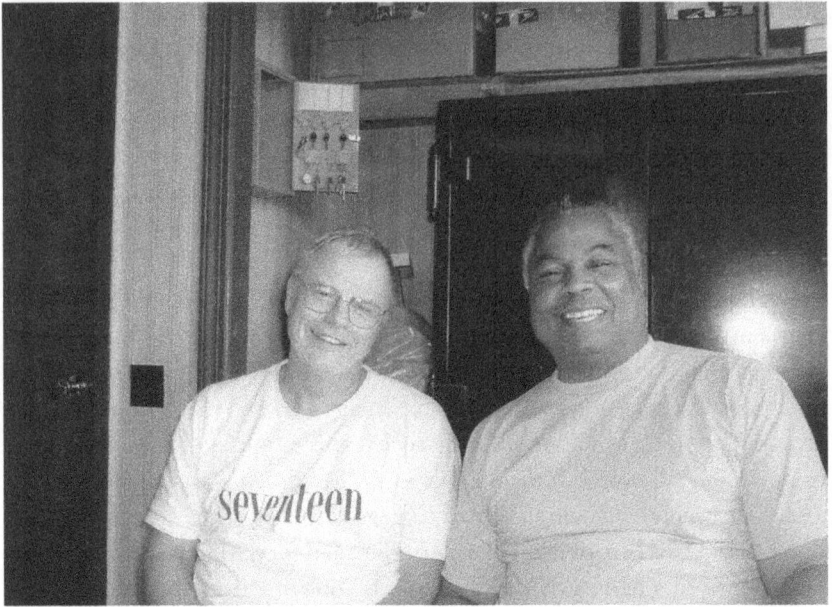

Richard Thomas (right) and Jeff Perry, retired mail handler union activists, in 2005. Thomas participated in the 1970 postal strike as a member of the MBPU. He later became a shop steward before being elected administrative vice president (and later branch president) of the New York City Branch of NPMHU Local 300. Perry began work at what is now called the New Jersey International Bulk Mail Center in Jersey City in 1974 and was a shop steward before being elected administrative vice president and treasurer of NPMHU Local 300. Photograph by the author.

do it, or whatever we decided to do, and then if we got some kind of write up, the shop steward would be called."[8]

Thomas's recollection of "taking it in their own hands" could easily be applied to the 1970 strike as well. The two highly visible, influential, and charismatic strike leaders, Vincent Sombrotto and Moe Biller, similarly recalled those dramatic events twenty-five years later. Writing in February 1995, NALC president Sombrotto looked back at the strike his branch had initiated, when he had gone from a non-active union member to rank-and-file strike leader of NALC Branch 36: "The strike itself was one of those rarities in American labor history—an actual uprising of rank-and-file workers who forged what was a revolutionary act with courage and conviction despite the resistance of their elected leaders."[9] In March 1995, APWU president Biller spoke before a panel discussion at the National Postal Museum in Washington, D.C., commemorating that strike exactly twenty-five years from the eve of its beginning. "Let me begin by saying," observed Biller, "that nobody can artificially manufacture the ingredients for the type of strike we had in 1970. The objective conditions must exist. . . . You had to have the elements necessary for spontaneous combustion; and believe me, we did. Wages were pitiful." Biller noted how urban postal workers were forced to keep up with rising costs by moonlighting, with many others even qualifying for welfare as the ultimate indignity. He also pointed to other important issues: "And working conditions were deplorable—ancient dungeons for postal facilities, with no heat in the winter, no air conditioning in the summer, and minimal indoor plumbing year-round. . . . It was downright medieval."[10]

Biller also recalled what he had predicted in 1969 to the *New York Times* when he used a Viet Nam War metaphor to criticize Nixon's 4.1 percent postal pay raise as something that "hit postal workers like a napalm bomb and they're really burning. . . . The Post Office thinks we're kidding when we warn about possible wildcat strikes. But anything could light the tinderbox."[11] Together Biller and Sombrotto came to symbolize strong executive leadership of formidable postal unions. Yet both came into national office and prominence by virtue of being at the head of the rank and file. Both men also came from powerful New York City union locals with long democratic and anti–Jim Crow traditions, combined with black members playing a significant role—especially in the case of the MBPU. The leadership that emerged from the strike was based on performance under fire, and it was these leaders who would direct the unions into the future.

"The reason we went on strike," recalled Frank Orapello in 2004 when he was NALC Branch 36 president, "is because we just couldn't live in New York City with the amount of money we made as a postal employee. Everybody had two or three jobs."[12] Eleanor Bailey, then an MBPU shop steward, concurred: "We really did not have the things that were necessary." The strike was indeed called primarily over issues of pay. Starting pay for postal workers in 1970 was $6,176 per year, reaching top pay of only $8,442 after twenty-one years. The pay was so low that many postal workers in New York City were eligible for food stamps.[13]

Yet salary and benefits were more than the common cause of the strike. They were also signifiers of collective frustration at being denied first-class labor citizenship. These were workers whose jobs personified public service, whose community status was compromised by low pay and ill treatment, and who seemed to be the only labor sector of society that had not publicly protested in a forceful fashion. The strike, as Branch 36 vice president Herman Sandbank told the *New York Times* in 1970, represented insistence on being treated like "first class citizens"—a common demand used by blacks in the civil

Vincent Sombrotto (NALC) (left) and Morris "Moe" Biller (APWU), two key leaders in the 1970 New York City postal strike, were elected presidents of their organizations in 1978 and 1980, respectively. Courtesy of the Metro Area Postal Workers Union Photographs Collection, Tamiment Library, New York University.

rights movement. For male heads of household especially, Aaron Brenner notes, there were issues of masculinity wrapped up in the combination of low salaries in an important government service that often treated them badly and where employees had to beg Congress for raises—especially in New York, a city known for labor militancy.[14]

The strike, then, became a kind of national postal worker referendum on their work-life status quo, with New York making the first motion. Many sensed that it was their turn, as Sombrotto put it: "Protests were everywhere. People were looking at government in many cases as an enemy not a friend. In our immediate area, workers, whether they were teachers, sanitation workers, transportation workers, all of them were taking some sort of job action of one kind or another to satisfy their needs and their salaries and benefits, and in many cases broke the law. . . . And the carriers were looking at: 'When do we get our just rewards for our labor? And how are we ever gonna get a raise?' . . . Other people were making advances while we were not."[15]

THE STRIKE BEGINS

The strike began in Manhattan at GCS and the GPO in the early hours of Wednesday, March 18, 1970, and spread across the country for eight days. By the time it ended almost one-third of the nation's postal workforce had joined the strike. It was an expression of rank-and-file militancy (with a vital legacy of civil rights industrial unionism) in a key communications industry that was unique in having unionized installations throughout the United States. Blacks constituted key organizers and large numbers of strikers across craft lines. According to media accounts and postal management status reports, the strike affected thirteen states and spread to as many as 200 cities and towns involving 671 stations across the country—mostly in the Northeast, Midwest, and Far West. The strike was also not coordinated. For example, postal workers in Chicago went out over the weekend but returned to work the following Monday—the same day that many Los Angeles postal workers went out. Detroit postal workers went out right after New York did and stayed out until the end.

While disorganization might have hindered the strike's effectiveness, it also reflected power seized by the rank and file from union officials. The resulting chaos not only forced those officials to "play catch up" but created uncertainty and hesitation on the government side as well. Postmaster General Winton Blount reacted to the nationwide walkout by temporarily embargoing mail to New York City and the surrounding communities, in addition to suspending the private express statutes that normally prohibited private carriers from handling first-class mail. (Blount rescinded both statutes by March 27 after the strike had ended.) On March 23 President Nixon declared a state of emergency and called out 22,000 federal troops to try to move the mail in New York City, where the wildcat was having the most serious financial consequences. Troops were also called out in Detroit but remained at the National Guard armory. Even in cities where postal workers did not strike, many took votes to strike if no settlement was reached by Saturday, March 28. Altogether, the strike involved between 152,000 and 209,000 postal workers out of a total of 750,000 workers: almost 28 percent of all postal workers, 36 percent of those being letter carriers, with the remaining 64 percent clerks and workers in other crafts.[16]

Initiating the strike were letter carriers belonging to the nation's largest postal union, the NALC. Strikers also belonged to another major AFL-CIO affiliate that did not authorize this strike, the UFPC; the NPMHU, another AFL-CIO affiliate; members of the Alliance, which did not vote to strike but advised its members not to cross picket lines; and members of the militant, independent, industrial NPU, the only union to officially sanction the strike with 53,000 of its 80,000 members walking out, comprising between one-fourth and one-third of all strikers. Strike participation varied, but no city surpassed New York, which went out for eight days with almost 100 percent solidarity.[17] Thirty-five years later, a retired Durham, North Carolina, letter carrier exclaimed to me with awe: "New York bailed us out—we were sweating bullets back then!"[18]

New York strike veterans have described the months leading up to the strike during which they could watch palpable tension rising "like a volcano." Eleanor Bailey described the Tour 1 (the "nightshift") letter carriers whom she credited with launching the strike as "the most progressive" and who were always being harassed or fired "left and right" for no reason.[19] NALC Branch 36, the largest in the nation at 6,700, had voted March 12 to hold a strike vote the following week. They had outmaneuvered their branch president, Gus Johnson, who had tried to sidetrack and co-opt it by scheduling a vote instead of a meeting where strike advocates could further argue their positions. By now, according to Aaron Brenner, Branch 36 rank-and-file organizing led by Vince Sombrotto, Tom Germano, and others had resulted in an increase in the branch's monthly meeting attendance from less than 100 in November 1969 to over 800 at the March 12 meeting. (Ironically, that same day the House Committee on Post Office and Civil Service approved a compromise postal reform package by a 17–6 vote that included full collective bargaining for the first time.) Rank and filers had assembled a platform that included a full government pension, hospitalization, life insurance for active and retired carriers, retirement available at twenty (not thirty) years, "area wages" adjusted for regions with higher costs of living, and the right to strike.[20]

Frank Orapello described union officers' attempts to prevent a strike on March 17: "Voting was to take place at the Manhattan Center. . . . I guess our local officers figured it was out of the way for most Bronx and Manhattan carriers, and also had a 6:00 P.M. voting time. . . . At about 6:45 the crowd [of carriers outside] got out of hand. . . . The doors finally opened. . . . [They] set up chairs on both sides of the room for carriers to [vote and] . . . exit. They wanted the carriers to go home. . . . I believe if we had voted and went home, there would never have been a strike. . . . I started to rearrange the chairs, to make sure that any letter carrier who wanted to stay [could do so]. . . . At about 11 P.M. . . . the result was 1,555 to strike and 1,055 not to strike. . . . They said we were going on strike March 18, 1970, at 12:01 A.M."[21]

Organizational merger that had eluded postal unions for years now emerged in practical terms among the rank and file. Just hours before, on the night of March 17, one of the Tour 1 NALC letter carrier "routers" had asked Eleanor Bailey what she thought about the strike that they had just called, and she replied that she was with them. In fact, according to a management study, all Tour 1 routers failed to report to their 10:30 P.M. shift that night—half an hour before the NALC Branch 36 strike tally had even been announced! The strike had begun with the nation's largest NALC branch, followed by the huge MBPU (biggest in the NPU) respecting the NALC's picket line before voting to join the strike on March 21. Members of smaller unions like the NPMHU and NAPFE also played key roles.[22] Among black rank-and-file strikers was Cleveland Morgan from NALC Branch 36 setting up picket lines, and Eleanor Bailey from the MBPU patrolling picket lines to make sure no one crossed them. "Folks at that time . . . were much more militant," Bailey later reflected, "and we were together. The only thing they needed was a leader."[23] Rank-and-file postal workers rejected union leaders who tried to tell them to continue to be patient, that raises were forthcoming, or that corporatization was the wave of the future. Biller and Sombrotto became prominent leaders as most top postal union officials lost credibility.[24]

As the early morning hours of March 18 arrived, Vincent Sombrotto and Cleveland Morgan were among the first striking letter carriers from Branch 36 to assemble picket signs and improvise strike barriers out of wooden police barricades that had been used in the St. Patrick's Day parade the day before.[25] At the start, a few hundred letter carriers and clerks began picketing outside post offices in Manhattan and the Bronx. Within two days about 200,000 postal workers, from big cities and small towns alike, had walked out. Aaron Brenner points out: "They did so of their own volition. There was no national strike coordination, since national postal union officials actively opposed the strike." The network consisted of personal phone calls, newspaper coverage, and face-to-face activity across craft, race, gender, and age lines.[26]

NALC Branch 36's strike vote was announced at 11 P.M., but the handful of letter carrier "routers" scheduled to begin work at 10:30 had already refused to show up for the start of their shift. Letter carriers threw up picket lines and barricades outside post offices in Manhattan and the Bronx at 12:01 A.M.—just in time for the clerks' shift—as the vast majority of carriers did not start

Postal workers on strike in New York City on a picket line behind police barricades, March 1970. NALC Branch 36—the largest in the NALC—was the first union to vote to strike, voting 1,555 to 1,055. About 200,000 postal workers struck nationwide. Courtesy of the Metro Postal Union Photographs Collection, Tamiment Library, New York University.

reporting until 6 A.M. Eleanor Bailey was one of thousands of clerks who walked out or refused to cross the Branch 36 picket lines, and soon voted to join the strike themselves. As a GPO shop steward, Bailey spent hours on the picket line making sure that clerks were not sneaking through the underground tunnels to get around the picket lines and go to work. MBPU mail handler Richard Thomas did the same: "We stayed there all night making sure people didn't go in, didn't cross the picket line. . . . Everything was done word of mouth. . . . It was definitely rank and file. We marched around the GPO . . . for basically five days."[27]

Just as Bailey and Thomas were emblematic of many young black unionists who helped enforce strike solidarity, Bailey's own family represented a division among postal workers. Another MBPU steward had told Bailey that her father, a World War II veteran and longtime postal mail handler in Manhattan, was crossing the picket lines. "My father loved his post office job," Bailey remembers, and when she confronted him he protested: "You don't know what the government did for me! I was a soldier and they gave me a job." But she was insistent: "Dad, I promise you—cross the picket line, I will break your legs!" Bailey's father was aghast at her threat, she recalls, but he would later repeat that story to friends with pride. Like many older workers, he used sick leave to stay home during the strike instead. The picket lines included many younger workers like Joann Flagler, with less than a year at the post office. Asked if she was scared, Flagler laughed: "I was young—I was nineteen years old! Who's afraid at that age? There was a *lot* of young people."[28]

Fear and excitement mingled in these uncharted waters. NALC Branch 36 strike veteran Frank Orapello remembers that "everybody was scared." Echoing this sentiment among strikers in the Los Angeles area, Raydell Moore, an African American who during the strike was a local NPU official, noted the number of postal workers in both Los Angeles and San Francisco who crossed picket lines, and made this observation based on his experience that reveals the mutually necessary work between leadership and rank and file: "You just don't come in being militant. You have to have a reason. Somebody's got to be strong enough to lead you to do what you want to do. The leaders had to be strong to have people to follow them when they called a strike. And don't think that the leaders weren't scared to death during that strike! 'Cause if you lost your job, where were you going to?"[29]

Meanwhile, three key figures in the NALC Branch 36 strike leadership whom I interviewed—Vincent Sombrotto, Al Marino, and Frank Orapello—at the time were ages forty-six, thirty-nine, and thirty-eight, respectively. Older strikers in New York, including those close to retirement, were telling newspaper reporters: "We haven't got anything now. So what can we lose?" Many of them chose to walk the picket lines rather than simply use up their sick or annual leave.[30]

On March 18, after MBPU president Moe Biller had urged his members to respect the carriers' picket lines, the MBPU was ready to walk out that night.[31] This is how the March 19 *New York Times* covered the MBPU strike meeting: "About 3,000 members of the Manhattan and Bronx Postal Union, which has 25,000 members, demanded an immediate sympathy strike [with Branch 36 of the NALC already out] at a tumultuous meeting at the Statler Hilton Hotel last night. Shouting 'Strike! Strike! Strike!' the union members swarmed over the speakers' platform and forced the local president Moe Biller to flee through a kitchen. They refused to listen to his argument that union bylaws required a secret ballot in any strike vote."[32]

The Associated Press and oral history accounts put that crowd at about 6,500—more than double the *Times*' more conservative figures.[33] John Walsh and Garth Mangum called this "one of the wildest meetings in postal labor

Three NALC Branch 36 1970 postal strike rank-and-file leaders in New York City in 2004. *Left to right*: NALC national president emeritus Vincent Sombrotto, former executive vice president and financial secretary/treasurer Al Marino, and former Branch 36 president Frank Orapello. After the strike, Sombrotto also won black support in his successful 1970 bid for the presidency of this historically progressive NALC branch. He was elected national president in 1978, serving from 1979 to 2002. Photograph by the author.

union history."[34] Biller demonstrated more sympathy with the strike than Gus Johnson, his NALC Branch 36 counterpart. But like all union leaders, Biller was concerned with the threat of fines, jail terms, and mass firings, as well as with maintaining proper procedures at a time when emotions ran so high as to make a secret ballot strike vote almost impossible. Walsh and Mangum also reported: "There were also militants from the SDS, the Black Panthers. . . . Three Young Lords [a Puerto Rican revolutionary group] in crimson berets were patrolling the platform which had been more or less surrounded by agitators. . . . 'Power to the People,' shouted the crowd (the sixties had finally arrived at the Post Office)."[35]

Biller himself later recalled: "The situation on the platform was becoming more menacing by the minute." His request for a secret ballot vote was shouted down. Someone pulled a knife on him before another member got in the way and blocked the assailant. Chairs were thrown from the balcony, MBPU financial secretary Milt Rosner remembers. Clearly, the majority of the crowd was angry and ready to vote to strike. Biller had to be escorted by supporters

Militants take over the stage at the New York City MBPU-NPU strike meeting on March 18, 1970, as President Moe Biller tries to call for a secret ballot vote. The MBPU voted by acclamation that night to join NALC Branch 36 in the strike and three days later voted in a secret ballot by a count of 8,242 to 940 to strike. Photograph by Donal F. Holway. Courtesy of the Metro Area Postal Workers Union Photographs Collection, Tamiment Library, New York University.

and city police for his own safety, with secret balloting now scheduled for three days later, where a strike vote carried by the lopsided margin of 8,242–940. Hundreds of new MBPU recruits signed up as the MBPU conducted a candlelight vigil in front of the GPO. Carriers and clerks had now shut down the New York City post office. Biller had been willing to risk jail and lead an illegal wildcat strike—as long as the union's bylaws were followed![36]

The strike caught many by surprise—including postal workers—though there had been many warning signs. Moe Biller later admitted with embarrassment that despite his popular image as a labor radical, striking had not even occurred to him until the late 1960s.[37] Richard Thomas recalls the lack of collective strike experience: "Everybody talking saying, 'We're not crossing the picket lines!' And everybody said, 'What's a picket line?' But they understood what the term meant." He also observed that "it was the rank and file who went on strike."[38] The strike began in New York because that city's labor culture was unique, but it spread because New York's post office was representative of all postal workers' grievances, as well as their willingness to take risks and to defy authority in order to win fairness and better treatment. Black agency played a crucial part.

THE STRIKE SPREADS

"It just snowballed throughout the whole country." That was how Frank Orapello described the strike, looking back in 2004. It was the phrase most commonly used at the time and to this very day.[39] And his branch, NALC Branch 36 in New York, had gotten it rolling. The variance of strike activity across the nation and even within cities still defies many preconceived notions of militant behavior by region, craft, or race. The strike especially spread to urban areas that had a history of militant black, labor, and left movement activity. Critical to the strike's success were these urban post offices that were in many cases central postal distribution centers. A Chicago strike veteran, Countee Abbott, then age twenty-nine with eleven years in the post office and the president of the Alliance's District Seven, told me: "The reason why the strike worked was because, contrary to what people thought, you didn't have to shut down every post office. If you just shut down the major metropolitan areas, you stopped the flow of mail, and that's exactly what happened. It wouldn't have been sufficient just for New York. But when New York, and Chicago, Philadelphia, Los Angeles, other major areas shut down, mail just backed up, and that idea that . . . 'we'll get the troops to come and move the mail,' well, that didn't work. And as a result of that, the mail backed up. And they were put in a position where they had to work something out."[40]

The appearance of this wildcat "snowball" getting bigger was inspiring to strikers, impressive to observers, and shocking to government and union officials. The media tended to portray this as mainly a "mailman's strike," but in most cities clerks and mail handlers together actually outnumbered carriers among those striking, as they did numerically in the workforce.[41] Postal workers began striking all along the eastern seaboard, from Long Island and up-state New York to Hartford, Boston, Newark, and Philadelphia, and then into the Midwest.

Detroit postal workers went out at 3 P.M. on March 18, according to Doug Holbrook, then president of the Detroit NPU. A formal vote was taken in a mass meeting in downtown Cobo Hall on Sunday, March 22, that included some three thousand postal workers from all postal unions except the rural letter carriers. The resolution to strike was unanimously carried after a fifteen-minute meeting, as Holbrook recalls: "I announced that we were officially on strike, and that we would not return to work until it was resolved." Holbrook also noted the UAW's backing of the local strike, and the UAW background of many postal workers—including Holbrook himself and Harry Tapsico, an African American and veteran of the bitter Ford "overpass strike" of 1941. Holbrook said he had appointed Tapsico executive vice president in 1966 to diversify local leadership over the objections of many white members. Even the small UFPC Local 295 led by a black president, Ivory Tillman, backed the strike.[42] Detroit was unique with strike unity that included the local Alliance branch—whose national office as well as local leadership in New York and other cities promised to honor picket lines but did not actively back the strike.[43] Not every Alliance member agreed with that position.

For example, Chicago Alliance official Countee Abbott proudly pro-claimed: "I participated in it. . . . The letter carriers' union [NALC] was in the forefront. . . . A large number of the letter carriers were black. The Alliance took the position that we would not cross picket lines of another labor organization. That was the position we took and we stayed out in support of that strike. And the postal inspectors came by the union and visited us, and tried to threaten us."[44] The Chicago Alliance represented about one-quarter of that city's 25,000 postal workers, and it voted to honor the picket lines that were thrown up by NALC Branch 11. The Alliance's Chicago president William S. Lewis told the *Chicago Tribune*: "We deplore the situation in which the carriers have found themselves; a situation in which the strikers have been forced to jeopardize their jobs to secure just wages." Another longtime Alliance member, Chicago postmaster Henry W. McGee, was quoted as having "empathy" with the strikers, although he called the strike itself "inexcusable."[45]

Meanwhile, roughly half of the largely black 6,000 member Chicago NALC

Branch 11 filled the hall of the Plumbers Union (which had long excluded blacks), chanting, "Postal power—strike!" The impromptu slogan reflected the widespread influence of the Black Power movement. "Our members are so militant, so upset, so frustrated they will stay out till hell freezes over," declared NALC Branch 11 president Henry S. Zych after his branch voted almost unanimously to strike. No media coverage was provided of other unions, but a management official said only 627 of the 1,827 clerks and mail handlers reported for duty at the main office on March 21, while just 127 of 1,484 clerks at branch stations showed up to work.[46]

Also striking in the Midwest was Cleveland. "I wasn't surprised because I was part of it," William H. Burrus Jr., then vice president of the Cleveland Postal Union-NPU, told me. "I think we went out the following day [after New York]." As a major mail hub Cleveland was crucial, he said. UFPC Local 72—with roughly 2,000 members, making it perhaps the UFPC's largest local—called a meeting with the Cleveland NPU that had about 300 members, at least fifty percent black, and with a black president, George Wade. The UFPC president, William F. Crocket, who was also black, declared that there would be no strike. But the NPU had other ideas. "We wanted workers to get engaged," recalls Burrus. "We just had a strong core." Though never credited in the local media with its leading role in the Cleveland wildcat, the NPU walked out on Thursday, March 19, according to Burrus. On Friday morning, letter carriers from NALC Branch 40 walked out as well, overwhelmingly voted to strike that night over the objections of their branch president, and began picketing Saturday. UFPC members, already wildcatting, formally voted to strike on Sunday, with Local 1 of the Special Delivery Messengers going out as well. Strikers in Cleveland did not return until Tuesday, March 24.[47]

The *Washington Post*, while observing that there was little if any strike activity in the nation's capital, noted the effectiveness of the Chicago and Philadelphia strikers, especially clerks, in slowing the nation's mail to a crawl. In Los Angeles, a major national distribution center, the Los Angeles Postal Union (LAPU-NPU) with 3,000 members voted to strike. The 2,200-member UFPC local voted not to strike. But fewer than fifty percent of all clerks arrived at work March 23 at the city's huge Terminal Annex. Those who did report to work moved the mail with NALC Branch 24 letter carriers, who had been unable to judge the results of a voice vote at a bitter strike meeting over the weekend, although that 3,500-member branch did vote that they would strike on April 15 if NALC president James Rademacher asked them to do so. In this majority-black post office blacks played leadership roles on all sides of the strike: LAPU president Leroy Armstead defiantly proclaimed his local to be on strike, NALC Branch 24 president Halline Overby publicly opposed it while expressing sympathy for the strikers, and the director of postal operations for Los Angeles, Tillman Thomas, a former clerk and supervisor once praised by the Alliance (he may have been a member), conceded to the press that it would be hard for 600 supervisors to handle the mail that 8,500 workers normally processed every day in that city. Suburban stations often walked out while city stations still worked. In San Francisco letter carriers voted to strike, while fewer than half of all clerks reported to work in the city by the bay.[48]

The strike was strongest in cities with the largest concentrations of black postal workers but was still limited to northern and western states. In Washington, D.C., the Alliance branch—D.C.'s largest postal union—voted not to strike, although its president, Robert White, expressed support for the strikers. Post office status reports and the local media described postal workers in D.C. as quiet and loyal during the strike. But contemporary and subsequent narratives have missed the remarkable story of NALC Branch 142 in Washington, D.C. It apparently voted to strike even before New York did, although it never went out.[49]

Branch 142 by 1970 was about 60 percent black, having absorbed many local Alliance members—many of whom still maintained dual Alliance/NALC membership. Branch meetings were mostly made up of black members, according to then-President Joseph Henry when I interviewed him in 2005. The March 1970 strike vote in D.C.—taken a few days before New York voted—was close. "I was quite upset," recalled Henry, who was ready to strike. "A letter carrier in 1970, with two members of the family, qualified for food stamps here in D.C. and New York City and your major metropolitan areas. . . . I probably worked an amount of overtime almost equal to my regular time. I made $7,200 [in annual salary]." "At each station the shop steward was responsible for polling the letter carriers, and the majority ruled." Anacostia Station, where he worked, voted to strike along with other large stations. Henry claims that the D.C. vote to strike was misrepresented as rejection to the membership by branch president Elliot Peacock—a veteran of the anti–Jim Crow fight in the NALC. But Henry said shop stewards discovered the apparent deception too late.[50]

Other postal union locals in the South and throughout the country sympathized with the wildcat but did not join, largely out of loyalty to the national union leadership of the NALC and the UFPC—both of which promised to lead a strike on April 15 if their demands were not met. But some southern union branches and locals considered striking before later voting it down (Charlotte and Houston), or voted to strike the following Saturday, March 28, if there was no settlement (Richmond and New Orleans). NALC branches in the latter two cities had black presidents who in fact made those very declarations. Richmond NALC Branch 492 president Lawrence G. Hutchins told the *Richmond*

Joseph Henry presides over a branch meeting in 2005. An NALC Branch 142 member since 1962, after the two segregated Washington, D.C., branches integrated, Henry was president from 1998 to 2008. He was also a supporter of the 1970 postal strike, but a questionable local vote count kept him and other strike supporters from walking out in D.C. Courtesy of Joseph Henry.

Times-Dispatch on March 24, after his union voted unanimously to strike in that city on March 28: "We will have pickets at the main post office at 12:01 A.M., Saturday if an agreement is not reached."[51] And in New Orleans the president of NALC Branch 124 was Clarence Acox, a former member of that city's segregated black NALC branch and veteran of the campaigns against Jim Crow branches. Many southern NALC branches now had elected black presidents, indicating that they either had a black majority or at least a large black minority able to work with and influence the white majority.

But while many black postal workers helped lead the strike, many others played key roles in ensuring that their branches did *not* strike. Atlanta, for example, had no reported strike activity, as current National Alliance District Three president Samuel Lovett still calls the strike "crazy," believing that strikers should have "stuck to the law" to resolve outstanding issues, while also noting that the South's lack of unionism contributed to the strike's failure there. In Miami, meanwhile, there was no strike vote by the Alliance branch according to Sam Armstrong (currently District Three's director of retirees), who proclaimed his pride in National Alliance president Smith's role ending the walkout. The failure of the South to walk out in fact reflected a number of issues: a history of workforce racial divisions; ambivalence on the part of southern postal workers (including African Americans); alienation from the tactics and wage demands of the strike leadership and northern urban strikers in general; and loyalty to their respective national union leaderships, all of whom officially opposed the strike with the exception of the NPU.

Yet in Washington, D.C., Joseph Henry said that race was no indicator for how his NALC branch voted. Nor have I found evidence anywhere else in the South that strike advocacy or opposition ran along racial lines. Henry also recalled having joint pre-strike meetings with the "far more militant" Washington Area Postal Union (WAPU-NPU).[52] It is remarkable in itself that strike votes were even taken in cities like Houston, Atlanta, New Orleans, Baltimore, Miami, Nashville, Chattanooga, Knoxville, Birmingham, Memphis, Washington, D.C., Charleston (West Virginia), Wilmington, Winston-Salem, and Charlotte.[53] The Richmond UFPC Local 199, an urban local in the weakest labor region of the country, took not one but two strike votes. Historian Vern Baxter, himself a former postal worker in that city, remembers: "Many Richmond postal workers walked off the job in solidarity with the wildcat post office strike in March 1970. I joined the strike in the middle of its second day, returning mail from a special delivery detail after someone reminded me on the street that I was a 'scab.'"[54]

Joyce Robinson, an African American postal clerk who in 2005 served as the APWU education director, was a member of Richmond UFPC Local 199 in 1970.

She did not recall any strike activity there but does remember that "we took two strike votes," adding that "we would have gone out" in Richmond if the strike had continued.[55] The *Richmond Times-Dispatch*, covering the strike votes taken by the local NALC and National Alliance branches, expressed concern over the local NALC's vote to strike March 28 if a settlement was not reached. In Charlotte, the NALC members voted against striking, but nearly half publicly expressed enthusiasm for it, alarming their branch leadership.[56] The rank-and-file debate also revealed some divisions, especially between regions.

In the months after the strike, one of the most bitter debates ever to appear in the pages of the NALC *Postal Record* ensued on all sides of the issue—the most contentious being the South's putative lack of action. Branch scribe John Susleck of San Francisco, a strike veteran, taunted the South in the May 1970 edition: "I would ask of my fellow branch scribes in the southland, 'will the south rise again' or were you too busy drinking those mint juleps."[57] Art Miller of the Buffalo NALC told how a patron actually heckled him for cowardice in going back to work before the wildcat ended: the best comeback he could manage was "you should see my Southern brothers."[58]

And from Flushing, New York, came this retort to a March entry in the *Postal Record* from a Madisonville, Kentucky, scribe who had objected to higher "area wages" proposed by strikers for the urban North: "Well the areas are divided, as shown in the recent strike we just had. I didn't hear of any Southern State going out with us, in sympathy or otherwise. Seems like you are living pretty good on $8,000 a year."[59]

On the other hand, a Michigan scribe called the "area wage" proposal divisive, seconded by a Winston-Salem, North Carolina, scribe who noted his branch had split on striking. The latter's loyalty to the national office and defensiveness over not striking was a common reaction among NALC southern scribes: "Since when do the [NALC union] Brothers in New York, Chicago, Detroit, etc. think they should get more for carrying mail than we do here in the South? . . . Some of you think that just because we did not walk out and you did, you deserve more; well, you don't. And put this in your pipe and smoke it—if our National Officers (all of them, not just Gus Johnson), call a walkout, we will be right there, pounding the pavement just as all the good [union] brothers here in the South will be doing."[60]

Taking a cue from NALC president Rademacher's charges of "communist influence" in the strike, the NALC scribe for the once-segregated Albany, Georgia, branch—a city that was a battleground in the early 1960s civil rights struggle—cautioned letter carriers to beware of "SDS and Weatherman" militants who had "wormed" their way into the post office and the NALC.[61] Incensed that their patriotism and autonomous actions were under question,

Herman Sandbank of New York proudly praised the strike, denounced Rademacher for red-baiting them, and proposed that Rademacher and other "old school" national officers needed to be taught a lesson "by the rank and file."[62]

Despite popular alienation with the "area wages" proposal combined with loyalty to President Rademacher and misgivings or opposition to striking the federal government, there nonetheless appeared in the pages of the *Postal Record* some southern support for a strike if the NALC leadership called it. Interestingly, this conditional strike support included Birmingham and Houston—cities that had Jim Crow branches just ten years before. And an oft-forgotten element in the settling of the strike was the threat by many NALC branches to join a planned nationwide strike—first on March 28 and subsequently on April 15—one that national union leaders felt compelled to support if postal workers' demands were not met.[63] The extraordinary strike had now provoked the previously unthinkable official response: an offer by the federal government to negotiate if the strikers returned to work.

TURNING POINT

In making his March 20 offer of negotiation to James Rademacher and other postal union leaders, Secretary of Labor George Shultz reminded them of what he argued were their common interests: "There's only one thing worse than a wildcat strike—a wildcat strike that succeeds." Meanwhile, Rademacher had assembled more than 300 NALC branch leaders and state association presidents who gave him negotiating power, provided that he propose action within the week if an agreement was not reached. Rademacher asked for their help in getting carriers back to work. But absent any concrete proposals, many rank and filers, especially in New York, refused to budge. This led President Nixon to declare a national emergency along with the unprecedented act of calling up troops to replace federal civilian workers on Monday, March 23, at the same time acknowledging that postal workers were "underpaid" and also had "other grievances."[64] Most mainstream media editorials called the strike harmful to the nation, echoing Nixon that the strike threatened the very "survival" of the government.[65] The government itself was not threatened, but it had lost control of a significant sector of government labor. Nixon sent unarmed troops to try to demoralize and break the strike at its epicenter and thus also send a message to any federal workers contemplating similar actions. But strikers in New York were contemptuous of Nixon's move that also increased the ire of postal workers elsewhere who had hesitated or even opposed the strike. And while government and military sources praised the troops for "moving" millions of pieces of mail, soldiers often practiced worker solidarity and passive protest, including deliberately sabotaging the processing of mail and openly fraternizing with strikers.[66]

MBPU strike veteran Eleanor Bailey, among others, pointed out that many postal and other union members belonged to the National Guard and thus had little incentive to break the strike. A standard mainstream media strike narrative depicted the troops overwhelmed by the work despite genuine attempts to try to move mountains of mail. But NALC Branch 36 strike veteran Al Marino laughed as he remembered: "Nixon claimed the National Guard was moving the mail, and the Guardsmen said 'Yes, we moved it from here to there!'"[67] Photos taken of military personnel during the strike also reveal the troops' frustration facing rows of "pigeonhole cases," unable to match the speed and ability required of the clerks' job—with tons of mail still requiring processing, not to mention delivery. Avoiding public displays of antipathy toward the troops also provided postal workers an opportunity to demonstrate their loyalty as public workers whose jobs were vital to national communications and finance. Indeed, polls showed the public backing the strikers despite also supporting Nixon's sending troops to New York. And postal workers were cheered by patrons when they did return.[68]

It also helped the strikers' cause to have struck at a vulnerable time for Nixon, who had already widened the war in Viet Nam by secretly bombing Cambodia for months before deciding to invade it in April 1970.[69] The sight of U.S. troops "invading" New York to break a postal strike provided a disturbing parallel to the U.S. occupation of the Indochinese peninsula, and the media even used Viet Nam War metaphors like "escalation" to describe the spreading of the strike. But strikers turned this military "occupation" to their advantage as a way to demonstrate their patriotism, public service, and courage. Richard Thomas said he and his colleagues were not intimidated by Nixon's sending in the military: "We were already former troops! Some of them were former postal workers—the ones that were in the National Guard. We were standing our ground!"[70]

Postal workers, their skepticism notwithstanding, returned to work not because of the troops' presence, but because NALC officials James Rademacher and Gus Johnson told them (falsely) that an attractive agreement had been reached with the administration. They understood that the threat of court-imposed fines could have financially crippled their unions that had begun the wildcat with no strike funds. Al Marino observed that Branch 36 went back to work without even taking a vote, hopeful that the agreement was authentic. And Detroit NPU strike veteran Doug Holbrook remembers: "Moe Biller called me . . . and he told me that this strike has got to end because we can't afford to lose our dues check off."[71]

Wildcat strikes are limited in what they can accomplish given the structure of union-management relations. In this case the federal government was acting as management with the laws and courts on its side. Yet its brief military occupation of the post office became bad theater. Intended by Nixon to remind postal workers that they were governed by federal law, the occupation instead revealed that the post office could not easily find willing or able replacements—even among the most ostensibly loyal federal workers, namely the troops. Photographs of postal workers cheering the departing troops on March 25 before returning to work the following day in fact suggested a strike victory, not the "crumbling" announced by the mass media—a narrative further contradicted by their own photographs of letter carriers smiling and hugging patrons, walking out of their respective post offices to their mail routes smiling and laughing with New York postmaster John Strachan and Chicago postmaster Henry W. McGee. Meanwhile, strikers were defiantly threatening to strike again if their demands were not met.[72] The strike had started, ended, and been the most sustained in New York, but across the nation postal workers had asserted themselves.

LESSONS

Aaron Brenner offered this cogent speculation for New York's central role in the strike: "worst working conditions . . . highest cost of living . . . most willing to strike . . . [Branch 36 elected leaders' lack of] experience and respect of the membership . . . the rank-and-file . . . well organized."[73] To that list could be added the various militant traditions within New York's local unions that combined with the black labor protest and civic traditions. Yet many of those same conditions also existed elsewhere. Labor relations scholar J. Joseph Loewenberg has pointed to the post office's indecisive reaction to the New York walkout as having unintentionally encouraged the "spread" of "strike fever" as soon as the "spell—and the law—of not striking against the government had been broken."[74] And even though the National Alliance leadership lagged behind their own rank and file, the civil rights movement of which it was a key ingredient had indirectly influenced the strike. Sociologists Larry Isaac and Lars Christiansen point to the civil rights movement's role in helping revive labor movement militancy in the 1960s, especially in the public sector.[75] Black postal workers in 1970 were among the most militant strikers— as well as some of the most cautious union leaders.

"It is obvious that blacks played a major part" in the strike, said former Chicago Alliance president Countee Abbott, "because . . . in major metropolitan areas . . . [such as] Chicago we were like 75 percent or more, other major cities we were probably 50–60 percent. New York and Philadelphia of course played a major part in making the strike a success."[76] Not only did blacks form majorities or at least large minorities in urban post offices (including almost 40 percent of New York City), but they were also highly unionized and militant. By the 1960s, two-thirds of African Americans were living in urban areas.[77] The *National Alliance* published the percentages of blacks in major cities in 1972 that read like a roll call of the 1970 strike, including New York, Chicago, Detroit, Cleveland, Philadelphia, Newark, and Oakland.[78]

But during the postal strike, the major media only occasionally paid special attention to black participation other than in a few photographs. Feature stories on individual black postal workers never reflected any unique black experience. Photographs and texts, however, were telling two different stories to newspaper readers across the country: the former communicated that this was a highly integrated workforce that had struck together (with blacks playing key roles at strike meetings in New York), while the latter implied that this was mainly white mailmen on strike. If we speculate that the media's failure to discuss postal office inequality was because no interviewed strikers who were interviewed brought it up when asked, we can also safely assume that had they at least asked any Alliance members, the latter would have gladly done so.[79]

It may seem counterintuitive that the strike would be led by letter carriers, with a historically more conservative union (the NALC) that included many older white men in a craft considered privileged, the work often solitary. Why was the strike not initiated by the unions of workers whose jobs were more socialized, namely clerks and mail handlers, many of whom were black, female, veterans, and young? Would the MBPU have gone out first if the NALC had not struck? There is no way to know that now. But as anger among postal workers had risen so high in March 1970—especially in New York and in particular following an inadequate and delayed pay raise—it is likely that some kind of walkout there would have occurred. Whether that walkout would have spread and become as successful as the one that really happened is also speculative. But what is certain is how crucial to the ultimate success of the 1970 postal wildcat strike was the cross-craft cooperation in many largely black urban postal facilities that had effective shop floor leadership. Equally certain is that the alienation felt by carriers in Branch 36 and the NALC in general paved the way for NALC strikers' defiance of their union and federal law in wildcatting. As then NALC Branch 36 vice president Herman Sandbank exclaimed following the strike: "They finally changed the N.A.L.C. from an Association to a Union."[80]

Although the MBPU was militant, its leadership could not legally call a strike.

It had to respond to its members, who generally respected and followed the leadership. But once the strike began, unity and leadership were crucial. Even the small UFPC New York City Local 10 struck over their national union's objections.[81] MBPU mail handler and strike veteran Richard Thomas's narrative provides insight into a number of issues: the overcoming of racial divisions among the strikers; the strike's rank-and-file character as well as its leadership across craft lines; and the key role of mail handlers, many of whom were young, angry black veterans who often wore their military fatigues on the shop floor: "We controlled the means of production," Thomas said. "So we didn't go in and the trucks couldn't go out." Thomas also credits NALC strike leader Vincent Sombrotto: "The reason the strike happened in New York was because of Sombrotto, my belief. . . . Basically he was very militant. His leadership was very good as far as I was concerned. . . . We just felt that we were going to stick together. Color or anything like that kind of went out the window at that particular time. We weren't thinking on that particular level at that particular time. We were only thinking about the benefits that could be gained, which is better salary. . . . And that's really what sparked it."[82]

Meanwhile, NALC national leaders were able to both corral the wildcat and exploit it before and after it had ended, as it set a March 28 deadline—then another for April 15 (when income tax returns are typically due) for Congress and the Nixon administration to act.[83] During the month of March, the postal wildcat competed for headlines with the Viet Nam War, the Cambodian military coup that overthrew the government of Prince Norodom Sihanouk, and clashes between the NAACP and President Nixon over what he called "forced school integration." Newspaper editorials denounced the postal wildcat strike as part of urban "lawlessness" ("law and order" having been a Nixon campaign slogan). But the media also had to consider public sympathy, as strikers maintained good public relations, including an avoidance of violence.[84]

Anticommunism, still used by opponents of progressive politics, had lost its ability to paralyze labor and civil rights movements—including the red-baiting of strikers by NALC president Rademacher. By all accounts, in fact, strikers rejected offers by the organized left to help leaflet and picket.[85] On the other hand, it was not just black postal workers who were influenced by the black freedom movement. For example, Ben Zemsky, president of UFPC Local 251 in Brooklyn, declared himself in favor of the strike and cited the civil rights movement as an inspiration. Zemsky's local, in fact, was one of the first and among the few UFPC locals to strike—most of the original Brooklyn Local 251 members having left the NFPOC in 1959 to help form the Brooklyn Postal Union-NPU.[86] And NALC Branch 36 strike leader Tom Germano had allied himself with black militant leaders Julius Lester and H. Rap Brown when he was at Queens College prior to entering the post office, and he had become involved in grassroots politics.[87]

Historical activism also helped prepare the strikers with their prior daily confrontations with management on the shop floor. Eleanor Bailey recalls Arthur Ryland, a prominent black MBPU official, active since the 1930s: "Oh my God, that was my idol! . . . His English was so impeccable! . . . He was my mentor. . . . He knew our contract backwards and forwards. . . . Phil Seligman was our master parliamentarian. These gentlemen that we had when I came in were masters at whatever they did. . . . They wanted to make the union a powerful force. . . . '*You didn't mess with Metro.*' . . . We had that reputation."[88]

Bailey's observation highlights how historical change includes both continuity and upheaval, and in the case of black postal workers it combines all the events and struggles of the 1940s and 1960s in the post office and its unions. The popular notion of "New York exceptionalism"—whereby social movements in that city have often served as a model for the rest of the nation—was both an overstated cliché and an actual phenomenon. As Eleanor Bailey put it: working conditions in New York were especially bad and "the lines were blurred" between postal workers of all ethnicities: "We were quite a militant group, whites and blacks," she said of New York City postal workers. "I don't think we even thought about color." Joann Flagler, originally from a working-class background in South Carolina, put it succinctly: "This is a labor city."[89]

The unity found in the New York postal unions and on the shop floor made New York City crucial to the strike's initiation and success. There was no magic in New York City air that blew away racial divides at the post office. The unity found on the strike picket lines also emerged from prior battles among workers. Cleveland Morgan recalls that when he started at the post office in the early 1960s there were far fewer black letter carriers than in 1970, and he actually encountered more problems with bigoted behavior by white coworkers than white managers: "I experienced a lot," he said; "I fought back." But after the strike he said that Sombrotto, whom he called more advanced on civil rights than the NALC national office, won election as Branch 36 president with black support: "He had a vision. There wasn't that many blacks on the slate before, but then when he came in he had . . . a lot of blacks with him."[90]

The merger that postal unions had been unable to formally accomplish over the decades was now being accomplished in practice by the rank and file, led by the one city that actually did have a historically functioning coalition of union locals. Occupational segregation still assigned blacks to the lower-paid crafts (levels one through four), such as the mail handlers. But Richard

Thomas expressed how relatively trivial those differences seemed when no craft job paid a living wage: "Just twenty cents more an hour" is how he summed up the wage differential between largely black and Puerto Rican mail handlers on the one hand versus clerks and mainly white carriers on the other: "We just felt that we couldn't live off of that kind of salary. . . . We made $2.75, they made $2.95. . . . We were all in the same pot. . . . This was a strike that involved everyone."[91]

For black New York postal workers like Richard Thomas, Joann Flagler, and Eleanor Bailey to argue that the strike "was not about color" indicates a diminished effectiveness played by white supremacy in the daily work life of that city's post office; the possibility of worker coalition across crafts; and a common awareness of similar economic needs despite barriers built on race, gender, and craft. By contrast, Countee Abbott—a National Alliance strike veteran despite his organization's ambivalent official posture—emphasized, as have seen, the particular role played in the strike by blacks. Postal workers were forging practical unity out of historical struggles that included the fight for equality and labor rights.

The strike represented an interest convergence on the part of all postal workers. For black strike participants, this action seemingly represented a common struggle—overall successful despite the fact that black workers had every reason to be "thinking about color" as long as racial differentials continued to operate in daily work life. The strike flourished where blacks and whites had already coalesced on the shop floor; where white supremacist practice by white workers had been marginalized; and where the local labor atmosphere encouraged militant labor activity. Where the strike failed to take hold often tended to be where postal salaries were at least adequate for local standards of living; where loyalty to union leadership prevailed; and where white supremacy had historically flourished, including Jim Crow branches and locals.

Preconceived notions of striker militancy would be just as wrong to portray blacks in the struck areas as having been universally militant as they would to claim that blacks merely followed whites in the strike. Both would miss the point of the fusion of militant labor traditions that made the strike successful in the North, Midwest, and parts of the Far West.[92] Similarly, regional preconceptions would dismiss the South as "too backward and divided" to participate in this militant labor action, ignoring how largely black postal union locals in cities such as Richmond, Charlotte, Miami, and Houston were actually picking up interest in the strike even as other regions were returning to work. Southern postal workers were among those especially angered after Nixon called troops to New York to move the mail.[93] And assumptions about regional disparities in terms of postal worker militancy and economic desperation have also been overstated. The economic situation of postal workers in the urban North may have indeed been worse than that of their colleagues in the South or the West. But southern cities also saw postal workers forced to augment their income with second jobs and welfare, as Joseph Henry in D.C. pointed out. The same week that postal workers went on strike, Atlanta sanitation workers also struck for a living wage—a year after the Atlanta National Alliance had organized a march with the NAACP and the National Urban League demanding that postal salaries approximate similar public service jobs.[94]

Postal unionists were influenced by more militant unions, and were often more progressive than organized labor in general. The example of D.C. is especially instructive: a city without a history of industrial labor militancy and long saddled by Jim Crow divisions between workers nonetheless saw black and white postal workers voting to strike. There the local NALC president, Elliot Peacock, an African American who had for years been part of the fight for equality in that union, like many officials did his best to muffle a rank-and-file upsurge that threatened the status quo for both the government and the union leadership.

Postal workers defied the government and their own union leadership, and African Americans played crucial roles on all sides of the strike. They were the letter carriers who stopped mail delivery, the urban clerks and mail handlers who halted mail processing, the union leaders opposed to it, and postmasters of installations affected most by it. Blacks and other postal workers joined a widespread labor insurgency in staging the largest wildcat strike in U.S. labor history, demonstrating workers' power at a time when layoffs, plant closings, and automation were already hurting private sector workforces and unions. But civil rights unionism faced major challenges in the reorganized post office, revealing limitations as well as strengths of the strike.

The black labor protest tradition that has been referred to as "civil rights unionism" in the mid-twentieth century in fact helped fuel what on the surface appeared to have been a "colorblind" spontaneous rank-and-file labor protest. There was a "New York exceptionalism" based on that city's mixed protest traditions, including southern U.S. black migrants, Caribbean immigrants, Irish, Germans, Italians, and Jews, combined with the northeast region's left-labor industrial struggle traditions.[95]

Out of that unique fusion emerged the engine that started and drove the nationwide strike. But the strike also depended on other regions that have received far less publicity for their role—the West, Midwest, and South. The strike itself was significant as it represented an unprecedented defiance of the ban on strikes for federal workers; their rejection of postal union leadership in creating and sustaining an unauthorized strike; and an escalation of social movement militancy by federal workers in a largely black sector, willing to paralyze the nation's means of communication and finance in order to achieve a living wage and recognition equal to that of private sector workers. Postal workers' previous shop floor clashes with management should have already contradicted a popular image (and self-image) of postal worker "docility," but the strike shattered that image for good.[96]

Rank-and-file militancy and civil rights unionism helped galvanize the 1970 postal strike as a protest against government treatment despite the conservatism of many union leaders. The old postal labor relations lobbying process had broken down. Leaders of the National Alliance had fallen behind their members, many of whom joined this mass uprising. The outcome of the strike also revealed limitations in launching direct actions even as it exposed the vulnerability of the status quo to popular protest. The strike's aftermath also created a dilemma for the Alliance as well as the NPU—the only union to officially support the strike. To win a place at the bargaining table for both unions would mean giving up their independence. Could they afford to do that?

CHAPTER ELEVEN

POST-STRIKE
(1970—1971)

The nationwide postal wildcat strike was over by March 25, 1970. Now what? "Euphoria" is how William H. Burrus Jr., then vice president of the Cleveland NPU local of the NPU, described the feeling of having taken on the federal government and won.[1] Richard Thomas, a mail handler strike participant then with the MBPU-NPU, remembers: "After the strike, after we went back to work, everything was, 'OK what's next?' . . . And everything was left in the hands of the Congress, and the powers that be to formulate what they were gonna do. We felt that our message was heard."[2]

"We were lost sheep!" exclaimed National Association of Letter Carriers (NALC) Branch 36 activist Al Marino. "No information! I'm surprised it went the way it did without leadership. It was just amazing!"[3] "The Postal Reorganization Act [PRA] could not have passed without the strike," concluded Branch 36 strike leader Vincent Sombrotto, noting that the original 1969 postal reform bill had only covered pay raises and corporatization, and that strikers had not even demanded full collective bargaining.[4] William Burrus concurred: "We had no idea what collective bargaining meant at the time. We basically wanted more money. But it was a good punch line to say you wanted collective bargaining rights, too. . . . We didn't get a formal seniority system until 1971 with bargaining. Prior to that we had an informal system, but it was ignored."[5]

The heads of the "exclusive" postal unions met January 21 and March 25 to craft demands for full collective bargaining and binding arbitration if any future contract negotiations broke down.[6] Meanwhile, a change in the workplace atmosphere could be detected, as MBPU strike leader Eleanor Bailey remembers: "We had a lot more power because . . . lower level and the middle level supervisors . . . they were so happy that we got what we got because of the fact that they were going to get more money. . . . And when it came down to actual discipline, they stayed off it for a while."[7] Frank Orapello similarly observed that "management was rooting for us. . . . And you know, after the strike . . . they started respecting us."[8] Thomas, Sombrotto, Marino, Orapello,

Bailey and other postal workers waited on the federal government to decide their fate. But there were also post-strike repercussions within and between the postal unions.

In D.C., Joseph Henry, then NALC Branch 142, told me in 2005 that his branch had been "greatly satisfied" with the post-strike wage increase and the fact that the new USPS would be government-owned and not a private corporation.[9] On the other hand, Countee Abbott, strike leader with the NAPFE, remembers how the Alliance and the NPU had to fight just to keep what collective bargaining rights they had previously enjoyed, as they watched full collective bargaining rights go exclusively to the AFL-CIO postal unions: "In the Postal Service's zeal to get a collective bargaining agreement, they had to have somebody to bargain with. . . . What happened is that . . . the [National] Labor Relations Act requires that in collective bargaining . . . the Labor Department has to define what is an appropriate bargaining unit. . . . After the transitional period they just pushed the organizations into 'exclusive' [status], they never held elections. . . . We [the Alliance and the NPU] went into court to sue, a compromise was worked out, there was an amendment to the Postal Reorganization Act [PRA] . . . that grandfathered the National Alliance [and] the NPU . . . that we would maintain . . . the right to address new employees, . . . bulletin boards, . . . [and] dues check-off for our members."[10]

The 1970 postal wildcat strike has been chronicled as a total triumph by virtually every labor historian and postal union writing on the subject. But the two industrial postal unions—the Alliance and the NPU—now warned of pitfalls with the reorganized post office. There is no doubt that the outcome of the postal wildcat strike represented a tremendous victory for postal workers. Yet it was also a qualified victory for blacks and indeed all postal workers. I argue that a more balanced view than is usually promoted would profit scholars and activists looking for lessons on both the strike's possibilities and limitations.[11]

Rank-and-file militancy had forced change in the post office and the unions, winning what the unions had been unable to accomplish in years of lobbying, bargaining, and pleading: substantial pay increases that were comparable to similar occupations and that brought some measure of pride to the job; a shorter length of time to top pay; and full collective bargaining rights. The mere fact of a rank-and-file nationwide wildcat strike was the product of an era, which inspired disempowered workers everywhere and altered power dynamics at the post office and in its unions. Most wildcats are spontaneous and local, but this one began with actual strike votes at local union meetings in New York before going nationwide.

Yet the rank-and-file strike momentum was quickly co-opted as the balance of power shifted back to the bargaining table between union and government

Countee S. Abbott (left), a 1970 postal strike participant in Chicago, with Ashby Smith (center) and Snow Grigsby, ca. 1969. Abbott was president of the National Alliance of Postal and Federal Employees (NAPFE) District Seven (Illinois, Michigan, Minnesota, and Wisconsin) until 1974, Smith was the national president of NAPFE until 1970, and Grigsby was the editor of the *National Alliance* until 1973. Courtesy of the National Alliance of Postal and Federal Employees.

leaders. There was good and bad news, and the good news was twofold. First, postal workers won many of their demands and set a precedent of strike action that could (and would) be subsequently used as a threat by postal union officials during contract negotiations. Second, the success of the strike encouraged democratic militant tendencies in the participating unions that challenged and in some cases overturned their respective entrenched leaderships. The bad news, however, was significant: the failure to win the right to strike and the exclusion from representation of the two unions that had championed equality and industrial unionism—the National Alliance and the NPU.

The union hierarchies and the federal government channeled the 1970 nationwide postal wildcat strike—an astonishing rank-and-file action—into a handful of exclusively recognized unions within the reorganized quasi-government USPS. Under the PRA that President Nixon signed into law on August 12, 1970, the USPS became an "independent establishment" within the executive branch, administered by an appointed Board of Governors. It was empowered to set postage rates and mandated to continue to provide universal service as a profitable business without government subsidies. Following the strike, postal workers, still under civil service, were provided substantial pay raises (6 percent retroactive to December 1969, with 8 percent added when the law was signed) and were required to work far fewer years (eight instead of twenty-one) to reach top pay. The PRA granted full collective bargaining rights to seven of the post office's nine unions (the six AFL-CIO unions plus the independent NRLCA) during this transitional period before the first contract was ultimately signed in 1971. The first contract was signed between the USPS and just four unions: the NRLCA and three AFL-CIO unions, the NALC, the NPMHU, and the APWU, the last a fusion of the UFPC, its former rival the NPU, and three smaller craft unions. Much had changed from 1970 to 1971 in the post office.

The National Alliance and NPU picketed postal contract negotiations in 1970 and again in 1971 while filing suit in court against the USPS and the other unions for excluding them. In 1971, after the lawsuit failed to win them a place at the table, the NPU suddenly joined its former rival the UFPC and three smaller unions in forming the APWU. The Alliance and the NPU severed ties as the Alliance defiantly remained independent, active, and outside the collective bargaining process. The Alliance avoided collapse by shifting gears to focus especially on EEO (equal employment opportunity) advocacy along with other forms of worker representation, with its official literature also taking on a more militant rank-and-file labor tone. In the months following the strike's end, New York's postal unions pressed the case for rank-and-file demands such as "area wages" and the right to strike. They also tried to form a joint local bargaining committee as debates over militancy raged in the NAPFE, the NALC, and the APWU. Just as they had during the strike, blacks figured largely among rank-and-file leaders in the strike's aftermath that saw the USPS shifting operations to white suburban areas, hoping to cut costs as well as to attract a more docile workforce less inclined to strike or challenge their authority.[12]

MANAGING MILITANCY

If federal officials were surprised by the wildcat strike, they were quick to take advantage of the negotiations that postal union leaders were using to convince strikers to return to work. Those negotiations threatened to marginalize the independent industrial unions as well as the efforts of rank-and-file postal strikers. The day before the strike ended, a March 24 press conference in Washington, D.C., saw Postmaster General Winton M. Blount peppered with questions from the press challenging the shifting positions taken by Congress, the Nixon administration, and Blount himself during the strike. One reporter asked if Blount would make a pledge to postal workers who had been saying they would go back to work upon receiving some assurance, in the reporter's words, "that there was a general sympathy for their plight in terms of wages and if they also got a pledge that you were going to do something to improve their lot." Blount's reply revealed the dilemma that he and other government officials faced, as well as his own actual powerlessness: "Let me make this clear. As Secretary [of Labor] Shultz said, there is only one thing worse than a wildcat strike, and that is a successful wildcat strike. We are not going to make any prior commitments to any specific legislation. But I think that it must be understood that the President very clearly said that he understood the problems that were concerning the postal employees."[13]

Blount finished the press conference by connecting postal workers' pay and other grievances that had precipitated the strike to what he called "postal reform," by which he and other government officials meant corporatist reorganization. Clearly not happy with the chain of events, or that postal workers had achieved more leverage by striking, Blount, like Nixon, was forced to concede the postal workers' justifiable anger that had led them to strike. Blount had no actual negotiating power, although he subsequently tried but failed to impose a gag order on postal workers testifying before Congress. In a press statement just two days before, he had even alluded to his own pre-strike warnings about low postal pay. Yet at the March 24 press conference he denied "that pay is hostage for [postal] reform."[14]

For his part, Nixon, despite having been elected a little over a year before on a platform of law and order, was not in a good position politically to actually enforce that program here, given the mass support the postal workers enjoyed. And despite their denials, the Nixon administration in fact had been holding postal pay raises hostage for postal reform. It was postal workers who forced the issue. But Blount and Nixon were not the only ones concerned with this dangerous precedent of postal worker empowerment.

An undated memo (probably issued soon after the strike ended) was circulated from Brian J. Gillespie in the USPS's Labor Relations Division of the Bureau of Personnel to the division's director, John N. Remissong. In it, Gillespie discussed the options of punishing the 1970 strikers while on the whole urging caution. Gillespie wanted to set an example to prevent "another wildcat walkout," but not "turn the clock back" or "tear the fabric" of postal labor relations. After all, he wrote, the strike had been really aimed more at the Nixon administration and Congress, not at postal management. To cancel "striking union recognition," he warned, could produce "raiding" between the unions. Gillespie also recommended against canceling "local agreements" because that could hamper labor relations, despite what he thought would be a potential benefit of doing so: "Eliminate NPU and Alliance in struck locals."[15]

Why did the strikers return to work without ironclad agreements and assurances of representation for all unions? It must be remembered that these were loyal union members who did not have a lot of options. They had already taken a huge leap by striking when for years the mantra of postal workers had been "you don't strike the federal government." Union leadership had rushed to make promises to their members to catch up with the militant rank and file. Even then, many strikers were reluctant to return to work because the agreements were not in writing.[16] This was not the first strike to unite workers previously divided along race, gender, or craft lines using the common denominator of pay and labor rights. Yet now there was still no movement within the AFL-CIO postal unions to include the NPU and the National Alliance.

The strike had forced a sea change in the post office. Black postal workers had played a significant role as part of a rank-and-file insurgency that had forced the federal government to negotiate. This put both the administration and postal union leadership in a bind. The administration did not want to reward defiance of its authority and federal law. Nor did it want to appear cruel in the public imagination in the way it treated underpaid and popular public servants. A postal management report written in September 1970 acknowledged in retrospect that its strike contingency plan had not only been vague, but had not even provided for the actual contingency of all post offices going out on strike simultaneously, much less staying out eight days.[17] For that matter the strikers had no contingency plan either: some who walked out early also returned early, others debated on the sidelines whether to walk out, while still others were determined to stay out indefinitely. But as soon as the last strikers returned to work on March 25, the battleground shifted from the picket line to the negotiating table, with officials of both the AFL-CIO postal unions and the federal government looking nervously over their shoulders at the union rank and file. The suddenness and strength of the strike had been sufficient to scare the administration and postal union leaders to negotiate to get strikers back to work. Now union leaders saw the rank and file as a bargaining chip they could call upon in future contract talks.[18]

Yet as broken as the previous system had been, that prior combination of "collective begging" and limited collective bargaining for postal unions had at least provided an opportunity for the two militant industrial unions—the NPU and the Alliance—to negotiate with management and challenge the AFL-CIO postal unions for representation rights on a local, regional, and even national basis, as well as pushing them to take tougher stands on behalf of postal workers. That was about to change. The new process threatened to exclude the NPU and Alliance from the bargaining table. Negotiations were underway between the post office, the AFL-CIO unions, and the NRLCA using the private sector winner-take-all model, where individual unions fight to become exclusive bargaining agents.[19]

During the 1970 strike negotiations, AFL-CIO president George Meany intervened and secured an agreement from the six AFL-CIO postal unions and the independent NRLCA to negotiate solely on pay raises—and even then he urged Congress to drop the retroactive part of the 8 percent postal pay raise.[20] Anger had now grown among many strikers who sensed that they had been forced by Meany and the AFL-CIO postal union heads to accept postal reorganization in exchange for pay raises that were not as much as they had been promised. The final "Memorandum of Agreement" between the post office and its unions provided for "pay increases of 14 percent—6 percent retroactive to December 27, 1969, and another 8 percent effective" when the PRA was passed; support for the new postal corporation; collective bargaining to govern wages, hours, and working conditions, with binding arbitration to handle all impasses; and fewer years required for postal workers to reach their pay grade's top level, from twenty-one to eight.[21]

NALC president James Rademacher, meanwhile, had supported President Nixon's postal corporation but was willing now to separate that question from issues of pay because the opposition within his union to corporatization was so overwhelming. That issue separation did not last long. After negotiating for about a week with the Nixon administration, all the AFL-CIO postal unions by April 2, 1970, had agreed to link pay raises to postal reorganization. Yet the founding of the USPS as an independent establishment within the federal government's executive branch (with Congress now removed from mediating or setting policy) was essentially the original postal corporation proposal of Presidents Johnson and Nixon—but with an important difference. The USPS expected great productivity gains and corporate autonomy in exchange for labor's salary increases. The unions, on the other hand, according to Vern Baxter, while winning pay raises in exchange for reorganization, still fought to keep collective bargaining rights over technological changes (mechanization) that would affect jobs and working conditions.[22]

New York City postal workers were the last to go back to work, and many considered walking out later that spring and still again the following year.[23] The MBPU's April 1970 Union Mail congratulated its members for gains won during the strike while condemning the leaders of the AFL-CIO postal unions: "You Did It," the headline proudly proclaimed to its members. "But . . . National Craft Union Leaders Sold Out New York Postal Workers."[24]

NALC leaders had exaggerated the agreement reached with the administration that turned out to be a 6 percent rather than a 12 percent retroactive raise plus full health benefits and area wages, and mere "negotiations on amnesty" rather than guaranteed full amnesty for strikers (although no one was fired for striking). New York NALC and MBPU branches and locals threatened to strike again. Industrial unionism was threatening the craft structure as the MBPU claimed that it had admitted over a thousand former NALC Branch 36 letter carriers into its ranks. Discussions of the MBPU merging with Branch 36, interrupted once before in June 1970, were terminated for good when NALC president Rademacher placed Branch 36 under trusteeship (i.e., temporarily assumed control over their affairs) in 1971 for planning a new strike vote in conjunction with the MBPU.[25] Meanwhile, National Alliance president Ashby Smith at a March 25, 1970, press conference made the dubious threat that his membership would walk off the job if EO 11491 was not amended. Citing the support of the NAACP and the National Urban League in this new struggle against discrimination, Smith noted the historic role his union played in representing all black postal workers, with 40,000 still claiming Alliance membership.[26]

Then, on October 21, 1970, after months of denouncing the AFL-CIO craft unions for exclusionary tactics, the Alliance, MBPU, and the NPU (the MBPU's parent union) filed a petition in U.S. District Court against the postmaster general and the seven "exclusive" unions to halt their bargaining and include the Alliance and NPU. This was an explicitly antidiscrimination, civil rights–based challenge to postal management and organized labor, reminiscent of the NAACP's protest of the National Labor Relations Act (NLRA) in 1935 that enshrined white AFL unions as exclusive bargaining agents in the private sector. This was a challenge now that arguably should have been done long before in both the private and public sectors. The Alliance's new president, Robert L. White, noted in the November *Postal Alliance* that their progressive coalition was far from being a minor player among the postal unions: "The NPU and the Alliance are unaffiliated industrial unions. NPU has 600 local affiliates, the Alliance 147. Our two unions respectively are the third and fourth largest in the postal service."[27]

The 1970–71 NPU–National Alliance coalition was a united front of independent militant industrial postal unions. When post-strike negotiations began on March 26, 1970, between the exclusive unions and the post office at the headquarters of the NPMHU's parent union, the Laborers International Union of North America (LIUNA), the reaction by the NPU and the Alliance was a kind

ALLIANCE PICKETS SELL OUT MEETING

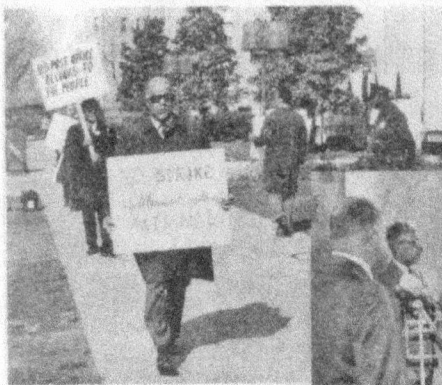

Alliance Pres. Smith leads picket line at sellout site.

Sellout story told to reporters by D.C. Pres. Robert White.

Sellout told to T.V., radio and press by Pres. Smith.

A montage of photos shows the National Alliance, joined by the NPU, at the Sonesta Hotel in Washington, D.C., picketing post-strike negotiations between the post office and postal unions with national "exclusive" representation status, March 27, 1970. Shown are the Alliance's national president Ashby Smith (left and center photos) and D.C. branch president Robert White, who would be elected national president later that year. Courtesy of the National Alliance of Postal and Federal Employees.

of wildcat strike reenactment, as Moe Biller and other NPU officials disrupted the meeting by demanding entry. The next day the NPU and the Alliance picketed the new meeting site at the Sonesta Hotel. (They would do so again yet again in February 1971 when they were excluded from postal union negotiations at USPS headquarters.)[28] But while the NPU was joining the Alliance in suing the other unions, it was also holding merger talks with the UFPC.[29]

On March 3, 1971, the NPU joined with the UFPC and three smaller craft unions in announcing the formation of the APWU. That ended the NPU's role as part of the independent government employee union coalition that had included the Alliance. Previously, there had even been hints of an Alliance and NPU merger. Just the month before, in fact, the *National Alliance* had published photos of the Alliance-NPU joint picketing of the negotiations in Washington, D.C., between the AFL-CIO unions and postal management, from which they were both excluded. But now as a result of the UFPC-NPU merger, Alliance president Robert L. White wrote tersely in the March 1971 *National Alliance* that "it has been decided to terminate the partnership between the National Alliance and the National Postal Union."[30] Relegated to a marginal role for the first time, the Alliance was determined to continue advocating for black workers, as well as for equality at the post office and the other federal agencies.[31]

Was the NPU unprincipled to abandon its coalition with the Alliance and join the APWU? Longtime APWU activist and union officer Doug Holbrook concurs with the NPU's *Progressive* in its final 1971 editions: the merger was a step toward greater industrial unionism. However, for the first decade of its existence, the content of the *American Postal Worker* and APWU convention resolutions resembled the old UFPC *Union Postal Clerk* more than the old NPU's *Progressive*. While the final issues of the *Progressive* gave prominence to the NPU's fight for equality for both people of color and women, the new *American Postal Worker* provided little or no such coverage.[32] The *Progressive*'s sudden 1971 optimistic declaration of imminent industrial postal union merger came after almost a year of accusing AFL-CIO postal union leaders of "selling out." But the political terrain had changed, as the *Progressive* itself pointed out.[33] Postal unions were now governed not just by the PRA but also by EO 11491, which put them under the same federal labor provisions as those in private industry (including the 1947 Taft-Hartley Act), although they were still denied the right to strike.[34] No exclusive representation rights meant no place at the collective bargaining table. It was either join or be left out.

Alliance president White was emphatic in March 1971 that "the National Alliance has no intentions of even discussing merger with any other union." To do so, he said, would destroy the autonomous black character of their union along with their historical commitment to always defend black postal workers when other unions let them down.[35] Yet National Alliance labor relations director Countee Abbott has revealed that the APWU actually offered the Alliance a berth within the APWU: "We were like the civil rights arm of the postal service," he recalls, adding: "The idea was that the Alliance would be the 'enforcement of civil rights' arm of APWU." Abbott also remembered President White in 1971 immediately rejecting the idea with the declaration: "We wouldn't be merged, we'd be *submerged*."[36] Merger with an AFL-CIO postal union would have been their only way to avoid being excluded from collective bargaining, as those unions displayed no interest in supporting an independent militant black industrial union. For its part, the Alliance leadership only threatened to strike when about to lose their official recognition. In sum, what the postal unions gained in immediate pay raises and full collective bargaining rights was far greater than what they lost in public policy lobbying—at which the Alliance especially had excelled. The Alliance now had to adapt to the new format.

CRISIS IN THE ALLIANCE

Soon after the strike, the May 1970 edition of the *National Alliance* published something seldom seen in its pages: a letter critical of its national leadership. This particular letter seemed to speak for Alliance members throughout the country who had joined other strikers while wondering where their union officials had been. There was growing concern throughout the organization that they were going to be permanently squeezed out of the new collective bargaining arrangements. Some said this could have been avoided. "If the Alliance had been in the forefront of this strike, calling out its members in key postal installations, much long-delayed recognition and representation could have been gained at the Washington talks," charged the letter writer—an angry and disappointed New York City member who signed only the initials "G.M.W." The writer had participated in the strike and wondered why the Alliance had not joined it.[37] In that same issue, President Smith responded with a three-page position paper that called the strike "the wrong tactic at the wrong time." At the same time, referring to the Alliance as "*probably* the most militant union of government workers," Smith declared that "if further negotiations failed, it would call a march on Washington, and, if necessary a strike to protect itself from the adverse effects of Executive Order 11491."[38]

A month later Smith used much of that same language in testifying against exclusion before the House Post Office Committee. At the same time, this former author of the militant "Civil Rights Trail" *Postal Alliance* column now condemned striking as a tactic and blamed Nixon's order for damaging the Alliance in abolishing "formal recognition" because it "played into the hands of the more militant and less responsible members of the black community." Trying in vain to preserve his union's status as a "reasonable" federal employee lobby, Smith sounded every bit as conservative as the AFL-CIO postal union presidents.[39]

But "G.M.W." was not the only frustrated Alliance member. Smith's May 1970 position paper concluded on the same page as the regular column by Cleveland Alliance official Loraine M. Huston, who sympathetically offered that the strike, "unauthorized though it was, served as no other method could to expose the plight of postal employees to the general public."[40] And in the April 1970 *National Alliance*, its longtime editor Snow Grigsby employed evocative images and indirect language to identify with the strikers and criticize union officials (possibly including Smith): "While union leadership made every effort to get their members to stop picketing and return to their jobs, the work stoppage continued to spread from city to city. This action was interpreted by many people to mean that the union leadership was out of touch with the rank-and-file union member. . . . This has been a criticism leveled against union leadership. Plush carpeting, soft leather chairs, and walnut paneled desks in union offices, can make one forget what it's like to carry a mail bag, throw letters in slots in dusty old cases, and drag mail sacks, and take home a check every two weeks which doesn't cover all of the expenses."[41]

At its 1970 national convention a groundswell that blamed Smith for the Alliance's loss of official recognition made his presidency the first casualty of rank-and-file rebellions in the postal unions following the strike. Smith lost a close race to D.C.'s activist branch president Robert White, and activist Wesley Young was elected national vice president. Smith died the following year, having presided over the organization at both its strongest and most critical junctures.[42] Ironically, the National Alliance, D.C.'s largest postal union, had voted not to strike during the nationwide wildcat when White had been branch president. White had even taken credit for preventing a strike in D.C. Nevertheless, White and Young now took more active stands than Smith had in his final years to make the Alliance a more militant labor and civil rights organization. Young, for example, blasted the AFL-CIO unions for collaborating with what he called the Nixon administration's "anti-labor actions" that included maintaining a ban on postal employees' right to strike.[43] And when the NPU announced its upcoming merger with APWU in March 1971, White cited this as proving the need for black autonomy: "Black workers still need a black controlled national labor union," he declared in the March 1971 *National Alliance*.[44]

Yet more black postal workers were joining unions that could represent them at the bargaining table. Black NALC officials Cleveland Morgan and Joseph Henry in New York City and Washington, D.C. (respectively), connected black Alliance-NALC dual membership with what Morgan called the post-strike "downsizing" of the Alliance. "Symbolism" was how Morgan explained black NALC members who simultaneously maintained Alliance membership despite the latter's inability to conduct grievance representation: "This [the Alliance] is something that fought racism throughout the years in the federal government and you wanted to keep it going." But in practical terms for letter carriers in New York, he added, the NALC was "your bread and butter."[45] In D.C., Joseph Henry remembers how many black Alliance members reacted after reorganization: "There were a number of Alliance people who still went to the old shop steward, seeking to have their grievances taken care of, and were certainly upset from time to time when they realized that their old steward could no longer represent them on the workroom floor, and they had to go to the NALC representative in order to represent them. That was something that they begrudgingly let go. And that was one reason why you began to see dual memberships creep up, because they realized that they could only go to the NALC shop steward."[46] Dual membership that had once been about pride and activism was now for many more about loyalty and nostalgia.

The Alliance, formed from exclusion in the early twentieth century, was considerably weakened but still active. Black postal workers created new spaces in other postal unions to fight for jobs, justice, and equality. If the most progressive force historically in the post office and its unions had been the Alliance, they were absent as an organization during postal workers' greatest upsurge during the period of March 18–25, 1970—the "days the mail stopped." Caution and hesitation at the top had cost them in ways that had not hurt the NALC or UFPC, to say the least. The Alliance's decades-old identity conundrum between labor union and civil rights organization had essentially been resolved for them over their objections. Without collective bargaining or grievance representation rights in the post office, they literally became the civil rights union.

The Alliance was still the go-to postal union for EEO cases. But even as other unions referred their members to the Alliance for EEO cases, those other unions were also becoming proficient at handling those cases themselves, as two retired APWU national offices, Raydell Moore from Long Beach, California, and Walter Kenney Sr., from Richmond, Virginia, informed me.[47] The Alliance did win elections to become the exclusive bargaining agent in government agencies like the Centers for Disease Control (CDC), the GSA, and a group of workers at the USPS national headquarters in Washington, D.C.[48] And in protesting systemic inequities like the movement of postal operations from the cities to the suburbs, the Alliance endured and reformed itself through crises over militancy and democracy as had the AFL-CIO postal unions—but with profoundly different results. They had lost members and collective bargaining status. For postal workers, then, striking over the common denominator of low pay had produced an unprecedented unity and a progressive future, yet without resolving ongoing issues of inequality and representation.

EPILOGUE

"We were working six, seven days a week—ten, twelve hours [a day]. . . . Conditions were very rough. The place was a powderkeg. The day after the contract expiration, it actually didn't take much to pull people out, it was so hot and oppressive."[1] Jeff Perry, a retired NPMHU activist and official, was describing the July 21, 1978, wildcat strike at the New York Bulk & Foreign Mail Center (NYB&FMC) in Jersey City, New Jersey. It came four years after the one-day 1974 wildcat at that same bulk mail center (BMC) over an arbitrary work shift change that postal management had tried to impose.

But the 1978 wildcat by NPMHU and APWU members lasted four days, and came just a day after 6,000 NALC and APWU members picketed USPS Headquarters in D.C. in protest of lagging contract negotiations. Wildcat strikes quickly hit the BMC in Kearney, New Jersey, and the San Francisco Bulk and Foreign Mail Facility (SFB&FMC) in Richmond, California, with reports of small walkouts at other BMCs. BMC pickets even went into Manhattan and marched around the GPO (now called the James A. Farley Building). Between five and six thousand clerks, mail handlers, maintenance, and other postal workers struck over safety issues, mandatory overtime, and what many postal workers regarded as an unsatisfactory contract. Several hundred were fired. An amnesty movement within the unions was only partially successful in getting full union backing to restore jobs to all those who had been terminated. But Perry cautioned against a "romanticized view" of the wildcat. In fact, what he called "our main base"—NPMHU Local 300 members on Tour 3 (approximately 3:30 P.M. until midnight)—had voted *not* to strike the night before because of the obvious tactical risks. Striking was still illegal for federal employees, as it remains today.[2]

Unlike the 1970 strike, workers did not formally vote to strike before wildcatting, although this time NALC Branch 36 letter carriers voted to strike if the APWU went out. Many of those striking these mail facilities were black, although blacks were still a minority at these industrial facilities built in suburban areas to attract what postal officials thought would be a whiter, more docile workforce. And many strikers were skeptical, like Jeff Perry and Monroe Head—veteran activist of the 1968 United Black Brothers caucus and wildcat at the Mahwah, New Jersey, Ford plant. So how did the limited postal wildcat happen this time? Overheated contract rhetoric by management and union officials created a situation where spontaneous anger could start a wildcat. This time postal management seemed well prepared, with postal inspectors videotaping strikers and news media already on the scene when the day shift (Tour 2) started. The acrimony from the inability (or as some charge, unwillingness) of the APWU and NPMHU to get all the 1978 wildcat firings rescinded lingers to this day. On the other hand, SFB&FMC workers caught management off-guard by voting overwhelmingly to set up picket lines on July 22, disrupting operations until the following Saturday in defiance of a court order.[3]

Broader questions remain as well, including maintenance of a black and white differential in job and union opportunities. For example, how did two industrial civil rights postal unions lose their seats at the collective bargaining table after the 1970 strike (the National Postal Union [NPU] deciding to merge into the APWU while the National Alliance of Postal and Federal Employees [NAPFE] chose to remain independent), while the smaller NPMHU found itself at that same table? The latter, predominantly black and increasingly militant, had also essentially been taken over in 1968 by the reputedly mob-influenced LIUNA, and in 1988 temporarily lost its autonomy to a trusteeship imposed by LIUNA's white male leadership.[4] And a decade after the 1970 postal strike, whether in Jersey City or Charlotte, there was evidence of whites fast-tracked into supervisory positions (often via temporary "details" that became permanent), while blacks with more education and seniority were routinely disqualified. The black experience at the post office always was, and still remains, fundamentally a fight for justice for themselves as well as all postal workers.

The post-1970 strike era saw a mixture of management accommodation and retaliation in dealing with its workers and unions, which in turn inspired more militant rank-and-file activity—up to a point. Postal workers had proven their ability with no official organization to shut down the largest federal communication network. But the 1970 strike at the same time followed union organizational lines. Subsequently the historical memory of the 1970 wildcat strike became a weapon invoked by top union officials dealing with management, as well as by rank-and-file postal unionists challenging their own officers.

The Alliance was now, in the words of Paul Tennassee, the "institutional memory" of black agency at the post office as well as the leading EEO (Equal Employment Opportunity) advocate in the ongoing fight for fairness. Even with automation taking its toll on postal employment, Noel V. S. Murrain, Alliance National Secretary and District Eight president in New York, told me: "The Alliance acts as an employment pool, particularly here in New York City." With postal jobs paying about $17,000 a year in 1976, the year Murrain finished his pre-law degree at City College of New York that he estimated would have earned him a $9,000 annual salary, he decided to stick with the postal job he had taken when he came out of the army in 1971. He was unequivocal about the role of Afro-Caribbean membership, education, and activism in the Alliance: "In New York, in particular, yes," he said of Afro-Caribbean influence. Even without collective bargaining rights, Murrain built local membership from 700 to over 2,000 during his term as Local 813 president from 1983 to 1992; he noted, "I work in Morgan [Mail Processing Facility], and whenever my members have problems, they come to me."[5]

Following a trend in private industry, the post office after the 1970 strike began constructing new facilities in the suburbs and taking jobs out of urban areas, beginning with thirty preferential mail facilities and twenty-one BMCs. Postmaster General Winton Blount announced on March 11, 1971, a one billion dollar plan to construct this network of factory-like automated BMCs in suburban areas near air, rail, and truck lines that would potentially save the USPS up to $500 million a year and improve efficiency, making it more competitive with the United Parcel Service. To keep letter processing and bulk mail in the same facility, Blount put it, was "like trying to manufacture tractors and sports cars on the same assembly line."[6]

The Alliance was among the first of many to charge that this move was both economically disastrous and racist. In 1971 Alliance officials and Rep. Abner J. Mikva (D-Ill.) presented evidence to the House Subcommittee on Postal Facilities and Mail, which they said demonstrated that postal management was insensitive to the flight of mail processing facilities and thousands of postal jobs from the mainly black inner-city center to the white suburbs.[7] Five months after Blount's announcement, Alliance president White attacked "the moving of postal services . . . where blacks and other minorities are situated to suburban areas."[8] A year later, Vice President Wesley Young warned that "60 per cent of the jobs already lost thru attrition and consolidation of the Postal Service's 15 regions into five had been held by blacks. . . . This is going to be a disaster for the Negro and for the country. The Postal Service has long been a place where Negroes who were denied jobs in the private sector could earn a decent living. But with the loss of this many jobs, you'll just about break the back of the black middle class."[9]

By 1974 the BMCs had already become inefficient, wasteful, dangerous workplaces. They were so dangerous, in fact, that in 1979, a young NYB&FMC mail handler named Michael McDermott was crushed by a conveyor belt whose safety device had been disabled in order to speed production. The resulting scandal later prompted President Jimmy Carter in 1980 to issue Executive Order 12196 that imposed Occupational Safety and Health Administration (OSHA) standards on federal agencies. In 1974, the *American Postal Worker* cau-

Robert White (left), National Alliance president, along with John W. White, Alliance
legislative aide and former District Two president from Baltimore, before a congressional
subcommittee (probably in April 1972). They testified in support of legislation that would
have restored the collective bargaining rights lost during postal reorganization in 1970
that only recognized the AFL-CIO postal unions and the independent NRLCA. During the
early 1970s, Alliance officials also testified against the post office's plans to move
operations from urban to suburban areas, thereby eliminating many postal jobs and job
opportunities for African Americans. Courtesy of the National Alliance of
Postal and Federal Employees.

tiously editorialized their "grave doubts" as to the future of BMCs, especially
their "site selection policies . . . contrary to the interests of minority employees
in particular."[10]

BMCs also became sites of wildcat strikes by clerks and mail handlers in 1974
and 1978 that saw blacks again playing critical roles. But as Jeff Perry reminds
us, it was the shop floor activism outside of those wildcats that was more
significant. The 1974 "Battle of the Bulk" at the NYB&FMC facility was a combination wildcat strike and management lockout over the latter's arbitrary
scheduling policies. Many who participated in the 1978 New Jersey and San

Francisco wildcat did not get their jobs back, and blamed Moe Biller for encouraging the strike and then abandoning them (both of which Biller later regretted). A strike was averted finally when APWU members ratified the contract in October.

Meanwhile, Vincent Sombrotto, the NALC Branch 36 strike leader in 1970, won the election for the national NALC presidency in 1978 with support from his Rank and File Caucus and began instituting union reforms the following year. Biller, who later regretted not having called a strike then, used the rank-and-file upsurge to win the APWU presidency in 1980. Joining Biller on that ticket as executive vice president was William H. Burrus Jr., along with John Richards as director of industrial relations. According to Burrus: "We ran against the status quo, and we revolutionized the political process and the collective bargaining mindset. . . . We thought that everything was possible."[11]

Besides economics, safety, and work rule issues, black postal workers were particularly concerned with ongoing discrimination, especially in disciplinary procedures and promotions. Twelve years after the 1970 wildcat, Postmaster General William F. Bolger conceded to black Representative William Clay (D-Mo.) that blacks in the USPS were being fired or suspended almost four times as often as whites. By the 1990s, with black "removals from service" double that of whites, there was still work for the Alliance—now led by a younger generation that included Wendy Kelly-Carter, the first woman elected New York and Bronx Local 813 president.[12]

But pro-equality work was also a hallmark of black APWU activists following the 1970 strike. Black APWU activists like Eleanor Bailey and Josie McMillian in the 1970s formalized their advocacy for women postal workers in the Post Office Women for Equal Rights (POWER) and in the Coalition of Labor Union Women (CLUW). Opposition to South African apartheid was popular in the 1980s among APWU activists in New York and elsewhere. The 1990s editions of the monthly *Local 300 Mail Handler News* in New York and New Jersey advocated for mail handlers and postal workers and against postal privatization, as well as against sweatshops in the private sector.

In the 2000s, APWU activist leaders like retired local president Ajamu Dillahunt in Raleigh, North Carolina, and Gregory Wilson in New York performed radical community work in addition to their shop floor advocacy. Reminiscent of historical Alliance practice, Joseph Henry tells how black members of suburban D.C. branches have asked his NALC Branch 142 in D.C. to represent them because of their own branches' prejudiced practices, which he notes also led to clashes at Virginia state NALC meetings well into the 1990s.[13] And the Alliance affirmed its support for the "peace candidate" in the 1972 election, Sen. George McGovern (D-S.D.). So did the Coalition of Black

Trade Unionists, formed in large part out of frustration with the AFL-CIO's refusal to endorse a presidential candidate that year and seeing President Nixon continuing to wage war in Vietnam while implementing anti-black policies at home. When Title VII was amended in 1972 to allow federal employees to file civil suits for discrimination, the Alliance publicized it.[14]

It was also in 1972 that Napoleon Chisholm, a black college-educated military veteran and letter carrier from Charlotte, told me that he filed a complaint on his own against the exclusive promotion of whites for the positions of finance examiner and budget assistant after failing to find support from any of the postal unions. A year later, he retained the law firm of NAACP Legal Defense Fund attorney Julius Chambers to file a class-action lawsuit (led by attorney Jonathan Wallas) against the USPS; the suit resulted in a $2 million affirmative action judgment in 1980 after a court found patterns and practice of management favoritism toward whites and discrimination toward blacks in areas of promotion and discipline. This was in a city where blacks could not join any postal union except the National Alliance until around 1961. In 1972, blacks made up about 45 percent of the Charlotte post office, including 419 of 922 nonsupervisory levels 1–6 (43 percent) but only about 9 percent (10 of 114) of the mostly supervisory level 7 and higher slots. A discriminatory supervisor's test as late as 1974 saw a passing rate of 58 percent for whites and 25.3 percent for blacks. From 1973 to 1978, blacks were fired at a rate of more than two to one over whites (69 percent to 31 percent), and blacks made up almost 60 percent of suspensions.[15]

Chisholm v. USPS documented management discrimination at the Charlotte post office, revealing a higher education level for black candidates rejected over whites (forty-six blacks versus twenty-one whites in 1974 had four-year college degrees, considered a qualification for higher level promotions). Chisholm, who told oral history interviewer Elizabeth Gritter in 2006 that he did not consider himself an activist, initially pursued a do-it-yourself approach that wound up including plaintiffs and witnesses on both sides who were Alliance and other postal union members. In many ways, what he told her was a microcosm of how hundreds of similar cases arose of ordinary workers determined to get justice: "My total feelings were for the postal service. I never intended to be antagonistic. . . . I was disappointed in the presentation of the postal service, which was almost my heart at the time as far as an employer. What was on trial . . . was the rules and regulations of personnel practices of the post office."[16]

The USPS EEO regional office did not support his claim, and the subsequent USPS EEO hearing examiner's partial finding in his favor was not much better—recommending only that he be granted relief with the first available promotion opening. Chisholm told me that he refused a level 20 position offered to him if he dropped the case. To his credit, he refused this individual solution in solidarity with his black coworkers because of the documented disparities in promotions and discipline that he wanted to change. The court found that this "system whereby favored whites were groomed to fill vacancies through the detailing [temporary assignment] process not only gave those whites additional income while they served on the details and the higher level jobs but discouraged blacks from even applying for jobs for which they were qualified." Temporary details (such as whites being appointed at a 68 percent higher rate than blacks in 1972) had become permanent assignments for whites. One black applicant was told by management in 1968 when applying for a supervisor's position in customer relations: "You're a good carrier but you're colored and Charlotte is not ready for colored to have this job."[17]

White allies over the years have also played important roles in keeping the fight for equality prominent—from the 1940s to the present day, from the NALC's Philip Lepper and the MBPU's Moe Biller to today's activists like mail handler Jeff Perry. Perry, who has confronted white supremacy in the post office and his own union, told me: "The best work we did was in the middle 80's at the Bulk Mail Center. . . . Every issue that we took on, we looked at in terms of how white supremacy was shaping it."[18]

In Mississippi, James Newman, a white clerk/mail handler and disabled veteran, was drawn to the Alliance for its support of postal workers' disability rights. Formerly an APWU member in Florida, then an NALC and NPMHU member in Mississippi, Newman is president of the Alliance's Gulfport, Mississippi, branch that is about 60 percent black and 40 percent white. He described being harassed by a white supervisor for belonging to the Alliance. Members of Newman's family at first thought he "was crazy" to belong to a black union, he told me, but they now support it, as he described the high level of EEO and MSPB (Merit Systems Protection Board) training he and other Alliance officials receive and the pride he feels in the organization. Visibly moved, he recalled the ninetieth anniversary of the Alliance's founding that he attended in 2003: "To stand in Chattanooga, Tennessee, where twenty-six men were willing to die for what they believed in was a distinct honor."[19]

Emblematic of ongoing post-strike direct action protests by black, white, and Latino postal workers was a situation that developed at the GPO in New York in 1971 after the LSM-ZMT (Letter Sorting Machine–Zip Mail Translator) was implemented. Management pushed clerks to key in zip codes at the rate of one letter per second. Josie McMillian, the first black woman elected president of New York Metro–APWU in 1981, had been an MBPU steward in 1971 when workers took action one day after a supervisor pressured a LSM-ZMT operator to

Twenty-first-century equipment. Two people operate a delivery barcode sorter, one feeding in stacks of letters, the other "sweeping" sorted letters into trays in delivery order.

key faster until the clerk shouted out: "I can't take it anymore." McMillian remembers: "And when that happened, everybody just stood up in the middle of the work room floor and said, 'That's it. *We*'re not doing it anymore.' Postal workers don't have the right to strike so naturally, me being the representative, the management called me over wanting me to order them back to work. We didn't go back to work that night. We proved our point."[20]

Meanwhile, automation remains a relentless challenge to postal work. "When I started off in the sixties," recalls mail handler Richard Thomas, "everything was done manually. . . . Eventually the mail went on wheels [large metal carts that ran on tracks]. . . . Now it comes containerized, and all we have to do is take it off the truck, put it on the elevator. . . . It's a vast improvement." Thomas also has noticed more people of color now in lower and middle management positions, but "higher level management still appears to be white."[21] Black job mobility has increased through years of pressure and embarrassing outside studies. In 1998, former Norfolk letter carrier Clarence E. Lewis was appointed chief operating officer—the third-highest USPS position.[22] "There's minority membership in every level of management [yet] there are thousands of offices that have never hired a minority," noted William H. Burrus Jr. In 2001 Burrus was the first African American elected

William H. Burrus Jr. in 2009. Burrus began working at the post office in 1958, participated in the 1970 postal strike in Cleveland as a member of the NPU, and in 2000 was the first African American elected president of the APWU. Photograph by the author.

president of the APWU (about one-third black and the world's largest postal union at 260,000 members), whose executive board, like that of the National Postal Mail Handlers Union, is about fifty percent people of color.[23] Economists Leah Platt Boustan and Robert Margo reported that "by 2000, the [statistical] mean black postal worker remained in the top 25 percent of black earners and above the median for the nation."[24]

The post office has long been a job magnet—especially for African Americans. In 1980s New York City, Gregory Wilson and Frederick John, now both GPO clerks at Morgan and APWU members, emerged from college and the U.S. Marine Corps (in Wilson's case) to pursue careers in business and the recording industry, respectively. "What I really wanted to do was to be in business," Wilson told me, "and I got a job at Chase Manhattan being a bank teller. . . . I was usually cashing post office people's checks, and I see how much they made. . . . I'm making $340 every two weeks. I look at the post office people's checks and they were making *thousands of dollars* every two weeks." He describes the day in 1986 that he came home from work to find a letter calling him to work as a USPS clerk. Frederick John was also surprised when he received a similar letter in 1985: "I got into the recording industry [as an engi-

NALC Branch 142 stewards being sworn in at branch headquarters, Washington, D.C., 2002. On the shop floor, postal union stewards represent coworkers in their respective crafts during management disciplinary proceedings and also file grievances when deemed necessary. Courtesy of Joseph Henry.

neer]. . . . I had taken the postal exam years ago. . . . I had forgotten about it, and they sent me the letter and I said, you know, this would be a good way to subsidize my recording [work]. . . . I can have a steady check coming in while I'm in the recording industry. . . . I'll work at the post office for a short time. . . . But the musical industry thing kind of waned. Next thing you know, it's twenty years later and I'm still here! . . . It was a good steady job. . . . You could do other ventures. . . . It got my son through college."[25]

But how secure is work at the post office today for blacks and other postal workers? Wilson and John, like Burrus and many other postal union activists, worry about their coworkers becoming too complacent in defending what past struggles and negotiations by unionists at the post office have won for them, including health benefits, retirement, a no-layoff clause for those with at least six years of service, and top pay now about $52,000 annually.[26] "The post office has been unique. . . . We shaped America," notes Burrus, who warns that "our country will lose something" without universal postal service: "It will also put an end to the relationship between the people of color and their opportunity to climb up the ladder of success in our country. . . . The postal service has permitted millions of African Americans . . . to better themselves."[27]

Facing massive deficits, volume drops, and Internet competition, however, the USPS from 2008 to 2009 proposed extensive privatization and has even suggested cutting one day of delivery per week. The USPS (opposed by the NALC and other postal unions) has closed over fifty airport mail facilities since 2006 and hopes to "outsource" some BMC work, "thus freeing up the BMCs for other postal operations."[28] Burrus has pressured Postmaster General John Potter and the USPS to bring back outsourced jobs and pay to retrain postal workers whose jobs were lost to technology, adding there is "nothing left now but manual activity." With overtime cuts, attrition, and "early out" retirements, postal workers are "now at 700,000 and dropping every day," says Burrus.[29]

Ironically, this attrition comes at a time when the U.S. Postal Service (the nation's second largest employer) justifiably claims to be "one of the leading employers of minorities and women." In 2008, 39 percent of the workforce was minorities and over 37 percent were women. The 39 percent minority figure included 21 percent African American, 8 percent Hispanic, and 8 percent Asian American. That diversity came about primarily as a result of the fight led over the years by African American postal workers for jobs, justice, and equality at the post office.[30]

CONCLUSION

A. L. Glenn made this observation in his 1956 history of the NAPE: "The line of demarcation is so finely drawn between civil rights affecting the entire race and those directly concerned with postal workers, that it becomes difficult at times to separate them."[1] Without the historical movement for equality in the post office that was led by black postal workers since the Civil War, the 1970 nationwide postal wildcat strike would not have happened on the scale that it did, nor could it have been successful in achieving its goals of economic and union empowerment.

"I worked [in the 1960s Cleveland post office] with [black] college graduates performing the rudimentary tasks of a postal employee," recalls APWU president William H. Burrus Jr. "People that had masters degrees. They couldn't get jobs as school teachers. They shared with me all of their wisdom. Postal jobs were not mentally challenging, so we spent a lot of time talking about different subjects. And I was a twenty-one, twenty-two-year-old man. These were forty-five-year-old, fifty-year-old men that had been in the war, gone to college . . . had skills way beyond the tasks they were performing. And we just talked all the time. I was basically like a sponge, soaking up wisdom."[2]

In whatever unions they happened to join—with the Alliance leading the way—black postal workers, with their combined labor protest and civic traditions, fused with other militant labor and community traditions. New York was unquestionably the crucible of this fusion that exploded on March 18, 1970, with the postal strike. But that fusion, the strike, and postal reforms have benefited from the continuity of struggle described by William Burrus. That was established among African Americans across generations in large part through migration from the South, and then dispersed across the country to mingle with other militant elements. As Felix Bell, then president of Jackson, Mississippi, National Alliance Local 405, told me in 2004: "If we had not fought for change, it would not have happened."[3]

Black postal workers have historically found themselves in a dance of survival with and against their employer, their own unions, and white coworkers —while their influence extends beyond the post office and its unions to the civil rights and labor movements. Putting the fight for equality first, they provided a legacy for any future rank-and-file success and black upward mobility.

NOTES

ABBREVIATIONS

Biller Files — American Postal Workers Union–Moe Biller Files, Tamiment Library/Robert F. Wagner Archives, Bobst Library, New York University, New York, N.Y.

Branch 36 interview — Interview by author with Al Marino, Frank Orapello, and Vincent Sombrotto, October 15, 2004, New York, N.Y.

BTV — Behind the Veil: Documenting African American Life in the Jim Crow South, Center for Documentary Studies Collection, Duke University Rare Book, Manuscript, and Special Collections Library, Durham, N.C.

FEPC Records — *Selected Documents from Records of the Committee on Fair Employment Practice*, Record Group 228 in the custody of the National Archives, edited by Bruce I. Friend (Glen Rock, N.J.: Microfilming Corporation of America, 1970), microfilm (Bobst Library, New York University, New York, N.Y.)

Local 251 Minutes — *American Postal Workers Union—Brooklyn Local 251 Minutes, 1918–1977*, microfilm

NAACP Collection — Manuscript—Education, *Sweatt v. Painter*, NAACP Collection, 1945–1950 (Primary Source), <http://cis.lexis.nexis.com> (May 21, 2006)

NAACP Papers — *Papers of the NAACP*, edited by John H. Bracey Jr. and August Meier (Baltimore: University Press of America, 1992), microfilm

New York Metro interview — Interview by author with Eleanor Bailey, Joann Flagler, Frederick John, Carlton Tilley, and Gregory Wilson, October 14, 2004, New York, N.Y.

NYMAPUC — American Postal Workers Union–New York Metro Area Postal Union Collection, Tamiment Library/Robert F. Wagner Archives, Bobst Library, New York University, New York, N.Y.

UNIA Records — *Universal Negro Improvement Association Records of the Central Division (New York), 1918–1959*, Schomburg Library Collection (Wilmington, Del.: Scholarly Resources, 1995), microfilm

USPS Archives — U.S. Postal Service Archives and Library, Washington, D.C.

1. In *Hollywood Shuffle* the grandmother and mother of Townsend's character, Bobby Taylor, get into an argument over whether he should have accepted the role of a stereotypical black pimp and gang leader in a film. Bobby's mother defends his decision to take the role, because "it's work," to which the grandmother retorts, "There's work at the post office!" Her point is that despite his desire to practice his craft, the demeaning stereotypes of such Hollywood roles are dishonest. Furthermore, an honest occupational alternative for African Americans, both historically and at present, exists at the post office. Bobby tells himself that he needs the work, but he also harbors doubts over the ethics of taking these kinds of roles. The film climaxes with Bobby resolving his dilemma by walking out in the middle of filming a scene (with his grandmother, mother, and younger brother watching). In response to another black actor's rationalization of needing the work, Bobby retorts with his grandmother's line about the post office. The movie concludes with Bobby in a letter carrier's uniform filming a short recruitment advertisement for the U.S. Postal Service: "Through rain, sleet, and snow, I deliver your mail. I'm a U.S. postman, and you can be one, too. I deliver people's dreams. And more importantly, I have the respect and admiration of the entire community. And that makes me proud. So if you can't take pride in your job, remember—there's always work at the post office!" See *Hollywood Shuffle*, dir. Robert Townsend, 1987.

This was not the first time postal work was singled out as a dignified job for African Americans. Evoking the upsurge of black movement culture in the postwar era and the leadership roles played by black professionals, the 1953 film *Bright Road*—Harry Belafonte's film debut—includes a scene where Belafonte's character, a school principal in the South, is taking the postal exam. See *Bright Road*, dir. Gerald Mayer, 1953. I am indebted to Paul Tennassee for this reference. On the other hand, one is hard pressed to find black postal workers in classic Hollywood films with postal workers in well-known roles, such as *Miracle on 34th Street* (dir. George Seaton, 1947). In contrast, black postal workers appear in more recent films such as *Jingle All the Way* (dir. Brian Levant, 1996), with the comedian Sinbad (more in line with the recent stereotype of the volatile postal worker), as well as *Poetic Justice* (dir. John Singleton, 1993), in which Tupac Shakur's character probably represents the most extreme example (fictional or otherwise) of a letter carrier deviating from his route (to use official postal jargon)—driving his postal vehicle several hundred miles between Los Angeles and Oakland. Black female postal workers are rarely seen in American films. The only film that comes to mind is *The Blues Brothers* (dir. John Landis, 1980), where a female postal clerk wearing a postal uniform shirt sits in the Chicago diner run by singer Aretha Franklin —and suddenly turns into one of Aretha's backup singers as they perform her classic rhythm and blues song "Think." Finally, comedian Keenan Ivory Wayans, who co-wrote *Hollywood Shuffle* with Townsend, plays a kind of Greek chorus in his role as a letter carrier in the film comedy *Don't Be a Menace to South Central While Drinking Your Juice in the Hood* (dir. Paris Barclay, 1995). The film spoofs coming-of-age "hood" films of the 1990s (especially *Boyz N the Hood*, dir. John Singleton, 1991). Wayans's character appears periodically after other characters' dramatic lines are uttered; speaking to the camera he shouts: "Message!" to remind the audience that that indeed is what they just heard. He also spoofs Shakur's character in *Poetic Justice*.

2. See David Barsamian, interview with Danny Glover, *Progressive* (December 2002), <http://www.progressive.org/dec02/intv1201.html> (February 25, 2006); and Ann Ger-

hart, "Actor in An Activist Role: Danny Glover Gives $1 Million to TransAfrica Forum," *Washington Post*, April 20, 1999, C1.

3. See Keith W. Medley, *We as Freemen: Plessy v. Ferguson* (Gretna, La.: Pelican, 2003).

4. *Sweatt v. Painter*, 339 U.S. 629 (1950); White and Sweatt family information quoted in A. L. Glenn, *History of the National Alliance of Postal Employees, 1913–1955* (Washington, D.C.: National Alliance of Postal Employees, 1956), 25, 38–40. Walter White was also the brother-in-law of A. L. Glenn, who was one of the first presidents of the National Alliance. See Paul Tennassee, "NAPFE: A Legacy of Contributions and Resistance," *National Alliance* (October 1999), 12. On William Monroe Trotter and his father see Stephen R. Fox, *The Guardian of Boston: William Monroe Trotter* (New York: Atheneum, 1970), 3–10, 89–97.

5. See <http://www.archives.gov/publications/prologue/2005/spring/weaver.html> (February 25, 2006); and "Editor's Notebook," *National Alliance* (January 1966), 4. See also John Hope Franklin and Alfred A. Moss Jr., *From Slavery to Freedom: A History of African Americans*, 8th ed. (1947; Boston: McGraw-Hill, 2000), 430, 450, where they note that Robert C. Weaver, a member of President Franklin D. Roosevelt's "Black Cabinet," was later named head of the Housing and Home Finance Agency by President John F. Kennedy in 1961. In 1965, President Lyndon B. Johnson named Weaver to head the new Department of Housing and Urban Development, making him the first black to hold a cabinet office.

6. Telephone conversation with Barbara Jeanne Fields, March 24, 2004, New York, N.Y.

7. David Barsamian, interview with June Jordan, "Childhood Memories, Poetry & Palestine," Boulder, Colorado, October 11, 2000, <http://www.alternativeradio.orgJordan02 .html> (February 25, 2006); "Voices from the Gaps: Women Writers of Color, University of Minnesota, June Jordan (1936–2002) Biography-Criticism," <http://voices.cla.umn.edu/ authors/JORDANjune.html> (February 25, 2006); and June Jordan, *Soldier: A Poet's Childhood* (New York: Basic Books, 2000), 5. According to Jordan, her father moved to New York City from Jamaica and was an admirer of UNIA founder Marcus Garvey.

8. Telephone interview with former SNCC activist Donald P. Stone, February 12, 2005, Snow Hill, Ala.

9. Leon Litwack, "The Road from Rentiesville" (interview with John Hope Franklin), *American Legacy* (Summer 2002), 35–45; and Buck Colbert Franklin, *My Life and an Era: The Autobiography of Buck Colbert Franklin*, ed. John Hope Franklin and John Whittington Franklin (Baton Rouge: Louisiana State University Press, 1997), 172–73, 180–81.

10. On Charles Rangel and Percy Sutton see author interview with John Adams and Dorothea Hoskins, longtime National Alliance officials from New York City, August 11, 2004, Washington, D.C. Coleman Young's father had also been a postal worker, and so was Coleman's brother George. Coleman himself worked and organized for less than a year at the Detroit post office, although as youths he and his brother often had to cover for their father when he could not make it in to work. See Coleman Young and Lonnie Wheeler, *Hard Stuff: The Autobiography of Coleman Young* (New York: Viking, 1994), xvii and 19–113, passim. See also Wilbur C. Rich, *Coleman Young and Detroit Politics: From Social Activist to Power Broker* (Detroit: Wayne State University Press, 1989), esp. 62.

11. Adams and Hoskins interview; author interview with Samuel Lovett and Sam Armstrong, August 11, 2004, Washington, D.C.

12. See also Aldon D. Morris, *The Origins of the Civil Rights Movement: Black Communities Organizing for Change* (1984; New York: Free Press, 1986), 58; and *New York Times*, March 26, 1997, <http://www.unbrokencircle.org/nytimes.htm> (February 25, 2006). See also

Glenn, *History of the National Alliance*, 422, where he noted that in November 1955, all black postal employees in Montgomery belonged to the National Alliance.

13. Jan Skutch and Kate Wiltrout, "Willing to Pay Whatever Price He Had to Pay to Stand Firm," *Savannah Morning News*, July 30, 2002, <http://www.savannahnow.com> (February 25, 2006). I am indebted to Charles M. Payne for making me aware of W. W. Law.

14. Charles M. Payne, *I've Got the Light of Freedom: The Organizing Tradition and the Mississippi Freedom Struggle* (Berkeley: University of California Press, 1995), 31–34. See also John Dittmer, *Local People: The Struggle for Civil Rights in Mississippi* (Urbana: University of Illinois Press, 1994), 72–73, 102–3. Moore retired from the post office in 1968. See Amzie Moore oral history, Civil Rights in Mississippi Digital Archive, <http://www.lib.usm.edu/ ~spcol/ crda/oh/index.html> (September 6, 2008).

15. See <http://www.dickgregory.com/about_dick_gregory.html> (February 25, 2006).

16. Keneth Kinnamon and Michel Fabre, eds., *Conversations with Richard Wright* (Jackson: University Press of Mississippi, 1993), 39 (see also 36–39, 173). This article is a reprint of Roy Wilder, "Wright, Negro Ex–Field Hand, Looks Ahead to New Triumphs," *New York Herald Tribune*, August 17, 1941, 6:4. I am indebted to Myrna Adams for this story. Wright came to the Chicago post office in 1927, and in 1934 he became a member of the CPUSA. After he left the post office, he moved to New York City and quit the CPUSA in 1942. See Mark Naison, *Communists in Harlem during the Depression* (Urbana: University of Illinois Press, 1983), 210; and Earl Ofari Hutchinson, *Blacks and Reds: Race and Class in Conflict, 1919–1990* (East Lansing: Michigan State University Press, 1995), 149–51.

17. Harry Haywood, *Black Bolshevik: Autobiography of an Afro-American Communist* (Chicago: Liberator Press, 1978), 99–116.

18. Jeffrey B. Perry, *Hubert Harrison: The Voice of Harlem Radicalism, 1883–1918* (New York: Columbia University Press, 2009), 83–87; and Naison, *Communists in Harlem*, 99. See also Hutchinson, *Blacks and Reds*, 149–51; and Keith P. Griffler, *What Price Alliance? Black Radicals Confront White Labor, 1918–1938* (New York: Garland, 1995).

19. "News, Reviews, and Commentary on Lesbian and Bisexual Women in Entertainment and the Media," <http://www.afterellen.com/archive/Ellen/People/2006/10/randle.html> (September 6, 2008), italics added; Charles Mingus biography by Gene Santoro, *Myself When I Am Real* (New York: Oxford University Press, 2000), 72–74, 84–85, 102–3.

20. Freddie Gorman (1939–2006) worked for the post office in both Detroit and Los Angeles. See Tim Allis, "Wait a minute, Mr. Postman—Aren't You Freddie Gorman, Who Co-wrote Please Mr. Postman?," *People Weekly*, March 7, 1988, 53–54; Pierre Perrone, from *The Independent*, <http://www.spectropop.com/remembers/FreddieGorman.htm> (November 24, 2008); Nelson George, *Where Did Our Love Go? The Rise and Fall of the Motown Sound* (New York: St. Martin's Press, 1985), 35, 40–41; Daisy Ridgway, "Researchers Find That Postal and Mail Themes Strike a Chord with Composers," *Research Reports* 82 (Autumn 1995), National Postal Museum, Smithsonian Institution website, <http://www.si.edu> (September 6, 2008). See also the Originals website, <http://www.soulwalking.co.uk/Originals.html> (February 25, 2006). See also the official U.S. Postal Service history, *The United States Postal Service: An American History, 1775–2006* (Washington, D.C.: USPS Publication 100, 2007), 10, that includes in its list of "other famous postal workers" the following, in addition to Richard Wright: "Charles R. Drew, Scientist and surgeon, part-time special delivery messenger, Washington, D.C.; Samuel L. Gravely, First African-

American admiral, railway mail clerk; Sherman Hemsley, Actor, clerk, Philadelphia, PA, and New York, NY."

21. On black mariners see W. Jeffrey Bolster, " 'To Feel Like a Man': Black Seamen in the Northern States, 1800–1860," *Journal of American History* 76, no. 4 (March 1990), 1173–99; and *Black Jacks: African American Seamen in the Age of Sail* (Cambridge, Mass.: Harvard University Press, 1997). Mobility, relative workplace autonomy, and interdependence were among the common features of the occupation of mariners, porters, and postal workers. See for example this observation by Naison, *Communists in Harlem*, 33–34: "[A] sizable minority of Harlem's population, though suspicious of Communists intentions, carefully scrutinized what Communists said. Harlem's working class contained a small but influential group of skilled and sophisticated men and women who had been exposed to radical ideologies and who were resolutely secular in their approach to politics. Longshoremen and seamen, printers and apparel workers, postmen and musicians, these individuals often had traveled widely (many were veterans) and had been educated far beyond the jobs they actually held. Along with Harlem's intellectuals and small businessmen, they had been the mainstay of the Garvey movement and other militant groups that proliferated after the war, and they relished the street-corner debates that were a feature of Harlem's life." See also Peter Rachleff, electronic communication to author, October 1, 2001. See also Paul Tennassee, conversation with author, November 23, 2001, for similar observations. On Pullman porters see Beth Tompkins Bates, *Pullman Porters and the Rise of Protest Politics in Black America, 1925–1945* (Chapel Hill: University of North Carolina Press, 2001).

22. "Postal Employees," *Ebony* (November 1949), 15; see also 16–18, which included a discussion of black postal workers active in the Alliance, NFPOC, and NALC, as well as the work of John T. Risher, an African American working for a Senate committee investigating charges of Jim Crowism in southern post offices that year. The *Ebony* article is also quoted in Glenn, *History of the National Alliance*, 428.

23. See E. Franklin Frazier, *Black Bourgeoisie* (1957; London: Collier, 1969), 50–51, for his inclusion of black postal workers as part of the black middle class.

24. Adam Fairclough, *Better Day Coming: Blacks and Equality, 1890–2000* (New York: Viking, 2001), 183. Fairclough's assignment of black postal workers to the "middle class rather than the working class" is, I think, an overstatement and an unnecessary dichotomy; I would argue both were true. Education, income, and social status place them sociologically in the middle class, but selling their labor power to produce goods and literally deliver services make them working class (or "proletarian"). In Marxian terms they would not be petit-bourgeois (the rough approximation of middle class) because they are not entrepreneurs.

25. See John Walsh and Garth Mangum, *Labor Struggle in the Post Office: From Selective Lobbying to Collective Bargaining* (Armonk, N.Y.: M. E. Sharpe, 1992), 214.

26. M. Brady Mikusko, *Carriers in a Common Cause: A History of Letter Carriers and the NALC* (Washington, D.C.: NALC, 1989), 65. See also Aaron Brenner, "Rank-and-File Rebellion, 1966–1975" (Ph.D. diss., Columbia University, 1996), 112–46. Virtually the only piece of literature by the NPMHU is the eighteen-page pamphlet, *We're the Hidden Heroes of the Postal Service* (Washington, D.C.: NPMHU, 1990). The official history of the National Rural Letter Carriers Association (NRLCA) is by a former president, Lester F. Miller, *The National Rural Letter Carriers Association: A Centennial Portrait* (Encino, Calif.: Cherbo Publishing, 2003). I am indebted to the NRLCA for that text.

27. See Glenn, *History of the National Alliance*; O. Grady Gregory, *From the Bottom of the*

Barrel: A History of Black Workers in the Chicago Post Office from 1921 (Chicago: National Alliance of Postal and Federal Employees, 1977). See also Henry W. McGee, *The Negro in the Chicago Post Office: Henry W. McGee Autobiography and Dissertation* (Chicago: VolumeOne Press, 1999) (originally "The Negro in the Chicago Post Office," master's thesis, University of Chicago, 1961); and telephone conversation with McGee's son, Professor of Law Henry W. McGee Jr., April 10, 2004, Seattle, to whom I am indebted for his insights as well as a copy of this combination thesis reprint and autobiography by his late father. I am also indebted to Paul Tennassee for making available to me his articles in the National Alliance from 1998 to 2004 on Alliance history, also available at their website, <http://www.napfe .com> (September 6, 2008). See also Historian, U.S. Postal Service, esp. "African-American Postal Workers in the 19th Century," <http://www.usps.com/postalhistory> (July 15, 2009); and Deanna Boyd and Kendra Chen, "The History and Experience of African Americans in America's Postal service," Smithsonian National Postal Museum, Washington, D.C., <http://www.postalmuseum.si.edu/AfricanAmericans/index.html> (September 6, 2008).

28. Vincent Harding, "History: White, Negro and Black," *Southern Exposure* (Winter 1974), 57.

29. Leon Fink and Brian Greenberg, *Upheaval in the Quiet Zone: A History of Hospital Workers' Union, Local 1199* (Urbana: University of Illinois Press, 1989), xv (see also x, on Local 1199's merging the civil rights and labor struggle in creating a strong union out of a once weak workforce by 1968; and xi, on 1199 "as an overwhelmingly black union led by secular-Jewish radicals"). See also Michael Keith Honey, *Black Workers Remember: An Oral History of Segregation, Unionism, and the Freedom Struggle* (Berkeley: University of California Press, 1999), introduction; and Robert Rodgers Korstad, *Civil Rights Unionism: Tobacco Workers and the Struggle for Democracy in the Mid-Twentieth Century South* (Chapel Hill: University of North Carolina Press, 2003).

30. See Walsh and Mangum, *Labor Struggle*; and Brenner, "Rank-and-File Rebellion," introduction and chap. 3.

31. Important examples of studies on public workers include Fink and Greenberg, *Upheaval in the Quiet Zone*; Sam Zagoria, ed., *Public Workers and Public Unions* (Englewood Cliffs, N.J.: Prentice-Hall, 1972); and Robert Shaffer, "Where Are the Organized Public Employees? The Absence of Public Employees Unionism from U.S. History Textbooks, and Why It Matters," *Labor History* 43, no. 3 (August 2002), 315–34.

32. Paul Johnston, *Success While Others Fail: Social Movement Unionism and the Public Workplace* (Ithaca, N.Y.: ILR Press, 1994), 4.

33. See Tennassee, "Legacy," 12. On NAPFE history, see also Paul Tennassee, NAPFE historian, personal conversation with author, November 23, 2001, NAPFE national headquarters, Washington, D.C. The National Alliance of Postal Employees (NAPE) became the National Alliance of Postal and Federal Employees, or NAPFE, in 1965, and is still active. Whether I refer to it as NAPE or NAPFE depends on the historical period that I am discussing, but for the sake of convenience I generally call it by its popular name, the National Alliance, or simply the Alliance. Ironically, the "National Alliance" is also the name of a white supremacist group, but I make no references here to that organization.

34. Black nationalism is something that I conceptualize broadly, drawing on scholars like Wahneema Lubiano and others in analyzing the broad spectrum of possibilities from race solidarity to pan-Africanism. See Wahneema Lubiano, "Black Nationalism and Black Common Sense," in *The House That Race Built: Black Americans, U.S. Terrain*, ed. Wahneema

Lubiano (New York: Pantheon Books, 1997), 232–52, esp. 232–34, where she addresses black nationalism as an "everyday ideology," that "in its broadest sense, is . . . an analytic, describing a range of historically manifested ideas about black American possibilities that include any or all of the following: racial solidarity, cultural specificity, religious, economic, and political separatism." See also John H. Bracey Jr., August Meier, and Elliott Rudwick, eds., *Black Nationalism in America* (Indianapolis: Bobbs-Merrill, 1970), xxvi, arguing for a broad definition ranging from "racial solidarity" to "sophisticated . . . Pan-Africanism."

35. McGee, *Negro in the Chicago Post Office (Autobiography)*, 8.

36. Honey, *Black Workers Remember*, 237. See also Korstad, *Civil Rights Unionism*, esp. 3, where he borrows Rosemary Feurer's term "civic unionism" to describe his study of 1940s black tobacco factory workers "who combined class consciousness with race solidarity and looked to cross-class institutions such as the black church as a key base of support." On the black labor protest tradition, see for example Payne, *I've Got the Light*; Earl Lewis, *In Their Own Interests: Race, Class, and Power in Twentieth-Century Norfolk, Virginia* (Berkeley: University of California Press, 1993); and Bates, *Pullman Porters*.

37. See Payne, *I've Got the Light*; and Fredrick C. Harris, "Will the Circle Be Unbroken? The Erosion and Transformation of African-American Civic Life," in *Civil Society, Democracy, and Civic Renewal*, ed. Robert K. Fullinwider (Lanham, Md.: Rowman and Littlefield, 1999), 319. See also Harris, *Something Within: Religion in African-American Political Activism* (New York: Oxford University Press, 1999); Charles M. Payne and Adam Green, eds., *Time Longer than Rope: A Century of African American Activism, 1850–1950* (New York: New York University Press, 2003); Robin D. G. Kelley, "Integration: What's Left?," *Nation*, December 14, 1998; Bruce Nelson, *Divided We Stand: American Workers and the Struggle for Black Equality* (Princeton, N.J.: Princeton University Press, 2001); John C. Leggett, *Class, Race, and Labor: Working-Class Consciousness in Detroit* (New York: Oxford University Press, 1968); and William H. Harris, *The Harder We Run: Black Workers since the Civil War* (New York: Oxford University Press, 1982).

38. See Glenn, *History of the National Alliance*, 118, quoting National Alliance president James B. Cobb's August 1955 news release that combined the themes of civil rights and justice for labor (with a pun on childbirth labor) and evoked the union's founders. On the Southern Christian Leadership Conference (SCLC), founding in 1957 under the slogan "To save the soul of America," see Martin Luther King Jr.'s recollections in "Beyond Vietnam: A Time to Break the Silence," speech delivered on April 4, 1967, at a meeting of Clergy and Laity Concerned at Riverside Church in New York City, <http://mlk-kpp01.stanford.edu> (November 24, 2008). See also Glenn, *History of the National Alliance*, 431, for Glenn's employing the slogan "Lift as we climb" to refer to black labor's influence on the labor movement and the larger society. That phrase is usually associated with turn-of-the-century black middle-class "uplift" ideology, an important strand in the history of black community organizing.

39. For the "old labor history" see John R. Commons, *History of Labour in the United States* (1918; New York: Macmillan, 1935). A good representative example of leading civil rights literature that focuses on black middle-class leadership of a struggle for civil rights apart from black working-class economic and social demands is Taylor Branch, *Parting the Waters: America in the King Years, 1954–63* (New York: Simon and Schuster, 1988). For a critique of the "old labor history" see David Roediger, *Towards the Abolition of Whiteness: Essays on Race, Politics, and Working Class History* (London: Verso, 1994), 21–38. For the "new labor history" and its differences with the "whiteness scholarship" of Roediger and others, see for example

Eric Arnesen, "Whiteness and the Historians' Imagination," *International Labor and Working-Class History* 60 (October 2001), 3–32. For a critique of the white blindspot of the "new labor history" see Nell Irvin Painter, "The New Labor History and the Historical Moment," *International Journal of Politics, Culture and Society* 2, no. 3 (Spring 1989), 367–70; and Herbert Hill, "Myth-Making as Labor History: Herbert Gutman and the United Mine Workers of America," *International Journal of Politics, Culture, and Society* 2, no. 2 (Winter 1988), 132–200. For a critique of "black and white unite and fight" left-labor history and of Philip Foner, see Noel Ignatiev [né Ignatin], "A Golden Bridge," *Political Discussion* 2 (April 1976), 17–45. Examples of unifying the black-left-labor narrative include Tennessee, "Legacy," 12–15; Robin D. G. Kelley, *Hammer and Hoe: Alabama Communists during the Great Depression* (Chapel Hill: University of North Carolina Press, 1990); Lewis, *In Their Own Interests*; Michael Keith Honey, *Southern Labor and Black Civil Rights: Organizing Memphis Workers* (Urbana: University of Illinois Press, 1993); and Noel Ignatiev, *How the Irish Became White* (New York: Routledge, 1995). Besides W. E. B. Du Bois's magisterial *Black Reconstruction in America, 1860–1880* (1935; Cleveland: World Publishing, 1968), a fine collection of his work that highlights his influence in unifying the narratives of labor, left, and black history is the one edited by David Levering Lewis, *W. E. B. Du Bois: A Reader* (New York: Henry Holt, 1995). See also Roediger, *Working toward Whiteness: How America's Immigrants Became White* (New York: Basic Books, 2005), esp. chap. 7. For the "blame the Cold War" thesis see for example Jacquelyn Dowd Hall, "The Long Civil Rights Movement and the Political Uses of the Past," *Journal of American History* 91, no. 4 (March 2005), 1233–63, revised version of Professor Hall's presidential address, Organization of American Historians annual meeting, March 27, 2004, Boston, reported by historian Rick Shenkman, "Reporter's Notebook: Highlights from the 2004 OAH Convention," History News Network, <http://hnn.us/articles/4320.html> (March 30, 2004). Among those questioning that view are Steven F. Lawson, *Civil Rights Crossroads: Nation, Community, and the Black Freedom Struggle* (Lexington: University Press of Kentucky, 2003), 21–22; and Fairclough, *Better Day Coming*, 215–16. On black postal worker activists who were Republicans, see telephone conversation with black journalist Richard Peery, November 20, 2008, Cleveland.

40. McGee, *Negro in the Chicago Post Office (Dissertation)*, 81–85.

41. On euphemisms for "white supremacy" in popular culture, see Payne and Green, *Time Longer than Rope*, 11. The entire collection of essays also attacks the labor/civil rights history dichotomy, and traces the various forms of what Adam Green calls black "critical citizenship" struggles that blurred workplace and community distinctions as it challenged white supremacy. On the first federal law banning blacks in the post office see *Statutes at Large* 2, chap. 48, sec. 4, 1802, italics added. There is evidence that blacks carried the mail from the seventeenth century until the early nineteenth-century ban. See William Reed, "Post office has been best gateway for Black jobs, opportunities," *Michigan Chronicle*, November 20, 2001, A6, from ProQuest (Ethnic News Watch and Historical Newspapers) website, <http://proquest.umi.com> (February 25, 2006). See also David R. Roediger, ed., *Black on White: Black Writers on What It Means to Be White* (New York: Schocken, 1998). The idea of a "migration magnet" was inspired by my reading of Lerone Bennett Jr., *The Shaping of Black America* (1974; New York: Penguin, 1993). See also Roger Waldinger, *Still the Promised City? African-Americans and New Immigrants in Postindustrial New York* (Cambridge, Mass.: Harvard University Press, 1996).

42. Political activism was already common for black women's groups in places where black men were disenfranchised, and the Alliance's Women's Auxiliary was more political

than other postal unions. The 1939 Hatch Act severely curtailed all government worker political activism, but it did not stop their spouses. See Gary Max Halter, "The Hatch Act Reconsidered" (Ph.D. diss., University of Maryland, 1969). On the black industrial union tradition and its influence on that region see for example Ernest Obadele-Starks, *Black Unionism in the Industrial South* (College Station: Texas A&M University Press, 2000); as well as Adam Fairclough, *Race and Democracy: The Civil Rights Struggle in Louisiana, 1915–1975* (Athens: University of Georgia Press, 1995); and Nelson, *Divided We Stand*, chap. 3, on New Orleans black worker formations. For that matter, we might also ask why Los Angeles, with its history of postal activism, was not more active than it was during the 1970 postal strike. See also Gilbert J. Gall, *The Politics of Right to Work: The Labor Federations as Special Interests, 1943–1979* (New York: Greenwood, 1988). Charlotte, North Carolina, mail clerks voted to wait five days before striking and apparently never did after that, and a strike vote narrowly lost in Houston. See official strike log, March 18–31, 1970, USPS Archives; and *Houston Chronicle* during the same period.

43. See for example Jeremy Brecher, *Strike!*, revised and updated ed. (Boston: South End Press, 1997), esp. chap. 7. This is not to say that wildcat strikes are always positive events: wildcat strikes have also been used historically against black workers by white workers seeking to eliminate blacks from skilled positions or from the workplace entirely. See for example Hill, *Black Labor*; and Harris, *Harder We Run*.

44. See Gilbert Osofsky, *Harlem: The Making of a Ghetto* (1963; New York: Harper, 1966), 170–71, on the 1918 civil rights law crafted by New York's first black legislator, Edward Johnson, a lawyer who was originally from Raleigh, North Carolina. For state labor anti-discrimination laws, see State of New York Executive Department, New York State Division of Human Rights, *Annual Report 1970* (State of New York, 1970), i; and New York State Commission Against Discrimination, *1948 Report of Progress* (State of New York, 1948), 43; Hill, *Black Labor*, introduction; David N. Gellman and David Quigley, eds., *Jim Crow New York: A Documentary History of Race and Citizenship, 1777–1877* (New York: New York University Press, 2003); and Arthur Ryland, oral history transcript, Box 4, folder 1976, Biller Files.

45. On New York's significance to the rest of the country as well as particulars of its movements see Tony Martin, *Race First: The Ideological and Organizational Struggles of Marcus Garvey and the Universal Negro Improvement Association* (Westport, Conn.: Greenwood Press, 1976), chap. 1; Fink and Greenberg, *Upheaval in the Quiet Zone*; and Bates, *Pullman Porters*. See also *UNIA Records*.

46. See for example Scott A. Sandage, "A Marble House Divided: The Lincoln Memorial, the Civil Rights Movement, and the Politics of Memory," in *Time Longer than Rope*, 492–535. On Howard University see Kevin Chappell, "Howard University: Mecca of Black Education," *Ebony* (May 2003), 60–68, 73; Franklin and Moss, *From Slavery to Freedom*, 130–31, 509, 523; Charles Reagan Wilson and William Ferris, eds., *Encyclopedia of Southern Culture* (Chapel Hill: University of North Carolina Press, 1989), xv, 1019, 1040, 1044, 1045, 1063; Jonathan Scott Holloway, *Confronting the Veil: Abram Harris, Jr., E. Franklin Frazier, and Ralph Bunche, 1919–1941* (Chapel Hill: University of North Carolina Press, 2002), esp. chap. 1; Mark Robert Schneider, *"We Return Fighting": The Civil Rights Movement in the Jazz Age* (Boston: Northeastern University Press, 2002), chap. 19. Despite its lack of industry that had attracted southern black migrants at a higher rate to urban northern centers like New York, Chicago, and Detroit, by 1930 Washington had become not only "the fifth largest city in African-America," but also "had the highest African-American percentage of the population. The District was 27 percent African-American while New York was 5 percent black

and Chicago 7 percent." See also Pauli Murray, *The Autobiography of a Black Activist, Feminist, Lawyer, Priest, and Poet* (1987; Knoxville: University of Tennessee Press, 1990), chap. 17, on the power of symbolic protest against Washington, D.C., Jim Crow in the 1940s.

47. See Paul Tennassee, "NAPFE: A Legacy of Contributions and Resistance," *National Alliance* 55, no. 10 (October 1999), 12–15, for his observation that the choice of Washington, D.C., in the early 1920s as headquarters for the Alliance was deliberate, because Washington "was where power resided and had to be lobbied constantly." It was also one of the first black organizations or postal unions to choose Washington as headquarters, and A. Philip Randolph even used the office at times. In addition to expanding the Alliance into an industrial organization open to all, during his tenure as president A. L. Glenn also created networks with black media and black organizations. The NRLCA headquarters is now in suburban D.C., in Alexandria, Virginia.

CHAPTER ONE

1. See "NALC Pioneer William Carney: From Runaway Slave to Civil War Hero," *Postal Record* (February 2001) (monthly journal of the National Association of Letter Carriers), <http://www.nalc.org/news/precord/0201-civilwar.html> (September 18, 2008). See also Frederick Douglass, *Narrative of the Life of Frederick Douglass, An American Slave* (1960; Cambridge, Mass.: Harvard University Press, 2001), 152; and "Black Postal Personnel, History," *Dual Charters and Blacks* folder, NALC Historical Files, National Association of Letter Carriers Library, Washington, D.C. See also Chandra Manning, *What This Cruel War Was Over: Soldiers, Slavery, and the Civil War* (New York: Alfred A. Knopf, 2007). I am also indebted to Carl Cruz, William Carney's great-great-great-nephew, for sharing family history with me.

2. See "NALC Pioneer William Carney." The article also notes: "Many early letter carriers were veterans, since appointments often were based on local political connections and it was common for a town's prominent citizens, and often the postmaster himself, to have been Union officers. There were just four letter carriers in New Bedford at the time of Carney's appointment in 1869. He was the only black." See also Historian, U.S. Postal Service, "African-American Postal Workers in the 19th Century," 4, <http://www.usps.com/postalhistory> (July 15, 2009). See also Deanna Boyd and Kendra Chen, "The History and Experience of African Americans in America's Postal Service," Smithsonian National Postal Museum, Washington, D.C., <http://www.postalmuseum.si.edu/AfricanAmericans/index.html> (September 6, 2008).

3. See John Walsh and Garth Mangum, *Labor Struggle in the Post Office: From Selective Lobbying to Collective Bargaining* (Armonk, N.Y.: M. E. Sharpe, 1992), 44. The first colonial post office was founded in 1639 in Massachusetts, and Pennsylvania followed in 1683. The southern colonies had no regular post offices, and instead utilized private messenger services between plantations, most of those messengers being enslaved African Americans. Benjamin Franklin was appointed the first U.S. postmaster of the new republic in 1775 by the Second Continental Congress, having already served as colonial Philadelphia postmaster from 1737 to 1753, and intra-colonial postmaster from 1753 until the American Revolution. See Kathleen Conkey, *The Postal Precipice: Can the U.S. Postal Service be Saved?* (Washington, D.C.: Center for the Study of Responsive Law, 1983), chap. 2; and M. Brady Mikusko, *Carriers in a Common Cause: A History of Letter Carriers and the NALC* (Washington, D.C.: National Association of Letter Carriers, 1989), 2.

4. See Historian, U.S. Postal Service, "African-American Postal Workers." See also Boyd and Chen, "History and Experience." See also Eric Foner, *Freedom's Lawmakers: A Directory of Black Officeholders during Reconstruction* (New York: Oxford University Press, 1993), 275–87. Six of the forty-three black postmasters that Foner lists were Union Army veterans, three of them also Freedmen's Bureau officials.

5. Kelly Barton Olds, "Public Service and Privatization in Antebellum America" (Ph.D. diss., University of Rochester, 1993), 4–5.

6. Ibid., 13.

7. Leon F. Litwack, *North of Slavery: The Negro in the Free States, 1790–1860* (1961; Chicago: University of Chicago Press, 1969), 31, 50, 57–59.

8. Ibid., 58. There is evidence that blacks carried the mail from the seventeenth century until the early nineteenth-century federal ban. See William Reed, "Post Office Has Been Best Gateway for Black Jobs, Opportunities," *Michigan Chronicle*, November 20, 2001, A6. See also Boyd and Chen, "History and Experience."

9. For white South Carolinians' reactions to Denmark Vesey's 1822 planned slave uprising see Vindex, *On the Liability of the Abolitionists to Criminal Punishment and on the Duty of the Non-Slave-Holding States to Suppress Their Efforts* (Charleston: A. E. Miller, 1835), 7 (Duke University Rare Book, Manuscript, and Special Collections Library); and Bertram Wyatt-Brown, "The Abolitionists' Postal Campaign of 1835," *Journal of Negro History* 50, no. 4 (October 1965), 227–38.

10. Litwack, *North of Slavery*, 57. Proslavery authorities especially kept a watchful eye on the integrated mariner workforce for any suspicious abolitionist activity. On black mariners see W. Jeffrey Bolster, " 'To Feel Like a Man': Black Seamen in the Northern States, 1800–1860," *Journal of American History* 76, no. 4 (March 1990), 1173–99; Bolster, *Black Jacks: African American Seamen in the Age of Sail* (Cambridge, Mass.: Harvard University Press, 1997); Marcus Rediker, *Between the Devil and the Deep Blue Sea: Merchant Seamen, Pirates, and the Anglo-American Maritime World, 1700–1750* (1987; Cambridge: Cambridge University Press, 1993); Marcus Rediker and Peter Linebaugh, "The Many Headed Hydra: Sailors, Slaves and the Atlantic Working Class in the Eighteenth Century," in *Gone to Croatan: Origins of North American Dropout Culture*, ed. Ron Sakolsky and James Koehnline (Brooklyn: Autonomedia, 1993), 129–60; and Herbert Aptheker, "Militant Abolitionism," *Journal of Negro History* 26, no. 4 (October 1941), 438–84.

11. Public Law, Post-Roads, *Statutes at Large* 2, chap. 48, sec. 4, 191, 1802, italics added. See also Reed, "Post Office."

12. Public Law, Post-Office, *Statutes at Large* 2, chap. 592, sect. 4, 594, 1810.

13. Litwack, *North of Slavery*, 31, 50.

14. See Public Law, Post-Office, *Statutes at Large* 4, chap. 64, sect. 7, 104, 1825, italics added. It is also interesting to note the reference to "persons" and not "men," suggesting that there was room for white women to serve as postal workers in the antebellum United States.

15. Litwack, *North of Slavery*, 58.

16. On the spoils system and the post office see Mikusko, *Carriers in a Common Cause*, 2–3. On Jacksonian democracy as "white affirmative action" see for example Theodore W. Allen, *The Invention of the White Race*, vol. 1, *Racial Oppression and Social Control* (London: Verso, 1995), 186. Allen has pointed out how historians continue "to ignore the most historically relevant fact about the [Jacksonian] spoils system, namely that it was first of all a 'white-race' spoils system." On the idea of the "white race" being a "white club" see Noel Ignatiev, *How the Irish Became White* (New York: Routledge, 1995).

17. W. E. B. Du Bois, *Black Reconstruction in America, 1860–1880* (1935; Cleveland: World Publishing, 1968), 102.

18. See *Dred Scott v. Sandford*, 60 U.S. 393 (1857). The Fourteenth Amendment in 1868 legally overturned the *Dred Scott* decision, but even by 1862 the U.S. attorney general was not treating it as legally enforceable. See Don E. Fehrenbacher, *The Dred Scott Case: Its Significance in American Law and Politics* (New York: Oxford University Press, 1978). The first letter carrier uniforms that appeared in 1868 were produced by the same manufacturer that had supplied uniforms to the Union Army. On postal uniform history see for example "Dressed for Success: The Evolution of Letter Carrier Uniforms," *Postal Record* (October 1986), 10–17, and *Postal Record* (February 1997), 6–13. Congress adopted the first official uniform for letter carriers in 1868, and manufacturers who had supplied military uniforms during the Civil War to the Union Army were now looking for business and eager to provide standardized clothing for postal employees. Early regulations and descriptions also refer to the uniform as being "cadet gray." I am indebted to Candace Main Rush, retired NALC historian, for this reference and background history in an electronic communication, October 6, 2003. See also Donald R. Shaffer, *After the Glory: The Struggles of Black Civil War Veterans* (Lawrence: University Press of Kansas, 2004), esp. 160–63: Shaffer importantly notes a unique Civil War memory among black military veterans and notes the leading roles of William Carney and James Trotter (both black postal workers) in the autonomous reunions of black Civil War veterans from 1885 to 1887.

19. Jacqueline Jones, *American Work: Four Centuries of Black and White Labor* (New York: W. W. Norton, 1998), 259. At the time it was still referred to as the U.S. Post Office Department.

20. See Historian, U.S. Postal Service, "List of Known African-American Post Office Clerks, 1800s," <http://www.usps.com/postalhistory> (July 15, 2009); and Jennifer M. Lynch, electronic communication to author, July 2, 2008.

21. Nell was an integrationist to the point of even opposing exclusively black churches, somewhat reminiscent of the Frederick Douglass and Martin Delaney debates of that period over assimilation versus black nationalism in general. On Nell, see Dorothy Porter Wesley, "Integration versus Separatism: William Cooper Nell's Role in the Struggle for Equality," in *Courage and Conscience: Black and White Abolitionists in Boston*, ed. Donald M. Jacobs (Bloomington: Indiana University Press, 1993), 207–24. On Nell's work against the New York property qualification, see David N. Gellman and David Quigley, eds., *Jim Crow New York: A Documentary History of Race and Citizenship, 1777–1877* (New York: New York University Press, 2003), 271–77, documents taken from William C. Nell, *Property Qualification or No Property Qualification: A Few Facts from the Record of Patriotic Services of the Colored Men of New York during the Wars of 1776 and 1812, with a Compendium of Their Present Business and Property Statistics* (New York, 1860). On the Douglass-Delaney debates, see *The Life and Writings of Frederick Douglass*, ed. Philip S. Foner, vol. 4, *Reconstruction and After* (New York: International Publishers, 1955), 276–81.

22. Litwack, *North of Slavery*, 58–59; and Robert P. Smith, "William Cooper Nell: Crusading Black Abolitionist," *Journal of Negro History* 55, no. 3 (July 1970), 194.

23. Historian, U.S. Postal Service, "African-American Postal Workers," <http://www.usps.com/postalhistory> (July 15, 2009). See also Boyd and Chen, "History and Experience." The U.S. Postal Service article differs from the NALC's official history that claims Curry in 1867 as the first black carrier in the nation. See Mikusko, *Carriers in a Common Cause*, 64–65. See also Eric Foner, *Reconstruction: America's Unfinished Revolution, 1863–1877* (New York: Harper, 1988), 240. See also "A Veteran Gone," *Postal Record* (June 1899), 156,

which wrote that Curry suffered paralysis at work in 1897 and died in April 1899. The NALC honored him as "the first colored letter carrier ever appointed in America." Born in Baltimore in 1840, he had served in Washington, D.C., at the Quartermaster General's office at the outbreak of the Civil War, becoming a messenger for the Postmaster General in 1866, sexton in 1868, clerk in 1869, messenger in 1870, and finally a carrier in 1871 (Lynch, electronic communication to author, July 2, 2008, citing *Boyd's Directory of Washington*).

24. John Hope Franklin and Alfred A. Moss Jr., *From Slavery to Freedom: A History of African Americans*, 8th ed. (1947; Boston: McGraw-Hill, 2000), 230.

25. Public Law, Post-Office Department, *Statutes at Large* 13, chap. 96, 515, 1865, italics added. See also *Statutes at Large* 13, chap. 90, 1865; "A Veteran Gone"; Historian, U.S. Postal Service, "African-American Postal Workers," 4–5; Branch 142 [NALC], <http://www.branch142.com> (December 31, 2008); "Disqualification of Color," 63, *Congressional Globe* online, December 19, 1864, American Memory website, Library of Congress, <http://memory.loc.gov> (September 22, 2008); and Smith, "William Cooper Nell," 199n67.

26. See also Paul P. Van Riper, *History of the United States Civil Service* (Evanston, Ill.: Row, Peterson, and Company, 1958), 162, who notes: "There are no figures showing the precise extent to which veterans came into the public service before 1900." But see also Department of Commerce and Labor Bureau of the Census, S. N. D. North Director, *Statistics of Employees: Executive Civil Service of the United States 1907*, Bulletin 94 (Washington, D.C.: Government Printing Office, 1908), 9, 46, 152–54, 159–61, that reveals, among other things, that 286,902 people worked in the federal government in civil service jobs, of whom 180,336 were postal workers and postmasters; Civil War veterans still working for the post office by 1907 (most by then would have been in their sixties at least) numbered 3,557, compared to 8,464 throughout the civil service (including 194 blacks, 83 in the District of Columbia alone); of 53,157 male postmasters (244 of them black), 4,977, or almost 10 percent, were Civil War veterans. (Female postmasters, incidentally, according to this survey numbered 9,057, or just under 7 percent, with 36 of them black.) See also Historian, U.S. Postal Service, "African-American Postal Workers"; and Boyd and Chen, "History and Experience."

27. See Historian, U.S. Postal Service, "Post Office Clerks, 1800s"; Barbara A. Gannon, "The Won Cause: Black and White Comradeship in the Grand Army of the Republic" (Ph.D. diss., Pennsylvania State University, 2005), 152–53; and electronic communication from Gannon to author, August 9, 2007.

28. Stephen R. Fox, *The Guardian of Boston: William Monroe Trotter* (New York: Atheneum, 1970), 8.

29. Historian, U.S. Postal Service, "African-American Postal Workers," 6; and "Stand By Their Colored Associate," *New York Times*, April 17, 1893. See also William H. Harris, *The Harder We Run: Black Workers since the Civil War* (New York: Oxford University Press, 1982).

30. See "Report of Proceedings of First Annual Convention, National Association of Letter Carriers of the United States," *Postal Record* (August / September 1890), 196, 198, 199; and "Branches," *Postal Record* (June / July 1891), 111. See also Historian, U.S. Postal Service, "List of Known African-American Letter Carriers, 1800s," which indicates that Washington started work with the post office in 1874, Moss in 1886. See also Paula J. Giddings, *Ida, A Sword among Lions: Ida B. Wells and the Campaign against Lynching* (New York: Amistad, 2008), 71, 171–83, 260. See also Peter Dodson, "Affairs at Coon City," *Postal Record* (November 1889), 14, and *Postal Record* (February 1890), 67. The latter included this passage: "At a recent meeting of the Coon City Association of Eminent Crap Shooters there was received

the application for membership, of Prof. Thomas Dillberry Rice." See also "A Letter Carrier Discharged on Complaint of Two Negroes," *Postal Record* (November 1891), 177, regarding a Nashville, Tennessee, carrier fired after assaulting and using racial epithets against two blacks while on the job.

31. Boyd and Chen, "History and Experience"; Historian, U.S. Postal Service, "African-American Postal Workers," which points out that the actual number of black postal workers was probably much higher.

32. Historian, U.S. Postal Service, "African-American Postal Workers," 3, and "List of Known African-American Employees, 1800s: Headquarters Employees, Railway Mail Service Employees, U.S. Mail Carriers, Contractors, and others," <http://www.usps.com/postalhistory> (July 15, 2009).

33. Vern K. Baxter, *Labor and Politics in the U.S. Postal Service* (New York: Plenum, 1994), 57.

34. Leon F. Litwack, *Trouble in Mind: Black Southerners in the Age of Jim Crow* (New York: Alfred A. Knopf, 1998), 161.

35. "The Colored Postmaster," *New York Times*, April 18, 1869, 9; "War on Negro Officials," *New York Times*, September 18, 1897, 1; "Lake City Wants Post Office," *New York Times*, May 22, 1899, 5.

36. "A Colored Postmaster's Trials," *Washington Post*, September 6, 1889, 2; "Colored Men in Office," *Washington Post*, October 29, 1889, 4; and "The Colored Postmaster," *Washington Post*, April 16, 1891, 4.

37. William H. Chafe et al., eds., *Remembering Jim Crow: African Americans Tell about Life in the Segregated South* (New York: New Press, 2001), 107–15. See also Franklin and Moss, *From Slavery to Freedom*, 342.

38. See "Black Postal Personnel, History"; Willard B. Gatewood, "Theodore Roosevelt and the Indianola Affair," *Journal of Negro History* 53, no. 1 (January 1968), 48–69; and Boyd and Chen, "History and Experience."

39. Litwack, *Trouble in Mind*, 162.

40. Historian, U.S. Postal Service, "List of Known African-American Employees"; and Boyd and Chen, "History and Experience."

41. See A. L. Glenn, *History of the National Alliance of Postal Employees, 1913–1955* (Washington, D.C.: National Alliance of Postal Employees, 1956), 25. It was taken from an article that appeared in the *Postal Alliance*, December 1941, by John Wesley Dobbs, Atlanta, "Negroes as Federal Employees in the State of Georgia." Alonzo L. Glenn had been president of the Alliance from 1921 to 1925. Anne Firor Scott conversation with author, May 10, 2003, and electronic message to author, July 12, 2003.

42. Hartford Boykin Sr. interview and tape summary by Karen Ferguson, July 16, 1993, Wilmington, N.C., BTV.

43. "Abe Whitess, mayor of Douglasville," *Born in Slavery: Slave Narratives from the Federal Writers Project, 1936–1938, Alabama Narratives*, 1:423–24, online collection, Library of Congress, <http://memory.loc.gov> (February 25, 2006).

44. Baxter, *Labor and Politics*, chap. 3.

45. A similar tendency in private sector unionism played out in the National Labor Union that was formed in 1866, where white unions vacillated over whether to allow blacks to join their unions or suggest that they form their own. That kind of treatment led to the formation of the Negro National Labor Union in 1869, although both collapsed soon after. See Lerone Bennett Jr., *The Shaping of Black America* (1974; New York: Penguin, 1993), 259–64; and Harris, *Harder We Run*, 25–26.

46. An early issue of the *Postal Alliance* paid tribute to Henry Boyd of Selma, Alabama. Retired in 1920 after forty-seven years of service, Boyd was possibly the oldest living black railway postal clerk and one of the first recorded black postal railway clerks, having been hired in 1873. See Glenn, *History of the National Alliance*, 348. That same year Jesse C. Duke, also of Selma, was himself hired as a railway postal clerk. Duke, a prominent outspoken local Republican Party and Baptist church leader, was removed from the post office in 1886 for his political activism, at which time he began his crusading journalism career. See Allen W. Jones, "The Black Press in the New South: Jesse C. Duke's Struggle for Justice and Equality," *Journal of Negro History* 64, no. 3 (Summer 1979), 215–28. While the "local" is the standard term for the local unit of most national and international union organizations, the Alliance referred to them as "branches" until after the 1970 national convention. See *New York Alliance Leader*, September–October 1970, 8. The NALC still calls local organizations "branches." See also Historian, U.S. Postal Service, "Post office clerks, 1800s," that has James Elias Rector of Little Rock, Arkansas, appointed as a clerk in 1872.

47. Du Bois, *Black Reconstruction*, 708.

48. See Mikusko, *Carriers in a Common Cause*, 31, 64–65; and Sterling D. Spero, *Government as Employer* (1948; Carbondale: Southern Illinois University Press, 1972), chap. 7. On African Americans and the Grand Army of the Republic (that included Jim Crow branches in the South), see Gannon, "Won Cause." See also Stuart McConnell, *Glorious Contention: The Grand Army of the Republic, 1865–1900* (Chapel Hill: University of North Carolina Press, 1992); and Mary R. Dearing, *Veterans in Politics: The Story of the G.A.R.* (Baton Rouge: Louisiana State University Press, 1952). See also a synopsis of the Grand Army of the Republic (GAR) on the website of the Sons of Union Veterans of the Civil War, <http://www.suvcw.org/gar.htm> (July 10, 2007). The GAR's evolution into a powerful political lobby and fraternal order became a model for the NALC, especially among the postal unions. On Augustus "Gus" Richmond and Henry F. Thompson, see "National Association of U.S. Post-office Clerks," *Postal Record* (February 1890), 88; and Historian, U.S. Postal Service, "List of Known African-American Employees."

49. See Van Riper, *United States Civil Service*, 161–62; and Historian, U.S. Postal Service, "African-American Postal Workers." See also Boyd and Chen, "History and Experience"; and their statistical graphs of U.S. Postal Service historian Jennifer Lynch's "known" black appointees that chart three periods: 1865–1876, 1877–1889, and 1890–1900. New black carrier appointments numbered 62, 53, and 23, respectively; black clerk appointments were 42, 42, and 3, respectively; and postmasters were 37, 34, and 42, respectively. Lynch made extensive use of newspapers and postal records, among other things. Electronic communication from Lynch to author, July 1, 2008. Civil Service examinations began for clerks and carriers in 1883. See Civil Service Act, *Statutes at Large* 22, chap. 27, 403 (1883)

50. Spero, *Government as Employer*, 107.

51. Franklin and Moss, *From Slavery to Freedom*, 432. See also Van Riper, *United States Civil Service*, 104. The "rule of three" ("rule of four" originally, from 1883 to 1888) has to be one of the more arcane features still extant in the civil service. Its establishment, according to Van Riper, was originally meant to "offer some discretion for the appointing officer."

52. Glenn, *History of the National Alliance*, 23.

53. See also Rayford W. Logan, *The Betrayal of the Negro: From Rutherford B. Hayes to Woodrow Wilson*, new enlarged ed. (1954; New York: Collier, 1965), and *The Negro in American Life and Thought: The Nadir, 1877–1901* (New York: Dial, 1954). On the origins of the civil service (with its roots in 1871 in the administration of President Ulysses S. Grant, 1869–

1877), its built-in inequality, its adoption by states and municipalities after the 1883 Pendleton Act, and the importance of the term "merit" to the act's passage, see Frances Gottfried, *The Merit System and Municipal Civil Service: A Fostering of Social Inequality* (New York: Greenwood, 1988), 7, and chap. 5.

54. See Kathleen L. Wolgemuth, "Woodrow Wilson and Federal Segregation," *Journal of Negro History* 44, no. 2 (April 1959), 158–73, esp. 162–65; Nancy J. Weiss, "The Negro and the New Freedom: Fighting Wilsonian Segregation," *Political Science Quarterly* 84, no. 1 (March 1969), 63–79; August Meier and Elliott Rudwick, "The Rise of Segregation in the Federal Bureaucracy, 1900–1930," *Phylon* 28, no. 2 (2nd Qtr., 1967), 178–84; Logan, *Betrayal of the Negro*, chap. 17; David Levering Lewis, *W. E. B. Du Bois: Biography of a Race, 1868–1919* (New York: Henry Holt, 1993), 423–24; Boyd and Chen, "History and Experience"; and Litwack, *Trouble in Mind*, 373. Litwack describes the Wilson administration: "Black men were dismissed from office, or their positions were downgraded. Jim Crow, already triumphant in Washington, D.C., was now extended to government departments, much to the relief of Wilson's wife Ellen, who had expressed shock at seeing black men and white women working in the same room in the Post Office Department." See also Du Bois, from his "Another Open Letter to Woodrow Wilson" (from the September 1913 *Crisis*), protesting cages built to segregate black workers within white areas when work areas could not be separated due to the nature of the work. Reprinted in David Levering Lewis, ed., *W. E. B. Du Bois: A Reader* (New York: Henry Holt, 1995), 446. Henry W. McGee has pointed to the demands by white southern congressmen at the time for Wilson to declare such an order after they had failed to pass similar legislation, in *The Negro in the Chicago Post Office: Henry W. McGee Autobiography and Dissertation* (Chicago: VolumeOne Press, 1999) (originally "The Negro in the Chicago Post Office," master's thesis, University of Chicago, 1961), 9–10, 25 *(Dissertation)*. See also Fox, *Guardian of Boston*, 168–86; and Richard Marius, *A Short Guide to Writing about History* (New York: HarperCollins, 1995), 105–28.

55. See Wolgemuth, "Woodrow Wilson and Federal Segregation," esp. 159–61; Weiss, "Fighting Wilsonian Segregation"; Meier and Rudwick, "Rise of Segregation"; and McGee, *Negro in the Chicago Post Office*.

56. Allan H. Spear, *Black Chicago: The Making of a Negro Ghetto, 1890–1920* (Chicago: University of Chicago Press, 1967), 23n., 37, 109; and McGee, *Negro in the Chicago Post Office (Dissertation)*, chap. 2. McGee also notes (16–17) that the Phalanx Forum was engaged in a "bitter rivalry" with the National Alliance of Postal Employees, as the latter was a trade union and the former a lobbying group but also a self-aggrandizing middle-class organization.

57. See for example Glenn, *History of the National Alliance*, esp. chap. 29.

58. Ellen Wright and Michel Fabre, eds., *Richard Wright Reader* (New York: Harper and Row, 1978), 352. "Throwing the scheme" involves rapidly placing addressed mail into designated case compartments. The civil service examination for clerks and carriers measures one's ability to quickly memorize and answer questions relating to a sample "scheme" as well as being able to quickly differentiate correct from incorrectly typed addresses. For a sample of the written exam for a would-be "substitute railway mail clerk," see James C. O'Brien and Philip P. Marenberg, *Your Federal Civil Service* (New York: Funk and Wagnalls, 1940), 1.

59. McGee, *Negro in the Chicago Post Office*; and Paul Tennassee, "NAPFE: A Legacy of Contributions and Resistance," *National Alliance* (October 1999), 12. The Railway Post Office was officially terminated in 1977 (replaced by air and truck transportation). By the early 1960s it had already been in sharp decline. Moving mail by rail received a near-fatal

blow with the Transportation Act of 1958 that allowed the discontinuance of passenger trains that were losing money—including those carrying mail. The post office then began moving away from urban rail terminals toward suburban distribution post offices, although some mail is still moved by rail today. See Baxter, *Labor and Politics*, 50–53; and U.S. Postal Service, *The United States Postal Service: An American History, 1775–2006* (Washington, D.C.: USPS Publication 100, 2007), 16–18. See also "RR Drops Mails; NPU Battles For MVS Jobs," *Progressive* (July 1963), 1, which began: "The Reading [Pennsylvania] Railroad has become the first railroad to drop transportation of the mails."

60. See for example Harris, *Harder We Run*, chap. 2.

61. Tennessee, "Legacy," 12. The evidence indicates that railroad mail clerking was done almost exclusively by men. In 1965 the NAPE became the National Alliance of Postal and Federal Employees (NAPFE), incorporating other federal workers. Tennessee is their resident historian.

62. Glenn, *History of the National Alliance*, chap. 1; and Tennessee, "Legacy," 12.

63. See for example Franklin and Moss, *From Slavery to Freedom*, chaps. 14–18; David R. Roediger, *Working toward Whiteness: How America's Immigrants Became White* (New York: Basic Books, 2005); Matthew Frye Jacobson, *Whiteness of a Different Color: European Immigrants and the Alchemy of Race* (Cambridge, Mass.: Harvard University Press, 1998); and Philip F. Rubio, *A History of Affirmative Action, 1619–2000* (Jackson: University Press of Mississippi, 2001), chaps. 3 and 7.

64. Glenn, *History of the National Alliance*, 45. The 1913 constitution was reprinted in its entirety.

65. Ibid., 50, italics added. Rituals and initiations have always been standard union practices. On white unions and their exclusionary rituals and initiations see for example Herbert Hill, *Black Labor and the American Legal System: Race, Work, and the Law* (1977; Madison: University of Wisconsin Press, 1985).

66. Glenn, *History of the National Alliance*, 50–51, 75.

67. Ibid., 45. See also author interview with Jackson, Mississippi, NAPFE branch president (at that time) Felix Bell, August 11, 2004, Washington, D.C.

68. Paul Tennessee, "A Book in the Making: African Americans: An Untold Story, NAPFE, 1913–2000," *National Alliance* (April 1998), 16. See also Glenn, *History of the National Alliance*. A few other law schools were represented in the Alliance's membership, such as Indiana University and the University of Michigan.

69. Tennessee, "Research and Education Corner: Individuals to Remember: James Foster Spencer, Henry T. Ellington, Ernest M. Thomas, Henry Lincoln Johnson," *National Alliance* (June 1999), 12. The National Alliance's monthly magazine had been founded in 1915 as the *Postal Alliance*, and kept that name until 1966 when it was changed to the *National Alliance*.

70. Paul Ortiz, "'Eat Your Bread without Butter, But Pay Your Poll Tax!': Roots of the African American Voter Registration Movement in Florida, 1919–1920," in *Time Longer than Rope: A Century of African American Activism, 1850–1950*, ed. Charles M. Payne and Adam Green (New York: New York University Press, 2003), 196–97. The year 1919 also saw the National Alliance holding its national convention in Jacksonville. See Glenn, *History of the National Alliance*, 54.

71. See for example Robert Zieger, *The CIO: 1935–1955* (Chapel Hill: University of North Carolina Press, 1995), 246–48. "Right to work" laws, with an anti-union bias built into the very term, typically outlawed the union shop, although some also outlawed public worker

union recognition. See for example Gilbert J. Gall, *The Politics of Right to Work: The Labor Federations as Special Interests, 1943–1979* (New York: Greenwood, 1988).

72. The Alliance's first branches came from railway mail clerk "clubs" in Houston, Kansas City, St. Louis, Memphis, Atlanta, Birmingham, Jacksonville, and Washington, D.C. (in other words, urban areas, the Deep South, and border states). Their inaugural convention in Chattanooga, Tennessee, in 1913 found nine of the original thirteen delegations representing southern states that Glenn called the "thirteen original colonies." They included Alabama, Arkansas, Florida, Georgia, Illinois, Indiana, Kansas, Louisiana, Mississippi, Missouri, North Carolina, Tennessee, and Texas. A number of subsequent conventions were held in the South as well. See Glenn, *History of the National Alliance*, 17, 20. Glenn's history includes not just his narrative but also verbatim reprints of selected articles from the *Postal Alliance*, official documents, and union correspondence. For black worker industrial organizing on the Texas Gulf Coast see Ernest Obadele-Starks, *Black Unionism in the Industrial South* (College Station: Texas A&M University Press, 2000).

73. National Alliance co-founder and first president Henry L. Mims of Houston, Texas, had earlier referred to himself as president of a local predecessor to the Alliance, the "Progressive Postal League." Glenn, *History of the National Alliance*, 19. On white supremacy in the Progressive movement, see Robert Allen, *Reluctant Reformers: Racism and Social Reform Movements in the United States* (Washington, D.C.: Howard University Press, 1983), chap. 4.

74. On speedup, the gag order, and the Lloyd–La Follette Act see Walsh and Mangum, *Labor Struggle*, 75–77. On RMA exclusion see Tennassee, "Legacy," 12.

75. Hubert Harrison, once an associate of Marcus Garvey and also a member of the IWW, was born in St. Croix, Virgin Islands. After Harrison wrote publicly against the accommodationist politics of Booker T. Washington in 1911, friends of Washington used their influence to get Harrison fired from his postal job. See Jeffrey B. Perry, ed., *A Hubert Harrison Reader* (Middletown, Conn.: Wesleyan University Press, 2001), 164–65; and Perry, *Hubert Harrison: The Voice of Harlem Radicalism, 1883–1918* (New York: Columbia University Press, 2009), 83–87. See also Sterling D. Spero and Abram L. Harris, *The Black Worker: The Negro and the Labor Movement* (1931; New York: Atheneum, 1969), 331: "During the active part of its life the I.W.W. issued about one million membership cards. About 100,000 of these cards were issued to Negroes." See also Winston James, *Holding Aloft the Banner of Ethiopia: Caribbean Radicalism in Early Twentieth-Century America* (London: Verso, 2000), 122–25, 183.

76. See James, *Holding Aloft the Banner*; and *UNIA Records*, esp. reel 5, series E, box 12, e88, for a good example of coalition: a letter from the Joint Committee Against Discrimination (JCAD), of which the UNIA was a member, and dated April 16, 1936, requesting a UNIA representative to serve on a community to investigate relief distribution in Harlem. The JCAD included forty-six organizations, including the BSCP, CPUSA, Socialist Party, Father Divine's Mission, NAACP, and black fraternity Alpha Phi Alpha. One small connection I have found between UNIA and the National Alliance is in Glenn, *History of the National Alliance*, 66–67: Henry Johnson, the National Alliance attorney for about two decades, had also represented Marcus Garvey in 1923. See Tennassee, "Legacy."

77. Glenn, *History of the National Alliance*, 422. Glenn also discusses (72–73) James B. Cobb, who became NAPE president in 1953, and who was a Durham, North Carolina, native and Howard Law School graduate. See also Glenn's mention (68) of Augusta, Georgia, letter carrier Thomas P. Bomar, who became a Howard Law School graduate and was later elected NAPE national secretary in 1939. On Charles Hamilton Houston and Howard Law

School's historic evolution of activism see Genna Rae McNeil, *Groundwork: Charles Hamilton Houston and the Struggle for Civil Rights* (Philadelphia: University of Pennsylvania Press, 1983). The reference to Washington, D.C., as a "transitional" city comes from William Ferris, conversation with author following talk at Duke University, Durham, North Carolina, September 3, 2003. On Howard University and Washington, D.C., as black intellectual centers see Jonathan Scott Holloway, *Confronting the Veil: Abram Harris, Jr., E. Franklin Frazier, and Ralph Bunche, 1919–1941* (Chapel Hill: University of North Carolina Press, 2002), esp. chap. 1.

78. Glenn, *History of the National Alliance*, 10, introduction. See for example Arthur Ryland, black member of MBPU and before that NFPOC New York City Local 10, interview with Dana Schecter, oral history transcript, November 19, 1976, Box 4, 1976, Biller Files, recalling entering the post office in 1927 at a time when he and other blacks were not allowed to hold clerk jobs that had contact with the public. On discrimination against black women in retail jobs, see for example Spear, *Black Chicago*, 155. See also Michael Keith Honey, *Black Workers Remember: An Oral History of Segregation, Unionism, and the Freedom Struggle* (Berkeley: University of California Press, 1999), 156, for black labor activist George Holloway's recollection of 1940s Memphis: "Blacks couldn't do any [postal] job accept [*sic*] letter carrier, because they wouldn't let us handle money. I quit the post office because I had a high test score, and they would only let me be a mail carrier."

79. Spero and Harris, *Black Worker*, 122. See also Daniel M. Johnson and Rex R. Campbell, *Black Migration in America: A Social Demographic History* (Durham, N.C.: Duke University Press, 1981).

80. Glenn, *History of the National Alliance*, 56.

81. Ibid., 54, 94.

82. Spero and Harris, *Black Worker*, 123. In *History of the National Alliance*, 54, 56, and 94, Glenn acknowledged the 1920s passivity on the part of the Alliance, but he also emphasized the absence of interest that the post office had in the welfare of the Alliance and black postal workers in general. The Alliance probably was circumspect then in dealing with postal management, while at the same time it was engaged in membership recruitment.

83. Spero and Harris, *Black Worker*, 124.

84. Glenn, *History of the National Alliance*, 87.

85. Ibid., 105–7; and Walsh and Mangum, *Labor Struggle*, 54.

86. Glenn, *History of the National Alliance*, chap. 5. See also Bates, *Pullman Porters*, 36–41, 126; and Paul Tennassee, "Governance, The House of Labor and Black Nationalism: A Review," *National Alliance* (March 2001), 24. The nationwide black nationalist 1924 "Negro Sanhedrin" convention in Chicago that hosted over 500 delegates invited the National Alliance—but not Randolph. The conference, according to historian Jonathan Scott Holloway, was part of Howard University professor Kelly Miller's "pro-American," "conservative," and "middle-class" vision that deliberately excluded socialists and communists, and ultimately was deemed a failure. The black intellectual center to the left of Miller built around Howard University, which Holloway notes included Ralph Bunche, Abram Harris, and E. Franklin Frazier, actually parallels the experience of many National Alliance officers. Many of the latter like President James B. Cobb held undergraduate or advanced degrees from Howard, and National Alliance headquarters and Howard University are located in the same Washington, D.C., neighborhood. See Glenn, *History of the National Alliance*, 326, for an account of the Alliance's participation in the 1924 Negro Sanhedrin or All-Race Conference in Chicago, where "nearly every Negro organization in the country

was represented," although the Alliance protested the lack of labor groups. Sanhedrin is "a reference to the Great Sanhedrin, the highest court of justice in ancient Jerusalem." See Holloway, *Confronting the Veil*, 25, introduction; and Bates, *Pullman Porters*, 38.

87. "Objectives," *Postal Alliance* (January 1942), 1. The only issue of the journal published before the 1940s that I have been able to find was the February 1934 edition, which did not contain any set of objectives, so they must have either appeared sometime between then and the January 1942 issue, or the latter in fact was the first appearance. See also Glenn, *History* of the National Alliance, chap. 14.

88. Glenn, *History of the National Alliance*, 18, 70, 76, 78. The districts approved at the 1923 Fort Worth convention were (1) Texas, New Mexico, and Arizona; (2) Louisiana and Mississippi; (3) Alabama and Florida; (4) Arkansas and Oklahoma; (5) Georgia and South Carolina; (6) Maryland, Washington, D.C., Virginia, West Virginia, and North Carolina; (7) Indiana, Illinois, Ohio, western Pennsylvania, Michigan, and Wisconsin; (8) Tennessee and Kentucky; (9) Missouri and Minnesota; (10) Iowa, Kansas, Nebraska, Colorado, North Dakota, and South Dakota; and (11) Delaware, eastern Pennsylvania, New Jersey, New York and the Northeast.

89. Ibid., 43.

90. On Kansas City and Detroit see ibid., 74, 301. On Chicago see ibid., 82; and Harry Haywood, *Black Bolshevik: Autobiography of an Afro-American Communist* (Chicago: Liberator Press, 1978), 98–99. It is interesting to see Haywood, coming from Houston, finding similar Republican Party patronage "connections," as he put it, with the "[Martin] Madden political machine" in Chicago. Madden, a member of the House Postal Committee, was a white congressman who helped many black constituents get postal jobs. Haywood was able to take the exam (with ten extra veteran points) through "S. L. Jackson of the Wabash Avenue YMCA, who at that time was a Black Republican stalwart." Haywood, *Black Bolshevik*, 98, 649. See also Glenn, *History of the National Alliance*, 94, on Alliance absorption of local clubs.

91. There is little discussion in Glenn's history, however, of direct action by branch members before 1940, although it was not uncommon for Alliance members publicly confronting postal officials. See for example Glenn, *History of the National Alliance*, 91, where delegates to the Alliance's 1925 convention challenged First Assistant Postmaster-General Bartlett on discrimination at the post office. See also Glenn, *History of the National Alliance*, chap. 19, "Branches and Their Activities."

92. Ibid., 78. "Eligibles" were employees with enough seniority who were therefore "eligible" to bid an open postal job for which they were considered qualified.

93. Author interview with William H. Burrus Jr., January 16, 2009, Washington, D.C.; and Mikusko, *Carriers in a Common Cause*, 64–65.

94. John Dittmer, *Local People: The Struggle for Civil Rights in Mississippi* (Urbana: University of Illinois Press, 1994), 20, 30, 42, and 229. Black postal workers who were NAACP members in Jackson included A. W. Wells, A. J. Noel, John W. Dixon, R. L. T. Smith, Percy Greene, Carsie Hall, and Jack Young. The Jackson NALC Branch 207 (later to become Branch 217 in 1962) included Dixon, Young, and Hall—the latter two becoming the state's first civil rights lawyers, providing continuity in the 1950s and 1960s civil rights struggles. Hall and Wells were both Alliance officials, and it is possible that some or all of the others were Alliance members as well. See also Glenn, *History of the National Alliance*, 295; George Bell, "Mississippi," *Postal Record* (September 1941), 412; and convention proceedings, *Postal Record* (October 1941), 567. A telephone conversation with Willenham Castilla, lifetime

National Alliance and NAACP activist, January 26, 2009, revealed that Castilla, who holds a master's degree, worked for the post office from 1951 to 1985. White NALC members, he said, during the first half of the twentieth century formed the separate Mississippi Association based in the eastern part of the state.

95. In 1930 the Urban League reported: "The National Federation of Post Office Clerks admits all Negroes to membership, and in 1926 had only two locals composed entirely of Negroes. These locals were located in Washington, D.C., Local No. 148, and Jacksonville, Florida, Local No. 492." National Urban League, *Negro Membership in American Labor Unions* (New York: Alexander Press, 1930). This is the earliest record I have found of Jim Crow NFPOC locals, but they probably began earlier than 1926. Both locals were in Alliance strongholds, and Jacksonville had seen white terrorism against black voting rights advocates who often were black postal workers. See Paul Ortiz, *Emancipation Betrayed: The Hidden History of Black Organizing and White Violence in Florida from Reconstruction to the Bloody Election of 1920* (Berkeley: University of California Press, 2005), esp. 173.

96. Convention proceedings, *Postal Record* (September 1917), 294–95. Unknown is the Michigan delegate who sponsored the "additional charter" resolution, as it was called. He was mistakenly identified in the official proceedings (295) as S. W. Ankenbrandt of Detroit, who at the 1919 convention not only denied having done so but also denounced the resolution. See convention proceedings, *Postal Record* (October 1919), 331–32. Convention proceedings were published within the *Postal Record* through 1941. After that, only summaries were published in the *Postal Record*, and the proceedings were published separately.

97. Convention proceedings, *Postal Record* (October 1935), 510. It was in the 1919 debate that "separate charter" was first heard. See convention proceedings, *Postal Record* (October 1919), 332. In 1935 I have found the first reference to "dual charters"—by opponents and in the published minutes. See convention proceedings, *Postal Record* (October, 1935), 509–10. By 1939, Jim Crow proponents (the Louisiana and Alabama State Associations) used the term "dual charters" in their resolution calling for segregation. See convention proceedings, *Postal Record* (October 1935), 499.

98. *Buchanan v. Warley*, according to the *Postal Alliance*, involved William Warley, a black letter carrier and local NAACP branch president in Louisville who filed suit against a city ordinance segregating housing by race. See "Editor's Notebook: Post Office Employees Make Great Contributions to Civil Rights," *Postal Alliance* (July 1950), 4. See *Buchanan v. Warley*, 245 U.S. 60 (1917): Charles Buchanan was a white man trying to enforce a contract on the sale of his house to Warley, whom the Court said had used the Louisville ordinance as a kind of escape clause. Buchanan's lawsuit argued that the ordinance violated the Fourteenth Amendment, while Warley ostensibly argued that the ordinance properly followed *Plessy v. Ferguson*. Buchanan's case, argued by Clayton Blakey of Louisville and the NAACP's president Moorfield Storey of Boston, prevailed. But in fact this was an NAACP-backed arranged litigation between Buchanan, a sympathetic white real estate agent, and Warley to test and try to overturn the law. See Roger L. Rice, "Residential Segregation by Law, 1910–1917," *Journal of Southern History* 34, no. 2 (May 1968), 179–99.

99. The resolution to ban separate charters was brought by Jacksonville, Florida, Branch 52; Yazoo City, Mississippi, Branch 986; and Pasadena, California, Branch 228. Convention proceedings, *Postal Record* (October 1919), 331–32.

100. National State Vice-Presidents, *Postal Record* (November 1917), 408.

101. Spero and Harris, *Black Worker*, 123. The NALC resolution was referring to the National Alliance by its journal name at the time, the *Postal Alliance*, which was a common

mistake. The singling out of the Alliance with the word "especially" here evokes more than the standard trade union rejection of the threat of any dual union acting as a kind of "Trojan horse" within its ranks, although many AFL unions had no problem raiding other unions. White carriers plainly saw them as a special threat, even as many whites saw all black carriers as a threat to their job monopoly.

102. Convention proceedings, *Postal Record* (October 1927), 408.

103. Ibid.

104. Ibid.

105. Ibid., italics added.

106. Ibid., italics added. The RMA's actual name was the Railway Mail Association. Casey's renaming of the RMA to include "white" anticipated a later period when African Americans commonly referred to the 1950s–1960s white supremacist Citizens Councils as the "White Citizens Councils" so often that it became (and remains) standard in American vocabulary and literature. I am indebted to Charles M. Payne for this observation.

107. Ibid., 408–9, italics added. Judging from the applause recorded as part of the transcript, Casey's sardonic, ironic constitutional reference to being "as white as any man in here" worked as a rhetorical device. Both Hill's and Casey's speeches could also be compared to many political speeches given during Reconstruction by African American elected officials.

108. Ibid., 409.

109. Convention proceedings, *Postal Record* (October 1935), 509.

110. Ibid., 510. The exact biblical verse was not cited by Stevens here, but the story, he said, related to disputes between Abraham and his nephew Lot's herdsmen, prompting the need to separate—the analogy being clear to blacks and whites. On W. J. Massey see ibid., 511. See also ibid., 517, for the rejection of Waco, Texas, Branch 404's attempt to enact dual branches as a constitutional amendment.

111. Convention proceedings, *Postal Record* (October 1939), 499.

112. See for example Frederick Douglass's May 30, 1881, speech in remembrance of John Brown reprinted in Louis Ruchames, *John Brown: The Making of a Revolutionary* (New York: Grosset and Dunlap, 1969), 278–99, and Part 2. In coining the term "Union Army Americanism" I do not romanticize the white army that President Abraham Lincoln initially put in the field to preserve the union without abolishing slavery, but rather the Union Army that African American activists like P. M. E. Hill remembered as finally—albeit belatedly and with discrimination and segregation intact—becoming the chief agent of African American slave emancipation with the vital entry of African American soldiers into the war. For African American memory and celebration of the armed struggle that overthrew slavery and their pivotal role in it, see for example Thavolia Glymph, " 'Liberty Dearly Bought': The Making of Civil War Memory in Afro-American Communities in the South," in *Time Longer than Rope: A Century of African American Activism, 1850–1950*, ed. Charles M. Payne and Adam Green (New York: New York University Press, 2003), 111–40, esp. 117. In postal union convention floor and journal debates, African American activists like Hill skillfully invoked that memory and found like-minded white allies.

113. "Carriers of U.S. Mail in Convention," *Chicago Defender*, September 15, 1923, 3.

114. Convention proceedings, *Postal Record* (October 1939), 499.

115. Ibid. For Bernstein's 1935 speech see convention proceedings, *Postal Record* (October 1935), 510. Barret from Arkansas was probably black.

116. Convention proceedings, *Postal Record* (October 1939), 511.

117. See also *Proceedings and Summaries of Proceedings of the Convention of the National Federation of Post Office Clerks* (1939), 129. "Civil Service—Appointment of First Eligible; Abolition of Photograph" was Resolution 411's self-explanatory title that challenged the civil service's discriminatory use of both the photograph and the discretion allowed civil service officers to choose from among the "top three" eligibles (based on high examination scores), and thus to frequently screen out African Americans. It was passed without objection. But no resolutions were raised against Jim Crow locals at that convention. In the handful of antidiscrimination resolutions that passed, there were no sectional differences heard, and only one objection—recorded anonymously—to the anti-lynching resolution. See "Anti-Lynching Bill," 103; "Discrimination Against Members," 103; "Dictatorship—Opposed to," 108; "Minorities—Persecution of," 112; all in *Proceedings and Summaries of Proceedings of the Convention of the NFPOC* (1939).

118. Between 1941 and 1962, besides debating Jim Crow branches, NALC convention delegates argued over whether the correct term was "separate" or "dual" charters. Both "separate" and "dual" were used in NALC publications, and commonly heard roughly the same on the convention floor, although defenders generally preferred the former while opponents tended to use the latter. President William Doherty liked to argue that there had been "separate," not "dual," charters in the NALC. See *Official Proceedings of the Forty-second Biennial Convention of the National Association of Letter Carriers, Cincinnati, Ohio, August 21–26, 1960*, 72. But in fact, the amended 1941 NALC Constitution, Article II, Section 1, referred neither to "dual" or "separate" but rather "second" charters. Convention proceedings, *Postal Record* (October 1941), 533. The last time "separate charters" was introduced by southerners was in 1935, as we have seen. In 1939 they introduced the term "dual charters" in their defeated amendment. Convention proceedings, *Postal Record* (October 1939), 499. By the time their "second charter" amendment passed in 1941, "separate" and "dual" had both become the accepted terms of debate.

119. Spero and Harris, *Black Worker*, 123. The term "white blindspot" I have borrowed from Allen, *Invention of the White Race*, 1:22–23.

120. See for example Glenn, *History of the National Alliance*, 307, from a *Postal Alliance* article written in 1943: "O. Grady Gregory of the Chicago branch reminds us. . . . 'A few years ago we sought admission into the A.F. of L. and were refused. At the 1937 convention in Baltimore we considered joining the C.I.O. but no action taken. . . . We have been skeptical of this organization, and the cry of our enemies of the taint of communism in its ranks. Down South if a Negro is aggressive and demands his rights, they call him crazy, whereas, in the North, he is a communist. I believe more sympathy would have been given the question at Baltimore had the organization been interested.' " In 1935 the CIO formed as a "Committee of Industrial Organizations" within the AFL. The CIO was suspended and then expelled from the AFL in 1936 for doing so. The CIO held its first convention in 1938 as the Congress of Industrial Organizations. On the CIO formation see Zieger, *CIO*, 88; and Paul Le Blanc, *A Short History of the U.S. Working Class: From Colonial Times to the Twenty-first Century* (Amherst, N.Y.: Humanity Books, 1999), 85. See also "The Urban League and the A.F. of L.: A Statement on Racial Discrimination," delivered July 9, 1935, online version of original *Opportunity* publication, <http://newdeal.feri.org/opp/opp35 247.htm> (November 12, 2005).

121. Hill, *Black Labor*, 23.

122. Franklin and Moss, *From Slavery to Freedom*, 438–39.

123. Charles Lionel Franklin, *The Negro Labor Unionist of New York: Problems and Conditions*

among *Negroes in the Labor Unions in Manhattan with Special Reference to the N.R.A. and Post-N.R.A. Situations* (New York: Columbia University Press, 1936), 7: "One of the phases of this research project dealt with the problems involved in the employment of Negroes and the necessarily related consideration of their status in the local organized labor movement—a tremendously important issue, for trade unions, broadening their jurisdictional activities to cover many professional and 'white-collar' occupations as well as the skilled craftsmen and unskilled common laborers, have increased their scope to such an extent that union membership is now a prerequisite for almost any kind of employment."

124. Ibid., see table 12, 176–77. Total black public sector employment in New York City rose from 1.9 percent in 1910, to 4.9 percent in 1920, to 7.8 percent in 1930. Ibid., see table 7, 40. The NFPOC formed out of a split with the "company union" (deferential to management) UNAPOC in 1906 and affiliated with the AFL that same year. See Spero, *Government as Employer*, 128–29.

125. Franklin, *Negro Labor Unionist*, 379.

126. Ibid., 380. The names of the black officers and delegates were not provided.

127. Spero, *Government as Employer*, 160–61. See also David Sheldon Hasson, "The Historical Development of Public Employee Unionism: The Performance and Effectiveness of The American Postal Unions" (Ph.D. diss., University of California–Riverside, 1974), 77. After the CIO refused entry to the PWA in 1937, the PWA collapsed as a viable union, but apparently CPUSA members moved into work in the CIO's United Federal Workers, which later became the United Public Workers, which in turn was purged by the CIO in 1950 along with nine other "communist-dominated" unions. See Ellen Schrecker, *Many Are the Crimes: McCarthyism in America* (Princeton, N.J.: Princeton University Press, 1998), 338–40.

128. Some PWA correspondence and newsletters can be found in *The CIO Files of John L. Lewis, Part I: Correspondence with CIO Unions*, ed. Robert Zieger (Frederick, Md.: University Publications of America, 1988), reels 5, 6, 9, microfilm, Perkins Library. See for example, in reel 6, frames 294–95, the PWA's self-reference in their publication *Unity Forum* (June 1937), "The one and only industrial union . . . in the postal service," in a front-page article titled "Big Increase in Postal Workers of America: Local 9 Reports 1,400 Members." On the next page there is a list of "all" postal unions that manages to omit the National Alliance and again contain this self-reference, this time announcing in capital letters: "THE ONLY ORGANIZATION IN THE WHOLE FIELD THAT SEEKS TO UNITE ALL POSTAL EMPLOYEES INTO ONE BIG UNION. 3,000 members. Formed in Cleveland, Ohio, 1933. C.I.O. Charter applied for. Began the movement for ONE organization."

129. *Postal Sub* (January–February 1934), 22–23, unprocessed box, Folder 42, Biller Files. In the case of the NASPOE, that a predominantly white industrial postal union would put their opposition to lynching in print in the early 1930s before the CIO was even conceived (and also took up that fight, at least nominally) is a marker of at least some CPUSA internal or external influence. Samuel Cohen, the editor of the NASPOE's *Postal Sub*, wrote an article in 1934 blasting the sudden rise in lynching and white acquiescence or apologetics for it. Cohen's critique (citing the Scottsboro case) referred to "legal lynch law" and concluded that the root cause was "economic suffering" that required "a new social order where the present economic chaos will not exist." Other features shared by both the NASPOE and the PWA with the CPUSA included the latter's "mass slogans" like "30 for 40" (30 hours work for 40 hours pay), popular communist and leftist jargon like "progressive" and "reactionary," and a mass approach coupled with some sectarian positions on pending postal legislation that were atypical for a trade union. Left or communist mass

literature often introduced radical ideas in circumspect fashion, thereby avoiding the risk of alienating potential allies who could be later won over to adopting more militant left and antiracist positions during personal contact.

130. From the photographs in the subsequent issue of the NASPOE's organ the *Postal Sub*, slogans on the signs included: "We need relief not promises"; "Millions for subsidies and starvation for substitutes"; and "Abolish the speed-up and stretch-out in the Post Office." (The last slogan was a reference to militant contemporary factory worker demands in auto and textiles, respectively.) Elsewhere in the same issue a writer from Hampton, Virginia, identifying himself as white, wrote how gratified he was to see the NASPOE protesting, as he said, Warner Bros. studios' request for white substitute postal workers. See *Postal Sub*; and 1934 Freeze March Photos, Box 2, Folder The Postal Sub, 1934; and Box 3, Folder Subs 1933–34, Biller Files. Some of the photos in this collection cited here did not make it into that issue, including those with signs identifying marchers from Brooklyn. Other signs protested the "stretch out"—originally a textile mill term for one worker having to run multiple machines simultaneously. (Nineteen thirty-four was the year of nationwide textile and other industry strikes.) One might imagine that the NASPOE and the PWA made common cause, given their similarities. Yet the differences between those two unions highlight a typical problem in U.S. left historiography, namely a lack of differentiation among left groups. The CPUSA may have been the biggest but it was certainly not the only left influence. See for example Nelson Lichtenstein, *Labor's War at Home: The CIO in World War II* (1982; Philadelphia: Temple University Press, 2003), xxiii n. 2, on the International Socialists' 1940 split with the Socialist Workers Party, a Trotskyist group. On the latter see Fred Stanton, ed., *Fighting Racism in World War II: C. L. R. James, George Breitman, Edgar Keemer, and Others* (New York: Monad, 1980). The choice by the CPUSA to occasionally hurl the charge "Uncle Tom" at black groups that did not agree with its political line arguably demonstrated a left version of white paternalism. See Mark Naison, *Communists in Harlem during the Depression* (Urbana: University of Illinois Press, 1983); Earl Ofari Hutchinson, *Blacks and Reds: Race and Class in Conflict, 1919–1990* (East Lansing: Michigan State University Press, 1995); and Keith P. Griffler, *What Price Alliance? Black Radicals Confront White Labor, 1918–1938* (New York: Garland, 1995). Whether the two left postal unions were rivals or allies, CPUSA "fronts" or merely groups with CPUSA members, the PWA did support some of NASPOE's campaigns despite their differences over the PWA's industrial unionism, as noted by New York City postal union veteran Max Epstein who had actually been at the PWA founding convention in Cleveland in 1934 as an observer. Max Epstein, 1976 oral history transcript, Box 4, Folder 1976, Max Epstein oral history 1/23/76.

131. Max Epstein in Arthur Ryland 1976 oral history transcript, Box 4, Folder 1976, Biller Files.

132. See Naison, *Communists in Harlem*; Hutchinson, *Blacks and Reds*; and Griffler, *What Price Alliance?*

133. Arthur Ryland in 1976 oral history transcript, APWU collection, Box 4, Folder 1976, Biller Files.

134. Ibid. Coincidentally, another jazz musician/postal worker was New York's first black postmaster, John Strachan. His tenure as postmaster was from 1966 to 1979. Born in Harlem in 1916, Strachan was himself the son of a postal clerk. Strachan, a well-known jazz saxophone player, worked as post office clerk in 1941 while pursuing bachelors and master's degrees from New York University and served in the Army from 1942 to 1946. See

unprocessed box, Folder 119, John Strachan obituary, October 1, 1982; and "John R. Stra-chan: New York's Postmaster Retires," *Postscript: The Voice of the New York Post Office* (Janu-ary 1979); Box 2, Folder 1979, Postscript, Biller Files. Strachan had also been a member of the National Alliance since 1954. See "New York City Branch—New Members," *Postal Alliance* (January 1955), 17; and "Editor's Notebook," *National Alliance* (November 1966), 4. Meanwhile, the minutes of the Brooklyn postal clerks union from 1918 to 1977 reveals a concern with issues related to equality. In particular we see increasing awareness of the contradictions involved in the late 1930s and early 1940s with the United States' hardening posture toward global fascism combined with a tolerance for white supremacy at home; an interest in the movement for "one big union" and requests for relations by left dual unions like the NASPOE (which, like the PWA, did not object to members belonging to other unions); and relations with the local branch of the National Alliance. See *Local 251 Minutes.* See also the *Postal Sub* (April 1933), 7, Biller Files, Box 3, Folder Subs 1933–34, where an item from the "Tidbits and Echoes" column reveals: "Brooklyn is interested in our pro-gram to the extent that they have formed a committee, with a view towards joining the SPOEA. They expect to continue their affiliation with the Feds. Belonging to the SPOEA does not prohibit membership in any other regular organization." The SPOEA or Sub-stitute Post Office Employees Association was the original name of the NASPOE. Some-time in the following year the name evidently changed, as this was their volume 1, number 4, and by 1934 they were calling themselves the NASPOE. See *Local 251 Minutes*, May 9, 1933, however for a different story: they voted to reject dual membership with SPOEA, as that would have violated the NFPOC constitution.

135. Walsh and Mangum, *Labor Struggle*, 84–85. The use of the term "federal union" here refers to federal employees. It is not the same as what the AFL called "federal unions," that is, AFL local affiliates of any kind without backing from the parent unions.

136. On Detroit, see for example "Detroit Shows the Way," *Progressive Fed: Official Pub-lication of the "Progressive Feds" Within the National Federation of Post Office Clerks* (April 1958), 1, Box 81, NYMAPUC. The Chicago Postal Union may have been in the CIO as well. See Naison, *Communists in Harlem*, 99, 210; Griffler, *What Price Alliance?*; and Hutchinson, *Blacks and Reds*, 149–51. On contemporary examples of "one big postal union" proponents, see for example Peter Rachleff, "Machine Technology and Workplace Control: The U.S. Post Office," in *Critical Studies in Organization and Bureaucracy*, ed. Frank Fischer and Carmen Sirianni (Philadelphia: Temple University Press, 1984), 143–56. On the Boston CIO postal union, see *Local 251 Minutes*, reel 2. See also Roediger, *Working toward Whiteness*, esp. chap. 7 for his critique of labor histories that see the CPUSA's work in the CIO in the 1930s and 1940s as the unrequited labor and civil rights model. I would argue also that both the PWA and the NASPOE embody Roediger's definition of "nonracial syndicalism."

137. See *Local 251 Minutes*, reel 1 (no frames numbered); and *UNIA Records*, reel 5; and John Baxter Streater Jr., "The National Negro Congress, 1936–1947" (Ph.D. diss., Univer-sity of Cincinnati, 1981), 359. See also Harris, *Harder We Run*, 110–12, 116.

138. See *Local 251 Minutes*, reel 1; and *UNIA Records*, reel 5. The left political tone of Local 251 meetings does progressively advance beginning in the early 1930s. See also Karl Baarslag, *History of the National Federation of Post Office Clerks* (Washington, D.C.: NFPOC, 1945), 184–86. Baarslag considered himself an "expert" on communism and warned "am-ateurs" who might miss the CPUSA's "innocent-looking facade. . . . Experts spot Commu-nists not so much by what they say or do, but by *how* they talk and *how* they do things. All communist literature no matter how artfully disguised and all communist acts no matter

how innocent and honest on their face, always conforms to the most recent shift in Party Line" (185, italics in original). Nineteen forty was evidently the first time Local 251 discussed sending a delegate to the NNC, which had begun in 1936.

139. Walsh and Mangum, *Labor Struggle*, 57–59. See for example Samuel S. Cohen, "Human Nature," *Postal Sub* (April 1933), 6, Box 3, Folder Subs 1933–34, Biller Files: "Forced to undergo the same vicissitudes of economic existence, the college man finds a common bond uniting him to the post office worker in the precariousness of their struggle for a livelihood. Today the college man in the Post Office is taking the lead in the fight for a living wage for subs. He makes use of his education by writing, editing, advising, drawing up bills to present to Congress, etc., all with a view toward furthering the interests of subs. The college man has thus changed his nature. He has learned that his lot must be thrown in with that of the worker." This also suggests a possible CPUSA intervention. See also Harry Blacksin (college graduate and activist in the leftist furriers union) oral history transcript, March 22, 1977, unprocessed box, Folder 114, Harry Blacksin answers, Biller Files. There was an economic determinism in Cohen's 1934 narrative, "Human Nature," common also to the CPUSA and the left CIO. Walsh and Mangum's references in *Labor Struggle* to white "college boys" treat college background in the post office as a new phenomenon, forgetting the long history of black college graduate activism in the post office.

140. Figures on blacks in the NALC and NFPOC are hard to find. The unions apparently did not keep such records. But outside groups like the Urban League help provide some of this information, for example: between 1926 and 1928 1,376 blacks belonged to the NALC, whose total membership then was no more than 60,000. The NFPOC by contrast had 356 blacks in an organization of about 38,000 during that period. See *Negro Membership*, 101–2; and *Labor Fact Book*, 130–31. Overall, according to First Assistant Postmaster General J. H. Bartlett, in 1925 there were 2,400 black letter carriers out of a national total of 46,739. "Bartlett Describes Negro Opportunity in Postal Service," *Washington Post*, November 15, 1925, 12. See also Samuel Krislov, *The Negro in Federal Employment: The Quest for Equal Opportunity* (Minneapolis: University of Minnesota Press, 1967), 22: blacks made up 15–30 percent of postal workers in major post offices. See Boyd and Chen, "History and Experience."

CHAPTER TWO

1. A. L. Glenn, *History of the National Alliance of Postal Employees, 1913–1955* (Washington, D.C.: National Alliance of Postal Employees, 1956), 72. Cobb entered Howard Law School in 1945 and earned his degree two years later. During this same period Charles Hamilton Houston, dean of the Howard University Law School, used it as a practice forum to launch an attack on segregation laws. See Genna Rae McNeil, *Groundwork: Charles Hamilton Houston and the Struggle for Civil Rights* (Philadelphia: University of Pennsylvania Press, 1983); and Pauli Murray, *The Autobiography of a Black Activist, Feminist, Lawyer, Priest, and Poet* (Knoxville: University of Tennessee Press, 1990), 180–88.

2. James B. Cobb, "Action Demanded," *Postal Alliance* (July 1943), 4. Also quoted in Glenn, *History of the National Alliance*, 308.

3. Ashby Carter, "1941 Behind—1942 Ahead," *Postal Alliance* (December 1941), 7.

4. For example, the June 1942 *Postal Alliance* featured guest articles by leftist Local 600 UAW-CIO (United Automobile Workers–Congress of Industrial Organizations) president Paul St. Marie, its black recording secretary Sheldon Tappes, and George R. Grigsby, the first black elected to the Executive Board of the leftist International Fur and Leather

Workers Union–CIO. All three union officials talked about the importance of union democracy and fighting discrimination. See "Object Lesson in Democracy" (14); George R. Grigsby, "Food for Thought" (14); Shelton Tappes, "The Integration of the Negro in the Labor Movement" (15); and Paul Ste. Marie, "What Does the Ford Local 600 UAW-CIO Mean to Its Negro Members" (15), *Postal Alliance* (June 1942), 14–15. For more on Local 600 and the Fur and Leather Workers, see for example Judith Stepan-Norris and Maurice Zeitlin, *Left Out: Reds and America's Industrial Unions* (Cambridge: Cambridge University Press, 2003), chap. 4 and epilogue. See also *Postal Alliance* (January 1942), 4, for "Last Minute Flash": "All Negro National organizations were summoned to New York City on the 10th of January for a conference to coordinate their efforts in getting the best possible results for equal opportunities on all jobs paid out of public funds." The January issue also featured a guest column by Negro History Week founder Carter G. Woodson, "Negro History Week, the Seventeenth Celebration, February 8 to 15," 13. First elected editor in 1940, Snow Grigsby served until 1973—the longest in Alliance history. See conversation by author with Jacquelyn Moore (*National Alliance* editor, 1974–2004), July 17, 2009, Washington, D.C.

5. "The 1942 Program for N.A.P.E.," *Postal Alliance* (January 1942), 4.

6. "Hit Jim Crow in St. Louis Post Office," *Postal Alliance* (January 1942), 5; and Glenn, *History of the National Alliance*, 308 (the September 1942 *Postal Alliance* article is quoted on 163).

7. Glenn, *History of the National Alliance*, 163; and Henry W. McGee, *The Negro in the Chicago Post Office: Henry W. McGee Autobiography and Dissertation* (Chicago: VolumeOne Press, 1999) (originally "The Negro in the Chicago Post Office," master's thesis, University of Chicago, 1961), chap. 8 (*Dissertation*) and "Appendix I: A Brief of Unfair Practices in the Chicago Post Office"—the January 1942 NAPE petition to the FEPC.

8. Despite the no-strike pledges made by private industry workers to government and industry through their AFL and CIO unions, World War II saw a record number of strikes, most of them wildcat strikes, and many of them also "hate strikes" by whites against black worker entry and promotion in industry—as well as a substantial number of retaliatory protest strikes by black workers. On strikes in World War II see Jeremy Brecher, *Strike!* revised and updated ed. (1972; Boston: South End Press, 1997), chap. 6; Herbert Hill, *Black Labor and the American Legal System: Race, Work, and the Law* (1977; Madison: University of Wisconsin Press, 1985), 263–64 and chap. 11; August Meier and Elliot Rudwick, *Black Detroit and the Rise of the UAW* (Oxford: Oxford University Press, 1981); Robert C. Weaver, *Negro Labor: A National Problem* (New York: Harcourt, 1946), 222–23; and Nelson Lichtenstein, *Labor's War at Home: The CIO in World War II* (1982; Philadelphia: Temple University Press, 2003). Lichtenstein's analysis of World War II–era hate strikes (125–26) is limited to Detroit and on page 126 he pronounces: "After 1943, hate strikes almost vanished." But for a record of the dozens of nationwide hate strikes throughout the war (including those after 1943), see *FEPC Records*, esp. Field Letter No. 47 dated February 14, 1945, from FEPC Director Will Maslow to the Division of Field Operations, listing a total of 92 "strikes involving inter-racial issues from July 1943 through December 1944." Most of these would qualify as "hate strikes"—like the one at the Brown Shoe Co., in St. Louis on October 27, 1944, over "Resistance of whites to Negro girl on machine work." Approximately sixteen of these strikes reflected black resistance, like the strike at the Carnegie-Illinois Steel Co. in Clairton, Pennsylvania, on February 26, 1944: "Negroes struck over failure to upgrade." The fact that about two-thirds of hate strikes (and two-thirds of all "race related" strikes)

listed here came after 1943—after black entrance into war industry reached substantial levels via the FEPC—reveals a more prolonged process of struggle with white workers than Lichtenstein's optimistic conclusion suggests. Of the ninety-two total strikes, the FEPC helped settle thirty-nine: eight in 1943 and thirty-one in 1944, no small feat for a mere "advisory" agency.

9. McGee, *Negro in the Chicago Post Office (Dissertation)*, 96 and chaps. 8–9.

10. Carol Anderson, *Eyes off the Prize: The United Nations and the African American Struggle for Human Rights, 1944–1955* (Cambridge: Cambridge University Press, 2003); Dominic J. Capeci Jr., "The Harlem Bus Boycott of 1941," in *Civil Rights since 1787: A Reader on the Black Struggle*, ed. Jonathan Birnbaum and Clarence Taylor (New York: New York University Press, 2000), 298–302; Capeci, *Harlem Riot of 1943* (Philadelphia: Temple University Press, 1977); and Nat Brandt, *Harlem at War: The Black Experience in WWII* (Syracuse: Syracuse University Press, 1996).

11. Cobb, "Action Demanded," 4–5. On Detroit riots of 1943 see also Dominic J. Capeci Jr. and Martha Wilkerson, *Layered Violence: The Detroit Rioters of 1943* (Jackson: University Press of Mississippi, 1991); John Hope Franklin and Alfred A. Moss Jr., *From Slavery to Freedom: A History of African Americans*, 8th ed. (1947; Boston: McGraw-Hill, 2000), 496; Meier and Rudwick, *Black Detroit*; and Thomas J. Sugrue, *The Origins of the Urban Crisis: Race and Inequality in Postwar Detroit* (Princeton, N.J.: Princeton University Press, 1996).

12. 1943 NAPE Convention minutes, *Postal Alliance* (August 1943), 32. See also "Segregation in P.O. Cafeteria Draws Protests: Race Worker in Clash with Café Manager," *Atlanta Daily World*, December 23, 1941, 1. There was no report in this article on the outcome of this incident, other than to say that the NAACP was protesting his treatment and the segregation of that federal facility.

13. *Postal Alliance* (August 1943), 32.

14. Ibid., 33.

15. Ibid., 49–51.

16. Ibid., 35.

17. Ibid., 55.

18. See Elmer E. Armstead, "What I Saw In St. Louis," *Postal Alliance* (October 1943), 11. Also cited in Glenn, *History of the National Alliance*, 167, emphasis in original. Jerry Gilliam was active in the Norfolk, Virginia, branch of the NAPE, its former national president, as well as president of the local NAACP and Grand Exalted Leader of the Eureka Lodge of the Elks. See Earl Lewis, *In Their Own Interests: Race, Class, and Power in Twentieth-Century Norfolk, Virginia* (Berkeley: University of California Press, 1993), 147–48.

19. Glenn, *History of the National Alliance*, 166, italics added. Glenn took some minor editorial liberties with quotes from Henry W. McGee's original article that appeared as "I Saw Uncle Tom Die," *Postal Alliance* (September 1943), 16, from which McGee's quotes are taken.

20. Glenn, *History of the National Alliance*, 103. Ironically, the Alliance apparently enrolled Postmaster Jackson as a member ("honorary"?) just four months before his death in December 1943 (Glenn, *History of the National Alliance*, 430).

21. On the FEPC see Louis Ruchames, *Race, Jobs, and Politics: The Story of the FEPC* (New York: Columbia University Press, 1953); Hill, *Black Labor*, chap. 4; but especially the standard work: Merl E. Reed, *Seedtime for the Modern Civil Rights Movement: The President's Committee on Fair Employment Practice, 1941–1946* (Baton Rouge: Louisiana State University Press, 1991). See also Reed, "FEPC and the Federal Agencies in the South," *Journal of Negro*

History 65, no. 1 (Winter 1980), 43–56, esp. 46–47, on increased black hiring due to FEPC pressure on southern post offices.

22. Adam Clayton Powell, "Making American Safe for Democracy First," *Postal Alliance* (June 1941), 6.

23. "Reprint from New Orleans Sentinel," *Postal Alliance* (January 1942), 11. The ratings report form also includes this information: "The period of eligibility is ordinarily 1 year, unless the District Manager finds it desirable to extend the eligibility of the entire register for an additional period. All honorably discharged soldiers, sailors, and marines, and the widows of such, and the wives of injured soldiers, sailors, and marines who themselves are not qualified but whose wives are qualified to hold such positions, are entitled to preference under the act of July 11, 1919." Beginning with the *Veterans Preference Act of 1944, Statutes at Large 58 (1944)*, chap. 268, 387–91, military veterans, their spouses, and their unmarried widows or widowers could receive five extra points (ten if they had a disability) when taking the civil service examination. Veterans could also apply military service years toward government service.

24. "Meet a Man of Action," *Postal Alliance* (May 1947), 18. See also Adam Fairclough, *Race and Democracy: The Civil Rights Struggle in Louisiana, 1915–1975* (Athens: University of Georgia Press, 1995), 57. The "core" of "The Group," according to Fairclough, included letter carrier Arthur J. Chapital, also an Alliance member, and postal clerk Donald Jones, probably also in the Alliance.

25. *FEPC Records*, reel 72. See also reel 66, L. A. Moyer, Executive Director and Chief Examiner, "Circular Letter No. 3148," September 18, 1941, 2.

26. John Hope Franklin notes that "after personal interviews, hiring officials sometimes avoided hiring Negroes by availing themselves of the Civil Service Commission's 'rule of three,' by which they could select a white who ranked second or third over a black who ranked first. A high test score and other qualifications like a college education did not and still do not automatically provide entry into the post office. In many cases a black applicant with the highest qualifications of the three would be bypassed in favor of a white applicant in that same batch with fewer qualifications below him or her." Franklin and Moss, *From Slavery to Freedom*, 432. See also *FEPC Records*, reel 72, "The Facts about Negro Employment in the Federal Government," 8; reel 66, "A Study of Complaints of Discrimination against the Federal Government Because of Race, Creed, Color or National Origin Originating with the Civil Service Commission" (1941–1943), 2; and McGee, *Negro in the Chicago Post Office (Dissertation)*, 9–10.

27. *Code of Federal Regulations, Title 3: The President, 1938–1943 Compilation* (Washington, D.C.: Government Printing Office, 1968), 824–30; and Executive Order 8587.

28. *New York Times*, November 7, 1940.

29. Glenn, *History of the National Alliance of Postal Employees*, 92, notes that the January 1941 *Postal Alliance* heralded the abolition of the application photograph requirement. See also "Along the N.A.A.C.P. Battlefront," *Crisis* (December 1940), 390. See also "President's Order Prohibits Civil Service Discrimination," *Pittsburgh Courier*, November 23, 1940, 3, Duke University Perkins/Bostock Library, microfilm. See also the *New York Times* for the period November 8–30, 1940, in that same collection.

30. *Annual Report of the Postmaster General, 1945–1949* (Washington, D.C.: Government Printing Office, 1946–1950), table 84, 13 (1946): the deficits had been as high as $205.6 million in 1932 and as low as $14.1 million in 1942. The surpluses from fiscal years 1943 to 1945 were $13.7 million, $43.9 million, and $169.1 million, respectively. On employment see

table 61, 158 (1949). Air mail miles increased also during this time tremendously: from 99,500 miles in 1928 to 97.5 million miles in 1949 (table 47, 150). Also, by 1949 veterans outnumbered non-veterans for the first time in modern postal history, making up 53.2 percent of all "field personnel" (i.e., anyone not considered "temporary") (23).

31. Vern K. Baxter, *Labor and Politics in the U.S. Postal Service* (New York: Plenum, 1994), 51–53.

32. See for example Melvin L. Oliver and Thomas M. Shapiro, *Black Wealth / White Wealth: A New Perspective on Racial Inequality* (New York: Routledge, 1997).

33. See for example Arthur Ryland oral history interview with Dana Schecter, November 19, 1976, New York, Biller Files.

34. Franklin and Moss, *From Slavery to Freedom*, 432.

35. Glenn, *History of the National Alliance*, 91, based on a speech by a senior postal official to the 1943 NAPE national convention. There were 353,156 postal employees in 1940 according to the *Annual Report* (1945), 158.

36. See for example William E. Leuchtenburg, *Franklin D. Roosevelt and the New Deal, 1932–1940* (New York: Harper and Row, 1963).

37. McGee, *Negro in the Chicago Post Office (Dissertation)*, 84. McGee also noted the problems management had with disciplining many of these newly hired black employees in this industrialized post office, giving us some evidence of individual and worker collective action the post office was not used to seeing. McGee's rise to Chicago Alliance leadership was combined with his taking over the reins of the local NAACP as part of a black working-class upsurge. See also Christopher Robert Reed, *The Chicago NAACP and the Rise of Black Professional Leadership, 1910–1966* (Bloomington: Indiana University Press, 1997), 4.

38. Remarkably, not only was Hamner never charged, but the white man later actually apologized to him. See Neil McMillen, "Fighting for What We Didn't Have: How Mississippi's Black Veterans Remember World War II," in *Remaking Dixie: The Impact of World War II on the American South* (Jackson: University Press of Mississippi, 1997), 93–188, esp. letter carrier Dabney Hamner's story: 100–103, 185n8, 186nn22,26,32. See also Timothy B. Tyson, *Radio Free Dixie: Robert F. Williams and the Roots of Black Power* (Chapel Hill: University of North Carolina Press, 1999). Hamner represented Clarksdale, Mississippi, Branch 1195 at the NALC convention in Cleveland in 1954: see *Official Proceedings of the Thirty-ninth Biennial Convention of the National Association of Letter Carriers, Cleveland Ohio, August 30– September 4, 1954*, 4a.

39. Author interview with Sam Armstrong and Samuel Lovett, August 11, 2004, Washington, D.C.

40. Leah Platt Boustan and Robert A. Margo, "Race, Segregation, and Postal Employment: New Evidence on Spatial Mismatch," *Journal of Urban Economics* (forthcoming, revised version of NBER Working Paper 13462), 8–9.

41. Henry W. McGee, *Negro in the Chicago Post Office (Dissertation)*, 83–85. But seniority was not an ironclad practice until the 1971 contract between postal unions and the USPS. See author interview with William H. Burrus Jr., January 16, 2009, Washington, D.C.

42. See A. Philip Randolph's speeches and resolutions to the 1938 and 1943 AFL conventions, respectively, in Philip S. Foner and Ronald L. Lewis, eds., *The Black Worker: A Documentary History from Colonial Times to the Present*, vol. 7, *The Black Worker from the Founding of the CIO to the AFL-CIO Merger, 1936–1955* (Philadelphia: Temple University Press, 1983), 427–37; 467–75. Randolph in 1943 identified at least twenty-four AFL affiliates and nine non-AFL affiliates that practiced exclusion or segregation. See also David R. Roediger, *Working*

toward Whiteness: How America's Immigrants Became White (New York: Basic Books, 2005), esp. chap. 7; and Herbert Hill, "The AFL-CIO and the Black Worker: Twenty-Five Years after the Merger," *Journal of Intergroup Relations* 10, no. 1 (Spring 1982), 5–79 (Reprint No. 241, Industrial Relations Research Institute, University of Wisconsin–Madison). See also Stepan-Norris and Zeitlin, *Left Out*, 236: by the late 1940s, twenty-nine of the CIO's thirty-six unions (81 percent) guaranteed membership to all eligible workers regardless of race or color, compared to the AFL's 13 of 89 (14.6 percent) major affiliates. CIO unions that had Jim Crow locals at any one time included the oil workers, textile workers, men's clothing workers, United Auto Workers, United Rubber Workers, United Steel Workers, longshoremen, and the Mine Mill and Smelter's Union. See also Martha Biondi, *To Stand and Fight: The Struggle for Civil Rights in Postwar New York City* (Cambridge, Mass.: Harvard University Press, 2003).

43. See *Union Postal Clerk* during this period. See also "Century of progress: 100-year-old NALC member blazed trail for blacks," *Postal Record* (January 1989), 10. That article on black history in the NALC added that once the separate charters were abolished, the union found that it actually picked up members, both black and white, including members of the National Alliance.

44. Glenn, *History of the National Alliance*, 293. The term "raiding" refers to a practice where a union either induces members of another union to join it instead, or tries to replace another union's jurisdiction with its own in a given workplace. See Paul Le Blanc, *A Short History of the U.S. Working Class: From Colonial Times to the Twenty-first Century* (Amherst, N.Y.: Humanity Books, 1999), 173.

45. The *Postal Record*, the official organ of the NALC, was established in 1888, the year before the formation of the NALC itself. Personal communication with Candace Main Rush, Information Center Director, NALC, Washington, D.C., April 5, 2001. Its format has expanded since the 1940s to include more feature articles. But during the 1940s its content was limited to editorials and brief news features of interest to letter carriers (such as pending federal legislation relating to the post office and postal workers), summaries of state association business such as elections, as well as "Branch Items" and "Ladies Auxiliary" notes—still regular features of today's *Postal Record*, although "Ladies Auxiliary" is now referred to simply as the "Auxiliary" with the rise of female letter carriers and male or female spouses of those carriers added to the Auxiliary.

46. Jervis Anderson, *A. Philip Randolph: A Biographical Portrait* (New York: Harcourt, 1973), 247–61.

47. Convention proceedings, *Postal Record* (October 1941), 533. See also Paul P. Van Riper, *History of the United States Civil Service* (Evanston, Ill.: Row, Peterson, and Company, 1958), 345.

48. Convention proceedings, *Postal Record* (October 1941), 533. Chicago's Barney B. Bernstein did not hesitate to condemn the resolution as "a ripsaw" against the NALC: "Brothers, if you have one spark of decency in you and the blood of American democracy is flowing in your veins, vote against approval of the committee's report." Emanuel Kushelewitz from New York's Branch 36—a branch that later took the lead in the 1970 postal wildcat strike—supported Bernstein's position while curiously expressing indifference at the outcome: "I don't care who wins, but I hope it doesn't bounce back here again." Detroit's Raymond Lieberman, however, was livid, demanding that Michigan's name be struck from the Georgia-authored resolution, claiming that his state convention had "never endorsed it and some trickery has been pulled here. I want the state of Michigan's name stricken off here 1,000 percent." Convention proceedings, *Postal Record* (October 1941), 534. D. L.

Morgan (white) from Baton Rouge, Louisiana, retorted: "In my part of the country we have a condition that is peculiar only to our country, and the states in that part of the country. The people of the southern States, of which I am a part, have a great desire . . . to be able to solve their own problem. . . . We only ask that the dual charter be granted for one primary purpose . . . that these men who are denied membership under the present set-up in these localities be given protection of the National Association of Letter Carriers. . . . Furthermore, it would advance the revenues of the National Association of Letter Carriers. . . ." Convention proceedings, *Postal Record* (October 1941), 534–35. See also "Unions Charge Post Office with Purge," *Postal Alliance* (January 1949), 19—a reprint from the Detroit Federation of Labor January 7, 1949, edition—where the Alliance noted that Ray Lieberman, now a member of the Postal Supervisors and who had taken such a strong stand for equality at the 1941 NALC convention, had been brought up on "letters of charges" for presumed disloyalty, along with NALC Detroit Branch 1 delegate James Nonen —both "outspoken liberals."

49. Convention proceedings, *Postal Record* (October 1941), 535.

50. The Alliance also became an unintended beneficiary of the NALC's 1941 approval of Jim Crow charters. In the following year sixty-five black letter carriers in Newport News, Virginia, including future NALC delegate John W. Lee, formed a new Alliance branch in that city. See "New Branch Established," *Postal Alliance* (June 1942), 13.

51. See *Postal Record* (October 1941), 535. In 1943 he was listed as "Peter H. Craig, Jr.," a Detroit delegate to the 1943 NALC national convention. See *Postal Record* (October 1943), 329. An apparently low-profile National Alliance member, Craig submitted an article to the *Postal Alliance* after he had retired. See Peter H. Craig, "Intra-Group Unity," *Postal Alliance* (October 1964), 29. In it he used similar language to warn against totalitarian and racist threats to democracy as in the 1941 NALC speech. Meanwhile, what had happened to P. M. E. Hill and Bernard Casey, the black NALC delegates who had helped block the last attempt at separate branches in 1939? They were not even listed among the delegates to the 1941 convention. It is possible that they had both retired or otherwise left the post office, as Hill had been an NALC convention delegate as far back as at least 1917, where he successfully argued against the separate charters. Casey for his part had been carrying mail since 1906, and may well have retired by 1941. It is possible that one or both were not selected as delegates that year. See also "Negro Clerks Rejected by New Orleans," *Postal Alliance* (April 1948), 19, for the campaign by the Alliance and the NAACP against discrimination in that city, where there were 283 black and 66 white carriers, and 451 white and 74 black clerks. On Casey see G. P. Hamilton, *The Bright Side of Memphis* (Memphis: Burke's Book Store, 1908), 198, in History Files, Folder Dual Charters and Blacks, NALC Library, Washington, D.C.

52. The welcoming address at this convention was provided by a member of the Jackson College faculty identified as a "Professor Dansby" (actually its former president, B. Baldwin Dansby) who, the report notes, "assured us that we were not only welcome to the entire buildings and its campus, but it was a very great pleasure to have the honor of being of some service to the members of the Mississippi State Association." George Bell, "Mississippi," *Postal Record* (September 1941), 412. In fact, black postal union and civil rights activists Carsie Hall, Jack H. Young, and J. W. Dixon were all Jackson College alumni, and Dixon was on its Board of Trustees. See B. Baldwin Dansby, *A Brief History of Jackson College: A Typical Story of the Survival of Education among Negroes in the South* (Jackson, Miss.: Jackson College, 1953), 125, 203, 207, and 233.

53. Telephone conversation with Willenham Castilla, January 26, 2009, Ridgeland, Miss. Castilla was also a military veteran and Jackson State alumnus.

54. On B. P. Newman's Alliance membership see 1943 NAPE Convention minutes, *Postal Alliance* (November 1943), 47.

55. *Postal Record* (September 1941), 534.

56. Ibid., 412. See also Glenn, *History of the National Alliance*, 295; convention proceedings, *Postal Record* (October 1941), 567; and John Dittmer, *Local People: The Struggle for Civil Rights in Mississippi* (Urbana: University of Illinois Press, 1994), 30.

57. See for example Ellwood Fredericks, "Wheeling, W. Va.," *Postal Record* (November 1941), 649: "The granting of dual charters in special instances was a step forward. This question has been much misunderstood in the past." See also I. H. Brooks, "Chattanooga, Tenn," 688: "Well, well, so the dual charter came through! Very simple wasn't it? The shortest course around one of 'them things.' The point is, it took so many years to get it simplified to where it would hold whatever it is supposed to hold. The necessity of a dual charter isn't that any group is predominantly selfish. It is only that neither group trusts the other. *And human nature is still such that they are right!*" (italics added). S. P. Cartier from New Orleans connected the dual charter amendment with NALC growth in the South and white southern bloc voting in the NALC: "The 'second charter' amendment, for which we have fought since 1931, will open up the way for the strengthening and growth of the N.A.L.C in this beautiful southland of ours. We shall be in Denver [at the next NALC convention in 1943] *as a solid, compact force* demanding and getting our rightful share of representation on the board of officers" (695, italics added). That reference was to the scheduled Denver convention of 1943, where Mayor Benjamin F. Stapleton would be the official host. Stapleton was elected governor of Colorado in 1923 with Klan support, but he broke with the Klan two years later. See William Chalmers, *Hooded Americanism: The First Century of the Ku Klux Klan, 1865–1965* (Garden City, N.Y.: Doubleday, 1965), 127, 132; and Robert Alan Goldberg, *Hooded Empire: The Ku Klux Klan in Colorado* (Urbana: University of Illinois Press, 1981), 29–35, 107.

58. Convention proceedings, *Postal Record* (October 1941), 488.

59. In fact, William Doherty, elected NALC president for the first time during that 1941 landmark convention, offers in his 1960 memoirs no reflections on the fight over dual charters or racism in the union. See William C. Doherty, *Mailman USA* (New York: David McKay, 1960).

60. M. E. Diggs, "Norfolk, Va.," *Postal Record* (November 1941), 696. This also raises the interesting possibility that, in spite of Jim Crow in the South, blacks dominated the NALC Virginia State Association in 1941, similar to how they possibly dominated the Mississippi NALC up until this time. See for example "Virginia," *Postal Record* (October 1941), 45, the report from the Virginia state NALC July convention by Secretary John W. Lee, one of several black state officers listed.

61. *Union Postal Clerk* (May 1941), 17; and John Walsh and Garth Mangum, *Labor Struggle in the Post Office: From Selective Lobbying to Collective Bargaining* (Armonk, N.Y.: M. E. Sharpe, 1992), 213.

62. *Union Postal Clerk* (July 1941), 76.

63. Convention proceedings, *Union Postal Clerk* (October 1941), 141.

64. Ibid., 84.

65. Ibid., 140. A resolution by Berkeley, California, Local No. 47 "favoring unity of the American labor movement into one federation" passed as well. See ibid., 139.

66. Ibid., 147–48.

67. Ibid., 140.

68. The 1941 NFPOC convention also approved a resolution in line with the AFL's continued opposition to easing immigration and naturalization laws that restrict "Asiatic" workers—shortly before passing a resolution supporting administration policy "to aid Great Britain and her allies who are fighting Fascist aggression." Ibid., 151. For a history of the AFL active opposition to Asian labor presence in America, not just in the trade unions, see for example Alexander Saxton, *The Indispensable Enemy: Labor and the Anti-Chinese Movement in California* (Berkeley: University of California Press, 1971). The alienation that many postal clerk radicals felt almost two decades later arguably goes back to the 1941 defeat of a resolution against Jim Crow locals.

69. The 1943 NFPOC convention was cancelled after the majority of locals voted in compliance with requests by the federal government and the postmaster general for limitations on nonmilitary travel during wartime. The NFPOC met in 1944, which now put their biennial meetings into even rather than odd years. See *Union Postal Clerk* (July 1943), 14–16. On the 1944 NFPOC Jim Crow locals resolution defeat see *Proceedings of the Twenty-third Convention of the National Federation of Post Office Clerks, Indianapolis, Indiana, July 24–29, 1944*, 128–29. See also *Proceedings*, 18, for Resolution 159 (Anti-Lynch Legislation) that passed without debate; and *Proceedings*, 118–20, for Resolution 8 (Discriminatory Practices—Condemning) that hypocritically put the NFPOC on record as opposing racial and religious discrimination everywhere—except, in fact, their own organization.

70. *Proceedings of the Twenty-third Convention of the National Federation of Post Office Clerks, Indianapolis, Indiana, July 24–29, 1944*, 119. See also *NAACP Papers*, Part 13, Series C, reel 6, frames 939 and 954. The first frame has Henry McWright's name on the Cleveland NAPE letterhead as vice president; and in the second frame, he appears as a twenty-seven-year veteran of the post office, and as one of twenty-six mostly black postal workers filing a 1949 civil suit against the federal government for attempting to remove them from the post office on charges of "disloyalty."

71. *1944 NFPOC Proceedings*, 133–34. McHugh's narrative suggests he was black, but I have not found proof that he was.

72. Conversation with Paul Tennassee, National Alliance headquarters, Washington, D.C., November 23, 2001.

73. "President's Memo No. 63" reference in "Discriminatory Technique," *Postal Alliance* (June 1942), 23.

74. *FEPC Records*, reel 70, Kahn, "Summary," 3. On Alice Kahn see Reed, *Modern Civil Rights Movement*, 208.

75. On the *National Labor Relations Act (1935)* and its debates see Hill, *Black Labor*, chap. 3.

76. On Reconstruction evocations see for example Robin D. G. Kelley, *Hammer and Hoe: Alabama Communists during the Great Depression* (Chapel Hill: University of North Carolina Press, 1990); and Philip F. Rubio, *A History of Affirmative Action, 1619–2000* (Jackson: University Press of Mississippi, 2001), chap. 2. For FEPC and white southern official awareness of parallels see for example *FEPC Records*, reel 70, Marjorie W. Lawson to Malcom Ross, "Staff Comments on Your Chicago Speech," December 28, 1943, 3, on Will Maslow's recommendation that Ross read W. E. B. Du Bois's *Black Reconstruction*; and reel 71, "Job Discrimination Debated in South" from "FEPC Clipping Digest (1942)." See also *FEPC Records*, reel 70, Alice Kahn memorandum to John A. Davis, "Summary of WPB Report on Detroit," alluding to coalitions forming to fight racism after the 1943 riots, which included

Alliance members and were credited with cutting the incidence of hate strikes during the war. (The WPB was the War Production Board.)

77. See *NAACP Papers*, Part 13, Series B, reels 22–23. It was President Truman in 1948 who ordered the nation's armed forces integrated in 1948 with Executive Order 9981, Title 3, CFR, 1943–1948. But Henry McGee told how he and other Chicago activists staged their own "march on Washington" after the larger one was cancelled, and lobbied federal officials—including those in the post office—against discrimination: "Therefore, in the spring of 1941, just before the date set to descend on Washington, President Roosevelt issued the famous executive order establishing a Fair Employment Practices Committee. In return Randolph called off the march on Washington. However, in Chicago, the Southside Council of Organizations continued its efforts and organized a miniature march on Washington. A large group of representatives of church and civic organizations went to Washington and visited with the heads of many governmental agencies to vent the frustration of blacks at being excluded from the war effort. I was personally involved in a group that met with the Federal Housing Administrator to protest the failure of blacks to secure FHA insured mortgages. One specific result was we were able to secure a FHA mortgage for a man named Basil Brown, who was trying to buy a home in Maywood, Illinois, a suburb just west of Chicago. This was the first such loan granted and it was followed by many more which enabled blacks for the first time to move to the suburbs. I was also with the committee that met with the post office department to protest discrimination against black postal workers." McGee, *Negro in the Chicago Post Office* (Dissertation), 16–17.

78. Paul Tennassee, "NAPFE: A Legacy of Contributions and Resistance," *National Alliance* (October 1999), 12–13; and *FEPC Records*, reel 66, "A Study of Complaints" (1941–1943). See also "Federal Protest of Unfair Discrimination Made to FDR in Form of Resolutions," *Atlanta Daily World*, July 22, 1941, 2.

79. See Hill, *Black Labor*; Biondi, *To Stand and Fight*; Reed, *Modern Civil Rights Movement*; and Ruchames, *Race, Jobs, and Politics*. Scholarly debates over the meaning of landmark policies and agencies often pit the founders of these institutions against the grassroots efforts that brought them into being. Too often those grassroots efforts are forgotten, as their advocates argue. But the contemporary meaning of those policies and agencies are also underappreciated. Small victories like the abolition of the photo application and Supreme Court decisions against Jim Crow were neither seen as millennial nor insignificant by black postal workers and their white allies, but rather as a series of successive important cracks in the Jim Crow system, with some surely more important than others. Similarly, while the FEPC in retrospect has been judged by most historians to have been both disappointing as well as precedent-setting, an even more important lesson for us should be how the FEPC was perceived by activists and public policy makers at the time, and how even its left critics reacted to its demise as being significant.

80. *FEPC Records*, reel 66, "Attachment A and B": Executive Order 8802 (June 25, 1941); and Executive Order 9346 (May 27, 1943).

81. The CSC at one point clashed with the FEPC, with tense memos being exchanged between the two agencies—the FEPC inquiring of the CSC how it could be that so few discrimination disputes were being resolved. The CSC and the post office were ranked third and fourth, respectively, in discrimination complaints in wartime federal service—the first- and second-place "awards" going to the Army and Navy, respectively. See *FEPC Records*, reel 72, "A Study of Complaints" (1941–1946). On the FEPC as a contested site, see

Reed, *Modern Civil Rights Movement*, esp. chaps. 3–4, where the black press, the NAACP, and left-labor unions fought to maintain the FEPC as a viable institution.

82. See for example a National Alliance complaint to the FEPC dated May 9, 1944, listing eighty-two clerks in the Los Angeles post office passed over for promotion to "foreman" by whites with less seniority. The dates of entering service for the black clerks ranged from 1906 to 1929. *NAACP Papers*, Part 13, Series C, reel 6, frames 946–50.

83. *FEPC Records*, reel 72, "Facts," 5–6.

84. McGee, *Negro in the Chicago Post Office (Dissertation)*, chaps. 8–9. On seniority and white privilege see Hill, *Black Labor*, introduction.

85. Quoted in Glenn, *History of the National Alliance*, 168.

86. Garrott quoted in ibid., with Karl Marx's quote in italics added. Not an exact quote of Marx, Garrott's words were very close to the original language of Marx's 1867 summary of America's past and Marx's prophetic prediction of the inevitable outcome of white workers' failure to connect with the struggles of black workers. The original quote comes from Karl Marx, *Capital: A Critique of Political Economy*, vol. 1, *The Process of Capitalist Accumulation*, ed. Frederick Engels, trans. Samuel Moore and Edward Aveling (1867; New York: International Publishers, 1979), 301: "In the United States of North America, every independent movement of the workers was paralysed so long as slavery disfigured a part of the Republic. *Labour cannot emancipate itself in the white skin where in the black it is branded*" (italics added).

87. After the FEPC lost congressional funding and went out of existence in 1946, the Alliance became involved in the campaign to restore it as a permanent commission, which in 1948 led to President Truman issuing Executive Order 9980 providing for a Fair Employment Board (FEB) of the Civil Service Commission. See Pauli Murray, *States Laws on Race and Color* (Cincinnati: Woman's Division of Christian Service, 1951), 565–85. The FEB was popularly known as the "little FEPC," no doubt referring to its reduced scale compared to the FEPC.

88. Beth Tompkins Bates, " 'Double V for Victory' Mobilizes Black Detroit," in *Freedom North: Black Freedom Struggles outside the South, 1940–1980*, ed. Jeanne Theoharis and Komozi Woodard (New York: Palgrave, 2003), 19. To avoid confusion with the Civil Rights Congress (CRC), I use the CRC initials to refer to the Congress only, and spell out any references to the Civic Rights Committee, itself an interesting suggestive precursor to the modern "civil rights movement."

89. Richard W. Thomas, *Life for Us Is What We Make It: Building Black Community in Detroit, 1915–1945* (Bloomington: Indiana University Press, 1992), 236.

90. Sugrue, *Origins of the Urban Crisis*, 110.

91. See Joshua B. Freeman, *Working-Class New York: Life and Labor Since World War II* (New York: New Press, 2000), 68–71. The Quinn-Ives Act was used, among other things, to pressure Major League Baseball to integrate in 1947. See also Murray, *States Laws*, 9: By the end of the 1940s, the following states had FEPC laws: Connecticut, Massachusetts, New Jersey, New Mexico, New York, Oregon, Rhode Island, and Washington. Indiana and Wisconsin had FEPC laws but without significant enforcement powers. Kansas and Nebraska had appointed a commission to study employment discrimination, and the following cities had FEPC ordinances: Chicago, Cincinnati, Cleveland, Milwaukee, Minneapolis, Philadelphia, Phoenix, and Richmond, California. Cities that later became hubs of postal activism resulting in the 1958 NFPOC split and subsequently the 1970 nationwide

postal wildcat strike included Cleveland, New York, Detroit, Minneapolis, and Chicago—all of which had included local pro-FEPC resolutions as well as having a history of black, labor, and left activism.

92. Tennassee, "Legacy," 12–13.

93. See McGee, *Negro in the Chicago Post Office.*

94. John Hope Franklin quoted in Shenkman, "Reporter's Notebook." See also Louis Lautier, "Jim Crow in the Nation's Capital," *Crisis* (April 1940), 125, which also included a report of the coalition formed to fight Jim Crow, "a united front organization representing 75 religious, fraternal and civic bodies," known as the Washington Civil Rights Committee. By 1948 "civil rights" had become the phrase of choice for legislation and programs relating to the fight for equality by African Americans. The Civil Rights Congress had adopted that name in 1946, the same year that President Truman's committee was convened and also used the term. See Gerald Horne, *Communist Front?: The Civil Rights Congress, 1946–1956* (Rutherford, N.J.: Fairleigh Dickinson University Press, 1988); and President's Committee on Civil Rights, *To Secure These Rights: The Report of the President's Committee on Civil Rights* (Washington, D.C.: Government Printing Office, 1947). A November 1, 1940, *New York Times* article (14L) quoted UMW-CIO leader John L. Lewis calling for protection of labor members' "civil rights" as a synonym for *individual* civil liberties—at a time when antiracist civil rights activists were more typically referring to their struggle as "anti–Jim Crow" or "antidiscrimination." In 1941 neither the original call nor the program for a nationwide March on Washington by A. Philip Randolph made any reference to civil rights but rather an end to "Jim Crow–ism." See reprint from original call in Thomas R. Frazier, ed., *Readings in African-American History,* 3rd ed. (Belmont, Calif.: Wadsworth, 2001), 271–78. Randolph's article "Why We March" the following year alluded to a continuing campaign for "civil, economic, and social rights." Randolph in Birnbaum and Taylor, *Civil Rights since 1787,* 305. A 1939 letter from Walter White to Gunnar Myrdal also made use of the term, but it was still far from popular usage. See Anderson, *Eyes off the Prize,* 18. We also should not underestimate the value of forceful rhetoric used in the World War II period against "Jim Crow" and "Uncle Toms" as well as comparisons made between white supremacy and European fascism, or black middle-class leadership accommodation strategies to Neville Chamberlain's 1938 "appeasement" of Hitler's territorial conquests in Eastern Europe. See Fred Stanton, ed., *Fighting Racism in World War II: C. L. R. James, George Breitman, Edgar Keemer, and Others* (New York: Monad, 1980), 25. A. Philip Randolph included the term Jim Crow in his 1948 movement to integrate the military: "Committee Against Jim Crow [sic] in Military Service and Training." Black postal worker activists and their white allies used it. NAACP national correspondence and press releases commonly used the term, as did the black press and white leftists as well. By the 1940s "Jim Crow" was commonly used among African Americans to "personalize" southern white supremacy and American white supremacy in general. It was uncommon for whites (especially in the South) to use the term unless they were opponents of white supremacy or were reporting it with quotation marks. See Hugh H. Smyth, "The Concept 'Jim Crow,' " *Social Forces* 27, no. 1 (October 1948–May 1949), 45–48.

95. See also Tennassee, "Legacy," 13.

96. Biondi, *To Stand and Fight,* 17.

97. Ibid., 26.

98. Detroit's CIO left included notable black radicals like the Reverend Charles Hill and a young autoworker, activist, and one-time postal worker organizer for the leftist United

Public Workers (UPW-CIO) named Coleman Young, who in 1974 would become the first African American to be elected mayor of Detroit. Coleman himself worked and organized for less than a year at the Detroit post office, although as adolescents he and his brother often went in to work for their father when he was unable to. See Coleman Young and Lonnie Wheeler, *Hard Stuff: The Autobiography of Coleman Young* (New York: Viking, 1994), xvii and 19–113, passim. See also Wilbur C. Rich, *Coleman Young and Detroit Politics: From Social Activist to Power Broker* (Detroit: Wayne State University Press, 1989), esp. 62–63: "In 1933, while Young was in high school, a group of Negro unionists formed the Federation of Negro Labor (FNL) and played a founding role in organizing the postal union with which Young was later associated." Rev. Charles Hill was also a founder of the NNC.

99. Thomas, *Life for Us*, 24.

CHAPTER THREE

1. See interview with Milt Rosner by Dana Schecter, April 27, 1977, New York, transcription, Biller Files. Rosner joined the NAACP at the post office where he worked: Times Square Station. It is intriguing to consider that he may have been recruited by an Alliance member.

2. Rosner interview with Schecter. Rosner joined the breakaway NPCU when the NFPOC split in 1959. See also Martha Biondi, *To Stand and Fight: The Struggle for Civil Rights in Postwar New York City* (Cambridge, Mass.: Harvard University Press, 2003), 16.

3. See Carol Anderson, *Eyes off the Prize: The United Nations and the African American Struggle for Human Rights, 1944–1955* (Cambridge: Cambridge University Press, 2003); and Mary L. Dudziak, *Cold War Civil Rights: Race and the Image of American Democracy* (Princeton, N.J.: Princeton University Press, 2000). See also Fred Stanton, ed., *Fighting Racism in World War II: C. L. R. James, George Breitman, Edgar Keemer, and Others* (New York: Monad, 1980), 25. Arguably the more crucial compromises on the part of the NAACP national office were acquiescence in anticommunism, deemphasis on mass mobilization, and their downgrading of issues of "economic equality"—the latter left to their labor secretary and "civil rights unions" like the National Alliance to champion and keep on the front burner, so to speak. See also H. M. Rollins, "A Christmas Message," *Postal Alliance* (December 1948), 13: "Civil Rights, the right to vote, to work and earn a decent wage, to be unmolested in ones private person, to seek redress for wrongs, to get equal value for ones money, to have an education equal to any other citizen, and many other basic human rights." See also excerpt from letter by Acting Secretary of State Dean Acheson to the FEPC on May 8, 1946: "The existence of discrimination against minority groups in this country has an adverse effect upon our relations with other countries. . . . Frequently we find it next to impossible to formulate a satisfactory answer to our critics." Quoted in William L. Patterson, ed., *We Charge Genocide: The Historic Petition to the United Nations for Relief from a Crime of the United States Government against the Negro People* (1951; New York: International Publishers, 1970), 162.

4. See Ellen Schrecker, *Many Are the Crimes: McCarthyism in America* (Princeton, N.J.: Princeton University Press, 1998), and Robert Rodgers Korstad, *Civil Rights Unionism: Tobacco Workers and the Struggle for Democracy in the Mid-Twentieth Century South* (Chapel Hill: University of North Carolina Press, 2003). See also National States' Rights Democrats Campaign Committee, *States' Rights Information and Speakers Handbook* (Jackson, Miss.: National States' Rights Democrats Campaign Committee, 1948). For an excellent, frank, and even-handed treatment of the CPUSA's blunders, see for example George Lipsitz,

Rainbow at Midnight: Labor and Culture in the 1940s (Urbana: University of Illinois Press, 1994), chap. 8. See also Steve Rosswurm's introduction in Rosswurm, ed., *The CIO's Left-Led Unions* (New Brunswick, N.J.: Rutgers University Press, 1992). Social movement studies usually focus on progressive movements, too often failing to consider the importance of mass-based reactionary movements. The literature on reactionary white movements has curiously omitted this period. For studies on those movements after the *Brown* decisions see for example Neil R. McMillen, *The Citizens' Council: Organized Resistance to the Second Reconstruction, 1954–64* (Urbana: University of Illinois Press, 1971); Dan T. Carter, *From George Wallace to Newt Gingrich: Race in the Conservative Counterrevolution, 1963–1994* (Baton Rouge: Louisiana State University Press, 1996); and Alan Draper, *Conflict of Interests: Organized Labor and the Civil Rights Movement in the South, 1954–1968* (Ithaca, N.Y.: ILR Press, 1994). Of those three, only Draper's focuses on white *workers*.

5. The debate over "origins" of the "civil rights movement" includes a discussion over whether even that term in retrospect is appropriate or is too restrictive. See for example Charles M. Payne and Adam Green, eds., *Time Longer than Rope: A Century of African American Activism, 1850–1950* (New York: New York University Press, 2003), 143; Neil McMillen, ed., *Remaking Dixie: The Impact of World War II on the American South* (Jackson: University Press of Mississippi, 1997); Biondi, *To Stand and Fight*; and Anderson, *Eyes off the Prize*. See also Adam Fairclough, *Race and Democracy: The Civil Rights Struggle in Louisiana, 1915–1975* (Athens: University of Georgia Press, 1995); Aldon D. Morris, *The Origins of the Civil Rights Movement: Black Communities Organizing for Change* (New York: Free Press, 1986); and Michael Keith Honey, *Black Workers Remember: An Oral History of Segregation, Unionism, and the Freedom Struggle* (Berkeley: University of California Press, 1999).

6. See for example Lance E. Hill, *The Deacons for Defense: Armed Resistance and the Civil Rights Movement* (Chapel Hill: University of North Carolina Press, 2004); Timothy B. Tyson, *Radio Free Dixie: Robert F. Williams and the Roots of Black Power* (Chapel Hill: University of North Carolina Press, 1999); and Jonathan Birnbaum and Clarence Taylor, eds., *Civil Rights since 1787: A Reader on the Black Struggle* (New York: New York University Press, 2000).

7. Morris, *Origins*, xi.

8. See Richard W. Thomas, *Life for Us Is What We Make It: Building Black Community in Detroit, 1915–1945* (Bloomington: Indiana University Press, 1992), 248. See also Robert Korstad and Nelson Lichtenstein, "Opportunities Found and Lost: Labor, Radicals, and the Early Civil Rights Movement," *Journal of American History* 75, no. 3 (December 1988), 786–811. See also Henry W. McGee, *The Negro in the Chicago Post Office: Henry W. McGee Autobiography and Dissertation* (Chicago: VolumeOne Press, 1999), 1–2 (*Dissertation*), for this insight on a familiar conundrum: "One of the most frustrating dilemmas which face the Negro in his struggle for equality in all areas of the national life is the problem of using segregated organizations to fight for integration. This has posed serious questions for many Negro groups and has been a special enigma to the Chicago branch of the Alliance. Although this association does not exclude any postal worker from membership, it has remained an almost entirely Negro organization. This factor has been a strength in that it has kindled the fires of racial pride and motivated the development of leadership which otherwise would have lain dormant. On the other hand, it has been a weakness in that it has alienated those Negroes who believe that segregated organizations are self-defeating when the ultimate goal is integration." Compare McGee's statement to some of those by Kwame Ture (Stokely Carmichael) in his autobiography on the difference between "integrated" and "black" organizations. See Stokely Carmichael, with Ekwueme Michael Thelwell,

Ready for Revolution: The Life and Struggles of Stokely Carmichael (Kwame Ture) (New York: Scribner, 2003), chap. 4.

9. On the importance of campaigns for more black postal supervision, see for example A. L. Glenn, *History of the National Alliance of Postal Employees, 1913–1955* (Washington, D.C.: National Alliance of Postal Employees, 1956); O. Grady Gregory, *From the Bottom of the Barrel: A History of Black Workers in the Chicago Post Office from 1921* (Chicago: National Alliance of Postal and Federal Employees, 1977); and McGee, *Negro in the Chicago Post Office.* For examples of various union officials fighting racism within their own rank and file, see for example August Meier and Elliot Rudwick, *Black Detroit and the Rise of the UAW* (Oxford: Oxford University Press, 1981); and Dan Georgakas and Marvin Surkin, *Detroit: I Do Mind Dying: A Study in Urban Revolution*, 2nd ed. (1975; Boston: South End Press, 1998). For examples of white management's battles ostensibly in favor of equality versus white labor's opposition during the 1940s, see for example Robert C. Weaver, *Negro Labor: A National Problem* (New York: Harcourt, 1946).

10. Morris, *Origins*, xi.

11. "Now's the Time," *Charlie Parker, Original Bird: The Beat of Bird on Savoy*, Savoy Jazz, 1988 (original recording November 26, 1945, New York), LP recording. See also John Hope Franklin and Alfred A. Moss Jr., *From Slavery to Freedom: A History of African Americans*, 8th ed. (1947; Boston: McGraw-Hill, 2000), chap. 21.

12. See Jacquelyn Dowd Hall, "The Long Civil Rights Movement and the Political Uses of the Past," *Journal of American History* 91, no. 4 (March 2005), 1233–63, revised version of Professor Hall's presidential address, Organization of American Historians annual meeting, March 27, 2004, Boston, reported by historian Rick Shenkman, "Reporter's Notebook: Highlights from the 2004 OAH Convention," History News Network, <http://hnn.us/articles/4320.html> (March 30, 2004). Professor Hall directs the University of North Carolina–Chapel Hill Southern Oral History Program. See SOHP website, <http://www.sohp.org/news/hall_address.htm> (September 10, 2008): "Hall heralded the work of historians whose research allows us to locate the roots of the movement as early as the 1930s; a black-left-labor alliance in the 1940s, she noted, advanced a critique of racialized capitalism that was far more profound in its implications than the narrower racial equality movement of the Cold War 1950s and 1960s." Shenkman's article included this summary: "So how can we account for the conservative triumphs that ended in a shredded safety net, the loss of high-paying blue collar jobs, and all the rest of the sorry milestones that have come to be identified with the twentieth century? Blame the Cold War, Hall told the group. That may have come as a shock to some in the audience, who just last night were told at the church meeting on *Brown* that the Cold War put pressure on the government to end segregation in order to take away from the communists an obvious symbol of American backwardness. But Hall argued that the movement was actually a casualty of the Cold War, which empowered red-baiting conservatives in both parties and led to the collapse of the black-labor-left alliance." Red-baiting opportunism was also engaged in by liberals as well as conservatives, yet many black and left-leaning activists also became alienated from CPUSA cadres and the party as a whole despite its progressive work, and often expressed angry annoyance with communists for packing mass organizations and coalitions with "concentrations" of disciplined cadres; placing a priority on the CPUSA party line and defending the Soviet Union's foreign and domestic policies at all costs; assuming a vanguard status; alternating between opportunism and sectarianism; and often attacking criticism of themselves and the Soviet Union as "red-baiting." See for example Lipsitz, *Rainbow at Midnight*, chap. 8; Pauli

Murray, *The Autobiography of a Black Activist, Feminist, Lawyer, Priest, and Poet* (Knoxville: University of Tennessee Press, 1990); Herbert Hill, "Communist Party—Enemy of Negro Equality," *Crisis* (June–July 1951), 365–71; Mark Naison, *Communists in Harlem during the Depression* (Urbana: University of Illinois Press, 1983); Earl Ofari Hutchinson, *Blacks and Reds: Race and Class in Conflict, 1919–1990* (East Lansing: Michigan State University Press, 1995); Keith P. Griffler, *What Price Alliance? Black Radicals Confront White Labor, 1918–1938* (New York: Garland, 1995); Athan G. Theoharis, *Chasing Spies: How the FBI Failed in Counterintelligence but Promoted the Politics of McCarthyism in the Cold War Years* (Chicago: Ivan R. Dee, 2002); and Stanton, *Fighting Racism in World War II*. For similar arguments to those advanced by Hall, see for example Judith Stepan-Norris and Maurice Zeitlin, *Left Out: Reds and America's Industrial Unions* (Cambridge: Cambridge University Press, 2003), epilogue; Schrecker, *Many Are the Crimes*, esp. 369, 389–91; Korstad and Lichtenstein, "Opportunities Found and Lost"; Korstad, *Civil Rights Unionism*, esp. 11–12; and Manning Marable, *Race, Reform, and Rebellion: The Second Reconstruction in Black America, 1945–1990* (1984; Jackson: University Press of Mississippi, 1991). For other views of the NAACP see Dona Cooper Hamilton and Charles V. Hamilton, *The Dual Agenda: Race and Social Welfare Policies of Civil Rights Organizations* (New York: Columbia University Press, 1997); August Meier and John H. Bracey Jr., "The NAACP as a Reform Movement, 1909–1965: 'To Reach the Conscience of America,'" *Journal of Southern History* 59, no. 1 (February 1993), 3–30; and Herbert Hill, "The Racial Practices of Organized Labor: The Contemporary Record," in *The Negro and the American Labor Movement*, ed. Julius Jacobson (Garden City, N.Y.: Archer, 1968), 286–357. For E. P. Thompson's 1983 Berkeley, California, speech and his observation on the average lifespan of social movements, see Korstad and Lichtenstein, "Opportunities Found and Lost," 811. For an extensive critique of the "long civil rights movement" thesis and an excellent survey and critique of civil rights and Black Power movement literature generally, see Sundiata Keita Cha-Jua and Clarence Lang, "The 'Long Movement' as Vampire: Temporal and Spatial Fallacies in Recent Black Freedom Studies," *Journal of African American History* 92, no. 2 (Spring 2007): 265–88, the quote here appearing on 265.

13. See Thomas J. Sugrue, *The Origins of the Urban Crisis: Race and Inequality in Postwar Detroit* (Princeton, N.J.: Princeton University Press, 1996); Hutchinson, *Blacks and Reds*; Lipsitz, *Rainbow at Midnight*, chap. 8; David R. Roediger, *Working toward Whiteness: How America's Immigrants Became White* (New York: Basic Books, 2005), chap. 7; Herbert Hill, *Black Labor and the American Legal System: Race, Work, and the Law* (1977; Madison: University of Wisconsin Press, 1985); and Nelson Peery, *Black Radical: The Education of an American Revolutionary* (New York: New Press, 2007).

14. See for example Paul Tennassee, "NAPFE: A Legacy of Contributions and Resistance," *National Alliance* (October 1999), 14–17; and Glenn, *History of the National Alliance*. The National Postal Workers Council (NPWC), an antiracist left postal union, is intriguing in that no record exists of them in the recorded history of the APWU and its predecessor unions. The NPWC is presumed to be leftist not only because of its affiliation with a left-wing CIO affiliate, the United Public Workers (later purged from the CIO by 1950), but also because it was engaged in organizing a conference against President Truman's executive order on loyalty cases. They wrote to the NAACP on May 17, 1949, to invite Walter White to join them. Notwithstanding the NAACP leadership's anticommunist leanings, a handwritten note, presumably by White himself, is scrawled at the bottom of that letter: "Very sorry, notice too short. Have speaking engagements in W. Va and NY that weekend." The

headquarters of the NPWC was listed as Detroit, with officers also based in Chicago, San Francisco, and Minneapolis. *NAACP Papers*, Part 13, Series C, reel 6, frame 1250.

15. *Annual Report of the Postmaster General, 1945–1949* (Washington, D.C.: Government Printing Office, 1946–1950), 23 (1949): "As of June 30, 1949, 53.2 percent of such employees were veterans."

16. Glenn, *History of the National Alliance*, 158, 168.

17. Paul P. Van Riper, *History of the United States Civil Service* (Evanston, Ill.: Row, Peterson, and Company, 1958), 144, 162, 269–70, 423, 436. Disabled veterans received federal government hiring preferences after the Civil War. They received five extra civil service examination points with the 1883 Pendleton Act. By World War I all veterans, their widows, and wives of veterans too disabled to work received preference points, adjusted to today's levels by President Warren G. Harding in 1923: five extra points for all veterans and ten points for disabled veterans. By 1934 one-fourth of federal employees were veterans, and almost half by the end of World War II. See also U.S. Civil Service Commission, *History of Veteran Preference in Federal Employment* (Washington, D.C.: Government Printing Office, 1955).

18. " 'Quota' Halts Enlistments," *Pittsburgh Courier*, August 17, 1946, 1; and Executive Order 9981.

19. See *Veterans Preference Act of 1944*; *Statutes at Large* 58, chaps. 286, 387 (1944); *Servicemen's Readjustment Act of 1944*, *Statutes at Large 58* , chaps. 268, 284 (1944); and Philip F. Rubio, *A History of Affirmative Action, 1619–2000* (Jackson: University Press of Mississippi, 2001), chaps. 4–5.

20. James Hill Jr., "Meet the New York Post Office," *Postal Alliance* (December 1948), 10. See also author interview with James Morris, longtime National Alliance member and practicing attorney from Brooklyn, New York, August 11, 2004, Washington, D.C.

21. "Object Lesson in Civil Rights in the Post Office," in *Postal Alliance* (December 1948), 16.

22. Glenn, *History of the National Alliance*, chap. 25. See also *NAACP Papers*, Part 13, Series C, reel 6, frame 1300, the *Postal Alliance* editor's report from the 1949 NAPE national convention, where "the Women's Auxiliary . . . pledged itself to . . . intensify their activity in promoting legislation and measures designed to help the men [recently purged from the post office for 'disloyalty']." The repeated use of the word "purge" was probably a deliberate comparison to common political practice and terminology in totalitarian states, as "purge" has long been popularly associated with the Communist Party's arbitrary firings (and worse) of officials in the USSR, especially under Josef Stalin. Schrecker, *Many Are the Crimes*, 20–21, 138.

23. "Letter Carriers Reject Resolution for FEPC: Liberals Out-Voted," *Pittsburgh Courier*, September 14, 1946, 5; and "NAPE Seeks No-Bias Policy for Employees," *Pittsburgh Courier*, June 22, 1946, 13.

24. Biondi, *To Stand and Fight*, 10; and Glenn, *History of the National Alliance*, 314, 328.

25. "Object Lesson in Civil Rights in the Post Office," *Postal Alliance* (December 1948), 10.

26. Ibid. The late 1940s also saw an annual labor education summer institute held at Ohio State University in Columbus, which included unions from the CIO, AFL, and the post office. The Alliance contributed the greatest number, according to one observer. "Alliance Participates in Summer School Session for Office Workers and White Collar Workers at Ohio State University," *Postal Alliance* (August 1948) 2, 8–9; and Glenn, *History of the National Alliance*, 316. On the American Labor Education Service see for example

Wiley A. Hall, "Adult Education Programs of Labor Unions and Other Workers Groups," *Journal of Negro Education* 14, no. 3 (Summer 1945), 407–11; Eleanor G. Coit and John D. Connors, "Agencies and Programs in Workers' Education," *Journal of Educational Sociology* 20, no. 8 (April 1947), 520–28; and Eleanor G. Coit and Orie A. H. Pell, "Labor Education and Intergroup Relations," *Journal of Educational Sociology* 25, no. 6 (February 1952), 319–20.

27. Thomas, *Life for Us*, 248.

28. *Postal Alliance* (January 1948), table of contents, 3.

29. Charles M. Payne, " 'The Whole United States is Southern!': *Brown v. Board* and the Mystification of Race," *Journal of American History* 91, no. 1 (June 2004), 83. Payne also notes: "In 1940, the percentage of all southern blacks who were registered to vote was estimated at below 5 percent. In 1947 the percent registered jumped to 12 percent, by 1952 to 20 percent. The increase seems directly attributable to the black voter registration drives that occurred across the South following Smith." See also *Smith v. Allwright*, 321 U.S. 649 (1944); and Darlene Clark Hine, *Black Victory: The Rise and Fall of the White Primary in Texas* (Millwood, N.Y.: KTO Press, 1979). On LeFlore see for example Bruce Nelson, "Organized Labor and the Struggle for Black Equality in Mobile during World War II," *Journal of American History* 80, no. 3 (December 1993), 952–88. See also "Press Release Entitled 'Next Step Is Drive for Registration of Southern Voters,' April 6, 1944," available at Manuscript—Voting Rights, Texas Primaries Cases, NAACP Collection, 1938–1946 (Primary Source), LexisNexis website, <http://cis.lexis-nexis.com> (November 12, 2005).

30. Clarissa Myrick-Harris, "Atlanta in the Civil Rights Movement," available at Atlanta Regional Council for Higher Education, <http://www.atlantahighered.org> (September 7, 2008); "John Wesley Dobbs," <http://www.aaregistry.com> (September 7, 2008); and Gary M. Pomerantz, *Where Peachtree Meets Sweet Auburn: The Saga of Two Families and the Making of Atlanta* (New York: Scribner, 1996), esp. chap. 9.

31. In Los Angeles, black postal workers in 1943 filed a grievance against "one of the most liberal post offices in the United States," as Postmaster Mary Briggs had described it in welcoming the NALC to their 1941 convention. See convention proceedings, *Postal Record* (October 1941), 463. The Alliance alleged that eighty-one qualified black clerks were passed over for a promotion given to a white man and accused her in 1943 of appointing only whites as supervisors and of calling blacks "incompetent" (see *NAACP Papers*, Part 13, Series C, reel 6, frame 949). Briggs responded by reiterating the post office's commitment to nondiscrimination in hiring and promotion. See Glenn, *History of the National Alliance*, 166. Los Angeles Alliance activists added this observation: "As an example of the outstanding background of some of the Negro clerks we wish to cite: Robert L. Robinson who entered the service 1-21-24. This man's service record is spotless and creditable. He is a university graduate who has received his Master's Degree and is now working toward his Doctorate." *NAACP Papers*, Part 13, Series C, reel 6, frame 948. National Alliance members in Los Angeles fought to advance black postal clerks who held virtually no supervisory or "desk jobs," despite accounting for "over 60 percent" of the clerk workforce in that city. That point was made by the Alliance's Special Committee to Investigate Promotional Discrimination in notifying the FEPC in 1944 that, while the "hiring policy of the administration would appear to be imminently [*sic*] fair," promotion is another story. *NAACP Papers*, Part 13, Series C, reel 6, frame 989. See also Glenn, *History of the National Alliance*, chap. 28.

32. *NAACP Papers*, Part 13, Series C, reel 6, frames 1049–50, italics added. By 1947 the "white problem" trope was already being used popularly to counter the standard "Negro problem" paradigm. It had most famously been advanced by such noted writers as George

S. Schuyler, Bayard Rustin, Richard Wright, and Lillian Smith. On Richard Wright's counter that "America has a white problem" in response to a French reporter's question about his opinion of the "Negro problem" in the United States, see George Lipsitz, "The Possessive Investment in Whiteness: Racialized Social Democracy and the 'White' Problem in American Studies," *American Quarterly* 47, no. 3 (September 1995), 369. The reporter's question had to do with the subtitle of the new book by Gunnar Myrdal, *An American Dilemma: The Negro Problem and Modern Democracy* (New York: Harper, 1944). Despite that book's unfortunate subtitle, Myrdal's conclusion was essentially the same as that of Wright, Smith, Rustin, and Schuyler—all prominent writers and/or activists who used the term "white problem." For Lillian Smith's use of the term, see *Pittsburgh Courier*, August 4, 1945, 1. See also the variation by George S. Schuyler, "The Caucasian Problem," in *What the Negro Wants*, ed. Rayford W. Logan (Chapel Hill: University of North Carolina Press, 1944), 281–97. And see Bayard Rustin, *Louisiana Weekly*, April 1, 1947: "Unjust social laws and patterns do not change because supreme courts deliver just decisions. One needs merely to observe the continued practice of Jim Crow in interstate travel, six months after the Supreme Court's decision, to see the necessity of resistance. Social progress comes from struggle; all freedom demands a price. . . . But if anyone at this date in history believes that the 'white problem,' which is one of privilege, can be settled without some violence, he is mistaken and fails to realize the ends to which men can be driven to hold on to what they consider their privileges." See <http://www.spartacus.schoolnet.co.uk/USAcore.htm> (May 21, 2006).

33. Glenn, *History of the National Alliance*, 105. In addition, a letter was subsequently circulated among Alliance members suggesting that they all quote from it as often as possible. Fanning himself later appeared on a cover of the *Postal Alliance*. See *NAACP Papers*, Part 13, Series C, reel 6, frame 1054; *Postal Alliance* (April 1948), cover; and "Editorial," *Postal Alliance* (January 1948), 4. In the latter reference, Fanning's challenge to other postmasters is included, as well as his resolute response to a white letter carrier who had expressed concern with Fanning's appointing so many black supervisors.

34. Glenn, *History of the National Alliance*, 417. See also telephone interview with Raydell Moore, January 13, 2006, Pahrump, Nev., and interview with John Adams, former New York City–Bronx branch National Alliance (NAPE) local president, Washington, D.C., August 11, 2004.

35. Glenn, *History of the National Alliance*, 105. Additional remarks of Fanning's included these: "One of the bulwarks of the battle to secure justice and fair treatment for the Negro race is the National Alliance of Postal Employees. . . . As postmaster of the fourth largest postoffice in the U.S., I never make a move without counseling with your organization and with the other organizations of postal employees. You make my work easier."

36. John A. Diaz, "Letter Carriers Retain Jim Crow," *Postal Alliance* (November 1948), 16 (reprint from the *Pittsburgh Courier*).

37. Convention proceedings, *Postal Record* (November 1948), 17. See also Leon Samis, "New York, N.Y.," *Postal Record* (December 1948), 28–29. Miami, a city that practiced segregation in the 1940s, was clearly on Samis's mind in one of the tabled resolutions. The Miami convention, which stuck mainly to issues of pay raises, benefits, and work rules, also featured a speech by Kansas congressman Edward H. Rees denouncing communism, followed by the convention's very first resolution (which was approved and adopted), titled "Elimination of Subversive Elements within the Postal Service." See *Postal Record* (November 1948), 6–7. Just two years earlier the parent AFL had voted down resolutions banning

Jim Crow locals. See Richard Thomas, "Blacks and the CIO," in Birnbaum and Taylor, *Civil Rights since 1787*, 293.

38. Convention proceedings, *Postal Record* (November 1948).

39. Diaz, "Letter Carriers Retain Jim Crow."

40. "Mail Carrier on Constitution Revision Committee," *Postal Alliance* (January 1947), 16. See also Convention report, *Postal Record* (October 1948), 47. NALC Branch 525 had been operative since 1923 in Norfolk. See Earl Lewis, *In Their Own Interests: Race, Class, and Power in Twentieth-Century Norfolk, Virginia* (Berkeley: University of California Press, 1993), 60.

41. *Official Proceedings of the Thirty-sixth Biennial Convention of the National Association of Letter Carriers, Miami, Florida, Oct. 11–16, 1948*, 36. Joining Diggs in opposing Jim Crow branches were Delegates C. E. Sullivan of Atlanta Branch 172 and Fred C. Byrd of Little Rock, Arkansas, Branch 35, who proudly pointed to his branch as one of the first NALC branches and also one that was not segregated. In opposition were white Delegates Dan Young, Branch 569 Texarkana, Arkansas, and R. H. Peacock of Jacksonville, Florida, Branch 3944 (incorrectly listed as a member of black Atlanta Branch 172!).

42. M. E. Diggs, "Virginia," *1948 NALC Proceedings*, appendix, 9a.

43. "Attention Letter Carriers Special Meeting!" *Postal Alliance* (November 1948), 16–17.

44. Ibid.; and "A Message to Our Fellow Letter Carriers," *Postal Alliance* (November 1948), 17.

45. John L. Stokes, "Uncle Tom's Chillun," *New York Alliance Leader* (May 1949), 1, 4, reprinted verbatim in the *Postal Alliance* (May 1949), 12.

46. Stokes, "Uncle Tom's Chillun," 1. Also quoted in Glenn, *History of the National Alliance*, 185.

47. For 1946 convention resolutions against discrimination see convention proceedings, *Union Postal Clerk* (September 1946), 14–19. See also *Local 251 Minutes*, 1946, reel 2. See also minutes for May 15, 1940: Local 251 sent a delegate to the April 1940 convention of the National Negro Congress, which by then had become communist-dominated. "Brother Clarke" (presumably black but not identified as such) reported back that among the resolutions passed were those in opposition to U.S. entry into World War II, the activities of the Dies Committee (the House Un-American Activities Committee), "and the elimination of photos on applications for Civil Service positions." On the National Negro Congress see for example Philip S. Foner and Ronald L. Lewis, eds., *The Black Worker: A Documentary History from Colonial Times to the Present*, vol. 7, *The Black Worker from the Founding of the CIO to the AFL-CIO Merger, 1936–1955* (Philadelphia: Temple University Press, 1983), 139–68; and William H. Harris, *The Harder We Run: Black Workers since the Civil War* (New York: Oxford University Press, 1982), 110–12, 116. On Maxwell's involvement with the National Alliance see available issues from 1945 to 1946 of its regular newsletter, the *Alliance Leader*, New York City Branch of the National Alliance of Postal Employees, 1945–1982, reel 1, microfilm, borrowed from State Historical Society of Wisconsin. The *Alliance Leader* (called the *New York Alliance Leader* until April 1946) published monthly or bimonthly over the years, and officers' names can usually be found on page 2: Maxwell's middle initial "O" was apparently corrected from "R" by the March 1946 issue.

48. Convention coverage, *Union Postal Clerk* (October 1946), 18. The resolution included an unnamed amendment by Local 10 delegate Nathan Weisburd, and the resolution was seconded by Chicago delegate George Wachowski. Local No. 140 was Washington, D.C.'s white local, and was mute on the subject. On the 1948 convention proceedings and the "Progressive Program" see *Union Postal Clerk* (October 1948), 14, 21–27. In 1952 the

NFPOC's national convention was reminded by New York Local 10 activists that the NFPOC had "unanimously adopted a resolution which recommended an amicable solution for abolition of dual locals . . . and that no separate dual charters shall ever again be issued." That 1946 equivocation by the national union helped give birth to the NFPOC's Progressive caucus that same year, which was organized to promote union democracy and an end to Jim Crow locals. See *Union Postal Clerk* (October 1952), 44. Members of the New York City local, including Morris "Moe" Biller, who would later become president of the APWU, would later remind the 1952 St. Paul convention of that unkept promise. Walsh and Mangum's study includes no specifics about the birth of the Progressives, but I found the reference to its birth and rationale in the 1974 "Notes on History of NY Metro Area Local, Women Stewards Meeting, June 13," Box 2, Folder 1974, NYMAPUC. NFPOC convention proceedings were included in the monthly *Union Postal Clerk* until 1954. See John Walsh and Garth Mangum, *Labor Struggle in the Post Office: From Selective Lobbying to Collective Bargaining* (Armonk, N.Y.: M. E. Sharpe, 1992).

49. See *1948 NALC Proceedings*, 37.

50. Ibid., 35, 44. See also M. Brady Mikusko, *Carriers in a Common Cause: A History of Letter Carriers and the NALC* (Washington, D.C.: NALC, 1989), 13. The first 50 branches of the NALC were formed by August 1890, 231 by August 1891, and 333 by August 1892.

51. *1948 NALC Proceedings*, 37, italics added. Doherty cited nine cities with segregated branches but could only name eight: Jackson, Charleston, Memphis, Norfolk, New Orleans, Atlanta, Montgomery, and Washington, D.C. That would mean that separate charters were later issued to Birmingham, Mobile, Jacksonville, St. Petersburg, Albany (Ga.), Baton Rouge, Shreveport, Greenville (S.C.), Houston, Lubbock, and Portsmouth (Va.), unless Doherty had forgotten to include one of those other charters in his original list of nine.

52. Ibid., 36.

53. *NAACP Papers*, Part 13, Series C, reel 6, frame 1038. See Carmichael, *Ready for Revolution*, chaps. 6–7, for Ture's discussion of the history of "contradictions" of Howard University both as Jim Crow critic and middle-class "uplift" promoter. Johnson had also been one of the NAACP team of attorneys who prevailed in *Smith v. Allwright*, 322 U.S. 649 (1944).

54. *NAACP Papers*, Part 13, Series C, reel 6, frame 1126. It is not known if Hall had been a member of the Alliance or any other postal union. See also Mikusko, *Carriers in a Common Cause*, 49.

55. See Steven F. Lawson, *Running for Freedom: Civil Rights and Black Politics in America since 1941* (New York: McGraw-Hill, 1991), 33–39. See also Executive Order 9981 and coverage of this and Executive Order 9980 on the Truman Library (TL) website, <http://www.trumanlibrary.org> (October 12, 2008), including an oral history interview with Truman's special counsel (1946–50), Clark M. Clifford. TL entries are more celebratory of Truman as one might expect, while Lawson shows Truman having to be pushed to the left on civil rights by liberal Democrats. For text of both executive orders and in later instructions, see Pauli Murray, *States Laws on Race and Color* (Cincinnati: Woman's Division of Christian Service, 1951), 571–85.

56. President's Committee on Civil Rights, *To Secure These Rights: The Report of the President's Committee on Civil Rights* (Washington, D.C.: Government Printing Office, 1947).

57. Biondi, *To Stand and Fight*, 59.

58. Ashby Carter, "A Statement on Civil Rights by the National Alliance of Postal Employees," *Postal Alliance* (February 1948), 11–20.

59. *Postal Alliance* (April 1948), 5, reprint from *Detroit Free Press*, April 1, 1948, and also described in Lipsitz, *Rainbow at Midnight*, 340.

60. *NAACP Papers*, Part 13, Series B, reel 25, frames 778–81. This press release was issued by the NCNW, CIO, Odd Fellows, Beauty Culture League, UAW-CIO, Alpha Kappa Alpha, American Jewish Committee, National Association of Colored Graduate Nurses, Friends Committee on National Legislation, American Veterans Committee, ACLU, National Council for a Permanent FEPC, ADL/B'nai B'rith, National Association of Negro Milliners, Hair Stylists and Dress Designers, National Alliance, National Medical Association, ILGWU-AFL, American Jewish Congress, and the NAACP, with the AFL and the National Catholic Welfare Conference observing. This conference in D.C. deliberately excluded the communist-dominated Civil Rights Congress (CRC). See also Darlene Clark Hine, "Black Professionals and Race Consciousness: Origins of the Civil Rights Movement, 1890–1950," *Journal of American History* 89, no. 4 (March 2003), 1279–94, especially where she refers to the National Association of Colored Graduate Nurses and the National Medical Association as a significant part of the black middle-class involvement in the 1940s civil rights struggle.

61. The NECRM in turn became the Leadership Conference on Civil Rights (LCCR), the National Alliance being a major organizer of both. See Biondi, *To Stand and Fight*, 170; and Tennessee, "Legacy," 14. For the CRC's reaction to being excluded from the civil rights coalition, see *NAACP Papers*, Part 13, Series B, reel 25, frames 842–45, "An Open Letter from William L. Patterson, Executive Secretary of the Civil Rights Congress, to the National Association for the Advancement of Colored People," November 14, 1949. The CRC and other left groups had good reason to be annoyed at the exclusion: according to Biondi, it was a United Public Workers delegate to the 1949 NAACP national convention who first put the resolution (later approved) on the floor to conduct a mass civil rights coalition lobbying effort called the National Emergency FEBC Mobilization. At the Mobilization's first D.C. conference in 1950, CIO officials who controlled the credentials committee excluded hundreds of mostly black leftists who wanted to participate. Biondi also notes the virulent anticommunism that NAACP head Roy Wilkins shared with FBI director J. Edgar Hoover, as well as the tricky position that LCCR member A. Philip Randolph was put in with the LCCR's strategy of combining lobbying with white liberal coalition. Biondi, *To Stand and Fight*, chap. 8. NAACP Labor Secretary Clarence Mitchell Jr., became a chief strategist and civil rights legislation architect of the LCCR, to the extent that he became known as the "101st Senator." Mitchell was also director of the NAACP's Washington Bureau. See John Hope Franklin and Alfred A. Moss Jr., *From Slavery to Freedom: A History of African Americans*, 8th ed. (1947; Boston: McGraw-Hill, 2000), 524–25. See *NAACP Papers*, Part 13, Series B, "Scope and Content," xi, for this analysis: "In 1949, the NAACP, dissatisfied with Randolph's handling of matters, broke away from the National Committee for a Permanent FEPC and created the Emergency Civil Rights Mobilization. . . . Finally in 1952, this NAACP-led coalition took Leadership Conference on Civil Rights (LCCR) as its title. The LCCR carried on the work of the National Committee for a Permanent FEPC and the Civil Rights Mobilization." See also *Local 251 Minutes*, reel 2 (no frame numbers), January 18, 1950, meeting minutes of Brooklyn Local 251 NFPOC, where delegate Harry Stewart reported on the national Civil Rights Mobilization of "5000 delegates from 33 states converged on Washington, D.C in the greatest demonstration of its kind in history." Local 251 was unique among predominantly white AFL postal unions in that it actively

participated in the campaign against lynching and maintained fraternal relations with local National Alliance and NAACP branches.

62. McGee, *Negro in the Chicago Post Office (Autobiography)*, 15–19. McGee related an ongoing struggle—including the Southside Council of Organizations' decision to march on Washington, D.C., in 1941 even after the March on Washington Movement had cancelled the nationwide march, as well as his struggle with the local NAACP over their investing large sums of branch funds to fight restrictive housing covenants.

63. Ibid., 17, italics added.

64. "On Adding Some Black to the Southern Scene, 'The Sweatt Case,'" *Postal Alliance* (January 1950), 11.

65. See Richard Kluger, *Simple Justice: The History of Brown v. Board of Education and Black America's Struggle for Equality* (New York: Vintage, 1977), 260–66, 275–78, 282. Houston black postal workers were crucial to the founding of the NAPE, and the Houston branch of the NAACP, which included a number of Alliance members, was also the branch that had launched the *Smith v. Allwright* voting rights lawsuit in 1940, and backed Sweatt in his legal campaign, as did the national Alliance office. See Tennassee, "Legacy"; Glenn, *History of the National Alliance*, chap. 1; and esp. "Editor's Notebook: Postal Employees Make Great Contributions to Civil Rights," *Postal Alliance* (May 1950), 4–6, 8 (undoubtedly Snow Grigsby's writing). Heman Sweatt had applied to the University of Texas law school, was rejected because he was black, and subsequently filed suit. The Texas legislature responded by trying to change the name of Prairie View College (a historically black college) to Prairie View University in order to establish the fiction of a "separate but equal" law school for blacks. With the help of the NAACP Sweatt took his case to the Supreme Court, which ruled that where an inadequate graduate school existed for blacks, they must then be allowed admission to white graduate schools. The decision chipped away at *Plessy* although it left its core intact: if a public university graduate school could not provide "equal" facilities, it was compelled to admit black students to a previously all-white one. Sweatt dropped out of Texas Law after the first year, reportedly from stress, but he continued to work with the NAPE, attending labor education seminars at Ohio State University as an NAPE representative. In the 1950s Sweatt moved to Cleveland, where he became branch president. In 1954 he earned a master's degree in social work at Atlanta University, where he later taught and was also assistant director of the National Urban League's Southern Regional Office. See Vivé Griffith, "'Courage and the Refusal to Be Swayed': Heman Marion Sweatt's Legal Challenge That Integrated the University of Texas," <http://txtell.lib.utexas.edu/stories/s0010-full.html> (May 21, 2006). Amilcar Shabazz, *Advancing Democracy: African Americans and the Struggle for Access and Equity in Higher Education in Texas* (Chapel Hill: University of North Carolina Press, 2004), discusses Sweatt and his case, although he does not mention his postal career or Alliance membership.

66. In a series of ironies, the NAACP national office responded to an appeal from Lulu White, Houston NAACP head, that Wesley and others were hedging their bets on segregation. But according to Richard Kluger, Marshall and the LDF were at that point still not prepared to make a direct attack on legal segregation. See Kluger, *Simple Justice*, 260–66, 275–78, 282. It appears that a number of disparate elements conspired to push the NAACP to use *Sweatt* as launching pad against *Plessy* and segregation, including the specter of southern school boards and states being willing to create phony equal educational facilities; the Justice Department's agreement to join in repudiating *Plessy*; and the willingness by

some black Houstonians to settle for "equal" but separate facilities if that is all that whites would seemingly grant (a concession that was anathema to the NAACP national office). See "Press Release Entitled 'Separate Not Equal, U.S. Insists,' February 16, 1950," and "Press Release Entitled 'End of Jim Crow Seen By Marshall,' June 8, 1950," Manuscript—Education, *Sweatt v. Painter*, NAACP Collection, 1945–1950 (Primary Source), <http://cis.lexis-nexis.com> (May 21, 2006), hereafter referred to as NAACP Collection. Wesley quit the NAACP in 1947 because he said that national officers like Thurgood Marshall and local officers like Lulu White had accused him and his organization, the Texas Conference for the Equalization of Educational Opportunities, of supporting segregated education. See "Carter Wesley, NAACP membership resignation, January 17, 1947," in Manuscript—Education, *Sweatt v. Painter*, NAACP Collection, 1945–1950. When Wesley in that same letter cautioned against communist influence in the NAACP, he may have been making a veiled reference to Lulu White, who was also at the time co-chair of the CRC. See Gerald Horne, *Communist Front? The Civil Rights Congress, 1946–1956* (Rutherford, N.J.: Fairleigh Dickinson University Press, 1988), 138–39. Wesley's position recalls Du Bois's January and March 1934 *Crisis* editorials. See David Levering Lewis, ed., *W. E. B. Du Bois: A Reader* (New York: Henry Holt, 1995), 557–62. See also *Smith v. Allwright*, 322 U.S. 649 (1944). Correspondence between Texas and the national office of the NAACP ("NAACP Legal Arguments in Texas Primary Case, 1938–1946," *Sweatt v. Painter*, NAACP Collection) offers a fascinating glimpse into the process by which fighting segregation came to be the NAACP's main target in the mid-1940s, between the *Smith v. Allwright* decision and the campaign to win *Sweatt v. Painter*. For example, in his "Letter to Carter W. Wesley, May 15, 1945," Thurgood Marshall emphasized the need to "secure equalization of educational opportunities," fresh on the heels of winning the *Smith* voting discrimination case, and made no mention of fighting segregation. But just a little over one year later found Marshall angrily writing in "Letter to Carter W. Wesley, October 25, 1946" that every segregated school "is a monument to the perpetuation of segregation." On Lulu White and the defeat of the Texas white primary see Darlene Clark Hine, *Black Victory: The Rise and Fall of the White Primary in Texas* (1979; Columbia: University of Missouri Press, 2003). See also Merline Pitre, *In Struggle against Jim Crow: Lulu B. White and the NAACP, 1900–1957* (College Station: Texas A&M University Press, 1999). According to Pitre (70), White's effectiveness as a civil rights leader, red-baited as she was by both Carter Wesley and the white media, was "closely connected to the work of such labor movement advance men as Richard Grovey, Sidney Hasgett, Heman Marion Sweatt, and Moses Leroy."

67. Thurgood Marshall, "Letter to William Hastie," April 3, 1947, *Sweatt v. Painter*, NAACP Collection.

68. Ibid. Marshall wrote William Hastie (who had become governor of the Virgin Islands) that based on Texas's attempts to equalize separate schools, the time had come to start confronting segregation: "The interesting thing is that the court refused to rule as a matter of law that segregation was invalid and the Chief Justice made the statement from the bench that it was the appellant's position that segregation and discrimination were tied up together."

69. Sweatt's "Letter to Walter Francis White, November 8, 1946," *Sweatt v. Painter*, NAACP Collection. See also "Editor's Notebook," *Postal Alliance* (May 1950), 6, for Lulu White's comments after having accompanied Sweatt to Austin that year along with other NAACP officials and confronted Texas state officials over what she called their "fascist

ideas" of white supremacy. See also Kluger, *Simple Justice*, 260–66, 275–78, 282; and Griffith, "Courage and the Refusal."

70. Marshall Letter to Heman Marion Sweatt, July 26, 1950, *Sweatt v. Painter*, NAACP Collection.

71. J. Luzine LeFlore, "John LeFlore Exonerated," *Postal Alliance* (January 1947), 16. John LeFlore's photo was also on the cover of that issue. See also Nelson, "Organized Labor."

72. See also McGee, *Negro in the Chicago Post Office*. On the insurgent NAPE officers in the 1940s—Ashby Carter, James Cobb, William Jason, and Snow Grigsby—see also Tennassee, "Legacy," 13.

73. McGee, *Negro in the Chicago Post Office (Dissertation)*, chaps. 5 and 7. McGee was not saying here that the Alliance lost its civil rights focus, but rather that it operated in a different sphere as before. I would argue more that it did both, leaning toward being a labor union in this period, but still lobbying and litigating like a civil rights group.

74. "Editor's Notebook: Postal Employees Make Great Contributions to Civil Rights," *Postal Alliance* (July 1950), 4. See also *Shelley v. Kraemer* 334 U.S. 1 (1948).

75. "Editor's Notebook," *Postal Alliance* (May 1950), 5.

76. "Prince Hall Grand Master's Resolution Hits Jim Crow," *Postal Alliance* (May 1950), 5.

77. Ibid., 6.

78. "Editor's Notebook," *Postal Alliance* (November 1948), 4. The *Postal Alliance* had also interviewed Progressive Party candidate Henry Wallace in their February issue on page 10.

79. See Glenda Gilmore, *Gender and Jim Crow: Women and the Politics of White Supremacy in North Carolina, 1896–1920* (Chapel Hill: University of North Carolina Press, 1996).

80. See Mary Church Terrell's legal and direct action coalition against public accommodation segregation in the nation's capital from 1950 to 1953. See Beverly Washington Jones, "Before Montgomery and Greensboro: The Desegregation Movement in the District of Columbia, 1950–1953," *Phylon* 43, no. 2 (2nd Qtr., 1982), 144–54. Terrell enjoyed close relations with the Alliance, and was also a signer of the Civil Rights Congress's petition to the United Nations in 1951, *We Charge Genocide*. See also Paul Tennassee, personal conversation, November 23, 2001. On New York City labor politics in the McCarthy era see Joshua B. Freeman, *Working-Class New York: Life and Labor since World War II* (New York: New Press, 2000), 90–101.

81. "Postal Employees," *Ebony* (November 1949), 15–18.

82. Tennassee, "Legacy."

83. One might even call this the Alliance's (more dedicated) version of the CIO's ill-fated "Operation Dixie." See Glenn, *History of the National Alliance*, 177; and Lewis, *In Their Own Interests*, 60.

84. Executive Order 9835.

CHAPTER FOUR

1. On McLean see *NAACP Papers*, Part 13, Series C, reel 6, frame 1212: he listed himself as "chairman of the Post Office Investigation Committee" of the local branch. See also William H. Harris, *The Harder We Run: Black Workers since the Civil War* (New York: Oxford University Press, 1982), chap. 2; H. Leon Prather Sr., *We Have Taken a City: Wilmington Racial Massacre and Coup of 1898* (Rutherford, N.J.: Fairleigh Dickinson University Press, 1984); and

David S. Cecelski and Timothy B. Tyson, eds., *Democracy Betrayed: The Wilmington Race Riot of 1898 and Its Legacy* (Chapel Hill: University of North Carolina Press, 1998).

2. See Ashby Carter, "National Roundup," *Postal Alliance* (November 1948), 13; Robert Rodgers Korstad, *Civil Rights Unionism: Tobacco Workers and the Struggle for Democracy in the Mid-Twentieth Century South* (Chapel Hill: University of North Carolina Press, 2003); and Michael Keith Honey, *Black Workers Remember: An Oral History of Segregation, Unionism, and the Freedom Struggle* (Berkeley: University of California Press, 1999). See also "Lost Record," *Alliance Leader* (April 1950), 1, presumably written by its editor, James Hill, concerning his role that year cooperating with the investigation by John T. Risher (launched by Sen. Langer) into discrimination in the federal service, especially in the Memphis post office. The *Postal Record* (October 1946), 516, shows the first NALC national convention appearance of Memphis all-white Branch 3856 alongside the original, now all-black Branch 27. By the 1954 convention blacks in Memphis had formed Branch 837, and by 1962 a reunified Branch 27 was restored. See *NALC Proceedings* for 1954 and 1962. See also items on Memphis in "Dual Charters and Blacks" Folder, NALC Library, Washington, D.C., and "Report of Proceedings of First Annual Convention, National Association of Letter Carriers of the United States," *Postal Record* (August / September 1890), 196, 198.

3. See Korstad, *Civil Rights Unionism*; and Honey, *Black Workers Remember*.

4. "McCarthyism" was originally coined as a negative expression by *Washington Post* editorial cartoonist Herbert Block less than a month after Sen. McCarthy gave his February 9, 1950, speech in Wheeling, West Virginia, warning of communist infestation in the government. McCarthy himself later proudly used it as a book title. In the words of journalist Richard Rovere, it was first an "oath then an affirmation." See Richard Rovere, *Senator Joe McCarthy* (1959; New York: Harper, 1973), 7. On J. Edgar Hoover's anticommunist campaign see for example Merl E. Reed, "The FBI, MOWM, and CORE, 1941–1946," *Journal of Black Studies* 21, no. 4 (June 1991), 465–79. The popularity and free reign of McCarthy and his Permanent Investigating Subcommittee of the Government Operations Committee reflected a concern in ruling circles about the volatility of American labor that had forced changes in labor law in the 1930s. The power of unions over closed shops was ended with the 1947 Taft-Hartley Act, which passed over Truman's veto. The act also required communist labor unions or members to register with the federal government. The House Committee on Un-American Activities (HUAC) that began its work in 1938 focused much of its attention on the "loyalty" of workers, specifically federal government workers. Sen. Pat McCarran's Senate Internal Security Subcommittee (SISS) performed much the same function as HUAC and the Permanent Investigating Subcommittee. See Ellen Schrecker, *The Age of McCarthyism: A Brief History with Documents*, 2nd ed. (Boston: Bedford / St. Martin's Press, 2002), esp. 64, 73, and *Many Are the Crimes: McCarthyism in America* (Princeton, N.J.: Princeton University Press, 1998). See also David Caute, *The Great Fear: The Anti-Communist Purge under Truman and Eisenhower* (New York: Simon and Schuster, 1978); Rovere, *Senator Joe McCarthy*; Albert Fried, ed., *McCarthyism: The Great American Red Scare: A Documentary History* (New York: Oxford University Press, 1997); Executive Order 9835, March 21, 1947 (also known as Truman's "Loyalty Oath" or *Federal Employees' Loyalty Program*), CFR, Title 3, 1943–1948 (issued March 21, 1947); and the 1947 Taft-Hartley Act (Labor Management Relations Act), Title 29, Chapter 7, U.S.C. See also Athan Theoharis, "The Politics of Scholarship: Liberals, Anti-Communism, and McCarthyism," <http://www.english.upenn.edu/~afilreis/50s/theoharis.html> (September 10, 2008).

5. Carol Anderson, *Eyes off the Prize: The United Nations and the African American Struggle for Human Rights, 1944–1955* (Cambridge: Cambridge University Press, 2003), 159. The Alliance, significantly, did not follow the NAACP or CIO internal witch-hunting model.

6. President's Committee on Civil Rights, *To Secure These Rights: The Report of the President's Committee on Civil Rights* (Washington, D.C.: Government Printing Office, 1947), 89.

7. See "American Federation of Labor Adopts Resolution Favoring Rescinding of Loyalty Executive Order," *Postal Alliance* (January 1949), 23; and Anderson, *Eyes off the Prize*. See also postal union journals during this period, for example: convention summary, *Union Postal Clerk* (October 1952), 44; and "Postal Alliance President Issues Statement on Loyalty Order," *Postal Alliance* (January 1949), 8.

8. George Lipsitz, *Rainbow at Midnight: Labor and Culture in the 1940s* (Urbana: University of Illinois Press, 1994), chaps. 4–8; A. L. Glenn, *History of the National Alliance of Postal Employees, 1913–1955* (Washington, D.C.: National Alliance of Postal Employees, 1956); Martha Biondi, *To Stand and Fight: The Struggle for Civil Rights in Postwar New York City* (Cambridge, Mass.: Harvard University Press, 2003); and Jeanne Theoharis and Komozi Woodard, eds., *Freedom North: Black Freedom Struggles outside the South, 1940–1980* (New York: Palgrave, 2003).

9. See Joshua B. Freeman, *Working-Class New York: Life and Labor since World War II* (New York: New Press, 2000).

10. See for example an article with a photo of a summer labor education seminar at Ohio State University in Columbus that included Alliance members meeting with representatives from the more liberal AFL to leftist CIO unions: some of the latter, in fact, were denied seats on the CIO Executive Board the following year and purged a year later. See "Alliance Participates," *Postal Alliance* (August 1948), 8–9. Two of those ten expelled unions represented at the Ohio State seminar included the United Public Workers and the United Office and Professional Workers. Among the Alliance members represented there was Heman Marion Sweatt, the plaintiff in *Sweatt v. Painter*. On the expulsion of "red" unions see for example Schrecker, *Many Are the Crimes*, esp. 338–40. Besides the two already named, they included the United Electrical, Radio and Machine Workers of America; International Union of Mine, Mill, and Smelter Workers; American Communications Association; Food, Tobacco, Agricultural and Allied Workers of America; Fur and Leather Workers; International Fisherman's Union, International Longshoremen's and Warehousemen's Union; and the National Union of Marine Cooks and Stewards. See also Judith Stepan-Norris and Maurice Zeitlin, *Left Out: Reds and America's Industrial Unions* (Cambridge: Cambridge University Press, 2003), 265; Steve Rosswurm, ed., *The CIO's Left-Led Unions* (New Brunswick, N.J.: Rutgers University Press, 1992), introduction; *Proceedings of the Eleventh Constitutional Convention of the Congress of Industrial Organizations* (Cleveland: CIO, 1949); and *Proceedings of the Twelfth Constitutional Convention of the Congress of Industrial Organizations* (Cleveland: CIO, 1950).

11. Glenn, *History of the National Alliance*, 179.

12. David Levering Lewis, ed., *W. E. B. Du Bois: A Reader* (New York: Henry Holt, 1995), 759–60. Reprinted from the 1949 proceedings of the House Committee on Foreign Affairs. Du Bois testified against the Military Assistance Act of 1949 as potentially provoking war with the Soviet Union, and noted how minority positions like his were treated: "We are afraid. For we stop logical thinking. We invent witch hunts. If in 1850 an American disliked slavery, the word of exorcism was 'abolitionist.' He was a 'nigger lover.' . . . Today the word

is 'Communist.' . . . If anybody questions the power of wealth . . . advocates civil rights for Negroes, he is a Communist, a revolutionist, a scoundrel, and is liable to lose his job or land in jail."

13. Biondi, *To Stand and Fight*, 140, italics added.

14. Ibid., 141. Biondi cites twenty-five black postal workers as having lost their jobs. The National Alliance at one point cited twenty-nine as having won them back, including Fred Turner in Brooklyn. See Paul Tennassee, "NAPFE: A Legacy of Contributions and Resistance," *National Alliance* (October 1999), 13.

15. "Bias at Post Office Charged by Negro in Loyalty Hearing," *Postal Alliance* (November 1948), 23. Washington also denied membership in the CPUSA, as did all his coworkers who had also been charged with disloyalty. The Alliance commonly noted with some bitterness the presumption of disloyalty toward African Americans by either those who supported Jim Crow or were ostensibly its foes. See for example "Resume of Known Facts in Connection with the Operation of the Loyalty Program of the Post Office Department," *Postal Alliance* (November 1948), 8: "It is highly significant that to date no news is had of any employee of the Government who has been cited for affiliation with or sympathy for the Ku Klux Klan. Yet here is the one organization which makes no secret of its aims to deprive American citizens of their constitutional rights through force and violence." Besides being hypocritically enforced, the language of the loyalty oath was vague and broad, as the Alliance and other critics pointed out. For example, Part 5, Section 1, called "Standards," stated: "The standard for the refusal of employment in an executive department or agency on grounds relating to loyalty shall be that, on all the evidence, reasonable grounds exist for belief that the person involved is disloyal to the Government of the United States." Section 2 laid out the criteria for "disloyalty": "Membership in, affiliation with or sympathetic association with any foreign or domestic organization, association, movement, group or combination of persons, designated by the Attorney General as fascist, communist, or subversive, or as having adopted a policy of advocating the commission of acts of force or violence to deny other persons their rights under the Constitution of the United States, or as seeking to alter the form of government of the United States by unconstitutional means." See Executive Order 9835. See also *1949 CIO Proceedings*, where a virtual parade of anti-communists ritualistically opposed leftist union nominees for Executive Board in paraphrasing those lines from the Loyalty Oath's Section one: "I have a firm conviction that — is ineligible under the constitution to serve." Alliance members noted bitterly that employees could be discharged not even on the basis of proven membership, but simply on the basis of having been charged with membership in a "subversive" organization, even if they belonged to that organization before it was so termed by the federal government. See *NAACP Papers*, Part 13, Series C, reel 6, frame 1300, and reel 5, frames 832–35 for a version of the Attorney General's List of Subversive Organizations that besides the CPUSA included groups like the Abraham Lincoln Brigade, the Civil Rights Congress, and the National Negro Congress. See also author interview with John Adams, former New York City–Bronx branch National Alliance local president, Washington, D.C., August 11, 2004. See also the case of Joseph Bryant, a window clerk and Cleveland Alliance member framed for overcharging a patron after he had been assigned to the previously all-white Shaker Square post office. Acquitted in January 1948, he energized that Alliance chapter. See "Resume of Known Facts," 7; and "The Branch That Hate Could Not Destroy: Remarks of Ashby G. Smith, President, NAPFE, at Testimonial Honoring Mary Guen, Cleveland, Ohio, September, 28, 1968," *National Alliance* (October 1968), 9. The fraud

charges against Bryant actually preceded the postal disloyalty purges. Bryant was defended by the Cleveland chapter of the CRC, according to Gerald Horne, *Communist Front? The Civil Rights Congress, 1946–1956* (Rutherford, N.J.: Fairleigh Dickinson University Press, 1988), 284.

16. See for example AFL president William Green cited in an article titled "AFL Seeks Integration" in the *Pittsburgh Courier*, September 21, 1946, 5, for a speech made at the AFL national convention: "Declaring that Communists are out to foment revolution in America and regard Negroes as candidates for front-line positions in the hoped-for revolution, he warned all Negroes to be aware of their sugar-coated promises." That convention also voted to keep Jim Crow union locals. See Richard Thomas, "Blacks and the CIO," in *Civil Rights since 1787: A Reader on the Black Struggle*, ed. Jonathan Birnbaum and Clarence Taylor (New York: New York University Press, 2000), 293. See also for example "Memorandum for the Attorney General" from FBI Director J. Edgar Hoover, September 17, 1943, warning of collaboration between FEPC representative Jack Burke in Detroit and reported communist organizer Jack Raskin. The former had allegedly urged the latter to "find Negro women who were to go to war plants and seek jobs with the possibility that racial discrimination might develop and an issue raised." See *FEPC Records*, reel 66. Also see a report by the ACLU that called discrimination against blacks the "most numerous and publicized" civil liberties issue of 1944–45 and noted "that of thirty-three persons serving prison sentences under war laws for speeches or publications, twenty-five are members of obscure Negro antiwar religious sects." *Pittsburgh Courier*, "ACLU Finds Discrimination Biggest Issue of 1944–45," August 4, 1945, 1.

17. *NAACP Papers*, Part 13, Series C, reel 5, frames 664–873; Anderson, *Eyes off the Prize*, 167; and Tennassee, "Legacy."

18. From 1947 to 1952 about 6.6 million persons were investigated. No espionage cases were found, and 500 lost their jobs for "questionable loyalty." Howard Zinn, *A People's History of the United States* (1980; New York: Harper, 1990), 420. See also Schrecker, *Many Are the Crimes*, 40.

19. Charlie Cherokee, "National Grapevine," *Chicago Defender*, November 6, 1948, excerpt, *NAACP Papers*, Series C, reel 6, frame 883; see also frames 843–83 and esp. frame 1300, in which Snow Grigsby, in his "Editor's Notebook" from the August 1949 *Postal Alliance*, notes the purge "peculiarly has struck at militant NAPE leaders and Jews." See also "Resume of Known Facts in Connection with the Operation of the Loyalty Program of the Post Office Department," *Postal Alliance* (November 1948), 2: "In Cleveland, as far as can be determined, 24 Negro Postal Employees, of whom 22 are members of the Cleveland Branch, NAPE, 8 of whom are member of the Executive Board; 4 Jews, 2 white gentiles." The article also noted NAACP leadership positions and veteran status held by several of the black victims, and "in Philadelphia it appears that the majority of those cited are Jews." A consistent theme in the black press was the highlighting of white allies whenever they could be found. Sometimes there would be a conflation of "Jews" as "whites." But Jewish allies were also noted for suffering ethno-religious discrimination, especially related to the loyalty purge. Alliance attorney O. John Rogge, for example, estimated that "nearly 90%" of those purged were blacks and Jews, and "virtually all are active spokesmen against racial and religious discrimination." See Glenn, *History of the National Alliance*, 244. See also the article datelined Shreveport, Louisiana, titled "Supported FEPC; Army Breaks White Officer: Championed Negro Cause," *Pittsburgh Courier*, September 22, 1945, 18. The *Chicago Defender* and the *Pittsburgh Courier* were probably the two largest nationally circulated black

newspapers at the time. See also telephone conversation with Richard Peery, longtime Cleveland journalist (and brother of longtime activist Nelson Peery), November 20, 2008, who argued that the 1948 postal purge was in part revenge against the Alliance by the Truman administration and his newly appointed postmaster general, Jesse M. Donaldson, former postmaster of New Orleans postmaster, because the Alliance (especially in Cleveland) and the NAACP had vigorously protested Donaldson's appointment. Documents in the *NAACP Papers*, Part 13, Series C, reel 6, frames 1056–1175, chronicle that campaign and support Peery's explanation.

20. *NAACP Papers*, Part 13, Series C, reel 5, frame 838.

21. Ibid., frame 871.

22. Ibid., frames 883, 887.

23. "NAACP Votes to Support Loyalty Purge Victims," *Postal Alliance* (January 1949), 14. The board passed that resolution on November 8, 1948.

24. *NAACP Papers*, Part 13, Series C, reel 5, frames 935–36.

25. Ibid., frames 934–1085. Co-plaintiffs with Bertram A. ("Bert") Washington included Henry McWright, Vernon Thomas, Curtis Cassel Garvin, Thomas Williams, Theodore Milner, Louis Joseph Bolden, Joseph Robbins, Albert B. Bolden (all from Cleveland); John C. Lymas, James L. Braxton, Isidore N. Cohen, Ralph Pepper, Morris B. Moses, Arthur L. Drayton, William D. Ridgeway (all from Philadelphia); Louis Stovack, Raymond Lieberman, Herbert Samuel Polson (all from Detroit); Benjamin Rice (New York), Albert Di Dario, Gino Di Dario, Lyndoors E. Grey, Lawrence Sarsfield Dowling, Arnold Garald Dowling, and James A. Bruno (all from New Jersey): all were Alliance members or supporters. See also ibid., reel 6, frame 1300, for *Postal Alliance* editor Snow Grigsby's August 1949 report from the just concluded NAPE national convention: "A message was received from Roy S. Wilkins, acting secretary of the NAACP, through Clarence Mitchell, NAACP labor secretary, stating that the NAACP would enter the cases of some twenty suspended postal workers in Cleveland." See also "High Court Fails to Review President's Loyalty Case," *Atlanta Daily World*, May 2, 1951, 2. See also "Accused in Post Office Purge," *Cleveland Call and Post*, October 16, 1948, 3-A: five Alliance members charged with disloyalty in Cleveland were also NFPOC members: Bert Washington, Albert Bolden, Curtis Garvin, Disraeli Henderson, and Henry McWright. The article further noted the Cleveland Alliance's activism in 1944 against unfair labor practices by Cleveland Postmaster O'Donnell, who later resigned; and their successful antidiscrimination campaign against Superintendent D. B. Snow of that city's postal garage. See also "Loyalty Hearings Resumed Here for Post Office Clerks," *Cleveland Call and Post*, December 11, 1948, 1, 9-A: to date only six discharges had been upheld by the Loyalty Review Board out of 335 cases.

26. Adam Fairclough, *Race and Democracy: The Civil Rights Struggle in Louisiana, 1915–1975* (Athens: University of Georgia Press, 1995), xviii. This may be a hard argument for many to accept, especially considering the virulence of Roy Wilkins's anticommunism. But see also Anderson, *Eyes off the Prize*, chap. 1, for a discussion of the NAACP's alienation with the CPUSA's prior attacks on them, and NAACP distrust of CPUSA pro-Soviet politics.

27. National Alliance's Statement on Loyalty Program, *NAACP Papers*, Part 13, Series C, reel 6, frame 882.

28. *NAACP Papers*, Part 13, Series C, reel 5, frame 881. See also "Negro Publishers Pledge Aid to Fight 'Purge,' " *Postal Alliance* (August 1949), 2–3, in *NAACP Papers*, Part 13, Series C, reel 6, frame 1299. The lead article in the Alliance's August 1949 issue of the *Postal Alliance* was titled "Negro Publishers Pledge Aid to Fight 'Purge.' " The black press departed from

their conservative stance of a few years earlier, and at least for the time being many were forthright where the NAACP's stance was equivocal. See for example Harvard Sitkoff, "African American Militancy in the World War II South: Another Perspective," in *Remaking Dixie: The Impact of World War II on the American South*, ed. Neil McMillen (Jackson: University Press of Mississippi, 1997), 70–92; and Gerald Horne, *Black and Red: W. E. B. Du Bois and the Afro-American Response to the Cold War, 1944–1963* (Albany: State University of New York Press, 1986), 1.

29. For example, the Alliance kept the Progressive-era term "comrade" despite worries by some members that it would cause people to connect the Alliance with the CPUSA, for whom that term was standard use. Glenn, *History of the National Alliance*, 107, taken from an unnamed edition of the *Postal Alliance* in 1950.

30. One of the few studies on the white worker mass base of Jim Crow is Alan Draper, "Brown v. Board of Education and Organized Labor in the South," *Historian* 57, no. 1 (Autumn 1994), 75–88.

31. The first "history" of the NFPOC—one of the predecessors to today's APWU—was written by Karl Baarslag, *History of the National Federation of Post Office Clerks* (Washington, D.C.: NFPOC, 1945). The author's photograph page introduces him as "Lt. Commander Karl Baarslag, U.S.N.R." (U.S. Naval Reserve). He was a former member of NFPOC Brooklyn Local 251 who became a naval intelligence officer specializing in communist affairs, and part of the anticommunist network of informants established in the 1940s and 1950s by the FBI. Baarslag, who had also been a part of small maritime radio-telegraphers union that became dominated by a communist faction, devoted several pages in his NFPOC history detailing how he saw the CPUSA trying to insinuate itself into the labor movement in general and his former postal union in particular. He later worked for Sen. McCarthy, and he was also part of the nationwide anticommunist network recruited from what the FBI called "trusted representatives." That network included the members of the AFL, Daughters of the American Revolution, right-wing radio broadcasters like Bishop Fulton J. Sheen, and former communists like Ben Mandel. See Schrecker, *Many Are the Crimes*, chap. 2, esp. 42–46, as well as chap. 7, passim.

32. See for example Resolution 654, "Civil Rights," brought by Local 10 that included defending trial rights of federal employees accused of disloyalty; and Resolution 740A "Membership-Discriminatory Practices," brought by Local 251 in *Resolutions to Be Acted Upon by the Twenty-ninth Convention of the National Federation of Postal Clerks, August 27 to September 1, 1956, Chicago, Illinois*, 165, 191. On the 1950 and 1955 loyalty case suspensions of Local 10 members see John Walsh and Garth Mangum, *Labor Struggle in the Post Office: From Selective Lobbying to Collective Bargaining* (Armonk, N.Y.: M. E. Sharpe, 1992), 59–60. See also for example *Summary of Proceedings of Twenty-sixth Biennial Convention of National Federation of Post Office Clerks*, in *Union Postal Clerk* (September 1950), 2–34, that included speeches and resolutions against communism. There is an interesting juxtaposition on page 14: the passage of a strong resolution in favor of postal union recognition and a rather weak one "asking that any employees involved in loyalty proceedings be granted the right to confront their accusers."

33. See "Transcript of Hearing before Postmaster General on April 5, 1949," esp. 7; and letter from Harold Buckles to Ephraim Handman, June 5, 1949; in Box 45, Folder Loyalty Case #99—Local 10, NFPOC, 1948–49—transcript of hearing, correspondence, NYMAPUC. Buckles was an aide to Rep. Klein. It is not known what attorney he is referring to here, as none was listed as present at the hearing that also included Edgar B. Jackson, chairman of the

departmental loyalty board. The transcript itself reads like a seventeenth-century Salem, Massachusetts, witchcraft trial.

34. Elmer E. Armstead, "An Open Letter to the Editor of the New York Fed," *Alliance Leader* (August 1951), 4.

35. While the Alliance typically prided itself on principled stands for the civil liberties of all, even the Alliance could find themselves drawn into liberal anticommunism, as can be seen in "Editor's Notebook," *Postal Alliance* (March 1949), 4, where Snow Grigsby, who for years had worked in coalition with leftists and communists, now would write: "No real American will deny that there is a definite Red menace among us, and none will oppose the seeking out of the elements. The opposition is to the method being employed." See also regular coverage of activist social clubs in the Baltimore and Washington *Afro-American* and *New York Amsterdam News*, also reflected in the *Postal Alliance*. While coverage in the black press often was in line with the positions of the NAACP, it could also be critical from both the left and the right.

36. On coverage of Du Bois, Robeson, and the Korean War, see for example Ashby G. Smith, "Civil Rights—The May Trail," *Postal Alliance* (June 1958), 12. See also these front-page articles in the *Washington Afro-American*: James L. Hicks, "Integration a Fact as We Fight Koreans" and "DuBois Gets Permit to Go Abroad," August 12, 1950; "Can't Get Passport, Robeson to Fight," August 26, 1950; and Woody L. Taylor, "McArthur Given No Credit for Integration in Korea," May 12, 1951. For oral histories and coverage of the black Korean War experience see John Biewen's American Radio Works' documentary and website at <http://www.americanradioworks.publicradio.org/features/korea/indix.html> (November 12, 2005). See also oral history interview with Jessie Johnson by Blair Murphy, Norfolk, Va., August 11, 1995, BTV. Johnson was a black Korean War veteran who scoffed at the notion of Truman's executive order integrating the military: what finally forced integration, he noted, was having an entire regiment go out into combat "and come back in a jeep," meaning there were only enough survivors to fit in a small military vehicle.

37. See for example coverage of the "Summit Meeting of the NNPA in Washington, D.C.," in *Postal Alliance* (June 1958), 7.

38. Glenn, *History of the National Alliance*, 253.

39. Ibid., 108. Dean George Johnson spoke at the 1951 convention on "Are Federal Employees Being Reduced to Second Class Citizenship?" Attorney Howard Jenkins in 1953 spoke in Atlantic City, at one point proclaiming: "I neither defend nor apologize for organizations composed primarily of Negroes." Ibid., 111.

40. Jason in *Postal Alliance* (February 1952), quoted in ibid., 253.

41. Ibid., 253.

42. Ibid., 254–55.

43. Ibid., 255. See also Executive Order 10450 (1953).

44. Jason in *Postal Alliance* (February 1952), 256.

45. "Postal Alliance Wins $37,000 Back Pay for 'Purge' Victims," *Postal Alliance* (September 1953), 4.

46. Walsh and Mangum, *Labor Struggle*, 59. See also "Employe [*sic*] Security Programs," *Union Postal Clerk* (November 1954), 6. Compared to 500 federal employee terminations (not even counting the many more forced resignations) between 1947 and 1952 under Truman's EO 9835 and EO 10241, 2,611 terminations between 1953 and 1954 is an astounding figure for a "reformed" EO 10450. See also EO 10450; and Zinn, *People's History*, 420.

47. Glenn, *History of the National Alliance*, 110–11. After conferring with both Democratic

candidate Adlai Stevenson and Republican Dwight Eisenhower, Alliance president Carter declared the "assurances" given by Eisenhower to be "the most positive." The Alliance's lobbying "operation" continued after Eisenhower's election in November 1952. The term "Operation Contact" must have seemed especially appropriate with former generals Eisenhower and Abrams now serving as president of the United States and assistant post-master general. Later issues of the *Postal Alliance* would criticize the new president as well as list his black appointments as positive accomplishments. See "Excerpts from the President's Address," *Postal Alliance* (October 1953), 5–6. See also *Postal Alliance* (October 1954), back page. "Operation Contact" was part of the Alliance's mode of operation: file petitions, complaints or lawsuits; hold fact-finding tours or meetings with postal officials, get the black press to cover it (preferably with a photograph), and then report on the results to its readers. See regular *Postal Alliance* criticisms of organized labor throughout 1950s and 1960s: for example in Ashby G. Smith, "Civil Rights—The December Trail; 1959 Review," *Postal Alliance* (January 1960), 10: "The Labor Movement in America that has done much to advance the cause of civil rights is not yet ready to make the all-out fight that must be made and there is a serious question if in this age of accelerated change we can wait until, unaided, it makes up its mind to move."

48. Bert Washington, the prominent black Cleveland activist forced to fight for his job over disloyalty charges, was also a United Public Workers–CIO member and an NNLC charter member. But I have found no references to the NNLC or the CRC in any issue of the *Postal Alliance*, although Alliance members worked with CRC members at various times in coalition. See Mindy Thompson, "The National Negro Labor Council: A History," *Occasional Paper No. 27* (New York: American Institute for Marxist Studies, 1978), 11. The *Washington Afro-American*'s coverage included grudging admiration for the NNLC in the regular column written by Clarence Mitchell, the NAACP Washington, D.C., Bureau Director. Mitchell called the formation of the NNLC proof that "the race question is still a No. 1 item on the agenda of some of the so-called left-wing unions. . . . Unless the major unions can be more vigorous than they have been on civil rights matters in recent months, the public will get the impression that only left-wing labor spokesmen want civil rights." See "Clarence Mitchell's Work Bench," *Washington Afro-American*, November 3, 1951, 15. In 1952 the *Baltimore Afro-American* scornfully employed words like "colored" and "right wing" to express their contempt for the founding convention of the Negro Labor Committee (NLC), the NNLC's anticommunist counterpart. The Alliance was not formally involved with either group, although individual Alliance members were part of the NNLC. At the NLC convention, according to one source, anticommunist white CIOers checked credentials of black delegates at the door. The CIO, following its purge of 1949–1950, reportedly had few black delegates at its convention in 1951. See "Tan Right Wing Labor Body Set Up," *Baltimore Afro-American*, March 8, 1952, 14. The article noted that the group meeting in Harlem passed resolutions against lynching and for affiliation with any trade union body that was not communist. It also contained this excerpt suggesting the newspaper's con-tempt for the NLC: "The group did not make any stand for the full civil rights program advocated by the President's Committee on Civil Rights, nor did it mention the barbaric treatment accorded colored people in Florida." On the same page was an article titled "NAPE Asks More P.O. Integration," which also appeared the same day in the *New York Amsterdam News* as "Seek Top Negro Position in PO." That issue of the *Amsterdam News* contained favorable coverage of the NLC, including its actual name, and noted the creden-tials check at the door without further comment. See "Labor Meet at Theresa Draws 350,"

2, *New York Amsterdam News*, March 8, 1952. Martha Biondi has argued that "the NNLC constituted a bridge between black-labor-left formations of the 1940s, and those of the 1960s, 1970s, and beyond, such as the Negro American Labor Council and the Coalition of Black Trade Unionists." See Biondi, *To Stand and Fight*, 264. Generally speaking she is correct. But the fire drawn by the NNLC for their militancy reveals a more complex line of political descent—from their inception to their disbanding in 1956 after coming under continuous attack from government and even mainstream civil rights and black labor leaders like A. Philip Randolph. The earlier National Negro Congress that had also seen black postal worker participation had in fact become dominated by communists by the 1940s. The NNLC, on the other hand, seems to have been more independent and black nationalist in contrast to the more conservative, ideologically "color-blind" NLC.

49. Telephone conversation with Vivian Grubbs, January 7, 2009. See also Nelson Peery, *Black Radical: The Education of an American Revolutionary* (New York: New Press, 2007), 103–54; and Biondi, *To Stand and Fight*, 263–67, 283. The NNLC disbanded after the Subversive Activities Control Board in 1956 demanded its membership list. Ironically, Randolph probably borrowed as much from the NNLC as he did the NLC in forming the Negro American Labor Council as a kind of angry but loyal black opposition in the AFL-CIO. He left the Negro American Labor Council in 1966. See Harris, *Harder We Run*, 162. Randolph, it could be argued, combined the black nationalism of the NNLC with the anticommunism of the NLC in creating the Negro American Labor Council in the 1960s.

50. See *Local 251 Minutes*, March 19, 1952, p. 2, reel 2.

51. Ibid., April 1952, p. 3, reel 2.

52. Biondi, *To Stand and Fight*, 240. The Eisenhower administration itself decided, as Ellen Schrecker points out, to bring McCarthy down for investigating disloyalty in the U.S. Army by releasing documents showing McCarthy trying to pull strings in the army for a close friend of his associate Roy Cohn. The nationally televised March–June 1954 Army-McCarthy hearings resulted in McCarthy alienating much of his public as well as congressional support, resulting in his censure by the Senate in December of that year. McCarthy drank himself to death three years after his censure. Schrecker, *Many Are the Crimes*, 262–65.

53. A few scholars of Jim Crow's demise have given credit to W. E. B. Du Bois's prediction in the wake of the *Brown* decision that Cold War political embarrassment would ultimately compel the U.S. government to abolish Jim Crow. See for example the argument by Derrick Bell, *Silent Covenants: Brown v. Board of Education and the Unfulfilled Hopes for Racial Reform* (Oxford: Oxford University Press, 2004), 67, based on comments made by Du Bois in *The Autobiography of W. E. B. Du Bois: A Soliloquy on Viewing My Life from the Last Decade of Its First Century* (New York: International Publishers, 1968), 333. See esp. chap. 6 of Bell, *Silent Covenants*, "Brown as an Anticommunist Decision." See also Horne, *Black and Red*. On the Cold War and Jim Crow's demise see also Mary L. Dudziak, *Cold War Civil Rights: Race and the Image of American Democracy* (Princeton, N.J.: Princeton University Press, 2000); and Anderson, *Eyes off the Prize*.

54. See Glenn, *History of the National Alliance*; Henry W. McGee, *The Negro in the Chicago Post Office: Henry W. McGee Autobiography and Dissertation* (Chicago: VolumeOne Press, 1999) (originally "The Negro in the Chicago Post Office," master's thesis, University of Chicago, 1961); and Tennessee, "Legacy," 12–15.

55. On black postal workers—especially the Alliance—in the black news media, see for example the *Chicago Defender*, the *Amsterdam News*, the *Pittsburgh Courier*, or the following examples from the *Afro-American*: "NAPE Asks More P.O. Integration," March 8, 1952, 14;

"Dean of Baltimore Mailmen Ends 45 Years of Service," May 17, 1952; "Postal Clerk Named Foreign Service Aide," April 5, 1952; or the *Atlanta Daily World*: "More Postal Gains Made in the South," April 8, 1952, 4; "Albany Branch NAPE Organized Here," November 22, 1952, 8; "Les Pavot Fete Guests with Valentine Bridge Party; Postal Alliance [National Alliance] Ball," February 17, 1954, 3; and E. N. Davis, "Atlanta Postal Men's Program Very Good," May 12, 1932, 1. In the last article the Alliance hosted its first annual branch meeting in Atlanta, hearing the Rev. Howard Thurman characterize black postal workers as, according to Davis's paraphrase, "the best nucleus for the substantial middle class that will necessarily from [*sic*] the backbone of the future Negro race in America."

56. Woody L. Taylor, "Inside Your Government," *Washington Afro-American*, June 9, 1951, 23.

57. Vivian Nucles, "Communist Bond Denied by Norfolk NAACP head," *Washington Afro-American*, March 31, 1951. The 1948 "Mundt Bill" or "Mundt-Nixon Bill," named for Senator Karl Mundt (R-S.D.) and Representative Richard M. Nixon (R-Calif.), "attempted to outlaw the CPUSA without naming it, by making it unlawful to remain a member of any organization that failed to register as a Communist political organization within 120 days after the Attorney General had issued a final order that it do so." The Bill passed the House as the "Communist Control Bill," but it died in the Senate Judiciary Committee, although it was later revived. See Caute, *Great Fear*, 563n16. Gilliam became national organizer for the NAPE in September 1953. See Glenn, *History of the National Alliance*, 112.

58. Glenn, *History of the National Alliance*, 254, from the *Postal Alliance* of February 1952. A similar response was told to me by National Alliance Brooklyn local member and attorney James Morris, August 11, 2004, Washington, D.C.

59. See for example this 1953 NAPE convention coverage in the *Cleveland Call and Post*, August 29, 1953, cited in Glenn, *History of the National Alliance*, 112: "They voted overwhelmingly to continue its all-out fight on the 'postal purge' which it began in 1949. Attorney Howard Jenkins of the Howard University Law School faculty declared that federal employees were faced with a 'sinister' threat to their security . . . and that prejudiced officials were using the threat of Communist hysteria as a weapon with which to silence Negroes who demanded their rights as first-class citizens."

60. Schrecker, *Age of McCarthyism*, 85. Sen. Joe McCarthy's witch-hunting base of operations was the Permanent Investigating Subcommittee of the Government Operations Committee, operating in tandem with SISS, "both of which conducted exactly the same kinds of investigations as HUAC." Schrecker, *Age of McCarthyism*, 64. On the post office being "much tougher" than even the State Department in their implementation of the loyalty-security program, see Schrecker, *Age of McCarthyism*, 45; as well as 178–82 for an anonymous case study of a postal worker's unsuccessful fight in 1954–1955 to regain the job he lost over alleged CPUSA membership.

61. Schrecker, *Many Are the Crimes*, 203, 211. Schrecker cogently argues that McCarthyism could better have been called "Hooverism" after FBI director J. Edgar Hoover, as FBI involvement was crucial before, during, and after McCarthy's brief but highly destructive reign.

62. For a critical look at the CPUSA and CIO see for example David Roediger, *Working toward Whiteness: How America's Immigrants Became White* (New York: Basic Books, 2005), esp. chap. 7. On the CPUSA see for example the CPUSA's critics: Theodore Draper, *The Roots of American Communism* (New York: Viking, 1957); Nathan Glazer, *The Social Basis of American*

Communism (New York: Harcourt, 1961); Harvey Klehr, *The Heyday of American Communism: The Depression Decade* (New York: Basic, 1984); and Harvey Klehr, John Earl Haynes, and Fridrikh Igorevich Firsov, *The Secret World of American Communism* (New Haven, Conn.: Yale University Press, 1995). Reacting to the negative historiography and helping to lead the way to a more sympathetic if somewhat critical view that has become the standard in the "new labor history" is Maurice Isserman, *Which Side Were You On? The American Communist Party during the Second World War* (Middletown, Conn.: Wesleyan University Press, 1982). See also Earl Ofari Hutchinson, *Blacks and Reds: Race and Class in Conflict, 1919–1990* (East Lansing: Michigan State University Press, 1995); and Michael Kazin, "The Agony and Romance of the American Left," *American Historical Review* 100, no. 5 (December 1995), 1488–1512. See also Juan Williams, *Thurgood Marshall: American Revolutionary* (New York: Times Books, 1998), chap. 24. See also Dudziak, *Cold War Civil Rights*.

63. "Address of Assistant Postmaster General Norman R. Abrams to the Alliance's 21st National Convention," *Postal Alliance* (October 1953), 9; and Committee on Post Office and Civil Service, House of Representatives, *Towards Postal Excellence: The Report of the President's Commission on Postal Reorganization, June 1968*, 94th Cong., 2nd sess. (Washington, D.C.: Government Printing Office, 1976), 100–101.

64. Glenn, *History of the National Alliance*, 114, 195, based on a January 1954 *Postal Alliance* article.

65. Horne, *Communist Front?*, 256–58.

66. See for example: " 'I'm Not a Red'—Mrs. Bethune; Scores Accusers," *Baltimore Afro-American*, May 5, 1952, 1. Both Robeson and Terrell had signed the 1951 "We Charge Genocide" petition presented to the United Nations by the Civil Rights Congress. See William L. Patterson, ed., *We Charge Genocide: The Historic Petition to the United Nations for Relief from a Crime of the United States Government against the Negro People* (1951; New York: International Publishers, 1970).

67. See for example "Postal Alliance Opens War on Bias," *Pittsburgh Courier*, September 7, 1946, 11; "D.C. Meet Draws 900 Delegates," *New York Amsterdam News*, February 23, 1952, M1; and Williams, *Thurgood Marshall*, 239–40. See *New York Alliance Leader* (October–November 1945), 3, for Elmer Armstead's being elected NAPE president of District Eight, and *New York Alliance Leader*, available issues (1952–54), reel 1, for his New York branch presidency during the early 1950s.

68. Jack Greenberg, *Crusaders in the Courts: How a Dedicated Band of Lawyers Fought for the Civil Rights Revolution* (New York: Basic Books, 1994), 220–21; and Biondi, *To Stand and Fight*, chap. 7.

69. See Paul Tennassee, "Alliance Opposition to the Loyalty-Security Programs, 1947–1959" (master's thesis, Johns Hopkins University, 2002); and Highpockets, "Quaker City Quips," *Postal Alliance* (May 1954), 2, esp. photo of National Alliance back-pay recipients at the Philadelphia law office of Rufus S. Watson, including Reese J. Brown, William D. Ridgway, Felix A. Titus, Clarence H. Haughton, Arthur Drayton, and I. N. Cohen—all from Philadelphia. Eight other National Alliance back-pay recipients included Frank Barnes (Santa Monica), Howard Jones (Los Angeles), Edward A. Smith (Philadelphia), Joseph Clark (St. Louis), Horace Elkins (Cleveland), Lee Jackson (Newark), and James Keys and William Ward (Chicago). See also "Postal Alliance Wins 37,000 Back Pay for Purge Victims," in "Editor's Notebook," *Postal Alliance* (September 1953), 4. George M. Johnson and Howard Jenkins, both of Howard Law School, also handled the suit, along with Charles A. Chandler of Cleveland and Josiah F. Henry of Baltimore. The lead up to this

latest attempted removal can be seen in "New Postal Purge Hits 5 in Philly," *Baltimore Afro-American*, March 15, 1952, 3, regarding the five previously reinstated black postal workers (all with fifteen or more years of service), who had all been previously charged with disloyalty in 1950 and subsequently cleared, and were now being charged again: Brown was a former local Alliance branch president. Drayton, Cohen, and Ridgeway had also been part of Bert Washington's 1949 civil suit against the government loyalty hunt. See also coverage in the *New York Amsterdam News*: "Philly 5 Face 'Postal Purge,'" March 15, 1952, 1. See also Adam Fairclough, *Better Day Coming: Blacks and Equality, 1890–2000* (New York: Viking, 2001), 215, recording Jason having been forced out of the Alliance in 1955, for reasons I have been unable to ascertain.

70. Convention summary, *Union Postal Clerk* (October 1952), 44.

71. The Committee on Organization speaker was identified as "Mr. Frasier," and these were his introductory remarks: "Mr. Frasier: I have one resolution on which I definitely called in the representatives of the local that was mentioned in the resolution. I would feel remiss if I didn't make a report on this. After all, they extended the courtesy to me, to my committee, to come before us, and I would like to see you proceed on the question of dual locals." Frasier then went on to tell delegates that "you might as well get your pencils out and start scratching from there on, because this is our recommendation." See NFPOC, *Official Proceedings of the Twenty-seventh Convention, 1952, St. Paul, Minnesota*, 140.

72. Ibid., 141.

73. Ibid., and Convention summary, *Union Postal Clerk* (October 1952), 44. Crickenberger had earlier cryptically alluded to an unidentified "nearby" local that Filbey noted resembled Baltimore. Besides the geographical coincidence, Crickenberger's mention that there were "approximately 800 clerks that are not represented in any A.F. of L. union" indicates that he was referring to Baltimore—as there were that many members of the Baltimore National Alliance branch by 1960, according to the Alliance's estimate. Apparently the 1950 NFPOC convention "tabled" any discussion of dual locals. See Committee on Organization, *Union Postal Clerk* (September 1950), 17. See also *Progressive Fed*, no. 1, NYMAPUC; and "Statement of John H. White Before Baltimore City Council," *Postal Alliance* (June 1960), 14.

74. *1952 NALC Proceedings*, 88. If Lepper's rhetorical question was ironic given his aid along with several black and white postal unionists in setting up Washington, D.C.'s segregated NALC Branch 4022 in 1948 (discussed in chapter 3), no one mentioned it on the convention floor.

75. *1952 NALC Proceedings*, 89.

76. Ibid.

77. Convention delegates, *Postal Record* (October 1948), 67.

78. *1952 NALC Proceedings*, 90. This "criticism" that Butler alludes to indicates a developed anti–Jim Crow consciousness in the city. If whites were included among those labor and media outlets he cited who were critical of his NALC black branch accepting Jim Crow status, it becomes all the more remarkable.

79. Ibid., 89, italics added.

80. Ibid., 89, italics added. For Doherty's support for separate charters see the official proceedings for NALC conventions in 1941, 1943, 1946, and 1948.

81. *1952 NALC Proceedings*, 94. There is no record of a walkout in the NALC's 1952 convention *Proceedings* or the *Postal Record*. But there is a reference to it in Glenn, *History of the National Alliance*, 417. Just two years earlier, a photo in the *Postal Record* revealed that

blacks made up half of the assembled Virginia state NALC officers. See "Virginia State Association," *Postal Record* (August 1950), 48.

82. Convention coverage, *Postal Record* (October 1952), 39.

83. A. L. Glenn, *History of the National Alliance*, 417. In this same July 1952 *Postal Alliance* entry, an NALC official protested that those leaving had been unfair to label the NALC as being discriminatory, given that "so many Negroes voted to support the union's board recommendation in this issue." If any black NALC members supported "dual charters," I have found no corroborating evidence.

CHAPTER FIVE

1. See "Staten Island Withdraws; Suspended By Pres. House," *Progressive Fed* (October 1958), 1; Herman Berlowe, "House Suspends 8 Prog-Fed Locals," *Progressive Fed* (November–December 1958), 1; Herman Berlowe, "Secession Move Spreads; Feds Flock to New Locals," *Progressive Fed* (January 1959), 1; and "Hail New Union!," *Progressive* (February 1959), 1; all from Box 81, NYMAPUC. The eight "suspended" locals, placed in trusteeship by the NFPOC, were New York Local 10, Philadelphia Local 89, Brooklyn Local 251, Boston Local 100, Los Angeles Local 64, Detroit Local 295, Minneapolis Local 125, and the Newark Local. See "House Suspends," 1.

2. Herman Berlowe, "NPCU Adopts Constitution; 115 Locals Join in 90 Days," *Progressive* (May 1959), 1, NYMAPUC.

3. Ibid. The NPU began its existence as the NPCU, or National Postal Clerks Union, before changing its name in 1960 to reflect its industrial character. Under NFPOC rules, no local—even the 10,000 member New York City local—could have more than ten delegates to a national convention. See John Walsh and Garth Mangum, *Labor Struggle in the Post Office: From Selective Lobbying to Collective Bargaining* (Armonk, N.Y.: M. E. Sharpe, 1992), 63, 67. See also Local 10, 1958 resolution; letter from Local 10 president Bernard Schwartz to J. Cline House, November 10, 1958; and letter from House to Schwartz, November 17, 1958, Box 1, Folder Resolutions, Correspondence, Memos 1952, 1958, NYMAPUC. The ad that evidently first provoked Schwartz's ire involved a white clerk from Washington, D.C., wishing to trade or transfer to Southern California. Postal unions have traditionally run "mutual trade/transfer" advertisements in the back of their monthly journals for union members interested in "swapping assignments" or transferring to other post offices subject to the approval of the postmasters involved. See also author interview with former Detroit postal union president Douglas C. Holbrook, then APWU director of retirees, August 16, 2005, Washington, D.C. Holbrook, who is white, estimated that the NPU was about one-quarter African American.

4. "NPCU Constitution," *Progressive* (July 1959), 4; Box 81, NYMAPUC.

5. See "Meany Attacks Union Dualism," *Federation Digest* (February 1959), 1; and "Security Risks Swaying Dual Union Leadership," *Federation Digest* (April 1959), 1; Box 81, NYMAPUC. See esp. *Progressive* (September 1959), including "Full Text of Noreen Case Debate on Senate Floor," 2, over the post office's removal of Walter Noreen, NPU first vice president, who had protested the post office's hiring part-time Christmas help from among those with full-time jobs elsewhere. Noreen was defended by Sen. Hubert Humphrey (D-Minn.) but viciously attacked by Sen. Everett Dirksen (R-Ill.), who called the NPU "a national independent union composed of extreme leftwing elements." Noreen was later

reinstated. See author telephone interview with Raydell Moore, January 13, 2006, Pahrump, Nevada. Moore, a former NPU official, agreed that the NPU was a civil rights union.

6. See Martha Biondi, *To Stand and Fight: The Struggle for Civil Rights in Postwar New York City* (Cambridge, Mass.: Harvard University Press, 2003); Joshua B. Freeman, *Working-Class New York: Life and Labor since World War II* (New York: New Press, 2000); Beverly Washington Jones, "Before Montgomery and Greensboro: The Desegregation Movement in the District of Columbia, 1950–1953," *Phylon* 43, no. 2 (2nd Qtr., 1982), 144–54. See also New York Metro interview.

7. Explicit opposition to Jim Crow locals expressed in NFPOC resolutions by certain Progressive locals, for example, was absent from the 1952 "Progressive Platform." See *Progressive Fed*, January 23, 1952, unprocessed Box 81; and "Progressive Platform, January 20, 1952," Box 60, Folder NFPOC NPC 1952–53, NYMAPUC. See also Walsh and Mangum, *Labor Struggle*, 59–62, for political differences apparently (and strangely) based on what were called the hurt feelings of Local 10 president Patrick Fitzgerald. Fitzgerald's red-baiting of liberal Local 10 members Ephraim "Frank" Handman, Moe Biller, Sidney Goodman, David Edelson, Joseph Ecker, and Henry Berman led to their suspensions from the post office from December 1955 until June 1956, when the suspensions were lifted based on a Supreme Court decision relating to federal employees in nonsensitive areas. It was widely believed that Fitzgerald charged the six based on revenge for their part in his defeat for the local presidency in 1953.

8. See for example "Editor's Notebook," "The 'One Big Union' Sales Pitch," *Postal Alliance* (February 1960), 4; "Highlights of Eighth District Convention," *Postal Alliance* (November 1960), 10–11; and W. F. Thomas, "Atlanta, Georgia," *Postal Alliance* (September 1960), 21.

9. Executive Order 10590, Establishing the President's Committee on Government Employment Policy, *Code of Federal Regulations, Title 3—The President: 1954–1958 Compilation* (Washington, D.C.: Government Printing Office, 1961), 237.

10. Karl Korstad, "Black and White Together: Organizing in the South with the Food, Tobacco, Agricultural, & Allied Workers Union (FTA-CIO), 1946–1952," in *The CIO's Left-Led Unions*, ed. Steve Rosswurm (New Brunswick, N.J.: Rutgers University Press, 1992), 94. Karl Korstad was the father of labor historian Robert Korstad.

11. Ashby Carter, "Resurrection—An Easter Message For Postal Employees," *Postal Alliance* (April 1953), 5.

12. "Alliance Calls on Senator to Straighten Out Bias Postmaster," ibid., 9.

13. Ashby G. Smith, "Civil Rights—The Jan. Trail," *Postal Alliance* (February 1952), 4. The column and even the title itself, whether intentionally or not, evoked Charles Hamilton Houston's weekly column inaugurated in the *Baltimore Afro-American* in 1946. (Houston was formerly the dean of the Howard University Law School and chief legal counsel for the NAACP.) Houston's column had initially been called "The Highway," then "Along the Highway," and finally "Our Civil Rights." The NAACP's national organ, the *Crisis*, for years also ran a regular column called "Along the NAACP Battlefront" that evoked mainstream American newspaper coverage of global armed conflicts. Similar civil rights–oriented newspaper columns that did not necessarily invoke these themes in their titles also appeared in the *Baltimore* and *Washington Afro-American* throughout the 1950s. These columns showed a sense of collective mission. But for the NAACP there was also a suggestion of its leadership if not actual ownership of the struggle.

14. Ashby G. Smith, "Civil Rights—The June Trail," *Postal Alliance* (July 1953), 6–7.

15. Ashby G. Smith, "Civil Rights—The July Trail," *Postal Alliance* (August 1953), 9. See also Aldon D. Morris, *The Origins of the Civil Rights Movement: Black Communities Organizing for Change* (1984; New York: Free Press, 1986), 17–18. The 1953 Baton Rouge city bus ordinance passed by the city council responding to black leaders' protest petitions reserved the very front seats for whites and the very rear seats for blacks, with all other seats open. White bus drivers struck against the ordinance.

16. Ashby G. Smith, "Civil Rights—The January Trail," *Postal Alliance* (February 1956), 9, italics added.

17. See for example the article and even the headline "End of JC [Jim Crow] in Sight," *Baltimore Afro-American*, June 17, 1950, 1, noted in also Juan Williams, *Thurgood Marshall: American Revolutionary* (New York: Times Books, 1998), 195 and 418n1. The reference was to the *Sweatt v. Painter* (1950) decision.

18. See speech by Dr. Martin Luther King Jr. printed in the *Postal Alliance*: "Address of Dr. M. L. King, Jr., Delivered at the First Annual Institute on Non-Violence and Social Change under the Auspices of the Montgomery Improvement Association, Montgomery, Alabama [December 1956]," in *Postal Alliance* (January 1957), 6, 18. See also James B. Cobb's speech in *Postal Alliance* (December 1956), 1–2, 6–7. King's personification of "old man segregation" was synonymous with phrases "old Jim Crow" commonly used during this postwar period to describe the historical and total system of white supremacy, simultaneously suggesting its mortality. But at other times King's emphasis on the struggle against segregation reflected a movement strategy that prioritized defeating what he and others considered the most vulnerable and anomalous aspect of that system.

19. Charles M. Payne, *I've Got the Light of Freedom: The Organizing Tradition and the Mississippi Freedom Struggle* (Berkeley: University of California Press, 1995), bibliographical essay; and Charles M. Payne and Adam Green, eds., *Time Longer than Rope: A Century of African American Activism, 1850–1950* (New York: New York University Press, 2003), introduction.

20. And often forgotten during this period was the influential black trade union coalition called the Negro American Labor Council that was established in 1960, which included the National Alliance. On the Negro American Labor Council, including the anticommunism promoted within it by its founder A. Philip Randolph, see for example William H. Harris, *The Harder We Run: Black Workers since the Civil War* (New York: Oxford University Press, 1982), 141, 150, 152. The letter carriers union has the same initials (NALC). To avoid confusion I spell out the Negro American Labor Council whenever I cite it.

21. Ashby G. Smith, "The June Trail," 6.

22. Biondi, *To Stand and Fight*, 275.

23. See ibid.; Myrlie B. Evers, *For Us, the Living* (1967; Jackson: University Press of Mississippi, 1996), chap. 11; Barbara Ransby, *Ella Baker and the Black Freedom Movement: A Radical Democratic Vision* (Chapel Hill: University of North Carolina Press, 2003), 161–62; and Robert A. Caro, *Master of the Senate* (New York: Alfred A. Knopf, 2002), 702–3. See also Amzie Moore, interview with Mike Garvey, April 13, 1977, Cleveland, Mississippi, at "Civil Rights" in Mississippi Digital Archive, <http://www.lib.usm.edu/~spcol/crda/oh/index.html> (September 10, 2008). Moore recalled the significance to black southerners that whites would even be tried for murdering Till, even with the outcome a certain farce.

24. Dona Cooper Hamilton and Charles V. Hamilton, *The Dual Agenda: Race and Social Welfare Policies of Civil Rights Organizations* (New York: Columbia University Press, 1997), 109.

25. See author interview with former National Alliance Washington, D.C., branch presi-

dent, Tommie Wilson, Washington, D.C., August 11, 2004. See also "Summit Meeting of Negro Leaders," May 12–13, 1958, Washington, D.C., *Postal Alliance* (June 1958), 6–7.

26. See Meier and Bracey, "NAACP as a Reform Movement"; Ashby G. Smith, "Civil Rights—The August Trail," *Postal Alliance* (September 1960), 14; Snow Grigsby, "Editor's Notebook," *Postal Alliance* (June 1954), 4; Ashby G. Smith, "Civil Rights—The February Trail," *Postal Alliance* (March 1960), 10; J. W. Meddling, "Greensboro, N.C.," *Postal Alliance* (March 1960), 17; Cherry Brown, "From the Annals of Labor," *Postal Alliance* (April 1960), 10; Ashby G. Smith, "Civil Rights—The April Trail," *Alliance* (May 1960), 12; Ashby G. Smith, "Civil Rights—The May Trail," *Postal Alliance* (June 1960), 10; and Loraine M. Huston, "Comments from Cleveland," *Postal Alliance* (September 1963), 20.

27. See "Summary of Proceedings—28th National Convention of the National Federation of Post Office Clerks," *Union Postal Clerk* (October 1954), 10. The 1954 NFPOC convention also voted 316–208 for Resolution 781-A that favored "the following Civil Rights program," which included an anti-lynching law, anti-poll tax law, a "fair employment practice law," bans on "discrimination and segregation" in the public and private sectors, in the military, and in public accommodations, and finally "full trial rights for federal employees whose loyalty has been challenged." See "Summary of Proceedings," 8. That same page also saw the adoption of a resolution supporting legislation that would outlaw the Communist Party.

28. "The 'Progressive Fed's' Report of the NFPOC in Convention at Cincinnati Ohio," *Bulletin No. 2*, August 24, 1954, Box 60, Folder Progressive Fed Convention 1958, NYMAPUC.

29. *Postal Record* (October 1954), 33; and John Hope Franklin and Alfred A. Moss Jr., *From Slavery to Freedom: A History of African Americans*, 8th ed. (1947; Boston: McGraw-Hill, 2000), 453, 617.

30. The NAACP was not the only organization putting pressure on the trade unions for white supremacist practices. For example, as Komozi Woodard points out: "In 1951, more than one thousand militant black workers, representing tens of thousands more, met to form the National Negro Labor Council (NNLC). . . . The NNLC organized itself into twenty-three local councils, challenged the Jim Crow policies of many of the big companies, and fought in hundreds of local struggles on political, economic, and social fronts." See Komozi Woodard, *A Nation within a Nation: Amiri Baraka (LeRoi Jones) and Black Power Politics* (Chapel Hill: University of North Carolina Press, 1999), 36.

31. "Editor's Notebook," *Postal Alliance* (April 1959), 4.

32. Cobb quotation from "Highlights," *Postal Alliance* (November 1960), 10. District Eight includes Connecticut, Massachusetts, New York, and the Virgin Islands. See also the *Concise Columbia Encyclopedia*, 2nd ed., s.v. "Liberia." The popular idea within the National Alliance that it served as a refuge for black postal workers is another interesting possible reason for Cobb's reference to Liberia.

33. *Postal Record* (October 1954), 31. See also Henry W. McGee, *The Negro in the Chicago Post Office: Henry W. McGee Autobiography and Dissertation* (Chicago: VolumeOne Press, 1999) (originally "The Negro in the Chicago Post Office," master's thesis, University of Chicago, 1961), 91 (*Dissertation*). By 1960, Boston had one of the smallest black postal employee percentages of any major U.S. city with a substantial black population: 3.4 percent.

34. *Postal Record* (October 1954), 33. See also *Official Proceedings of the Thirty-ninth Biennial Convention of the National Association of Letter Carriers, Cleveland, Ohio, August 30–September 4, 1954*, 116–17.

35. *1954 NALC Proceedings*, 116–17.

36. Ibid. See also "Editor's Notebook," *Postal Alliance* (September 1954), 4. The *Postal Alliance* claimed that Chicago's Branch 11 did not take a stand, but they were in fact listed among those in opposition in the proceedings, and delegate Kinsella did second Sullivan's amendment. Nor did the *Postal Alliance* mention that the compromise amendment that was passed had been brought to the floor by a black carrier.

37. *1954 NALC Proceedings*, 117, italics added.

38. Ibid., 117–18.

39. Ibid., 117.

40. Convention coverage, *Postal Record* (October 1954), 11.

41. *Postal Record* (August 1954), 30.

42. *Postal Record* (September 1954), 46. See also Earl Lewis, *In Their Own Interests: Race, Class, and Power in Twentieth-Century Norfolk, Virginia* (Berkeley: University of California Press, 1993), 60; and *1954 NALC Proceedings*, appendix. Also attending was black Mississippi World War II veteran Dabney Hamner, representing Clarksdale Branch 1195. *1954 NALC Proceedings*, 4a.

43. "Editor's Notebook," *Postal Alliance* (September 1954), 4. The vote was based on the parliamentary procedure of "calling for division," or counting votes when the voice vote appears too close to call.

44. McGee, *Negro in the Chicago Post Office (Dissertation)*, 91.

45. Leon Samis, "Highlights of the Cleveland Convention," *Postal Record* (November 1954), 28.

46. See for example "Labor Convention Adopts Program of P.O. Workers," *Union Postal Clerk* (September 1949), 9; "American Federation of Labor to Meet in December," *Union Postal Clerk* (September 1955), 13; and Philip S. Foner and Ronald L. Lewis, eds., *The Black Worker: A Documentary History from Colonial Times to the Present*, vol. 7, *The Black Worker from the Founding of the CIO to the AFL-CIO Merger, 1936–1955* (Philadelphia: Temple University Press, 1983), 613–14. See also Hamilton and Hamilton, *Dual Agenda*, 113–20.

47. A. L. Glenn, *History of the National Alliance of Postal Employees, 1913–1955* (Washington, D.C.: National Alliance of Postal Employees, 1956), 319. See also Stanley Levey, "Meany Vows Fight on Bias When Labor's Ranks Unite," *New York Times*, February 27, 1955, reprinted in Foner and Lewis, eds., *Black Worker*, 7:615–16; and *Report of the First Constitutional Convention Proceedings, New York, N.Y., December 5–8, 1955* (Washington, D.C.: AFL-CIO, 1955). See also James B. Cobb, "Administrator's Portfolio: The Negro and the Merger," *Postal Alliance* (January 1956), 2, 8.

48. Cobb, "Administrator's Portfolio," 2.

49. Ibid. See also "This Month's Cover," *Union Postal Clerk* (November 1948), 8.

50. Cobb, "Administrator's Portfolio," 3, italics added.

51. George Meany speech in convention coverage, *Postal Record* (October 1956), 15.

52. Edmund F. Wehrle, "Guns, Butter, Leon Keyserling, the AFL-CIO, and the Fate of Full-Employment Economics," *Historian* 66, no. 4 (Winter 2004), 730–48.

53. See Francis M. Wilhoit, *The Politics of Massive Resistance* (1954; New York: George Braziller, 1973); Alan Draper, "Brown v. Board of Education and Organized Labor in the South," *Historian* 57, no. 1 (Autumn 1994), 75–88; and George Lewis, *The White South and the Red Menace: Segregationists, Anticommunism, and Massive Resistance, 1945–1965* (Gainesville: University Press of Florida), 2004.

54. See for example Michael Keith Honey, *Black Workers Remember: An Oral History of*

Segregation, Unionism, and the Freedom Struggle (Berkeley: University of California Press, 1999); and Draper, "Brown v. Board of Education." See also Alan Draper, *A Rope of Sand: The AFL-CIO Committee on Political Education, 1955–1967* (New York: Praeger, 1989), chap. 5.

55. Robert Allen, *Reluctant Reformers: Racism and Social Reform Movements in the United States* (Washington, D.C.: Howard University Press, 1983), 195–99.

56. Drew Pearson, "Jury-Trial Battle Swung By Labor," *Postal Alliance* (August 1957), 2 (reprinted from the *Washington Post*); and "Editor's Notebook," *Postal Alliance* (August 1957), 4. See also *Postal Alliance* (October 1957), cover, 3, and 24, and Caro, *Master of the Senate*, chaps. 33–41, esp. 702–3, 870–72, and 991.

57. See "Declaration of Constitutional Principles: The Southern Manifesto (March 12, 1956)," in Steven F. Lawson and Charles M. Payne, *Debating the Civil Rights Movement, 1945–1968* (Lanham, Md.: Rowman and Littlefield, 1998), 54–59; and "Morrison Bill H.R. 9531 Overwhelmingly Approved in Committee," *Postal Record* (September 1962), 5. The other three signers of the Southern Manifesto who were also on the House Post Office and Civil Service Committee were Joel T. Broyhill (R-Va.), Tom Murray (D-Tenn.), and James C. Davis (D-Ga.).

58. Pearson, "Jury-Trial Battle."

59. "Editor's Notebook," *Postal Alliance* (October 1957), 4.

60. See Stanley Levey, "Meany Vows Fight on Bias When Labor's Ranks Unite," *New York Times*, February 27, 1955, reprinted in Foner and Lewis, eds., *Black Worker*, 7:615–16. According to this article, Meany in his speech "hailed the Supreme Court decision on desegregation in public schools as a 'milestone in civil rights.' And he urged that the states seeking to avoid the law by 'legal and technical device,' be deprived of any Federal aid to education. Mr. Meany disclosed that he had received a letter recently from a member of the South Carolina State Senate urging him to 'mind your own business' on desegregation."

61. The 1956 NFPOC convention included "Civil Rights" resolution 654 brought by New York Local 10, an expansion of the 1954 "Civil Rights program" resolution 781-A that passed at that convention, including support for the *Brown* decisions. Resolutions 739, 740, 740A, 741, and 741A, all backed by the New York State Federation and Brooklyn Local 251 as well as Local 10, called for an end to "discriminatory practices" and "dual locals" in the NFPOC; they were joined by D.C. Local 148 in Resolution 742 calling for abolition of dual locals. See *Resolutions to Be Acted Upon by the Twenty-Ninth Convention of the National Federation of Post Office Clerks*, August 27–September 1, 1956, Chicago, Ill., 165, 191–92. (A resolution banning communist membership in the NFPOC, brought by the Illinois delegates, was also listed on 191–192.) See also *Resolutions to Be Acted Upon by the Thirtieth Convention of the National Federation of Postal Clerks, August 25 to August 30, 1958, Boston, Massachusetts*, 209, that included Resolutions 812, 813, and 814 brought by Locals 10 and 148. Both Resolution booklets (1956 and 1958) found at NYMAPUC, Box 60, Loose material. See also "Two S.F. Postal Clerks Fired for Picketing P.O.," "Didn't Strike, They Say," "National Referendum Chance for Members," and "Detroit Shows the Way," *Progressive Fed*, (March 1958), 1, Box 81, Folder Progressive Feds within NFPOC, NYMAPUC. See Bob White, "Washington, D.C.," *Postal Alliance* (September 1956), 13, where he noted: "Just recently, in a referendum ballot held by the all white local of the A.F. of L. clerks local here, the vote against integrating the two locals was some lopsided figure like 407 to 66. Even after this voting result was made known, our boys are still clinging to their little jim crow set up, and this is also true of the carriers local." See also "The Answer House Would Not Print," *Progressive Fed* (November-Decem-

ber 1958), 4, Box 81, Folder Progressive Feds within NFPOC, NYMAPUC. See also "Summary of Proceedings-30th National Convention of the National Federation of Post Office Clerks," *Union Postal Clerk* (October 1958).

62. See White, "Washington, D.C.," 13. See *Washington Afro-American* editorial, May 17, 1958, reprinted as "Don't Be Fooled By Words," *Postal Alliance* (June 1958), 11.

63. McGee, *Negro in the Chicago Post Office (Dissertation)*, 97–98.

64. Glenn, *History of the National Alliance*, 112.

65. "Camera Catches Exciting Moments at NPCU Convention," *Progressive* (May 1959), 4. Strangely enough, no mention was made of this historic convention in the *Postal Alliance*.

66. See *Progressive*, 1959–1971.

67. Harold L. Keith, "Moment of Truth for Negroes in American Labor Movement: 'Phony' Liberals Named as Targets," from *Pittsburgh Courier*, January 9, 1960, reprinted in *Postal Alliance* (January 1960), 5.

68. "Editor's Notebook," *Postal Alliance* (June 1960), 4; and from the same issue, Charles R. Braxton, "Jim Crow Fight Is Ours Alone: The Negro American Labor Council's Founding Convention," 8; "Grievance Registered at NALC Convention on Promotional Policies in Post Offices," 9; Norman Vasconcellos, "What the Negro American Labor Council Means," 9; Ashby G. Smith, "Civil Rights—The May Trail," 10; and Rufus P. Knighton, "N.A.L.C. Founding Convention," 11. An article in the *Postal Alliance* the following year noted the significance of the fact that President Kennedy's Executive Order 10925 against racial bias in federal contracts was signed just three weeks after a Negro American Labor Council workshop on that very subject in the nation's capital. "Greater New York NALC Holds Action Conference," *Postal Alliance* (July 1961), 8. The close proximity of Kennedy's executive order and the February 1961 Workshop and Institute on Race Bias in the Unions, Industry, and Government was reminiscent of President Truman's issuing his 1948 executive orders against discrimination in federal employment and segregation in the military just a few weeks after a similar civil rights summit conference in Washington, D.C. On the Little Rock Nine, see for example Daisy Bates, *A Long Shadow of Little Rock: A Memoir* (Little Rock: University of Arkansas Press, 1987).

69. "The Negro's Dual Role" [editorial], *Alliance Leader* (April–May 1956), 4. Also notable (reflecting the Alliance's stance on women's role in the organization and the fight for equality) was the parenthetical inclusion here of the female pronoun "herself" alongside what was then a commonly assumed male/female (but male-identified) pronoun "himself." See also W. E. B. Du Bois, *The Souls of Black Folk* (1903; New York: Penguin Books, 1989), 5: "One ever feels his two-ness—an American, a Negro; two souls, two thoughts, two unreconciled strivings; two warring ideals in one dark body, whose dogged strength alone keeps it from being torn asunder."

70. "Picture-story" [editorial], *Alliance Leader*, (November–December 1956), 1.

71. See for example Kathleen L. Wolgemuth, "Woodrow Wilson and Federal Segregation," *Journal of Negro History* 44, no. 2 (April 1959), 158–73; reprinted with the same title in *Postal Alliance* (July 1959), 4.

72. "Organizer Jerry O. Gilliam Starts Out"; and James B. Cobb, "The Alliance Then and Now," *Postal Alliance* (October 1953), 22.

73. "White Citizens Councils' Unionists," editorial from *Pittsburgh Courier*, March 7, 1959, reprinted in *Postal Alliance* (March 1959), 2, alongside John W. King, "A Letter to an Editor."

74. James Hill, "We Have Just Begun to Fight," *Postal Alliance* (October 1954), 9.

75. Elmer E. Armstead, "The Incomparable Parallel," *Alliance Leader* (June 1954), 3, reel

1, microfilm; edited and reprinted in the June 1954 *Postal Alliance* and quoted in Glenn, *History of the National Alliance*, 198, italics added. See also *Postal Alliance* (October 1954), 9.

76. The New York City NAACP meanwhile had moved its headquarters to Harlem in 1952 under the direction of its president, Ella Baker, whereupon, according to her biographer Barbara Ransby, the "branch built coalitions with other groups in the city and carried out aggressive campaigns focused primarily on school reform and desegregation and police brutality." See Ransby, *Ella Baker*, 149. Baker would go on to help found two pivotal civil rights organizations in 1957 and 1960: the SCLC and SNCC, respectively. See also author interview with John Adams and Dorothea Hoskins, August 11, 2004, Washington, D.C.

77. Biondi, *To Stand and Fight*, 219; Rolland Dewing, "The American Federation of Teachers and Desegregation," *Journal of Negro Education* 42, no. 1 (Winter 1973), 79–92; Leon Fink and Brian Greenberg, *Upheaval in the Quiet Zone: A History of Hospital Workers' Union, Local 1199* (Urbana: University of Illinois Press, 1989); and *New York Alliance Leader* (1945–46, available issues), New York City Branch of the National Alliance of Postal Employees, 1945–1982, reel 1, microfilm, borrowed from State Historical Society of Wisconsin.

78. See Biondi, *To Stand and Fight*, 246; and "Educators Condemn 'Segregated' Schools," *Alliance Leader* (May 1954), reel 1. See also Ransby, *Ella Baker*, 152–53: Baker was also part of that committee originally convened by the Board of Education, with which she lobbied for several years along with Kenneth and Mamie Clark before helping to launch Parents in Action against Educational Discrimination, a grassroots coalition.

79. Biondi, *To Stand and Fight*, chap. 8.

80. Ibid., chap. 12. The Bronx NAACP was founded and led by a black postal worker whose son, Jesse Davidson, has also worked with that organization, the Urban League, and other community organizations to this day. See Mark Naison, "The Bronx African American History Project," *OAH [Organization of American Historians] Newsletter* 33, no. 3 (August 2005), 14; and electronic communication from Peter Derrick, Bronx Historical Society, September 12, 2005.

81. See Daniel M. Johnson and Rex R. Campbell, *Black Migration in America: A Social Demographic History* (Durham, N.C.: Duke University Press, 1981), 116–17; Richard Kluger, *Simple Justice: The History of Brown v. Board of Education and Black America's Struggle for Equality* (New York: Vintage, 1977), 508; and Henry McGee, *Negro in the Chicago Post Office (Dissertation)*, 91.

82. See author interviews with D. James Pinderhughes, July 17, 2004, Washington, D.C., and Tommie Wilson, August 11, 2004, Washington, D.C. See also "Bartlett Describes Negro Opportunity in Postal Service: [First] Assistant [Postmaster General] Tells Musolit Club 24 Per Cent of Local Mail Workers Colored," *Washington Post*, November 15, 1925, 12. MuSoLit was Washington, D.C.'s "Music, Social, Literary" black social club. Four top National Alliance union leaders also spoke to the group. On MuSoLit, see book review by Sarah J. Shoenfeld of Audrey Elisa Kerr, *The Paper Bag Principle: Class, Colorism, and Rumor and the Case of Black Washington, D.C.* (Knoxville: University of Tennessee Press), 2006, H-Net (Humanities and Social Sciences Online), H-DC, August, 2007, <http://www.h-net.org/reviews/showrev.php?id=13464> (July 1, 2008).

83. See Glenn, *History of the National Alliance*, 296–98; and Cindy George, "[June] Campbell, pioneer of rights, dies," *Raleigh News and Observer*, August 20, 2004, 1B, 7B. In the late 1950s and early 1960s, noted civil rights leader Ralph Campbell was president of the Raleigh NAACP, the Raleigh-Wake Citizens Association, and the Raleigh Alliance branch.

84. See author interview with George Booth Smith, former local president of Durham

National Alliance branch, August 27, 2004, Durham, North Carolina. I am indebted to André Vann and Jerry Gershenhorn for information on Dr. Boulware. See also Glenn, *History of the National Alliance*, 296, showing thirty-five members in the Durham branch by the 1956 publication date, evidently the branch's first or second year. Smith thought 1957 was the year he was hired by the post office, but he was not positive. It is likely that he started either in 1955 or 1956.

85. See "Task Force Says 84% of Postal Employees Are in Unions," *Progressive* (December 1961), 4; and Miles E. Hoffman, *Labor Monograph No. 5: A Contemporary Analysis of a Labor Union* (Philadelphia: Temple University, 1963), 6.

86. Kluger, *Simple Justice*, chap. 21. Kluger's story of black activist Gardner Bishop, the "U Street barber," highlights some of those differences.

87. "Editor's Notebook," *Postal Alliance* (September 1956), 2. In New York City, meanwhile, black teachers challenged Jim Crow union locals in the South as early as 1952. See Dewing, "American Federation of Teachers." The expressed preference for an all-black union by Alliance members should not be confused with a segregated, white-privileged labor movement.

88. See Walter P. Holmes, interview with Karen Ferguson, June 15, 1993, Charlotte, N.C., BTV. Holmes also noted that he was married to the first black principal of Charlotte's first integrated school, Wellmore Elementary School. See also Zecharaiah Alexander, interview with Rhonda Mawhood, June 11, 1993, Charlotte, N.C. Alexander noted the relative ease of obtaining postal employment in New York City compared to Charlotte in the 1920s and 1930s, as well as his family's having suffered political persecution in Charlotte during the McCarthy era. Yet in Durham, the NALC did not accept blacks until the early 1970s. See author interviews with Jimmy Mainor, January 5, 2004, and George Booth Smith, August 27, 2004.

89. McGee, *Negro in the Chicago Post Office (Dissertation)*, 102.

90. See Arthur Ryland oral history interview with Dana Schecter, New York City, November 19, 1976, APWU-Moe Biller Files, Box 4, Folder 1977, Tamiment/Wagner Archives. See also Berlowe, "NPCU Adopts Constitution"; and Walsh and Mangum, *Labor Struggle*, 67–70.

91. Branch 36 interview. Sombrotto guessed that Branch 36 by the time of the 1970 strike had roughly the same demographics as the population of New York City as a whole. In 1970 blacks made up 21.2 percent of the city's population of nearly 7.9 million. "Editor's Notebook," *National Alliance* (January 1972), 4.

CHAPTER SIX

1. *Official Proceedings of the Forty-third Biennial Convention of the National Association of Letter Carriers, Denver, Colorado—September 2–7, 1962*, 131. See also "Convention Committees Report," *Postal Record* (October 1962), 34, for a photograph of the committee reading their report. Loy Bell, who had once spoken out for dual charters at the 1948 convention, was not there on the stage with the rest of the Committee, and his absence was not explained. See also *1952 NALC Proceedings*, 94. Durant's dual NAPFE/NALC membership wass discussed in a telephone conversation with Noel V. S. Murrain, NAPFE District Eight president, and current national secretary, September 24, 2008, New York. On Oscar Durant's National Alliance activism, Durant was listed in the pages of the *Alliance Leader* as a committee member in the Alliance from 1955 through 1959. For example, in 1955 Durant was appointed to both

the National Alliance's Audit Committee and the Education and Legislative Committee, and in 1956 to the Housing Committee. See "1955 Presidential Committee Appointments," *Alliance Leader* (December–January 1955), 7; "Standing Committees 1956–57," *Alliance Leader* (February–March 1956), 7; and the Audit Committee, in the last reference I have found in the *Alliance Leader* to his membership, *Alliance Leader* (January–February 1959), 6; reel 1, microfilm, borrowed from the State Historical Society of Wisconsin.

2. See for example *Proceedings of the Fourth Constitutional Convention of the AFL-CIO, vol. 1, Daily Proceedings, Miami Beach, Florida, December 7–13, 1961* (Washington, D.C.: AFL-CIO, 1961). This convention saw numerous overlapping references to civil rights, EO 10925, and the Cold War by President Kennedy, Martin Luther King Jr., Walter Reuther, and A. Philip Randolph, among others. If the message was not made clearly enough in other speeches, then a black delegate from the Transport Workers Union of America, Louis Manning, did so here: "Brothers and sisters, the eyes of the world are watching America. And every time a Negro is lynched and every time a Negro is denied his civil rights, communistic Russia and the satellites are looking on. You are giving them food and you are giving them ammunition to use against us" (509). See *Proceedings*, 488–516, for the debate over Resolution 33 outlawing AFL-CIO discrimination and segregation, brought by A. Philip Randolph and Milton Webster. It passed.

3. Branch 36 interview.

4. See also Lester F. Miller, *The National Rural Letter Carriers Association: A Centennial Portrait* (Encino, Calif.: Cherbo Publishing, 2003). I am grateful to the NRLCA for furnishing me with this text.

5. On the various postal unions see for example Committee on Post Office and Civil Service, House of Representatives, *Towards Postal Excellence: The Report of the President's Commission on Postal Organization, June 1968*, 94th Cong., 2nd sess., November 24, 1976 (Washington, D.C.: Government Printing Office, 1976), 19, 112–20.

6. M. Brady Mikusko, *Carriers in a Common Cause: A History of Letter Carriers and the NALC* (Washington, D.C.: NALC, 1989), 61.

7. See Steven F. Lawson, *Running for Freedom: Civil Rights and Black Politics in America Since 1941* (New York: McGraw-Hill, 1991), 79–81; and Charles M. Payne, *I've Got the Light of Freedom: The Organizing Tradition and the Mississippi Freedom Struggle* (Berkeley: University of California Press, 1995), 124, 173–74.

8. See Lawson, *Running for Freedom*, 75–79; "Greater New York NALC Holds Action Conference," *Postal Alliance* (July 1961), 8; and Tennessee, "NAPFE: A Legacy of Resistance and Contributions, 1913–1999," *National Alliance* (October 1999), 14. See also EO 10925 and EO 10988, <http://www.eeoc.gov> (September 10, 2008).

9. "The Kennedy-Alliance Conference," *Postal Alliance* (November 1960), 2.

10. Cobb letter to Kennedy, *Postal Alliance* (December 1960), 4. On Fulbright see Taylor Branch, *Parting the Waters: America in the King Years, 1954–63* (New York: Simon and Schuster, 1988), 397.

11. See Ashby G. Smith, "Civil Rights—The April Trail," *Postal Alliance* (May 1960), 12, which included a salute to black civil rights demonstrators in the United States as well as "the Algerians for self-determination," and Turkish students fighting their government's repression and "creating an embarrassment in this portion of the 'Free World.'"

12. The quotation is from a letter from James K. Baker to James Cobb, February 8, 1961, frames 633–34. See also letter from James K. Baker to Roy Wilkins, February 15, 1961, frame 0631; and letter from James Cobb to Chester Moore (president of the Philadelphia

branch of the NAPE), May 12, 1960, frames 631–32; all in *NAACP Papers*, Supplement to Part 13, reel 13.

13. Paul Tennassee, "The Smith Presidency Part I," *National Alliance* (February 2002), 17. See also *New York Alliance Leader* during this period.

14. Telephone interview with Donald P. Stone, February 12, 2005, Snow Hill, Ala. Stone also remembers there being quite a few college graduates like himself among the black postal workers in Atlanta and, by contrast, no white college graduates. Stone also relates that there were many other graduates of Atlanta's historically black colleges working at the Atlanta post office: Morehouse College, Spelman College, Atlanta University (now Clark Atlanta University), and Morris Brown College.

15. Address by John Gronouski, 1965, Box 6, Folder EO 10925 (Discrimination), NYMAPUC. See also John Hope Franklin and Alfred A. Moss Jr., *From Slavery to Freedom: A History of African Americans*, 8th ed. (1947; Boston: McGraw-Hill, 2000), 529–30.

16. Letter from Roy Wilkins, NAACP Executive Secretary, to Jerry R. Holleman, Executive Vice-Chairman of the President's Committee on Equal Employment Opportunity, March 24, 1961, frame 350; and letter from Jerry R. Holleman to Roy Wilkins, April 6, 1961, frame 352, *NAACP Papers*, Supplement to Part 13, reel 13, italics added. See also Lawson, *Running for Freedom*; and Executive Orders 10925 and 10590. EO 10925 included the standard legal term that has since become a household word for civil rights law enforcement—"affirmative action."

17. See John Walsh and Garth Mangum, *Labor Struggle in the Post Office: From Selective Lobbying to Collective Bargaining* (Armonk, N.Y.: M. E. Sharpe, 1992), 92; and Major David C. Davies, "Grievance Arbitration within Department of the Army under Executive Order 10988," *Military Law Review* 46, Headquarters, Department of the Army (October 1969), 1–30, <http://www.loc.gov/rr/frd/Military_Law/Military_Law_Review/pdf-files/27 687F~1.pdf> (September 10, 2008).

18. *Congressional Record* 107-pt. 1, (January 17, 1961), 864–65.

19. I am grateful to NALC historian Nancy Dysart for locating and sending me a copy of the Rhodes-Johnston bill. It was reprinted as "Employee-Relation Legislation Introduced in Senate and House of Representatives" in the *Postal Record* (February 1961), 9–10, in addition to the comments from the *Congressional Record* by the bill's Senate sponsors on pages 8, 11, and 20. Also known in the Senate as S. 473, or the "Recognition of Federal Employee Unions" bill, this bill was "practically identical," in the opinion of the *Postal Record* editor at that time, to H.R. 12 introduced by George M. Rhodes (D-Pa.) at the opening of the 87th Congress (1961–1962). See also Walsh and Mangum, *Labor Struggle*, 90. The Task Force included "the Secretary of Labor (Chairman), Secretary of Defense, Postmaster General, Director of the Bureau of the Budget, Chairman of the Civil Service Commission, and Special Counsel to the President."

20. See Ashby G. Smith, "Address to Convention," *Alliance Leader* (September–October 1963), 1.

21. Paul Nehru Tennassee, "NAPFE Battles for Union Recognition, 1945–1965, Part II," *National Alliance* (August 2001), 12–13. Tennassee notes that President Kennedy named an Advisory Committee to the new postmaster general, J. Edward Day, which included among others NALC president William Doherty and NAACP board of directors member Carl Murphy, publisher of the weekly *Afro-American* in Baltimore and Washington, D.C., and NAPE ally.

22. Ibid. See also Walsh and Mangum, *Labor Struggle*, 88–93, and Mikusko, *Carriers in a*

Common Cause, 61–62, the latter sharing the assessment of Vern K. Baxter, *Labor and Politics in the U.S. Postal Service* (New York: Plenum Press, 1994), 69, that Kennedy "preempted" the bill with his task force and subsequent executive order. See also Davies, "Grievance Arbitration," 4.

23. The section quoted was titled "Collective Bargaining." See "Post Office Department New York Region Orientation of Postmasters to Union Recognition: The Purposes and Objectives of the Conference" (n.d., but from its wording probably late 1962; unsigned, but probably from New York City postmaster Robert Christenberry himself), Box 3, Folder 10988, NYMAPUC. See also EO 10988; and Rhodes-Johnston. Rhodes-Johnston's "collective bargaining" powers were also limited by the strike ban on all federal employees. See also the contract language here that evokes collective bargaining without ever using the term in the first *Agreement between United States Post Office Department* and the six national "exclusives" during that time (April 1, 1963–March 31, 1964): the NALC, NAPOGSME, NASDM, NFPOMVE, NRLCA, and UFPC; Folder Unions: Agreements, USPS Archives. The NPMHU would not win national exclusive recognition for its craft until 1964 (previously it had "formal" status).

24. Mikusko, *Carriers in a Common Cause*, 61–62.

25. One of few postal labor historians to note this important feature of EO 10988 is Paul Nehru Tennassee, "NAPFE Battles for Union Recognition, 1945–1965," *National Alliance* (September 2001), 13.

26. Sen. Johnston, when governor of South Carolina, had defied the 1944 *Smith v. Allwright* decision, calling the state legislature into special session to delete every law that had to do with state primaries in order to keep Democratic primaries exclusively white "private clubs." See Richard Kluger, *Simple Justice: The History of Brown v. Board of Education and Black America's Struggle for Equality* (New York: Vintage, 1977), 299. See also Martin Halpern, *Unions, Radicals, and Democratic Presidents: Seeking Social Change in the Twentieth Century* (Westport, Conn.: Praeger, 2003), chap. 5; and Jeff Woods, *Black Struggle, Red Scare: Segregation and Anti-Communism in the South, 1948–1968* (Baton Rouge: Louisiana State University Press, 2004), 55, 67.

27. EO 10988, Sec. 6 (b).

28. EO 10988, Sec. 2 (3). See also *Official Proceedings of the Thirty-ninth Biennial Convention of the National Association of Letter Carriers, Cleveland, Ohio, August 30–September 4, 1954*, 116, for the compromise resolution that passed that convention with similar language, although not consummated in practice until 1962: "No letter carrier shall be denied membership in any Branch because or race, creed, color, or national origin."

29. See Rhodes-Johnston bill, esp. Title II, Section 310 (d). Johnston and Humphrey's silence on civil rights during this bill's presentation came during a year where civil rights was frequently debated on the floor of Congress. Humphrey also acknowledged in his remarks that federal workers did not and should not have the right to strike, and this bill would not alter that fact. See Congress, Senate, Senator Johnston of South Carolina and Senator Humphrey of Minnesota, speaking for the Recognition of Federal Employee Unions bill, S.473, 87th Cong., 1st sess., *Congressional Record* 107-pt. 1 (January 17, 1961), 863–65.

30. See electronic communications from Paul Nagle, Robert Gabrielsky, and Frank R. Scheer, August 20–23, 2009. I am indebted to their recollections and information. Paul Nagle had fought the Article III ban on blacks for years (along with Gabrielsky's father, Irving, who was a close friend, coworker, and union brother of Nagle's in Philadelphia).

Former NPTA president Nagle lamented the "racial myopia among some railway mail clerks." He presided over the 1958 San Francisco convention that missed banning Article III by just two votes. Still president in 1960, Nagle presided over the vote to revoke Article III at its 1960 Kansas City, Missouri, convention, a vote that Dr. Scheer, curator of the Railway Mail Service (RMS) Library in Boyce, Virginia, also confirmed. "The latter event is notably honorable," Nagle wrote me, "because the vote came on Yom Kippur, with a significant number of observant Jews participating." I am also indebted to Robert Gabrielsky for contact with Nagle and information on white railway mail clerks like his father and Paul Nagle, fighting Jim Crow in the RMA/NPTA. In 1964 Nagle was appointed by President Johnson to be in charge of EEO compliance in the post office. The RMA became the NPTA in 1949 after the RMS became the Postal Transportation Service (PTS). The PTS was eliminated in 1960, and the NPTA joined with the NFPOC and the UNAPOC to form the UFPC in 1961. See also APWU website <http://www.apwu.org> (September 15, 2008). See also premature accounts of Article III's 1958 "demise": "Hear Ye! Hear Ye!," *Alliance Leader* (November–December 1958), 4; and "Fed Briefs," *Progressive Fed* (January 1959), 2. According to Herbert Northrup's 1943 study, the constitution of the NRLCA only allowed blacks to belong to segregated locals. See Philip S. Foner and Ronald L. Lewis, eds., *The Black Worker: A Documentary History from Colonial Times to the Present*, vol. 7, *The Black Worker from the Founding of the CIO to the AFL-CIO Merger, 1936–1955* (Philadelphia: Temple University Press, 1983), 471–72. The NRLCA constitution also provided that "only white members are eligible to serve as delegates to conventions or to hold office." Quoted in Tennassee, "Perspectives on African American History: 12th and 13th Compromise, Part V," *Guyana Journal* (October 2000), 34. A search of back issues of the *National Rural Letter Carrier* turns up no resolutions since 1943 abolishing either provision. But in the February 10, 1962, issue there suddenly appeared a reprint of EO 10988 titled "Policy on Employee-Management Cooperation," 90–93. Their April 7 issue subsequently ran an article "Rural Letter Carriers Will Ballot," 202, that concluded with this paragraph: "It has also been emphatically stated that employee organizations have certain obligations which must be met before recognition of any type can be extended. The first is the requirement that the organizations not discriminate because of race, color, religion, or national origin. It is not sufficient that their Constitution and By-Laws indicate that no discrimination exists but the actual day by day operation of the employee organization must indicate that discrimination does not in fact exist. It has been repeated that all forms of recognition will be withdrawn from any employee organization practicing discrimination." Their constitutional provisions against black delegates and for segregated locals may have been quietly and suddenly dropped after EO 10988. Ironically, the NRLCA was the first union to sign a national exclusive contract with the post office on July 12, 1962. See *National Rural Letter Carrier*, July 21, 1962, "NRLCA Signs First Agreement under Labor-Management Program," 439. See also Miller, *National Rural Letter Carriers Association*, who makes no mention in this official union history of blacks or racial policies in the NRLCA.

31. "Senate Bill 1135-House Bill 554 and You," *Alliance Leader* (May 1952), 3. At the time the NLRA or Wagner Act was passed, organized labor consisted of one federation—the AFL. Many if not most of its unions excluded, segregated, or discriminated in some way against black workers. In the 1940s, 26 of the AFL's 100 unions excluded blacks outright, while many others like the NALC and NFPOC had Jim Crow locals. See for example Labor Research Association, *Labor Fact Book 5* (1941; New York: Oriole Editions, 1972), chap. 7; and Thomas R. Brooks, *Toil and Trouble: A History of American Labor*, 2nd ed., revised

and enlarged (1964; New York: Delta, 1971), 255–65. At their 1941 convention, the AFL had urged protesting black workers to be "grateful" for mere membership. See David R. Roediger, *Working toward Whiteness: How America's Immigrants Became White* (New York: Basic Books, 2005), 209. I found no record of support or opposition to the 1961 Rhodes-Johnston bill in the *Postal Alliance*. I did discover two articles seven years apart in the *Alliance Leader* that supported it under certain conditions. A March 1952 editorial noted that the Alliance had been responsible for amending Rhodes-Withrow (an earlier version of Rhodes-Johnston), whereby the clause that called for recognition of federal unions "representing a majority of employees" was deleted. (Ironically, the chair of the House Post Office and Civil Service Committee that backed their amendment was Rep. Tom Murray [D-Tenn.], who in 1957 joined with other white southern members of Congress in signing the Southern Manifesto opposing integration.) In 1959, John Adams of the New York Alliance editorialized in favor of "HR-6—Rhodes—Union Recognition—Labor Management is most essential today and it could help in our progress with management." See John H. Adams, "Here and There," *Alliance Leader* (April–May 1959), 5.

32. "Perspective on Executive Order 10988," *Postal Alliance* (April 1962), 9. In the same issue see also "Editor's Notebook," 4. On the Wagner Act see Herbert Hill, *Black Labor and the American Legal System: Race, Work, and the Law* (1977; Madison: University of Wisconsin Press, 1985), chap. 2, esp. 74–86.

33. Charles Braxton, "The Gift of Red Tape," *Postal Alliance* (April 1962), 8. See also "Employee-Relation Legislation Introduced," 9. The Rhodes-Johnston bill proclaimed that a federal union "shall not include any organization whose basic purpose is purely social, fraternal, or limited to a single special interest objective which is only incidentally related to conditions of employment." That description did not fit the Alliance—except in caricature by its opponents in Congress, postal management, and other postal unions. Given the Alliance's working relationship with the Kennedy administration, it is hard to imagine liberal Democratic backers of this bill like Sen. Humphrey sponsoring a bill that suggested exclusion of the Alliance. And the wording probably was more likely aimed at fraternal lodges like the (Irish) Emerald Society, the (Italian) Columbian Society, and the Jewish Postal Workers. But given the widespread attacks on the Alliance as a "narrow" social advocacy group, it is possible that the Alliance could have been excluded from further representation had the bill become law, whether or not that was the intent of its framers. EO 10988, by contrast, included any "employee organization" that functioned as a union.

34. See Executive Order 10988 (1962), esp. Secs. 4b and 5a, <http://www.eeoc.gov> (September 10, 2008).

35. See "Biggest Postal Clerk Convention Opens on Note of Hope for New Era of Labor Relations in Postal Service," *Union Postal Clerk* (September 1962), 7; "Exclusive Union Contract Signed by Philadelphia Postmaster," *Postal Alliance* (July 1963), 18; "A Sweep for Industrial Unionism," *Union Mail* (July–August 1962), 1; and "Feds Fail, But NPU Scores among MH, MV, Custodians," *Progressive* (August 1962), 3. The NPU won in New York, Los Angeles, Philadelphia, Brooklyn, Newark, St. Paul, Jersey City, Jamaica, N.Y., Tucson, Long Beach, and Fresno. See also Committee on Post Office and Civil Service, *Towards Postal Excellence*, 19, 112–20. According to Post Office Department figures, cited by the Kappel Commission in June 1968 as "estimated membership," the NALC's membership was 190,000, and they were allowed to represent 195,386 employees (including non-union carriers and Alliance members); UFPC's membership was only 143,000, but they were now able to represent 308,078 employees. Other AFL-CIO postal unions included the

NAPOGSME, with 21,500 members representing 22,473 employees; the NFPOMVE, with 8,000 members representing 11,433 employees; the NASDM, with 2,500 members representing 5,540 employees; and the National Association of Post Office Mail-Handlers, Watchmen, Messengers, and Group Leaders, with 35,000 members. The independent craft NRLCA, with 40,000 members, represented 30,753 employees (18,317 substitute rural carriers were excluded from coverage under the national agreement). The AFL-CIO postal unions plus the NRLCA by this time enjoyed national "exclusive recognition." The two independent unions (the NPU and the Alliance) only had national "formal recognition." The National Alliance is listed here as having 32,000 members, although the organization routinely listed itself as having enrolled 40,000 members. These nine organizations are the only ones that could legitimately be called labor unions—the three supervisor associations by definition were part of management but nonetheless participated in the representation elections, as EO 10988 allowed for any "employee organizations" that were not strictly "social." Winning national formal recognition, then, were the National Association of Post Supervisors, the National League of Postmasters, and the National Association of Postmasters of the United States, the latter relinquishing its recognition in 1967. See also Walsh and Mangum, *Labor Struggle*, 91, on what they call the first "unique and historic" postal representation election, held from June 1 to July 16, 1962. Ballots were mailed to 520,000 eligible employees in 93,000 voting units at 35,000 post offices.

36. EO 10988; EO 10987; Rhodes-Johnston bill. Rhodes-Johnston omitted any mention of the right to strike (although its authors assumed it in public statements), but the explicit anti-strike provision of EO 10988 bluntly reminded federal workers that they still did not enjoy all the labor rights of private sector workers. Postal unions argued against some of EO 10988's provisions, such as whether supervisors should be represented by the unions, or whether union dues could still only be collected by union officials "on the clock" (during work hours) on the shop floor. Executive Order 10987 accompanied 10988 and included many of the grievance procedure provisions from the Rhodes-Johnston bill. See "Editor's Notebook," *Postal Alliance* (December 1963), 4. A December 13, 1963, agreement was signed under terms provided by EO 10988 and to take effect January 1, 1964, whereby union members' dues could be deducted from their paychecks, thus saving union shop stewards the trouble of getting permission from supervisors to go out on the shop floor and collect dues from each member once a month. See also *Agreement between United States Post Office Department and National Association of Letter Carriers AFL-CIO, National Association of Post Office and General Services Maintenance Employees, National Association of Special Delivery Messengers AFL-CIO, National Federation of Post Office Motor Vehicle Employees AFL-CIO, National Rural Letter Carriers Association, United Federation of Postal Clerks AFL-CIO, April 1, 1963–March 31, 1964* (POD Publication 53), Folder Unions: Agreements, USPS Archives.

37. Author interview with Sam Armstrong and Samuel Lovett, August 11, 2004, Washington, D.C.

38. On "separate charter" abolition in the NALC, see *1962 NALC Proceedings*, 129–31. On the AFL-CIO Committee on Civil Rights, see *1962 NALC Proceedings*, 111. On Randolph, Meany, the AFL-CIO, and the Negro American Labor Council, see William H. Harris, *The Harder We Run: Black Workers since the Civil War* (New York: Oxford University Press, 1982), 161–62; and Paula F. Pfeffer, *A. Philip Randolph, Pioneer of the Civil Rights Movement* (Baton Rouge: Louisiana State University Press, 1990), 112–13. See also 1962 Negro American Labor Council minutes, *Papers of A. Philip Randolph*, reel 23, microfilm. On black student movement in the South see for example Barbara Ransby, *Ella Baker and the Black Freedom*

Movement: A Radical Democratic Vision (Chapel Hill: University of North Carolina Press, 2003). See also J. W. Meddling, "Greensboro, N.C.," *Postal Alliance* (March 1960), 17. Telephone conversation with C. C. Draughn, January 5, 2009.

39. James Forman, *The Making of Black Revolutionaries* (1972; Seattle: University of Washington Press, 1997), 224.

40. Ibid., 294.

41. "Agreement Reached on Merger," *Union Postal Clerk* (November 1960), 2–3. See also "Kennedy Orders Ties Cut with Dual Unions," *Progressive* (July 1961), 8; Box 81, NYMAPUC. There was no response from the UFPC to the NPU's charge, and I have found no public evidence of UFPC's formal abolition of Jim Crow locals, leading me to conclude that they abolished them quietly.

42. Author interview with William H. Burrus Jr., January 16, 2009, Washington, D.C.

43. *Official Proceedings of the Forty-second Biennial Convention of the National Association of Letter Carriers, Cincinnati, Ohio—August 21–26, 1960*, 71.

44. Ibid., 72.

45. Ibid., italics added. See also "Appendix to Proceedings," in *Official Proceedings of the Thirty-eighth Biennial Convention of the National Association of Letter Carriers, New York, N.Y.— September 1st to 6th, 1952*, 9a. See also "Resolution No. 2—Dual Charters," convention proceedings, *Postal Record* (October 1941), 533, for the constitutional wording. See also *Official Proceedings of the Thirty-sixth Biennial Convention of the National Association of Letter Carriers, Miami Florida, October 11th–16th, 1948*, 37. See also duplicates of original charter certificates in Atlanta: Branch 72 (black), Branch 3837 (white), and Branch 73 (merged), at NALC Library, Washington, D.C.

46. Author interviews with D. James Pinderhughes, July 17, 2004, Washington, D.C., and Joseph Henry, August 15, 2005, Washington, D.C. Henry also mentioned that before merger the all-white Branch 142 had held their monthly meetings at a prestigious spot indeed— the NALC national headquarters (recently named after President Emeritus Vincent R. Sombrotto), located downtown near the Capitol building.

47. "Report of the Committee on Separate Charters," *1962 NALC Proceedings*, 131; and "Committee on Separate Charters," *Postal Record* (February 1961), 28.

48. "Report of the Committee."

49. Ibid., 130. On black migration see Daniel M. Johnson and Rex R. Campbell, *Black Migration in America: A Social Demographic History* (Durham, N.C.: Duke University Press, 1981), esp. 117. In the years 1940–1950, while the overall black migration pattern was to the North, Midwest, and Far West, of the cities listed above with Jim Crow branches only Birmingham shows a net black population loss, while Atlanta, Memphis, and St. Petersburg show modest black population increases, and Houston and Norfolk show substantial increases.

50. See Harold L. Keith, "All Postal Votes Sought by Letter Carriers on Ballot," *New Pittsburgh Courier*, January 23, 1962, 12.

51. "Statement by National President Robert L. White at the Federal Bar Association's Seminar on Executive Order 11491," *National Alliance* (May 1971), 2.

52. See *1941 NALC Proceedings*, 555; *1948 NALC Proceedings*; *1952 NALC Proceedings*, 2a, 4a. See also *1954 NALC Proceedings*; *1960 NALC Proceedings*, 28a; *Postal Alliance* (April 1957), 23; and *Postal Alliance* (September 1959), 11.

53. Committee on Post Office and Civil Service, *Towards Postal Excellence*, 19; and APWU website, <http://www.apwu.org> (September 15, 2008).

54. Henry interview. All unions also printed in their journals copies of their respective recognition statuses, replete with the government-conferred italic script title lettering. See also *1952 NALC Proceedings*, 2a, 4a; *1960 NALC Proceedings*, 28a; *1962 NALC Proceedings*, 12a; *Postal Alliance* (April 1957), 23; *Postal Alliance* (September 1959), 11–13; "Beaumont, Texas," *Postal Alliance* (July 1960), 18.

55. See "This is 'Victory?' " *Progressive* (August 1962), 2; and Tennassee, "NAPFE Battles for Union Recognition, 1945–1965, Part II," *National Alliance* (September 2001), 15. See also Leon A. Wheeler, "The President's Desk: Unity and Strength in Action," *Alliance Leader* (March–April 1962), 2; Wheeler, "The President's Desk: In the Face of Adversity We Continue to Grow," *Alliance Leader* (September–October 1962), 2; and John H. Adams, "The President's Desk," *National Alliance* (November–December 1963), 2, New York City Branch of the National Alliance of Postal Employees, 1945–1982, reel 2, microfilm, borrowed from State Historical Society of Wisconsin. The NPU was also the fastest growing of all the postal unions at the time: it would later gain about 10,000 members between 1967 and 1970. See author interview with former Detroit Postal Union president Douglas C. Holbrook, then APWU Director of Retirees, August 16, 2005, Washington, D.C. Holbrook, who is white, believes that had the NPU, UFPC, and three other unions not merged into the APWU, the NPU's inroads at the time into UFPC's strength would have put the UFPC in serious jeopardy of losing its exclusive representation of the clerk craft.

56. Ashby G. Smith, "Civil Rights Trail," *Postal Alliance* (March 1960), 10, and other columns in the *Postal Alliance* each month during 1960–61. See also *Rebel without a Cause* (dir. Nicholas Ray, 1955), the classic film about youth rebellion referenced by Smith.

57. Ashby G. Smith, "Civil Rights Trail," *Postal Alliance* (June 1961), 10.

58. Author interview with George Booth Smith, former local president of Durham National Alliance branch, August 27, 2004, Durham, N.C.

59. Ashby G. Smith, "Civil Rights—The July Trail," *Postal Alliance* (August 1961), 11.

60. See "Yeah, That's Right!, *Progressive* (June 1962), 2.

61. See *Agreement between United States Post Office Department*. See also Baxter, *Labor and Politics*, 75.

62. Baxter, *Labor and Politics*, 76.

63. See Franklin and Moss, *From Slavery to Freedom*, 538; and Edward Conrad Smith, ed., *The Constitution of the United States*, 11th ed. (1936; New York: Barnes and Noble, 1979), 57. "Norfolk, Virginia Branch Stresses Use of Vote," *Postal Alliance* (March 1961), 19. For Wallace S. Hayes, see "Editor's Notebook," *National Alliance* (November 1966), 4; and "Century of Progress," *Postal Record* (January 1989), 10. Alfonso W. Davis is listed as a member of the Board of Directors of the New York–Bronx branch, *Alliance Leader* (February 1965), 2. Davis's name can be found as Branch Chaplain in *Alliance Leader* (November–December 1959), 2; and a member of the Women's Auxiliary Committee and Sick Committee, in *Alliance Leader* (January–February 1960), 7. His visit to Jacksonville, Florida, in 1941 was noted in the branch item from L. C. Moman, "Jacksonville Branch," *Postal Alliance* (October 1941), 7, that Davis was "now an active member of the New York City Branch," and "gave a word of encouragement to all." Paul Ortiz has found Alliance members in 1919–1920 Jacksonville leading efforts to defy Jim Crow bars against blacks voting in that state. See Paul Ortiz, *Emancipation Betrayed: The Hidden History of Black Organizing and White Violence in Florida from Reconstruction to the Bloody Election of 1920* (Berkeley: University of California Press, 2005), 173. In the same month that President Kennedy signed EO 10988—January 1962—the *Postal Alliance* published a voting chart listing all thirty-two states where

they had members and including the electoral races being held, dates of primaries, registration deadlines, and, where applicable, the last day to pay the poll tax. See "Pittsburgh Branch Hits Office on Bias" and election guide, *Postal Alliance* (January 1962), 17, 23.

64. Amzie Moore, second part interview with Mike Garvey, April 13, 1977, Cleveland, Mississippi, at Civil Rights in Mississippi Digital Archive, <http://www.lib.usm.edu/~spcol/crda/oh/index.html> (September 10, 2008). Moore corrected the date of his firing (as well as some other chronological discrepancies) to 1961 in this part of the interview. See also Payne, *I've Got the Light*, 31; and John Dittmer, *Local People: The Struggle for Civil Rights in Mississippi* (Urbana: University of Illinois Press, 1994), 72–73, 102–3. Moore also helped found the Regional Council of Negro Leadership in 1951 and worked closely with SNCC in the 1960s.

65. The post office had fired Law for what it called "insufficient execution of his duties": conducting civil rights work on government time, misdelivering a letter seven years before, and urinating behind a bush on his route because of his kidney ailment and refusal to use Jim Crow toilets. See Paul D. Bolster, "Civil Rights Movements in Twentieth Century Georgia" (Ph.D. diss., University of Georgia, 1972), chap. 6, esp. 240n27. See also articles in *Savannah Morning News*, <http://www.savannahnow.com> (September 10, 2008), for example: Jan Skutch and Kate Wiltrout, "Willing to Pay Whatever Price He Had to Pay to Stand Firm," *Savannah Morning News*, July 30, 2002; Trezzvant W. Anderson, "W. W. Law Reinstated as Carrier—But: Postmaster's Rebuke is 'Vicious,' " *New Pittsburgh Courier*, November 4, 1961; "Upsetting Georgian, One of 'God's Angry Men': The Explosive Case of Westley Law," in *New Pittsburgh Courier*, October 28, 1961; and "Senator Case, NAPE Show Interest: Protests Mount against Firing of Westley W. Law," in *New Pittsburgh Courier*, September 30, 1961. Two months earlier, Postmaster General Day had appeared at the national convention of the NRLCA. The Harvard-educated Springfield, Illinois, native was deferential to this gathering in Atlanta of probably the whitest union in the post office. With convention entertainment provided by an antebellum southern belle fashion show, Day proudly noted the centennial of the Confederate Post Office on June 1 of that year (during the "War of Secession," as he deferentially called it), and praised it as having been a model of efficiency. See NRLCA, *Proceedings of the 57th National Convention, August 15–18, 1961, Atlanta Georgia*, in *National Rural Letter Carrier* (October 7–14, 1961), 615–19. That same convention passed a resolution "that we approve and endorse our Association stand against one big Postal Union" (629). See also cover and pages 74–75 of the NRLCA's *52nd Annual Convention Proceedings, August 14–17, Louisville, Kentucky*, in *National Rural Letter Carrier* (September 22, 1956), that included huge flags of both the United States and the Confederacy. See also author interview with Don Cantriel, August 17, 2005, Alexandria, Virginia, at NRLCA national headquarters. Cantriel, who is white and originally from Arkansas, was vice president of the NRLCA at the time. He first worked at a rural Missouri post office in 1980 after working in a Missouri auto factory and belonging to the UAW. He described the NRLCA as historically having been a family organization. He had not heard of any exclusionary or segregationist policies in the union's past. See also "New Postmaster General West Coast Insurance Executive," *Postal Alliance* (January 1961), 3.

66. See Payne, *Light of Freedom*, 116; Dittmer, *Local People*, 108–9; and Bolster, "Civil Rights Movements," chap. 6.

67. See Louis M. Kohlmeier, "Administration to Remove Postal Stations from Stores with Segregated Facilities," from a June 1963 *Wall Street Journal* article reprinted in *Postal Alliance* (July 1963), 12. See also Tennassee, "Legacy," 14. Los Angeles was then the nation's (and the

world's) third-largest post office. Shaw was appointed acting postmaster on April 15, 1963, and received his permanent appointment on October 1, 1964. See "Named Head of World's Third Largest Post Office," (Memphis) *Tri-State Defender*, April 13, 1963, 1; and Deanna Boyd and Kendra Chen, "The History and Experience of African Americans in America's Postal Service," Smithsonian National Postal Museum, Washington, D.C., <http://www .postalmuseum.si.edu/AfricanAmericans/index.html> (September 6, 2008).

68. "Miami Four Make Hard Trip," *Progressive* (March 1962), 8; "Are You One?," *Progressive* (July 1966), 3; and "Act on Strike Prohibition," *Progressive* (August–September 1966), 3: the NPU debated the right to strike before other postal unions did so.

69. "New Los Angeles P.M." and "Outstanding Supervisor," photos and captions, *Progressive* (July 1963), 2; "NPU Wins Exclusive in Boston," *Progressive* (December 1963), 1; and "Charlotte Has Formal," *Progressive* (June 1964), 4; Holbrook interview; and Herman Berlowe, "NPU Wins after UFPC Rebuffs Fired Workers," *Progressive* (January 1963), 1. Frazier had charged the post office with discrimination, and Gallegos's case was described by the union as "harassment."

70. See author interviews with Cleveland Morgan, July 18, 2005, New York, and with Felix Bell, National Alliance District Four president, August 11, 2004, Washington, D.C. Bell saw his entry into the Jackson, Mississippi, post office in 1969 as part of a collective black social and cultural movement: "We were scoring high [on the civil service exam] because we were brought up with the ideology that education opened up doors, so we were *educated*; we knew how to take aptitude tests."

71. "3 Promotions in Dallas, Texas Post Office Causes Stir," *Postal Alliance* (June 1963), 10.

72. See "JFK Death Great Loss to P.O. Unions," *Progressive* (November 1963), 1; "Editor's Notebook," *Postal Alliance* (December 1963), 4; *Postal Record* (December 1963), cover story; *Union Postal Clerk*, (December 1963), cover story; and Mary Stanton, *Freedom Walk: Mississippi or Bust* (Jackson: University Press of Mississippi, 2003).

73. "Here's Civil Rights Key," *Progressive* (December 1963), 3. The article reported the bill would direct the Commerce Department to "compile figures on denial of voting rights" and possibly enforce one of the Fourteenth Amendment's "little-known provisions" proportionally disenfranchising any discriminating states—but because the bill had been delayed by House Rules Committee chairman Howard Smith (D-Va.), the House Judiciary Committee was "now circulating a discharge petition, a device used successfully in the past by postal unions."

CHAPTER SEVEN

1. Philip Seligman, "How about More Training, Better Facilities for Them," *Union Mail* (May 1966), 6. Box 50, Folder Women, NYMAPUC.

2. Ibid.

3. Interview with Philip Seligman by Dana Schecter, June 29, 1976, New York, Box 4, Biller Files. Seligman recalled that in New York there was a rise from "perhaps 500 women" in the 1940s to "thousands" in the 1960s.

4. See New York Metro interview. Eleanor Bailey is not sure of the date she gave this speech or where. It had to have been between 1972 (based on past-tense references to USPS-APWU childcare surveys and Nixon's veto of the Brademus childcare bill in 1971 for which she had advocated) and Nixon's resignation on August 9, 1974. See Box 8, Folder

Officer's File—Drafts of Speeches, NYMAPUC. Her speech was probably given in New York City in early 1974 given the references to their local women's committee, whose work was written about in Georgia Dullea, "Women Unionists: Learning How to Be Heard," *New York Times*, April 18, 1974 (n.p.). See Box 50, File Women, NYMAPUC.

5. The term "Jane Crow" was coined by black feminist legal scholar Pauli Murray. See her book *The Autobiography of a Black Activist, Feminist, Lawyer, Priest, and Poet* (1987; Knoxville: University of Tennessee Press, 1990), 362, referencing her December 1965 *George Washington Law Review* article with Mary Eastwood titled "Jane Crow and the Law: Sex Discrimination and Title VII."

6. U.S. Civil Service Commission Manpower Statistics Division, *Study of Employment of Women in the Federal Government 1969* (Washington, D.C.: Government Printing Office, 1970), 1. See also "Women Mail Carriers—History," from USPS Historian's Office (probably Rita Moroney), August 1986, Box History, Folder Women, NALC Library, Washington, D.C.; Alice Kessler-Harris, *Out to Work: A History of Wage-Earning Women in the United States*, 20th anniversary ed. (New York: Oxford University Press, 2003), 143.

7. Historian, U.S. Postal Service, "African-American Postal Workers," 3, and "List of Known African-American Employees, 1800s: Headquarters Employees, Railway Mail Service Employees, U.S. Mail Carriers, Contractors, and others," <http://www.usps.com/postalhistory> (July 15, 2009). See also Department of Commerce and Labor Bureau of the Census, S. N. D. North, Director, *Statistics of Employees, Executive Civil Service of the United States 1907*, Bulletin 94 (Washington, D.C.: Government Printing Office, 1908), 47. In this record 2,294 women were listed as clerks (no listings by race), 4 as railway clerks, and 116 as rural carriers. Out of 9,057 female postmasters, 36 were listed as "Negro," 8 as "Indian," and 3 as "Mongolian," the latter intriguing given the repressive anti-immigrant 1882 Chinese Exclusion Act (161).

8. *Fourteenth Census of the United States, 1920*, vol. 4, *Population Occupations* (Washington, D.C.: Government Printing Office, 1923), 735. The first female NRLCA convention delegates appeared in 1908, but it is not known when black females first joined the NRLCA or served as convention delegates. See Lester F. Miller, *The National Rural Letter Carriers Association: A Centennial Portrait* (Encino, Calif.: Cherbo Publishing, 2003), 22. See also John Hope Franklin and Alfred A. Moss Jr., *From Slavery to Freedom: A History of African Americans*, 8th ed. (1947; Boston: McGraw-Hill, 2000), 390.

9. Historian, U.S. Postal Service, "List of Known African-American Post Office Clerks, 1800s." See also A. L. Glenn, *History of the National Alliance of Postal Employees, 1913–1955* (Washington, D.C.: National Alliance of Postal Employees, 1956), 50–51, 75. See also "The First Convention Meeting, Chattanooga, Tennessee, October 3, 1913," *Postal Alliance* (August 1963), 9, photo caption of what the Alliance calls their "founding fathers," including "Mrs. A. K. Bruce, Hostess," the wife of Chattanooga founding member and later president A. K. Bruce.

10. Ashby G. Smith, "The President's Desk . . . A Salute to the Fair Ladies," *Postal Alliance* (October 1963), 2. See also "Cherry Brown, President of Indianapolis, Indiana Alliance branch," photo caption, Postal Alliance (April 1962), 8; and "An Open Letter by Mrs. Essie L. Fellows, President Los Angeles Branch NAPE," *Postal Alliance* (February 1964), 15. See also "Mary F. Guen, Co-Chairman," Membership Committee, *Postal Alliance* (April 1965), 17.

11. See Milton Holmes, "Baltimore, Maryland," *National Alliance* (July 1966), 12–13, praising the Women's Auxiliary for its part in the joint Alliance-CORE march in Baltimore "addressed to the problems of open occupancy, rent control, school budget, and the shoot-

ing of [civil rights activist] James Meredith [in Mississippi by a white supremacist]." See also "Women Count," *Washington Area Postal Employee* (June 1963), 25, Box 81, NYMAPUC.

12. Paul Tennassee, "NAPFE: A Legacy of Contributions and Resistance," *National Alliance* 55, no. 10 (October 1999); Kessler-Harris, *Out to Work*, 219–24, 273–74, 291–96; and Elsie Resnick, interviewed by Milt Rosner, November 26, 1976, Biller Files.

13. See Henry W. McGee, *The Negro in the Chicago Post Office: Henry W. McGee Autobiography and Dissertation* (Chicago: VolumeOne Press, 1999) (originally "The Negro in the Chicago Post Office," master's thesis, University of Chicago, 1961), 84–85 (*Dissertation*); and 1943 NAPE Convention minutes, *Postal Alliance* (August 1943), 32.

14. "They're Coming In!!!," *New York Alliance Leader* (January–February 1945), 3; and "1959 Standing Committees," *Alliance Leader* (January–February 1959), 6.

15. Kessler-Harris, *Out to Work*. See also Historian, U.S. Postal Service, "Women Mail Carriers," 6n12: "The Vietnam War, which led to fewer male applicants for postal jobs, also contributed to the rise in the employment of women." During the Viet Nam War, approximately 8,615,000 Americans—mostly men—served in the military. See Lawrence M. Baskir and William A. Strauss, *Chance and Circumstance: The Draft, the War, and the Vietnam Generation* (New York: Vintage Books, 1978), 5.

16. New York Metro interview. See also author interview with Jeff Perry and Richard Thomas, July 18, 2005, New York.

17. M. Brady Mikusko, *Carriers in a Common Cause: A History of Letter Carriers and the NALC* (Washington, D.C.: NALC, 1989), 69; "Female Postal Employees," *The Chief: The Civil Employees' Weekly*, August 13, 1965, 4, found in Box 50, Folder Women, NYMAPUC; and U.S. Civil Service Commission, Manpower Statistics Division, *Study of Employment of Women in the Federal Government 1970 Prepared for the Federal Women's Program* (Washington, D.C.: Government Printing Office, 1971), table A-1, 12–13. Women numbered 4,573—almost a third of D.C.'s 13,006 postal workers.

18. Donald Singleton, "Gals Put Their Stamp on the PO: Lady Clerks Are Now Carrying the Mail," *New York Daily News*, February 17, 1966, 4.

19. Adam Fairclough, *Better Day Coming: Blacks and Equality, 1890–2000* (New York: Viking, 2001), chap. 12.

20. Franklin and Moss, *From Slavery to Freedom*, 530: "Between June 1961 and June 1962 federal employment of blacks increased by only 11,000, with most of these new workers getting jobs only at the lower levels, while the total number of federal employees increased by more than 62,000."

21. To date the best and most balanced discussion of the PCSW is by Dorothy Sue Cobble, *The Other Women's Movement: Workplace Justice and Social Rights in Modern America* (Princeton, N.J.: Princeton University Press, 2004), chap. 6. Cobble reveals the influence of black and white "labor feminists" (her term) inside the commission, and the particular interest black middle-class women leaders like Dorothy Height displayed in working women's issues. Irving Bernstein, in *Promises Kept: John F. Kennedy's New Frontier* (New York: Oxford University Press, 1991), does argue, 200–201, on the significance of the PCSW, but on 204 he declares the 1963 Equal Pay Act was a "symbolic triumph," that is to say, a "victory with little substance," adding this sweeping claim: "But the civil rights movement was fully engaged in achieving this goal for blacks without assuming the added responsibility for women. Black women were far more concerned with race than with sex." His assessment of the EPA is shared by Walter Fogel, *The Equal Pay Act: Implications for Comparable Worth* (New York: Praeger, 1984), who argues that there was little unequal pay for equal

work when the EPA was passed based on hourly income—but annual income was another story. Jo Freeman, *The Politics of Women's Liberation: A Case Study of an Emerging Social Movement and Its Relation to the Policy Process* (New York: David McKay, 1975), 52–53, 170–77, sees the PCSW as important although its findings were ignored, and agrees that the EPA was not particularly useful. Nancy Gabin has written on UAW activist women's struggle to include sex discrimination as part of state fair employment practice committees and how these women contested "protective legislation" for women that was in fact discriminatory. She notes the PCSW's refusal in their final report to consider sex discrimination as a separate category. See Gabin, "Women and the United Automobile Workers' Union in the 1950s," in *Women, Work and Protest: A Century of U.S. Women's Labor History*, ed. Ruth Milkman (Boston: Routledge and Kegan Paul, 1985), 270–71. But see also New York Metro interview. Eleanor Bailey stressed the practical and symbolic significance of the EPA for female federal workers and civil service applicants. See also Duchess Harris, "From the Kennedy Commission to the Combahee Collective: Black Feminist Organizing, 1960–1980," in *Sisters in the Struggle: African American Women in the Civil Rights–Black Power Movement*, ed. Bettye Collier-Thomas and V. P. Franklin (New York: New York University Press, 2004), 280–305. The Equal Pay Act (EPA) became law in June 1963. It was sandwiched between the President's Commission on the Status of Women (PCSW, established by Executive Order 10980, issued December 14, 1961) and Kennedy's Committee and Council Relating to the Status of Women (established by Executive Order 11126, issued November 1, 1963). Both the 1961 and 1963 PCSW committees included the chairman of the Civil Service Commission as part of these interdepartmental committees established, among other things, for the purpose of "evaluation of the progress of Federal departments and agencies in advancing the status of women." President Kennedy's Executive Orders 10925 and 10988 banning discrimination in federal employment and contracts both used the decades-old language that forbade discrimination based on "race, color, creed, or national origin." The EPA combined with the PCSW could be seen as a precursor to the inclusion of sex discrimination as a prohibited labor activity in Title VII of the 1964 Civil Rights Act. For texts of Executive Orders 10925, 10988, 10980, 11126, the Equal Pay Act of 1963, and the Civil Rights Act of 1964, see the EEOC website, <http://www.eeoc.gov> (September 10, 2008). An account revealing the PCSW as a contested site is the personal recollection of the Rev. Dr. Pauli Murray—an influential researcher and member of a PCSW advisory committee: the Committee on Political and Civil Rights. See Murray, *Autobiography*, 347–57, 364. See also Leon Hillman, "Chicago Branch President Proposes Child Care Aid for Working Mothers," *Postal Alliance* (October 1962), 13. Except for Cobble's work, what little literature exists on the PCSW and the EPA consistently underestimates their significance. Equal pay having been part of the Fair Labor Standards Act of 1938, this reform carried the imprimatur of President Roosevelt through his widow, Eleanor Roosevelt, who died in 1962 during her tenure on the PCSW. The EPA was actually seen as a showcase by the PCSW, just as the post office under Kennedy became an intended showcase for gender as well as racial equality. This public policy was in part a product of the momentum for equal rights measures generated by the 1960s black freedom movement as well as Cold War exigencies. Dissenting voices from the corporate world notwithstanding, the consensus among labor, government, women's professional groups, and business officials at both the House and Senate subcommittee hearings on the EPA in 1963 was that unequal pay based on gender was a "serious social problem." Labor leaders complained to Congress how foreign communist labor leaders at the meetings of the International Labor Organization (ILO, affiliated with the United Nations) were scoring propaganda points on gender inequality in the United States just as they had done previously on racial inequality. See *Equal Pay Act: Hearings Before the Special Subcommittee on Labor of the Committee on Education and Labor, House of Representatives, Eighty-eighth Congress, First Session on H.R. 3861 and Related Bills to Prohibit Discrimination, on Account of Sex, in the Payment of Wages by Employers Engaged in Commerce or in the Production of Goods for Commerce and to Provide for the Restitution of Wages Lost by Employees by Reason of Any Such Discrimination, Hearings Held in Washington, D.C., March 15, 25, 26, and 27, 1963, Adam C. Powell, Chairman* (Washington, D.C.: Government Printing Office, 1963). See also *Equal Pay Act of 1963: Hearings Before the Subcommittee on Labor of the Committee on Labor and Public Welfare, United States Senate, Eighty-eighth Congress, First Session, on S. 882 and S. 910, to Amend the Equal Pay Act of 1963, April 2, 3, and 16, 1963* (Washington, D.C.: Government Printing Office, 1963), esp. the testimony of Caroline Davis, UAW Women's Department, including this comment: "In the last 10 years, 39 nations have accepted the 'equal pay for equal work' convention of the International Labor Organization, among them nine Iron-Curtain [communist] countries. The United States is conspicuously absent from the rolls. You may be certain that American labor hears about this failure when it attends ILO meetings. You may also be certain that lack of an equal pay law and U.S. failure to adhere to the ILO convention has been grist for the Communist mills."

22. "All Postmasters: Employment of Women," *Postal Bulletin*, 20288, January 11, 1962, Washington, D.C., 1; in Box 50, Folder Women, NYMAPUC. Yet as regards Equal Employment Opportunity executive orders, even President Lyndon B. Johnson's 1965 Executive Order 11246 that replaced EO 10925 did not change the long-standing "race, creed, color, or national origin" language. That would have to wait until 1967 with President Johnson's Executive Order 11375 providing "equal opportunity in Federal employment and employment by Federal contractors on the basis of merit and without discrimination because of race, color, religion, sex or national origin." President Jimmy Carter's Executive Order 11478 in turn prohibited discrimination "because of race, color, religion, sex, national origin, handicap, or age." See EEO website.

23. Postal job announcements in Box 50, Folder Women, in NYMAPUC.

24. Author interview with William H. Burrus Jr., January 16, 2009, Washington, D.C. According to Burrus, when he entered the Cleveland post office in 1958 there were only about 50 women out of 2,000 clerks—ironically, mostly widows of servicemen and hired from the male register. It was also during this time that his father entered the Detroit post office.

25. Letter from Philip Seligman to John F. McNally, Chairman Labor-Management Safety and Health Committee, April 27, 1966, Box 50, Folder Women, NYMAPUC.

26. Author interview with Daisy Strachan, August, 11, 2004, Washington, D.C.

27. Ibid. John Strachan was born in Harlem, but his family came from the Bahamas. See also correspondence in Box 50, Folder Women, NYMAPUC.

28. New York Metro interview. New York City NALC Branch 36 letter carrier Cleveland Morgan also recalls taking that exam and thinking it easy compared to the New York University placement exam he had taken not long before. See author interview with Cleveland Morgan, July 18, 2005, New York: For a look into the civil service exam for postal workers, see a "how-to" manual prepared with CSC approval: James C. O'Brien and Philip P. Marenberg, *Your Federal Civil Service* (New York: Funk and Wagnalls, 1940).

29. Author interview with John Adams and Dorothea Hoskins, August 11, 2004, Washington, D.C. Hoskins came to the post office in 1970. Unfortunately, nowhere does Herbert

Hill (NAACP labor secretary from 1953 to 1977) in his voluminous writings discuss his work on behalf of black postal workers. See also Russell P. Crawford, "Rep. A. C. Powell, Jr.: 'I Will Be Alert,'" *New York Alliance Leader* (January–February 1945), 1, New York City Branch of the National Alliance of Postal Employees, 1945–1982, reel 1, microfilm. The Alliance also printed a letter from Rep. Powell. "I can assure you, my friends of the Postal Alliance," Powell wrote to the *New York Alliance Leader*, "whenever legislation comes before me favoring a post office worker I will be in the forefront supporting him." Crawford was both editor of the *New York Alliance Leader* and head of the local NAACP. See also McGee, *Negro in the Chicago Post Office (Autobiography)*, 19; *(Dissertation)*, 40, 68. According to McGee, Rep. Dawson's secretary Fred Wall was the main factor behind Dawson's support for the Alliance, which included securing more promotions for blacks, especially black women.

30. Adams and Hoskins interview. See also author interview with Noel V. S. Murrain, August 12, 2004, Washington, D.C. On Percy Sutton see <http://www.aaregistry.com> (November 12, 2005).

31. Adams and Hoskins interview. See also photo feature, *National Alliance* (August 1967), 18. Strachan had previously been sworn in as Acting Postmaster on November 4, 1966. See "Editor's Notebook," *National Alliance* (November 1966), 4; Murrain interview. On New York postmaster Vinnie Malloy see for example "Local 813 January 1999, Alexander Edwards, Retirees Report," <http://www.napfe.com> (November 12, 2005). The *Postal Alliance* became the *National Alliance* in 1966, following an organizational name change from NAPE to NAPFE, or National Alliance of Postal and Federal Employees, in 1965.

32. New York Metro interview. As Eleanor Bailey remarked to a group of APWU women in 1974: "My involvement with the postal service came in 1964 under Executive Order 10988." See Eleanor Bailey typed remarks before APWU women's meeting (location and event unknown and n.d., but almost certainly 1974), Box 8, Folder Legislative Director Eleanor Bailey, NYMAPUC. From 1965 to 1967 the number of black postal workers went up 43 percent to a total of 18.9 percent of the total workforce, while Latino workers increased from 1 to 3 percent—a 185 percent rise. Of the 716,000 employees working at the post office in 1967, 88 percent, or almost 630,000, were concentrated in only 15 percent (4,868) of the nation's post offices. There were a little over 20,000 African Americans working for the post office in New York City's five boroughs out of about 70,000 postal workers altogether—more than in any other post office in the country. At just under thirty percent of New York's post office, that represented more than a 100 percent jump from 1955. Figures on the Manhattan post office are in Committee on Post Office and Civil Service, House of Representatives, *Towards Postal Excellence: The Report of the President's Commission on Postal Reorganization June 1968*, 94th Cong., 2nd sess. (Washington, D.C.: Government Printing Office, 1976), 101–4 (also known as the Kappel Commission). On Manhattan-Bronx combining as of January 7, 1963, see T. A. Vanterpool, "Uptown in Bronx Central," *Alliance Leader* (September–October 1962), 6. See also "Editor's Notebook," *National Alliance* (February 1968), 4, for figures on blacks in urban post offices, including 20,796 in greater New York City out of about 70,000 workers, or approximately 28.5 percent. But New York Alliance branch president John Adams estimated that figure to be 34.1 percent. See John H. Adams, "President's Desk," *Alliance Leader* (September–October 1967), 1. On 1955 figures for blacks in the New York City post office see Glenn, *History of the National Alliance*, 424. See also McGee, *Negro in the Chicago Post Office (Dissertation)*, 91. See also occasional Alliance articles in Spanish, for example Evelio Bello, "La Alliance y Comunidades (The Alliance and Communities)," *Alliance Leader* (July 1964), 4.

33. Percentages from 1972 of women employed by the post office from *Federal Civilian Employment by Minority Group and Sex, United States Civil Service Commission*, November 30, 1972. See also "Chicago, Illinois" and "Washington, D.C.," *Postal Alliance* (March 1960), 20; and "Welcome! New Alliance Members" (figures for September 1960–January 1961) *New York Alliance Leader* (March–April 1961), 7.

34. Bailey in our interview referred to John Strachan in the present tense despite the fact that he was deceased, which I think reflected a mutually respectful and cordial relationship even when they had been workplace adversaries—something not uncommon between postal managers and union activists. See New York Metro interview. See also Box 29, Folder GPO, Inc. 9/11/72–7/25/74, NYMAPUC, for a sample of the many grievances filed by Bailey in NYMAPUC archives. The sample is a "Grievance Appeal—Step 2," appealing, in her words, a contract "Violation of XIV—Section I." She filed the grievance on behalf of Special Delivery clerks, protesting: "The lack of heat in the Spec Delivery section of PO. It is unbearable."

35. Apart from letter carriers and those in a few smaller crafts, who are required to wear uniforms, most postal employees are allowed to choose their own work clothing, and it is instructive of expressive culture that Bailey looks back nostalgically on having conducted a sit-in wearing clothing that was both popular and controversial. The media's typical voyeuristic treatment of mini-skirts extended to the post office: young, attractive mini-skirted female letter carriers emptying mail collection boxes. See letter from Acting Postmaster John Strachan to Moe Biller, Box 50, Folder Women, NYMAPUC. See also New York Metro interview; "Women's Day," *Alliance Leader* (July–August 1967), 6; Hillman, "Chicago Branch President Proposes," "All Postmasters: Employment of Women," and "More Opportunities Assured Women in Federal Service," *Postal Alliance* (October 1962), 12; Ashby G. Smith, "Let's Use What We Have," *Postal Alliance* (August 1962), 2; "Statement of National Alliance of Postal and Federal Employees to Advisory Committee to Post Office Department on Equal Employment Opportunity in Postal Service, June 4, 1968," *National Alliance* (June 1968), 8–9; Box 50, Folder Women, NYMAPUC; and *Alliance Leader* (July–August 1967), 6. The article reads at one point: "ALLIANCE FOUGHT FIRST FOR HIRING WOMEN IN THE POSTAL SERVICE." See also "Portrait of Leadership," *Alliance Leader* (September–October 1967), 3.

36. See for example Loraine M. Huston, "Comments From Cleveland," *Postal Alliance* (December 1963), 15; "President's Commission Asks New Rights For Women," *Postal Alliance* (November 1963), 14; "Strictly Speaking Post Office," *Alliance Leader* (March-April 1963), 3; and Seligman, "How about More?"

37. See ". . . from the Executive Board W.A.P.U.," Washington Area Postal Employee (December 1963), 25, Box 81, NYMAPUC. Of thirteen board members, two were women: Jean Powell was "Sub. Representative" and Sarah Fowell was recording secretary.

38. "Washington Gets Woman 'Mailman,'" *Postal Alliance* (February 1963), 7. See also author interview with Joseph Henry, August 15, 2005, Washington, D.C.; and Historian, U.S. Postal Service, "Women Mail Carriers."

39. Author interview with D. James Pinderhughes, July 17, 2004, Washington, D.C.; and Henry interview. See also telephone conversation with Joyce Robinson, APWU national office, July 1, 2005, Washington, D.C.

40. See Josie McMillian oral history tapelog and summary (n.d., c. 1981, original tape damaged), New Yorkers at Work Oral History Collection: Project Files, 142, no. 1, Tamiment/Wagner Archives; and New York Metro interview.

41. Strachan interview; and Adams and Hoskins interview.

42. New York Metro interview.

43. See Cobble, *Other Women's Movement*, 3, for her discussion of what she calls "labor-feminists" in the post-1940s labor movement.

CHAPTER EIGHT

1. Paul N. Tennassee, "The Smith Presidency Part II," *National Alliance* (March 2002), 17. William Jason, whom the post office had once tried to remove for "disloyalty," also spoke.

2. James Cobb, "Strength Is in the Bargaining Power," *Alliance Leader* (May 1966), 5. In calling the Alliance a "civil rights union" I disagree with the assessment of the pre-1970 Alliance made by Aaron Brenner, "Striking against the State: The Postal Wildcat of 1970," *Labor's Heritage* (Spring 1996), 26n12: "It . . . functioned more like a Civil Rights Organization than a union." At the time it was still processing grievances and adverse actions besides lobbying Congress—very much like a postal union.

3. On the tendency of the black civic tradition in the Alliance to become overly accommodating, see for example Henry W. McGee, *The Negro in the Chicago Post Office: Henry W. McGee Autobiography and Dissertation* (Chicago: VolumeOne Press, 1999) (originally "The Negro in the Chicago Post Office," master's thesis, University of Chicago, 1961). Also addressing that 1965 convention was Rep. Adam Clayton Powell Jr. (D-N.Y.), longtime Alliance ally. Powell proclaimed the congruency of his and the Alliance's campaigns for equality within both the labor movement and the larger society that was at odds with the practice of what he caustically referred to as "the traditional American values" of white supremacy. Quoted in Tennassee, "The Smith Presidency Part II." The Alliance later came to Powell's defense in 1967 when he was blocked from taking his longtime seat in the House of Representatives because of charges of misappropriating funds. He was later seated with the loss of twenty-two years of seniority and a $40,000 fine. The Alliance also excoriated liberal Democrats who refused to back him. See also " 'Discrimination' in Congressional Ouster of Powell," *National Alliance* (March 1967), 10.

4. Herbert Hill, "The AFL-CIO and the Black Worker: Twenty-Five Years after the Merger," *Journal of Intergroup Relations* 10, no. 1 (Spring 1982), 35 (Reprint No. 241, Industrial Relations Research Institute, University of Wisconsin–Madison). I am indebted to the late Herbert Hill for this and other pamphlets of his journal writings. On Alliance support for Hill and his challenges to unions, see for example "NAACP Labor Head Charges Union Bias," *National Alliance* (July 1967), 12; and Rodgers C. Birt, "The Moment of Truth," *National Alliance* (April 1968), 14.

5. "Editor's Notebook," *Postal Alliance* (December 1963), 4.

6. John Walsh and Garth Mangum, *Labor Struggle in the Post Office: From Selective Lobbying to Collective Bargaining* (Armonk, N.Y.: M. E. Sharpe, 1992).

7. "Dictation by David Silvergleid—February 8, 1961," Box 61, Folder Merger Joint Letter 1961, NYMAPUC. See there earlier talks in June 1960 between the NALC and MBPU, and in January 1961 as well, with the Alliance observing, as they did in February of that year.

8. "National Alliance Convention," *Alliance Leader* (September–October 1961), 7.

9. See "New York Postal Workers in Orderly Visual Demonstration for Pay Increase," Metropolitan Postal Council News Release, March 5, 1964, Box 54, Folder MPC Outdoor Demo, NYMAPUC. The April 19, 1952, edition of the *Progressive Fed* monthly national

newsletter (produced in New York City by NFPOC Local 10) reported: "A protest rally held by the NYC letter carriers drew an overflow crowd. Carriers were protesting elimination of collections [mail pickups] which would cause the transfer of 300 regular carriers. The rally was attended by the entire Board of Officers of Local 10." The article noted that the publicity resulting from "this militant action" embarrassed the post office into rescinding the order. It also noted that the NFPOC would never sanction such direct action. See "NYC Letter Carriers Win Fight for Assignments," *Progressive*, April 19, 1952, 2.

10. "All PO Unions Rally in Brooklyn," *Progressive* (May 1965), 1.

11. Ironically, the same union—the NALC—whose members would begin the 1970 wild-cat strike, was later blamed for its narrow craft orientation being the major obstacle to postal union merger, in the opinion of William Burrus, the first black president of the APWU. See Walsh and Mangum, *Labor Struggle*, 101.

12. See "Big Federation Victory: UFPC Wins EXCLUSIVE Rights for All Clerks," *Union Postal Clerk* (August 1962), 2. See also "Biggest Postal Clerk Convention Opens on Note of Hope for New Era of Labor Relations in Postal Service," *Union Postal Clerk* (September 1962), 7.

13. Kenneth C. Groves [Kansas City, Mo.], "Dual Unionism," *Postal Alliance* (December 1963), 10.

14. See for example "Case for One Union," *Progressive* (November 1961), 2; and "Merger —One Union a Must," *Washington Area Postal Employees*, 5.

15. See "Editor's Notebook," *Postal Alliance* (June 1963), 4. Snow Grigsby's report, "Promotions in Dallas," actually alluded to "two large national AFL-CIO affiliated post office unions," suggesting the UFPC *and* the NALC, although this is the only mention I have seen of the NALC, and I have found no record of such an action. The same page also noted a scheduled march in Detroit on June 23 of 100,000 people "expected to participate in a 'Freedom Walk' to focus attention on Civil Rights" and support Dr. Martin Luther King Jr. and the SCLC. The 1963 Detroit "Walk to Freedom March" of 200,000 people was con-ducted several weeks before the national March on Washington and surprisingly still finds little mention in civil rights historiography, especially as it involved debates between civil rights and black nationalist forces. See for example Angela D. Dillard, "Religion and Radicalism: The Reverend Albert B. Cleage, Jr., and the Rise of Black Christian National-ism in Detroit," in *Freedom North: Black Freedom Struggles outside the South, 1940–1980* (New York: Palgrave, 2003), ed. Jeanne Theoharis and Komozi Woodard, 166–67. See also "3 Promotions in Dallas Texas Causes Stir," *Postal Alliance* (June 1963), 10. In the introduction to the latter, the *Postal Alliance* editor wrote, "Here, the fact of real merit is separated from the fiction of racial superiority." Murphy, as a department spokesman, wrote this to the *Dallas Daily News*, June 12, 1963: "After carefully reviewing the actions taken, it is the Department's position that no groups of individuals may be completely excluded from promotional opportunities so long as qualified members have passed the supervisory exam-ination, have the required minimum number of years of service and are successfully per-forming their duties in their current position." See also Paul Tennassee, "NAPFE: A Leg-acy of Resistance and Contributions, 1913–1999," *National Alliance* (October 1999), 14. See also L. H. Moses Jr., "Report on Hearing," 41; and "Postal Promotions Rescinded," 58, *Washington Area Postal Employee* (December 1963). Moses told his readers how congressional committee members grilled Murphy as to whether President Kennedy, the Justice Depart-ment, or Vice President Johnson had pressured him to appoint blacks as supervisors in Dallas, which Murphy denied. "But one of the most outstanding facts I heard," mused

Moses, "was that these same men in question were on the exam list during the year of 1956 and were deliberately passed over because of their color. . . . The promotions of the three Negroes were way overdue." Another article in the journal reported that the black promotions had been rescinded.

16. See "Alliance Pickets March in Support of Equal Opportunities," *Postal Alliance* (August 1963), 22; and Ashby G. Smith, "Address to Convention," *New York Alliance Leader* (September–October 1963), 1. The same page noted that then First Vice President John Adams was stepping up to New York branch president, as Leon Wheeler had received a postal management promotion, which Adams told me was common. Author interview with John Adams and Dorothea Hoskins, August 11, 2004, Washington, D.C.

17. See "Alliance Pickets 'Fed' Rally," *Washington Reports*, August 2, 1963, Box 71 (A-15), Folder NPU and NPCU misc. bulletins and leaflets, 1959–1963, NYMAPUC.

18. See Lorraine Huston, "Comments From Cleveland," *Postal Alliance* (December 1963), 15; Joe Wachtman, "Broadside Accuses Postal Union of Bias," *Postal Alliance* (February 1962), 13, reprinted from the *Baltimore News-Post*, February 1, 1962; and Ashby G. Smith, "No Time for Myths," *Postal Alliance* (October 1963), 17. Most craft employees at that time were classified as a "level five" or lower, so a "level seven" indicated management status.

19. Telephone conversation with Walter T. Kenney Sr., January 24, 2009. Kenney was elected to Richmond's city council in 1977 and to the mayor's office in 1990.

20. William H. Harris, *The Harder We Run: Black Workers since the Civil War* (New York: Oxford University Press, 1982), 161–62; and Dona Cooper Hamilton and Charles V. Hamilton, *The Dual Agenda: Race and Social Welfare Policies of Civil Rights Organizations* (New York: Columbia University Press, 1997), 123–28. Herman Yarbrough, president of the Alliance New Orleans branch writing in 1960 on Labor Day, argued that the Negro American Labor Council "was organized with more in mind than the simple bread and butter aspects of the worker. It will apparently seek to encompass the total welfare of all workers." See Herman Yarbrough, "Labor's Goals," *Postal Alliance* (September 1960), 5. In 1962 George Meany was a featured speaker at the Council's convention, and Herbert Hill has argued that the Council, which began with more than 10,000 members, now "embraced a program of accommodation with the AFL-CIO. The NALC [Negro American Labor Council] abandoned its original attack on discriminatory patterns within organized labor; soon thereafter its membership declined and it ceased to be an effective voice for black workers." Hill, "AFL-CIO and the Black Worker," 8–9. By 1964 the *Postal Alliance* had stopped referring to the Council in its pages.

21. See "NAPE Joins Successful March on Washington for Jobs and Freedom," *Postal Alliance* (September 1963), 18, which reprinted the entire text of Dr. Martin Luther King Jr.'s famous speech from that August 28, 1963, march. See also "Taking Off to Join the Freedom March," photo and caption, *Union Mail* (September–October 1963), 1. See also *Local 251 Minutes:* at this point the majority of 251 had left to join the Brooklyn Postal Union–NPU. Their positions were usually the same on civil rights and labor issues as MBPU: for example, their monthly meeting minutes reveal that, among other things, they sent telegrams to President Kennedy and New York senators Javits and Keating in support of the Freedom Riders (June 20, 1961); a fifty dollar donation to the family of white Alliance civil rights martyr William Moore (May 21, 1963); the same amount to the NAACP Medgar Evers scholarship fund after Evers's assassination (June 18, 1963); a telegram to New York congressional representatives urging their support of the civil rights bill (September 17, 1963); and acceptance of the National Alliance's invitation to attend their district convention

luncheon (October 15, 1963). On blacks in the UFPC see *Union Postal Clerk* (September 1962), 31: in Chicago, six of seventeen local officers sworn in that month to begin their two-year terms were black. See also *Union Postal Clerk* (September 1962), 30, for a photo caption of a Detroit labor symposium that included a cross-section of AFL-CIO leaders, sponsored by Local 295 and its president, William B. McCain, who was African American. Individual AFL-CIO unions like the UAW backed the March on Washington, but the federation's Executive Council did not. See Hill, "The AFL-CIO," 35.

22. Tennassee, "The Smith Presidency Part IV," 21, *National Alliance* (May 2002). King made not infrequent use of the black nationalist "we as a people" theme in his speeches and sermons, including his very last one, "I've Been to the Mountaintop" on April 3, 1968, in Memphis; see Martin Luther King Jr., Research and Education Institute website, <http://mlk-kppo1.stanford.edu> (November 24, 2008).

23. Tennassee, "The Smith Presidency Part IV," 16–17. The "Objectives" published just below the *National Alliance*'s masthead every month were changed slightly to reflect the transition and these remain the same today: "To keep the membership informed as to what transpires in the Postal *and other branches of the Federal Service.*" Interestingly, these longtime objectives did not alter their longtime assertion that "none need any peculiar arrangements set aside for them to hold any certain positions within the Government service" even as the organization supported affirmative action. The Alliance adamantly argued that affirmative action, unlike white privilege, did not constitute "reverse racism," as charged by the UFPC and conservative legislators, but rather was a corrective to the tradition of white privilege in the post office, its unions, and American society at large. Construction site clashes such as the one cited earlier went on for years with contractors and construction unions at odds with civil rights demonstrators over white privilege and black exclusion in construction work. Many of those protests were led by Harlem activist Jim Haughton and his Harlem Fightback organization. Together they were part of the early struggle for affirmative action as a form of civil rights law enforcement and historic black compensation.

24. "What Everyone Should Know about the National Alliance of Postal Employees," *Postal Alliance* (April 1965), 17. Italics added.

25. See for example *Postal Alliance* and *Progressive*, 1963–1964. Many back issues of these journals are available at the USPS Archives, except for the *Progressive*, available in part on microfilm through the Wisconsin Historical Society, or hard copy at NYMAPUC.

26. President Kennedy's EO 10925 first mandated federal agencies to develop studies and recommendations for equal employment opportunities. The Civil Service and Post Office established affirmative action EEO committees. Title VII of the 1964 Civil Rights Act established the EEOC for private sector employees only. Federal workers used their respective agency's EEO until the 1972 Employment Opportunity Act allowed federal workers to use both EEOC and the courts for discrimination complaints. See Tennassee, "Legacy," 14; and EO 10925.

27. Author interview with James Morris, August 11, 2004, Washington, D.C.

28. Adams and Hoskins interview; author interview with Countee Abbott, August 12, 2004, Washington, D.C.

29. Author interview with Felix Bell Sr., August 11, 2004, Washington, D.C.; telephone conversation with Willenham Castilla, January 26, 2009.

30. A coalition of civil rights groups including SNCC picked up where Meredith was shot and injured by a white supremacist soon after beginning his solo trek. See MBPU *News Flash!*, June 10, 1966, a periodic bulletin board posting. The letterhead referred to the

MBPU as "A Democratic Trade Union." Box 46, Folder Equal Opportunity and Civil Rights, NYMAPUC. The same folder also includes the Post Office Department's General Release no. 167 of October 31, 1965, highlighting the increased number of black promotions in the previous fiscal year. There is also a June 9, 1966, letter from the Afro American Civil Service Employees, Inc., thanking Biller for attending their "Testimonial Luncheon honoring Assemblyman Percy E. Sutton and Postmaster Robert K. Christenberry." Sutton himself had once been a postal worker. See Adams and Hoskins interview. On the March Against Fear see for example the recollections of two former SNCC leaders: Stokely Carmichael with Ekwueme Michael Thelwell, *Ready for Revolution: The Life and Struggles of Stokely Carmichael (Kwame Ture)* (New York: Scribner, 2003), 501–8.

31. Ashby G. Smith, "From the President's Desk," *Postal Alliance* (September 1963), 2. This was probably part of the same civil rights coalition that began a summer of picketing construction sites beginning at the one at Harlem Hospital on June 13, 1963—the day after black civil rights leader Medgar Evers was assassinated in Mississippi. See Herbert Hill, "The Racial Practices of Organized Labor: The Contemporary Record," in *The Negro and the American Labor Movement*, ed. Julius Jacobson (Garden City, N.Y.: Archer, 1968), 303–4. The 1963 protests were led by the Joint Committee for Equal Employment Opportunity and included members of the NAACP, CORE, the Urban League, the Negro American Labor Council (of which the Alliance was a member), the Association of Catholic Trade Unionists, and the Workers Defense League.

32. See "Mississippi Freedom Democratic Party," and "Have You Heard the Voice of Any Congressman of Mississippi Concerning These Facts," *Postal Alliance* (January 1965), 19, the latter discussing recent black church bombings; and "Women of the Year," *Postal Alliance* (January 1965), 21. The Mississippi Freedom Democratic Party was, as civil rights scholar John Dittmer called it, "an independent, movement-led political party" that emerged in 1964 from a coalition of civil rights organization "to challenge the state Democratic party's delegation at the national convention . . . in August," as well as to run candidates in the state's congressional primary. Denied seating at the national convention, they demonstrated and dramatized Mississippi's denial of black suffrage and representation in front of a national audience, resulting in nearly the entire all-white Mississippi delegation walking out. See John Dittmer, *Local People: The Struggle for Civil Rights in Mississippi* (Urbana: University of Illinois Press, 1995), 237, 285–302.

33. See also Mary Stanton, *Freedom Walk: Mississippi or Bust* (Jackson: University Press of Mississippi, 2003); and Taylor Branch, *Parting the Waters: America in the King Years, 1954–63* (New York: Simon and Schuster, 1988), 748–50, 764–65. See also Moe Biller letter to Albert Goodman, Treasurer NAACP, August 15, 1963, Box 46, Folder Civil Rights, NYMAPUC. Biller also noted in the letter that the MBPU had voted to send a delegation to the March on Washington for Jobs and Freedom, and Biller expressed pride that Goodman was also a member of the MBPU. Similar to NFPOC Local 10 maintaining a small loyalist local with the same name within the NFPOC after the 1959 split (then becoming the UFPC a year later), and keeping that name when reunification occurred in 1971 as the APWU, the NFPOC loyalists in Brooklyn kept the Local 251 name while the NPU branch in Brooklyn called itself the Brooklyn Postal Union. Both were also reunited within APWU in 1971. It was actually the Brooklyn NPU that made the NAACP donation, not the UFPC (formerly NFPOC) Local 251, whose records are not available in this collection during the "split years" of 1959–71.

34. See New York Metro interview; and Adams and Hoskins interview. When postal

workers leave their craft occupation to take a management position, besides being congratulated, in addition they are often considered by some of their former coworkers to have "gone over to the other side." The post office even has a two-year temporary management transition position known as "204B" where one can return to one's previous craft position, as many have, if they decide that management is not for them. Those who leave crafts for management, however, often encounter jibes from coworkers. John Adams, himself a former Alliance president who become an EEO specialist, noted how New York postmaster Albert Goldman had a policy of trying to convert union presidents into supervisors—as one can see from reading the *Alliance Leader* over the years. The Alliance in fact is the only postal union with a management division. In 1964, despite being contested by the NPU, the NPMHU finally won national exclusive rights to represent mail handlers after having lost the first one in 1962. On the NPMHU winning a 1964 "national exclusive" election, see "Mailhandler Election," *Progressive* (December 1964), 1.

35. Jeffrey O. G. Ogbar, *Black Power: Radical Politics and African American Identity* (Baltimore: Johns Hopkins University Press, 2004), 157.

36. Ibid. See also Duke University undergraduate paper by Charisse Williams based on her oral history interviews with Ajamu Dillahunt, retired postal clerk and local president of the APWU, Raleigh, North Carolina, 2005, Center for Documentary Studies collection at Duke University Special Collections library. A "black nationalist" analysis of the Alliance's history is made by Paul Tennassee in "Legacy." Telephone conversation with Paul Tennassee, June 10, 2004. Tennassee argues that the Alliance comprised pro-integration black nationalists. Tennassee establishes black autonomy as the determining factor in his definition, which also challenges strict conceptions of black nationalism as separatist. Tennassee's definition becomes problematic, however, in that most Alliance public pronouncements put distance between themselves and black nationalists of their day. See also Charles M. Payne on the narrow popular framing of "civil rights" as normative, compared to the broader democratic and economic implications associated with that term and/or the movement's ultimate goals by many black freedom movement veterans. See Payne in Steven F. Lawson and Charles M. Payne, *Debating the Civil Rights Movement, 1945–1968* (Lanham, Md.: Rowman and Littlefield, 1998), 99–140, esp. 128–31. The Alliance also found itself fighting off a new "red scare" that used Black Power as a scare tactic. See Roger C. Birt Jr., "Letters to the Editor: 'Disrupting Mail?,'" *National Alliance* (January 1969), 17.

37. See Martin Luther King Jr. (originally from his book *Where Do We Go From Here?*), reprinted in James M. Washington, ed., *A Testament of Hope: The Essential Writings and Speeches of Martin Luther King, Jr.* (1986; San Francisco: HarperSanFrancisco, 1991), 573. In Dr. King's recollection of his 1966 discussion with a group of Black Power advocates including Stokely Carmichael (Kwame Ture) of SNCC and Floyd McKissick of CORE, King expressed sympathy for the term's "denotative" meaning but opposition to its "connotative" meaning that the white press had already conflated with violence. Carmichael refused to abandon the slogan, arguing: "Power is the only thing respected in this world. . . . Martin, you know as well as I do that practically every other ethnic group in America has done this. The Jews, the Irish, and the Italians did it, why can't we?" King's rejoinder on the same page was: "That is just the point. . . . No one has ever heard the Jews publicly chant a slogan of Jewish power, but they have power. Through group unity, determination and creative endeavor, they have gained it. The same thing is true of the Irish and Italians." What King left out of this analysis, though, was the absorption and empowerment of

various European American ethnic groups as white and therefore privileged. Indicative of the slogan's currency was the number of other disempowered groups of color that quickly adapted slogans such as "Chicano Power" and "Red Power" for, respectively, Mexican Americans and Native Americans.

38. Author interview with Cleveland Morgan, July 18, 2005, New York; Bell interview.

39. Author interview with Jeff Perry and Richard Thomas, July 18, 2005, New York. On black caucuses in auto and steel, respectively, see Dan Georgakas and Marvin Surkin, *Detroit: I Do Mind Dying: A Study in Urban Revolution*, updated ed. (1975; Boston: South End Press, 1998); and Ruth Needleman, *Black Freedom Fighters in Steel: The Struggle for Democratic Unionism* (Ithaca, N.Y.: Cornell University Press, 2003).

40. See Moe Biller, "Straight from the Shoulder," *Union Mail* (May 1966), italics added. See also John H. Adams, "The President's Desk," *New York Alliance Leader* (March 1966), 1, subheaded "Merger with the Alliance." There were further public arguments on this issue from both sides. See also New York Metro interview.

41. See for example "Taking Off to Join"; "We Salute S. Wesley Henderson," *Union Mail* (March 1960), 10. See also *Union Mail* (July–August 1966), 4, for two African American clerks, Rebecca Daniels and Juanita Stamper, in photo caption: "Getting Briefed on union activities at headquarters last month were two distaff delegates representing the new and growing leadership in MBPU. Female reps are most welcome as ranks of women keep growing." See also Henry Reese, "Unions and the Negro Revolt," *Union Mail* (May 1968), 6.

42. See for example Wyatt C. Williams, "The National Office," *National Alliance* (November 1966), 8.

43. See the following articles and issues of the *Postal Alliance*: "Baltimore Branch Pickets City Hall" (March 1963), 13; "Austin, Texas," photo caption (June 1964), 22; "Write in for rights campaign moves to Post Office," photo caption (January 1964), 22; and "Charge Discrimination in Pittsburgh Post Office Jobs" (January 1965), 11. The article noted that the Alliance picketed in conjunction with CORE, the NAACP, the National Urban League, and the Negro Protest Committee. The protests in Baltimore were against the segregated Northwood Theater located near the historically black Morgan College (now Morgan State University). Black postal workers picketed City Hall on their lunch hour after several hundred black college students were jailed for their part in the protest, with bail collectively set at nearly a quarter million dollars. The page 13 photograph in the June *Postal Alliance* shows that city's mayor and Alliance pickets smiling and tearing up their picket signs after the theater agreed to integrate.

44. "Leaders of Rights Groups Seek Curb on Mass Demonstrations," *Postal Alliance* (August 1964), 16, italics added.

45. "NAACP Branches Move to Avert Race Riots," *Postal Alliance* (August 1964).

46. Tennassee, "The Smith Presidency Part VI," *National Alliance* (July 2002), 20–21.

47. See author interview with Jimmy Mainor, January 5, 2004, Durham, N.C.; and Bell interview.

48. Telephone interview with Donald P. Stone, February 12, 2005, Snow Hill, Ala.

49. The swing room is where postal workers take breaks. See author interviews with George Booth Smith, August 27, 2004, Durham, N.C.; Joseph Henry, August 15, 2005, Washington, D.C.; and D. James Pinderhughes, July 17, 2004, Washington, D.C.

50. Author interview with Doug Holbrook, August 16, 2005, Washington, D.C.

1. Author interview with Jeff Perry and Richard Thomas, July 18, 2005, New York. Thomas's father was a police officer, his mother a telephone operator. Perry, whose father was a pipe fitter, started with the post office in 1974. See also New York Metro interview.

2. Perry and Thomas interview. Delegates to a special 1968 NPMHU convention voted to merge with the Laborers International Union of North America (LIUNA) in a disputed election, whereupon many mail handlers left for the National Alliance or the MBPU. See "Mail Handler Union Torn Asunder," *Progressive* (November 1968), 1; "Mail Handler Leaders Flock to NPU," *Progressive* (August 1969), 1; John Walsh and Garth Mangum, *Labor Struggle in the Post Office: From Selective Lobbying to Collective Bargaining* (Armonk, N.Y.: M. E. Sharpe, 1992), 112–13; and Perry and Thomas interview. LIUNA was later condemned for reported mob ties, and possibly having illegally assumed control over the NPMHU. See also H. H. Hubert, "An Open Letter to All Mail Handlers Who Oppose Racism and Mob Control of Our Union: The Mail Handler Struggle for Democracy and Autonomy," draft pamphlet in possession of author. See also telephone conversation with Jeff Perry based on documents in his possession, August 22, 2009.

3. Paul Nehru Tennassee, "NAPFE: A Legacy of Resistance and Contributions, 1913–1999," *National Alliance* (October 1999), 15. To reflect its new commitment to organizing all federal employees, the Alliance changed its name officially at its 1965 convention in Los Angeles from the National Alliance of Postal Employees; 1965 also was the Alliance's highest point of influence in the post office and among postal workers.

4. Committee on Post Office and Civil Service, House of Representatives, *Towards Postal Excellence: The Report of the President's Commission on Postal Organization, June 1968*, 94th Cong., 2nd sess. (1968; Washington, D.C.: Government Printing Office, 1976), 18–22, 119, and chap. 3.

5. Aaron Brenner, "Striking against the State: The Postal Wildcat of 1970," *Labor's Heritage* (Spring 1996), 6–7.

6. For Executive Order 11491 see EEOC website, <http://www.eeoc.gov> (September 8, 2008).

7. See "Moe Biller's Remarks for Panel Discussion," 25th Anniversary of the 1970 Postal Strike, National Postal Museum, Smithsonian Institution, Washington, D.C., March 17, 1995, National Association of Letter Carriers (NALC) Library, Washington, D.C.

8. See for example Raymond Weiss, "Flushing, N.Y.," branch item, *Postal Record* (May 1970), 76, supporting higher area wages in response to a letter written in opposition to area wages by a Madisonville, Kentucky, branch scribe in the March 1970 *Postal Record*.

9. Aaron Brenner, "Rank-and-File Rebellion, 1966–1975" (Ph.D. diss., Columbia University, 1996), 114; and Marvin J. Levine, "The U.S. Postal Service: A Labor Relations Hybrid," *Employee Relations Law Journal* 4, no. 2 (1978), 232.

10. "20,000 Detroiters Line Up for 60 Post Office Jobs," *Washington Area Postal Employees* (June 1963), 35. The article was reprinted form the *AFL-CIO News*, Box 81, NYMAPUC.

11. See for example Nelson Lichtenstein, Susan Strasser, and Roy Rosenzweig, eds., *Who Built America?: Working People and the Nation's Economy, Politics, Culture, and Society*, vol. 2, *Since 1877* (Boston: Bedford/St. Martin's Press, 2000), 627, 685; Thomas R. Brooks, *Toil and Trouble: A History of American Labor*, 2nd ed., revised and enlarged (1964; New York: Delta, 1971), 255–65. Brooks notes on 255: "Economists in the early 1960s were given to treating

unemployment in the United States as troublesome 'pockets' in an expanding economy. But to Negro workers, these 'pockets' were a sea of quicksand sucking them down to extinction." See New York Metro interview. On the rise of public sector jobs see Robert Shaffer, "Where Are the Organized Public Employees? The Absence of Public Employees Unionism from U.S. History Textbooks, and Why It Matters," *Labor History* 43, no. 3 (August 2002), 316; and Ray Marshall and Virgil L. Christian Jr., eds., *Employment of Blacks in the South: A Perspective on the 1960s* (Austin: University of Texas Press, 1978), 107. On black economic gains during this time see Melvin L. Oliver and Thomas M. Shapiro, *Black Wealth / White Wealth: A New Perspective on Racial Equality* (New York: Routledge, 1997), 24.

12. Tennassee, "Legacy," 15; "Take the Federal Service Entrance Examination," *Postal Alliance* (December 1965), 27.

13. Committee on Post Office and Civil Service, *Towards Postal Excellence*, 24.

14. "United Action Taken by NAACP, National Urban League and National Alliance of Postal and Federal Employees to Further Equal Employment Opportunity in Federal Agencies on an Area Basis," *National Alliance* (April 1968), 8.

15. Perry and Thomas interview. See also Vern K. Baxter, *Labor and Politics in the U.S. Postal Service* (New York: Plenum, 1994), 70–78, on LSMs, developed in 1957 and improved as MPLSMs (multiple position letter sorting machines) that were brought online in the early 1960s about the same time that five-digit zip codes were introduced in 1962 to mechanize mail processing. It was a technological change that postal unions protested because it essentially "Taylor-ized" or "Ford-ized" LSM operators by trying to make them extensions of their machines: they had to quickly key in letters for processing at machine speeds set by management at sixty letters per minute. On mail handlers' craft, see Baxter, *Labor and Politics*, 64–65.

16. Ibid., 67.

17. Author interview with William H. Burrus Jr., January 16, 2009, Washington, D.C.

18. Studs Terkel, *Working* (1972; New York: Avon Books, 1975), 362. Carrier work "standards" have included the so-called minimum of "18 and 8," or putting eighteen letters and eight flats per minute into a route "case." Management historically has also measured carriers' street performance during periodic "route inspections." See M. Brady Mikusko, *Carriers in a Common Cause: A History of Letter Carriers and the NALC* (Washington, D.C.: NALC, 1989).

19. David Montgomery, *Workers' Control in America: Studies in the History of Work, Technology, and Labor Struggles* (1979; Cambridge: Cambridge University Press, 1986); Mikusko, *Carriers in a Common Cause*, esp. 72–77; and Brenner, "Rank-and-File Rebellion."

20. Perry and Thomas interview.

21. I am grateful to John Roberts for the observation of interdependency of New York letter carriers' jobs. John was a friend and letter carrier colleague of mine at the West Durham post office and NALC Branch 382 in the 1990s.

22. Philip Seligman oral history interview by Dana Schecter, June 29, 1976, New York, transcription, Biller Files.

23. The post office's hierarchical structure (with military veterans occupying many craft and supervisory positions) and much of its official and informal terminology at times appears to have been borrowed from the nation's armed forces. Shifts are organized into three "tours of duty" (Tour 1, 12 A.M.–8 A.M.; Tour 2, 8 A.M.–4 P.M.; Tour 3, 4 :scp.m.–12 :sca.m., typically) using the twenty-four-hour clock shared by the government and the

military (where, for example, 2 :sca.m. becomes 0200 hours). "OD" is the "officer of the day," and a temporary assignment is called a "detail." The military's commissioned officers could be said to have counterparts at the post office in the latter's "tour superintendents," "station managers," and "supervisors." The military noncommissioned officer status could be roughly translated into the postal "clerk-in-charge" or the temporary supervisor (also known as a "204B"). Heavy "incoming" mail volume is commonly described as "getting hit hard" in language that evokes bombardment during wartime. "Insubordination," "refusing a direct order," and "going AWOL" (absent without leave) are also military-originated expressions used by postal management to describe "severe" labor discipline problems. And all postal employees are constantly urged by management to pull together "for the good of the service"—an expression with echoes of military service that is sometimes mocked by postal workers if they feel taken advantage of. Committee on Post Office and Civil Service, *Towards Postal Excellence*, 108–9. See also Perry and Thomas interview.

24. Committee on Post Office and Civil Service, *Towards Postal Excellence*, Study 3: Postal Manpower. See also Mikusko, *Carriers in a Common Cause*; and Walsh and Mangum, *Labor Struggle*.

25. In 1966 the MBPU and Alliance clashed over the MBPU's allegation of Alliance "separatism" in opposing the proposed (but later scrapped) UFPC-NPU merger that same year. See Moe Biller, "Straight from the Shoulder," *Union Mail* (May 1966), 3. See also merger talks and vote (the NPU voted for, the UFPC against): "Drive for Giant 'Yes' Vote in March Merger Referendum," *Progressive* (February 1966), 1; "Merger Talks Continue: Agreement Lacked Two-Thirds Majority," *Union Postal Clerk* (May 1966), 2; and Sidney Goodman, "An 'Open Letter' to the President of the United Federation Postal Clerks," *Progressive* (November 1966), 4, where the NPU president noted the merger's collapse and asked UFPC president Roy Halleck to explain their subsequent anti-NPU rancor.

26. See for example Philip S. Foner and Ronald L. Lewis, eds., *The Black Worker: A Documentary History from Colonial Times to the Present, vol. 7, The Black Worker from the Founding of the CIO to the AFL-CIO Merger, 1936–1955* (Philadelphia: Temple University Press, 1983), 471–72; Committee on Post Office and Civil Service, *Towards Postal Excellence*, 106; and Henry W. McGee, *The Negro in the Chicago Post Office: Henry W. McGee Autobiography and Dissertation* (Chicago: VolumeOne Press, 1999) (originally "The Negro in the Chicago Post Office," master's thesis, University of Chicago, 1961). See also Lester F. Miller, *The National Rural Letter Carriers Association: A Centennial Portrait* (Encino, Calif.: Cherbo Publishing, 2003), 83, who notes the NRLCA opposition to the abolition of patronage for postmasters and rural letter carriers because they felt that "a good caliber of employee was chosen by this method." President Nixon abolished the practice by executive order in 1969.

27. Tennassee, "Legacy."

28. See Committee on Post Office and Civil Service, *Towards Postal Excellence*; New York Metro interview; Perry and Thomas interview; Branch 36 interview; author interview with Cleveland Morgan, July 18, 2005, New York; Seligman interview by Schecter; and Moe Biller interview by Schecter, July 7, 1976, New York, Biller Files.

29. Committee on Post Office and Civil Service, *Towards Postal Excellence*, 11.

30. The Kappel Commission was preceded by a task force appointed by Postmaster General Lawrence F. O'Brien in 1966. O'Brien had just been appointed that year, and the following year he took the results of his task force and proposed that the position of postmaster general be abolished as a cabinet position and the post office replaced by a corporation. The *Postal Record*, the journal of the NALC, which later praised O'Brien when he resigned

in 1968, in 1966 charged him with orchestrating the Chicago mail crisis by cutting back on overtime. See Committee on Post Office and Civil Service, *Towards Postal Excellence*, iv. The commission included the dean of Harvard Business School, plus top executives from such corporate entities as the Ford Foundation, General Electric, Campbell Soup, and Bank of America. The sole labor representative on the commission was George Meany, who did express some reservations with the proposed change. According to postal scholar John Tierney, Meany was appointed as a labor "token" because the unions were opposed to the idea. However, it is possible that he was selected not only to provide "labor's voice," but to help "sell" the planned reorganization that had been first proposed by O'Brien. See John T. Tierney, *Postal Reorganization: Managing the Public's Business* (Boston: Auburn House, 1981), 11. See also Joseph F. Thomas, "Unhappy Employees—No Mystery," *Union Postal Clerk* (October 1966), 6; David Silvergleid, "From the Top," *Progressive* (November 1966), 4; James H. Rademacher, "New Postal Policies Shatter Morale," *Postal Record* (August 1966), 8; Tierney, *Postal Reorganization*; and Baxter, *Labor and Politics*, 81. On postal worker drop in morale and rising militancy see Mikusko, *Carriers in a Common Cause*, 66–67.

31. The backlog coverage began with "Seek to End Big Mail Backlog," *Chicago Tribune*, October 7, 1966, section 1, page 2: "McGee blamed the heavy accumulation, mostly advertising circulars and catalogs, on refusals by the administration to authorize overtime work. . . . McGee discounted rumors that employees disgruntled with the no-overtime order have created the backlog thru deliberately slow downs." The first appearance on the front page was "Mail Routed Thru St. Louis: Chicago Office Can't Keep Up with Flow," *Chicago Tribune*, October 13, 1966, 1; followed by "Ask Approval to Destroy Mail Pileups," *Chicago Tribune*, October 14, 1966, 1–2, with Hartigan's "emergency" warning and mention that twenty-five cities had been sent mail normally handled in Chicago, as that city was the nation's "most important mail processing point." See "Hire 350 to Reduce Mail Backlog: Weekend Crews Also Increased," *Chicago Tribune*, October 15, 1966, 1–2. Hartigan blamed holiday advertising circulars (the expired ones were destroyed upon mailer's permission with postage refunded) and "absenteeism." See "McGee to Report Today on City's Mail Jam: First Class Backlog Is Cleaned Up," October 17, 1966, section 1, page 3. But see also the post office news blackout in "Imposes News Suspension on Mail Logjam," *Chicago Tribune*, October 18, 1966, section 1B, page 2; "Mail Jam Solved: Officials," *Chicago Tribune*, October 19, 1966, section 1, page 3, claiming the logjam "over and operations are back to normal, postal officials reported yesterday," along with an investigation "to curb loafing and excessive absenteeism." There is no mention of the 1966 backlog in Baxter, *Labor and Politics*; or Walsh and Mangum, *Labor Struggle*. By contrast, Mikukso, *Carriers in a Common Cause*, 66, reports that during that month "the system broke down completely. Almost every major post office in the country reported huge backlogs of undelivered mail." I have not yet found any other account that corroborates this intriguing report. See also Silvergleid, "From the Top." The *Chicago Daily News* called it a "backlog" on October 7 with a page 5 story, "Big Backlog at Post Office Here; 1st-Class Jam on 4th-Class Mail"—the same day the *Tribune* first broke the story. The *Daily News* gave it sparse coverage from then on—and front-page coverage for the first and only time on October 18, when Hartigan announced: "The crisis is over." See Frank Maier, "138 Postal Aides Here Face Discipline," *Chicago Daily News*, October 18, 1966, 1. Ironically, a front-page article in the October 14, 1966, *Chicago Daily News* ("Lucas Fired by Post Office") that mentioned the backlog briefly also announced that McGee had fired mail handler Robert Lucas, "Negro civil rights leader" and chair of the Chicago CORE chapter. Lucas had been demanding that workers cleaning up

the backlog be paid at overtime rates. Lucas was fired for being AWOL from work the first week of September when he had been leading civil rights marchers into suburban Cicero to protest housing discrimination there.

32. James Rademacher, "New Postal Policies Shatter Morale," *Postal Record* (August 1966), 8.

33. Mikusko, *Carriers in a Common Cause*, 66–67.

34. "Act on Strike Prohibition," *Progressive* (August–September 1966), 3, italics added. The study later found that there was no constitutional basis for overturning that federal law. See "Strike Test Not Feasible," *Progressive* (February 1967), 3.

35. Ashby G. Smith, "From the President's Desk: What of the New Year? What of the Old?," *National Alliance* (January 1967), 2. Shortly after taking office as national president of the Alliance in 1961 Smith had begun writing a new regular monthly column titled "From the President's Desk."

36. " 'Employment and Politics: Cornerstone of Democracy': Address of State Representative Carl B. Stokes of Cleveland, Ohio, Before the National Alliance of Postal and Federal Employees Annual Congressional Dinner, Washington-Hilton Hotel, Washington, D.C.," *National Alliance* (May 1966), 15. See also "Ask Approval to Destroy," 2, in the October 14, 1966, *Chicago Tribune*, noting the appointment of McGee, "a career postal employee, was unusual since the job usually [has gone] to a politician with no postal experience, as a reward for political services."

37. See for example John David Skrentny, *The Ironies of Affirmative Action: Politics, Culture, and Justice in America* (Chicago: University of Chicago Press, 1996); and Philip F. Rubio, *A History of Affirmative Action, 1619–2000* (Jackson: University Press of Mississippi, 2001). See also "Stokes address," 16; and NYMAPUC, Box 6, Folder EO 10925 (Discrimination), for a January 11, 1967, meeting between the Postal Service Committee on Equal Employment Opportunity and MBPU representatives Arthur Ryland and Moe Biller that revealed a similar profile of the New York City post office in terms of job levels for blacks and Puerto Ricans: levels 1–3 were 56 percent black and 11 percent Puerto Rican; levels 4–6 were 31 percent black and 6 percent Puerto Rican; levels 7–11 were 9 percent black and 1 percent Puerto Rican; and levels 12–20 were 5 percent black and 0 percent Puerto Rican. The same file has a February 5, 1965, policy letter from New York Postmaster Robert K. Christenberry to all New York postal employees urging support for EO 10925. Committee on Post Office and Civil Service, *Towards Postal Excellence*, 19, cites 1967 Post Office Department figures, which listed the Alliance as having 32,000 members, while the Alliance usually claimed 40,000 during this period. The discrepancy may reflect the fact that the Alliance began representing other federal employees in 1965. See also McGee, *Negro in the Chicago Post Office (Dissertation)*, 96. See also author interview with Doug Holbrook, August 16, 2005, Washington, D.C.: Holbrook estimated that at its peak about one-quarter (roughly 18,000) of the NPU membership was black. Thomas Bomar of the Alliance in 1965 suggested that the UFPC had more black members than the NAPFE. That would put the UFPC somewhere between one-quarter about one-third black, with about 40,000 black members. Bomar's figures on the UFPC may be a slight overestimate, as that would not allow for hardly any black members of the NALC and NPMHU (at least 20,000 between them). See Tennessee, "The Smith Presidency Part V," *National Alliance* (June 2002), 21. For Executive Order 11246 see <http://www.eeoc.gov> (September 10, 2008); and "Agencies Must Establish, Maintain 'Positive Program' of Equal Opportunity," *National Alliance* (February 1966), 7.

38. McGee, *Negro in the Chicago Post Office (Autobiography)*, 27.

39. Ibid., 27–28.

40. Ibid., 28.

41. Author interview with Countee Abbott, August 12, 2004, Washington, D.C.

42. McGee, *Negro in the Chicago Post Office (Autobiography)*, 28.

43. "Seek to End Big Mail Backlog."

44. McGee, *Negro in the Chicago Post Office (Dissertation)*, 98–99; on seniority see 53–54.

45. See Jeffrey O. G. Ogbar, *Black Power: Radical Politics and African American Identity* (Baltimore: Johns Hopkins University Press, 2004). See also Enormel Clark, "Letter Box," *National Alliance* (February 1968), 11.

46. See author interview with John Adams and Dorothea Hoskins, August 11, 2004, Washington, D.C.

47. Telephone interview with Donald P. Stone, February 12, 2005, Snow Hill, Ala. See also Rubio, *History of Affirmative Action*.

48. Ibid. See also author interview with Sam Armstrong and Samuel Lovett, August 11, 2004, Washington, D.C.; and Clayborne Carson, *In Struggle: SNCC and the Black Awakening of the 1960s* (Cambridge, Mass.: Harvard University Press, 1981), 195–201.

49. Milton Holmes, "Baltimore, Maryland," *National Alliance* (July 1966), 12. See also electronic communication from Nishani Frazier to author, September 28, 2005. Frazier's mother was a Cleveland postal worker who left the post office to do full-time work with CORE in the early 1960s. Frazier's mother, aunt, and uncle also did CORE work in Baltimore, a CORE "target city." Telephone conversation with Frazier, November 9, 2005.

50. "Chicago Branch Urges Participation in Civic and Community Affairs," *National Alliance* (November 1966), 13. See also Steven F. Lawson, *Running for Freedom: Civil Rights and Black Politics in America Since 1941* (New York: McGraw-Hill, 1991), 118–21.

51. See "Objectives," *Postal Alliance* (January 1942), 1.

52. See Bobbie Barbee, " 'Big Daddy' Tells Church He Has 5,000 Judases; He Will Rise," *Jet*, April 11, 1968, 14–19. Urging the crowd to "think black," Rev. Powell had just returned to Harlem to a tumultuous reception after an eighteen-month self-imposed exile in Bimini. One photo caption read: "Powell pointedly assails Dr. Martin Luther King's 'nonviolence' programs as no longer useful." Coverage in *Jet* after King's assassination also revealed an upsurge in militant black activism.

53. Tennassee, "The Smith Presidency VII," *National Alliance* (August 2002), 12–14; and Charles H. King Jr., "Cities in Crisis," *National Alliance* (July 1969), 13.

54. Tennassee, "The Smith Presidency VI," *National Alliance* (July 2002), 17. Milton Holmes in particular was an active Baltimore Alliance and CORE member. See Louis C. Goldberg, "CORE in Trouble: A Social History of the Organizational Dilemmas of the Congress of Racial Equality Target City Project in Baltimore, 1965–1967" (Ph.D. diss., Johns Hopkins University, 1970), 255–56.

55. "Alliance Calls for Action on Equal Opportunity," *National Alliance* (June 1967), 5.

56. Clark, "Letter Box," 11, in response to an article by Eric Hoffer in the *Philadelphia Enquirer*. Capitals in original.

57. Tennassee has also noted a 1967 power struggle turning physical in the Detroit Alliance branch where "Black Power militants" reported to be "black Muslim" guards of one of the local Alliance leaders assaulted supporters of another local leader. See "The Smith Presidency Part VI," *National Alliance* (July 2002), 20; Ashby G. Smith, "Dr. King is Dead—Where to From Here?," *National Alliance* (April 1968), 2; and Tennassee, "A Book in the Making: African Americans, An Untold Story, NAPFE, 1913–2000," *National Alliance*

(April 1998), 16: "NAPFE is a unique 'black nationalist' union, which in practice is democratic, antiracist, integrationist and patriotic."

58. Wyatt C. Williams, "The National Office," *National Alliance* (February 1967), 5.

59. Wyatt C. Williams, "The National Office," *National Alliance* (November 1967), 8. See also "NAACP Labor Head Charges Union Bias," *National Alliance* (July 1967), 12.

60. See for example Alex Poinsett, "Crusade against the Craft Unions," *Ebony* (December 1969), 33–42; Holmes, "Baltimore, Maryland"; Philip S. Foner, Ronald L. Lewis, and Robert Cvornyek, eds., *The Black Worker: A Documentary History from Colonial Times to the Present*, vol. 8, *The Black Worker since the AFL-CIO Merger, 1955–1980* (Philadelphia: Temple University Press, 1984), esp. 368–70 and 456–66; Ogbar, *Black Power*, chap. 5; and Rubio, *History of Affirmative Action*, chaps. 6–7.

61. "Agencies Must Establish, Maintain 'Positive Program' of Equal Opportunity," *National Alliance* (February 1966), 7.

62. "Alliance Calls for Action."

63. See for example "United Action Taken," 8; and Armstrong and Lovett interview.

64. McGee, *Negro in the Chicago Post Office (Dissertation)*, 1–2.

65. Williams, "The National Office," *National Alliance* (February 1967), 7. The first Alliance chapters had been mostly southern; the February 1967 *National Alliance* now listed five northern cities along with two Deep South cities and three border South cities among the Alliance's ten biggest chapters, which were Chicago, Washington, D.C., New York City, Philadelphia, Baltimore, Detroit, St. Louis, Atlanta, New Orleans, and Cleveland.

66. See for example Leon Fink and Brian Greenberg, *Upheaval in the Quiet Zone: A History of Hospital Workers' Union, Local 1199* (Urbana: University of Illinois Press, 1989).

67. "Dulski to Push 'Slum Post Office' Probe," *Union Mail* (February 1969), in Box 3, Folder Officers Files, NYMAPUC; and Wyatt C. Williams, "The National Office," *National Alliance* (February 1967), 5. The latter column's subtitle pertaining to working conditions in the New York post office was "Visits: New York Post Office—Dirt, Decay, and Denial."

68. Perry and Thomas interview. See also author interview with Felix Bell, August 11, 2004, Washington, D.C.

69. "Project Transition," *National Alliance* (August 1970), 6. As of 1991 the revised plan became Operation Transition. See <http://www.dmdc.osd.mil/ot/index.html> (November 12, 2005). See also "A Message from the Postmaster General," *National Alliance* (March 1968), 5. The MBPU's December 1967 *Union Mail* reported that a civil service preparatory course was being offered at the Walter Reed Army Hospital in D.C. for hospitalized Viet Nam vets, expanded to some 30,000 veterans in 1968: see "Viet Nam Vets Get PO Prep Course," *Union Mail* (December 1967), 4. Ironically, Executive Order 11397 of February 9, 1968, was superseded by Executive Order 11521 on March 26, 1970—coming at the end of the postal strike. See the website of the National Archives and Records Administration, <http://www.archives.gov> (September 10, 2008).

70. "United Action Taken," italics added.

71. Mikusko, *Carriers in a Common Cause*, 66–69.

72. Michael Keith Honey, *Going Down Jericho Road: The Memphis Strike, Martin Luther King's Last Campaign* (New York: W. W. Norton, 2007), 65–69. Evers, a railway mail clerk, probably belonged to the National Alliance. At the time of his sanitation worker organizing, he was still fighting to get his postal job back, having been fired in 1959 for allegedly violating the Hatch Act when he ran for local public office that year. See Elizabeth Gritter, "Memories of H. T. Lockard," *Southern Cultures* 14, no. 5 (Fall 2008), 109–10; and "O. Z.

Evers to Run for Court Clerk," *Tri-State Defender*, June 30, 1962, 1. In *Evers v. Dwyer* 358 *U.S.* 202 (1958), the U.S. Supreme Court reversed and remanded the case to the lower court that had refused to rule on it.

73. Joan Turner Beifuss, *At the River I Stand: Memphis, the 1968 Strike, and Martin Luther King* (Brooklyn: Carlson Publishing, 1989), 157. Middlebrook was also featured in the film documentary of that strike, *At the River I Stand*, dir. David Appleby, Allison Graham, Steven Ross, 1993. The correct name of the church is the Greater Middle Baptist Church. Rev. Middlebrook is currently the pastor of the Canaan Baptist Church of Christ in Knoxville. Benjamin Hooks was a practicing attorney and minister who went on to become executive director of the NAACP from 1977 to 1992. See Manning Marable, *Race, Reform, and Rebellion: The Second Reconstruction in Black America, 1945–1990* (1984; Jackson: University Press of Mississippi, 1991), 184; and NAACP website, <http://www.naacp.org> (August 15, 2009).

74. Telephone conversation with Rev. Dr. Harold Middlebrook, June 9, 2005, Knoxville, Tenn. Rev. Middlebrook told me he left the post office before the 1970 strike.

75. Michael Eric Dyson, *I May Not Get There with You: The True Martin Luther King, Jr.* (New York: Free Press, 2000), chap. 4.

76. See for example "Report on The Poor Peoples Bus to Washington," *Alliance Leader* (August 1968), 5; "Unions and the Negro Revolt," *Union Mail* (May 1968), 6; "To Serve Humanity," *Union Mail* (May 1968), 3; "The Poor People's March—Solidarity P.O.," *Union Mail* (July–August 1968), 4–5; and "We Were There Because We Care!," *Union Mail* (July–August 1968), 1. For reactions to the King assassination see "Dr. King Is Dead" and "Editor's Notebook," *Union Mail* (July–August 1968), 4; photo caption page, *National Alliance* (April 1968), 6; "Alliance Offers Reward of $10,000 for King's Murderer" and "NAACP Mourns Slaying of Martin Luther King, Jr.," *National Alliance* (April 1968), 7. Ironically in 1968, the Civil Rights Act signed by President Johnson exactly one week after King's assassination also included anti-riot clauses aimed at SNCC activists. "Editor's Notebook," *National Alliance* (April 1968), 4. By contrast, tributes to Dr. King were extensive in the journals of the United Rubber Workers, AFSCME, and the United Auto Workers. See "Deep in Our Hearts . . . We Shall Overcome," *United Rubber Worker* (April 1968), 3; "To Curb the Agony and Bloodshed," *UAW Solidarity* (August 1968), 11; and "Memphis: The Tragedy and Triumph," [AFSCME] *Public Employee* (April 1968), 5.

77. See "Deliver Us From 'Friends,' " *National Alliance* (May 1967), 9. See also Tennassee, "The Smith Presidency Part VI," 19, and "The Smith Presidency Part VII."

78. Tennassee, "The Smith Presidency VIII," *National Alliance* (September 2002), 26–27; and Wyatt C. Williams, "Racism, Labor, and the Alliance," *National Alliance* (May 1968), 6.

79. See "Brooklyn, N.Y. Branch Protests Racial Innuendo," *National Alliance* (September 1969), 8. See also Ogbar, *Black Power*, esp. chap. 5, and Rodgers C. Birt (Indianapolis), "The Moment of Truth," *National Alliance* (January 1969), 14, where he accused the AFL-CIO (using the popular pejorative "Big Labor") of organizing federal workers to try to swallow up independent unions like the Alliance in order to shore up its sagging membership rolls.

80. See "Post Office Contingency Plan for Work Stoppages, July 15, 1968," Box 3, Folder Officers' Files—Presidents—Moe Biller—Kingsbridge—Postal Reform, NYMAPUC. The memo was issued by Deputy Postmaster Frederick C. Belen to "All Regional Directors, Postal Inspectors, All Postmasters (at FIRST CLASS OFFICES)." All capitals in original.

81. Richard J. Levine, "Restive Postal Workers Pose Mounting Threat of Wildcat Walkouts; Post Office Hopes to Cope with Stoppages; Unions Drop No Strike Pledges," *National Alliance* (September 1968), 18, reprinted from *Wall Street Journal*, September 9, 1968; and

"NPU Drops 'No Strike' Provision," National Postal Union *Washington Report*, September 4, 1968, 1. I have not found the text of the "strike deadline" resolution, but this same article seems to confirm the *Wall Street Journal*'s report of an averted strike deadline, as it concludes: "Two subsequent resolutions offered from the floor—which would have mandated *withholding* of labor and/or outright strike—were ruled out of order." Box 78, Washington Reports, 1968, NYMAPUC.

82. John Cramer, "Postal Unions Revolt over Strike Law," *Washington Daily News*, August 26, 1968, reprinted in *Postal Record* (October 1968), 23. See also Levine, "Restive Postal Workers." At 87 percent, the post office was one of the most highly unionized employers in the nation.

83. Cramer, "Postal Unions Revolt"; and Levine, "Restive Postal Workers."

84. *Postal Record* (September 1968), 63.

85. Cramer, "Postal Unions Revolt"; "Fourth Day," NALC 1968 convention summary, *Postal Record* (September 1968), 63; and Levine, "Restive Postal Workers."

86. James Rademacher, "Urgency of Militant Unionism More Clear Now," *Postal Record* (May 1968), 6.

87. Levine, "Restive Postal Workers." The only other record of the 1967 Newark wildcat that I have found is James McHugh, "150 post office workers protest cut in overtime," *Newark Star-Ledger*, December 18, 1967, 9.

88. Committee on Post Office and Civil Service, *Towards Postal Excellence*, 2. See also Kathleen Conkey, *The Postal Precipice: Can the U.S. Postal Service Be Saved?* (Washington, D.C.: Center for the Study of Responsive Law, 1983), 42–45, on Kappel's privatization aims, and for a critique of the Kappel Commission's conclusion that a postal corporation was the only alternative to another catastrophe like the one in Chicago in 1966.

89. See Tierney, *Postal Reorganization*, 16–20; and Conkey, *Postal Precipice*, 45–49. By 1968, Postmaster General O'Brien was replaced in 1968 by W. Marvin Watson, who was in turn replaced in 1969 by Winton M. Blount with the 1968 election of Nixon to the White House. Tierney, *Postal Reorganization*, 11. See also "PM General Names EEO Task Force," *National Alliance* (July 1968), 7. This three-person task force was sent around the country to "review promotions procedures and other employment practices." It included Evelyn B. Anderson, a black female former New York City postal clerk then with the Office of Equal Employment Opportunity.

90. See Max Siderman, "Growl of the Wildcat Heard in POs As CSC Proposes Mini-Sized 4.1% Pay Raise," *Union Mail* (March 1969), 4; and "Nixon Exec. Order Implements 4.1% 'Nothing' Increase," *Union Mail* (June 1969), 1. See also Levine, "Restive Postal Workers."

91. Mikusko, *Carriers in a Common Cause*, 66–70. See also Branch 36 interview: their collective recollection is that the Kingsbridge strikers were initially fired, then given two-week suspensions. See also Al Marino, "A Time of Fury: The Postal Strike of 1970," 2001 Research Paper Workshop, Empire State College, May 15, 1982, in author's possession; and Max Siderman, " 'Innocent of Concerted Action'; Incident Wiped from All PO Records," *Union Mail* (July–August 1969), 1, with the main headline reading: " 'KB'ers' Are Cleared ... They're Back on Job!" The article hailed this as a "smashing win for unionism." See also "Contingency Plan" and "UFPC Policy Statement Opposes Work Stoppages," *Federation News Service*, July 3, 1969, 1; Box 3, Folder Officer's Files, NYMAPUC. The "direct order" that managers were instructed to give to any strikers under the 1969 "contingency plan" may have had in mind management's ambiguous response in the 1967 Newark walkout.

92. Loraine M. Huston, "Comments from Cleveland," *National Alliance* (September 1969), 9; and Williams, "Racism, Labor, and the Alliance." EO 11491 more resembled the unsuccessful Rhodes-Johnston bill of 1961 than President Kennedy's EO 10988 that was issued in its place. For Executive Order 11491, effective January 1, 1970, see EEOC website, <http://www.eeoc.gov> (September 10, 2008).

93. Snow Grigsby, "Editor's Notebook," *National Alliance* (December 1969), 4. Grigsby in his arguments invoked Gilliam, who had died in February 1968. On Gilliam, see cover and "Jerry O. Gilliam, President Emeritus National Alliance of Postal and Federal Employees," *National Alliance* (March 1968), 5.

94. Ned Young, "Union Board OKs Strike," *National Alliance* (December 1969), 6, reprint from *Washington News American*, November 26, 1969, 4-A; and Mike Causey, "Work Stoppage Threatened by Union," *National Alliance* (December 1969), 5–6, reprinted from *Washington Post*, November 26, 1969, B-9. The coalition was formed to fight Nixon's order. This article also noted that Smith's strike call, while ostensibly illegal, was probably protected as "the U.S. District Court here has ruled that the government's 'no strike' oath is unconstitutional." See also David Holmberg, "Alliance Hits Nixon Order," *National Alliance* (December 1969), 5, reprinted from *Washington Evening Star*, November 25, 1969, A-2.

95. Branch 36 interview; "Pay Raise Rally in New York City," *National Alliance* (May 1967), 22; "Demonstration at the White House, Pay Raise, Equal Employment Opportunity," *National Alliance* (September 1967), 8; and Ashby G. Smith, "From the President's Desk: Let's Begin the Debate!" *National Alliance* (December 1967), 2.

96. See also "News Release, Metropolitan Postal Council, March 5, 1964 [and also] May 23, 1965," Box 54, Folder Metro Postal Council Outdoor demo, NYMAPUC. New York Metro interview. See also "NPU says 'Nuts to 4.1%,'" *Progressive* (April 1969), 1; "The Pay-Nut Rally," *Union Mail* (May 1969), 4–5; and oral histories, Biller Files. The "whistle-blowing" rally was in 1967. See "Historic Pay Rally Rouses Capital; Nat'l Pay Demos Week of June 16th," *Progressive* (June 1967), 2.

97. See for example Sidney Goodman (NPU president), "The Time Had Come," editorial; and "The Right to Strike," *Progressive* (November 1967), 3. See also "Outlines 1970 Program," *Progressive* (February 1970), 1.

98. Marino, "A Time of Fury," 5–6; Brenner, "Striking against the State," 11, 122–23; and Mikusko, *Carriers in a Common Cause*, 72.

CHAPTER TEN

1. Author interview with Cleveland Morgan, July 18, 2005, New York.

2. Aaron Brenner, "Rank-and-File Rebellion, 1966–1975" (Ph.D. diss., Columbia University, 1996), 112.

3. Ibid., 145, italics added.

4. See Aaron Brenner, "Striking against the State: The Postal Wildcat of 1970," *Labor's Heritage* (Spring 1996), 4–27, based on a chapter in his "Rank-and-File Rebellion," 112–46. As of this writing, no book-length scholarly study has been done on the 1970 strike. Some references to it are contained within larger studies: see J. Joseph Loewenberg, "The Post Office Strike of 1970," in *Collective Bargaining in Government: Readings and Cases*, ed. Loewenberg and Michael H. Moskow (Englewood Cliffs, N.J.: Prentice-Hall, 1972), 192–215; John Walsh and Garth Mangum, *Labor Struggle in the Post Office: From Selective Lobbying to Collective Bargaining* (Armonk, New York: M. E. Sharpe, 1992), part 1; M. Brady Mikusko, *Carriers in a*

Common Cause: A History of Letter Carriers and the NALC (Washington, D.C.: NALC, 1989); and Martin Halpern, *Unions, Radicals, and Democratic Presidents: Seeking Social Change in the Twentieth Century* (Westport, Conn.: Praeger, 2003), chap. 5. See also Stephen Shannon, "Work Stoppage in Government: The Postal Strike of 1970," *Monthly Labor Review* 101, no. 7 (July 1978), 14–22; Robert H. Zieger and Gilbert J. Gall, *American Workers, American Unions*, 3rd ed. (1986; Baltimore: Johns Hopkins University Press, 2002), 211–12; Jeremy Brecher, *Strike!*, revised and updated ed. (1972; Boston: South End Press, 1997), 258–60; and Stanley Aronowitz and Jeremy Brecher, "Notes on the Postal Strike," *Root and Branch* 1 (1970), 1–5. I am grateful to the authors for sharing their articles with me.

5. "Task Force Says 84% of Postal Employees Are in Unions," *Progressive* (December 1961), 4 (this refers to "President Kennedy's Task Force Report"). See also Committee on Post Office and Civil Service, House of Representatives, *Towards Postal Excellence: The Report of the President's Commission on Postal Organization, June 1968*, 94th Cong., 2nd sess. (1968; Washington, D.C.: Government Printing Office, 1976), 18–19; Rep. Carl B. Stokes (D-Ohio), "Employment and Politics: Cornerstone of Democracy," address to NAPFE annual congressional dinner, Washington, D.C., *National Alliance* (May 1966), 16; and John C. Leggett, *Class, Race, and Labor: Working-Class Consciousness in Detroit* (New York: Oxford University Press, 1968).

6. Brenner, "Rank-and-File Rebellion"; Walsh and Mangum, *Labor Struggle*, part 1; and Al Marino, "A Time of Fury: The Postal Strike of 1970" (1982 Empire State College research paper), 11. See also Patrick J. Nilan (then-UFPC Legislative Director), "Union Lobbying at the Federal Level," in *Collective Bargaining in Government*, 221–27. Lobbying "from below" included informational picketing and letter writing.

7. See Brenner, "Rank-and-File Rebellion," 122–23; and Mikusko, *Carriers in a Common Cause*, 72.

8. Author interview with Jeff Perry and Richard Thomas, July 18, 2005, New York. On mail handler figures see Committee on Post Office and Civil Service, House of Representatives, 94th Cong., 2nd sess., November 24, 1976, *Towards Postal Excellence*, 100. On mail handlers see United States Civil Service Commission, Manpower Statistics Division, *Occupations of Federal Blue-Collar Workers*, Pamphlet 59-2 (Washington, D.C.: Government Printing Office, October 31, 1960), 5.

9. "A Personal Narrative by NALC President Vincent R. Sombrotto, Written February 20, 1995: 1970 Postal Strike," NALC Library, Washington, D.C.

10. "Moe Biller's Remarks for Panel Discussion, 25th Anniversary of the 1970 Postal Strike, National Postal Museum, Smithsonian Institution, Washington, D.C., March 17, 1995," NALC Library, Washington, D.C., italics added. The APWU was the successor to the NPU and other clerk unions that merged in 1971.

11. The MBPU in 1973 became the New York Metro Area Postal Union of the American Postal Workers Union (NYMAPU-APWU), of which Biller in 1995 was its national president. Biller quotation originally appeared in Damon Stetson, "Postal Employees Protest 4% Raise," *New York Times*, June 21, 1969, and quoted in Brenner, "Rank-and-File Rebellion," 125.

12. See Branch 36 interview. Marino, Orapello, and Sombrotto hailed from immigrant Italian families, very common in the New York post office. Orapello and Sombrotto also both had fathers who were city workers.

13. See New York Metro interview. See also Stetson, "Union Chief"; and John Darnton, "Postman's Pay Just $2 a Week Too High for Welfare," *New York Times*, March 25, 1970, 31.

See also Murray Schumach, "Simmering Discontent Sparked Strike," in *New York Times*, March 25, 1970, 31, on Branch 36's 1967 campaigns against the "no-strike" clause for government employees.

14. Brenner, "Rank-and-File Rebellion," 137–38.

15. Branch 36 interview.

16. NALC president James Rademacher began his editorial in *Postal Record* (June 1970) by quoting Mahatma Gandhi: *"These are my people, I must hurry and try to keep up with them, for I am their leader."* For Nixon's emergency order see 1970 strike material, unprocessed box, USPS Archives. Figures vary somewhat on the total numbers of workers and offices involved in the strike. See for example "Status Report 12, Prepared by POD Control Room, 3/24/70, 1:00 PM," including 132,642 clerks and other crafts (64 percent), and 76,052 carriers, or 36 percent. The postal regions most affected (with numbers of local post offices struck in parentheses) included New York (220), Philadelphia (215), Chicago (84), San Francisco (51), Boston (31), followed by Cincinnati and Minneapolis (both with 14) and Denver (11). Regions unaffected included Atlanta, Dallas, Memphis, St. Louis, Seattle, Washington, D.C., and Wichita. See Status Reports, 1970 strike material, unprocessed box, USPS Archives. See also there "March 1970 Work Stoppage," unsigned postal management memo, July 17, 1970, that listed 671 offices and 152,000 workers as having been involved. That became the figure the post office publicized, but no reason was given for their revising downward the number of strikers. The troops were from the National Guard and the U.S. Army, Navy, Air Force, and Marines. See also Postmaster General Winton Blount press conference, March 24, 1970, Washington, D.C.; and Statement, March 19, 1970, USPS Archives. See also Walsh and Mangum, *Labor Struggle*, 70: they note that 14 percent of strikers were not in clerk or carrier crafts.

17. See Walsh and Mangum, *Labor Struggle*, 70. See also "More Than Ever—NPU," *Progressive* (April 1970), for estimates of their striking members, NPU's vital role in strike, and protest of NPU's exclusion along with NAPFE by the AFL-CIO unions. On the various postal unions see Committee on Post Office and Civil Service, *Towards Postal Excellence*, 19.

18. Conversation with anonymous retired letter carrier and NALC member, October 25, 2005, Durham, N.C.

19. New York Metro interview.

20. Brenner, "Rank-and-File Rebellion," 130–31; "Chronology of Legislative Events Affecting NALC, 1969–1970," *Postal Record* (May 1970), 13; and Harold E. Dolenga, "An Analytical Case Study of the Policy Formation Process (Postal Reform and Reorganization)" (Ph.D. diss., Northwestern University, 1973), esp. 229–32, 511–61.

21. Frank Orapello, "1970 Postal Strike," New York Letter Carriers Branch 36 website, <http://www.nylcbr36.org/history.htm> (September 10, 2008).

22. There are still differences of opinion between some NALC and APWU strike veterans in New York City. Some NALC officers believe that the APWU did not actually strike but did respect the NALC picket line. APWU officers insist that they joined the NALC-led strike. The records in the APWU collection at Tamiment/Wagner corroborate the APWU officers' narrative. See also Walsh and Mangum, *Labor Struggle*, chap. 2. See also *The Postal Strike—March 1970: Draft, September 21, 1970*, 30, in 1970 strike material, unprocessed box, USPS Archives.

23. See New York Metro interview and conversation with Cleveland Morgan, October 15, 2004, New York.

24. See Moe Biller interview with Dana Schecter, oral history transcript, July 7, 1976, New York, Box 4, Folder 1976, Biller Files. See also Branch 36 interview.

25. See Brenner, "Rank-and-File Rebellion," esp. 112; and Mikusko, *Carriers in a Common Cause*. See also New York Metro interview; Branch 36 interview; Morgan interview, 2005; and Morgan conversation, 2004. See also Orapello, "1970 Postal Strike."

26. Brenner, "Rank-and-File Rebellion," 132. See also Branch 36 interview.

27. See New York Metro interview; and Perry and Thomas interview.

28. New York Metro interview.

29. Telephone interview with Raydell Moore, January 13, 2006, Pahrump, Nev.

30. Branch 36 interview. See also "Slow Boil, Quick Blast, No Mail," *New York Daily News*, March 19, 1970 (n.p.), in 1970 strike material, unprocessed box, USPS Archives.

31. New York Metro interview; Walsh and Mangum, *Labor Struggle*, chap. 2.

32. Damon Stetson, "Letter Carriers Defy Injunction Ordering Them Back to Work," *New York Times*, March 19, 1970, 52. It was a fortuitous coincidence that this was a regularly scheduled meeting.

33. Biller oral history with Schecter; New York Metro interview. See also Walsh and Mangum, *Labor Struggle*, 22.

34. Walsh and Mangum, *Labor Struggle*, 21.

35. Ibid., 22.

36. Ibid., 23. See ibid., 22, for Biller's "vivid" memory of a "hard working" black shop steward "with tears rolling down his cheeks" pleading with him to leave the podium to avoid bloodshed. See also Biller interview with Schecter.

37. Biller interview with Schecter.

38. Perry and Thomas interview.

39. Branch 36 interview.

40. Author interview with Countee Abbott, August 12, 2004, Washington, D.C.

41. See for example Peter Kriss, "10,000 Mailmen Vote to Continue Walkout in 4 Large Cities," *New York Times*, March 24, 1970, 1; and "The Day the Mail Stopped." The Post Office Status Report number 7—a two-page summary report issued March 23, 1970, at 12 midnight, six days into the strike—lists the percentages of striking offices by region and city. Chicago, Denver, and San Francisco were exceptions. In Chicago, for example, 15,000 clerks struck versus 26,000 carriers. Looking at percentages by region as of March 23, 1970, two-thirds of Boston's clerks had returned, compared to 54 percent of its carriers; for New York it was 1 percent versus 4 percent; Philadelphia, 73 percent versus 79 percent; Cincinnati, zero versus 5 percent; Chicago, 12 percent versus 11 percent; Minneapolis, 16 percent versus 11 percent; Denver, 38 percent versus 96 percent; and San Francisco, 35 percent versus 44 percent. The city of Detroit reported 19 percent of its clerks and none of its carriers back at work by that date, Cleveland had 2 percent of its clerks and none of its carriers, Brooklyn had the same figures, Los Angeles had 68 percent of its clerks and 95 percent of its carriers, Denver 50 percent of its clerks and no carriers, while Minneapolis had no clerks or carriers back by then. See Report No. 7, Summary Report, 3/23/70, 12 midnight, 1970 Strike Folders, Status Reports, 1970 strike material, unprocessed box, USPS Archives.

42. Author interview with Doug Holbrook, August 16, 2005, Washington, D.C. See also photo caption, "Clenched fists indicate the feelings of 4,000 Detroit postal workers who shouted down a union leadership proposal that they return to their jobs today," *Cleveland Plain Dealer*, March 23, 1970, 1. See also the NALC Detroit Branch 1 voting 3–1 to return to work "after the Washington agreement was announced" in Lawrence Van Gelder, "Many Cities Hurt," *New York Times*, March 21, 1970, 12. On the 1941 Ford strike see August Meier

and Elliot Rudwick, *Black Detroit and the Rise of the UAW* (Oxford: Oxford University Press, 1981), 88–89. An interesting parallel to Detroit's strike vote came in the southern industrial center of Charleston, West Virginia, home of the United Mine Workers struggles for many years. Roger Kennedy, a *Postal Record* "branch scribe" from Charleston, announced in the May issue that the strike had brought local intercraft unity: "We have agreed in the future to present a united front to local management." Roger Kennedy, "Charleston, W. Va.," *Postal Record* (May 1970), 72.

43. Leo Brown, "President's Desk," *Alliance Leader* (March–April–May 1970), 1. Detroit's cross-craft unity is all the more remarkable given that few carriers worked out of the main post office.

44. Abbott interview.

45. "Mailmen Defy Plea; But Set Parley Today," *Chicago Tribune*, March 22, 1970, 2.

46. See James Strong, "City, Suburbs Face Shutting of All Service," *Chicago Tribune*, March 21, 1970, 1; and James Strong and Rudolph Unger, "6 Suburbs Vote to End Strike," *Chicago Tribune*, March 24, 1970, 4.

47. Author interview with William H. Burrus Jr., January 16, 2009, Washington, D.C. See also Status Reports, March 22–24, 1970, 1970 strike material, unprocessed box, USPS Archives.

48. Harry Bernstein, "Letter Carriers in L.A. to Back April 15 Walkout," *Los Angeles Times*, March 20, 1970, 1; Robert Kistler and Robert Rawitch, "Wildcat Mail Strike Spreading in L.A. Suburban Areas," *Los Angeles Times*, March 22, 1970, 1; "Restraining Order Issued in S. F. Tieup," in *Los Angeles Times*, March 22, 1970, 22; Kistler, "Central L.A. Tie-Up Possible Despite Union Leaders' Pleas," *Los Angeles Times*, March 23, 1970, 1. When Thomas was promoted to superintendent of compensation in the Los Angeles post office, it was publicized by the Alliance. See "Los Angeles, Calif.," photo caption, *Postal Alliance* (February 1964), 15. See also Doug Shuit, "Letter Carriers Return to Most Stations in L.A.," *Los Angeles Times*, March 24, 1970, 1; and "L.A. Mail Service Near Normal as Carriers Reject Walkout," *Los Angeles Times*, March 25, 1970, 3. See also Moore interview.

49. Walsh and Mangum, *Labor Struggle*, 145. See also author interview with Joseph Henry, August 15, 2005, Washington, D.C., and telephone conversation with Joseph Henry, August 18, 2005. See also Committee on Post Office and Civil Service, *Towards Postal Excellence*, 102, that makes the point that by July 1967, 88 percent of all postal workers worked at only 15 percent of its offices, and the ten largest offices employed more than 22 percent of all workers, in order from the largest: New York (Manhattan), 41,406; Chicago, 28,229; Boston, 14,195; Los Angeles, 13,588; Philadelphia, 12,014; Washington, D.C., 11,349; San Francisco, 10,228; Detroit, 9,865; Cleveland, 9,242; and Brooklyn, 8,638. By 1960 only Boston had a small percentage of blacks at the post office (3.4 percent); in Detroit it was 49.7 percent, Cleveland, 40.6 percent, and Philadelphia, 39.2 percent, while Chicago, Los Angeles, and D.C. were all majority-black. See Henry W. McGee, *The Negro in the Chicago Post Office: Henry W. McGee Autobiography and Dissertation* (Chicago: VolumeOne Press, 1999) (originally "The Negro in the Chicago Post Office," master's thesis, University of Chicago, 1961), 91 (*Dissertation*).

50. Henry interview. See also Holbrook interview. The Lanham, Maryland, NALC branch voted to strike at midnight on March 22, according to the 2 P.M. Post Office Status Report for that day, but the March 23, 10 A.M. Status Report reported no strike activity there. Status Reports, 1970 strike material, unprocessed box, USPS Archives. I have not seen any union sources to confirm this, however.

51. Frank Walin, "City Carriers Set Saturday Deadline," *Richmond Times-Dispatch*, March 24, 1970, 1. See also "No Area Postal Woes Forecast," *New Orleans Times-Picayune*, March 22, 1970, 1. See also "Postal Force Here Awaits Union Ruling," *Atlanta Constitution*, March 24, 1970, 8C; and James Roper, "25 Called Here: Air Reservists Activated; Memphis Carriers Vote to Stay on Job," *Memphis Commercial Appeal*, March 24, 1970, 1.

52. Author interview with Sam Armstrong and Samuel Lovett. See also Henry interview.

53. In the post office's "status report number 12," March 24, 1970, 1 P.M., on the seventh day of the strike 384 offices had returned to work out of 640: that is, 40 percent of the original striking offices were still on strike, 200 in the New York region alone (which includes New Jersey), 29 in the Philadelphia region, and the rest scattered around the country. The Philadelphia region includes Pennsylvania, Virginia, Maryland, Delaware, and West Virginia. There was either strike activity or strike votes reported in the Alliance strongholds of Baltimore, Richmond, and Philadelphia—also an NPU stronghold—with Virginia hosting historically black activist NALC branches as well. Folder Strike Report, unprocessed box, USPS Archives.

54. Vern K. Baxter, *Labor and Politics in the U.S. Postal Service* (New York: Plenum, 1994), 2.

55. Telephone conversation with Joyce Robinson, July 1, 2005, Washington, D.C., APWU headquarters. See also telephone conversation with retired Richmond Local 199 and national UFPC official Walter Kenney Sr., January 24, 2009. Kenney remembers discussion but not voting in Richmond.

56. See for example "City Carriers to Vote Tomorrow on Strike," *Richmond Times-Dispatch*, March 22, 1970, A-4; Walin, "City Carriers"; "Post Offices Hold Much N.C. Mail," *Charlotte Observer*, March 20, 1970, 1; "No Strike Likely Here," *Charlotte Observer*, March 21, 1970, 1; and Cheree Briggs, "Mailmen to Talk Work Stoppage," *Charlotte Observer*, March 22, 1970, 1.

57. John Susleck, "San Francisco, Ca.," *Postal Record* (May 1970), 92.

58. Art Miller, "Buffalo, N.Y.," ibid., 72.

59. Raymond Weiss, "Flushing, N.Y.," ibid., 76. The concept of "area wages" calls for higher wages for postal workers in regions with higher standards of living.

60. Ted R. Little, "Winston-Salem, N.C.," *Postal Record* (September 1970), 119. Among the NALC "loyalists" were the Fall River, Mass., branch, while Framingham, Mass., carriers proudly upheld it, noting shop floor issues as well as pay. *Postal Record* (September 1970), 76. Dubuque, Iowa, also opposed the strike, as did Toledo and Columbus, although Cleveland supported it. See "Branch Items," *Postal Record* (May 1970), 73–74, 95. Another interesting development was the appearance in the pages of the *Postal Record* of more Latino scribes, most in the West, and most supporting the strike. See for example John Mendez of San Fernando, *Postal Record* (May 1970), 92; David F. Ortega, "Oakland, Ca.," *Postal Record* (June 1970), 74–75; Jose Baltazar, "Houston, Tex.," *Postal Record* (June 1970), 69; and Tony Montanez, "Miami, Fla.," *Postal Record* (August 1970), 53, the latter being a conciliatory column.

61. Roland W. Pain, "Albany, Ga.," *Postal Record* (August 1970), 43–44. The reference is to the predominantly white radical-left Students for a Democratic Society that split in 1969, its ultra-left Weatherman faction being the last remnants of the organization and occupants of its national headquarters in Chicago. See for example Kirkpatrick Sale, *SDS* (New York: Vintage Books, 1974), and David Barber, *A Hard Rain Fell: SDS and Why It Failed* (Jackson: University Press of Mississippi, 2008).

62. Herman Sandbank, "New York, N.Y.," *Postal Record* (June 1970), 74. On Albany in

the civil rights movement see for example Aldon D. Morris, *The Origins of the Civil Rights Movement: Black Communities Organizing for Change* (New York: Free Press, 1986), 239–50.

63. In *Postal Record* (May 1970) see "Birmingham, Ala.," 72; Jose Baltazar, "Houston, Tex.," 79; and "Chronology of Legislative Events," 13.

64. Brenner, "Striking against the State," 17. See also Walsh and Mangum, *Labor Struggle*, 25–27; "Chronology of Legislative Events," 13–15; Grace Lichtenstein, "Military Worked in Other Strikes," *New York Times*, March 23, 1970, 36; and "President's Statement, Order and Proclamation," *New York Times*, March 24, 1970, 34.

65. See for example " 'Survival of Government,' " editorial, *New York Times*, March 24, 1970, 46.

66. New York Metro interview and Branch 36 interview. See also interview with Philip Seligman by Dana Schecter, June 29, 1976, New York, Box 4, Folder 1976, Biller Files: "My son-in-law happened to be in the national guard. . . . He was telling people to mis-box a lot mail." See also Elsie Resnick, interviewed by Milt Rosner, November 26, 1976, Biller Files: "And they threw mail into any bag just to get rid of the mail." See also Marino, "A Time of Fury," 9–10, in possession of author; Brenner, "Striking against the State," 17, 20; and Loewenberg, "Post Office Strike."

67. Marino, "Time of Fury"; Branch 36 interview; New York Metro interview.

68. "First Day on a New Job," front-page photo caption, *New York Times*, March 25, 1970. There were even stories that some carriers in New York took their "case strips" with them when they struck. Each mail route has a metal case with paper address labels connected in a long plastic strip called "case strips." Removing them would make it impossible to efficiently organize mail for delivery. Henry interview. See also "Women in Queens, N.Y., Welcome Back Carrier Victor Oleaga," front-page photo caption, *Atlanta Constitution*, March 26, 1970; and George Gallup, "80% Favor Higher Pay for Postmen," *Los Angeles Times*, March 26, 1970, 11.

69. See Howard Zinn, *A People's History of the United States* (1980; New York: Harper, 1990), chap. 18.

70. Perry and Thomas interview; Morgan interview.

71. Marino, "Time of Fury," 11; Holbrook interview.

72. See "Women in Queens." See also "Chicago: Henry McGee puts his arms around letter carriers starting rounds," photo caption, *New York Times*, March 25, 1970, 31; "New York Postmaster John N. Strachan leads Manhattan letter carriers down post office steps as deliveries resume," *Washington Post*, March 27, 1970, A1. See also "Troops Move Out: Leader of City Union That Began Strike Urged Return"; plus photo caption, "Postal workers wave to soldiers leaving main post office," *New York Times*, March 26, 1970, 1; Loewenberg, "Post Office Strike," 198; and Walsh and Mangum, *Labor Struggle*, 27. Gus Johnson told Moe Biller that Shultz's "agreement" called for a 12 percent pay raise retroactive to October 1969, paid health benefits, "compression" of top pay from twenty-one to eight years, area wage calculations, full collective bargaining, and amnesty for strikers. Fines were threatened both to Johnson and Biller and their respective locals beginning 5 P.M. March 25 if the unions did not agree to end the strike. Biller had wanted to phone Blount first to verify the offer, but he was unsuccessful. With Branch 36 heading back to work, Biller felt he had no choice but to recommend to an MBPU mass meeting that afternoon that they return to work while he went to Washington to verify the agreement's validity. Those in attendance voted to return.

73. Larry Isaac and Lars Christiansen, "How the Civil Rights Movement Revitalized

Labor Militancy," *American Sociological Review* 67, no. 5 (October 2002), 722–46, esp. 738. See also Brenner, "Striking against the State," 27n37; and Branch 36 interview.

74. Loewenberg, "Post Office Strike," 210.

75. Isaac and Christiansen, "How the Civil Rights Movement."

76. Abbott interview.

77. Daniel M. Johnson and Rex R. Campbell, *Black Migration in America: A Social Demographic History* (Durham, N.C.: Duke University Press, 1981), 154–55.

78. "Balance of Power," *National Alliance* (January 1972), 4.

79. See for example Patricia Stemper, "Letter Carriers Say Wages Put Them at Hardship Level," *Chicago Tribune*, March 22, 1970, 2; Al Prince, "City Mailmen Sitting Tight, May Vote on Strike Friday," *Houston Post*, March 25, 1970, 3, with accompanying photograph of a mass meeting showing a number of African American clerk union members, especially women; and, in the same issue, section 2, page 2, for a staged photo of three "postal wives"—symbolically framed as one white, one black, and one Latina—the latter Emily Baltazar, the wife of Houston NALC Branch 183 scribe Jose Baltazar. See also Peter Millones, "Postal Pay for Typical Carrier Falls below U.S. Standards Here," *New York Times*, March 20, 1970, 40; Neil Maurer, "D.C. Mailmen Air Complaints," *Washington Post*, March 24, 1970, A8; *New York Times*, March 18–28, 1970; *Washington Post*, March 21–28, 1970; *New York Amsterdam News*, "Independent Postal Union Has Own Fight," March 28, 1970, 59; *New York Times*, March 19, 1970, 1, 52; and Walsh and Mangum, *Labor Struggle*, chap. 2. By contrast, in their strike coverage the black press only demonstrated concern with the National Alliance's viability.

80. Herman B. Sandbank, "New York, N.Y.," *Postal Record* (May 1970), 85.

81. Homer Bigart, "Walkout Widens: Almost Half of Nation Is Affected—Clerks Here Vote to Strike," *New York Times*, March 22, 1970, 1.

82. Perry and Thomas interview.

83. "Chronology of Legislative Events," 13.

84. See Millones, "Postal Pay," about a Bronx black letter carrier with twenty-three years: James Troupe, forced to moonlight at a dry cleaners because of low postal pay. See also the daily "box" titled "Issues in the Postal Walkout," *New York Times*, March 22, 1970, 70, noting postal worker demands for pay commensurate with other civil servants and congressional and presidential motion in the direction of granting raises and turning the mails over to "an independent postal authority." See also Gallup, "80% Favor Higher Pay"; Walsh and Mangum, *Labor Struggle*, 24.

85. Brenner, "Rank-and-File Rebellion," 112. A contrast can be made here between the height of the Cold War in the early 1970s and the World War II antifascist and pre–Cold War anticommunist period. NALC president Rademacher accused SDS of infiltrating the union, but he failed miserably in his attempt to red-bait the strikers. Internally, postal management decried the presence in Los Angeles of "hippy types" from SDS, the Black Panther Party, and the Progressive Labor Party, who were "obviously not postal workers" picketing in support of the postal strikers. The Nixon administration tried to make sure that the media ran stories that this was Nixon's "domestic equivalent to the Cuban missile crisis." But if so they failed, as I have found no such reference from that period in the media. See "confidential memo" from Jeb S. Magruder to H. R. Haldeman, March 26, 1970, 1970 strike material, unprocessed box, USPS Archives.

86. Brenner, "Rank-and-File Rebellion," 124.

87. Ibid., 128. See also Donald Flynn, "$3 an hour to Start, $4 After 21 Years," *New York*

Daily News, March 19, 1970, 3–4: a "human interest" profile of four striking postal workers included Germano's story, as well as that of a black female clerk named Sylvia Cutts. NAPFE historian Paul Tennassee claims that members of the Black Panther Party and the Nation of Islam were involved in the New York strike vote. Paul Tennassee, conversation with author, November 23, 2001, Washington, D.C. The degree to which this is true, their influence on the vote, and whether they were present as union members or merely interested observers is still not clear.

88. New York Metro interview.

89. Ibid.

90. Morgan interview.

91. Perry and Thomas interview; New York Metro interview. At that time most postal workers were in the lowest four levels: clerks and carriers who today are mostly level 5 then were level 4, which is today's mail handler level, although they were just below clerks and carriers then. In fact, when mail handlers at level 3 step 3 in July 1969 were making $2.71 an hour, level 4 step 3 clerks and carriers were paid $2.80 an hour, a difference of only nine cents an hour. See "Post Field Service," *National Alliance* (September 1969), 8. Four years after Rep. Stokes noted how only slightly more than a thousand blacks worked above level 4, by April 1970 Snow Grigsby wrote: "There are 132,011 black employees in the postal service. Of this number 123,632 are concentrated in the low 1 through 4 pay grades." See "Editor's Notebook," *National Alliance* (April 1970), 4.

92. See for example a recollection by an anonymous strike veteran and member of the ultra-left Progressive Labor Party in "Black Workers Inspired 1970 Postal Workers' Wildcat," June 6, 1996, *Challenge* online edition <http://www.plp.org> (November 12, 2005).

93. Walin, "City Carriers"; and "Census Form Delay Looms If Mailmen Strike Here," *Richmond Times-Dispatch*, March 25, 1970, 1. An added worry for the government was the U.S. census forms for 1970 that were due to go out soon in the mail.

94. Henry interview. See also Michael Wright and Alex Coffin, "Union Rejects Offers by City, Goes on Strike," *Atlanta Constitution*, March 18, 1970, 1. City workers rejected Atlanta's offer of a 25 percent pay raise to $2.13 an hour. See also "Atlanta Branch Marches, Petitions Congressman," *National Alliance* (September 1969), 19. See also interview with Moore.

95. See Joshua B. Freeman, *Working-Class New York: Life and Labor since World War II* (New York: New Press, 2000); Winston James, *Holding Aloft the Banner of Ethiopia: Caribbean Radicalism in Early Twentieth-Century America* (London: Verso, 2000); Leon Fink and Brian Greenberg, *Upheaval in the Quiet Zone: A History of Hospital Workers' Union, Local 1199* (Urbana: University of Illinois Press, 1989); Bruce Nelson, *Divided We Stand: American Workers and the Struggle for Black Equality* (Princeton, N.J.: Princeton University Press, 2001), chap. 2; and Martha Biondi, *To Stand and Fight: The Struggle for Civil Rights in Postwar New York City* (Cambridge, Mass.: Harvard University Press, 2003).

96. Exploited workers may suddenly leap from resignation to rebellion in collective struggle, according to the social theory of Karl Marx, "Preface to a Contribution to the Critique of Political Economy," in Karl Marx and Frederick Engels, *Selected Works* (New York: International Publishers, 1974), 183. Narratives of pre-strike postal worker "docility" were commonplace. See also "The Day the Mail Stopped," *Newsweek*, March 30, 1970, 14: "And never in the 195 years of their history had the docile servants of the world's largest mail service raised so much as a pinky in organized protest."

1. Author interview with William H. Burrus Jr., January 16, 2009, Washington, D.C.

2. Author interview with Richard Thomas and Jeff Perry, July 18, 2005, New York.

3. Branch 36 interview.

4. Ibid.

5. Burrus interview.

6. The "exclusive" unions were those with that official status under Nixon's executive order: the six AFL-CIO postal unions and the independent National Association of Rural Letter Carriers. See also "Chronology of Legislative Events Affecting NALC, 1969–1970," *Postal Record* (May 1970), 8, 12, 13, 17. Collective bargaining rights were also included in the March 12, 1970, House Committee compromise.

7. New York Metro interview.

8. Branch 36 interview.

9. Author interview with Joseph Henry, August 15, 2005, Washington, D.C.; telephone conversation with Joseph Henry, August 18, 2005.

10. Author interview with Countee Abbott, August 12, 2004, Washington, D.C. See also Paul Tennassee, "The Smith Presidency Part XI," *National Alliance* (December 2002), 18–21.

11. Ibid. See also for example John Walsh and Garth Mangum, *Labor Struggle in the Post Office: From Selective Lobbying to Collective Bargaining* (Armonk, N.Y.: M. E. Sharpe, 1992); M. Brady Mikusko, *Carriers in a Common Cause: A History of Letter Carriers and the NALC* (Washington, D.C.: NALC, 1989); and Aaron Brenner, "Striking against the State: The Postal Wildcat of 1970," *Labor's Heritage* (Spring 1996), 4–27.

12. It took Congress five months to pass the PRA, in part because of two major "distractions": Nixon's Cambodia invasion and debates over "right to work" legislation. See Walsh and Mangum, *Labor Struggle*, chap. 3. On the NPU/NAPFE lawsuit, see Box 45, Folder Counsel Files *NPU et. al. v. Blount*, NYMAPUC. On the Alliance's losing battles for collective bargaining status after the strike, see for example Paul Nehru Tennassee, "NAPFE Battles in Congress, 1970–1976, Part I," *National Alliance* (May 2004), 17–19; and "NAPFE Battles in Congress, 1970–1976, Part II," *National Alliance* (June 2004), 12–14. On the APWU merger see "Five Postal Unions Sign Merger Agreement," [UFPC] *Federation News Service*, March 4, 1971, 1, Box 78, Folder 1971, NYMAPUC: included besides the NPU and the UFPC were the NAPOGSME, the NFPOMVE, and the NASDM. All but the NPU were AFL-CIO unions. African American presidents of postal unions included Monroe Crable of the Maintenance union and Lonnie Johnson of the NPMHU (not part of the APWU merger). See also Marvin J. Levine, "The U.S. Postal Service: A Labor Relations Hybrid," *Employee Relations Law Journal* 4, no. 2 (1978), 227. In the post office and other agencies covered by the Civil Service Act, "adverse actions" include suspensions and discharges, while grievances cover working conditions. After Executive Order 11491 went into effect, the Alliance lost those rights in the USPS, although they can still process EEO complaints, NLRB unfair labor practices, adverse action at the appeal level for veterans under the MSPB (Merit Systems Protection Board, begun in 1979), and judicial review. See Tennassee, "NAPFE Battles I"; "NAPFE Battles II"; and NAPFE website <http://www.napfe.com> (November 12, 2005).

13. Postmaster General Winton Blount, "Second Press Conference on Work Stoppage," March 24, 1970, Washington, D.C., transcript, unprocessed box, USPS Archives.

14. Ibid. New York postal workers I interviewed expressed having been surprised at the time that Nixon, while talking tough on television, was conciliatory behind the scenes, as Richard Thomas remembers: "It was a little shocking that President Nixon was pushing it, because he was a 'law and order' guy. We thought we'd have to bump heads. . . . The only thing we got penalized was five days of pay, but we were willing to go through it." Cleveland Morgan had a similar observation of Nixon: "Everybody talks about Nixon," he said, "but he did a favor to us by turning us around with the postal service." See interview with author Cleveland Morgan, July 18, 2005, New York; and author interview with Jeff Perry and Richard Thomas, July 18, 2005, New York. See also Walsh and Mangum, *Labor Struggle*, chap. 3.

15. Internal memo (n.d., probably late March 1970) from Brian Gillespie to John M. Remissong, Director, Labor Relations Division, Bureau of Personnel, 1970 strike material, unprocessed box, USPS Archives.

16. Aaron Brenner, "Rank-and-File Rebellion, 1966–1975" (Ph.D. diss., Columbia University, 1996), 112–46.

17. "Draft [of] 'The Postal Strike—March 1970,'" September 21, 1970, 1970 strike material, unprocessed box, USPS Archives.

18. An ardent opponent of the March 1970 wildcat, NALC president Rademacher vowed to the NALC March 20 Emergency Conference that he would lead an illegal walkout himself the following week if an agreement was not reached within five days. See Mikusko, *Carriers in a Common Cause*, 75. Years later, Rademacher was heard to boast during the 1975 contract negotiations that he had at his disposal "dial a strike"—letter carriers poised at his command to walk off the job if asked. In 1971, after nearly six months of negotiations without a single wage offer from management, the formation of the APWU in July 1971 helped break the management-imposed impasse during contract negotiations as MBPU 1970 strike veterans threatened to strike again. See Kathleen Conkey, *The Postal Precipice: Can the U.S. Postal Service Be Saved?* (Washington, D.C.: Center for the Study of Responsive Law, 1983), 143–49.

19. See for example Mikusko, *Carriers in a Common Cause*; Brenner, "Rank-and-File Rebellion"; Walsh and Mangum, *Labor Struggle*, 92–93; and Martin Halpern, *Unions, Radicals, and Democratic Presidents: Seeking Social Change in the Twentieth Century* (Westport, Conn.: Praeger, 2003), chap. 5. See also Jeremy Brecher, *Strike!*, revised and updated ed. (1972; Boston: South End Press, 1997); and Robert H. Zieger and Gilbert J. Gall, *American Workers, American Unions*, 3rd ed. (1986; Baltimore: Johns Hopkins University Press, 2002), 211–12. As far as the abolition of the "formal" recognition status that the Alliance and NPU both enjoyed, an executive order by President Johnson had eliminated the "informal" recognition category, but Nixon's elimination of "formal" recognition was much more serious. See also *Postal Reorganization Act [PRA]*, August 12, 1970, *Statutes at Large* 84; and Stephen Shannon, "Work Stoppage in Government: The Postal Strike of 1970," *Monthly Labor Review* 101, no. 7 (July 1978), 14–22. Shannon argues on page 21: "Two amendments were added to protect minority unions and to prevent the union shop." That was the intent but not the reality of the law. See for example an article by Sen. Charles Goodell (R-N.Y.) and Rep. Robert Nix (D-Pa.) titled "Congress Did Not Intend That the National Alliance Be Frozen Out during the Transitional Bargaining," *National Alliance* (April 1972), 7. The original Nixon administration postal reform bill (supported by the craft unions) provided for "national craft units." The PRA rejected that language in Sections 10, 1202, and 1203 in favor of the NLRB taking one to two years to determine appropriate bargaining units,

allowing the current seven "exclusive" craft unions the right to collectively bargain, while Section 1205 provided for voluntary dues deduction. Despite congressional support for the two industrial unions' right to compete, Section 1203 of the PRA accorded "exclusive recognition" to any union selected by the majority in a given unit. It did not allow for multiple forms of recognition, at most allowing for a new election if "at least 30 percent" of unit employees filed a protest petition. With no new elections held, the already exclusively recognized unions became a *fait accompli*. See also Executive Order 11491 at EEOC website, <http://www.eeoc.gov> (September 10, 2008); and "The Position of the National Alliance of Postal and Federal Employees on the Post Office Strike, Postal Corporation, Pay Increases and Union Representation," *National Alliance* (May 1970), 6.

20. Blount, "Second Press Conference." See also Clyde Young, "The Great 'Sellout,'" *National Alliance* (August 1970), 5. See also Halpern, *Unions, Radicals, and Democratic Presidents*, chap. 5. According to Halpern, the AFL-CIO had historically not demonstrated much interest in winning collective bargaining rights for federal workers—before the 1970 postal wildcat strike.

21. Mikusko, *Carriers in a Common Cause*, 76–77.

22. See PRA, part 1, chap. 2, sec. 201, 720; Vern K. Baxter, *Labor and Politics in the U.S. Postal Service* (New York: Plenum, 1994), 91–93; Shannon, "Work Stoppage in Government"; and Levine, "The U.S. Postal Service," 232–33. See also "Congress Clears Landmark Postal Reorganization Plan," 1970 *CQ Almanac* [Congressional Quarterly Almanac], 350, 1970 strike material, unprocessed box, USPS Archives. Nixon's aides then went to work selling the plan to Congress and the public. See "Appendix C: White House Plan to Sell New Postal Reorganization Legislation, Presented at 4/18/70 meeting in Herb Klein's office," unprocessed box, USPS Archives.

23. See for example Box 53, NYMAPUC; and Draft report, September 21, 1970, 68, 1970 strike material, unprocessed box, USPS Archives.

24. "You Did It, But . . . National Craft Union Leaders Sold Out New York Postal Workers," *Union Mail* (April 1970), 1, Box 4, Folder Union Mail April 1970 Strike Issue, NYMAPUC collection. See also Brenner, "Striking against the State," 20–22.

25. See "Branch 36 Temporarily Suspends Merger Talks with MBPU," [Branch 36] *Carriers' Flash*, June 15, 1970; and Damon Stetson, "Postal Local Here Put under Parent," *New York Times*, December 4, 1971, 35; in Folder 4/71 NALC Strike Vote, Box 54, NYMAPUC. See also Arthur Ryland, transcript of "Group tape, Ryland, Epstein, Salk, Rosner," by Dana Schecter, December 1, 1976, New York; Walsh and Mangum, *Labor Struggle*, chap. 3; and Shannon, "Work Stoppage in Government," 20. "Trusteeship" is where a union's national office takes over the operations of a local.

26. Ashby Smith press conference, March 25, 1970, Washington, D.C., 1970 strike material, unprocessed box, USPS Archives. Smith erroneously claimed here that there were 200,000 blacks in the post office. Snow Grigsby cited the post office's figures in his "Editor's Notebook," *National Alliance* (April 1970), 4, noting that of 132,011 black postal workers, 123,632 were still in the lower 1–4 pay grades.

27. MBPU "News Flash!," October 21, 1970, Box 45, Folder Postal Reform—Apr.—Sept. 1970, unprocessed, NYPMAPU collection; Robert White, "From the National Office— Operation 57," *National Alliance* (November 1970), 2; and "Alliance and Manhattan-Bronx in Joint Action on Bargaining," *Progressive* (November 1970), 1. On the 1935 NLRA debate see Herbert Hill, *Black Labor and the American Legal System: Race, Work, and the Law* (1977; Madison: University of Wisconsin Press, 1985), introduction.

28. "Alliance Pickets Postal Negotiations," *National Alliance* (May 1970), 5; and "National Alliance Demonstrates." See also Walsh and Mangum, *Labor Struggle*, chap. 3.

29. Blacks held prominent positions in both the NPU and UFPC hierarchy, and the NPU merger committee included Los Angeles strike veterans Ben Evans and Leroy Armstead. See "Court to Rule on Injunction to Halt Bargaining by Crafts," and "NPU, UFPC Merger Committees Meet as One Union Drive Makes Progress," *Progressive* (January 1971), 1. See also "NPU Merger Committee Ready," front-page photo caption, *Progressive* (November 1970); and *Biennial Report to the National Convention of United Federation of Postal Clerks-AFL-CIO, Los Angeles, California, August 10–15, 1970*, 11, showing photo of the ten UFPC delegates to the 1969 AFL-CIO national convention, including two black delegates, Wallace Baldwin of Atlanta and Charles Baker of Chicago, Box 71, Folder Publications, NYMAPUC. The report grudgingly praised the outcome of the postal strike and pointed to clerks' crucial role in it while also excoriating what it called "tough-talking militant unions" when no union leader, they said, had actually sanctioned a walkout. *Biennial Report*, 8.

30. "National Alliance of Postal and Federal Employees Demonstrates against Exclusion from Postal Negotiations," *National Alliance* (February 1971), 2. See also Robert L. White, "From the National Office," *National Alliance* (March 1971), 2; and "Merger Agreement Is Signed: Members Will Vote on Adoption of Constitution for New Union," *Progressive* (March 1971), 1.

31. Walsh and Mangum, *Labor Struggle*, chap. 2; and White, "From the National Office," *National Alliance* (March 1971), 2.

32. See monthly issues of the *American Postal Worker*, 1971–1978. See also author interview with Doug Holbrook, August 16, 2005, Washington, D.C.

33. "You Did It!"; "A New Kind of Ball Game," *Progressive* (July 1970), 2.

34. See EO 11491 and the PRA. In 1947 the Taft-Hartley Act replaced the 1935 Wagner Act or NLRA. See Hill, *Black Labor*, 87, 148.

35. White, "From the National Office," *National Alliance* (March 1971).

36. Author interview with Countee Abbott, August 12, 2004, Washington, D.C. The "submerged" reference is also found in White, "From the National Office," *National Alliance* (March 1971), 2.

37. Letter to the editor, *National Alliance* (May 1970), 11.

38. "Position of the National Alliance," ibid., 8, italics added.

39. "Statement of Ashby G. Smith, President, National Alliance of Postal and Federal Employees, Before the House Committee on Post Office and Civil Service on HR 17070," *National Alliance* (June 1970), 6.

40. "Position of Alliance"; Loraine M. Huston, "Comments from Cleveland," *National Alliance* (May 1970), 8.

41. "Editor's Notebook" (April 1970).

42. Tennassee, "The Smith Presidency Part XI." See also Tennassee, "NAPFE Battles Part I," and "NAPFE Battles Part II."

43. Wesley Young, "Collective Bargaining with Binding Arbitration vs. Collective Bargaining with the Right to Strike," *National Alliance* (January 1971), 6.

44. White, "From the National Office," (March 1971), 2.

45. Morgan interview; Morgan conversation, 2004.

46. Henry interview.

47. Telephone interview with Raydell Moore, January 13, 2006, Pahrump, Nev.; telephone conversation with Walter Thomas Kenney Sr., January 24, 2009, Richmond, Va.

48. "Atlanta, GA.—'They Got It All Together,' photo caption," *National Alliance* (April 1972), 15; and "National Alliance Signs Contracts with G.S.A. and U.S.P.S.," *National Alliance* (July and August 1973), 7. GSA is the General Services Administation.

EPILOGUE

1. See author interview with Jeff Perry and Richard Thomas, July 18, 2005, New York. Today, the NYB&FMC is known as the New Jersey International and Bulk Mail Center.

2. Ibid.

3. Ibid. Telephone conversation with Jeff Perry, September 10, 2008, and February 6, 2009. See also Michael Braun in "Dave Cline: Rank & File Rebel, Part 1," <http://firemtn.blogspot.com/2007/11/dave-cline-rebel-worker-i.html> (February 6, 2009) for other cities involved in the 1978 wildcat. APWU president William H. Burrus Jr. mentions that there was no wildcat in D.C. See Burrus interview, January 16, 2009. See also <http://www.judibari.org> (September 10, 2008). See also on the 1978 wildcat: Box 15, Folder New York Bulk Fired Workers Operation Defense that includes union bulletins, press releases, court transcripts, as well as documents and correspondence between unions and postal management, in NYMAPUC; *Amnesty Bulletin* (April 1980), Postal Workers Defense Committee [San Francisco], Box 2, Folder 1980, American Postal Workers Committee (APWU) collection, both at Tamiment/Wagner Archives, New York University. See also Pranay Gupte, "Postal Employees in Still More Cities Threaten to Strike," *New York Times*, July 24, 1978, A1; Gupte, "City Area Postmen Taking Strike Vote," *New York Times*, July 25, 1978, B9; "Rank and File Angered over New Contract," *San Francisco Examiner*, July 22, 1978, 1; "Richmond mail pickets defy order," in *San Francisco Examiner*, July 22, 1978, 3. See also John Walsh and Garth Mangum, *Labor Struggle in the Post Office: From Selective Lobbying to Collective Bargaining* (Armonk, New York: M. E. Sharpe, 1992), 114–16, 126–28, especially on the role of the "Outlaws," a leftist group heavily involved in organizing the wildcat. On Mahwah, see Komozi Woodard, *A Nation within a Nation: Amiri Baraka (LeRoi Jones) and Black Power Politics* (Chapel Hill: University of North Carolina Press, 1999), 129–30.

4. See for example Jeff Perry, "Getting White Workers Involved," in *A Troublemaker's Handbook 2: How to Fight Back Where You Work—and Win!*, ed. Jane Slaughter (1991; Detroit: Labor Notes, 2005), 170–72; H. H. Hubert, "An Open Letter to All Mail Handlers Who Oppose Racism and Mob Control of Our Union: The Mail Handler Struggle for Democracy and Autonomy," 1988 draft pamphlet in possession of author; Tom DiPiazza, "Discrimination Cited at Mail Facility," *Dispatch* [Hudson/Bergen Counties, New Jersey], 1, 18. I am indebted to Jeff Perry for these sources and analysis. See also Jack Anderson, "Mob Dominates Organized Labor, U.S. Report Says," *Washington Post*, October 3, 1981, E51; and Ed Barnes and Bob Windrem, "Six Ways to Take Over a Union," *Mother Jones* (August 1980); and President's Commission on Organized Crime, *Report to the President and the Attorney General, The Edge: Organized Crime, Business and Labor Unions* (Washington, D.C.: USGPO, 1986), section six. See also telephone conversation with Jeff Perry, from documents in his possession, August 22, 2009.

5. Paul Tennassee, during author interview with Noel Murrain, August 12, 2004, Washington, D.C.

6. John T. Tierney, *Postal Reorganization: Managing the Public's Business* (Boston: Auburn House, 1981), 59. On private industry relocation from urban to suburban areas, see for example Thomas Sugrue, *The Origins of the Urban Crisis: Race and Inequality in Postwar Detroit*

(Princeton, N.J.: Princeton University Press, 1996); and William Julius Wilson, *When Work Disappears: The World of the New Urban Poor* (New York: Alfred A. Knopf, 1997).

7. See "Working Conditions and Postal Construction Program—U.S. Postal Service," *Hearings before the Subcommittee on Postal Facilities and Mail of the Committee on Post Office and Civil Service, House of Representatives*, 92nd Congress, 1st and 2nd sessions, July 21, 28, September 22, October 28, November 9, December 7, 8, 9, 1971; March 1, 8, 9, June 14, September 13, 26, 27, 28, October 4, 1972, Serial No. 92–93 (Washington, D.C.: Government Printing Office, 1972), esp. 91–96. Postal scholars and activists have declared this to be the post office's "white flight" from a workforce considered by management to be largely "militant and black." The postal operations move occurred when the auto industry was closing some of its urban plants after black-led wildcats and were moving operations to predominantly white suburban southern plants or overseas. See Perry and Thomas interview; Peter Rachleff, *Moving the Mail: From a Manual Case to Outer Space* (Morgantown, W.Va.: Work Environment Project, 1982), 19–20; Dan Georgakas and Marvin Surkin, *Detroit: I Do Mind Dying: A Study in Urban Revolution*, updated ed. (1975; Boston: South End Press, 1998); Kathleen Conkey, *The Postal Precipice: Can the U.S. Postal Service Be Saved?* (Washington, D.C.: Center for the Study of Responsive Law, 1983), 79, 91, 162–63. In October 1971, Blount resigned as postmaster general, returning to his lucrative construction business in Alabama, and subsequently winning $91 million worth of contracts to build four of the BMCs that he planned.

8. Robert L. White, "From the President's Office," *National Alliance* (August 1971), 2.

9. "Negroes Fear Postal Job Losses," *National Alliance* (January 1972), 5, reprinted from *Washington Daily News*, January 6, 1972.

10. "Let's Get the Facts," editorial, *American Postal Worker* (March 1974), 4, in Box 29, Folder F, Battle of the Bulk, 1973–74, NYMAPUC; and Walsh and Mangum, *Labor Struggle*, 131–33.

11. See Burrus interview. See also Pranay Gupte, "Postal Employees in Still More Cities Threaten to Strike," *New York Times*, July 24, 1978, A1; Gupte, "City Area Postmen Taking Strike Vote," *New York Times*, July 25, 1978, B9; Walsh and Mangum, *Labor Struggle*, 114–16; and Perry and Thomas interview. Subsequent contract negotiations were characterized by frequent NALC and APWU strike threats, USPS stonewalling, and ultimately arbitrated settlements. Walsh and Mangum, *Labor Struggle*, 169–246. Perry telephone conversations.

12. Conkey, *Postal Precipice*, 163; Craig Zwerling and Hilary Silver, "Race and Job Dismissals in a Federal Bureaucracy," *American Sociological Review* 57, no. 5 (October 1992), 651–60; and conversation between Wendy Kelly-Carter and author, August 11, 2004, Washington, D.C. See also author interview with Doug Holbrook, August 16, 2005, Washington, D.C.: the APWU that a decade before stood at 334,000 members claimed only 218,000 members in 2005. New York Metro, still the largest branch, is down to about 7,000 members.

13. Box 50, Folder Women; and Box 8, Folder Officer's File-Drafts of Speeches, NYMAPUC. See also New York Metro interview; and author interview with Joseph Henry, president, Capital City Branch 142 NALC, August 15, 2005, Washington, D.C. See also *Local 300 Mail Handler News*, October and December 1995.

14. Philip S. Foner, Ronald L. Lewis, and Robert Cvornyek, eds., *The Black Worker: A Documentary History from Colonial Times to the Present*, vol. 8, *The Black Worker since the AFL-CIO Merger, 1955–1980* (Philadelphia: Temple University Press, 1984), 332–64; "Equal Employment Opportunity Act of 1972," *National Alliance* (April 1972), 12; Wesley Young, "What Is Our Public Posture?," *National Alliance* (November 1972), 8. Young blasted the

Federal Times for marginalizing their antiwar position by omitting the Alliance in an article on postal unions that backed McGovern: "It is apparent, from your view point, blacks are only newsworthy when they are calling white folk 'honky' or 'burning buildings.'"

15. See *Chisholm v. USPS*, 516 F. Supp. 810 (October 3, 1980), <http://web.lexis-nexis .com> (June 5, 2005); and telephone conversation with Napoleon Chisholm (no union affiliation), June 5, 2005. See also interview with Napoleon Bonaparte Chisholm by Elizabeth Gritter, May 10, 2006, Charlotte, North Carolina, Southern Oral History Program, in the Southern Historical Collection Manuscripts Department, Wilson Library, the University of North Carolina at Chapel Hill. Included in the transcript of Gritter's interview is Chisholm's case in *Employment Practices Decisions*, vol. 24, *1980–1981* (Chicago: Commerce Clearing House, 1980); see esp. 17,986, 17,993, 18,010, and 18,012. See also Charisse Williams, April 4 and 24, 2005, interviews with Ajamu Dillahunt, including field notes, tapelogs, and undergraduate paper, "Non-Violent Protests to the Point of Production: The Evolution of the Left in the Civil Rights Movement," Center for Documentary Studies Collection, Duke University Rare Book, Manuscripts, and Special Collections Library.

16. *Chisholm v. USPS*; and Gritter interview with Chisholm.

17. *Employment Practices Decisions*, esp. 18,010; author conversation with Chisholm; and Gritter interview with Chisholm.

18. Perry and Thomas interview.

19. Author interview with James Newman, August 12, 2004, Washington, D.C. See also author interview with Felix Bell, August 11, 2004, Washington, D.C. The Jackson, Mississippi, NAPFE branch is about 25 percent white. Felix Bell, president of the Jackson branch, contrasts white postal workers in Mississippi in the 1960s that would resign rather than work with blacks with a "new generation" in the late 1980s who had gone to school, socialized, and been in the military with blacks. The Civil Service Commission was abolished effective January 1, 1979, with the *Civil Service Reform Act of 1978*, its functions replaced by the MSPB, the Federal Labor Relations Authority, and the Office of Personnel Management. See "History" at "Records of the Merit Systems Protection Board" at National Archives and Records Administration website, <http://www.archives.gov/research/gui de-fed-records/groups/479.html> (September 15, 2008).

20. See Josie McMillian oral history tapelog and summary (n.d., ca. 1981, original tape damaged), New Yorkers at Work Oral History Collection: Project Files, 142, no. 1, Tamiment/Wagner Archives. MBPU became New York Metro in 1973.

21. Perry and Thomas interview.

22. Deanna Boyd and Kendra Chen, "The History and Experience of African Americans in America's Postal Service," Smithsonian National Postal Museum, Washington, D.C., <http://www.postalmuseum.si.edu/AfricanAmericans/index.html> (September 6, 2008).

23. Burrus interview. See also APWU and NPMHU websites.

24. Leah Platt Boustan and Robert A. Margo, "Race, Segregation, and Postal Employment: New Evidence on Spatial Mismatch," *Journal of Urban Economics* (forthcoming, revised version of NBER Working Paper 13462), 9.

25. NYMAPUC interview.

26. Ibid.; Burrus interview.

27. Burrus interview.

28. USPS, "Postal Accountability and Enhancement Act & 302 Network Plan June 2008," esp. 31, at the NPMHU website, along with NPMHU protests, <http://www

.npmhu.org> (September 10, 2008): during 2006–2007, forty-six Airport Mail Centers were closed, and eight more in 2008. See also "Delegates Vow to Fight Privatization of Parcel Post," APWU website, <http://www.apwu.org/index2.htm> (September 15, 2008); "Postal Workers Getting Early Retirement Offers," *Raleigh News and Observer*, August 21, 2008, 9B; and "Basic Standards for All Mailing Services: Private Express Statutes," <http://pe.usps.gov/cpim/ftp/manuals/QSG300/Q608.pdf> (September 15, 2008). See also "Privatization of Federal Jobs Wrong Approach," *National Alliance* online article (June 2003), <http://www.napfe.com/mg_cn.asp> (September 15, 2008), for NAPFE's combining with the NAACP's Federal Sector Task Force to stop federal job loss. See also "Postal Overhaul Becomes Law," <http://www.nalc.org/postal/reform/index.html> (September 15, 2008) regarding the NALC's successful efforts to help keep the 2006 Postal Accountability Act from changing "the basic structure and mission of the Postal Service." See also "Dripping with Red Ink, Post Office Pleads for Authority to Cut Out a Day of Mail Delivery," *Raleigh News and Observer*, January 29, 2009, 3A. See also Randolph E. Schmid, "Postal Service Will Cut Costs and Offices," *Raleigh News and Observer*, August 4, 2009, 5A.

29. Burrus interview.

30. See United States Postal Service, *Comprehensive Statement on Postal Operations 2008*, 26–27, <http://www.usps.com (August 21, 2009). U.S. Postal Service employment dropped from 816,886 in 1990 to 753,254 in 2007. See also Table 481, "Federal Civilian Employment by Branch and Agency: 1990 to 2007," 319, U.S. Census Bureau, *Statistical Abstract of the United States: 2009*, <http://www.census.gov> (August 21, 2009). The federal government as a whole is still the nation's largest employer, with almost 2.7 million civilian employees in 2007. But Wal-Mart is now the nation's single largest corporation and private employer, with over one million employees in the United States and 400,000 abroad. See United Food and Commercial Workers website, <http://www.ufcw.org> (August 21, 2009).

CONCLUSION

1. A. L. Glenn, *History of the National Alliance of Postal Employees, 1913–1955* (Washington, D.C.: National Alliance of Postal Employees, 1956), 315. The book actually includes 1956 references also.

2. Author interview with William H. Burrus Jr., January 16, 2009, Washington, D.C.

3. Author interview with Felix Bell Sr., August 11, 2004, Washington, D.C. Ten years before this interview, I later discovered, Myrlie Evers-Williams, the widow of black civil rights leader Medgar Evers, assassinated in 1963, had presided over the dedication of the Medgar Evers Post Office Building in Jackson—just two blocks away from the Hinds County Detention Center where her husband's killer, Byron De La Beckwith, had finally been convicted earlier that year. See Claudia Dreifus, "The Widow Gets Her Verdict," *New York Times*, November 27, 1994, sec. 6, 69.

BIBLIOGRAPHY

MANUSCRIPT COLLECTIONS

Duke University Rare Book, Manuscript, and Special Collections Library, Durham, N.C.
    Behind the Veil: Documenting African American Life in the Jim Crow South,
        Center for Documentary Studies Collection
    Civil Rights and Labor Struggles, Center for Documentary Studies Collection
National Association of Letter Carriers Library, Washington, D.C.
National Association of Letter Carriers Historical Files
North Carolina Central University Archives, Records and History Center
    C. Elwood Boulware file
Tamiment Library / Robert F. Wagner Archives, Bobst Library, New York University,
    New York, N.Y.
        American Postal Workers Union–New York Metro Area Postal Union Collection
        American Postal Workers Union–Moe Biller Files
U.S. Postal Service Archives and Library, Washington, D.C.
1970 Postal Strike Collection
University of North Carolina at Chapel Hill
Southern Oral History Program, Southern Historical Collection

ORAL HISTORY INTERVIEWS BY AUTHOR

Deposited in Center for Documentary Studies Collection, Duke University Rare Book,
    Manuscript, and Special Collections Library, Durham, N.C.

Countee Abbott, August 12, 2004, Washington, D.C.
John Adams and Dorothea Hoskins, August 11, 2004, Washington, D.C.
Sam Armstrong and Samuel Lovett, August 11, 2004, Washington, D.C.
Eleanor Bailey, Joann Flagler, Frederick John, Carlton Tilley, and Gregory Wilson,
    October 14, 2004, New York, N.Y.
Felix Bell Sr., August 11, 2004, Washington, D.C.
William H. Burrus Jr., January 16, 2009, Washington, D.C.
Don Cantriel, August 17, 2005, Alexandria, Va.
Joseph Henry, August 15, 2005, Washington, D.C.
Douglas C. Holbrook, August 16, 2005, Washington, D.C.
Jimmy Mainor (with assistance from Joy Ogunsile, Ryan Biernesser, Shannon
    Cambridge, Brocky Proxmire, Corey Sobel, and Claire Rauh), January 5, 2004,
    Durham, N.C.
Al Marino, Frank Orapello, and Vincent Sombrotto, October 15, 2004, New York, N.Y.
Raydell Moore, January 13, 2006, Pahrump, Nev. (telephone)

Cleveland Morgan, July 18, 2005, New York, N.Y.

James Morris (transcribed by Tiana Mack), August 11, 2004, Washington, D.C.

Noel Murrain, August 11, 2004, Washington, D.C.

James Newman, August 12, 2004, Washington, D.C.

Jeff Perry and Richard Thomas, July 18, 2005, New York, N.Y.

D. James Pinderhughes, July 17, 2004, Washington, D.C.

George Booth Smith, August 27, 2004, Durham, N.C.

Donald P. Stone, February 12, 2005, Snow Hill, Ala. (telephone)

Daisy Strachan, August 11, 2004, Washington, D.C.

Tommie L. Wilson, August 11, 2004, Washington, D.C.

OTHER ORAL HISTORY INTERVIEWS

Zecharaiah Alexander, by Rhonda Mawhood, June 11, 1993, Charlotte, N.C., Behind the Veil: Documenting African American Life in the Jim Crow South, Duke University Rare Book, Manuscript, and Special Collections Library, Durham, N.C.

Moe Biller, Elie Resnick, Milt Rosner, Arthur Ryland, Charles Salk, and Philip Seligman, by Dana Schecter, Cornell University Oral History Project, Box 4, 1976, American Postal Workers Union Collection, Tamiment Library/Robert F. Wagner Archives, Bobst Library, New York University, New York, N.Y.

Napoleon Bonaparte Chisholm, by Elizabeth Gritter, May 10, 2006, Charlotte, N.C., Southern Oral History Program, Southern Historical Collection Manuscripts Department, Wilson Library, University of North Carolina at Chapel Hill.

Ajamu Dillahunt, Duke University oral history and undergraduate paper by Charisse Williams, Raleigh, N.C., April 4 and 25, 2005, CDS Collection, Duke University Rare Book, Manuscript, and Special Collections Library, Durham, N.C.

Walter P. Holmes, by Karen Ferguson, June 15, 1993, Charlotte, N.C., Behind the Veil: Documenting African American Life in the Jim Crow South, Duke University Rare Book, Manuscript, and Special Collections Library, Durham, N.C.

Jessie Johnson, by Blair Murphy, August 11, 1995, Norfolk, Va.

Josie McMillian, by unknown, ca. 1981, New York, N.Y., Tamiment Library/Robert F. Wagner Archives, Bobst Library, New York University, New York, N.Y.

Amzie Moore, by Mike Garvey, March 29, 1977, Civil Rights in Mississippi Digital Archive, <http://www.lib.usm.edu/~spcol/crda/oh/index.html>.

D. James Pinderhughes, by Rhonda Jones, May 6, 2004, Washington, D.C., transcribed by Tiana Mack

"Abe Whitess, mayor of Douglasville," by unknown. Available in *Born in Slavery: Slave Narratives from the Federal Writers Project, 1936–1938, Alabama Narratives,* 1:423–24, online collection, Library of Congress, <http://memory.loc.gov>.

GOVERNMENT DOCUMENTS, STATUTES, AND COURT DECISIONS

Annual Report of the Postmaster General, 1945–1949. Washington, D.C.: Government Printing Office, 1946–1950.

Buchanan v. Warley, 245 U.S. 60 (1917).

Chisholm v. USPS, 516 F. Supp. 810 (October 3, 1980).

Civil Service Act. Statutes at Large 22 (1983).

Civil Service Reform Act of 1978, PL 95-454 (S 2640).

Committee on Post Office and Civil Service, House of Representatives. *Towards Postal Excellence: The Report of the President's Commission on Postal Reorganization, June 1968.* 94th Cong., 2nd sess. Washington, D.C.: Government Printing Office, 1976.

Department of Commerce and Labor Bureau of the Census, S. N. D. North, Director. *Statistics of Employees: Executive Civil Service of the United States 1907.* Bulletin 94. Washington, D.C.: Government Printing Office, 1908.

Dred Scott v. Sandford, 60 U.S. 393 (1857).

"Equal Pay Act." *Hearings Before the Special Subcommittee on Labor of the Committee on Education and Labor, House of Representatives, Eighty-eighth Congress, First Session on H.R. 3861 and Related Bills to Prohibit Discrimination, on Account of Sex, in the Payment of Wages by Employers Engaged in Commerce or in the Production of Goods for Commerce and to Provide for the Restitution of Wages Lost by Employees by Reason of Any Such Discrimination, Hearings Held in Washington, D.C., March 15, 25, 26, and 27, 1963, Adam C. Powell, Chairman.* Washington, D.C.: Government Printing Office, 1963.

"Equal Pay Act of 1963." *Hearings Before the Subcommittee on Labor of the Committee on Labor and Public Welfare, United States Senate, Eighty-eighth Congress, First Session, on S. 882 and S. 910, to Amend the Equal Pay Act of 1963, April 2, 3, and 16, 1963.* Washington, D.C.: Government Printing Office, 1963.

Evers v. Dwyer, 358 U.S. 202 (1958).

Executive Order 8587 (1940).

Executive Order 8802 (1941).

Executive Order 9346 (1943).

Executive Order 9835 (1947).

Executive Order 9980 (1948).

Executive Order 9981 (1948).

Executive Order 10450 (1953).

Executive Order 10590 (1955).

Executive Order 10926 (1961).

Executive Order 10980 (1961).

Executive Order 10988 (1962).

Executive Order 11126 (1963).

Executive Order 11246 (1965).

Executive Order 11397 (1968).

Executive Order 11491 (1970).

Executive Order 11521 (1970).

Fourteenth Census of the United States, 1920. Vol. 4, *Population Occupations.* Washington, D.C.: Government Printing Office, 1923.

Labor Management Relations Act (Taft-Hartley), Title 29, Chapter 7, U.S.C. (1947)

Labor-Management Reporting and Disclosure Act. Statutes at Large 73 (1959).

National Labor Relations Act. Statutes at Large 49 (1935).

Postal Reorganization Act. Statutes at Large 84 (1970).

President's Commission on Organized Crime. *Report to the President and the Attorney General, The Edge: Organized Crime, Business and Labor Unions.* Section six. Washington, D.C.: USGPO, 1986.

Public Law, Post-Office. Statutes at Large 2 (1810).

Public Law, Post-Office. Statutes at Large 4 (1825).

Public Law, Post-Office Department. *Statutes at Large* 13 (1865).

Public Law, Post-Roads. *Statutes at Large* 2 (1802).

Servicemen's Readjustment Act of 1944. Statutes at Large 58 (1944).

Shelley v. Kraemer, 334 U.S. 1 (1948).

Smith v. Allwright, 322 U.S. 649 (1944).

Sweatt v. Painter, 339 U.S. 629 (1950).

U.S. Census Bureau. *Statistical Abstract of the United States: 2009.* <http://www.census.gov> (August 21, 2009).

U.S. Civil Service Commission. *History of Veteran Preference in Federal Employment.* Washington, D.C.: Government Printing Office, 1955.

U.S. Civil Service Commission, Manpower Statistics Division. *Occupations of Federal Blue-Collar Workers.* Washington, D.C.: Government Printing Office, October 31, 1960.

——. *Study of Employment of Women in the Federal Government 1970 Prepared for the Federal Women's Program.* Washington, D.C.: Government Printing Office, 1971.

U.S. Congress, Senate, Senator Johnston of South Carolina and Senator Humphrey of Minnesota, speaking for the Recognition of Federal Employee Unions, S. 473, 87th Cong., 1st sess., *Congressional Record* 107, pt. 1 (17 January 1961).

U.S. Postal Service. *Comprehensive Statement on Postal Operations 2008.* <http://www.usps.com> (August 21, 2009).

——. *The United States Postal Service: An American History, 1775–2006.* Washington, D.C.: U.S. Postal Service Publication 100, 2007.

Veterans Preference Act of 1944. Statutes at Large 58 (1944).

"Working Conditions and Postal Construction Program—U.S. Postal Service." *Hearings before the Subcommittee on Postal Facilities and Mail of the Committee on Post Office and Civil Service, House of Representatives.* 92nd Cong., 1st and 2nd sess., July 21, 28, September 22, October 28, November 9, December 7, 8, 9, 1971; March 1, 8, 9, June 14, September 13, 26, 27, 28, October 4, 1972, Serial No. 92–93. Washington, D.C.: Government Printing Office, 1972.

NEWSPAPERS AND PERIODICALS

American Legacy

American Postal Worker

Atlanta Daily World

Baltimore Afro-American

Chicago Daily News

Chicago Defender

Chicago Tribune

Cleveland Call and Post

Cleveland Plain Dealer

Crisis

Dispatch (Hudson and Bergen Counties, N.J.)

Ebony

Federal Times

Houston Post

Jet

Louisiana Weekly

Michigan Chronicle
National Rural Letter Carrier
New York Alliance Leader
New York Amsterdam News
New York Post
New York Times
Opportunity
People Weekly
Philadelphia Inquirer
Pittsburgh Courier (and *New Pittsburgh Courier*)
Postal Alliance (*National Alliance* after 1965)
Postal Record
Postal Sub
Progressive
Progressive Fed
Public Employee (AFSCME)
Raleigh (N.C.) News and Observer
Savannah (Ga.) Morning News
Solidarity (UAW)
Tri-State Defender (Memphis, Tenn.)
Union Mail
Union Postal Clerk
United Rubber Worker
Unity Forum
Washington Afro-American
Washington Daily News
Washington Post

CONVENTION PROCEEDINGS

AFL-CIO. *Report of the First Constitutional Convention Proceedings, New York, N.Y., December 5–8, 1955*. Washington, D.C.: AFL-CIO, 1955.

"Minutes of the National Convention of the National Alliance of Postal Employees." *Postal Alliance* (August 1943). Schomburg Center for Research in Black Culture, New York Public Library, New York, N.Y.

Official Proceedings of the Convention of the National Association of Letter Carriers, 1890, 1917, 1919, 1927, 1933, 1935, 1937, 1939, 1941, 1943, 1946, 1948, 1952, 1954, 1956, 1958, 1960, 1962, 1968. National Association of Letter Carriers Library, Washington, D.C., and University of Wisconsin–Madison Library.

Proceedings of the Eleventh Constitutional Convention of the Congress of Industrial Organizations. Cleveland: CIO, 1949.

Proceedings of the Fifth Constitutional Convention of the AFL-CIO. Vol. 1, *Daily Proceedings, New York, New York, November 14–20, 1963*. Washington, D.C.: AFL-CIO, 1963.

Proceedings of the Fourth Constitutional Convention of the AFL-CIO. Vol. 1, *Daily Proceedings, Miami Beach, Florida, December 7–13, 1961*. Washington, D.C.: AFL-CIO, 1961.

Proceedings and Summaries of Proceedings of the Convention of the National Federation of Post Office Clerks 1939, 1941, 1944, 1946, 1948, 1950, 1952, 1954, 1958. U.S. Postal Service Library, Washington, D.C., and the State Historical Society of Wisconsin, Madison.

Proceedings of the Twelfth Constitutional Convention of the Congress of Industrial Organizations. Cleveland: CIO, 1950.

ARTICLES AND PAMPHLETS

Allis, Tim. "Wait a Minute, Mr. Postman—Aren't You Freddie Gorman, Who Co-Wrote Please Mr. Postman?" *People Weekly*, March 7, 1988, 53–54.

Aptheker, Herbert. "Militant Abolitionism." *Journal of Negro History* 26, no. 4 (October 1941), 438–84.

Arnesen, Eric. "Whiteness and the Historians' Imagination." *International Labor and Working-Class History* 60 (October 2001), 3–32.

Aronowitz, Stanley, and Jeremy Brecher. "Notes on the Postal Strike." *Root and Branch* 1 (1970), 1–5.

Bolster, W. Jeffrey. " 'To Feel Like a Man': Black Seamen in the Northern States, 1800–1860." *Journal of American History* 76, no. 4 (March 1990), 1173–99.

Boustan, Leah Platt, and Robert A. Margo. "Race, Segregation, and Postal Employment: New Evidence on Spatial Mismatch." *Journal of Urban Economics*. Forthcoming. Revised version of NBER Working Paper 13462.

Brenner, Aaron. "Striking against the State: The Postal Wildcat of 1970." *Labor's Heritage* (Spring 1996), 4–27.

Cha-Jua, Sundiata, and Clarence Lang. "The 'Long Movement' as Vampire: Temporal and Spatial Fallacies in Recent Black Freedom Studies." *Journal of African American History* 92, no. 2 (Spring 2007), 265–@88.

Cherny, Robert W. "Prelude to the Popular Front: The Communist Party in California, 1931–35." *American Communist History* 1, no. 1 (June 2002), 5–42.

Coit, Eleanor G., and John D. Connors. "Agencies and Programs in Workers' Education." *Journal of Educational Sociology* 20, no. 8 (April 1947), 520–28.

——, and Orie A. H. Pell. "Labor Education and Intergroup Relations." *Journal of Educational Sociology* 25, no. 6 (February 1952), 319–20.

Dewing, Rolland. "The American Federation of Teachers and Desegregation." *Journal of Negro Education* 42, no. 1 (Winter 1973), 79–92.

Draper, Alan. "Brown v. Board of Education and Organized Labor in the South." *Historian* 57, no. 1 (Autumn 1994), 75–88.

Gatewood, Willard B. "Theodore Roosevelt and the Indianola Affair." *Journal of Negro History* 53, no. 1 (January 1968), 48–69.

Gregory, O. Grady. *From the Bottom of the Barrel: A History of Black Workers in the Chicago Post Office from 1921*. Chicago: National Alliance of Postal and Federal Employees, 1977.

Gritter, Elizabeth. "Memories of H. T. Lockard." *Southern Cultures* 14, no. 5 (Fall 2008), 106–16.

Hall, Jacquelyn Dowd. "The Long Civil Rights Movement and the Political Uses of the Past." *Journal of American History* 91, no. 4 (March 2005), 1233–63.

Hall, Wiley A. "Adult Education Programs of Labor Unions and Other Workers Groups." *Journal of Negro Education* 14, no. 3 (Summer 1945), 407–11.

Harding, Vincent. "History: White, Negro and Black." *Southern Exposure* (Winter 1974), 52–62.

Hill, Herbert. "The AFL-CIO and the Black Worker: Twenty-Five Years after the

Merger." *Journal of Intergroup Relations* 10, no. 1 (Spring 1982), 5–79. Reprint No. 241, Industrial Relations Research Institute, University of Wisconsin–Madison.

——. "Lichtenstein's Fictions Revisited: Race and the New Labor History." *New Politics* (Winter 1999), 149–63.

——. "Myth-Making as Labor History: Herbert Gutman and the United Mine Workers of America." *International Journal of Politics, Culture, and Society* 2, no. 2 (Winter 1988), 132–200.

Hine, Darlene Clark. "Black Professionals and Race Consciousness: Origins of the Civil Rights Movement, 1890–1950." *Journal of American History* 89, no. 4 (March 2003), 1279–94.

Hoffman, Miles E. *Labor Monograph No. 5: A Contemporary Analysis of a Labor Union.* Philadelphia: Temple University, 1963.

Hubert, H. H. "An Open Letter to All Mail Handlers Who Oppose Racism and Mob Control of Our Union: The Mail Handler Struggle for Democracy and Autonomy." Draft pamphlet in possession of author, 1988.

Ignatiev [né Ignatin], Noel. "A Golden Bridge." *Political Discussion* 2 (April 1976), 17–45.

——. "The White Worker and the Labor Movement in Nineteenth-Century America." *Race Traitor: Journal of the New Abolitionism* 3 (Spring 1994), 100–107.

Isaac, Larry, and Lars Christiansen. "How the Civil Rights Movement Revitalized Labor Militancy." *American Sociological Review* 67, no. 5 (October 2002), 722–46.

Jones, Allen W. "The Black Press in the New South: Jesse C. Duke's Struggle for Justice and Equality." *Journal of Negro History* 64, no. 3 (Summer 1979), 215–28.

Jones, Beverly Washington. "Before Montgomery and Greensboro: The Desegregation Movement in the District of Columbia, 1950–1953." *Phylon* 43, no. 2 (2nd Qtr., 1982), 144–54.

——. "Race, Sex, and Class: Black Female Tobacco Workers in Durham, North Carolina, 1920–1940, and the Development of Female Consciousness." *Feminist Studies* 10, no. 3 (Fall 1984), 441–51.

Kazin, Michael. "The Agony and Romance of the American Left." *American Historical Review* 100, no. 5 (December 1995), 1488–1512.

Kelley, Robin D. G. "Integration: What's Left?" *Nation*, December 14, 1998, 17–19.

Korstad, Robert, and Nelson Lichtenstein. "Opportunities Found and Lost: Labor, Radicals, and the Early Civil Rights Movement." *Journal of American History* 75, no. 3 (December 1988), 786–811.

Levine, Marvin J. "The U.S. Postal Service: A Labor Relations Hybrid." *Employee Relations Law Journal* 4, no. 2 (1978), 220–40.

Lipsitz, George. "The Possessive Investment in Whiteness: Racialized Social Democracy and the 'White' Problem in American Studies." *American Quarterly* 47, no. 3 (September 1995), 369–87.

Meier, August, and John H. Bracey Jr. "The NAACP as a Reform Movement, 1909–1965: 'To Reach the Conscience of America.'" *Journal of Southern History* 59, no. 1 (February 1993), 3–30.

Meier, August, and Elliott Rudwick. "The Rise of Segregation in the Federal Bureaucracy, 1900–1930." *Phylon* 28, no. 2 (2nd Qtr., 1967), 178–84.

National Postal Mail Handlers Union. *We're the Hidden Heroes of the Postal Service.* Washington, D.C.: NPMHU, 1990.

National States' Rights Democrats Campaign Committee. *States' Rights Information and Speakers Handbook.* Jackson, Miss.: National States' Rights Democrats Campaign Committee, 1948.

Nelson, Bruce. "Organized Labor and the Struggle for Black Equality in Mobile during World War II." *Journal of American History* 80, no. 3 (December 1993), 952–88.

Painter, Nell Irvin. "The New Labor History and the Historical Moment." *International Journal of Politics, Culture and Society* 2, no. 3 (Spring 1989), 367–70.

Payne, Charles M. " 'The Whole United States is Southern!': *Brown v. Board* and the Mystification of Race." *Journal of American History* 91, no. 1 (June 2004), 83–91.

Reed, Merl E. "The FBI, MOWM, and CORE, 1941–1946." *Journal of Black Studies* 21, no. 4 (June 1991), 465–79.

———. "FEPC and the Federal Agencies in the South." *Journal of Negro History* 65, no. 1 (Winter 1980), 43–56.

Rice, Roger L. "Residential Segregation by Law, 1910–1917." *Journal of Southern History* 34, no. 2 (May 1968), 179–99.

Shaffer, Robert. "Where Are the Organized Public Employees? The Absence of Public Employee Unionism from U.S. History Textbooks, and Why It Matters." *Labor History* 43, no. 3 (August 2002), 315–34.

Shannon, Stephen. "Work Stoppage in Government: The Postal Strike of 1970." *Monthly Labor Review* 101, no. 7 (July 1978), 14–22.

Smith, Robert P. "William Cooper Nell: Crusading Black Abolitionist." *Journal of Negro History* 55, no. 3 (July 1970), 182–99.

Smyth, Hugh H. "The Concept 'Jim Crow.' " *Social Forces* 27, no. 1 (October 1948–May 1949), 45–48.

Tennassee, Paul Nehru. "Perspectives on African American History: 12th and 13th Compromise, Part V." *Guyana Journal* (October 2000), 34–40.

Thompson, Mindy. "The National Negro Labor Council: A History." *Occasional Paper No. 27.* New York: American Institute for Marxist Studies, 1978.

Vindex. *On the Liability of the Abolitionists to Criminal Punishment and on the Duty of the Non-Slave-Holding States to Suppress Their Efforts.* Charleston: A. E. Miller, 1835. Pamphlet originally published in the *Charleston Courier.* Duke University Rare Book, Manuscript, and Special Collections Library, Durham, N.C.

Weaver, Robert. *Seniority and the Negro Worker.* Chicago, ca. 1945.

Wehrle, Edmund F. "Guns, Butter, Leon Keyserling, the AFL-CIO, and the Fate of Full-Employment Economics." *Historian* 66, no. 4 (Winter 2004), 730–48.

Weiss, Nancy J. "The Negro and the New Freedom: Fighting Wilsonian Segregation." *Political Science Quarterly* 84, no. 1 (March 1969), 63–79.

Wolgemuth, Kathleen L. "Woodrow Wilson and Federal Segregation." *Journal of Negro History* 44, no. 2 (April 1959), 158–73.

Wyatt-Brown, Bertram. "The Abolitionists' Postal Campaign of 1835." *Journal of Negro History* 50, no. 4 (October 1965), 227–38.

Zwerling, Craig, and Hilary Silver. "Race and Job Dismissals in a Federal Bureaucracy." *American Sociological Review* 57, no. 5 (October 1992), 651–60.

BOOKS AND CHAPTERS IN BOOKS

Allen, Robert. *Reluctant Reformers: Racism and Social Reform Movements in the United States.* Washington, D.C.: Howard University Press, 1983.

Allen, Theodore W. *The Invention of the White Race*. Vol. 1, *Racial Oppression and Social Control*. London: Verso, 1995.

Anderson, Carol. *Eyes off the Prize: The United Nations and the African American Struggle for Human Rights, 1944–1955*. Cambridge: Cambridge University Press, 2003.

Anderson, Jervis. *A. Philip Randolph: A Biographical Portrait*. New York: Harcourt, 1973.

Baarslag, Karl. *History of the National Federation of Post Office Clerks*. Washington, D.C.: NFPOC, 1945.

Barber, David. *A Hard Rain Fell: SDS and Why It Failed*. Jackson: University Press of Mississippi, 2008.

Baskir, Lawrence M., and William A. Strauss. *Chance and Circumstance: The Draft, the War, and the Vietnam Generation*. New York: Vintage Books, 1978.

Bates, Beth Tompkins. " 'Double V for Victory' Mobilizes Black Detroit, 1941–1946." In *Freedom North: Black Freedom Struggles outside the South, 1940–1980*, ed. Jeanne Theoharis and Komozi Woodard, 17–40. New York: Palgrave, 2003.

——. *Pullman Porters and the Rise of Protest Politics in Black America, 1925–1945*. Chapel Hill: University of North Carolina Press, 2001.

Bates, Daisy. *A Long Shadow of Little Rock: A Memoir*. Little Rock: University of Arkansas Press, 1987.

Baxter, Vern K. *Labor and Politics in the U.S. Postal Service*. New York: Plenum, 1994.

Beifuss, Joan Turner. *At the River I Stand: Memphis, the 1968 Strike, and Martin Luther King*. Brooklyn: Carlson Publishing, 1989.

Bell, Derrick. *Silent Covenants: Brown v. Board of Education and the Unfulfilled Hopes for Racial Reform*. Oxford: Oxford University Press, 2004.

Bennett, Lerone, Jr. *Before the Mayflower: A History of Black America*. 1962. 5th ed. New York: Penguin, 1984.

——. *The Shaping of Black America*. 1974. Reprint, New York: Penguin, 1993.

Bernstein, Irving. *Promises Kept: John F. Kennedy's New Frontier*. New York: Oxford University Press, 1991.

Biondi, Martha. *To Stand and Fight: The Struggle for Civil Rights in Postwar New York City*. Cambridge, Mass.: Harvard University Press, 2003.

Bolster, W. Jeffrey. *Black Jacks: African American Seamen in the Age of Sail*. Cambridge, Mass.: Harvard University Press, 1997.

Bracey, John H., Jr., August Meier, and Elliott Rudwick, eds. *Black Nationalism in America*. Indianapolis: Bobbs-Merrill, 1970.

Branch, Taylor. *Parting the Waters: America in the King Years, 1954–63*. New York: Simon and Schuster, 1988.

Brandt, Nat. *Harlem at War: The Black Experience in WWII*. Syracuse: Syracuse University Press, 1996.

Brecher, Jeremy. *Strike!* 1972. Revised and updated ed., Boston: South End Press, 1997.

Brooks, Jennifer E. *Defining the Peace: World War II Veterans, Race, and the Remaking of Southern Political Tradition*. Chapel Hill: University of North Carolina Press, 2004.

Brooks, Thomas R. *Toil and Trouble: A History of American Labor*. 1964. 2nd ed., New York: Delta, 1971.

Capeci, Dominic, Jr. "The Harlem Bus Boycott of 1941." In *Civil Rights since 1787: A Reader on the Black Struggle*, ed. Jonathan Birnbaum and Clarence Taylor, 298–302. New York: New York University Press, 2000.

——. *The Harlem Riot of 1943*. Philadelphia: Temple University Press, 1977.

Capeci, Dominic, Jr., and Martha Wilkerson. *Layered Violence: The Detroit Rioters of 1943.* Jackson: University Press of Mississippi, 1991.

Carmichael, Stokely (Kwame Ture), and Charles V. Hamilton. *Black Power: The Politics of Liberation in America.* New York: Vintage, 1967.

——, with Ekwueme Michael Thelwell. *Ready for Revolution: The Life and Struggles of Stokely Carmichael (Kwame Ture).* New York: Scribner, 2003.

Caro, Robert A. *Master of the Senate.* New York: Alfred A. Knopf, 2002.

Carson, Clayborne. *In Struggle: SNCC and the Black Awakening of the 1960s.* Cambridge, Mass.: Harvard University Press, 1981.

Carter, Dan T. *From George Wallace to Newt Gingrich: Race in the Conservative Counterrevolution, 1963–1994.* Baton Rouge: Louisiana State University Press, 1996.

Caute, David. *The Great Fear: The Anti-Communist Purge under Truman and Eisenhower.* New York: Simon and Schuster, 1978.

Cecelski, David S., and Timothy B. Tyson, eds. *Democracy Betrayed: The Wilmington Race Riot of 1898 and Its Legacy.* Chapel Hill: University of North Carolina Press, 1998.

Chafe, William H., Raymond Gavins, Robert Korstad, with Paul Ortiz, Robert Parrish, Jennifer Ritterhouse, Keisha Roberts, and Nicole Walgora-Davis, eds. *Remembering Jim Crow: African Americans Tell about Life in the Segregated South.* New York: New Press, 2001.

Chalmers, William. *Hooded Americanism: The First Century of the Ku Klux Klan, 1865–1965.* Garden City, N.Y.: Doubleday, 1965.

Cobble, Dorothy Sue. *The Other Women's Movement: Workplace Justice and Social Rights in Modern America.* Princeton, N.J.: Princeton University Press, 2004.

Commons, John R. *History of Labour in the United States.* 1918. Reprint, New York: Macmillan, 1935.

Conkey, Kathleen. *The Postal Precipice: Can the U.S. Postal Service Be Saved?* Washington, D.C.: Center for the Study of Responsive Law, 1983.

Curry, George E., ed. *The Affirmative Action Debate.* Reading, Mass.: Addison-Wesley, 1996.

Dansby, B. Baldwin. *A Brief History of Jackson College: A Typical Story of the Survival of Education among Negroes in the South.* Jackson, Miss.: Jackson College, 1953.

Dearing, Mary R. *Veterans in Politics: The Story of the G.A.R.* Baton Rouge: Louisiana State University Press, 1952.

Dillard, Angela D. "Religion and Radicalism: The Reverend Albert B. Cleage, Jr., and the Rise of Black Christian Nationalism in Detroit." In *Freedom North: Black Freedom Struggles outside the South, 1940–1980,* ed. Jeanne Theoharis and Komozi Woodard, 153–76. New York: Palgrave, 2003.

Dittmer, John. *Local People: The Struggle for Civil Rights in Mississippi.* Urbana: University of Illinois Press, 1994.

Doherty, William C. *Mailman USA.* New York: David McKay, 1960.

Douglass, Frederick. *Narrative of the Life of Frederick Douglass, an American Slave.* 1960. Reprint, Cambridge, Mass.: Harvard University Press, 2001.

Draper, Alan. *Conflict of Interests: Organized Labor and the Civil Rights Movement in the South, 1954–1968.* Ithaca, N.Y.: ILR Press, 1994.

——. *A Rope of Sand: The AFL-CIO Committee on Political Education, 1955–1967.* New York: Praeger, 1989.

Draper, Theodore. *The Roots of American Communism.* New York: Viking, 1957.

Dubofsky, Melvyn. *We Shall Be All: A History of the Industrial Workers of the World.* Chicago: Quadrangle, 1969.

Du Bois, W. E. B. *The Autobiography of W. E. B. Du Bois: A Soliloquy on Viewing My Life from the Last Decade of Its First Century*. New York: International Publishers, 1968.

———. *Black Reconstruction in America, 1860–1880*. 1935. Reprint, Cleveland: World Publishing, 1968.

———. *The Souls of Black Folk*. 1903. New York: Penguin Books, 1989.

Dudziak, Mary L. *Cold War Civil Rights: Race and the Image of American Democracy*. Princeton, N.J.: Princeton University Press, 2000.

Dyson, Michael Eric. *I May Not Get There with You: The True Martin Luther King, Jr*. New York: Free Press, 2000.

Employment Practices Decisions. Vol. 24, *1980–1981*. Chicago: Commerce Clearing House, 1981.

Evers, Myrlie B. *For Us, the Living*. 1967. Reprint, Jackson: University Press of Mississippi, 1996.

Fairclough, Adam. *Better Day Coming: Blacks and Equality, 1890–2000*. New York: Viking, 2001.

———. *Race and Democracy: The Civil Rights Struggle in Louisiana, 1915–1975*. Athens: University of Georgia Press, 1995.

Fehrenbacher, Don E. *The Dred Scott Case: Its Significance in American Law and Politics*. New York: Oxford University Press, 1978.

Fink, Leon, and Brian Greenberg. *Upheaval in the Quiet Zone: A History of Hospital Workers' Union, Local 1199*. Urbana: University of Illinois Press, 1989.

Fogel, Walter. *The Equal Pay Act: Implications for Comparable Worth*. New York: Praeger, 1984.

Foner, Eric. *Freedom's Lawmakers: A Directory of Black Officeholders during Reconstruction*. New York: Oxford University Press, 1993.

———. *Reconstruction: America's Unfinished Revolution, 1863–1877*. New York: Harper, 1988.

Foner, Philip S., ed. *The Life and Writings of Frederick Douglass*. Volume 4, *Reconstruction and After*. New York: International Publishers, 1955.

Foner, Philip S., and Ronald L. Lewis, eds. *The Black Worker: A Documentary History from Colonial Times to the Present*. Volume 7, *The Black Worker from the Founding of the CIO to the AFL-CIO Merger, 1936–1955*. Philadelphia: Temple University Press, 1983.

Foner, Philip S., Ronald L. Lewis, and Robert Cvornyek, eds. *The Black Worker: A Documentary History from Colonial Times to the Present*. Volume 8, *The Black Worker since the AFL-CIO Merger, 1955–1980*. Philadelphia: Temple University Press, 1984.

Forman, James. *The Making of Black Revolutionaries*. 1972. Seattle: University of Washington Press, 1997.

Fox, Stephen R. *The Guardian of Boston: William Monroe Trotter*. New York: Atheneum, 1970.

Franklin, Buck Colbert. *My Life and an Era: The Autobiography of Buck Colbert Franklin*. Ed. John Hope Franklin and John Whittington Franklin. Baton Rouge: Louisiana State University Press, 1997.

Franklin, Charles Lionel. *The Negro Labor Unionist of New York: Problems and Conditions among Negroes in the Labor Unions in Manhattan with Special Reference to the N.R.A. and Post-N.R.A. Situations*. New York: Columbia University Press, 1936.

Franklin, John Hope, and Alfred A. Moss Jr. *From Slavery to Freedom: A History of African Americans*. 1947. 8th ed., Boston: McGraw-Hill, 2000.

Frazier, E. Franklin. *Black Bourgeoisie*. 1957. London: Collier, 1969.

Frazier, Thomas R., ed. *Readings in African-American History.* 3rd ed. Belmont, Calif.: Wadsworth, 2001.

Freeman, Jo. *The Politics of Women's Liberation: A Case Study of an Emerging Social Movement and Its Relation to the Policy Process.* New York: David McKay, 1975.

Freeman, Joshua B. *Working-Class New York: Life and Labor since World War II.* New York: New Press, 2000.

Fried, Albert, ed. *McCarthyism: The Great American Red Scare: A Documentary History.* New York: Oxford University Press, 1997.

Gabin, Nancy. "Women and the United Automobile Workers' Union in the 1950s." In *Women, Work and Protest: A Century of U.S. Women's Labor History,* ed. Ruth Milkman. Boston: Routledge and Kegan Paul, 1985.

Gall, Gilbert J. *The Politics of Right to Work: The Labor Federations as Special Interests, 1943–1979.* New York: Greenwood, 1988.

Gellman, David N., and David Quigley, eds. *Jim Crow New York: A Documentary History of Race and Citizenship, 1777–1877.* New York: New York University Press, 2003.

Georgakas, Dan, and Marvin Surkin. *Detroit: I Do Mind Dying: A Study in Urban Revolution.* 1975. Updated ed., Boston: South End Press, 1998.

George, Nelson. *Where Did Our Love Go? The Rise and Fall of the Motown Sound.* New York: St. Martin's Press, 1985.

Giddings, Paula J. *Ida, A Sword among Lions: Ida B. Wells and the Campaign against Lynching.* New York: Amistad, 2008.

Gilmore, Glenda. *Gender and Jim Crow: Women and the Politics of White Supremacy in North Carolina, 1896–1920.* Chapel Hill: University of North Carolina Press, 1996.

Gitlin, Todd. *The Sixties: Years of Hope, Days of Rage.* New York: Bantam, 1987.

Glazer, Nathan. *The Social Basis of American Communism.* New York: Harcourt, 1961.

Glenn, A. L. *History of the National Alliance of Postal Employees, 1913–1955.* Washington, D.C.: National Alliance of Postal Employees, 1956.

Glymph, Thavolia. " 'Liberty Dearly Bought': The Making of Civil War Memory in Afro-American Communities in the South." In *Time Longer than Rope: A Century of African American Activism, 1850–1950,* ed. Charles M. Payne and Adam Green, 111–40. New York: New York University Press, 2003.

Goldberg, Robert Alan. *Hooded Empire: The Ku Klux Klan in Colorado.* Urbana: University of Illinois Press, 1981.

Gottfried, Frances. *The Merit System and Municipal Civil Service: A Fostering of Social Inequality.* New York: Greenwood, 1988.

Greenberg, Jack. *Crusaders in the Courts: How a Dedicated Band of Lawyers Fought for the Civil Rights Revolution.* New York: Basic Books, 1994.

Griffler, Keith P. *What Price Alliance? Black Radicals Confront White Labor, 1918–1938.* New York: Garland, 1995.

Halpern, Martin. *Unions, Radicals, and Democratic Presidents: Seeking Social Change in the Twentieth Century.* Westport, Conn.: Praeger, 2003.

Hamilton, Dona Cooper, and Charles V. Hamilton. *The Dual Agenda: Race and Social Welfare Policies of Civil Rights Organizations.* New York: Columbia University Press, 1997.

Harris, Duchess. "From the Kennedy Commission to the Combahee Collective: Black Feminist Organizing, 1960–1980." In *Sisters in the Struggle: African American Women in the Civil Rights–Black Power Movement,* ed. Bettye Collier-Thomas and V. P. Franklin, 280–305. New York: New York University Press, 2004.

Harris, Fredrick C. *Something Within: Religion in African-American Political Activism*. New York: Oxford University Press, 1999.

——. "Will the Circle Be Unbroken? The Erosion and Transformation of African-American Civic Life." In *Civil Society, Democracy, and Civic Renewal*, ed. Robert K. Fullinwider, 317–38. Lanham, Md.: Rowman and Littlefield, 1999.

Harris, William H. *The Harder We Run: Black Workers since the Civil War*. New York: Oxford University Press, 1982.

Haywood, Harry. *Black Bolshevik: Autobiography of an Afro-American Communist*. Chicago: Liberator Press, 1978.

Hill, Herbert. "Black Labor and Affirmative Action: An Historical Perspective." In *The Question of Discrimination: Racial Inequality in the U.S. Labor Movement*, ed. Steven Shulman and William Darity Jr., 190–267. Middletown, Conn.: Wesleyan University Press, 1989.

——. *Black Labor and the American Legal System: Race, Work, and the Law*. 1977. Reprint, Madison: University of Wisconsin Press, 1985.

——. "The Racial Practices of Organized Labor: The Contemporary Record." In *The Negro and the American Labor Movement*, ed. Julius Jacobson, 286–357. Garden City, N.Y.: Archer, 1968.

Hill, Lance E. *The Deacons for Defense: Armed Resistance and the Civil Rights Movement*. Chapel Hill: University of North Carolina Press, 2004.

Hine, Darlene Clark. *Black Victory: The Rise and Fall of the White Primary in Texas*. 1979. Reprint, Columbia: University of Missouri Press, 2003.

Holloway, Jonathan Scott. *Confronting the Veil: Abram Harris, Jr., E. Franklin Frazier, and Ralph Bunche, 1919–1941*. Chapel Hill: University of North Carolina Press, 2002.

Honey, Michael Keith. *Black Workers Remember: An Oral History of Segregation, Unionism, and the Freedom Struggle*. Berkeley: University of California Press, 1999.

——. *Going Down Jericho Road: The Memphis Strike, Martin Luther King's Last Campaign*. New York: W. W. Norton, 2007.

——. *Southern Labor and Black Civil Rights: Organizing Memphis Workers*. Urbana: University of Illinois Press, 1993.

Horne, Gerald. *Black and Red: W. E. B. Du Bois and the Afro-American Response to the Cold War, 1944–1963*. Albany: State University of New York Press, 1986.

——. *Communist Front?: The Civil Rights Congress, 1946–1956*. Rutherford, N.J.: Fairleigh Dickinson University Press, 1988.

Hutchinson, Earl Ofari. *Blacks and Reds: Race and Class in Conflict, 1919–1990*. East Lansing: Michigan State University Press, 1995.

Ignatiev, Noel. *How the Irish Became White*. New York: Routledge, 1995.

Isserman, Maurice. *Which Side Were You On? The American Communist Party during the Second World War*. Middletown, Conn.: Wesleyan University Press, 1982.

Jacobs, Harriet. *Incidents in the Life of a Slave Girl*. 1861. New York: Oxford University Press, 1988.

Jacobson, Matthew Frye. *Whiteness of a Different Color: European Immigrants and the Alchemy of Race*. Cambridge, Mass.: Harvard University Press, 1998.

James, Winston. *Holding Aloft the Banner of Ethiopia: Caribbean Radicalism in Early Twentieth-Century America*. London: Verso, 2000.

Johnson, Daniel M., and Rex R. Campbell. *Black Migration in America: A Social Demographic History*. Durham, N.C.: Duke University Press, 1981.

Johnston, Paul. *Success While Others Fail: Social Movement Unionism and the Public Workplace*. Ithaca, N.Y.: ILR Press, 1994.

Jones, Jacqueline. *American Work: Four Centuries of Black and White Labor*. New York: W. W. Norton, 1998.

Jordan, June. *Soldier: A Poet's Childhood*. New York: Basic Books, 2000.

Kelley, Robin D. G. *Hammer and Hoe: Alabama Communists during the Great Depression*. Chapel Hill: University of North Carolina Press, 1990.

Kessler-Harris, Alice. *Out to Work: A History of Wage-Earning Women in the United States*. 20th anniversary ed. New York: Oxford University Press, 2003.

Kinnamon, Keneth, and Michel Fabre, eds. *Conversations with Richard Wright*. Jackson: University Press of Mississippi, 1993.

Klarman, Michael J. *From Jim Crow to Civil Rights: The Supreme Court and the Struggle for Racial Equality*. Oxford: Oxford University Press, 2004.

Klehr, Harvey. *The Heyday of American Communism: The Depression Decade*. New York: Basic, 1984.

Klehr, Harvey, John Earl Haynes, and Fridrikh Igorevich Firsov, *The Secret World of American Communism*. New Haven, Conn.: Yale University Press, 1995.

Kluger, Richard. *Simple Justice: The History of Brown v. Board of Education and Black America's Struggle for Equality*. New York: Vintage, 1977.

Korrol, Virginia E. Sanchez. *From Colonia to Community: The History of Puerto Ricans in New York City*. Berkeley: University of California Press, 1994.

Korstad, Karl. "Black and White Together: Organizing in the South with the Food, Tobacco, Agricultural, & Allied Workers Union (FTA-CIO), 1946–1952." In *The CIO's Left-Led Unions*, ed. Steve Rosswurm, 69–94. New Brunswick, N.J.: Rutgers University Press, 1992.

Korstad, Robert Rodgers. *Civil Rights Unionism: Tobacco Workers and the Struggle for Democracy in the Mid-Twentieth Century South*. Chapel Hill: University of North Carolina Press, 2003.

Krislov, Samuel. *The Negro in Federal Employment: The Quest for Equal Opportunity*. Minneapolis: University of Minnesota Press, 1967.

Labor Research Association. *Labor Fact Book 5*. 1941. Reprint, New York: Oriole Editions, 1972.

Lawson, Steven F. *Civil Rights Crossroads: Nation, Community, and the Black Freedom Struggle*. Lexington: University Press of Kentucky, 2003.

——. *Running for Freedom: Civil Rights and Black Politics in America since 1941*. New York: McGraw-Hill, 1991.

Lawson, Steven F., and Charles Payne. *Debating the Civil Rights Movement, 1945–1968*. Lanham, Md.: Rowman and Littlefield, 1998.

Le Blanc, Paul. *A Short History of the U.S. Working Class: From Colonial Times to the Twenty-first Century*. Amherst, N.Y.: Humanity Books, 1999.

Leggett, John C. *Class, Race, and Labor: Working-Class Consciousness in Detroit*. New York: Oxford University Press, 1968.

Leuchtenburg, William E. *Franklin D. Roosevelt and the New Deal, 1932–1940*. New York: Harper and Row, 1963.

Lewis, David Levering. *W. E. B. Du Bois: Biography of a Race, 1868–1919*. New York: Henry Holt, 1993.

——, ed. *W. E. B. Du Bois: A Reader*. New York: Henry Holt, 1995.

Lewis, Earl. *In Their Own Interests: Race, Class, and Power in Twentieth-Century Norfolk, Virginia*. Berkeley: University of California Press, 1993.

Lewis, George. *The White South and the Red Menace: Segregationists, Anticommunism, and Massive Resistance, 1945–1965*. Gainesville: University Press of Florida, 2004.

Lichtenstein, Nelson. *Labor's War at Home: The CIO in World War II*. 1982. Reprint, Philadelphia: Temple University Press, 2003.

Lichtenstein, Nelson, Susan Strasser, and Roy Rosenzweig, eds. *Who Built America?: Working People and the Nation's Economy, Politics, Culture, and Society*, vol. 2, *Since 1877*. American Social History Project. Boston: Bedford/St. Martin's Press, 2000.

Lipsitz, George. *Rainbow at Midnight: Labor and Culture in the 1940s*. Urbana: University of Illinois Press, 1994.

Litwack, Leon F. *North of Slavery: The Negro in the Free States, 1790–1860*. 1961. Reprint, Chicago: University of Chicago Press, 1969.

———. *Trouble in Mind: Black Southerners in the Age of Jim Crow*. New York: Alfred A. Knopf, 1998.

Loewenberg, J. Joseph. "The Post Office Strike of 1970." In *Collective Bargaining in Government: Readings and Cases*, ed. J. Joseph Loewenberg and Michael H. Moskow, 192–215. Englewood Cliffs, N.J.: Prentice-Hall, 1972.

Logan, Rayford W. *The Betrayal of the Negro: From Rutherford B. Hayes to Woodrow Wilson*. 1954. New enlarged ed., New York: Collier, 1965.

———. *The Negro in American Life and Thought: The Nadir, 1877–1901*. New York: Dial, 1954.

Lubiano, Wahneema. "Black Nationalism and Black Common Sense." In *The House That Race Built: Black Americans, U.S. Terrain*, ed. Wahneema Lubiano, 232–52. New York: Pantheon Books, 1997.

Manning, Chandra. *What This Cruel War Was Over: Soldiers, Slavery, and the Civil War*. New York: Alfred A. Knopf, 2007.

Marable, Manning. *Race, Reform, and Rebellion: The Second Reconstruction in Black America, 1945–1990*. 1984. Reprint, Jackson: University Press of Mississippi, 1991.

Marius, Richard. *A Short Guide to Writing about History*. New York: HarperCollins, 1995.

Marshall, Ray, and Virgil L. Christian, Jr., eds. *Employment of Blacks in the South: A Perspective on the 1960s*. Austin: University of Texas Press, 1978.

Martin, Tony. *Race First: The Ideological and Organizational Struggles of Marcus Garvey and the Universal Negro Improvement Association*. Westport, Conn.: Greenwood Press, 1976.

Marx, Karl. *Capital: A Critique of Political Economy. Vol. 1: The Process of Capitalist Accumulation*. Ed. Frederick Engels, trans. Samuel Moore and Edward Aveling. 1867. New York: International Publishers, 1979.

Marx, Karl, and Frederick Engels. *Selected Works*. New York: International Publishers, 1974.

McConnell, Stuart. *Glorious Contention: The Grand Army of the Republic, 1865–1900*. Chapel Hill: University of North Carolina Press, 1992.

McGee, Henry W. *The Negro in the Chicago Post Office: Henry W. McGee Autobiography and Dissertation*. Chicago: VolumeOne Press, 1999.

McMillen, Neil. *The Citizens' Council: Organized Resistance to the Second Reconstruction, 1954–64*. Urbana: University of Illinois Press, 1971.

———, ed. *Remaking Dixie: The Impact of World War II on the American South*. Jackson: University Press of Mississippi, 1997.

McNeil, Genna Rae. *Groundwork: Charles Hamilton Houston and the Struggle for Civil Rights*. Philadelphia: University of Pennsylvania Press, 1983.

Medley, Keith W. *We as Freemen: Plessy v. Ferguson.* Gretna, La.: Pelican, 2003.

Meier, August, and Elliot Rudwick. *Black Detroit and the Rise of the UAW.* Oxford: Oxford University Press, 1981.

Mikusko, M. Brady. *Carriers in a Common Cause: A History of Letter Carriers and the NALC.* Washington, D.C.: National Association of Letter Carriers, 1989.

Milkman, Ruth, ed. *Women, Work and Protest: A Century of U.S. Women's Labor History.* Boston: Routledge and Kegan Paul, 1985.

Miller, Lester F. *The National Rural Letter Carriers Association: A Centennial Portrait.* Encino, Calif.: Cherbo Publishing, 2003.

Montgomery, David. *Workers' Control in America: Studies in the History of Work, Technology, and Labor Struggles.* 1979. Reprint, Cambridge: Cambridge University Press, 1986.

Moroney, Rita L. *History of the U.S. Postal Service, 1775–1982.* Washington, D.C.: Government Printing Office, 1983.

Morris, Aldon D. *The Origins of the Civil Rights Movement: Black Communities Organizing for Change.* 1984. Reprint, New York: Free Press, 1986.

Murray, Pauli. *The Autobiography of a Black Activist, Feminist, Lawyer, Priest, and Poet.* 1987. Reprint, Knoxville: University of Tennessee Press, 1990.

———. *States Laws on Race and Color.* Cincinnati: Woman's Division of Christian Service, 1951.

Myrdal, Gunnar. *An American Dilemma: The Negro Problem and Modern Democracy.* New York: Harper, 1944.

Naison, Mark. *Communists in Harlem during the Depression.* Urbana: University of Illinois Press, 1983.

National States' Rights Democrats Campaign Committee. *States' Rights Information and Speakers Handbook.* Jackson, Miss.: National States' Rights Democrats Campaign Committee, 1948.

National Urban League. *Negro Membership in American Labor Unions.* New York: Alexander Press, 1930.

Needleman, Ruth. *Black Freedom Fighters in Steel: The Struggle for Democratic Unionism.* Ithaca, N.Y.: Cornell University Press, 2003.

Nelson, Bruce. *Divided We Stand: American Workers and the Struggle for Black Equality.* Princeton: Princeton University Press, 2001.

Nilan, Patrick J. "Union Lobbying at the Federal Level." In *Collective Bargaining in Government: Readings and Cases,* ed. J. Joseph Loewenberg and Michael H. Moskow, 221–27. Englewood Cliffs, N.J.: Prentice-Hall, 1972.

Norrell, Robert J. "One Thing We Did Right: Reflections on the Movement." In *New Directions in Civil Rights Studies,* ed. Armstead Robinson and Patricia Sullivan, 65–80. Charlottesville: University of Virginia Press, 1991.

Obadele-Starks, Ernest. *Black Unionism in the Industrial South.* College Station: Texas A&M University Press, 2000.

O'Brien, James C., and Philip P. Marenberg. *Your Federal Civil Service.* New York: Funk and Wagnalls, 1940.

Ogbar, Jeffrey O. G. *Black Power: Radical Politics and African American Identity.* Baltimore: Johns Hopkins University Press, 2004.

Ogletree, Charles J., Jr. *All Deliberate Speed: Reflections on the First Half Century of Brown v. Board of Education.* New York: W. W. Norton, 2004.

Oliver, Melvin L., and Thomas M. Shapiro. *Black Wealth / White Wealth: A New Perspective on Racial Equality*. New York: Routledge, 1997.

Ortiz, Paul. " 'Eat Your Bread without Butter, But Pay Your Poll Tax!': Roots of the African American Voter Registration Movement in Florida, 1919–1920." In *Time Longer than Rope: A Century of African American Activism, 1850–1950*, ed. Charles M. Payne and Adam Green, 196–229. New York: New York University Press, 2003.

———. *Emancipation Betrayed: The Hidden History of Black Organizing and White Violence in Florida from Reconstruction to the Bloody Election of 1920*. Berkeley: University of California Press, 2005.

Osofsky, Gilbert. *Harlem: The Making of a Ghetto*. 1963. Reprint, New York: Harper, 1966.

Patterson, William L., ed. *We Charge Genocide: The Historic Petition to the United Nations for Relief from a Crime of the United States Government against the Negro People*. 1951. Reprint, New York: International Publishers, 1970.

Payne, Charles M. *I've Got the Light of Freedom: The Organizing Tradition and the Mississippi Freedom Struggle*. Berkeley: University of California Press, 1995.

Payne, Charles M., and Adam Green, eds. *Time Longer than Rope: A Century of African American Activism, 1850–1950*. New York: New York University Press, 2003.

Peery, Nelson. *Black Radical: The Education of an American Revolutionary*. New York: New Press, 2007.

Perry, Jeffrey. "Getting White Workers Involved." In *A Troublemaker's Handbook 2: How to Fight Back Where You Work—and Win!*, ed. Jane Slaughter, 170–72. 1991. Detroit: Labor Notes, 2005.

———, ed. *A Hubert Harrison Reader*. Middletown, Conn.: Wesleyan University Press, 2001.

———. *Hubert Harrison: The Voice of Harlem Radicalism, 1883–1918*. New York: Columbia University Press, 2009.

Pfeffer, Paula F. *A. Philip Randolph, Pioneer of the Civil Rights Movement*. Baton Rouge: Louisiana State University Press, 1990.

Pitre, Merline. *In Struggle against Jim Crow: Lulu B. White and the NAACP, 1900–1957*. College Station: Texas A&M University Press, 1999.

Pomerantz, Gary M. *Where Peachtree Meets Sweet Auburn: The Saga of Two Families and the Making of Atlanta*. New York: Scribner, 1996.

Prather, H. Leon, Sr. *We Have Taken a City: Wilmington Racial Massacre and Coup of 1898*. Rutherford, N.J.: Fairleigh Dickinson University Press, 1984.

President's Committee on Civil Rights. *To Secure These Rights: The Report of the President's Committee on Civil Rights*. Washington, D.C.: Government Printing Office, 1947.

Rachleff, Peter. "Machine Technology and Workplace Control: The U.S. Post Office." In *Critical Studies in Organization and Bureaucracy*, ed. Frank Fischer and Carmen Sirianni, 143–56. Philadelphia: Temple University Press, 1984.

———. *Moving the Mail: From a Manual Case to Outer Space*. Morgantown, W.Va.: Work Environment Project, 1982.

Ransby, Barbara. *Ella Baker and the Black Freedom Movement: A Radical Democratic Vision*. Chapel Hill: University of North Carolina Press, 2003.

Rediker, Marcus. *Between the Devil and the Deep Blue Sea: Merchant Seamen, Pirates, and the Anglo-American Maritime World, 1700–1750*. 1987. Reprint, Cambridge: Cambridge University Press, 1993.

Rediker, Marcus, and Peter Linebaugh. "The Many Headed Hydra: Sailors, Slaves and the Atlantic Working Class in the Eighteenth Century." In *Gone to Croatan: Origins of North American Dropout Culture*, ed. Ron Sakolsky and James Koehnline, 129–60. Brooklyn: Autonomedia, 1993.

Reed, Christopher Robert. *The Chicago NAACP and the Rise of Black Professional Leadership, 1910–1966*. Bloomington: Indiana University Press, 1997.

Reed, Merl E. *Seedtime for the Modern Civil Rights Movement: The President's Committee on Fair Employment Practice, 1941–1946*. Baton Rouge: Louisiana State University Press, 1991.

Rich, Wilbur C. *Coleman Young and Detroit Politics: From Social Activist to Power Broker*. Detroit: Wayne State University Press, 1989.

Roediger, David R., ed. *Black on White: Black Writers on What It Means to Be White*. New York: Schocken, 1998.

———. *Towards the Abolition of Whiteness: Essays on Race, Politics, and Working Class History*. London: Verso, 1994.

———. *Working toward Whiteness: How America's Immigrants Became White*. New York: Basic Books, 2005.

Rosswurm, Steve, ed. *The CIO's Left-Led Unions*. New Brunswick, N.J.: Rutgers University Press, 1992.

Rovere, Richard. *Senator Joe McCarthy*. 1959. Reprint, New York: Harper, 1973.

Rubio, Philip F. *A History of Affirmative Action, 1619–2000*. Jackson: University Press of Mississippi, 2001.

Ruchames, Louis. *John Brown: The Making of a Revolutionary*. New York: Grosset and Dunlap, 1969.

———. *Race, Jobs, and Politics: The Story of the FEPC*. New York: Columbia University Press, 1953.

Sale, Kirkpatrick. *SDS*. New York: Vintage Books, 1974.

Sandage, Scott A. "A Marble House Divided: The Lincoln Memorial, the Civil Rights Movement, and the Politics of Memory." In *Time Longer than Rope: A Century of African American Activism, 1850–1950*, ed. Charles M. Payne and Adam Green, 492–535. New York: New York University Press, 2003.

Santoro, Gene. *Myself When I Am Real*. New York: Oxford University Press, 2000.

Saxton, Alexander. *The Indispensable Enemy: Labor and the Anti-Chinese Movement in California*. Berkeley: University of California Press, 1971.

Schneider, Mark Robert. *"We Return Fighting": The Civil Rights Movement in the Jazz Age*. Boston: Northeastern University Press, 2002.

Schrecker, Ellen. *The Age of McCarthyism: A Brief History with Documents*. 2nd ed. Boston: Bedford/St. Martin's Press, 2002.

———. *Many Are the Crimes: McCarthyism in America*. Princeton, N.J.: Princeton University Press, 1998.

Schuyler, George S. "The Caucasian Problem." In *What the Negro Wants*, ed. Rayford W. Logan, 281–97. Chapel Hill: University of North Carolina Press, 1944.

Scott, James C. *Weapons of the Weak: Everyday Forms of Peasant Resistance*. New Haven, Conn.: Yale University Press, 1985.

Shabazz, Amilcar. *Advancing Democracy: African Americans and the Struggle for Access and Equity in Higher Education in Texas*. Chapel Hill: University of North Carolina Press, 2004.

Shaffer, Donald R. *After the Glory: The Struggles of Black Civil War Veterans*. Lawrence: University Press of Kansas, 2004.

Sitkoff, Harvard. "African American Militancy in the World War II South: Another Perspective." In *Remaking Dixie: The Impact of World War II on the American South*, ed. Neil McMillen, 70–92. Jackson: University Press of Mississippi, 1997.

Skrentny, John David. *The Ironies of Affirmative Action: Politics, Culture, and Justice in America.* Chicago: University of Chicago Press, 1996.

Slaughter, Jane, ed. *A Troublemaker's Handbook 2: How to Fight Back Where You Work—and Win!* 1991. Reprint, Detroit: Labor Notes, 2005.

Smith, Edward Conrad, ed. *The Constitution of the United States.* 1936. 11th ed., New York: Barnes and Noble, 1979.

Spear, Allan H. *Black Chicago: The Making of a Negro Ghetto, 1890–1920.* Chicago: University of Chicago Press, 1967.

Spero, Sterling D. *Government as Employer.* 1948. Reprint, Carbondale: Southern Illinois University Press, 1972.

Spero, Sterling D., and Abram L. Harris. *The Black Worker: The Negro and the Labor Movement.* 1931. Reprint, New York: Atheneum, 1969.

Stanton, Fred, ed. *Fighting Racism in World War II: C. L. R. James, George Breitman, Edgar Keemer, and Others.* New York: Monad, 1980.

Stanton, Mary. *Freedom Walk: Mississippi or Bust.* Jackson: University Press of Mississippi, 2003.

Stepan-Norris, Judith, and Maurice Zeitlin. *Left Out: Reds and America's Industrial Unions.* Cambridge: Cambridge University Press, 2003.

Sugrue, Thomas J. *The Origins of the Urban Crisis: Race and Inequality in Postwar Detroit.* Princeton, N.J.: Princeton University Press, 1996.

Sullivan, Patricia. *Days of Hope: Race and Democracy in the New Deal Era.* Chapel Hill: University of North Carolina Press, 1996.

Terkel, Studs. *Working.* 1972. Reprint, New York: Avon Books, 1975.

Theoharis, Athan G. *Chasing Spies: How the FBI Failed in Counterintelligence but Promoted the Politics of McCarthyism in the Cold War Years.* Chicago: Ivan R. Dee, 2002.

Theoharis, Jeanne, and Komozi Woodard, eds. *Freedom North: Black Freedom Struggles outside the South, 1940–1980.* New York: Palgrave, 2003.

Thomas, Richard W. *Life for Us Is What We Make It: Building Black Community in Detroit, 1915–1945.* Bloomington: Indiana University Press, 1992.

Thompson, Heather. *Whose Detroit? Politics, Labor, and Race in a Modern American City.* Ithaca, N.Y.: Cornell University Press, 2001.

Tierney, John T. *Postal Reorganization: Managing the Public's Business.* Boston: Auburn House, 1981.

Tyson, Timothy B. *Radio Free Dixie: Robert F. Williams and the Roots of Black Power.* Chapel Hill: University of North Carolina Press, 1999.

Van Riper, Paul P. *History of the United States Civil Service.* Evanston, Ill.: Row, Peterson, and Company, 1958.

Waldinger, Roger. *Still the Promised City? African-Americans and New Immigrants in Postindustrial New York.* Cambridge, Mass.: Harvard University Press, 1996.

Walker, Iain, and Heather J. Smith. *Relative Deprivation: Specification, Development, and Integration.* Cambridge: Cambridge University Press, 2002.

Walsh, John, and Garth Mangum. *Labor Struggle in the Post Office: From Selective Lobbying to Collective Bargaining.* Armonk, N.Y.: M. E. Sharpe, 1992.

Washington, James M., ed. *A Testament of Hope: The Essential Writings and Speeches of Martin Luther King, Jr.* 1986. Reprint, San Francisco: HarperSanFrancisco, 1991.

Weaver, Robert C. *Negro Labor: A National Problem*. New York: Harcourt, 1946.

Wesley, Dorothy Porter. "Integration versus Separatism: William Cooper Nell's Role in the Struggle for Equality." In *Courage and Conscience: Black and White Abolitionists in Boston*, ed. Donald M. Jacobs, 207–24. Bloomington: Indiana University Press, 1993.

Wilhoit, Francis M. *The Politics of Massive Resistance*. 1954. Reprint, New York: George Braziller, 1973.

Williams, Juan. *Thurgood Marshall: American Revolutionary*. New York: Times Books, 1998.

Wilson, Charles Reagan, and William Ferris, eds. *Encyclopedia of Southern Culture*. Chapel Hill: University of North Carolina Press, 1989.

Wilson, William Julius. *When Work Disappears: The World of the New Urban Poor*. New York: Alfred A. Knopf, 1997.

Woodard, Komozi. *A Nation within a Nation: Amiri Baraka (LeRoi Jones) and Black Power Politics*. Chapel Hill: University of North Carolina Press, 1999.

Woods, Jeff. *Black Struggle, Red Scare: Segregation and Anti-Communism in the South, 1948–1968*. Baton Rouge: Louisiana State University Press, 2004.

Wright, Ellen, and Michel Fabre, eds. *Richard Wright Reader*. New York: Harper and Row, 1978.

Young, Coleman, and Lonnie Wheeler. *Hard Stuff: The Autobiography of Coleman Young*. New York: Viking, 1994.

Zagoria, Sam, ed. *Public Workers and Public Unions*. Englewood Cliffs, N.J.: Prentice-Hall, 1972.

Zieger, Robert H. *The CIO: 1935–1955*. Chapel Hill: University of North Carolina Press, 1995.

Zieger, Robert H., and Gilbert J. Gall. *American Workers, American Unions*. 1986. 3rd ed., Baltimore: Johns Hopkins University Press, 2002.

Zinn, Howard. *A People's History of the United States*. 1980. Reprint, New York: Harper, 1990.

THESES, DISSERTATIONS, AND PAPERS

Bolster, Paul D. "Civil Rights Movements in Twentieth Century Georgia." Ph.D. diss., University of Georgia, 1972.

Brenner, Aaron. "Rank-and-File Rebellion, 1966–1975." Ph.D. diss., Columbia University, 1996.

Dolenga, Harold E. "An Analytical Case Study of the Policy Formation Process (Postal Reform and Reorganization)." Ph.D. diss., Northwestern University, 1973.

Farley, Abron. "Persuasion, Mediation and Conflict in the Postal Service before and after the Postal Reorganization Act." Master's thesis, California State University–Dominguez Hills, 1985.

Gannon, Barbara A. "The Won Cause: Black and White Comradeship in the Grand Army of the Republic." Ph.D. diss., Pennsylvania State University, 2005.

Goldberg, Louis C. "CORE in Trouble: A Social History of the Organizational Dilemmas of the Congress of Racial Equality Target City Project in Baltimore, 1965–1967." Ph.D. diss., Johns Hopkins University, 1970.

Halter, Gary Max. "The Hatch Act Reconsidered." Ph.D. diss., University of Maryland, 1969.

Hasson, David Sheldon. "The Historical Development of Public Employee Unionism:

The Performance and Effectiveness of the American Postal Unions." Ph.D. diss., University of California–Riverside, 1974.

Marino, Al. "A Time of Fury: The Postal Strike of 1970." 2001 Research paper workshop, Empire State College, May 15, 1982.

McGee, Henry W. "The Negro in the Chicago Post Office." Master's thesis, University of Chicago, 1961.

Olds, Kelly Barton. "Public Service and Privatization in Antebellum America." Ph.D. diss., University of Rochester, 1993.

Streater, John Baxter, Jr. "The National Negro Congress, 1936–1947." Ph.D. diss., University of Cincinnati, 1981.

Tennassee, Paul. "Alliance Opposition to the Loyalty-Security Programs, 1947–1959." Master's thesis, Johns Hopkins University, 2002.

Williams, Charisse. "Non-Violent Protests to the Point of Production: The Evolution of the Left in the Civil Rights Movement." Duke seminar paper, CDS collection at Duke University Rare Book, Manuscript, and Special Collections Library, Durham, N.C.

MICROFILM

Located at Duke University Perkins/Bostock Library and interlibrary loan.

American Postal Workers Union—Brooklyn NFPOC Local 251 Minutes, 1918–1977. Brooklyn, N.Y.: Mathias and Carr, 1987.

The CIO Files of John L. Lewis, Part I: Correspondence with CIO Union. Edited by Robert Zieger. Frederick, Md.: University Publications of America, 1988.

The Papers of A. Philip Randolph. Bethesda, Md.: University Publications of America, 1990.

Papers of the NAACP. Edited by John H. Bracey Jr. and August Meier. Baltimore: University Press of America, 1992.

Records of the Southern Christian Leadership Conference, 1954–1970. Edited by Randolph H. Boehm. Bethesda, Md.: University Publications of America, 1995.

Selected Documents from Records of the Committee on Fair Employment Practice. Record Group 228 in the custody of the National Archives. Edited by Bruce I. Friend. Glen Rock, N.J.: Microfilming Corporation of American, 1970.

Universal Negro Improvement Association Records of the Central Division (New York), 1918–1959. Schomburg Library Collection. Wilmington, Del.: Scholarly Resources, 1995.

FILMS AND VIDEOS

At the River I Stand, dir. David Appleby, Allison Graham, Steven Ross, 1993.

Boyz N the Hood, dir. John Singleton, 1991.

Bright Road, dir. Gerald Mayer, 1953.

Don't Be a Menace to South Central While Drinking Your Juice in the Hood, dir. Paris Barclay, 1995.

Hollywood Shuffle, dir. Robert Townsend, 1987.

Jingle All the Way, dir. Brian Levant, 1996.

Miracle on 34th Street, dir. George Seaton, 1947.

Poetic Justice, dir. John Singleton, 1993.

Rebel without a Cause, dir. Nicholas Ray, 1955.

Parker, Charlie. "Now's the Time." *Original Bird: The Beat of Bird on Savoy* (LP), Savoy Jazz, 1988. Original recording, November 26, 1945, New York.

INTERNET ARTICLES, WEBSITES, AND DIGITAL ARCHIVES

African American registry. <http://www.aaregistry.com> (November 12, 2005).

American Memory. Library of Congress. <http://memory.loc.gov> (September 22, 2008).

American Postal Workers Union. <http://www.apwu.org> (September 15, 2008).

Atlanta Regional Council for Higher Education. <http://www.atlantahighered.org> (September 7, 2008).

Bari, Judi. <http://www.judibari.org> (September 10, 2008).

Barnes, Ed, and Bob Windrem. "Six Ways to Take Over a Union." *Mother Jones* (August 1980), <http://www.laborers.org> (September 13, 2008).

"Basic Standards for All Mailing Services: Private Express Statutes." <http://pe.usps .gov/cpim/ftp/manuals/QSG300/Q608.pdf> (September 15, 2008).

Biewen, John. <http://www.americanradioworks.publicradio.org/features/korea/indix .html> (November 12, 2005).

"Black Workers Inspired 1970 Postal Workers' Wildcat." *Challenge*, June 6, 1996. <http:// www.plp.org> (November 12, 2005).

Boyd, Deanna, and Kendra Chen. "The History and Experience of African Americans in America's Postal Service." Smithsonian National Postal Museum, Washington, D.C. <http://www.postalmuseum.si.edu/AfricanAmericans/index.html> (September 6, 2008).

Branch 142 [National Association of Letter Carriers]. <http://www.branch142.com> (December 31, 2008).

Braun, Michael. "Dave Cline: Rank & File Rebel, Part 1." <http://firemtn.blogspot .com/2007/11/dave-cline-rebel-worker-i.html> (February 6, 2009).

Civil Rights in Mississippi Digital Archive. <http://www.lib.usm.edu/~spcol/crda/oh/ index.html> (September 10, 2008).

Davies, Major David C. "Grievance Arbitration within the Department of the Army under Executive Order 10988." *Military Law Review* 46 (October 1969), 1–30. Headquarters, Department of the Army. <http://www.loc.gov/rr/frd/Military _Law/Military_Law_Review/pdf-files/27788B~1.pdf> (September 10, 2008).

Equal Employment Opportunity Commission. <http://www.eeoc.gov> (September 10, 2008).

Glover, Danny. Interview by David Barsamian. *Progressive* (December 2002). <http:// www.progressive.org/dec02/intv1201.html> (February 25, 2006).

Gregory, Dick. <http://www.dickgregory.com/about_dick_gregory.html> (February 25, 2006).

Griffith, Vivé. "'Courage and the Refusal to Be Swayed': Heman Marion Sweatt's Legal Challenge That Integrated the University of Texas." <http://txtell.lib.utexas.edu/ stories/s0010-full.html> (May 21, 2006).

Hall, Jacquelyn Dowd. Organization of American Historians presidential address, March 27, 2004, Boston. Reported by Rick Shenkman, History News Network. <http:// hnn.us/articles/4320.html> (March 30, 2004).

Historian, U.S. Postal Service. <http://www.usps.com/postalhistory> (July 15, 2009). Includes following articles and databases: "African-American Postal Workers in the 19th Century"; "List of Known African-American Postmasters, 1800s"; "List of Known African-American Letter Carriers, 1800s"; "List of Known African-American Post Office Clerks, 1800s"; "List of Known African-American Employees, 1800s: Headquarters Employees, Railway Mail Service Employees, U.S. Mail Carriers, Contractors, and Others"; and "Women Mail Carriers."

Jordan, June. Interview by David Barsamian. "Childhood Memories, Poetry & Palestine." Boulder, Colo., October 11, 2000. <http://www.alternativeradio.org/Jordan02.html> (February 25, 2006).

King, Martin Luther, Jr. Research and Education Institute. <http://mlk-kppo1 .stanford.edu> (November 24, 2008).

Manuscript-Education. *Sweatt v. Painter*. NAACP Collection, 1945–1950 (Primary Source). <http://cis.lexis.nexis.com> (May 21, 2006).

National Alliance of Postal and Federal Employees. <http://www.napfe.com> (February 6, 2009).

National Archives and Records Administration. <http://www.archives.gov> (September 10, 2008).

National Association for the Advancement of Colored People. <http://www.naacp.org> (August 15, 2009)

National Association of Letter Carriers. <http://www.nalc.org> (September 18, 2008).

National Postal Mail Handlers Union. <http://www.npmhu.org> (September 10, 2008).

New York Letter Carriers Branch 36 [National Association of Letter Carriers]. "1970 Postal Strike." <http://www.nylcbr36.org/history.htm> (September 10, 2008).

"News, Reviews, and Commentary on Lesbian and Bisexual Women in Entertainment and the Media." <http://www.afterellen.com/archive/Ellen/People/2006/10/randle.html> (September 6, 2008).

Operation Transition. <http://www.dmdc.osd.mil/ot/index.html> (November 12, 2005).

Originals fan website. <http://www.soulwalking.co.uk/Originals.html> (February 25, 2006).

Perrone, Pierre. Article from *The Independent*. <http://www.spectropop.com/remembers/FreddieGorman.htm> (November 24, 2008).

Ridgway, Daisy. "Researchers Find That Postal and Mail Themes Strike a Chord with Composers." *Research Reports* 82 (Autumn 1995). National Postal Museum, Smithsonian Institution <http://www.si.edu> (September 6, 2008).

Shoenfeld, Sarah J. Review of Audrey Elisa Kerr, *The Paper Bag Principle: Class, Colorism, and Rumor and the Case of Black Washington, D.C.* Knoxville: University of Tennessee Press, 2006. H-Net (Humanities and Social Sciences Online), H-DC, August 2007, <http://www.h-net.org/reviews/showrev.php?id=13464> (July 1, 2008).

Sons of Union Veterans of the Civil War. <http://www.suvcw.org/gar.htm> (July 10, 2007).

Theoharis, Athan. "The Politics of Scholarship: Liberals, Anti-Communism, and McCarthyism." <http://www.english.upenn.edu/~afilreis/50s/theoharis.html> (September 10, 2008).

Truman Library. <http://www.trumanlibrary.org> (October 12, 2008).

United Food and Commercial Workers (UFCW). <http://www.ufcw.org> (August 21, 2009).

University of North Carolina–Chapel Hill Southern Oral History Program. <http://www.sohp.org/news/hall_address.htm> (September 10, 2008).

"The Urban League and the A.F. of L.: A Statement on Racial Discrimination." Paper delivered July 9, 1935 [*Opportunity*]. <http://newdeal.feri.org/opp/opp35247.htm> (November 12, 2005).

"Voices from the Gaps: Women Writers of Color, University of Minnesota, June Jordan (1936–2002) Biography-Criticism." <http://voices.cla.umn.edu/authors/JORDANjune.html> (February 25, 2006).

INDEX

www.ingramcontent.com/pod-product-compliance
Lightning Source LLC
Chambersburg PA
CBHW021806270326
41932CB00007B/70